VARIETIES
OF
EXPERIENCE

An Introduction to Philosophy

ALBERT WILLIAM LEVI
ASSOCIATE PROFESSOR OF PHILOSOPHY
WASHINGTON UNIVERSITY

THE RONALD PRESS COMPANY • NEW YORK

Library of Congress Catalog Card Number: 57–6807
PRINTED IN THE UNITED STATES OF AMERICA

To

TITA and ESTELLE

Preface

The Varieties of Experience introduces beginners in philosophy, whether college students or amateurs, to its chief areas. Starting with a section on the meaning and method of philosophy, it continues with sections dealing with the philosophy of nature, the philosophy of human experience, and the philosophy of religion.

Its method is to combine text and readings from the great philosophers, ancient and modern. The text comprises between one third and one fourth of the total. The last section of each chapter of text is a brief specific introduction to each of the selections for that chapter. In general, text and readings are intimately related.

The readings contain 35 selections from 27 philosophers, from Plato and Aristotle in the ancient world to Dewey and Whitehead among our contemporaries. The readings are not a history of philosophy, although I have tried to make them representative of the philosophic tradition as a whole. This, of course, does not mean that every school is represented on every issue. Nor could this wisely be done for introductory purposes. In choosing the selections, I have had this in mind: (a) that they should be important and significant treatments of their subject, (b) that they should be solid without being complex or overtechnical, (c) that they should be interesting.

No introduction to philosophy can be all things to all men. Nor need it be, for the chief gratification of an author is to please himself. But in these matters, "no man is an island . . . ," and in philosophy, even among the warring schools there is, after all, a certain consensus about what is genuinely important and dare not be neglected. I have tried to keep in mind and in balance both my own judgment of what is philosophically valuable and the canons of philosophic tradition which we must all respect.

In writing this text and choosing these selections, I have been guided by the following general considerations.

An introductory course should be *really* introductory and not terminal. A beginning course or textbook that tries to exhaust the field or to be ridiculously systematic is certain to repel or discourage the student. My aim, therefore, has been to whet the appetite, not sate it. This makes it possible to include selections which ask questions as well as answer them.

An introduction to philosophy should not be dogmatic or sectarian but presentational. Thus the important philosophical positions are reflected in this book, but few of them are either hotly defended or absolutely rejected. This approach is inevitable in a text which takes philosophy to be a reflection upon the *varieties* of human experience.

In this work the readings bear the main burden of the presentation. The great philosophers have the mellowest voice; why should they not speak? The text introduces the problems and the possibilities, but even the elementary student has the right to the undiluted beverage. Another way of saying this is that I believe in philosophical baptism not by sprinkling but by complete immersion.

It is difficult to put so much in so little space, but I have tried in the text to avoid too great condensation. Philosophizing demands time, and I have here and there tried to indicate this by a certain leisureliness of style. But sometimes, too, the pace is brisk. Such lack of uniformity reflects the simple fact that minds function moodily and not mechanically.

ALBERT WILLIAM LEVI

St. Louis, 1956

Contents

VARIETIES
OF
EXPERIENCE

CHAPTER 1

The Philosophic Enterprise

Philosophy is a discipline which has had a long and complicated history. Like science and art, historiography and religion, it goes back to the earliest times of recorded thought. It is a constant and, indeed, an indispensable feature of human culture.

But because of its antiquity, and because throughout its evolution its greatest exponents have been men of such different interests and capacities, it is difficult to find a simple formula which covers their diverse contributions. Some philosophers like Plato, Aristotle, Kant, and Hegel have been professional teachers who have made their living from their work. Some like Auguste Comte and Arthur Schopenhauer were connected with the academic world but not actually in it, either because they scorned it, or were unable to receive an appointment. Still others, like Socrates and Spinoza, have been amateurs by inclination, consciously and purposefully refusing to earn their living by teaching the ideas which were their main concern.

Similarly, philosophers have differed widely in the interests which have carried them into philosophy. Thomas Aquinas, Dominican friar of the thirteenth century, George Berkeley, bishop of the Irish Church in the eighteenth century, and Søren Kierkegaard, Danish divinity student in the nineteenth—all saw philosophy as the means to prove the truths of religion, to dispel the materialism which in their opinion resulted in atheism, and thereby to lead men's hearts to God. Others, like Pythagoras in the ancient world, René Descartes in the late Renaissance, and Bertrand Russell today, have been primarily mathematicians whose view of human knowledge and the universe has been vastly influenced by the concept of numbers and by the methods of deductive thinking. Some, like Protagoras, Thomas Hobbes, and John Stuart Mill, have been interested

1

in problems of social living and of politics, so that whatever else they have done in philosophy has been stimulated by a desire to understand the actions of men and the motives of their political behavior. Still others like Thales (the earliest Greek thinker of whom we know), the Elizabethan Francis Bacon, and in our own time Alfred North Whitehead, have begun with an interest in physical nature and have made their philosophies into something more closely allied to the natural sciences than to religion or society. How is it possible to find among these philosophers a single impulse or a single defining characteristic which covers the diversity of their interests and concerns?

If one looks for some simple content or subject matter common to them all, the search will not be rewarding. And even if one were to have all the great philosophers of past times by some miracle restored to life and standing before one, and then, like Socrates, were to question them: "And what then is philosophy?," they would answer in a chorus of conflicting voices, and perhaps no two answers would be exactly alike.

For "philosophy" is like the elephant in the ancient story, and "philosophers" are somewhat like the blind men who cannot see it as a whole, but who hold onto some one part and from this vantage point seek to describe the total beast. The man who has philosophy by the nose says: "Philosophy tries to provide us with a system of ultimate truths about the world—a complete set of general ideas applicable to all branches of our experience." The man who has philosophy by the feet says: "Philosophy is not the contemplation by pure intellects of their own abstract nature. It is the search for principles which are useful in a vigorous practical life." The man who has philosophy by the tail says: "Philosophy unlike science, has no business with facts. It can help us to analyze our meanings and perhaps to find the ultimate premises upon which all of our scientific knowledge rests. But that is all." The man who has philosophy by the ears says: "Philosophy is an attempt to deal with those difficult matters which are of the very deepest human concern: What are our reasons for living? How ought we to act? What can we ultimately hope for in our lives and after?" And the nose, feet, tail, and ears are only a few parts of the elephant!

Every attempt to define philosophy at the outset has two aspects. On the one hand, it seeks to explain what philosophers have done throughout the history of philosophy; it seeks to describe the philosophic past. And on the other hand, it tries to tell philosophers what they ought to do when they philosophize properly; it seeks to give a rule for the future. The dangers of both aspects are apparent. It is that of defining philosophy too narrowly so that the definition does not account for the many interests of philosophers in the past, or that it unduly restricts the activity of philosophers in the future. The best thing here (if define one must) is to risk the error of vagueness by being too broad rather than to strive for accuracy and leave out something important.

But there is an even easier way out of the difficulty. If we wish to know what an apple is, we do not look into a dictionary for its "definition," into the Bible for its symbolic meanings, or at a painting of Cézanne for its shape and color. We bite into it. Fortunately with philosophy we may do the same. This book is furnished with many examples of philosophers going about their business and philosophizing: John Stuart Mill presenting the "Evidence for A God"; Plato telling us about "Political Obligation"; F. H. Bradley asking "Why Should I Be Moral?"; William James trying to make sense out of "The Dilemma of Determinism." To consider the evidence for the existence of God, to examine the nature of our political obligations, to ask what is the rationale of moral behavior, and to consider in what sense human activity is free are examples of philosophical activity. Indeed, the selections which make up the greater part of this book together form a good denotative definition of philosophy. And to read them is to learn about philosophy not by description but by direct acquaintance. It is, so to speak, "biting into it."

Nevertheless, if one were to ask, "What is that quality which all of these examples share in common?," it would be possible to give an answer. *They are all examples of the activity of serious and able men reflecting upon, meditating, reasoning about, and considering deeply the nature of their experience.*

All philosophy begins with experience. We study science, fall in love, are called by our country to fight in its wars, hear beautiful music, attend church, read history, observe the plants and animals in nature. And, if we do not merely let these things happen to us like someone living in a dream, when the experience has passed the first absorbed and unconscious phase, we begin to question. What is the nature of the energy which composes the physical world? What is the meaning of the fact that people are blinded by "feeling"? What exactly does a man owe to his country? What is there in the music that makes us call it beautiful? Is it true that the God whom we worship is both completely perfect and all-powerful? Does history have a direction: is it going somewhere? Are the plants and animals in nature accidents or do their structures express some natural plan?

It is true that much of our experience is unreflective. It happens to us and we think no more about it. But in those who not only have experiences but reflect upon them, ponder them, try to make sense out of them, there is a philosophic impulse at work. *The activity which we call philosophizing is simply a reflecting upon experience.*

PHILOSOPHY AND EXPERIENCE

From this fact two very interesting consequences follow. The first is that unlike the sciences and the arts, philosophy has no specific subject matter of its own, but draws its materials from all the arts and sciences. It is not difficult to distinguish between physics, the study of radiant energy, and biology, the study of the function and structure of living organisms. Nor between political science, which studies the composition and incidence of power, and sociology, which studies the forms of human association. Nor between the music which delights when it is heard and the painting which delights when it is seen. These arts and sciences are each unique and separable from one another. But each one can be a source of philosophic reflection. Each one can contribute problems which philosophers attempt to solve.

Before there can be philosophy, there must be experience. And it must be the kind of experience which is immediately and directly presented to our consciousness. A deep reverence for God is not the philosophy of religion, but it may become, as in the case of St. Thomas Aquinas, the origin of a philosophy of religion. Profound knowledge of the facts of physical science is not the philosophy of science, but, as in the case of Alfred North Whitehead, it may be the foundation of a philosophy of science. A dedicated appreciation of works of art is not the philosophy of art, but it may, as in the case of George Santayana, be the source of a philosophy of art. The difference between religion and the philosophy of religion, or between art and the philosophy of art, is a difference between a direct or primary experience and a reflective or secondary experience in which the mind returns to a consideration of that which it has first experienced without reflection.

Long ago the great Greek philosopher Aristotle said that a young man is not a fit student of moral philosophy. Perhaps what he meant was that a young man has not lived long enough to have much moral experience or much appreciation of life's deeper ethical problems. He has not yet been faced with those serious moral choices which have to do with commitment to a vocation or the founding of a family or facing death in battle. Therefore his goodness, if good he is, is the result of good training and the early formation of good habits. But to be able to philosophize about morality, one must have had considerable contact with real moral situations.

It is perhaps the same with philosophy as a whole. Since it is a secondary experience, it is not likely to be of vital concern unless one has had some of the primary experiences upon which it reflects. If you are completely uninterested in art, it is unlikely that aesthetics will interest you. If you have little acquaintance with the facts of history, you will probably not be much concerned with the meaning and significance of historical processes. If you have no knowledge of politics and society, it is not probable that you will be interested in the proper relations of the state and its citizens or in the philosophy behind our civil liberties. Still, Aristotle's comment on the inadvisability of the young man's study of moral philosophy must be accepted only with qualifications, and to extend it to the field of philosophy in general would be a mistake. Surely there is no greater difficulty in teaching than presenting the student with all the answers, or a large variety of answers, before he himself has asked the questions. It is unlikely that those without experience will already have asked all the philosophic questions, but the mere opportunity to observe the questions which philosophers ask and their attempts at an answer may stimulate them to ask the same questions for themselves, and even perhaps to seek those primary experiences through which the answers may be suggested.

Philosophy, then, has this particular virtue: the more experience one accumulates, the more one has to speculate upon, and since our experiences continue until our death, the materials of philosophy grow richer with time. And this is why philosophy itself from the days of Thales has continued to ask the questions and to engage the minds of men. It is not only that philosophers make important statements about life and the operations of the mind and the universe. It is also that there are certain persistent problems of philosophy which are never definitively answered just because experience never comes to an end and because the human condition always suggests some questions which are inexhaustible to meditation. Anyone who wishes to pursue the philosophic enterprise may do so. It requires only a meditative cast of mind and the impulse to reflect upon the nature of human experience.

Of course it would be foolish to pretend that being reflective by nature is sufficient to turn one into a Plato or an Aristotle, a Spinoza or a Kant. But that is less perhaps a matter of inherent genius than of concentration. Above all it is a matter of time. Philosophizing takes time!

The society of Europe in the Middle Ages was divided into distinct classes with separate and distinct functions: the nobility, whose duty it was to fight and protect; the serfs and villeins, whose duty it was to work; and the clergy, whose duty it was to pray and to think. For the clergy were not only the religious leaders, but the custodians of learning, and it was they who constructed the picture of the world by which that age lived.

It is less congenial for us in the modern world with our democratic point of view to believe that there is a single class whose function it is to rule society, or a single class whose function it is to think for society. And yet the last is partly true. Our own society too has its necessary division of labor. Every man is not his own architect, his own lawyer, or his own physician. Neither is he necessarily his own poet, his own historian, or his own philosopher. For, just as there is a division of labor within business and the practical professions, so there is a division of labor within the arts and sciences. Therefore there is a sense in which T. S. Eliot, William Carlos Williams, and W. H. Auden and, of course, others are the poets who speak for the modern world. For who has time to be his own poet? And similarly, men like John Dewey, Bertrand Russell, and George Santayana are the philosophers who speak for us. For who has time to be his own philosopher? These are the men who express our perplexities, who reflect upon our age, who have taken the time to create the world views by which it is possible for modern men to order their lives. And in general, philosophers are the men whom a society sets apart to reflect upon its experiences— to spend their lifetime in constructing or discovering the images of meaning and aspiration by which the rest may live.

Nevertheless, there is an important sense in which every man must be his own philosopher, just as in a democratic society citizens exercise political choice and make political decisions even if they do not actively engage in politics or hold political office. For every man must live his own life in a universe which he did not create, in conflict with obstacles against which he must constantly push, and he must make choices and decisions which exhibit his values and appeal to his preferences. If our lives are not to be merely mindless, and if we refuse to permit our actions to be simply the result of drifting or the spineless acceptance of the values of others, then we must come to some conclusion about the values which we wish to prevail and the nature of the universe in which we live. Such conclusions are bound to be philosophical.

THE VARIETIES OF EXPERIENCE

If philosophizing is, indeed, but "a reflecting upon experience," then the more systematic body of writings which make up our philosophical heritage can be viewed in its totality as a critical review of the forms of human experience. And, since these writings have certain subdivisions and have been classified traditionally in certain ways, one might expect that these divisions would give us some clue to the divisions within experience itself. For "experience" is a huge and all-inclusive term, as big as life, and almost as confusing. How is it philosophically possible to give some order and organization to this concept?

The greatest Christian philosopher of the early Middle Ages was St. Augustine. And in his writings there is a passage in which he maps the geography of the universe. The totality of it all, he says, is divided into three parts. First, there is the realm of things below man, the realm of rocks and trees, mountains and rivers, climate and weather, plants and animals. This world would exist and be itself even if human individuals had never come into existence. We call it *Nature*.

Second, there is the realm of things on the level of man. This is the realm where man participates and whose character is given by his activities and his interests. It is the realm of family life, of social activity, of the political state and its laws. It is the realm in which men enjoy moral responsibility, create and appreciate beautiful objects, where they write and consider their own history. These activities may take place within a physical world, but they follow from the nature of man. They belong to the level of *the Human*.

Third, there is the realm of things above man. This is the realm of God in his perfect and all-powerful nature, of his acts and of the events which follow from his will. It is the realm of the saints, the domain of immortality, the transcendental universe of the values of truth, goodness, and beauty, not as these enter into human experience but as they may be in their own nature, guaranteed and authorized by God. This is the realm of *the Divine*.

The experience of *Nature*, the experience of *the Human*, the experience of *the Divine*, provide the first great demarcation of the map of experience, and, whether or not we agree with St. Augustine about the importance and the reality of all of these three areas of experience, they have surely been the subjects of the most intensive philosophic reflection. In fact, it has been customary even to distinguish the major philosophical positions or points of view according to which of these three areas forms their primary interest or, more exactly, whether they take one of these areas as ultimate and interpret the others in its terms. Thus, following the sense of Augustine's division, we may distinguish all philosophers roughly as (1) naturalists, (2) humanists, or (3) supernaturalists.

The concept of "Nature" is one of the most venerable ideas in the philosophical tradition of the Western world. The earliest Greek speculations about the physical world with the coming of age of science turned into controlled investigation of the forces operative within nature. Thus it is no accident that an interest in nature has become associated with the methods of inquiry which are used today in the observational and experimental natural sciences. One of the chief characteristics of naturalism as a philosophic point of view is its sympathy with the scientific method.

But the second and certainly most important character of naturalism is its effort either to reduce the other realms of experience to parts of nature, or to deny their validity. If the idea of a supernatural realm of being means that there is a form of experience which is not reachable by ordinary men using the methods of science, then the naturalist must deny that a supernatural realm of being exists. He would admit that men have an "idea" of God, but hold that this idea corresponds to nothing "real," much, indeed, as the great psychiatrist Sigmund Freud held that religion is a delusion —practically a neurotic symptom! Similarly in his treatment of the realm of the human, the naturalist tends to see man not as a creature uniquely outside of nature, but as a part of nature, living its life, subject to its laws, related to its other parts. The naturalist sees man's qualities as continuous with those of all animal life, and his special functions and abilities as simply the last and most elevated which have emerged from the seething creativity of nature.

Humanists in philosophy are those who take their point of departure from human nature and from man's unique activities. They consider human culture with its institutions, associations, arts, and sciences as the central philosophic fact, and they interpret all experience as the outgrowth of human need and human creation.

Humanists do not deny that there is a realm which is called "Nature," but, believing with the ancient Greek philosopher Protagoras that "Man is the measure of all things," they say that the concept of "Nature" is something which man himself has constructed, and they are interested in nature less for itself than for the ways in which it may be controlled, and its forces harnessed for human purposes. The humanistic point of view is not necessarily antiscientific, although it has sometimes been so in former ages, but it is mistrustful of all attempts to turn man into one of the "things" in nature. As Emerson has it:

> There are two laws discrete
> Not reconciled,—
> Law for man, and law for thing;
> The last builds town and fleet,
> But it runs wild,
> And doth the man unking.

Nor does the humanistic point of view deny the realm of religion. Only, it sees religion less as a clue to ultimate reality than as the expression of a stubborn human need, and it views the striving for a common faith as something inherent in the nature of man. This is the way that Dostoevski has Ivan express it in *The Brothers Karamazov:*

So long as man remains free he strives for nothing so incessantly and so painfully as to find some one to worship. But man seeks to worship what is established beyond dispute, so that all men would agree at once to worship it. For these pitiful creatures are concerned not only to find what one or the other can worship, but to find something that all would believe in and worship; what is essential is that all may be *together* in it. This craving for *community* of worship is the chief misery of every man individually and of all humanity from the beginning of time.

The point of view of the philosophical supernaturalist is most clearly expressed in the desire to understand and appreciate the divine nature, and it therefore produces works which are devoted to theology. St. Augustine's own work and that of St. Thomas Aquinas are of this kind. But here again, such an interest does not deny either a realm of nature or a realm of human activity. In the treatise on law which forms a small part of St. Thomas's great *Summa Theologica* he discourses and argues concerning the law of God, and in so doing he relates it both to human law and to what he calls the law of nature. Both of these are taken as realities, but as expressions of and subordinate to the law of God. When the supernaturalist considers nature, it is frequently a nature which is symbolic of powers which lie outside and transcend its own province. For him nature primarily testifies to the goodness and the power of its creator. And it is the same with man. His humanity the supernaturalist does not deny. But he finds man's importance to lie in the fact that he is a creature of God. In the drama of human choice and human accomplishment he finds the constant expression of divine purpose.

Naturalism, humanism, and supernaturalism are far from being tight categories of philosophy. But if one takes them as standpoints or attitudes toward experience, then they do in some sense conflict with one another. If, on the other hand, one takes them as an interest in different areas of experience (Nature, Man, God), then, indeed, one sees that they have been the enduring objects of philosophical reflection, and any account of what philosophy has been and can be must include them all.

This book is not written from the standpoint of either naturalism, humanism, or supernaturalism. Its function is not persuasive but presentational. If its materials seem drawn more largely from the area of the human, that is because such materials provide perhaps the best introduction to philosophy as a whole.

Nature, the Human, the Divine provide only a rough classification of experience. In nature and in the human there are multiple divisions, and it is these divisions which have given to philosophy its specific fields. The chart on page 11 tries to relate the area of experience, the field of philosophy which deals with it, and the chapter in this book devoted to that subject.

Characteristics of Philosophic Reflection

One of the great classics in the history of philosophizing is Plato's *Republic*. It is a long book and it is written in the form of a dialogue or discussion in which Socrates has the leading role. Sometimes the argument seems to wander or digress, but always miraculously it returns to the main thread. But this main thread is a curious one. It starts narrowly with a simple question: What do we really mean when we call a man "just"? But by the time we have come two-thirds through the book, we have arrived at the terribly broad and perplexing question: Of everything in the universe, what things are most real? When one looks back, one sees that the argument has progressed by reasonable and logical steps. Who is the just man? The man who lives in a just state. What is a just state? The state which has wise rulers. How are the rulers of a state made wise? By good education. What is a good education? Education which gives knowledge about things which are ultimately most valuable and most real. What things are ultimately most valuable and most real? And so, from a simple, specific, and fairly concrete issue we have pushed forward the argument further and further toward a complex, general, and fairly abstract conclusion. And, as we have done so, we have progressively brought more and more areas into the discussion: first ethics, then politics, then educational theory, then theory of knowledge, and finally metaphysics. This is one typical method of philosophic reflection.

	AREA OF EXPERIENCE	FIELD OF PHILOSOPHY	CHAPTER
	The Knowing Process	Epistemology or Methodology	2
Nature	Matter in Motion Living Things	Philosophy of Nature or Philosophy of Science	3
Nature	Mind The Universe As a Whole	Metaphysics or Cosmology	4
Man	Individual Decision	Ethics	5
Man	Social Living	Social Philosophy	6
Man	The Arts	Aesthetics	7
Man	History	Philosophy of History	8
God	God	Philosophy of Religion	9

One of the great classics of contemporary philosophy is the *Principia Ethica* of the late British philosopher G. E. Moore. This book is considerably shorter than the *Republic* and it is not written in dialogue form, but it too follows a line of reasoning. But Moore's method is almost the exact opposite of Plato's. He begins with the very general question: What is good? And he shows at once that the question is highly ambiguous. It can mean: (1) What individual things are good? (2) What is the list of human virtues (like courage or temperance or charity)? or (3) How can "good" be defined? Moore then accepts meaning (3), and goes on to point out that the word "definition" is also ambiguous. For example, "definition" could mean (1) an arbitrary stipulated definition, (2) a dictionary or customary definition, or (3) a real or descriptive definition. He then accepts meaning (3) and passes on to further consider the difference between "good" and "the good." And so the book continues, at each step analyzing meanings more and more minutely, growing narrower and narrower, but with the most modest sincerity striving for always greater clarity and precision. To one who has not read Moore in the original but only followed my account, his method may seem hair-splitting and tedious, but it too is one of the typical modes of philosophic reflection.

It is a matter of common experience that ordinary arguments very often follow either the method of Plato or of G. E. Moore. Sometimes they begin with a very specific subject, but this leads to something broader and more inclusive until finally we end up discussing the total nature of life or of the universe. At other times they begin with some argument which hinges upon the vagueness or ambiguity of the question or its terms, and then we try to analyze meanings, make distinctions, and in general bring some clarity into the controversy. And as we grow clearer, we are forced more and more to restrict the scope of our discussion.

It is not surprising that ordinary arguments often follow one of these two patterns. For the method of Plato and the method of G. E. Moore represent two different but universal and recurrent characteristics of philosophic reflection. On the one hand, there is a great philosophic impulse toward wholeness or completeness which causes us to try to bring together as much of our experience as we can, to unify it, to make it one thing. And on the other hand, there is a great philosophic impulse toward getting down to the part, isolating and examining it so that we may be absolutely certain and clear about this one thing at least.

The philosophic impulse toward wholeness and unity is very closely akin to the human desire to make sense out of diverse experiences by somehow making connections between them. But it is not so much making connection as one would connect two points by a straight line on a drafting board as it is as one would collect together in a basket a whole group of different kinds of mushrooms in the forest.

The historian who says, "In 220 B.C. the Chinese built a great wall and in A.D. 410 the Goths captured Rome," puzzles us for he seems to be saying nothing significant. Rome is far from China and six hundred years separate the two events. But when he goes on to tell us that this wall kept the Vandal hordes from expanding eastward and forced them in the other direction until finally after centuries they were actually at the gates of Rome, we understand perfectly. But this is not the way the philosopher makes connections. His procedure is better illustrated by Schopenhauer.

Schopenhauer asked: What is the real inner nature of *everything* which we experience in the universe? And he answered: Every force in nature, every impulsion, every activity, every movement is an expression of *Will*. The waters hurrying to the ocean are an expression of will, the magnet drawing its iron filings, the force of gravitation, the movement of plants toward the sun, the search of animals for food, the contraction of the pupil of the eye, the desire to reproduce, the crystal forming itself layer by layer, the instinct of wasps and bees, the nesting of birds; all these are aspects of a single thing—Will. It is not necessary to agree with Schopenhauer. It is only important to see that his efforts were one kind of philosophic reflection—the kind which strives for unity and wholeness, the kind which tries to relate all things to one another.

The impulse for unity and wholeness seems to spring from a very important capacity of the human mind; the ability to see that things which seem very different are really very much alike, perhaps even the same. This was Schopenhauer's genius, that, in the diverse manifestations of nature, he could find one single principle at work.

But the impulse to be clear and accurate seems to spring from just the reverse capacity of the mind; the ability to distinguish and to discriminate—the ability to see that things which seem much alike, even identical, are after all often very different. An average man looks at the following sentences:

1. Napoleon *is* Buonaparte.
2. God *is*.
3. A bird *is* a vertebrate.
4. Grass *is* green.
5. To weep *is* to be sad.

And he notices that they are all alike in that each contains the word
is. But any trained logician will tell you at once that in each of
these sentences the verb *is* performs a very different function and
has a very different meaning. In (1) *is* expresses *identity*, in (2)
it expresses *existence*, in (3) *class membership*, in (4) a *quality*, in
(5) *implication*. And when one senses this, one can change the
sentences into the different propositions they really are.

1. Napoleon and Buonaparte are identical.
2. God exists.
3. Birds belong to the class of vertebrates.
4. Grass has the quality of greenness.
5. Weeping implies being sad.

Such discriminations, based upon the ability to distinguish difference in apparent likeness and to gain therefrom in clarity and exacti-
tude is a second characteristic of philosophic reflection.

The two examples of philosophic reflection referred to were
Plato's *Republic* and G. E. Moore's *Principia Ethica*. The discussion
in the former starts with the question: What is justice? The discussion in the latter starts with the question: What is good? Although
their methods are so different, both Plato and G. E. Moore begin
with questions which are of the very greatest importance, which
would be of concern to every human individual. This is a third
characteristic of philosophic reflection—that it deals with those issues
which humanly matter most.

The brilliant German philosopher Immanuel Kant in the eighteenth century formulated the great philosophical questions: What
can I know? What ought I to do? What can I hope for? Other
philosophers may formulate them differently but sooner or later one
returns to them: What are the extensions and the limitations of
human knowledge? What things are ultimately of greatest value,
and how can they be maximized in human conduct? Is the universe
as a whole hostile or friendly to the purposes by which I rule my
life and is my death meaningless as well as inevitable?

The philosopher may be skilled in organizing experience, in analyzing assumptions, and in refining meanings, but sooner or later he
must return to consider the facts of our human condition. Men are
born not by their own free will. They live in a world of suffering.
Their dearest enterprises are subject to the whims of chance and
the accidents of misfortune. They are lonely and try in vain to make
contact with their fellows. Much of what they do is attended by
guilt. And in the end they die. These are the moments which provide the great questions. And to these questions also philosophy
devotes itself.

This does not mean that philosophy can provide dogmatic answers to all the true questions which it itself raises. It is true that, if one were to examine Kant's philosophy as a whole, one would find that he had, indeed, answered the three questions which he had asked. *What can I know?* I can know appearances—things as they seem, not what they really are. *What ought I to do?* Why, I ought to do my duty as is required of any reasonable and moral man. *What can I hope for?* I can hope that if I have been morally good (but not particularly fortunate) I may be rewarded by immortality.

But no one has believed either that Kant has answered the great questions once and for all, or that his answers are not themselves grounds for still further questions. There must always be a tentativeness about the answers to the great questions, a sense that perhaps the answer to some of them is beyond our powers, that we cannot hope to reach final conclusions. Nevertheless, if philosophers did not attempt to deal with them, their work would be unimportant. For mere clarity is hardly a virtue if the things about which we are clear are trivial.

Philosophical reflections, as the examples in this book will show, are as broad and diverse as the minds of men. But they all exhibit one or more of these characteristics: (1) They try to relate things in a fashion which will express the sense of wholeness or connectedness, (2) they try to refine meanings and analyze assumptions so as to produce the greatest accuracy and clarity, and (3) they raise just those questions of meaning and value which are of the greatest human importance.

The following selections, "Why Philosophize" by William James and "Critical and Speculative Thought" by C. D. Broad are written by modern philosophers who have lived and worked within the past seventy years. Both of them have made important contributions to modern philosophy although their temperaments and interests have been very different. There are many different views of the nature of the philosophic enterprise. Those of James and Broad have been included because they represent an interesting opposition of views. And yet, strangely enough, there is a certain basic agreement between them. Broad's central distinction between critical and speculative thought almost exactly parallels James's two philosophic impulses—the desire for unity and the desire for clearness. That two such diverse minds agree in this matter gives added weight to the account of philosophy which they propose.

• William James (1842–1910)

Why Philosophize?[1]

William James, one of the best loved of American philosophers, taught most of his life at Harvard. Along with C. S. Peirce he is a founder of the most influential American school of philosophy—"Pragmatism." Although James was trained as a physician and wrote one of the most influential modern treatises on psychology, his ultimate interests were always humanistic rather than scientific. He therefore views philosophy as the product less of cold thought than of intellectual passion. The clearness and simplicity which the philosopher seeks are for him warm human needs, and he sees philosophy as the satisfaction of a "craving" rather than as the impersonal spectator attitude at work. James always has great sympathy for emotion and the part which it plays in human life. He too agrees that philosophy is not a substitute for direct experience. *The Will To Believe, Pragmatism,* and *The Varieties of Religious Experience* are among the most important of his writings.

What is the task which philosophers set themselves to perform; and why do they philosophize at all? Almost every one will immediately reply: They desire to attain a conception of the frame of things which shall on the whole be more rational than that somewhat chaotic view which every one by nature carries about with him under his hat. But suppose this rational conception attained, how is the philosopher to recognize it for what it is, and not let it slip through ignorance? The only answer can be that he will recognize its rationality as he recognizes everything else, by certain subjective marks with which it affects him. When he gets the marks, he may know that he has got the rationality.

What, then, are the marks? A strong feeling of ease, peace, rest, is one of them. The transition from a state of puzzle and perplexity to rational comprehension is full of lively relief and pleasure.

But this relief seems to be a negative rather than a positive character. Shall we then say that the feeling of rationality is constituted merely by the absence of any feeling of irrationality? I think there

[1] From "The Sentiment of Rationality" (1896), published in *The Will to Believe.*

are very good grounds for upholding such a view. All feeling whatever, in the light of certain recent psychological speculations, seems to depend for its physical condition not on simple discharge of nerve-currents, but on their discharge under arrest, impediment, or resistance. Just as we feel no particular pleasure when we breathe freely, but a very intense feeling of distress when the respiratory motions are prevented—so any unobstructed tendency to action discharges itself without the production of much cogitative accompaniment, and any perfectly fluent course of thought awakens but little feeling; but when the movement is inhibited, or when the thought meets with difficulties, we experience distress. It is only when the distress is upon us that we can be said to strive, to crave, or to aspire. When enjoying plenary freedom either in the way of motion or of thought, we are in a sort of anaesthetic state in which we might say with Walt Whitman, if we cared to say anything about ourselves at such times, "I am sufficient as I am." This feeling of the sufficiency of the present moment, of its absoluteness—this absence of all need to explain it, account for it, or justify it—is what I call the Sentiment of Rationality. As soon, in short, as we are enabled from any cause whatever to think with perfect fluency, the thing we think of seems to us *pro tanto* rational.

Whatever modes of conceiving the cosmos facilitate this fluency, produce the sentiment of rationality. Conceived in such modes, being vouches for itself and needs no further philosophic formulation. But this fluency may be obtained in various ways; and first I will take up the theoretic way.

The facts of the world in their sensible diversity are always before us, but our theoretic need is that they should be conceived in a way that reduces their manifoldness to simplicity. Our pleasure at finding that a chaos of facts is the expression of a single underlying fact is like the relief of the musician at resolving a confused mass of sound into melodic or harmonic order. The simplified result is handled with far less mental effort than the original data; and a philosophic conception of nature is thus in no metaphorical sense a labor-saving contrivance. The passion for parsimony, for economy of means in thought, is the philosophic passion *par excellence;* and any character or aspect of the world's phenomena which gathers up their diversity into monotony will gratify that passion, and in the philosopher's mind stand for that essence of things compared with which all their other determinations may by him be overlooked.

More universality or extensiveness is, then, one mark which the philosopher's conception must possess. Unless they apply to an enormous number of cases they will not bring him relief. The

knowledge of things by their causes, which is often given as a definition of rational knowledge, is useless to him unless the causes con-
verge to a minimum number, while still producing the maximum
number of effects. The more multiple then are the instances, the
more flowingly does his mind rove from fact to fact. The phenomenal transitions are no real transitions; each item is the same old
friend with a slightly altered dress.

Who does not feel the charm of thinking that the moon and the
apple are, as far as their relation to the earth goes, identical; of
knowing respiration and combustion to be one; of understanding
that the balloon rises by the same law whereby the stone sinks; of
feeling that the warmth in one's palm when one rubs one's sleeve
is identical with the motion which the friction checks; of recognizing the difference between beast and fish to be only a higher degree
of that between human father and son; of believing our strength
when we climb the mountain or fell the tree to be no other than
the strength of the sun's rays which made the corn grow out of which
we got our morning meal?

But alongside of this passion for simplification there exists a sis-
ter passion, which in some minds—though they perhaps form the
minority—is its rival. This is the passion for distinguishing; it is the
impulse to be *acquainted* with the parts rather than to comprehend
the whole. Loyalty to clearness and integrity of perception, dislike
of blurred outlines, of vague identifications, are its characteristics.
It loves to recognize particulars in their full completeness, and the
more of these it can carry, the happier it is. It prefers any amount
of incoherence, abruptness, and fragmentariness (so long as the literal details of the separate facts are saved) to an abstract way of
conceiving things that, while it simplifies them, dissolves away at the
same time their concrete fulness. Clearness and simplicity thus set
up rival claims, and make a real dilemma for the thinker.

A man's philosophic attitude is determined by the balance in him
of these two cravings. No system of philosophy can hope to be
universally accepted among men which grossly violates either need,
or entirely subordinates the one to the other. The fate of Spinoza,
with his barren union of all things in one substance, on the one hand;
that of Hume, with his equally barren "looseness and separateness"
of everything, on the other—neither philosopher owning any strict
and systematic disciples today, each being to posterity a warning
as well as a stimulus—show us that the only possible philosophy
must be a compromise between an abstract monotony and a concrete heterogeneity. But the only way to mediate between diversity
and unity is to class the diverse items as cases of a common essence

which you discover in them. Classification of things into extensive "kinds" is thus the first step; and classification of their relations and conduct into extensive "laws" is the last step, in their philosophic unification. A completed theoretic philosophy can thus never be anything more than a completed classification of the world's ingredients; and its results must always be abstract, since the basis of every classification is the abstract essence embedded in the living fact—the rest of the living fact being for the time ignored by the classifier. This means that none of our explanations are complete. They subsume things under heads wider or more familiar; but the last heads, whether of things or of their connections, are mere abstract genera, data which we just find in things and write down.

When, for example, we think that we have rationally explained the connection of the facts A and B by classing both under their common attribute x, it is obvious that we have really explained only so much of these items as is x. To explain the connection of choke-damp and suffocation by the lack of oxygen is to leave untouched all the other peculiarities both of choke-damp and of suffocation—such as convulsions and agony on the one hand, density and explosibility on the other. In a word, so far as A and B contain l, m, n, and o, p, q, respectively, in addition to x, they are not explained by x. Each additional particularity makes its distinct appeal. A single explanation of a fact only explains it from a single point of view. The entire fact is not accounted for until each and all of its characters have been classed with their likes elsewhere. To apply this now to the case of the universe, we see that the explanation of the world by molecular movements explains it only so far as it actually is such movements. To invoke the "Unknowable" explains only so much as is unknowable, "Thought" only so much as is thought, "God" only so much as is God. $Which$ thought? $Which$ God?—are questions that have to be answered by bringing in again the residual data from which the general term was abstracted. All those data that cannot be analytically identified with the attribute invoked as universal principle, remain as independent kinds or natures, associated empirically with the said attribute but devoid of rational kinship with it.

Hence the unsatisfactoriness of all our speculations. On the one hand, so far as they retain any multiplicity in their terms, they fail to get us out of the empirical sand-heap world; on the other, so far as they eliminate multiplicity, the practical man despises their empty barrenness. The most they can say is that the elements of the world are such and such, and that each is identical with itself wherever found; but the question Where is it found? the practical man is left to answer by his own wit. Which, of all the essences, shall here and now be held the essence of this concrete thing, the fundamental philosophy never attempts to decide. We are thus led to the conclusion that the simple classification of things is, on the one hand, the best possible theoretic philosophy, but is, on the other, a most miserable and inadequate substitute for the fulness of the truth. It is a monstrous abridgment of life, which, like all all abridgments, is got by the absolute loss and casting out of real matter. This is why so few human beings truly care for philosophy. The particular determinations which she ignores are the real matter exciting needs, quite as potent and authoritative as hers. What does the moral enthusiast care for philosophical ethics? Why does the *Aesthetik* of every German philosopher appear to the artist an abomination of desolation?

> Grau, teurer Freund, ist alle Theorie
> Und grün des Lebens goldner Baum.

The entire man, who feels all needs by turns, will take nothing as an equivalent for life but the fulness of living itself. Since the essences of things are as a matter of fact disseminated through the whole extent of time and space, it is in their spread-outness and alternation that he will enjoy them. When weary of the concrete clash and dust and pettiness, he will refresh himself by a bath in the eternal springs, or fortify himself by a look at the immutable natures. But he will only be a visitor, not a dweller, in the region; he will never carry the philosophic yoke upon his shoulders, and when tired of the gray monotony of her problems and insipid spaciousness of her results, will always escape gleefully into the teeming and dramatic richness of the concrete world.

So our study turns back here to its beginning. Every way of classifying a thing is but a way of handling it for some particular purpose. Conceptions, "kinds," are teleological instruments. No abstract concept can be a valid substitute for a concrete reality except with reference to a particular interest in the conceiver. The interest of theoretic rationality, the relief of identification, is but one of a thousand human purposes. When others rear their heads, it must pack up its little bundle and retire till its turn recurs. The exaggerated dignity and value that philosophers have claimed for their solutions is thus greatly reduced. The only virtue their theoretic conception need have is simplicity, and a simple conception is an equivalent for the world only so far as the world is simple— the world meanwhile, whatever simplicity it may harbor, being also a mightily complex affair. Enough simplicity remains, however, and enough urgency in our craving to reach it, to make the theoretic function one of the most invincible of human impulses. The quest of the fewest elements of things is an ideal that some will follow, as long as there are men to think at all.

But suppose the goal attained. Suppose that at last we have a system unified in the sense that has been explained. Our world can now be conceived simply, and our mind enjoys the relief. Our universal concept has made the concrete chaos rational. But now I ask, Can that which is the ground of rationality in all else be itself properly called rational? It would seem at first sight that it might. One is tempted at any rate to say that, since the craving for rationality is appeased by the identification of one thing with another, a datum which left nothing else outstanding might quench that craving definitively, or be rational *in se*. No otherness being left to annoy us, we should sit down at peace. In other words, as the theoretic tranquillity of the boor results from his spinning no further considerations about his chaotic universe, so any datum whatever (provided it were simple, clear, and ultimate) ought to banish puzzle from the universe of the philosopher and confer peace, inasmuch as there would then be for him absolutely no further considerations to spin.

This in fact is what some persons think. Professor Bain says—

A difficulty is solved, a mystery unriddled, when it can be shown to resemble something else; to be an example of a fact already known. Mystery is isolation, exception, or it may be apparent contradiction: the resolution of the mystery is found in assimilation, identity, fraternity. When all things are assimilated, so far as assimilation can go, so far as likeness holds, there is an end to explanation; there is an end to what the mind can do, or can intelligently desire . . . The path of science as exhibited in modern ages is toward generality, wider and wider, until we reach the highest, the widest laws of every department of things; there explanation is finished, mystery ends, perfect vision is gained.

But, unfortunately, this first answer will not hold. Our mind is so wedded to the process of seeing an *other* beside every item of its experience, that when the notion of an absolute datum is presented to it, it goes through its usual procedure and remains pointing at the void beyond, as if in that lay further matter for contemplation. In short, it spins for itself the further positive consideration of a nonentity enveloping the being of its datum; and as that leads nowhere, back recoils the thought toward its datum again. But there is no natural bridge between nonentity and this particular datum, and the thought stands oscillating to and fro, wondering "Why was there anything but nonentity; why just this universal datum and not another?" and finds no end, in wandering mazes lost. Indeed, Bain's

words are so untrue that in reflecting men it is just when the attempt
to fuse the manifold into a single totality has been most successful,
when the conception of the universe as a unique fact is nearest its
perfection, that the craving for further explanation, the ontological
wonder-sickness, arises in its extremest form. As Schopenhauer says,
"The uneasiness which keeps the never-resting clock of metaphysics
in motion, is the consciousness that the non-existence of this world
is just as possible as its existence."

The notion of nonentity may thus be called the parent of the philosophic craving in its subtilest and profoundest sense. Absolute existence is absolute mystery, for its relations with the nothing remain
unmediated to our understanding. One philosopher only has pretended to throw a logical bridge over this chasm. Hegel, by trying
to show that nonentity and concrete being are linked together by a
series of identities of a synthetic kind, binds everything conceivable
into a unity, with no outlying notion to disturb the free rotary circulation of the mind within its bounds. Since such unchecked
movement gives the feeling of rationality, he must be held, if he has
succeeded, to have eternally and absolutely quenched all rational
demands.

But for those who deem Hegel's heroic effort to have failed,
nought remains but to confess that when all things have been unified to the supreme degree, the notion of a possible other than the
actual may still haunt our imagination and prey upon our system.
The bottom of being is left logically opaque to us, as something
which we simply come upon and find, and about which (if we wish
to act) we should pause and wonder as little as possible. The philosopher's logical tranquillity is thus in essence no other than the
boor's. They differ only as to the point at which each refuses to let
further considerations upset the absoluteness of the data he assumes.
The boor does so immediately, and is liable at any moment to the
ravages of many kinds of doubt. The philosopher does not do so
till unity has been reached, and is warranted against the inroads of
those considerations, but only practically, not essentially, secure
from the blighting breath of the ultimate Why? If he cannot exor-
cize this question, he must ignore or blink it, and, assuming the data
of his system as something given, and the gift as ultimate, simply
proceed to a life of contemplation or of action based on it. There
is no doubt that this acting on an opaque necessity is accompanied
by a certain pleasure. See the reverence of Carlyle for brute fact:
"There is an infinite significance in fact." "Necessity," says Dühring,
and he means not rational but given necessity, "is the last and highest point that we can reach. . . . It is not only the interest of ulti-

mate and definitive knowledge, but also that of the feelings, to find a last repose and an ideal equilibrium in an uttermost datum which can simply not be other than it is."

Such is the attitude of ordinary men in their theism, God's fiat being in physics and morals such an uttermost datum. Such also is the attitude of all hard-minded analysts and *Verstandesmenschen.* Lotze, Renouvier, and Hodgson promptly say that of experience as a whole no account can be given, but neither seek to soften the abruptness of the confession nor to reconcile use with our impotence.

But mediating attempts may be made by more mystical minds. The peace of rationality may be sought through ecstasy when logic fails. To religious persons of every shade of doctrine moments come when the world, as it is, seems so divinely orderly, and the acceptance of it by the heart so rapturously complete, that intellectual questions vanish; nay, the intellect itself is hushed to sleep—as Wordsworth says, "thought is not; in enjoyment it expires." Ontological emotion so fills the soul that ontological speculation can no longer overlap it and put her girdle of interrogation-marks round existence. Even the least religious of men must have felt with Walt Whitman, when loafing on the grass on some transparent summer morning, that "swiftly arose and spread round him the peace and knowledge that pass all the argument of the earth." At such moments of energetic living we feel as if there were something diseased and contemptible, yea vile, in theoretic grubbing and brooding. In the eye of healthy sense the philosopher is at best a learned fool.

Since the heart can thus wall out the ultimate irrationality which the head ascertains, the erection of its procedure into a systematized method would be a philosophic achievement of first-rate importance. But as used by mystics hitherto it has lacked universality, being available for few persons and at few times, and even in these being apt to be followed by fits of reaction and dryness; and if men should agree that the mystical method is a subterfuge without logical pertinency, a plaster but no cure, and that the idea of nonentity can never be exorcised, empiricism will be the ultimate philosophy. Existence then will be a brute fact to which as a whole the emotion of ontologic wonder shall rightfully cleave, but remain eternally unsatisfied. Then wonderfulness or mysteriousness will be an essential attribute of the nature of things, and the exhibition and emphasizing of it will continue to be an ingredient in the philosophic industry of the race. Every generation will produce its Job, its Hamlet, its Faust, or its Sartor Resartus.

• C. D. Broad (1887–   )

Critical and Speculative Thought[2]

C. D. Broad, who taught for many years in England at the University of Cambridge and elsewhere, has all his life been interested in the natural sciences and in their contributions to our understanding of the process of human knowing. Among his books are *Perception, Physics, and Reality; Scientific Thought; The Mind and Its Place In Nature*. Professor Broad, in contrast to the position in the text, sees philosophy as a science with a subject matter whose function is the clarification of meanings. His distinction between critical and speculative thought is important and universally accepted because it points to two different strains or, if you will, two different temperaments in philosophical thinking. He expresses, although temperately, a certain skepticism about the value of speculative thought. He himself and his works belong rather to the "critical" tradition.

I shall devote this introductory chapter to stating what I think Philosophy is about, and why the other sciences are important to it and it is important to the other sciences. A very large number of scientists will begin such a book as this with the strong conviction that Philosophy is mainly moonshine, and with the gravest doubts as to whether it has anything of the slightest importance to tell them. I do not think that this view of Philosophy is true, or I should not waste my time and cheat my students by trying to teach it. But I do think that such a view is highly plausible, and that the proceedings of many philosophers have given the general public some excuse for its unfavourable opinion of Philosophy. I shall therefore begin by stating the case against Philosophy as strongly as I can, and shall then try to show that, in spite of all objections, it really is a definite science with a distinct subject-matter. I shall try to show that it really does advance and that it is related to the special

[2] From C. D. Broad, *Scientific Thought* (1923), pp. 11-22. Copyright by the Humanities Press, Inc.

sciences in such a way that the cooperation of philosophers and scientists is of the utmost benefit to the studies of both.

I think that an intelligent scientist would put his case against Philosophy somewhat as follows. He would say: "Philosophers discuss such subjects as the existence of God, the immortality of the soul, and the freedom of the will. They spin out of their minds fanciful theories, which can neither be supported nor refuted by experiment. No two philosophers agree, and no progress is made. Philosophers are still discussing with great heat the same questions that they discussed in Greece thousands of years ago. What a poor show does this make when compared with mathematics or any of the natural sciences! Here there is continual steady progress; the discoveries of one age are accepted by the next, and become the basis for further advances in knowledge. There is controversy indeed, but it is fruitful controversy which advances the science and ends in definite agreement; it is not the aimless wandering in a circle to which Philosophy is condemned. Does this not very strongly suggest that Philosophy is either a mere playing with words, or that, if it has a genuine subject-matter, this is beyond the reach of human intelligence?"

Our scientist might still further strengthen his case by reflecting on the past history of Philosophy and on the method by which it is commonly taught to students. He will remind us that most of the present sciences started by being mixed up with Philosophy, that so long as they kept this connexion they remained misty and vague, and that as soon as their fundamental principles began to be discovered they cut their disreputable associate, wedded the experimental method, and settled down to the steady production of a strapping family of established truths. Mechanics is a case in point. So long as it was mixed up with Philosophy it made no progress; when the true laws of motion were discovered by the experiments and reasoning of Galileo it ceased to be a part of Philosophy and began to develop into a separate science. Does this not suggest that the subject-matter of Philosophy is just that ever-diminishing fragment of the universe in which the scientist has not yet discovered laws, and where we have therefore to put up with guesses? Are not such guesses the best that Philosophy has to offer; and will they not be swept aside as soon as some man of genius, like Galileo or Dalton or Faraday, sets the subject on the sure path of science?

Should our scientist talk to students of Philosophy and ask what happens at their lectures, his objections will most likely be strengthened. The answer may take the classical form: "He tells us what everyone knows in language that no one can understand." But, even if the answer be not so unfavourable as this, it is not unlikely to take the form: "We hear about the views of Plato and Kant and Berkeley on such subjects as the reality of the external world and the immortality of the soul." Now the scientist will at once contrast this with the method of teaching in his own subject, and will be inclined to say, if *e.g.* he be a chemist: "We learn what *are* the laws of chemical combination and the structure of the Benzene nucleus, we do not worry our heads as to what exactly Dalton thought or Kekule said. If philosophers really know anything about the reality of the external world why do they not say straightforwardly that it is real or unreal, and prove it? The fact that they apparently prefer to discuss the divergent views of a collection of eminent 'back-numbers' on the question strongly suggests that they know that there is no means of answering it, and that nothing better than groundless opinions can be offered."

I have put these objections as strongly as I can, and I now propose to see just how much there is in them. First, as to the alleged unprogressive character of Philosophy. This is, I think, an illusion; but it is a very natural one. Let us take the question of the reality of the external world as an example. Common-sense says that chairs and tables exist independently of whether anyone happens to perceive them or not. We study Berkeley and find him claiming to prove that such things can only exist so long as they are perceived by someone. Later on we read some modern realist, like Alexander, and we are told that Berkeley was wrong, and that chairs and tables can and do exist unperceived. We seem merely to have got back to where we started from, and to have wasted our time. But this is not really so, for two reasons. (i) What we believe at the end of the process and what we believed at the beginning are by no means the same, although we express the two beliefs by the same form of words. The original belief of common-sense was vague, crude and unanalysed. Berkeley's arguments have forced us to recognise a number of distinctions and to define much more clearly what we mean by the statement that chairs and tables exist unperceived. What we find is that the original crude belief of common-sense consisted of a number of different beliefs, mixed up with each other. Some of these may be true and others false. Berkeley's arguments really do refute or throw grave doubt on some of them, but they leave others standing. Now it may be that those which are left are enough to constitute a belief in the independent reality of external objects. If so this final belief in the reality of the external world is much clearer and subtler than the *verbally* similar belief with which we began. It has been purified of irrelevant factors, and is no longer a vague mass of different beliefs mixed up with each other.

(ii) Not only will our final belief differ in content from our original one, it will also differ in certainty. Our original belief was merely instinctive, and was at the mercy of any sceptical critic who chose to cast doubts on it. Berkeley has played this part. Our final belief is that part or that modification of our original one that has managed to survive his criticisms. This does not of course *prove* that it is true; there may be other objections to it. But, at any rate, a belief that has stood the criticisms of an acute and subtle thinker, like Berkeley, is much more likely to be true than a merely instinctive belief which has never been criticised by ourselves or anyone else. Thus the process which at first sight seemed to be merely circular has not really been so. And it has certainly not been useless; for it has enabled us to replace a vague belief by a clear and analysed one, and a merely instinctive belief by one that has passed through the fire of criticism.

The above example will suggest to us a part at least of what Philosophy is really about. Common-sense constantly makes use of a number of concepts, in terms of which it interprets its experience. It talks of *things* of various kinds; it says that they have *places* and *dates,* that they *change,* and that changes in one *cause* changes in others, and so on. Thus it makes constant use of such concepts or categories as thinghood, space, time, change, cause, etc. Science takes over these concepts from common-sense with but slight modification, and uses them in its work. Now we can and do *use* concepts without having any very clear idea of their meaning or their mutual relations. I do not of course suggest that to the ordinary man the words *substance, cause, change,* etc., are mere meaningless noises, like *Jabberwock* or *Snark.* It is clear that we mean something, and something different in each case, by such words. If we did not we could not use them consistently, and it is obvious that on the whole we do consistently apply and withhold such names. But it is possible to apply concepts more or less successfully when one has only a very confused idea as to their meaning. No man confuses place with date, and for practical purposes any two men agree as a rule in the places that they assign to a given object. Nevertheless, if you ask them what exactly they mean by *place* and *date,* they will be puzzled to tell you.

Now the most fundamental task of Philosophy is to take the concepts that we daily use in common life and science, to analyse them, and thus to determine their precise meanings and their mutual relations. Evidently this is an important duty. In the first place, clear and accurate knowledge of anything is an advance on a mere hazy general familiarity with it. Moreover, in the absence of clear knowledge of the meanings and relations of the concepts that we use, we are certain sooner or later to apply them wrongly or to meet with exceptional cases where we are puzzled as to how to apply them at all. For instance, we all agree pretty well as to the place of a certain pin which we are looking at. But suppose we go on to ask: "Where is the image of that pin in a certain mirror; and is it in this place (whatever it may be) in precisely the sense in which the pin itself is in *its* place?" We shall find the question a very puzzling one, and there will be no hope of answering it until we have carefully analysed what we mean by *being in a place*.

Again, this task of clearing up the meanings and determining the relations of fundamental concepts is not performed to any extent by any other science. Chemistry *uses* the notion of substance, geometry that of space, and mechanics that of motion. But they assume that you already know what is meant by *substance* and *space* and *motion*. So you do in a vague way; and it is not their business to enter, more than is necessary for their own special purposes, into the meaning and relations of these concepts as such. Of course the special sciences do in some measure clear up the meanings of the concepts that they use. A chemist, with his distinction between elements and compounds and his laws of combination, has a clearer idea of substance than an ordinary layman. But the special sciences only discuss the meanings of their concepts so far as this is needful for their own special purposes. Such discussion is incidental to them, whilst it is of the essence of Philosophy, which deals with such questions for their own sake. Whenever a scientist begins to discuss the concepts of his science in this thorough and disinterested way we begin to say that he is studying, not so much Chemistry or Physics, as the *Philosophy* of Chemistry or Physics. It will therefore perhaps be agreed that, in the above sense of Philosophy, there is both room and need for such a study, and that there is no special reason to fear that it will be beyond the compass of human faculties.

At this point a criticism may be made which had better be met at once. It may be said: "By our own admission the task of Philosophy is purely verbal; it consists entirely of discussions about the meanings of words." This criticism is of course absolutely wide of the mark. When we say that Philosophy tries to clear up the meanings of concepts we do not mean that it is simply concerned to substitute some long phrase for some familiar word. Any analysis, when once it has been made, is naturally *expressed* in words; but so too is any other discovery. When Cantor gave his definition of Continuity, the final result of his work was expressed by saying that you can substitute for the word "continuous" such and such a verbal phrase. But the essential part of the work was to find out exactly what properties are present in objects when we predicate continuity of them, and what properties are absent when we refuse to predicate continuity. This was evidently not a question of words but of things and their properties.

Philosophy has another and closely connected task. We not only make continual use of vague and unanalysed concepts. We have also a number of uncriticised beliefs, which we constantly assume in ordinary life and in the sciences. We constantly assume, e.g., that every event has a cause, that nature obeys uniform laws, that we live in a world of objects whose existence and behaviour are independent of our knowledge of them, and so on. Now science takes over those beliefs without criticism from common-sense, and simply works with them. We know by experience, however, that beliefs which are very strongly held may be mere prejudices. Negroes find it very hard to believe that water can become solid, because they have always lived in a warm climate. Is it not possible that we believe that nature as a whole will aways act uniformly simply because the part of nature in which the human race has lived has happened to act so up to the present? All such beliefs then, however deeply rooted, call for criticism. The first duty of Philosophy is to state them clearly; and this can only be done when we have analysed and defined the concepts that they involve. Until you know exactly what you mean by *change* and *cause* you cannot know what is meant by the statement that *every change has a cause*. And not much weight can be attached to a person's most passionate beliefs if he does not know what precisely he is passionately believing. The next duty of Philosophy is to test such beliefs; and this can only be done by resolutely and honestly exposing them to every objection that one can think of oneself or find in the writings of others. We ought only to go on believing a proposition if, at the end of this process, we still find it impossible to doubt it. Even then of course it may not be true, but we have at least done our best.

These two branches of Philosophy—the analysis and definition of our fundamental concepts, and the clear statement and resolute criticism of our fundamental beliefs—I call *Critical Philosophy*. It is obviously a necessary and a possible task, and it is not performed by any other science. The other sciences *use* the concepts and *assume* the beliefs; Critical Philosophy tries to analyse the former and to criticise the latter. Thus, so long as science and Critical Philosophy keep to their own spheres, there is no possibility of conflict between them, since their subject-matter is quite different. Philosophy claims to analyse the general concepts of substance and cause, *e.g.*, it does not claim to tell us about particular substances, like gold, or about particular laws of causation, as that *aqua regia* dissolves gold. Chemistry, on the other hand, tells us a great deal about the various kinds of substances in the world, and how changes in one cause changes in another. But it does not profess to analyse the general concepts of substance or causation, or to consider what right we have to assume that every event has a cause.

It should now be clear why the method of Philosophy is so different from that of the natural sciences. Experiments are not made, because they would be utterly useless. If you want to find out how one substance behaves in the presence of another you naturally put the two together, vary the conditions, and note the results. But no experiment will clear up your ideas as to the meaning of *cause* in general or of *substance* in general. Again, all conclusions from experiments rest on some of those very assumptions which it is the business of Philosophy to state clearly and to criticise. The experimenter assumes that nature obeys uniform laws, and that similar results will follow always and everywhere from sufficiently similar conditions. This is one of the assumptions that Philosophy wants to consider critically. The method of Philosophy thus resembles that of pure mathematics, at least in the respect that neither has any use for experiment.

There is, however, a very important difference. In pure mathematics we start either from axioms which no one questions, or from premises which are quite explicitly assumed merely as hypotheses; and our main interest is to deduce remote consequences. Now most of the tacit assumptions of ordinary life and of natural science claim to be true and not merely to be hypotheses, and at the same time they are found to be neither clear nor self-evident when critically reflected upon. Most mathematical axioms are very simple and clear, whilst most other propositions which men strongly believe are highly complex and confused. Philosophy is mainly concerned, not with remote conclusions, but with the analysis and appraisement of the original premises. For this purpose analytical power and a certain kind of insight are necessary, and the mathematical method is not of much use.

Now there is another kind of Philosophy; and, as this is more exciting, it is what laymen generally understand by the name. This is what I call *Speculative Philosophy*. It has a different object, is pursued by a different method, and leads to results of a different degree of certainty from Critical Philosophy. Its object is to take over the results of the various sciences, to add to them the results of religious and ethical experiences of mankind, and then to reflect upon the whole. The hope is that, by this means, we may be able to reach some general conclusions as to the nature of the Universe, and as to our position and prospects in it.

There are several points to be noted about Speculative Philosophy. (i) If it is to be of the slightest use it must presuppose Critical Philosophy. It is useless to take over masses of uncriticised detail from the sciences and from the ethical and religious experiences of men. We do not know what they mean, or what degree of certainty they possess till they have been clarified and appraised by Critical Philosophy. It is thus quite possible that the time for Speculative Philosophy has not yet come; for Critical Philosophy may not have advanced far enough to supply it with a firm basis. In the past people have tended to rush on to Speculative Philosophy, because of its greater practical interest. The result has been the production of elaborate systems which may quite fairly be described as moonshine. The discredit which the general public quite rightly attaches to these hasty attempts at Speculative Philosophy is reflected back on Critical Philosophy, and Philosophy as a whole thus falls into undeserved disrepute.

(ii) At the best Speculative Philosophy can only consist of more or less happy guesses, made on a very slender basis. There is no hope of its reaching the certainty which some parts of Critical Philosophy might quite well attain. Now speculative philosophers as a class have been the most dogmatic of men. They have been more certain of everything than they had a right to be of anything.

(iii) A man's final view of the Universe as a whole, and of the position and prospects of himself and his fellows, is peculiarly liable to be biased by his hopes and fears, his likes and dislikes, and his judgments of value. One's Speculative Philosophy tends to be influenced to an altogether undue extent by the state of one's liver and the amount of one's bank-balance. No doubt livers and bank-balances have their place in the Universe, and no view of it which fails to give them their due weight is ultimately satisfactory. But their due weight is considerably less than their influence on Speculative Philosophy might lead one to suspect. But, if we bear this in mind and try our hardest to be "ethically neutral," we are rather liable to go to the other extreme and entertain a theory of the Universe which renders the existence of our judgments of value unintelligible.

A large part of Critical Philosophy is almost exempt from this source of error. Our analysis of truth and falsehood, or of the nature of judgment, is not very likely to be influenced by our hopes and fears. Yet even here there is a slight danger of intellectual dishonesty. We sometimes do our Critical Philosophy, with half an eye on our Speculative Philosophy, and accept or reject beliefs, or analyse concepts in a certain way, because we feel that this will fit in better than any alternative with the view of Reality as a whole that we happen to like.

(iv) Nevertheless, if Speculative Philosophy remembers its limitations, it is of value to scientists, in its methods, if not in its results. The reason is this. In all the sciences except Psychology we deal with objects and their changes, and leave out of account as far as possible the mind which observes them. In Psychology, on the other hand, we deal with minds and their processes, and leave out of account as far as possible the objects that we get to know by means of them. A man who confines himself to either of these subjects is likely therefore to get a very one-sided view of the world. The pure natural scientist is liable to forget that minds exist, and that if it were not for them he could neither know nor act on physical objects. The pure psychologist is inclined to forget that the main business of minds is to know and act upon objects; that they are most intimately connected with certain portions of matter; and that they have apparently arisen gradually in a world which at one time contained nothing but matter. Materialism is the characteristic speculative philosophy of the pure natural scientist, and subjective idealism that of the pure psychologist. To the scientist subjective idealism seems a fairy tale, and to the psychologist materialism seems sheer lunacy. Both are right in their criticisms, but neither sees the weakness of his own position. The truth is that both these doctrines commit the fallacy of over-simplification; and we can hardly avoid falling into some form of this unless at some time we make a resolute attempt to think *synoptically* of all the facts. Our *results* may be trivial; but the *process* will at least remind us of the extreme complexity of the world, and teach us to reject any cheap and easy philosophical theory, such as popular materialism or popular theology.

SUGGESTED FURTHER READINGS

AYER, A. J. *Language, Truth and Logic.* 2nd ed.; New York: Dover Publications, 1951. Chap. ii, "The Function of Philosophy." A positivist view.

BERGSON, HENRI. *The Creative Mind.* Translated by M. L. ANDISON. New York: Philosophical Lib., Inc., 1946. Chap. iv, "Philosophical Intuition." An idealist view.

COLLINGWOOD, R. G. *Speculum Mentis.* London: Oxford University Press, 1924. Chap. vii, "Philosophy."

DEWEY, JOHN. *Experience and Nature.* New York: W. W. Norton & Company, Inc., 1935. Chap. i, "Experience and Philosophic Method." A pragmatic view.

JAMES, WILLIAM. *Some Problems of Philosophy.* New York: Longmans, Green & Company, Inc., 1928. Chap. i, "Philosophy and Its Critics."

LEWIS, C. I. *Mind and the World Order.* New York: Charles Scribner's Sons, 1929. Chap. i, "The Proper Method of Philosophy."

MARITAIN, JACQUES. *An Introduction to Philosophy.* London and New York: Sheed & Ward Ltd., 1930. pp. 102-42. A neo-scholastic view.

PEIRCE, C. S. "Philosophy and the Sciences: A Classification" in *The Philosophy of Peirce,* ed. JUSTUS BUCHLER. New York: Harcourt, Brace & Co., Inc. 1940.

RUSSELL, BERTRAND. *Mysticism and Logic.* London: G. Allen & Unwin, 1936. Chap. vi, "On Scientific Method in Philosophy."

SELSAM, HOWARD. *What Is Philosophy?* 2nd ed.; New York: International Publishers Co., Inc., 1938. Chap. i, "Philosophy For Whom?" A Marxist view.

WHITEHEAD, A. N. *Science and the Modern World.* New York: The Macmillan Co., 1925. Chap. ix, "Science and Philosophy."

CHAPTER 2

Philosophy and the Ways of Knowing

The Varieties of Knowledge

When Euclid tells us that "If two straight lines cut one another, the vertical or opposite angles will be equal" (Proposition 15, Book I of *The Elements*), we feel ourselves in the presence of knowledge. And we are sure that Sir Isaac Newton's remarks (conclusion of Book I, Part I of his *Optics*), made in the seventeenth century, represent the truth for astronomical experiment as that age saw it: "Long Telescopes may cause objects to appear brighter and larger than short ones can do, but they cannot be so formed as to take away that confusion of the rays which arises from the tremors of the atmosphere. The only remedy is a most serene and quiet air, such as may perhaps be found on the tops of highest mountains above the grosser clouds."

And what is true of the mathematical propositions of Euclid and the physical propositions of Newton, we feel holds for other sciences as well. For instance, we accept as authoritative this statement from Darwin's *Origin of Species:*

We will now turn to climbing plants. These can be arranged in a long series, from those which simply twine round a support, to those which I have called leaf-climbers, and to those provided with tendrils. In these two latter classes the stems have generally but not always, lost the power of twining, though they retain the power of revolving, which the tendrils also possess. The gradations from leaf-climbers to tendril-bearers are wonderfully close, and certain plants may be indifferently placed in either class . . .

We are prepared to believe Adam Smith when, in *The Wealth of Nations,* he speaks of the division of labor within society in this way:

The great increase of the quantity of work which, in consequence of the division of labour, the same number of people are capable of performing, is owing

34

to three different circumstances; first, to the increase of dexterity in every particular workman; secondly, to the saving of the time which is commonly lost in passing from one species of work to another; and lastly, to the invention of a great number of machines which facilitate and abridge labour, and enable one man to do the work of many . . .

Other statements, although they do not pretend to be scientific, also make some claim upon our belief. When the Prophet Isaiah quotes the word of God: "Zion shall be redeemed with judgment and her converts with righteousness. And the destruction of the transgressors and of the sinners shall be together, and they that forsake the Lord shall be consumed," there is a species of truth to be considered. And when Shakespeare's Brutus asserts:

> 'tis a common proof
> That lowliness is young ambition's ladder,
> Whereto the climber-upward turns his face;
> But when he once attains the upmost round,
> He then unto the ladder turns his back,
> Looks in the clouds, scorning the base degrees
> By which he did ascend . . .

something both significant and true has been uttered concerning the nature of mankind.

We sense at once that there is something similar in these statements of Newton, Darwin, and Adam Smith although the first is speaking of telescopes, the second of plants, and the third of human labor. The similarity is that they are all three "descriptive" statements, and that what they describe would be observable by the human senses of sight, touch, etc., and observable to anyone who directed his attention to telescopes, climbing plants, or workers in a factory. Such statements can be called "empirical."

For a moment we are even prepared to believe that the statement from Euclid is like the other three. It too seems descriptive. But what does it describe? Surely nothing perceptible to the senses. The intersection of straight lines, yes; but then we remember that, for Euclid, "A line is length without breadth." But a line totally without breadth is imperceptible to sight! And then we understand that the diagrams which always accompany Euclid's text are all falsifications. They all contain lines with breadth; they are not, therefore, really Euclidean lines at all, but lines through which the eyes *suggest* to the mind what a Euclidean line really is. Euclid's "points without magnitude" and "lines without breadth" are not objects of sense perception but concepts, and the statements about them are not "empirical" but "rationalistic."

With the passage from Isaiah there is real difficulty. How, for example, are we to interpret the sentence "and they that forsake the Lord shall be consumed"? The reference to God is unmistakable, but God is not empirically observable. Nor is it the case that to such a statement the mind gives assent automatically as it does once it understands the meaning of the proposition from Euclid. In fact, there is a real question as to what Isaiah really means, and until that meaning is made clear, the question of the truth of the proposition (and hence its claim to be considered knowledge) is in doubt. But this unclarity seems to be a native property of religious statements. Religious prophecy, "descriptions" of the acts of God, the statements in which faith are cloaked, are more often than not metaphorical and suggestive rather than literal and precise. And, far from being a stumbling block to religion, this is the very meat upon which the genuinely religious feed. There are those who live by the words of Isaiah who have never heard of Euclid or Isaac Newton. Does this mean that there is another form of knowledge, neither empirical nor rationalistic, which we could perhaps call "intuitive," and which is the source of our access to "religious truth"?

Shakespeare's assertion also presents certain problems as a claim to "knowledge." Of course we know that poetry is not science, and we should never dream of subjecting Brutus' reflection upon human experience and human nature to the same standards of rigorous conformity to what is observable by the senses which we would demand of Darwin or Adam Smith. Shakespeare's statement is made by a created character in a constructed play. It is presented to the imagination by the playwright; it makes a claim upon our emotions, but it is not an invitation to a process of scientific verification. Yet there *is* something in it which invites us to acceptance or rejection. We feel it either to be true or false to human nature. We are tempted to measure it against our own knowledge of the world. And the same is true of the "statements" made by poetic dramas as a whole. *Othello* does make some assertion about the tragedy of sexual jealousy. *Macbeth* asserts something about the consequences of immoderate ambition. *Lear* asserts something deep about the ultimate working-out of blindness in high places. In this way poetry also presents the truth, and its formulations also can make some claim to the title of knowledge.

So far there is no reason to find a serious conflict between the enterprises of Euclid, Newton, Darwin, Adam Smith, Isaiah, and Shakespeare. If there is a variety of areas of experience, there is no reason why each should not be approached in its own way. And if the term "knowledge" be granted a broad enough meaning, then it might be able to cover the results of mathematics and physics, natural and social science, poetry and religion. Unfortunately, this kind of peaceful coexistence has not been possible. Mathematicians and natural scientists have quarreled over the nature of the first principles of logic. In the seventeenth century, the great critic Boileau said of the rationalistic meditations of Descartes that "they had cut the throat of poetry." And the warfare between the natural sciences and religion has been a constant feature of Western culture.

The first difficulty arises when there is a dispute as to which methods of knowing have rightful domain over a certain realm of experience. St. Thomas Aquinas, in the thirteenth century, held that there is much truth about divine things which is attainable by reason, although he admitted that there are some articles of the Christian faith which cannot be understood by reason and must, therefore, be proposed to man as an object of faith. And he said, at any rate, that there are no truths of reason which are in opposition to the truth of Christian faith. But just five hundred years later, David Hume, in a devastating attack on the human belief in miracles, argued that a miracle is a violation of the laws of nature, and that, since experience has established these laws, to believe in miracles would be irrational, for it would subvert every principle of the human understanding. So long as faith and reason are acknowledged as separate sources of belief, valid for religion and science respectively, there is no conflict. But when religion disputes with science for a claim to "reasonableness," trouble ensues.

The second difficulty arises when the pluralism of areas of experience is superseded by a frantic search for a single infallible method. Consider the case of philosophy. I have said that philosophy is a reflection upon experience. But a reflection of what kind? Does it claim to *describe* the most significant of human experiences? Then it must be like the ventures of Newton, Darwin, and Adam Smith. But in that case how can it be distinguished from science? Does it attempt to *establish* the most basic truths of the reasoning process itself? But in that case how can it be distinguished from the mathematical work of Euclid? Does it attempt to lay down the *prescriptions* by which a man ought to live? But in that case how can it be distinguished from the moral passion of an Isaiah? Does it *present to the imagination* a major world view in which emotion plays an important role? But in that case how can it be distinguished from the poetry of a Goethe or a Dante?

There are some indeed, who like to think of philosophy as akin in its method to natural science; some who like to think of it as mathematics; some who think it is the handmaiden of religion; and still others who think of it as a kind of reasonable poetry. But whichever alternative is chosen is justified by some appeal to the validity and dignity of a certain kind of knowledge. Much dispute about philosophy is really a dispute about proofs, procedures, and techniques. And it reflects an age-old quest—the search for that way of knowing which shall give us reliable knowledge about the things that matter most.

ATTITUDES TOWARD KNOWLEDGE

Before turning to the chief "ways of knowing" which have been candidates for the honor of providing us with reliable knowledge, it is necessary to say something not about knowledge itself but about the human attitudes toward knowledge. To do this we must distinguish between logic and psychology, and between *propositions* and the *judgments* about whether they are true or false.

All knowledge is expressible in propositions, and these propositions may be asserted to be absolutely true, probably true, probably false, or absolutely false. For example the following are propositions: A straight line is the shortest distance between two points on any plane surface; under standard conditions water boils at 212° F.; the ancient Egyptians understood the principle of the aeroplane; 29,004 plus 18,621 equals 47,629. The first is true without qualification; the second is true with a very high degree of probability; the third is probably false; and the last is, without qualification, false. But it is obvious that people can mistakenly believe that true propositions are false or that false propositions are true. College physics students have been known to assert that water boils at 218° F., and elementary pupils in arithmetic that 29,004 plus 18,621 equals 47,629.

The distinction between the logical entities known as propositions which are true or false and the judgment or belief in someone's mind that such and such a proposition is true, permits us to formulate the rule which ought to guide the reasonable beliefs of men. And it is simply this: *Believe without qualification true propositions; reject without qualification false propositions; in the case of propositions which are neither certainly true nor certainly false, qualify your belief in direct proportion to the probability that the proposition is true, that is, according to the evidence available.*[1] This rule tries to bring about a certain congruence between the state of the facts and the state of human belief. It says that when there is no evidence, we are not entitled to believe, although we have an intel-

---

[1] A. M. Frye and A. W. Levi, *Rational Belief: An Introduction to Logic* (New York: Harcourt, Brace & Co., Inc., 1941), p. 456.

lectual obligation to keep an open mind. It says that when the evidence is clear we have a duty to believe, in short, to come to a verdict when the truth is beyond any reasonable doubt. This rule is the rule of rational belief, and the attitude of mind which it expresses may be called "provisionalism."

Now, it is a matter of the simplest observation when we examine our own practice and the practice of others that few individuals abide by the rule of rational belief. Although in theory almost everyone would agree that we should proportion our assent to the evidence, we nonetheless hold to the majority of our unquestioned beliefs although we have no direct observation of their truth and do not even make a pretense of weighing the testimony of those who assert them to be so.

I am convinced that the earth is round like a sphere although I have never acquainted myself with the astronomical evidence. I believe that the strip of water which separates Alaska and Siberia is very narrow although I have never seen it. I am convinced that there are really existing cities like Budapest, Moscow, and Prague although I have never been to them. And I am sure that Paris and Vienna and Istanbul are today exactly as they were yesterday and as they were when I saw them last. We all believe in our own birth although we have no recollection of its taking place, and we are convinced that we shall one day die although we can have no real experience of the future. The remotest figures of history have for us a reality which has nothing to do with our knowledge of the facts. Julius Caesar and Napoleon and Socrates are figures whose previous existence we never for a moment doubt. And there are times when it takes an act of will to disbelieve in the former existence of Ivan Karamazov and Don Quixote, D'Artagnan and Falstaff. Our "will to believe" seems to provide a reality for us which has little to do with logic, with probability, and with evidence.

Little of what we believe about the world is directly tested by our own reason, experience, and observation. We accept on trust nine-tenths of the truths to which we adhere. Some of our beliefs come from our parents, some from school, some from magazines and newspapers, and the vast majority we simply pick up from friends and the world at large. These beliefs gradually grow into a cohesive mass which form, so to speak, our capital of ideas.

Under these conditions there is a strong tendency to maintain our system of belief at all costs. Man is not only an extremely credulous animal who tends to believe what he is told, but once the idea has become a part of his system of beliefs, it is extremely difficult to dislodge. And the larger the number of people who hold the same belief, the more they are persons of prestige or reputation, and the more ancient and traditional the belief, the more difficult it will be to dislodge it. These are some of the causes of the natural conservatism of the human mind.

Since beliefs are generally acquired without a rigorous inquiry into their truth, they are not easily given up even in the face of convincing evidence that they are false. Since, when a belief is first presented to the mind, we do not conscientiously seek all the possible evidence which might disprove it, then, when later new facts appear, they will be fitted in with the beliefs currently held rather than be permitted to challenge them.

The fact that we rely so much upon the authority of others for our beliefs, that we accept them without criticism, and that we refuse to give them up, is one of the chief characteristics of the mind. And it is, from the standpoint of provisionalism, the principal form of human irrationality. We believe too easily in the first place. And we hold on to belief too stubbornly in the second. Believing without question the word of others is "authoritarianism." And holding a belief without seeking or yielding to evidence is "dogmatism."

If dogmatism amounts to a peculiar stubbornness in belief, then its opposite, "skepticism," amounts to a peculiar stubbornness in unbelief. It would indeed be neat if one were able to say that dogmatism and skepticism were equal excesses of the human mind—equal excesses of waywardness toward which thought is disposed when it strays from the reasonable position of provisionalism. It would be neat, but it is not quite in accord with the facts. Actually, dogmatism seems to be the more natural propensity, the more customary inclination of mankind. Perhaps this is the reason why skepticism has always seemed the more attractive position. At least it is the one of greater interest to philosophers.

In one sense skepticism is quite logically a consequence of a prior dogmatism in others. If it is natural for men to believe upon the evidence of authority, then it is equally natural for them to be doubtful in the presence of a vast number of conflicting authorities. And one of the common experiences of mankind is the recognition of the number of authorities which conflict and the hopeless diversity of beliefs even among "the experts." Each religion has its own signs of divine favor, of miraculous proofs, of special and individual revelation. But as the British philosopher David Hume saw, what is an argument for the truth of Buddhism is an argument against the truth of Christianity; what is an argument in favor of the chosen mission of the Jews casts some doubt upon the chosen mission of Mohammed.

In philosophy something like this has also occurred. From the earliest times there have been quarrels between Stoics and Epicureans in moral theory, realists and idealists in the theory of knowledge, materialists and spiritualists in the interpretation of values. Democritus and Plato were opponents in the ancient world; Marxists and Bergsonians perpetuate this opposition into the present day. With controversy continuing, little permanently settled, the intellectual battles still raging, some skepticism about the conclusions of philosophers must be inevitable.

If one source of skepticism is the conflict of authorities, another is the prevalence of error. In the passage about telescopes quoted at the beginning of the chapter, Sir Isaac Newton alluded to "the confusion of the rays which arises from the tremors of the atmosphere." It is a common experience for astronomers that what they see is distorted by the medium through which they see it. And it is no less common an experience of ordinary observation. But it is a disturbing thought. It is not the stars which "twinkle" but the atmosphere. If in so simple a case our knowledge of the objects is distorted, how much of the rest of our sense perception also gives us an inexact or erroneous picture of the world? Our processes of perception are very indirect, and this suggests the possibility that although we have experience of "appearances," we may have no true knowledge of the "realities" which lie behind them and to which we can never penetrate.

We are all commonly aware of the errors in sense perception which constantly occur, of our mistaken estimates about the size and distance of objects, of optical illusions, of our difficulty in discriminating the exact nature of odors and the real source of sounds. But if such are the errors to which immediate and direct perception is subject, what of our knowledge of the past, both through our own memory and the testimony of other eye-witnesses? Our own memories are notorious for the ease with which they play us false, and other witnesses, even when they have no desire to falsify the facts, are subject to the same errors of observation and memory as we ourselves. A reasonable skepticism might well suggest to us that all the data of history are of somewhat doubtful credibility.

The errors of observation cast doubt upon our knowledge of the present; the errors of memory upon our knowledge of the past. Can we have any more assurance in our knowledge of the future? Certainly not; even less, skepticism replies.

The knowledge of the past which we have through our own memory is at least a direct experience. But our anticipation of the future must always be an inference, a passage from the known to the unknown. What logical right have we to predict the future from the past? Obviously it is because of the *assumption* that what has held in the past will also hold in the future, and that the operations of nature are orderly and uniform. But even if nature has exhibited constancy in the past, what reason have we to believe that it will not shift and change in the future? The only honest answer is that we cannot be absolutely certain of our belief in the uniformity of nature. This belief is itself a generalization of our past experience. And it is, of course, the foundation of all our anticipations. But let us admit that it is far from certain. If we hold to it, it is because with all of its theoretical limitations it is the best of the alternatives available to guide our inferences. But this is ultimately a practical answer, not a sound theoretical one. And if our aim is absolute certainty, then the skeptic has a perfect right to call into question our knowledge of the future no less than that of the present and the past.

Absolute skepticism adopted as a practical creed would be impossible. It would be paralyzing and self-destructive. Imagine the consequences if we could not be convinced by any arguments that what was on our plate was really food; that the red light on the traffic signal was really red; or if we suddenly decided that the law of the uniformity of nature was untenable and, although we had never been able to overcome the pull of gravitation in the past, stepped out into space from our office on the sixteenth floor!

But there is another kind of skepticism, a theoretical skepticism —the initial use of doubt as a method by means of which we may make an investigation of the origin, the extent, and the validity of all our knowledge. And this is the kind which has been associated with philosophy and with two of the most acute of modern philosophers: René Descartes and Immanuel Kant.

Descartes is famous because one winter's day in a comfortable room and with nothing else to do, he pretended to take his mind apart, trying almost to become a newborn babe again by systematically doubting all the beliefs which he had acquired through his lifetime, and attempting to clean the slate of his intellect so that he might begin anew only with what was absolutely certain and indubitable. His account of this experience and the conclusions to which he finally came is one of the classics of modern philosophy.[2]

Kant's skepticism is less dramatic than Descartes', but perhaps more thoroughgoing. In his *Critique of Pure Reason*, published in

[2] Partially reproduced on page 48 below.

1781, he began not with universal doubt but with a critical attitude toward the possibilities of human knowledge. He did not insist upon "a clean slate." He simply was unwilling to begin with trust in the power of human reason without first investigating the grounds upon which reason staked her claim. And the outcome of his investigation, in a word, was that although reason was competent to provide us with knowledge of mathematics and natural science, that is, about "appearances," it was totally unable to provide knowledge about "things in themselves." Therefore reason can say nothing about those things in which the human individual has the greatest stake—God, freedom, immortality. Indeed, Kant saw that when reason tries to go beyond its limited powers and to make statements about the divine, about the universe as a whole, or about the inmost nature of the human self, it then falls into hopeless contradictions and insoluble paradoxes. This is a new mode of skepticism, for it is directed, not towards sense perception or our knowledge of the past and future, but to the very inmost workings of the reasoning process itself.

It is interesting to note that the skepticism of both Descartes and Kant is an initial attitude and not a final result. Descartes' first doubts slowly turn into an affirmation of our right to believe in "clear and distinct ideas." And Kant's denial that we may have rational knowledge of God and freedom then paves the way for his final assertion that we have the right to believe in these things through faith.

THREE METHODS OF HUMAN KNOWING

But upon which of the forms of knowledge should philosophy pattern itself? What way of knowing is the most reliable in establishing truths of the greatest importance and those of which we may have the greatest assurance? To these questions three traditional answers have been given. (1) We ought to rely upon that way of knowing by which the mind provides the ultimate principles of thought and by which it reasons to conclusions which are certain. (2) We ought to rely upon that way of knowing by which our senses observe the conditions which exist in the world, and which formulates experience on the basis of its observability. (3) We ought to rely upon that way of knowing which gives us deep, direct, and intuitive insight into art and religion, and which enlarges our vision of the world. The first mode of knowing is the method of mathematics, and its partisans are called "rationalists." The second mode of knowing is the method of natural science, and its partisans are called "empiricists." The third mode of knowing is the method of artistic, moral, and religious mysticism, and its partisans are called "intuitionists."

When we examine once again Euclid's proposition "If two straight lines cut one another, the vertical or opposite angles will be equal," we see that we have good reason for feeling that this is an item of knowledge in which we may have confidence. Indeed, we do not think of it as "very probably" true, but as "absolutely" true. It is *certain* because Euclid has *demonstrated* it to us. If we examine that demonstration, we find that it rests upon two premises: a prior proposition which Euclid has proved, "The angles which one straight line makes with another straight line on one side of it is equal to two right angles" (Proposition 13), and an axiom, "If equals be subtracted from equals, the results are equal" (Axiom 3). If these two are true, then the conclusion follows from them inevitably in precisely the same fashion as when one says: If "all X's are Y's," and if "this Z is an X," then it follows that "this Z is a Y." But where do Euclid's premises themselves come from?

Euclid begins with three kinds of assumptions which are called respectively *definitions, postulates,* and *axioms.* The definitions are simply a presentation of the elements of geometry. They prescribe what a line, a point, an angle, a right angle means. They are *relations of meanings* by which the chief concepts are mutually associated, as when he says, "An acute angle is one which is less than a right angle" (Definition 12). The nature of Euclid's postulates presents a more difficult problem, but let us turn to his axioms. Here are a few of them:

1. Things which are equal to the same thing are equal to one another.
2. If equals be added to equals, the results are equal.
6. Things which are double the same thing are equal to one another.
9. The whole is greater than its part.
11. All right angles are equal.

What are these statements, and how must we feel about their truth or falsity? A moment's reflection will convince us that they are necessarily true and their certainty stems from the fact that they express the laws of logic in general; that is, the very laws of thought by which any reasonable human mind operates.

Many more of these axioms or first principles are made explicit in the study of logic. Some of them may be called "laws of thought," some of them "principles of inference." Here are a few examples:

If A is greater than B and B is greater than C, then A is greater than C.

If any proposition is true, then it is true.

If no X's are Y's, then no Y's are X's.

No proposition can be both true and false.

If A is greater than B, then B is smaller than A.

A proposition must be either true or false.

These statements as well as the axioms above from Euclid have a peculiar status as knowledge. We not only know them to be certainly true, but we know them as such quite apart from any experiences which we have had in the world, quite apart from any observations which we have made. These truths have not been derived from our experience, for they are independent of experience. This means that in some sense they precede experience, and that no possible experience whatsoever could ever refute them. For this reason they have sometimes been called *universal, necessary,* and *a priori.*

Axioms, first principles, and principles of inference do not give us information about the world so much as about the mind and its reasoning powers. And we, in consequence, speak of them as *self-evident* not so much to indicate the strength of our conviction that they are true, as to record the fact that once their meaning is really understood, it is logically impossible to doubt them.

In the geometry of Euclid we have a perfect example of the rationalistic method of knowing, which is simply a deductive elaboration of principles that are self-evident. This means that we explore the implications of the a priori statements with which we begin through a method which amounts to a process of the substitution of equivalent concepts. Throughout the history of philosophy there have been thinkers who have idealized this form of knowing as the highest of which the mind is capable, and not a few of these have proposed it as the ideal method for the expression of philosophical experience.

There is an old distinction in philosophy, often associated with Leibniz, a contemporary of Descartes, between "truths of reason" and "truths of fact." The way of knowing beloved by rationalists gives us truths of reason. The way of knowing approved by empiricists gives us truths of fact. Each of the examples of knowledge quoted earlier from Newton, Darwin, and Adam Smith is an illustration of the truths of fact.

If one looks at these once again, it will be apparent that they deal with facts each in a somewhat different fashion. Newton makes a *generalization* about the difference between long and short telescopes, and although he does not cite the specific experiences which have led him to this conclusion, our knowledge of his busy life as a professional astronomer suggests the source of this generalization. Darwin's remarks also are based on the experiences of a practicing naturalist, but they lead less to a simple generalization than to a *classification* of climbing plants. And finally, Adam Smith, the observant economist, makes a classification too, but it is a classification which tries to establish a *causal connection* between the division of labor and the increase in the quantity of work performed which is its consequence. Generalization, classification, and the establishment of causal connection are all methods of dealing with the truths of fact. And they are alike in one crucial respect: they all reduce finally to some activity of making observations through our senses.

In this respect there is not much difference between the activity of science and that of common sense. We all observe (really generalize from observation) that stones are hard, trains whistle, the sky is blue, grapefruit is sour, dogs bite. It is only when we think critically about these statements that we recognize their looseness and need of greater specification. Only some kinds of stones are hard. The sky is blue only on some days and at certain times. Grapefruit ranges from quite sweet to extremely sour. Only when the need for greater accuracy of statement and for greater accuracy in the measurement of our observations is acknowledged does the passage from crude common sense to systematic science take place.

The method of the experimental sciences ultimately reduces to verification by the making of observations; but science, as it grows more systematic, not only introduces more refinements in its definitions of terms, and utilizes instruments which are themselves more accurate means of observation and measurement, but it also grows more abstract. Physics deals not with tables, chairs, and inkstands, but with bodies, masses, and forces. Biology abandons oak trees, spiders, and rosebushes to deal with vertebrates, reproduction, and nutrition. Science has always the aim of understanding the structure and functioning of the natural world, but more and more it turns from the conception of particular things to a correlation of abstract properties.

The prestige and success of natural science is enormous. And as Peirce notes,[3] its method has two great advantages: (1) Its conclusions are open to public verification and do not have the disadvantages of "merely private" truths, and (2) it is progressive —that is, its results are constantly subject to a process of improve-

[3] See pp. 61 ff.

ment and self-correction. It is small wonder then that, in science's method of observation of the world of facts, empiricists should find that method of knowing in which their confidence is unbounded.

There is a third way of knowing which is suggested by the passages from Isaiah and Shakespeare quoted earlier, although they are not precisely examples of it. This is the method of intuition. Religious prophecy and poetic statement approach it, but they fail to exemplify intuitive knowing in one important respect; however vague, metaphorical or symbolic their language, they do speak with words. The ultimate act of intuitive knowing, on the contrary, claims to dispense with language and with symbols.

The intuitionist claims that there is a form of knowing which is neither sense perception nor intellectual reasoning, but a deep, direct insight into experience which is above them both. There are truths which one learns here, but they are truths which concern the nature of God, or the universe in its wholeness, and the organ through which one learns these things is not easy to specify. But there is some capacity of the mind whereby one *becomes aware of* or, if you will, *acquainted with* cosmic energies, and through which the spirit of man can unite with the universe. Such claims have always been made by the great religious mystics, and the inner harmonies of feeling and imagination which they experience set them apart from the many who do not share this experience. And yet, the activity of those we call artists (be they painters, poets, or musicians) does provide something comparable. These men too possess *the integrative faculty* to an unusual degree, and they experience and present a vision of the nature of things which causes more prosaic minds to be moved and instructed. A great intuitive vision of the world can infect even the stodgy and the commonplace.

The intuitive experience is difficult to make intelligible, and there are those who describe it ironically as mere imagination tinged with dogmatism. But those [4] who most respect its claims tend to describe it by pairs of opposites. Intuition, they say, is direct rather than symbolic, integrative rather than analytic, vision rather than fact, a matter of feeling or sympathy rather than reasoning. And they say too that philosophy functions best when it adopts a method of intuition rather than that of logic or empirical science.

The following selections, "What We May Doubt" by René Descartes, "Inquiry and Belief" by Charles Sanders Peirce, and "Analysis and Intuition" by Henri Bergson, all illustrate one of the major concerns of Western philosophy since the Renaissance; the question

[4] Henri Bergson, for example. See pp. 76 ff.

of where our knowledge comes from, how wide it extends, how trustworthy we may really consider it. Descartes wrote in the seventeenth century, Peirce toward the end of the nineteenth, Bergson died during the Second World War.

A comparison of these contributions to the theory of knowledge may be instructive. Descartes illustrates skepticism as a method of testing the validity of knowledge, but he uses it to further his own rationalistic point of view. Peirce, in insisting upon the real, emotional character of "doubt" shows the artificiality of Descartes' procedure. But he also advocates the scientific method as the only adequate method for obtaining knowledge. Bergson in his espousal of intuition sets it in opposition to that very scientific knowledge favored by Peirce, but his treatment of the self as the most stable object of our intuitive knowledge has certain features in common with Descartes. In these men the three methods of knowing mentioned in the text are given more detailed exemplification.

• René Descartes (1596–1650)

What We May Doubt[5]

René Descartes, one of the most famous mathematicians and philosophers of the age of Louis XIII, has often been called "the father of modern philosophy." His interest in the theory of knowledge and his confidence in the clarity and fruitfulness of the methods of mathematics is reflected in almost everything he wrote, certainly in the *Meditations On First Philosophy* of which the first two are reproduced here. Descartes begins by noting the uncertainty of our sense perceptions when compared with the certainty of mathematical demonstrations. And he proposes to discard all beliefs which he can possibly doubt. He finally concludes that the absolute consciousness of self is the Archimedean lever upon which all else can pivot. From his own existence he then infers the existence of God and of the world. He even thought that our knowledge of bodies (the wax) comes less from sense perception than from an act of thought. Other valuable works of Descartes are: *Discourse On Method, The Principles of Philosophy, The Passions of the Soul.*

[5] From René Descartes, *Meditations on First Philosophy* (1641), trans. John Veitch (1879), Meditations I, II.

I

Several years have now elapsed since I first became aware that I had accepted, even from my youth, many false opinions for true, and that consequently what I afterwards based on such principles was highly doubtful; and from that time I was convinced of the necessity of undertaking once in my life to rid myself of all the opinions I had adopted, and of commencing anew the work of building from the foundation, if I desired to establish a firm and abiding superstructure in the sciences. But as this enterprise appeared to me to be one of great magnitude, I waited until I had attained an age so mature as to leave me no hope that at any stage of life more advanced I should be better able to execute my design. On this account, I have delayed so long that I should henceforth consider I was doing wrong were I still to consume in deliberation any of the time that now remains for action. Today, then, since I have opportunely freed my mind from all cares, (and am happily disturbed by no passions), and since I am in the secure possession of leisure in a peaceable retirement, I will at length apply myself earnestly and freely to the general overthrow of all my former opinions. But, to this end, it will not be necessary for me to show that the whole of these are false—a point, perhaps, which I shall never reach; but as even now my reason convinces me that I ought not the less carefully to withhold belief from what is not entirely certain and indubitable, than from what is manifestly false, it will be sufficient to justify the rejection of the whole if I shall find in each some ground for doubt. Nor for this purpose will it be necessary even to deal with each belief individually, which would be truly an endless labour; but, as the removal from below of the foundation necessarily involves the downfall of the whole edifice, I will at once approach the criticism of the principles on which all my former beliefs rested.

All that I have, up to this moment, accepted as possessed of the highest truth and certainty, I received either from or through the senses. I observed, however, that these sometimes misled us; and it is the part of prudence not to place absolute confidence in that by which we have even once been deceived.

But it may be said, perhaps, that, although the senses occasionally mislead us respecting minute objects, and such as are so far removed from us as to be beyond the reach of close observation, there are yet many other of their informations (presentations), of the truth of which it is manifestly impossible to doubt; as for example, that I am in this place, seated by the fire, clothed in a winter dress-ing-gown, that I hold in my hands this piece of paper, with other intimations of the same nature. But how could I deny that I possess these hands and this body, and withal escape being classed with persons in a state of insanity, whose brains are so disordered and clouded by dark bilious vapours as to cause them pertinaciously to assert that they are monarchs when they are in the greatest poverty; or clothed (in gold) and purple when destitute of any covering; or that their head is made of clay, their body of glass, or that they are gourds? I should certainly be not less insane than they, were I to regulate my procedure according to examples so extravagant.

Though this be true, I must nevertheless here consider that I am a man, and that, consequently, I am in the habit of sleeping, and representing to myself in dreams those same things, or even sometimes others less probable, which the insane think are presented to them in their waking moments. How often have I dreamt that I was in these familiar circumstances—that I was dressed, and occupied this place by the fire, when I was lying undressed in bed? At the present moment, however, I certainly look upon this paper with eyes wide awake; the head which I now move is not asleep; I extend this hand consciously and with express purpose, and I perceive it; the occurrences in sleep are not so distinct as all this. But I cannot forget that, at other times, I have been deceived in sleep by similar illusions; and, attentively considering those cases, I perceive so clearly that there exist no certain marks by which the state of waking can ever be distinguished from sleep, that I feel greatly astonished; and in amazement I almost persuade myself that I am now dreaming.

Let us suppose, then, that we are dreaming, and that all these particulars—namely, the opening of the eyes, the motion of the head, the forth-putting of the hands—are merely illusions; and even that we really possess neither an entire body nor hands such as we see. Nevertheless, it must be admitted at least that the objects which appear to us in sleep are, as it were, painted representations which could not have been formed unless in the likeness of realities; and, therefore, that those general objects, at all events,—namely, eyes, a head, hands, and an entire body—are not simply imaginary, but really existent. For, in truth, painters themselves, even when they study to represent sirens and satyrs by forms the most fantastic and extraordinary, cannot bestow upon them natures absolutely new, but can only make a certain medley of the members of different animals; or if it is so novel that nothing at all similar has ever been seen before, and such as is, therefore, purely fictitious and absolutely false, it is at least certain that the colours of which this is composed are real.

And on the same principle, although these general objects, viz. (a body), eyes, a head, hands, and the like, be imaginary, we are nevertheless absolutely necessitated to admit the reality at least of some other objects still more simple and universal than these, of which, just as of certain real colours, all those images of things, whether true and real, or false and fantastic, that are found in our consciousness (cogitatio), are formed.

To this class of objects seem to belong corporeal nature in general and its extension; the figure of extended things, their quantity or magnitude, and their number, as also the place in, and the time during, which they exist, and other things of the same sort. We will not, therefore, perhaps reason illegitimately if we conclude from this that Physics, Astronomy, Medicine, and all the other sciences that have for their end the consideration of composite objects, are indeed of a doubtful character; but that Arithmetic, Geometry, and the other sciences of the same class, which regard merely the simplest and most general objects, and scarcely inquire whether or not these are really existent, contain somewhat that is certain and indubitable; for whether I am awake or dreaming, it remains true that two and three make five, and that a square has but four sides; nor does it seem possible that truths so apparent can ever fall under a suspicion of falsity (or incertitude).

Nevertheless, the belief that there is a God who is all-powerful, and who created me, such as I am, has, for a long time, obtained steady possession of my mind. How, then, do I know that he has not arranged that there should be neither earth, nor sky, nor any extended thing, nor figure, nor magnitude, nor place, providing at the same time, however, for (the rise in me of the perceptions of all these objects, and) the persuasion that these do not exist otherwise than as I perceive them? And further, as I sometimes think that others are in error respecting matters of which they believe themselves to possess a perfect knowledge, how do I know that I am not also deceived each time I add together two and three, or number the sides of a square, or form some judgment still more simple, if more simple indeed can be imagined? But perhaps Deity has not been willing that I should be thus deceived, for He is said to be supremely good. If, however, it were repugnant to the goodness of Deity to have created me subject to constant deception, it would seem likewise to be contrary to his goodness to allow me to be occasionally deceived; and yet it is clear that this is permitted. Some, indeed, might perhaps be found who would be disposed rather to deny the existence of a Being so powerful than to believe that there is nothing certain. But let us for the present refrain from opposing this opinion, and grant that all which is here said of a Deity is fabulous: nevertheless in whatever way it be supposed that I reached the state in which I exist, whether by fate, or chance, or by an endless series of antecedents and consequents, or by any other means, it is clear (since to be deceived and to err is a certain defect) that the probability of my being so imperfect as to be the constant victim of deception, will be increased exactly in proportion as the power possessed by the cause, to which they assign my origin, is lessened. To these reasonings I have assuredly nothing to reply, but am constrained at last to avow that there is nothing of all that I formerly believed to be true of which it is impossible to doubt, and that not through thoughtlessness or levity, but from cogent and maturely considered reasons; so that henceforward, if I desire to discover anything certain, I ought not the less carefully to refrain from assenting to those same opinions than to what might be shown to be manifestly false.

But it is not sufficient to have made these observations; care must be taken likewise to keep them in remembrance. For those old and customary opinions perpetually recur—long and familiar usage giving them the right of occupying my mind, even almost against my will, and subduing my belief; nor will I lose the habit of deferring to them and confiding in them so long as I shall consider them to be what in truth they are, viz., opinions to some extent doubtful, as I have already shown, but still highly probable, and such as it is much more reasonable to believe than deny. It is for this reason I am persuaded that I shall not be doing wrong, if, taking an opposite judgment of deliberate design, I become my own deceiver, by supposing, for a time, that all those opinions are entirely false and imaginary, until at length, having thus balanced my old by my new prejudices, my judgment shall no longer be turned aside by perverted usage from the path that may conduct to the perception of truth. For I am assured that, meanwhile, there will arise neither peril nor error from this course, and that I cannot for the present yield too much to distrust, since the end I now seek is not action but knowledge.

I will suppose, then, not that Deity, who is sovereignly good and the fountain of truth, but that some malignant demon, who is at once exceedingly potent and deceitful, has employed all his artifice to deceive me; I will suppose that the sky, the air, the earth, colours, figures, sounds, and all external things, are nothing better than the illusions of dreams, by means of which this being has laid snares for my credulity; I will consider myself as without hands, eyes, flesh, blood, or any of the senses, and as falsely believing that I am possessed of these; I will continue resolutely fixed in this belief, and if indeed by this means it be not in my power to arrive at the knowledge of truth, I shall at least do what is in my power, viz., (suspend my judgment), and guard with settled purpose against giving my assent to what is false, and being imposed upon by this deceiver, whatever be his power and artifice.

But this undertaking is arduous, and a certain indolence insensibly leads me back to my ordinary course of life; and just as the captive, who, perchance, was enjoying in his dreams an imaginary liberty, when he begins to suspect that it is but a vision, dreads awakening, and conspires with the agreeable illusions that the deception may be prolonged; so I, of my own accord, fall back into the train of my former beliefs, and fear to arouse myself from my slumber, lest the time of laborious wakefulness that would succeed this quiet rest, in place of bringing any light of day, should prove inadequate to dispel the darkness that will arise from the difficulties that have now been raised.

· · · · ·

II

The Meditation of yesterday has filled my mind with so many doubts, that it is no longer in my power to forget them. Nor do I see, meanwhile, any principle on which they can be resolved; and, just as if I had fallen all of a sudden into very deep water, I am so greatly disconcerted as to be unable either to plant my feet firmly on the bottom or sustain myself by swimming on the surface. I will, nevertheless, make an effort, and try anew the same path on which I had entered yesterday, that is, proceed by casting aside all that admits of the slightest doubt, not less than if I had discovered it to be absolutely false; and I will continue always in this track until I shall find something that is certain, or at least, if I can do nothing more, until I shall know with certainty that there is nothing certain. Archimedes, that he might transport the entire globe from the place it occupied to another, demanded only a point that was firm and immoveable; so also, I shall be entitled to entertain the highest expectations, if I am fortunate enough to discover only one thing that is certain and indubitable.

I suppose, accordingly, that all the things which I see are false (fictitious); I believe that none of those objects which my fallacious memory represents ever existed; I suppose that I possess no senses;

I believe that body, figure, extension, motion, and place are merely fictions of my mind. What is there, then, that can be esteemed true? Perhaps this only, that there is absolutely nothing certain.

But how do I know that there is not something different altogether from the objects I have now enumerated, of which it is impossible to entertain the slightest doubt? Is there not a God, or some being, by whatever name I may designate him, who causes these thoughts to arise in my mind? But why suppose such a being, for it may be I myself am capable of producing them? Am I, then, at least not something? But I before denied that I possessed senses or a body; I hesitate, however, for what follows from that? Am I so dependent on the body and the senses that without these I cannot exist? But I had the persuasion that there was absolutely nothing in the world, that there was no sky and no earth, neither minds nor bodies; was I not, therefore, at the same time persuaded that I did not exist? Far from it; I assuredly existed, since I was persuaded. But there is I know not what being, who is possessed at once of the highest power and the deepest cunning, who is constantly employing all his ingenuity in deceiving me. Doubtless, then, I exist, since I am deceived; and, let him deceive me as he may, he can never bring it about that I am nothing, so long as I shall be conscious that I am something. So that it must, in fine, be maintained, all things being maturely and carefully considered, that this proposition (pronunciatum) I am, I exist, is necessarily true each time it is expressed by me, or conceived in my mind.

But I do not yet know with sufficient clearness what I am, though assured that I am; and hence, in the next place, I must take care, lest perchance I inconsiderately substitute some other object in room of what is properly myself, and thus wander from truth, even in that knowledge (cognition) which I hold to be of all others the most certain and evident. For this reason, I will now consider anew what I formerly believed myself to be, before I entered on the present train of thought; and of my previous opinion I will retrench all that can in the least be invalidated by the grounds of doubt I have adduced, in order that there may at length remain nothing but what is certain and indubitable. What then did I formerly think I was? Undoubtedly I judged that I was a man. But what is a man? Shall I say a rational animal? Assuredly not; for it would be necessary forthwith to inquire into what is meant by animal, and what by rational, and thus, from a single question, I should insensibly glide into others, and these more difficult than the first; nor do I now possess enough of leisure to warrant me in wasting my time amid subtleties of this sort. I prefer here to attend to the thoughts that sprung up of themselves in my mind, and were inspired by my own nature alone, when I applied myself to the consideration of what I was. In the first place, then, I thought that I possessed a countenance, hands, arms, and all the fabric of members that appears in a corpse, and which I called by the name of body. It further occurred to me that I was nourished, that I walked, perceived, and thought, and all those actions I referred to the soul; but what the soul itself was I either did not stay to consider, or, if I did, I imagined that it was something extremely rare and subtile, like wind, or flame, or ether, spread through my grosser parts. As regarded the body, I did not even doubt of its nature, but thought I distinctly knew it, and if I had wished to describe it according to the notions I then entertained, I should have explained myself in this manner: By body I understand all that can be terminated by a certain figure; that can be comprised in a certain place, and so fill a certain space as therefrom to exclude every other body; that can be perceived either by touch, sight, hearing, taste, or smell; that can be moved in different ways, not indeed of itself, but by something foreign to it by which it is touched (and from which it receives the impression); for the power of self-motion, as likewise that of perceiving and thinking, I held as by no means pertaining to the nature of body; on the contrary, I was somewhat astonished to find such faculties existing in some bodies.

But (as to myself, what can I now say that I am), since I suppose there exists an extremely powerful, and, if I may so speak, malignant being, whose whole endeavours are directed towards deceiving me? Can I affirm that I possess any one of all those attributes of which I have lately spoken as belonging to the nature of body? After attentively considering them in my own mind, I find none of them that can properly be said to belong to myself. To recount them were idle and tedious. Let us pass, then, to the attributes of the soul. The first mentioned were the powers of nutrition and walking; but, if it be true that I have no body, it is true likewise that I am capable neither of walking nor of being nourished. Perception is another attribute of the soul; but perception too is impossible without the body: besides, I have frequently, during sleep, believed that I perceived objects which I afterwards observed I did not in reality perceive. Thinking is another attribute of the soul; and here I discover what properly belongs to myself. This alone is inseparable from me. I am—I exist: this is certain; but how often? As often as I think; for perhaps it would even happen, if I should wholly cease to think, that I should at the same time altogether cease to be. I now admit nothing that is not necessarily true: I am therefore, precisely speaking, only a thinking thing, that is, a mind (mens sive animus), understanding, or reason,—terms whose signification was before unknown to me. I am, however, a real thing, and really existent; but what thing? The answer was, a thinking thing. The question now arises, am I aught besides? I will stimulate my imagination with a view to discover whether I am not still something more than a thinking being. Now it is plain I am not the assemblage of members called the human body; I am not a thin and penetrating air diffused through all these members, or wind, or flame, or vapour, or breath, or any of all the things I can imagine; for I supposed that all these were not, and, without changing the supposition, I find that I still feel assured of my existence.

But it is true, perhaps, that those very things which I suppose to be non-existent, because they are unknown to me, are not in truth different from myself whom I know. This is a point I cannot determine, and do not now enter into any dispute regarding it. I can only judge of things that are known to me: I am conscious that I exist, and I who know that I exist inquire into what I am. It is, however, perfectly certain that the knowledge of my existence, thus precisely taken, is not dependent on things, the existence of which is as yet unknown to me: and consequently it is not dependent on any of the things I can feign in imagination. Moreover, the phrase itself, I frame in image (effingo), reminds me of my error; for I should in truth frame one if I were to imagine myself to be anything, since to imagine is nothing more than to contemplate the figure or image of a corporeal thing; but I already know that I exist, and that it is possible at the same time that all those images, and in general all that relates to the nature of body, are merely dreams (or chimeras). From this I discover that it is not more reasonable to say, I will excite my imagination that I may know more distinctly what I am, than to express myself as follows: I am now awake, and perceive something real; but because my perception is not sufficiently clear, I will of express purpose go to sleep that my dreams may represent to me the object of my perception with more truth and clearness. And, therefore, I know that nothing of all that I can embrace in imagination belongs to the knowledge which I have of myself, and that there is need to recall with the utmost care the mind from this mode of thinking, that it may be able to know its own nature with perfect distinctness.

But what, then, am I? A thinking thing, it has been said. But what is a thinking thing? It is a thing that doubts, understands, (conceives), affirms, denies, wills, refuses, that imagines also, and perceives. Assuredly it is not little, if all these properties belong to my nature. But why should they not belong to it? Am I not that very being who now doubts of almost everything; who, for all that, understands and conceives certain things; who affirms one alone as true, and denies the others; who desires to know more of them, and does not wish to be deceived; who imagines many things, sometimes even despite his will; and is likewise percipient of many, as if through the medium of the senses. Is there nothing of all this as true as that I am, even although I should be always dreaming, and although he who gave me being employed all his ingenuity to deceive me? Is there also any one of these attributes that can be properly distinguished from my thought, or that can be said to be separate from myself? For it is of itself so evident that it is I who doubt, I who understand, and I who desire, that it is here unnecessary to add anything by way of rendering it more clear. And I am as certainly the same being who imagines; for, although it may be (as I before supposed) that nothing I imagine is true, still the power of imagination does not cease really to exist in me and to form part of my thought. In fine, I am the same being who perceives, that is, who apprehends certain objects as by the organs of sense, since, in truth, I see light, hear a noise, and feel heat. But it will be said that these presentations are false, and that I am dreaming. Let it be so. At all events it is certain that I seem to see light, hear a noise, and feel heat; this cannot be false, and this is what in me is properly called perceiving (sentire), which is nothing else than thinking. From this I begin to know what I am with somewhat greater clearness and distinctness than heretofore.

But, nevertheless, it still seems to me, and I cannot help believing, that corporeal things, whose images are formed by thought, (which fall under the senses), and are examined by the same, are known with much greater distinctness than that I know not what part of myself which is not imaginable; although, in truth, it may seem strange to say that I know and comprehend with greater distinctness things whose existence appears to me doubtful, that are unknown, and do not belong to me, than others of whose reality I am persuaded, that are known to me, and appertain to my proper nature; in a word, than myself. But I see clearly what is the state of the case. My mind is apt to wander, and will not yet submit to be restrained within the limits of truth. Let us therefore leave the mind to itself once more, and, according to it every kind of liberty, (permit it to consider the objects that appear to it from without), in order that, having afterwards withdrawn it from these gently and opportunely, (and fixed it on the consideration of its being and the properties it finds in itself), it may then be the more easily controlled.

Let us now accordingly consider the objects that are commonly thought to be (the most easily, and likewise) the most distinctly known, viz., the bodies we touch and see; not, indeed, bodies in general, for these general notions are usually somewhat more confused, but one body in particular. Take, for example, this piece of wax; it is quite fresh, having been but recently taken from the bee-hive; it has not yet lost the sweetness of the honey it contained; it still retains somewhat of the odour of the flowers from which it was gathered; its colour, figure, size, are apparent (to the sight); it is hard, cold, easily handled; and sounds when struck upon with the finger. In fine, all that contributes to make a body as distinctly known as possible, is found in the one before us. But, while I am speaking, let it be placed near the fire—what remained of the taste exhales, the smell evaporates, the colour changes, its figure is destroyed, its size increases, it becomes liquid, it grows hot, it can hardly be handled, and, although struck upon, it emits no sound. Does the same wax still remain after this change? It must be admitted that it does remain; no one doubts it, or judges otherwise. What, then, was it I knew with so much distinctness in the piece of wax? Assuredly, it could be nothing of all that I observed by means of the senses, since all the things that fell under taste, smell, sight, touch, and hearing are changed, and yet the same wax remains. It was perhaps what I now think, viz., that this wax was neither the sweetness of honey, the pleasant odour of flowers, the whiteness, the figure, nor the sound, but only a body that a little before appeared to me conspicuous under these forms, and which is now perceived under others. But, to speak precisely, what is it that I imagine when I think of it in this way? Let it be attentively considered, and, retrenching all that does not belong to the wax, let us see what remains. There certainly remains nothing, except something extended, flexible, and movable. But what is meant by flexible and movable? Is it not that I imagine that the piece of wax, being round, is capable of becoming square, or of passing from a square into a triangular figure? Assuredly such is not the case, because I conceive that it admits of an infinity of similar changes; and I am, moreover, unable to compass this infinity by imagination, and consequently this conception which I have of the wax is not the product of the faculty of imagination. But what now is this extension? Is it not also unknown? For it becomes greater when the wax is melted, greater when it is boiled, and greater still when the heat increases; and I should not conceive (clearly and) according to truth, the wax as it is, if I did not suppose that the piece we are considering admitted even of a wider variety of extension than I ever imagined. I must, therefore, admit that I cannot even comprehend by imagination what the piece of wax is, and that it is the mind alone (mens, Lat., entendement, F.) which perceives it. I speak of one piece in particular; for, as to wax in general, this is still more evident. But what is the piece of wax that can be perceived only by the (understanding or) mind? It is certainly the same which I see, touch, imagine; and, in fine, it is the same which, from the beginning, I believed it to be. But (and this it is of moment to observe) the perception of it is neither an act of sight, of touch, nor of imagination, and never was either of these, though it might formerly seem so, but is simply an intuition (inspectio) of the mind, which may be imperfect and confused, as it formerly was, or very clear and distinct, as it is at present, according as the attention is more or less directed to the elements which it contains, and of which it is composed.

But, meanwhile, I feel greatly astonished when I observe (the weakness of my mind, and) its proneness to error. For although, without at all giving expression to what I think, I consider all this in my own mind, words yet occasionally impede my progress, and I am almost led into error by the terms of ordinary language. We say, for example, that we see the same wax when it is before us, and not that we judge it to be the same from its retaining the same colour and figure: whence I should forthwith be disposed to conclude that the wax is known by the act of sight, and not by the intuition of the mind alone, were it not for the analogous instance of human beings passing on in the street below, as observed from a window. In this case I do not fail to say that I see the men themselves, just as I say that I see the wax; and yet what do I see from the window beyond hats and cloaks that might cover artificial machines, whose motions might be determined by springs? But I judge that there are human beings from these appearances, and thus I comprehend, by the faculty of judgment alone which is in the mind, what I believed I saw with my eyes.

The man who makes it his aim to rise to knowledge superior to the common, ought to be ashamed to seek occasions of doubting from the vulgar forms of speech; instead, therefore, of doing this, I shall proceed with the matter in hand, and inquire whether I had a clearer and more perfect perception of the piece of wax when I first saw it, and when I thought I knew it by means of the external sense itself, or, at all events, by the common sense (sensus communis), as it is called, that is, by the imaginative faculty; or whether I rather apprehend it more clearly at present, after having examined with greater care, both what it is, and in what way it can be known. It would certainly be ridiculous to entertain any doubt on this point. For what, in that first perception, was there distinct? What did I perceive which any animal might not have perceived? But when I distinguish the wax from its exterior forms, and when, as if I had stripped it of its vestments, I consider it quite naked, it is certain, although some error may still be found in my judgment, that I cannot, nevertheless, thus apprehend it without possessing a human mind.

But, finally, what shall I say of the mind itself, that is, of myself? For as yet I do not admit that I am anything but mind. What, then! I who seem to possess so distinct an apprehension of the piece of wax,—do I not know myself, both with greater truth and certitude, and also much more distinctly and clearly? For if I judge that the wax exists because I see it, it assuredly follows, much more evidently, that I myself am or exist, for the same reason: for it is possible that what I see may not in truth be wax, and that I do not even possess eyes with which to see anything; but it cannot be that when I see, or, which comes to the same thing, when I think I see, I myself who think am nothing. So likewise, if I judge that the wax exists because I touch it, it will still also follow that I am; and if I determine that my imagination, or any other cause, whatever it be, persuades me of the existence of the wax, I will still draw the same conclusion. And what is here remarked of the piece of wax, is applicable to all the other things that are external to me. And further, if the (notion or) perception of wax appeared to me more precise and distinct, after that not only sight and touch, but many other causes besides, rendered it manifest to my apprehension, with how much greater distinctness must I now know myself, since all the reasons that contribute to the knowledge of the nature of wax, or of any body whatever, manifest still better the nature of my mind? And there are besides so many other things in the mind itself that contribute to the illustration of its nature, that those dependent on the body, to which I have here referred, scarcely merit to be taken into account.

But, in conclusion, I find I have insensibly reverted to the point I desired; for, since it is now manifest to me that bodies themselves are not properly perceived by the senses nor by the faculty of imagination, but by the intellect alone; and since they are not perceived because they are seen and touched, but only because they are understood (or rightly comprehended by thought), I readily discover that there is nothing more easily or clearly apprehended than my own mind. But because it is difficult to rid one's self so promptly of an opinion to which one has been long accustomed, it will be desirable to tarry for some time at this stage, that, by long continued meditation, I may more deeply impress upon my memory this new knowledge.

• Charles Sanders Peirce (1839–1914)

Inquiry and Belief[6]

Charles Sanders Peirce, one of the most original minds of the nineteenth century, was educated at Harvard and was during his whole life interested in science and philosophy, although he never held a permanent university post. Known to a small circle for his work in mathematical logic, the philosophy of meaning (semantics), and the philosophy of science, his fame has constantly grown since his death in 1914. His more technical contributions appear in the six volumes of *The Collected Papers of Charles Sanders Peirce*. But he wrote many semipopular articles, one of which the following selection reproduces. Peirce views inquiry of all kinds as a struggle to gain belief, that is, to pass from the discomforts of doubt to a more settled state of mind. And he contrasts the various methods at our disposal for "fixing belief"—those of tenacity, authority, metaphysics, and science. He indicates the superiority of the method of science in terms which are eloquent, moving, and ironic.

Few persons care to study logic, because everybody conceives himself to be proficient enough in the art of reasoning already. But I observe that this satisfaction is limited to one's own ratiocination, and does not extend to that of other men.

We come to the full possession of our power of drawing inferences, the last of all our faculties; for it is not so much a natural gift as a long and difficult art. The history of its practice would make a grand subject for a book. The medieval schoolmen, following the Romans, made logic the earliest of a boy's studies after grammar, as being very easy. So it was as they understood it. Its fundamental

---

[6] From C. S. Peirce, "The Fixation of Belief," *Popular Science Monthly*, 1877. One paragraph is omitted.

principle, according to them, was, that all knowledge rests either on authority or reason; but that whatever is deduced by reason depends ultimately on a premiss derived from authority. Accordingly, as soon as a boy was perfect in the syllogistic procedure, his intellectual kit of tools was held to be complete.

To Roger Bacon, that remarkable mind who in the middle of the thirteenth century was almost a scientific man, the schoolmen's conception of reasoning appeared only an obstacle to truth. He saw that experience alone teaches anything—a proposition which to us seems easy to understand, because a distinct conception of experience has been handed down to us from former generations; which to him likewise seemed perfectly clear, because its difficulties had not yet unfolded themselves. Of all kinds of experience, the best, he thought, was interior illumination, which teaches many things about Nature which the external senses could never discover, such as the transubstantiation of bread.

Four centuries later, the more celebrated Bacon, in the first book of his *Novum Organum,* gave his clear account of experience as something which must be open to verification and reexamination. But, superior as Lord Bacon's conception is to earlier notions, a modern reader who is not in awe of his grandiloquence is chiefly struck by the inadequacy of his view of scientific procedure. That we have only to make some crude experiments, to draw up briefs of the results in certain blank forms, to go through these by rule, checking off everything disproved and setting down the alternatives, and that thus in a few years physical science would be finished up—what an idea! "He wrote on science like a Lord Chancellor," indeed, as Harvey, a genuine man of science, said.

The early scientists, Copernicus, Tycho Brahe, Kepler, Galileo, Harvey, and Gilbert, had methods more like those of their modern brethren. Kepler undertook to draw a curve through the places of Mars, and to state the times occupied by the planet in describing the different parts of that curve; but perhaps his greatest service to science was in impressing on men's minds that this was the thing to be done if they wished to improve astronomy; that they were not to content themselves with inquiring whether one system of epicycles was better than another, but that they were to sit down to the figures and find out what the curve, in truth, was. He accomplished this by his incomparable energy and courage, blundering along in the most inconceivable way (to us), from one irrational hypothesis to another, until, after trying twenty-two of these, he fell, by the mere exhaustion of his invention, upon the orbit which a mind well furnished with the weapons of modern logic would have tried almost at the outset.

In the same way, every work of science great enough to be well remembered for a few generations affords some exemplification of the defective state of the art of reasoning of the time when it was written; and each chief step in science has been a lesson in logic. It was so when Lavoisier and his contemporaries took up the study of Chemistry. The old chemist's maxim had been, "Lege, lege, lege, labora, ora, et relege." Lavoisier's method was not to read and pray, but to dream that some long and complicated chemical process would have a certain effect, to put it into practice with dull patience, after its inevitable failure, to dream that with some modification it would have another result, and to end by publishing the last dream as a fact: his way was to carry his mind into his laboratory, and literally to make of his alembics and cucurbits instruments of thought, giving a new conception of reasoning as something which was to be done with one's eyes open, in manipulating real things instead of words and fancies.

The object of reasoning is to find out, from the consideration of what we already know, something else which we do not know. Consequently, reasoning is good if it be such as to give a true conclusion from true premises, and not otherwise. Thus, the question of validity is purely one of fact and not of thinking. A being the facts stated in the premises and B being that concluded, the question is, whether these facts are really so related that if A were B would generally be. If so, the inference is valid; if not, not. It is not in the least the question whether, when the premises are accepted by the mind, we feel an impulse to accept the conclusion also. It is true that we do generally reason correctly by nature. But that is an accident; the true conclusion would remain true if we had no impulse to accept it; and the false one would remain false, though we could not resist the tendency to believe in it.

We are, doubtless, in the main logical animals, but we are not perfectly so. Most of us, for example, are naturally more sanguine and hopeful than logic would justify. We seem to be so constituted that in the absence of any facts to go upon we are happy and self-satisfied; so that the effect of experience is continually to contract our hopes and aspirations. Yet a lifetime of the application of this corrective does not usually eradicate our sanguine disposition. Where hope is unchecked by any experience, it is likely that our optimism is extravagant. Logicality in regard to practical matters (if this be understood, not in the old sense, but as consisting in a wise union of security with fruitfulness of reasoning) is the most useful quality an animal can possess, and might, therefore, result from the action of natural selection; but outside of these it is probably of more advantage to the animal to have his mind filled with pleasing and encouraging visions, independently of their truth; and thus, upon unpractical subjects, natural selection might occasion a fallacious tendency of thought.

That which determines us, from given premisses, to draw one inference rather than another, is some habit of mind, whether it be constitutional or acquired. The habit is good or otherwise, according as it produces true conclusions from true premisses or not; and an inference is regarded as valid or not, without reference to the truth or falsity of its conclusion specially, but according as the habit which determines it is such as to produce true conclusions in general or not. The particular habit of mind which governs this or that inference may be formulated in a proposition whose truth depends on the validity of the inferences which the habit determines; and such a formula is called a guiding principle of inference. Suppose, for example, that we observe that a rotating disk of copper quickly comes to rest when placed between the poles of a magnet, and we infer that this will happen with every disk of copper. The guiding principle is, that what is true of one piece of copper is true of another. Such a guiding principle with regard to copper would be much safer than with regard to many other substances—brass, for example.

A book might be written to signalize all the most important of these guiding principles of reasoning. It would probably be, we must confess, of no service to a person whose thought is directed wholly to practical subjects, and whose activity moves along thoroughly-beaten paths. The problems that present themselves to such a mind are matters of routine which he has learned once for all to handle in learning his business. But let a man venture into an unfamiliar field, or where his results are not continually checked by experience, and all history shows that the most masculine intellect will ofttimes lose his orientation and waste his efforts in directions which bring him no nearer to his goal, or even carry him entirely astray. He is like a ship in the open sea, with no one on board who understands the rules of navigation. And in such a case some general study of the guiding principles of reasoning would be sure to be found useful.

The subject could hardly be treated, however, without being first limited; since almost any fact may serve as a guiding principle. But it so happens that there exists a division among facts, such that in one class are all those which are absolutely essential as guiding principles, while in the others are all which have any other interest as objects of research. This division is between those which are necessarily taken for granted in asking why a certain conclusion is thought to follow from certain premises, and those which are not implied in such a question. A moment's thought will show that a variety of facts are already assumed when the logical question is first asked. It is implied, for instance, that there are such states of mind as doubt and belief—that a passage from one to the other is possible, the object of thought remaining the same, and that this transition is subject to some rules by which all minds are alike bound. As these are facts which we must already know before we can have any clear conception of reasoning at all, it cannot be supposed to be any longer of much interest to inquire into their truth or falsity. On the other hand, it is easy to believe that those rules of reasoning which are deduced from the very idea of the process are the ones which are the most essential; and, indeed, that so long as it conforms to these it will, at least, not lead to false conclusions from true premises. In point of fact, the importance of what may be deduced from the assumptions involved in the logical question turns out to be greater than might be supposed, and this for reasons which it is difficult to exhibit at the outset. The only one which I shall here mention is, that conceptions which are really products of logical reflection, without being readily seen to be so, mingle with our ordinary thoughts, and are frequently the causes of great confusion. This is the case, for example, with the conception of quality. A quality, as such, is never an object of observation. We can see that a thing is blue or green, but the quality of being blue and the quality of being green are not things which we see; they are products of logical reflections. The truth is, that common-sense, or thought as it first emerges above the level of the narrowly practical, is deeply imbued with that bad logical quality to which the epithet metaphysical is commonly applied; and nothing can clear it up but a severe course of logic.

We generally know when we wish to ask a question and when we wish to pronounce a judgment, for there is a dissimilarity between the sensation of doubting and that of believing.

But this is not all which distinguishes doubt from belief. There is a practical difference. Our beliefs guide our desires and shape our actions. The Assassins, or followers of the Old Man of the Mountain, used to rush into death at his least command, because they believed that obedience to him would insure everlasting felicity. Had they doubted this, they would not have acted as they did.

So it is with every belief, according to its degree. The feeling of believing is a more or less sure indication of there being established in our nature some habit which will determine our actions. Doubt never has such an effect.

Nor must we overlook a third point of difference. Doubt is an uneasy and dissatisfied state from which we struggle to free ourselves and pass into the state of belief; while the latter is a calm and satisfactory state which we do not wish to avoid, or to change to a belief in anything else. On the contrary, we cling tenaciously, not merely to believing, but to believing just what we do believe.

Thus, both doubt and belief have positive effects upon us, though very different ones. Belief does not make us act at once, but puts us into such a condition that we shall behave in some certain way, when the occasion arises. Doubt has not the least such active effect, but stimulates us to inquiry until it is destroyed. This reminds us of the irritation of a nerve and the reflex action produced thereby, while for the analogue of belief, in the nervous system, we must look to what are called nervous associations—for example, to that habit of the nerves in consequence of which the smell of a peach will make the mouth water.

The irritation of doubt causes a struggle to attain a state of belief. I shall term this struggle Inquiry, though it must be admitted that this is sometimes not a very apt designation.

The irritation of doubt is the only immediate motive for the struggle to attain belief. It is certainly best for us that our beliefs should be such as may truly guide our actions so as to satisfy our desires; and this reflection will make us reject every belief which does not seem to have been so formed as to insure this result. But it will only do so by creating a doubt in the place of that belief. With the doubt, therefore, the struggle begins, and with the cessation of doubt it ends. Hence, the sole object of inquiry is the settlement of opinion. We may fancy that this is not enough for us, and that we seek, not merely an opinion, but a true opinion. But put this fancy to the test, and it proves groundless; for as soon as a firm belief is reached we are entirely satisfied, whether the belief be true or false. And it is clear that nothing out of the sphere of our knowledge can be our object, for nothing which does not affect the mind can be the motive for mental effort. The most that can be maintained is, that we seek for a belief that we shall think to be true. But we think each one of our beliefs to be true, and, indeed, it is mere tautology to say so.

That the settlement of opinion is the sole end of inquiry is a very important proposition. It sweeps away, at once, various vague and

erroneous conceptions of proof. A few of these may be noticed
here.

1. Some philosophers have imagined that to start an inquiry it
was only necessary to utter a question whether orally or by setting
it down upon paper, and have even recommended us to begin our
studies with questioning everything! But the mere putting of a
proposition into the interrogative form does not stimulate the mind
to any struggle after belief. There must be a real and living doubt,
and without this all discussion is idle.

2. It is a very common idea that a demonstration must rest on
some ultimate and absolutely indubitable propositions. These, according to one school, are first principles of a general nature; according to another, are first sensations. But, in point of fact, an inquiry,
to have that completely satisfactory result called demonstration,
has only to start with propositions perfectly free from all actual
doubt. If the premises are not in fact doubted at all, they cannot
be more satisfactory than they are.

3. Some people seem to love to argue a point after all the world
is fully convinced of it. But no further advance can be made.
When doubt ceases, mental action on the subject comes to an end;
and, if it did go on, it would be without a purpose.

If the settlement of opinion is the sole object of inquiry, and if
belief is of the nature of a habit, why should we not attain the desired end, by taking as answer to a question any we may fancy, and
constantly reiterating it to ourselves, dwelling on all which may
conduce to that belief, and learning to turn with contempt and
hatred from anything that might disturb it? This simple and direct
method is really pursued by many men. I remember once being
entreated not to read a certain newspaper lest it might change my
opinion upon free-trade. "Lest I might be entrapped by its fallacies
and misstatements," was the form of expression. "You are not," my
friend said, "a special student of political economy. You might,
therefore, easily be deceived by fallacious arguments upon the subject. You might, then, if you read this paper, be led to believe in
protection. But you admit that free-trade is the true doctrine; and
you do not wish to believe what is not true." I have often known
this system to be deliberately adopted. Still oftener, the instinctive
dislike of an undecided state of mind, exaggerated into a vague
dread of doubt, makes men cling spasmodically to the views they
already take. The man feels that, if he only holds to his belief without wavering, it will be entirely satisfactory. Nor can it be denied
that a steady and immovable faith yields great peace of mind. It
may, indeed, give rise to inconveniences, as if a man should reso-

lutely continue to believe that fire would not burn him, or that he would be eternally damned if he received his ingesta otherwise than through a stomach-pump. But then the man who adopts this method will not allow that its inconveniences are greater than its advantages. He will say, "I hold steadfastly to the truth, and the truth is always wholesome." And in many cases it may very well be that the pleasure he derives from his calm faith overbalances any inconveniences resulting from its deceptive character. Thus, if it be true that death is annihilation, then the man who believes that he will certainly go straight to heaven when he dies, provided he have fulfilled certain simple observances in this life, has a cheap pleasure which will not be followed by the least disappointment. A similar consideration seems to have weight with many persons in religious topics, for we frequently hear it said, "Oh, I could not believe so-and-so, because I should be wretched if I did." When an ostrich buries its head in the sand as danger approaches, it very likely takes the happiest course. It hides the danger, and then calmly says there is no danger; and, if it feels perfectly sure there is none, why should it raise its head to see? A man may go through life, systematically keeping out of view all that might cause a change in his opinions, and if he only succeeds—basing his method, as he does, on two fundamental psychological laws—I do not see what can be said against his doing so. It would be an egotistical impertinence to object that his procedure is irrational, for that only amounts to saying that his method of settling belief is not ours. He does not propose to himself to be rational, and, indeed, will often talk with scorn of man's weak and illusive reason. So let him think as he pleases.

But this method of fixing belief, which may be called the method of tenacity, will be unable to hold its ground in practice. The social impulse is against it. The man who adopts it will find that other men think differently from him, and it will be apt to occur to him, in some saner moment, that their opinions are quite as good as his own, and this will shake his confidence in his belief. This conception, that another man's thought or sentiment may be equivalent to one's own, is a distinctly new step, and a highly important one. It arises from an impulse too strong in man to be suppressed, without danger of destroying the human species. Unless we make ourselves hermits, we shall necessarily influence each other's opinions; so that the problem becomes how to fix belief, not in the individual merely, but in the community.

Let the will of the state act, then, instead of that of the individual. Let an institution be created which shall have for its object to keep correct doctrines before the attention of the people, to reiterate them perpetually, and to teach them to the young; having at the same time power to prevent contrary doctrines from being taught, advocated, or expressed. Let all possible causes of a change of mind be removed from men's apprehensions. Let them be kept ignorant, lest they should learn of some reason to think otherwise than they do. Let their passions be enlisted, so that they may regard private and unusual opinions with hatred and horror. Then, let all men who reject the established belief be terrified into silence. Let the people turn out and tar-and-feather such men, or let inquisitions be made into the manner of thinking of suspected persons, and when they are found guilty of forbidden beliefs, let them be subjected to some signal punishment. When complete agreement could not otherwise be reached, a general massacre of all who have not thought in a certain way has proved a very effective means of settling opinion in a country. If the power to do this be wanting, let a list of opinions be drawn up, to which no man of the least independence of thought can assent, and let the faithful be required to accept all these propositions, in order to segregate them as radically as possible from the influence of the rest of the world.

This method has, from the earliest times, been one of the chief means of upholding correct theological and political doctrines, and of preserving their universal or catholic character. In Rome, especially, it has been practised from the days of Numa Pompilius to those of Pius Nonus. This is the most perfect example in history; but wherever there is a priesthood—and no religion has been without one—this method has been more or less made use of. Wherever there is an aristocracy, or a guild, or any association of a class of men whose interests depend, or are supposed to depend, on certain propositions, there will be inevitably found some traces of this natural product of social feeling. Cruelties always accompany this system; and when it is consistently carried out, they become atrocities of the most horrible kind in the eyes of any rational man. Nor should this occasion surprise, for the officer of a society does not feel justified in surrendering the interests of that society for the sake of mercy, as he might his own private interests. It is natural, therefore, that sympathy and fellowship should thus produce a most ruthless power.

In judging this method of fixing belief, which may be called the method of authority, we must, in the first place, allow its immeasurable mental and moral superiority to the method of tenacity. Its success is proportionately greater; and, in fact, it has over and over again worked the most majestic results. The mere structures of stone which it has caused to be put together—in Siam, for example, in Egypt, and in Europe—have many of them a sublimity hardly more than rivalled by the greatest works of Nature. And, except the geological epochs, there are no periods of time so vast as those which are measured by some of these organized faiths. If we scrutinize the matter closely, we shall find that there has not been one of their creeds which has remained always the same; yet the change is so slow as to be imperceptible during one person's life, so that individual belief remains sensibly fixed. For the mass of mankind, then, there is perhaps no better method than this. If it is their highest impulse to be intellectual slaves, then slaves they ought to remain.

But no institution can undertake to regulate opinions upon every subject. Only the most important ones can be attended to, and on the rest men's minds must be left to the action of natural causes. This imperfection will be no source of weakness so long as men are in such a state of culture that one opinion does not influence another —that is, so long as they cannot put two and two together. But in the most priest-ridden states some individuals will be found who are raised above that condition. These men possess a wider sort of social feeling; they see that men in other countries and in other ages have held to very different doctrines from those which they themselves have been brought up to believe; and they cannot help seeing that it is the mere accident of their having been taught as they have, and of their having been surrounded with the manners and associations they have, that has caused them to believe as they do and not far differently. Nor can their candour resist the reflection that there is no reason to rate their own views at a higher value than those of other nations and other centuries; thus giving rise to doubts in their minds.

They will further perceive that such doubts as these must exist in their minds with reference to every belief which seems to be determined by the caprice either of themselves or of those who originated the popular opinions. The willful adherence to a belief, and the arbitrary forcing of it upon others, must, therefore, both be given up. A different new method of settling opinions must be adopted, that shall not only produce an impulse to believe, but shall also decide what proposition it is which is to be believed. Let the action of natural preferences be unimpeded, then, and under their influence let men, conversing together and regarding matters in different lights, gradually develop beliefs in harmony with natural causes. This method resembles that by which conceptions of art have been brought to maturity. The most perfect example of it is to be found in the history of metaphysical philosophy. Systems of this sort have not usually rested upon any observed facts, at least not in any great degree. They have been chiefly adopted because their fundamental propositions seemed "agreeable to reason." This is an apt expression; it does not mean that which agrees with experience, but that which we find ourselves inclined to believe. Plato, for example, finds it agreeable to reason that the distances of the celestial spheres from one another should be proportional to the different lengths of strings which produce harmonious chords. Many philosophers have been led to their main conclusions by considerations like this; but this is the lowest and least developed form which the method takes, for it is clear that another man might find Kepler's theory, that the celestial spheres are proportional to the inscribed and circumscribed spheres of the different regular solids, more agreeable to his reason. But the shock of opinions will soon lead men to rest on preferences of a far more universal nature. Take, for example, the doctrine that man only acts selfishly—that is, from the consideration that acting in one way will afford him more pleasure than acting in another. This rests on no fact in the world, but it has had a wide acceptance as being the only reasonable theory.

This method is far more intellectual and respectable from the point of view of reason than either of the others which we have noticed. Indeed, as long as no better method can be applied, it ought to be followed, since it is then the expression of instinct which must be the ultimate cause of belief in all cases. But its failure has been the most manifest. It makes of inquiry something similar to the development of taste; but taste, unfortunately, is always more or less a matter of fashion, and accordingly metaphysicians have never come to any fixed agreement, but the pendulum has swung backward and forward between a more material and a more spiritual philosophy, from the earliest times to the latest. And so from this, which has been called the a priori method, we are driven, in Lord Bacon's phrase, to a true induction. We have examined into this a priori method as something which promised to deliver our opinions from their accidental and capricious element. But development, while it is a process which eliminates the effect of some casual circumstances, only magnifies that of others. This method, therefore, does not differ in a very essential way from that of authority. The government may not have lifted its finger to influence my convictions; I may have been left outwardly quite free to choose, we will say, between monogamy and polygamy, and, appealing to my conscience only, I may have concluded that the latter practice is in itself licentious. But when I come to see that the chief obstacle to the spread of Christianity among a people of as high culture as the Hindoos has been a conviction of the immorality of our way of treating women, I cannot help seeing that, though governments do not interfere, sentiments in their development will be very greatly determined by accidental causes. Now, there are some people, among whom I must suppose that my reader is to be found, who, when they see that any belief of theirs is determined by any circumstance extraneous to the facts, will from that moment not merely admit in words that that belief is doubtful, but will experience a real doubt of it, so that it ceases in some degree at least to be a belief.

To satisfy our doubts, therefore, it is necessary that a method should be found by which our beliefs may be determined by nothing human, but by some external permanency—by something upon which our thinking has no effect. Some mystics imagine that they have such a method in a private inspiration from on high. But that is only a form of the method of tenacity, in which the conception of truth as something public is not yet developed. Our external permanency would not be individual. It must be something which affects, or might affect, every man. And, though these affections are necessarily as various as are individual conditions, yet the method must be such that the ultimate conclusion of every man shall be the same. Such is the method of science. Its fundamental hypothesis, restated in more familiar language, is this: There are Real things, whose characters are entirely independent of our opinions about them; those Reals affect our senses according to regular laws, and, though our sensations are as different as are our relations to the objects, yet, by taking advantage of the laws of perception, we can ascertain by reasoning how things really and truly are; and any man, if he have sufficient experience and he reason enough about it, will be led to the one True conclusion. The new conception here involved is that of Reality. It may be asked how I know that there are any Reals. If this hypothesis is the sole support of my method of inquiry, my method of inquiry must not be used to support my hypothesis. The reply is this: 1. If investigation cannot be regarded as proving that there are Real things, it at least does not lead to a contrary conclusion; but the method and the conception on which it is based remain ever in harmony. No doubts of the method, therefore, necessarily arise from its practice, as is the case with all the others. 2. The feeling which gives rise to any method of fixing belief is a dissatisfaction at two repugnant propositions. But here already is a vague concession that there is some one thing which a proposition should represent. Nobody, therefore, can really doubt that there are Reals, for, if he did, doubt would not be a source of dissatisfaction. The hypothesis, therefore, is one which every mind admits. So that the social impulse does not cause men to doubt it. 3. Everybody uses the scientific method about a great many things, and only ceases to use it when he does not know how to apply it. 4. Experience of the method has not led us to doubt it, but, on the contrary, scientific investigation has had the most wonderful triumphs in the way of settling opinion. These afford the explanation of my not doubting the method or the hypothesis which it supposes; and not having any doubt, nor believing that anybody else whom I could influence has, it would be the merest babble for me to say more about it. If there be anybody with a living doubt upon the subject, let him consider it.

To describe the method of scientific investigation is the object of this series of papers. At present I have only room to notice some points of contrast between it and other methods of fixing belief.

This is the only one of the four methods which presents any distinction of a right and a wrong way. If I adopt the method of tenacity, and shut myself out from all influences, whatever I think necessary to doing this, is necessary according to that method. So with the method of authority: the state may try to put down heresy by means which, from a scientific point of view, seem very ill-calculated to accomplish its purposes; but the only test on that method is what the state thinks; so that it cannot pursue the method wrongly. So with the a priori method. The very essence of it is to think as one is inclined to think. All metaphysicians will be sure to do that, however they may be inclined to judge each other to be perversely wrong. The Hegelian system recognizes every natural tendency of thought as logical, although it be certain to be abolished by counter-tendencies. Hegel thinks there is a regular system in the succession of these tendencies, in consequence of which, after drifting one way and the other for a long time, opinion will at last go right. And it is true that metaphysicians do get the right ideas at last; Hegel's system of Nature represents tolerably the science of his day; and one may be sure that whatever scientific investigation shall have put out of doubt will presently receive a priori demonstration on the part of the metaphysicians. But with the scientific method the case is different. I may start with known and observed facts to proceed to the unknown; and yet the rules which I follow in doing so may not be such as investigation would approve. The test of whether I am truly following the method is not an immediate appeal to my feelings and purposes, but, on the contrary, itself involves the application of the method. Hence it is that bad reasoning as well as good reasoning is possible; and this fact is the foundation of the practical side of logic.

It is not to be supposed that the first three methods of settling opinion present no advantage whatever over the scientific method. On the contrary, each has some peculiar convenience of its own. The a priori method is distinguished for its comfortable conclusions. It is the nature of the process to adopt whatever belief we are inclined to, and there are certain flatteries to the vanity of man which we all believe by nature, until we are awakened from our pleasing dream by rough facts. The method of authority will always govern the mass of mankind; and those who wield the various forms of organized force in the state will never be convinced that dangerous reasoning ought not to be suppressed in some way. If liberty of speech is to be untrammelled from the grosser forms of constraint, then uniformity of opinion will be secured by a moral terrorism to which the respectability of society will give its thorough approval. Following the method of authority is the path of peace. Certain non-conformities are permitted; certain others (considered unsafe) are forbidden. These are different in different countries and in different ages; but, wherever you are, let it be known that you seriously hold a tabooed belief, and you may be perfectly sure of being treated with a cruelty less brutal but more refined than hunting you like a wolf. Thus, the greatest intellectual benefactors of mankind have never dared, and dare not now, to utter the whole of their thought; and thus a shade of prima facie doubt is cast upon every proposition which is considered essential to the security of society. Singularly enough, the persecution does not all come from without; but a man torments himself and is oftentimes most distressed at finding himself believing propositions which he has been brought up to regard with aversion. The peaceful and sympathetic man will, therefore, find it hard to resist the temptation to submit his opinions to authority. But most of all I admire the method of tenacity for its strength, simplicity, and directness. Men who pursue it are distinguished for their decision of character, which becomes very easy with such a mental rule. They do not waste time in trying to make up their minds what they want, but, fastening like lightning upon whatever alternative comes first, they hold it to the end, whatever happens, without an instant's irresolution. This is one of the splendid qualities which generally accompany brilliant, unlasting success. It is impossible not to envy the man who can dismiss reason, although we know how it must turn out at last.

Such are the advantages which the other methods of settling

opinion have over scientific investigation. A man should consider well of them; and then he should consider that, after all, he wishes his opinions to coincide with the fact, and that there is no reason why the results of those three first methods should do so. To bring about this effect is the prerogative of the method of science. Upon such considerations he has to make his choice—a choice which is far more than the adoption of any intellectual opinion, which is one of the ruling decisions of his life, to which, when once made, he is bound to adhere. The force of habit will sometimes cause a man to hold on to old beliefs, after he is in a condition to see that they have no sound basis. But reflection upon the state of the case will overcome these habits, and he ought to allow reflection its full weight. People sometimes shrink from doing this, having an idea that beliefs are wholesome which they cannot help feeling rest on nothing. But let such persons suppose an analogous though different case from their own. Let them ask themselves what they would say to a reformed Mussulman who should hesitate to give up his old notions in regard to the relations of the sexes; or to a reformed Catholic who should still shrink from reading the Bible. Would they not say that these persons ought to consider the matter fully, and clearly understand the new doctrine, and then ought to embrace it, in its entirety? But, above all, let it be considered that what is more wholesome than any particular belief is integrity of belief, and that to avoid looking into the support of any belief from a fear that it may turn out rotten is quite as immoral as it is disadvantageous. The person who confesses that there is such a thing as truth, which is distinguished from falsehood simply by this, that if acted on it should, on full consideration, carry us to the point we aim at and not astray, and then, though convinced of this, dares not know the truth and seeks to avoid it, is in a sorry state of mind indeed.

Yes, the other methods do have their merits: a clear logical conscience does cost something—just as any virtue, just as all that we cherish, costs us dear. But we should not desire it to be otherwise. The genius of a man's logical method should be loved and reverenced as his bride, whom he has chosen from all the world. He need not condemn the others; on the contrary, he may honour them deeply, and in doing so he only honours her the more. But she is the one that he has chosen, and he knows that he was right in making that choice. And having made it, he will work and fight for her, and will not complain that there are blows to take, hoping that there may be as many and as hard to give, and will strive to be the worthy knight and champion of her from the blaze of whose splendours he draws his inspiration and his courage.

• Henri Bergson (1859–1941)

Analysis and Intuition[7]

Henri Bergson was the most famous philosopher to appear in France between the Franco-Prussian and the Second World War. A distinguished lecturer at the College de France, Nobel Prize winner in literature, and creative mind, his philosophy has been a subject of great controversy. Beginning with an interest in biology, Bergson's work slowly became an attack upon the narrowness of scientific method and a defense of those forms of knowledge with which the artist and the religious mystic are familiar. In the following selection Bergson's aptness of illustration and literary ability show to excellent advantage. In it he attempts to distinguish scientific and intuitive methods of knowing and to explain his preference for the latter. He does this largely through his examination of self-knowledge and its two forms. Other important works of Bergson are: *Time and Free Will, Matter and Memory, Creative Evolution,* and *The Two Sources of Morality and Religion.*

A comparison of the definitions of metaphysics and the various conceptions of the absolute leads to the discovery that philosophers, in spite of their apparent divergencies, agree in distinguishing two profoundly different ways of knowing a thing. The first implies that we move round the object; the second that we enter into it. The first depends on the point of view at which we are placed and on the symbols by which we express ourselves. The second neither depends on a point of view nor relies on any symbol. The first kind of knowledge may be said to stop at the relative; the second, in those cases where it is possible, to attain the absolute.

Consider, for example, the movement of an object in space. My perception of the motion will vary with the point of view, moving or stationary, from which I observe it. My expression of it will vary with the systems of axes, or the points of reference, to which I relate it; that is, with the symbols by which I translate it. For this double reason I call such motion relative: in the one case, as in the other, I am placed outside the object itself. But when I speak of an abso-

[7] From Henri Bergson, *An Introduction to Metaphysics,* trans. T. E. Hulme, pp. 1-29. Copyright, 1912, by G. P. Putnam's Sons.

lute movement, I am attributing to the moving object an interior, and, so to speak, states of mind; I also imply that I am in sympathy with those states, and that I insert myself in them by an effort of imagination. Then, according as the object is moving or stationary, according as it adopts one movement or another, what I experience will vary. And what I experience will depend neither on the point of view I may take up in regard to the object, since I am inside the object itself, nor on the symbols by which I may translate the motion, since I have rejected all translations in order to possess the original. In short, I shall no longer grasp the movement from without, remaining where I am, but from where it is, from within, as it is in itself. I shall possess an absolute.

Consider, again, a character whose adventures are related to me in a novel. The author may multiply the traits of his hero's character, may make him speak and act as much as he pleases, but all this can never be equivalent to the simple and indivisible feeling which I should experience if I were able for an instant to identify myself with the person of the hero himself. Out of that indivisible feeling, as from a spring, all the words, gestures, and actions of the man would appear to me to flow naturally. They would no longer be accidents which, added to the idea I had already formed of the character, continually enriched that idea, without ever completing it. The character would be given to me all at once, in its entirety, and the thousand incidents which manifest it, instead of adding themselves to the idea and so enriching it, would seem to me, on the contrary, to detach themselves from it, without, however, exhausting it or impoverishing its essence. All the things I am told about the man provide me with so many points of view from which I can observe him. All the traits which describe him, and which can make him known to me only by so many comparisons with persons or things I know already, are signs by which he is expressed more or less symbolically. Symbols and points of view, therefore, place me outside him; they give me only what he has in common with others, and not what belongs to him and to him alone. But that which is properly himself, that which constitutes his essence, cannot be perceived from without, being internal by definition, nor be expressed by symbols, being incommensurable with everything else. Description, history, and analysis leave me here in the relative. Coincidence with the person himself would alone give me the absolute.

It is in this sense, and in this sense only, that absolute is synonymous with perfection. Were all the photographs of a town, taken from all possible points of view, to go on indefinitely completing one another, they would never be equivalent to the solid town in which we walk about. Were all the translations of a poem into all possible languages to add together their various shades of meaning and, correcting each other by a kind of mutual retouching, to give a more and more faithful image of the poem they translate, they would yet never succeed in rendering the inner meaning of the original. A representation taken from a certain point of view, a translation made with certain symbols, will always remain imperfect in comparison with the object of which a view has been taken, or which the symbols seek to express. But the absolute, which is the object and not its representation, the original and not its translation, is perfect, by being perfectly what it is.

It is doubtless for this reason that the absolute has often been identified with the infinite. Suppose that I wished to communicate to some one who did not know Greek the extraordinarily simple impression that a passage in Homer makes upon me; I should first give a translation of the lines, I should then comment on my translation, and then develop the commentary; in this way, by piling up explanation on explanation, I might approach nearer and nearer to what I wanted to express; but I should never quite reach it. When you raise your arm, you accomplish a movement of which you have, from within, a simple perception; but for me, watching it from the outside, your arm passes through one point, then through another, and between these two there will be still other points; so that, if I began to count, the operation would go on for ever. Viewed from the inside, then, an absolute is a simple thing; but looked at from the outside, that is to say, relatively to other things, it becomes, in relation to these signs which express it, the gold coin for which we never seem able to finish giving small change. Now, that which lends itself at the same time both to an indivisible apprehension and to an inexhaustible enumeration is, by the very definition of the word, an infinite.

It follows from this that an absolute could only be given in an intuition, whilst everything else falls within the province of analysis. By intuition is meant the kind of intellectual sympathy by which one places oneself within an object in order to coincide with what is unique in it and consequently inexpressible. Analysis, on the contrary, is the operation which reduces the object to elements already known, that is, to elements common both to it and other objects. To analyze, therefore, is to express a thing as a function of something other than itself. All analysis is thus a translation, a development into symbols, a representation taken from successive points of view from which we note as many resemblances as possible between the new object which we are studying and others which we believe we know already. In its eternally unsatisfied desire to embrace the object around which it is compelled to turn, analysis multiplies without end the number of its points of view in order to complete its always incomplete representation, and ceaselessly varies its symbols that it may perfect the always imperfect translation. It goes on, therefore, to infinity. But intuition, if intuition is possible, is a simple act.

Now it is easy to see that the ordinary function of positive science is analysis. Positive science works, then, above all, with symbols. Even the most concrete of the natural sciences, those concerned with life, confine themselves to the visible form of living beings, their organs and anatomical elements. They make comparisons between these forms, they reduce the more complex to the more simple; in short, they study the workings of life in what is, so to speak, only its visual symbol. If there exists any means of possessing a reality absolutely instead of knowing it relatively, of placing oneself within it instead of looking at it from outside points of view, of having the intuition instead of making the analysis: in short, of seizing it without any expression, translation, or symbolic representation—metaphysics is that means. Metaphysics, then, is the science which claims to dispense with symbols.

There is one reality, at least, which we all seize from within, by intuition and not be simple analysis. It is our own personality in its flowing through time—our self which endures. We may sympathize intellectually with nothing else, but we certainly sympathize with our own selves.

When I direct my attention inward to contemplate my own self (supposed for the moment to be inactive), I perceive at first, as a crust solidified on the surface, all the perceptions which come to it from the material world. These perceptions are clear, distinct, juxtaposed or juxtaposable one with another; they tend to group themselves into objects. Next, I notice the memories which more or less adhere to these perceptions and which serve to interpret them. These memories have been detached, as it were, from the depth of my personality, drawn to the surface by the perceptions which resemble them; they rest on the surface of my mind without being absolutely myself. Lastly, I feel the stir of tendencies and motor habits—a crowd of virtual actions, more or less firmly bound to these perceptions and memories. All these clearly defined elements appear more distinct from me, the more distinct they are from each other. Radiating, as they do, from within outwards, they form, collectively, the surface of a sphere which tends to grow larger and lose itself in the exterior world. But if I draw myself in from the periphery towards the centre, if I search in the depth of my being that which is most uniformly, most constantly, and most enduringly myself, I find an altogether different thing.

There is, beneath these sharply cut crystals and this frozen surface, a continuous flux which is not comparable to any flux I have ever seen. There is a succession of states, each of which announces that which follows and contains that which precedes it. They can, properly speaking, only be said to form multiples states when I have already passed them and turn back to observe their track. Whilst I was experiencing them they were so solidly organized, so profoundly animated with a common life, that I could not have said where any one of them finished or where another commenced. In reality no one of them begins or ends, but all extend into each other.

This inner life may be compared to the unrolling of a coil, for there is no living being who does not feel himself coming gradually to the end of his role; and to live is to grow old. But it may just as well be compared to a continual rolling up, like that of a thread on a ball, for our past follows us, it swells incessantly with the present that it picks up on its way; and consciousness means memory.

But actually it is neither an unrolling nor a rolling up, for these two similes evoke the idea of lines and surfaces whose parts are homogeneous and superposable on one another. Now, there are no two identical moments in the life of the same conscious being. Take the simplest sensation, suppose it constant, absorb in it the entire personality: the consciousness which will accompany this sensation cannot remain identical with itself for two consecutive moments, because the second moment always contains, over and above the first, the memory that the first has bequeathed to it. A consciousness which could experience two identical moments would be a consciousness without memory. It would die and be born again continually. In what other way could one represent unconsciousness?

It would be better, then, to use as a comparison the myriad-tinted spectrum, with its insensible gradations leading from one shade to another. A current of feeling which passed along the spectrum, assuming in turn the tint of each of its shades, would experience a series of gradual changes, each of which would announce the one to follow and would sum up those which preceded it. Yet even here the successive shades of the spectrum always remain external one to another. They are juxtaposed; they occupy space. But pure duration, on the contrary, excludes all idea of juxtaposition, reciprocal externality, and extension.

Let us, then, rather, imagine an infinitely small elastic body, contracted, if it were possible, to a mathematical point. Let this be drawn out gradually in such a manner that from the point comes a constantly lengthening line. Let us fix our attention not on the line as a line, but on the action by which it is traced. Let us bear in mind that this action, in spite of its duration, is indivisible if accomplished without stopping, that if a stopping-point is inserted, we have two actions instead of one, that each of these separate actions is then the indivisible operation of which we speak, and that it is not the moving action itself which is divisible, but, rather, the stationary line it leaves behind it as its track in space. Finally, let us free ourselves from the space which underlies the movement in order to consider only the movement itself, the act of tension or extension; in short, pure mobility. We shall have this time a more faithful image of the development of our self in duration.

However, even this image is incomplete, and, indeed, every comparison will be insufficient, because the unrolling of our duration resembles in some of its aspects the unity of an advancing movement and in others the multiplicity of expanding states; and, clearly, no metaphor can express one of these two aspects without sacrificing the other. If I use the comparison of the spectrum with its thousand shades, I have before me a thing already made, whilst duration is continually in the making. If I think of an elastic which is being stretched, or of a spring which is extended or relaxed, I forget the richness of color, characteristic of duration that is lived, to see only the simple movement by which consciousness passes from one shade to another. The inner life is all this at once: variety of qualities, continuity of progress, and unity of direction. It cannot be represented by images.

But it is even less possible to represent it by concepts, that is by abstract, general, or simple ideas. It is true that no image can reproduce exactly the original feeling I have of the flow of my own conscious life. But it is not even necessary that I should attempt to render it. If a man is incapable of getting for himself the intuition of the constitutive duration of his own being, nothing will ever give it to him, concepts no more than images. Here the single aim of the philosopher should be to promote a certain effort, which in most men is usually fettered by habits of mind more useful to life. Now the image has at least this advantage, that it keeps us in the concrete. No image can replace the intuition of duration, but many diverse images, borrowed from very different orders of things, may, by the convergence of their action, direct consciousness to the precise point where there is a certain intuition to be seized. By choosing images as dissimilar as possible, we shall prevent any one of them from usurping the place of the intuition it is intended to call up, since it would then be driven away at once by its rivals. By providing that, in spite of their differences of aspect, they all require from the mind the same kind of attention, and in some sort the same degree of tension, we shall gradually accustom consciousness to a particular and clearly-defined disposition—that precisely which it must adopt in order to appear to itself as it really is, without any veil. But, then, consciousness must at least consent to make the effort. For it will have been shown nothing: it will simply have been placed in the attitude it must take up in order to make the desired effort, and so come by itself to the intuition. Concepts on the contrary—especially if they are simple—have the disadvantage of being in reality symbols substituted for the object they symbolize, and demand no effort on our part. Examined closely, each of them, it would be seen, retains only that part of the object which is common to it and to others, and expresses, still more than the image does, a comparison between the object and others which resemble it. But as the comparison has made manifest a resemblance, as the resemblance is a property of the object, and as a property has every appearance of being a part of the object which possesses it, we easily persuade ourselves that by setting concept beside concept we are reconstructing the whole of the object with its parts, thus obtaining, so to speak, its intellectual equivalent. In this way we believe that we can form a faithful representation of duration by setting in line the concepts of unity, multiplicity, continuity, finite or infinite divisibility, etc. There precisely is the illusion. There also is the danger. Just in so far as abstract ideas can render service to analysis, that is, to the scientific study of the object in its relations to other objects, so far are they incapable of replacing intuition, that is, the metaphysical investigation of what is essential and unique in the object. For on the one hand these concepts, laid side by side, never actually give us more than an artificial reconstruction of the object, of which they can only symbolize certain general, and, in a way, impersonal aspects; it is therefore useless to believe that with them we can seize a reality of which they present to us the shadow alone. And, on the other hand, besides the illusion there is also a very serious danger. For the concept generalizes at the same time as it abstracts. The concept can only symbolize a particular property by making it common to an infinity of things. It therefore

always more or less deforms the property by the extension it gives
to it. Replaced in the metaphysical object to which it belongs, a
property coincides with the object, or at least moulds itself on it, and
adopts the same outline. Extracted from the metaphysical object,
and presented in a concept, it grows indefinitely larger, and goes
beyond the object itself, since henceforth it has to contain it, along
with a number of other objects. Thus the different concepts that
we form of the properties of a thing inscribe round it so many circles, each much too large and none of them fitting it exactly. And
yet, in the thing itself the properties coincided with the thing, and
coincided consequently with one another. So that if we are bent on
reconstructing the object with concepts, some artifice must be sought
whereby this coincidence of the object and its properties can be
brought about. For example, we may choose one of the concepts
and try, starting from it, to get round to the others. But we shall
then soon discover that according as we start from one concept or
another, the meeting and combination of the concepts will take place
in an altogether different way. According as we start, for example,
from unity or from multiplicity, we shall have to conceive differently the multiple unity of duration. Everything will depend on
the weight we attribute to this or that concept, and this weight will
always be arbitrary, since the concept extracted from the object
has no weight, being only the shadow of a body. In this way, as
many different systems will spring up as there are external points
of view from which the reality can be examined, or larger circles
in which it can be enclosed. Simple concepts have, then, not only
the inconvenience of dividing the concrete unity of the object into
so many symbolical expressions; they also divide philosophy into
distinct schools, each of which takes its seat, chooses its counters,
and carries on with the others a game that will never end. Either
metaphysics is only this play of ideas, or else, if it is a serious occupation of the mind, if it is a science and not simply an exercise, it
must transcend concepts in order to reach intuition. Certainly,
concepts are necessary to it, for all the other sciences work as a rule
with concepts, and metaphysics cannot dispense with the other sciences. But it is only truly itself when it goes beyond the concept,
or at least when it frees itself from rigid and ready-made concepts
in order to create a kind very different from those which we habitually use; I mean supple, mobile, and almost fluid representations,
always ready to mould themselves on the fleeting forms of intuition.
We shall return later to this important point. Let it suffice us for
the moment to have shown that our duration can be presented to
us directly in an intuition, that it can be suggested to us indirectly

by images, but that it can never—if we confine the word concept to its proper meaning—be enclosed in a conceptual representation.

Let us try for an instant to consider our duration as a multiplicity. It will then be necessary to add that the terms of this multiplicity, instead of being distinct, as they are in any other multiplicity, encroach on one another; and that while we can no doubt, by an effort of imagination, solidify duration once it has elapsed, divide it into juxtaposed portions and count all these portions, yet this operation is accomplished on the frozen memory of the duration, on the stationary trace which the mobility of duration leaves behind it, and not on the duration itself. We must admit, therefore, that if there is a multiplicity here, it bears no resemblance to any other multiplicity we know. Shall we say, then, that duration has unity? Doubtless, a continuity of elements which prolong themselves into one another participates in unity as much as in multiplicity; but this moving, changing, colored, living unity has hardly anything in common with the abstract, motionless, and empty unity which the concept of pure unity circumscribes. Shall we conclude from this that duration must be defined as unity and multiplicity at the same time? But singularly enough, however much I manipulate the two concepts, portion them out, combine them differently, practise on them the most subtle operations of mental chemistry, I never obtain anything which resembles the simple intuition that I have of duration; while, on the contrary, when I replace myself in duration by an effort of intuition, I immediately perceive how it is unity, multiplicity, and many other things besides. These different concepts, then, were only so many standpoints from which we could consider duration. Neither separated nor reunited have they made us penetrate into it.

We do penetrate into it, however, and that can only be by an effort of intuition. In this sense, an inner, absolute knowledge of the duration of the self by the self is possible. But metaphysics here demands and can obtain an intuition, science has none the less need of an analysis. Now it is a confusion between the function of analysis and that of intuition which gives birth to the discussions between the schools and the conflicts between systems.

Psychology, in fact, proceeds like all the other sciences by analysis. It resolves the self, which has been given to it at first in a simple intuition, into sensations, feelings, ideas, etc., which it studies separately. It substitutes, then, for the self a series of elements which form the facts of psychology. But are these elements really parts? That is the whole question, and it is because it has been evaded that the problem of human personality has so often been stated in insoluble terms.

It is incontestable that every psychical state, simply because it belongs to a person, reflects the whole of a personality. Every feeling, however simple it may be, contains virtually within it the whole past and present of the being experiencing it, and, consequently, can only be separated and constituted into a "state" by an effort of abstraction or of analysis. But it is no less incontestable that without this effort of abstraction or analysis there would be no possible development of the science of psychology. What, then, exactly, is the operation by which a psychologist detaches a mental state in order to erect it into a more or less independent entity? He begins by neglecting that special coloring of the personality which cannot be expressed in known and common terms. Then he endeavors to isolate, in the person already thus simplified, some aspect which lends itself to an interesting inquiry. If he is considering inclination, for example, he will neglect the inexpressible shade which colors it, and which makes the inclination mine and not yours; he will fix his attention on the movement by which our personality leans towards a certain object: he will isolate this attitude, and it is this special aspect of the personality, this snapshot of the mobility of the inner life, this "diagram" of concrete inclination, that he will erect into an independent fact. There is in this something very like what an artist passing through Paris does when he makes, for example, a sketch of a tower of Notre Dame. The tower is inseparably united to the building, which is itself no less inseparably united to the ground, to its surroundings, to the whole of Paris, and so on. It is first necessary to detach it from all these; only one aspect of the whole is noted, that formed by the tower of Notre Dame. Moreover, the special form of this tower is due to the grouping of the stones of which it is composed; but the artist does not concern himself with these stones, he notes only the silhouette of the tower. For the real and internal organization of the thing he substitutes, then, an external and schematic representation. So that, on the whole, his sketch corresponds to an observation of the object from a certain point of view and to the choice of a certain means of representation. But exactly the same thing holds true of the operation by which the psychologist extracts a single mental state from the whole personality. This isolated psychical state is hardly anything but a sketch, the commencement of an artificial reconstruction; it is the whole considered under a certain elementary aspect in which we are specially interested and which we have carefully noted. It is

not a part, but an element. It has not been obtained by a natural
dismemberment, but by analysis.

Now beneath all the sketches he has made at Paris the visitor
will probably, by way of memento, write the word "Paris." And as
he has really seen Paris, he will be able, with the help of the original
intuition he had of the whole, to place his sketches therein, and so
join them up together. But there is no way of performing the inverse operation; it is impossible, even with an infinite number of
accurate sketches, and even with the word "Paris" which indicates
that they must be combined together, to get back to an intuition
that one has never had, and to give oneself an impression of what
Paris is like if one has never seen it. This is because we are not
dealing here with real parts, but with mere notes of the total impression. To take a still more striking example, where the notation
is more completely symbolic, suppose that I am shown, mixed together at random, the letters which make up a poem I am ignorant
of. If the letters were parts of the poem, I could attempt to reconstitute the poem with them by trying the different possible arrangements, as a child does with the pieces of a Chinese puzzle. But I
should never for a moment think of attempting such a thing in this
case, because the letters are not component parts, but only partial
expressions, which is quite a different thing. That is why, if I know
the poem, I at once put each of the letters in its proper place and
join them up without difficulty by a continuous connection, whilst
the inverse operation is impossible. Even when I believe I am actually attempting this inverse operation, even when I put the letters
end to end, I begin by thinking of some plausible meaning. I
thereby give myself an intuition, and from this intuition I attempt
to redescend to the elementary symbols which would reconstitute
its expression. The very idea of reconstituting a thing by operations
practised on symbolic elements alone implies such an absurdity that
it would never occur to any one if they recollected that they were
not dealing with fragments of the thing, but only, as it were, with
fragments of its symbol.

Suggested Further Readings

Bergson, Henri. *Creative Evolution*. Translated by Arthur Mitchell. New
    York: Henry Holt & Co., Inc., 1911. Chaps. ii, iii.
Bradley, F. H. *Appearance and Reality*. London: Oxford University Press, 1947.
    Chaps. i-v, xxiv.
Dewey, John. *How We Think*. Boston: D. C. Heath & Co., 1910.
Ewing, A. C. *Reason and Intuition*. London: Oxford University Press, 1942.
Hume, David. *An Enquiry Concerning Human Understanding*. La Salle, Ill.: The
    Open Court Publishing Co., 1912.

KANT, IMMANUEL. *Prolegomena to Any Future Metaphysic.* New York: Liberal Arts Press, 1951.

LEIBNIZ, G. W. *New Essays Concerning Human Understanding.* La Salle: The Open Court Publishing Co., 1916.

LEWIS, C. I. *Mind and the World Order.* New York: Charles Scribner's Sons, 1929. Chaps. ii, v, vii.

LOCKE, JOHN. *Essay Concerning Human Understanding.* London: Oxford University Press, 1924. Bk. I.

MONTAGUE, W. P. *The Ways of Knowing.* New York: The Macmillan Co., 1925. Chaps. i, ii, iv.

RUSSELL, BERTRAND. *Mysticism and Logic.* New York: W. W. Norton & Co., Inc., 1929. Chaps. i, x.

———. *Our Knowledge of the Eternal World.* New York: W. W. Norton & Co., Inc., 1929. Chaps. iii, iv.

SANTAYANA, GEORGE. *Scepticism and Animal Faith.* New York: Charles Scribner's Sons, 1929. Chaps. i-vi.

CHAPTER 3

Matter and Life

COMMON SENSE AND THE NATURAL WORLD

All our philosophizing about nature begins with ordinary experience. The concept of what "Nature" is has varied with different historical epochs and according to the modes of interpretation which they have employed, but there is a certain first-hand knowledge which we all seem to have, and which appears to follow from our direct acquaintance with rivers and rocks, plants and animals, the planets and the seasons.

The first acquaintance of the child or the primitive man with the natural world must be—if, indeed, we can pretend to reconstruct it—as William James once put it "a blooming, buzzing confusion." For the earliest undiscriminating awareness is of a jumble of many things; all together, but at the same time all puzzlingly different. It is like looking into a strange kitchen after a large dinner party. All is multiplicity and confusion.

But it is amazing how quickly an efficient housekeeper can bring order out of this chaos. A few simple distinctions between leftovers and garbage, things to be washed and things to be laundered, between dishes, glasses and silverware, and the plan for action is given. Leftovers in the refrigerator, garbage in the incinerator, laundry in the basket, then dishes, glasses, silver sorted, washed and put in their respective places. Chaos has become neatness and order.

All philosophizing about nature begins when an initial multiplicity and confusion is confronted by the urge toward neatness and order; when we discriminate between kinds of natural existences; when we apply a system of categories to the objects within our experience so that we may better understand their natures and their operations. But when we deal with nature, what system of categories do we employ?

If we ask this question of different philosophers of nature—Aristotle, Spinoza, Hegel, or Whitehead for example—we should receive somewhat different answers according to their respective standpoints. But there is one place to which we may turn confident that the answer will have a certain universality, a certain freedom from merely individual bias. And that is the evidence of *language.* Words are useful because they symbolize or stand for things, and language has come into being to help us deal with and master our experiences. Naming is always closely associated with the experience of those who use the names. Investigation of language may thus lead to knowledge about things. Our new question then becomes: What categories of nature are implied in the existence of civilized languages?

The question is not as simple as it first seems, but for our purposes, it may be simply answered. All languages use nouns, verbs and adjectives. "Last night at the supper table father cut the tough meat with a sharp knife." "Father," "table," "meat," "knife" are nouns and they stand for things, persons, or *substances.* "Cut" is a verb and it stands for an act, a process, an *event.* "Supper," "tough," "sharp" are adjectives and they stand for aspects, descriptive characteristics, or *qualities.* Substance, event, quality are expressible in language because they are elements or categories of nature.

But there are two other important phrases in the sentence: "last night" and "at the supper table." The indefinite statement, "Father cut the tough meat with a sharp knife," needs completion with a reference to "where" and "when." No one is satisfied with experience in the void. It is useless to plan to meet someone "at any drugstore"; you must say where. It is absurd to invite a friend for supper "sometime"; you must say when. Therefore substances, events, and qualities must be localized. And all localization is accomplished by some specific reference to *space* and *time.* Substances do not *exist* unless they occur in space and time. Events do not happen except at certain times at certain places. And even qualities like *redness* or *hardness* to be "real" must be associated with substances which are spatially located. When redness or hardness appear, it is always as "this red patch of wall" or "this hard rock"; that is, in connection with spatial extension. Thus, from language itself we have inferred five basic categories for the ordering of nature: *substance, event, quality, space,* and *time.*

It must be admitted that each of these categories is extremely abstract, and ordinary common sense does not always invoke them in its functioning. Our usual distinctions between "now" and "then," "earlier" and "later" certainly imply *time,* but within a frame of reference bounded by limits like "today" or "the week end" or "this week." And in the same way our distinctions between "toward downtown," "toward the river," "to the left," "under my feet," "above my head" certainly imply *space,* but within a context of meaning provided by the city within which we live or the spot upon which we stand. Consciousness of *time* and *space* probably begins with purely local "times" and "places," and only later, when there is a need to correlate these with distant places and remote events, are all "places" and "times" oriented within a uniform three-dimensional space and given location in a single uniformly flowing time.

But the sense of time is given in still another fashion in our direct experience of nature, and this provides a somewhat different set of categories than are suggested by the grammatical parts of speech. Whitehead has said that in our apprehension of nature we experience "the things which occur," "the things which endure," and "the things which recur." Let us see to what this distinction leads.

That it is true is undeniable. A rabbit darts from behind a bush, and in a few seconds is again lost from sight. A streak of lightning flashes in the sky. A sudden scream pierces the air at night. These are "occurrences." They flash into experience and out of it again. They are brief, momentary, and generally without consequence.

But a tree "endures." If there is one outside the kitchen window, I may close my eyes for a moment as I look at it, but I do not expect it to be gone when I open them again. And when I look out again next month, I also expect it to be there. Still, I do know that trees die and are destroyed. Mountain ranges are more indestructible. The Alps have looked down upon the wars of European man since time began. The Appalachians were there a quarter of a billion years ago. That is endurance! And what about colors? The color blue seems to be outside time entirely, to be *eternal.* Different blue objects may appear and pass away like other occurrents, but the color blue itself seems somehow to remain; a permanent *possibility* for experience.

A more interesting aspect of nature are the things which recur. The sun rose yesterday morning, it has risen today; I am confident that it will rise tomorrow. The winter's cold and barrenness is followed by the spring's warmth and new life, and this progression of the seasons recurs each year. The rotation of the earth makes the recurrent days, the path of the earth around the sun makes the recurrent seasons. All aspects of nature seem to be dominated by the existence of *periodic events,* that is, by the succession of events so like one another, although they are not identical and differ slightly, that for all practical purposes they may be called repetitions of the same thing.

Periodicity dominates the larger universe of the solar system. It also dominates the mechanism of the life of the body. There is repetitive regularity in the beat of the heart, in the inhalations and exhalations of the breath. It is found no less in the phases of the moon, in the alternations of its light, and in the rise and fall of the tides. But from the point of view of the philosophy of nature a recognition of periodicity is of particular importance, for it is the very basis of two of our most important scientific and philosophic conceptions: the conception of *time* and the conception of *laws of nature*.

The first is obvious. The units of our measurement of time are the day, the week, the month, the year. The first and the last are simply the standard recurrences of two types of movement of the earth relative to the sun. And the week and the month are based on standard recurrences of the phases of the moon. Hour, minute, second are not based upon *natural time* but are mathematically arbitrary or *conceptual* divisions made within the span of natural time; the hour being one 24th of a day, the minute one 1,440th, and the second one 86,400th. But obviously without a recurrent regularity within nature, no concept of time could be standardized. And this is the reasonableness of the definition of time which Aristotle gave long ago, that it is simply *the measure of natural motion*.

Laws of nature also are dependent upon periodicity. For the laws of nature are simply the observed identities of pattern which persist through any series of observations.[1] It is impossible to conceive of a law of nature without being able to say: "This event has happened before, and it can happen again." In short, a universe in which there were merely occurrences could never be a world of ordered regularity. Our ability to formulate the "laws of nature" hinges on our ability to recognize that what are at first assumed to be mere occurrences are actually recurrences in between which time intervals are distinguishable and perhaps even finally measurable.

MEASUREMENT, ABSTRACTION, MATTER

For the extent to which our common sense experience of the natural world may be turned into scientific knowledge, we are indebted to two operations of the human mind; *abstraction* and *measurement*. The former is a process by which the mind may be directed to a selected aspect of experience rather than to its total given nature.

[1] This is based on A. N. Whitehead, *Adventures of Ideas* (New York: The Macmillan Co., 1933), chap. vii.

The latter depends upon our ability to relate different experiences or sets of things according to the idea of their *quantity*. How does the idea of quantity arise?

The most general urge of the human mind in its confrontation of nature is an urge for order. Already we have noted how the orderliness of mind leads to a system of categories on the one hand, and through the experience of periodicity to an ordering of occurrences to which we give the name of "time" on the other. But if one great fact of nature is *periodicity*, another is *continuity*. And as periodicity is the foundation of the concept of time, so continuity is the foundation of the concept of space.

The arc of the sun through the sky from sunrise to sunset is a continuous path through space. The distance which we walk from our home to school is a continuous, although doubtless irregular, path. The straight line which for Euclid is the shortest distance between any two points on a plane surface is a continuity. The "quantities" of geometry are "continuous" quantities. Of course, "lengths" are quantities of one kind, "areas" of another, and "volumes" of still a third, but whether we view the "spaces" with which we deal as one-, two-, or three-dimensional, they are continuous, and the geometry which deals with their ideal properties can be defined either as the *science of continuous quantity* or *the science of dimensional order*. It matters little which we say.

If geometry is the science of continuous quantity, arithmetic may be called *the science of discrete quantity*. This means that mathematics as the science of order has one branch based on the dimensional order which involves the idea of continuity and another based on the serial order represented in the system of integral numbers. The combination of these two is the brilliant discovery (now a commonplace of everyday thought and procedure) which is the foundation upon which rests the whole idea of scientific measurement. Consider the figures on page 93.

The line (a) is an example of geometrical quantity. It is continuous. It can be infinitely extended upon either side of the page. It can be thought of as composed of an infinite number of points. It can be thought of as a whole having parts. (b) is a series of integers or integral numbers. They are discrete and separable. They progress by regular additions of the unit 1. This series also can be thought of as a whole having parts. And it may go on 12,13,14,15 . . . to infinity. The regularly divided line (c) is the great discovery. It is the giving of discrete numbers to a continuous quantity so that the repetition of equal units becomes a new way of perceiv-

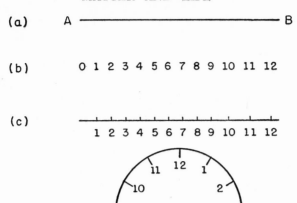

(a) A ——————————————— B

(b) 0 1 2 3 4 5 6 7 8 9 10 11 12

(c) 1 2 3 4 5 6 7 8 9 10 11 12

(d)

ing continuity. But obviously it will surprise nobody. For it is simply the principle which is expressed in the everyday ruler or yardstick. The last figure (d) is also familiar. It is the face of a clock with the hour hand alone showing. But note that it is also the regularly divided line (c) now shaped as the circumference of a circle so that the passage of the hour hand over it is endlessly repetitive or periodic. And here we have the instrument for the measurement of time.

Clocks and metrical instruments are the means of measurement, and the clock with its moving hand is particularly remarkable for the fashion in which it combines the qualities of periodicity and continuity. The small hand is like a planet moving in its orbit and, true to Kepler's second law of planetary motion, as the hand moves, it (the radius vector from center to circumference) sweeps out equal areas in equal times. And the circumference is simply a circular ruler! The clock is the great instrument for the measurement of time and space, and it demonstrates even better than the metaphors of Bergson that the time of natural science is little more than a species of spatial thinking. Clocks are the perfect symbols of science for in them are combined the concepts of space, time, and number.

The world of our everyday experience is full of qualitative distinctions: "This room is too hot"; "What a dark gray that flannel is!"; "Those seats are certainly hard." And an examination of these qualitative distinctions generally shows them to be meaningful in the context of some concept of opposite qualities. Too hot is related to too cold. Dark gray is related to light gray. Hard is related to soft. But even these oppositions give way to polarities. We see that not only space is continuous, but there are continuities in the qualitative manifestations of the world. Between the resistance of a diamond and that of porous sandstone there are numerous gradations. Between the elasticity of iron and that of rubber there are numerous stages. Between the hottest day of summer and the coldest day of winter there are many degrees of temperature. Between zinc-white and lamp-black there are many, many shades of grey.

When the qualitative differences of the natural world are recognized as imprecise, and when there is an attempt to specify them precisely by reducing them to the model of continuous quantity, science has supplanted common sense. The existence of chronometers (clocks), micrometers, photometers, and thermometers attests to the fact that differences of time, length, light, and temperature have become scientifically measurable. But there is one important fact which must be kept in mind. Science is only a selected aspect of the whole of experience. *The scientific replacement of qualitative distinctions by quantitative distinctions is possible only through an act of abstraction.*

Let us see how abstraction takes place. Let us begin with this actual pen which I hold in my hand, and let us analyze it roughly into the following elements, parts, or aspects, all of which in some sense compose or enter into the natural thing or event which this pen is. To call it a "pen" indicates that it is a member of a class of objects, and possibly that there exist others like it with which it shares some of its qualities. To call it "this" pen means that it is a specific individual, unlike all others in its markings, scars, its being mine, its having my initials and the like. Let us represent the various elements of the pen as follows:[2]

P: the qualities common to this pen and to others. These may in turn be analyzed into P1 (color), P2 (hardness), P3 (shape), P4 (size), P5 (weight), P6 (construction), P7 (material) P8, P9, P10, etc.

p: the qualities peculiar to my pen. These may in turn be analyzed into p1 (its blackness), p2 (its specific hardness),

p3 (its specific shape), p4, p5, p6, etc.

S: the property of being in space.

[2] This symbolism (with my own additions and modifications) follows W. P. Montague, *The Ways of Knowing* (New York: The Macmillan Co., 1925), p. 71.

s: the particular place where my pen is when it is observed (if space changes take place, this can be indicated by successive positions s1, s2, s3, etc.

T: the property of being in time.

t: the particular time when my pen is being observed (this can also be indicated by successive moments as t1, t2, t3, etc.).

Now it is clear that I may direct my attention to all of these aspects together as the total natural and conceptual event, or to only a few, or even one of the aspects at a time. When I attend to $P (P1, P2, P3 \ldots) p (p1, p2, p3 \ldots) S s T t$ I attend to the whole experience. When I attend to $P (P1, P2, P3 \ldots) p (p1, p2, p3 \ldots)$ $S T$, I attend to the enduring object. When I attend to $P S T$ it is to the class of pens, and when to just P to the abstract idea of being a pen. But I can also attend only to $p2, p3, p4, p5, t1, s1$, and this abstraction of hardness, shape, size, weight at a specific time and place will be the typical kind of abstraction from the total experienced event with which physical science customarily deals. On just such abstractions of time, space, and matter did the great physical theories of the seventeenth century depend.

The physical concept of matter rests upon a type of abstraction which is familiar to mathematicians but which is somewhat perplexing from the standpoint of common sense. The mathematician can deal with points knowing full well that Euclidean points have no size. And the physicist can deal with point-instants knowing that nothing so defined is observable, since there is no such thing as "nature at an instant." The perplexity then, is that the "mass points" which are sometimes loosely called "particles of matter" are aspects of rigid bodies and are said to "move" in continuous material media. But they are not observable in the sense that a rose is observable, and consequently one cannot meaningfully ask the question: "What is the color of mass points?" as one might ask the question: "What is the color of this rose?" The qualities of particles according to classical physical theory are mass, position, and velocity. Grosser bodies have these too, and that is one of the reasons for the meaningless question about color. But when one realizes that from the infinite variety of the qualities of material events, mechanics chooses a very few as being "of physical interest," the distinction between "real things" and "scientific objects" can be made and understood. One then sees that parts or aspects of the real (mass-points, particles, or "atoms") are not *actual* (apparent or observable) in the same way as the whole observable natural events which they compose.

THE STANDPOINT OF MATERIALISM

It is one of the ironies of time (many of which afflict philosophy) that a theory of physics which achieved immediate and startling success in the seventeenth century should seep down into philosophy and live on as a theory of the ultimate nature of the universe. The mechanical view of the physical world which began with Galileo, Boyle, and Descartes, which achieved its highest peak in the genius of Sir Isaac Newton in the seventeenth century, and which was worked out in its final details by Euler, Lagrange, and Laplace in the eighteenth, has lived on into the nineteenth and twentieth centuries as a metaphysical doctrine of the nature of ultimate reality. As such it is called *materialism*.

From this point of view materialism is a philosophic ghost which remains over from some previous scientific lifetime to haunt the human mind. But as an influence which seems compelling to some few professional philosophers and to many who philosophize unprofessionally, it is a ghost which is very much alive. It is necessary, then, to note those aspects of the doctrines of Newtonian physics which have become the foundation of the standpoint of materialism.

It is a great surprise to one who looks into Newton's *Mathematical Principles of Natural Philosophy* for the first time to find that the form of this work is exactly the same as Euclid's; that he begins with definitions of matter and motion, passes on to "axioms or laws of motion," and then begins his demonstrations. But, just as in Euclid, the presuppositions of Newton's system are all to be found in the definitions and axioms. I restate a few of these in modern language to give the flavor of the system:[3]

1. The quantity of matter is its mass.
2. The quantity of motion is its mass times its velocity.
3. There is an absolute mathematical time which is uniform.
4. There is an absolute space in which the motions of matter occur.
5. All motions are caused by forces impressed upon bodies.
6. Every change of motion is proportional to a force impressed.
7. To every action there is an equal opposed reaction.
8. We must not assign more causes to events than absolutely necessary to explain them.
9. To the same effects we must as far as possible assign the same causes.

[3] Isaac Newton, *Mathematical Principles of Natural Philosophy*, rev. trans. by Florian Cajori (Berkeley: University of California Press, 1934), pp. 1-27, 398-400.

10. The qualities of bodies found by experiment are to be thought of as universal qualities of all bodies whatsoever.

If one tries to put all of these together, to summarize the view of nature which they represent, it is readily apparent that the concept is that of a *machine*. Many of our views of experience are guided by analogy, and when we think in such general terms as "Nature," it is often the case that our final image is a metaphor. For this reason it is of the greatest appropriateness that someone should have called the physical world of the seventeenth century "The Newtonian world machine."

A machine has parts each of which has a specific location, and these parts are all related to one another in strict quantitative terms. The parts of a machine move regularly, and no motion takes place without its proper outside cause or without its proper determinable effect. Nothing happens by chance; all is so interrelated that the machine operates uniformly and with perfect regularity. Repeatable motions and hence predictability are of the essence of mechanical operations. Newton's world provided laws of motion mathematically expressible which should hold for bodies at the outermost regions of space as well as at the surface of the earth, which should govern the greatest spiral nebula as well as the smallest particle of matter. It is little wonder that he himself called it "this most beautiful system."

Modern materialism, too, bases its claims about the world upon the image of a machine, although it has passed beyond the Newtonian conceptions of matter, and also is more negative than was Newton himself about the ultimate purposiveness of the universe. Perhaps the most concise and at the same time fully developed statement of the materialist position occurs in Hugh Elliot.[4] The chief aspects of the materialist standpoint which he emphasizes are (1) the uniformity of law, (2) the denial that there exists any such thing as purpose in the universe, and (3) the denial of any form of existence which cannot be treated by physics and chemistry. Let us consider these in a little greater detail.

In some sense it is probably true that any age of science is an age of materialism. Others besides Elliot have emphasized that science by its very nature tends to be "mechanistic" and "deterministic" (that is, to view the universe as a machine and to hold to a doctrine of the universal reign of scientific law). And the concept of matter, the *abstract* concept which lies behind the observable appearance of objects is a part of this same system. There has been much talk

[4] *Modern Science and Materialism*, chaps. v, vi.

that modern physics with its abandonment of solid matter, its emphasis upon process and upon the behavior of energy in space-time has abandoned materialism. But this seems to be a complete misunderstanding of the nature of modern science. Materialism is not a theory of substance so much as a logical standpoint. For, its assertion that there is some abstract substratum behind appearances really remains unchanged whether this substratum is called space-time, energy, or matter. The heart of the materialist position, as Elliot says, lies in its belief in the uniformity of nature and the faith that the future can always be predicted on the experimental evidence of the past.

The denial that there is any ultimate goal or purpose in the universe is a more questionable matter. For it seems to be characteristic of nineteenth-century materialism rather than of the science of the seventeenth century. Newton, for example, conceived the world as a machine, but he never doubted that it was created by the hand of God, nor that its accuracy expressed the "counsel and domination of an intelligent and powerful Being." [5] And he admitted that the world as we know it is the product of God's "final causes" or divine purpose. In the end the assertion or denial of purposive striving in nature or goals of the universe cannot be dogmatically proved. Its denial is one of the more controversial tenets of the materialistic creed.

The denial that there is any form of existence which cannot be treated by physics and chemistry is, in effect, the denial of independent status to two other aspects of nature customarily distinguished—the domain of *living things* and the domain of *minds*. The materialist excludes from existence in experience not only souls and God, but also "mind," "consciousness," "will," "feeling," and all entities of a similar nature. It is not that the materialist denies that these terms are customarily used, or that there may be some actuality to which they refer. But if they have actual reference, it is always to some material existence or process, and is, therefore, expressible in the formulas of matter in motion. If it is not so expressible, then it refers to nothing real.

The same is true of the materialistic treatment of living beings. No materialist denies the existence of plant and animal life. Only, he denies that life is a phenomenon *different in kind* from matter in motion. Different in degree, probably. Different in complexity certainly. But the point is that the behavior of living things, like the rest of the natural world, is subject to the universal laws of cause and effect. Living things are composed of matter, and, although

[5] Newton, *op. cit.*, p. 544.

"organic" rather than "inorganic," they act according to chemical necessity. There is nothing in the domain of life which is not explicable by reference to the laws of physics and chemistry.

Materialism as a standpoint demanding the universal reign of causal law has a certain persuasiveness, for it appeals to the passion for orderliness which animates us all, and which the scientist possesses in unusual measure. But its denial of purposiveness to the universe, and its claim *to reduce* life and mind to physical and chemical experience has aroused bitter opposition. And it is around these issues that the philosophical battles continue to rage.

The Realm of Living Things

Against the standpoint of materialism two challenges have arisen. One has emerged from philosophy itself in the form of an alternative theory of reality termed *idealism,* a theory which takes seriously the distinction between matter and mind, and which asserts the latter as the type of experience which gives us the best insight into the ultimately real.

But the second challenge is more relevant here because it comes not from philosophy, but from science; that is, from another science besides physics, with its own subject-matter and its own authority— the science of biology. Or, to put it more accurately, the science which deals with the nature and properties of living things has become the battleground where are confronted the conflicting claims of *mechanists,* those who agree that living things are best explained as matter in motion, and *vitalists,* those who believe that the understanding of life demands principles totally different from those sufficient for the understanding of matter.

The cornerstone of the vitalist's argument is that life, by its very nature, behaves differently from matter, and this because of a difference in its principle of organization. Material bodies—rocks, minerals and the like—are *aggregates* of similar parts, and their cohesion is mechanical. This means that any change of mass by addition or subtraction brings about no significant transformation of the totality. But living beings are *organic wholes,* and the higher their degree of complication and differentiation, the more do the unlike parts need to cooperate in the service of the continued life of the organism. The grains of sand upon a beach constitute that beach by addition, and the loss of even a large number does not endanger the physical existence of the remainder. But the differentiated cells of the human body must live through organic cooperation, and the destruction of large cellular areas in crucial organs may mean the death of the whole. *Life, death, growth,* and *reproduction* have introduced new qualitative differences in the world which may involve atomic or energy changes, *but are not reducible to them.*

But the most philosophically interesting thing about living things is the fact that *time* is involved in them, not as it is involved in an equation of physics, but as it is involved in the writing of history. Organisms have a past which is not strictly repeatable, and a future never clearly foreseen. Birth, growth, youth, maturity, old age, death give time a *direction,* an arrow pointing into the future. In the lifetime of all living beings there seems to be a point of completeness or maximum effectiveness which we call the period of *maturity* and it is in connection with this that the concept of "purposiveness" (or *teleology* as it is sometimes called) makes it appearance. For it is as though there were some active force, some capacity, some vital principle (or *entelechy* as Aristotle called it) which directs this course of living things to the moments of life's maturest self-expression. Different forms of life have different life spans and different points of maturity, but it is at that point where living things express most completely their tendency, that is, express most completely the potentialities implicit within their natures, that the realm of the organic acquires the sense of purposiveness which the physical operations of nature so often appear to lack.

Purposiveness seems to characterize the life of individual animal beings. Does it equally well hold for the entire course of animal development which is called the evolutionary process? There is now very little disagreement over the main facts of evolution. The plants and animals existing today are the descendants of ancestors which were less complex in structure, and the entire process of development began with unicellular forms (protesta) which slowly, and over enormous periods of time, passed through the stages of coelenterates, from which one branch led to the arthropods (crustacea and insects) and another through the chordates up to the mammals and to man. According to Darwin chance variations in species occur and those varieties best suited to their environment tend to survive. According to Lamarck the environment changes and makes new demands, and those animal forms which are best able to adapt to new conditions survive and reproduce. In either case the process is viewed as mechanical and "purposeless."

But this "purposelessness" has been challenged by one of the great philosophers of the century, Henri Bergson in his classic *Creative Evolution.* If adaptation to environment were the only causal force in evolution, he asserted, then the process would have come to a standstill long ago. Inferior organisms often seem even better than complicated ones in adaptation. Why then does life which has succeeded quite well in adapting itself go on evolving toward further complication despite this? The answer, says Bergson, is that there is an impetus, a vital urge which drives it on, and this vital driving force is in its nature purposive. Life breaks into different species as an exploding shell bursts the material confines of its cartridge, and like the shell, the impulse comes from behind and from within. Every change is novel, unforeseen, and creative. The line of development, which began by the separation of plants and animals, continued in the separation of the vertebrates, who have developed intelligence, and the arthropods, who have remarkably developed instincts. These two purposive products of evolution—instinct and intelligence—need to merge into a kind of intuition (see selection on page 76), which can then be considered the purposive product of the entire evolutionary scheme. The universe is not something finished and perfected; it is a constant becoming which is at every moment creative. And this creativity is the purpose of life.

Bergson's position is very much like that of those biologists who call themselves "emergent evolutionists." These individuals see the whole realm of nature as a series of "levels" or "plateaus" in a continuous upward expansion. They hold that at each level new qualities *emerge* which cannot be reduced or explained by the levels preceding them, although they could not have come into existence unless the other levels had existed first. A merely "physical" level is followed by a chemical or "organic" level. This produces a vital level which, in turn, is the condition for a psychological level to emerge. This position leads directly into the next chapter. For it holds that out of the bountiful womb of nature there comes first *matter,* next *life,* and finally *mind.*

The following selections "The Nature of Matter" by Karl Pearson, "The Ideal of Pure Mechanism" by C. D. Broad, "Law and Purpose In Biology" by Morris Cohen, and "Nature and Life" by Alfred North Whitehead are all concerned with speculation about nature and particularly about our knowledge of "matter" and "life." All four philosophers have done their major writing since 1900.

The selections from Pearson and Broad have been included to illustrate in greater detail the nature of scientific abstractions and the standpoint of materialism; that from Morris Cohen to shed some light on scientific and philosophic problems in biology. Whitehead already illustrates a treatment of life which is not merely biological but also cosmic, and for this reason provides a fine transition to issues treated in the next chapter.

• Karl Pearson (1857–1936)

The Nature of Matter[6]

Karl Pearson, educated at Cambridge, was a well-known mathematician, physicist, and statistical biologist at the University of
London. He was not only a scientist, but a reflective man, and a
passionate advocate of the methods of the exact sciences. His
idealistic bent is obvious in *The Grammar of Science*, one of the
great semiphilosophical books about science which began a vogue
lasting to our own time. In this selection Pearson distinguishes between the "perceptions" of ordinary experience and the "conceptions" of science, and shows some of the difficulties when matter
is conceived as the hard, impenetrable substance which common
sense takes it to be.

"All things move"—but only in Conception

An old Greek philosopher, who lived perhaps some five hundred
years B.C., chose as the dictum in which he summed up his teaching
the phrase: "*All things flow.*" After-ages, not understanding what
Heraclitus meant—it is doubtful whether he understood himself—
dubbed him "Heraclitus the Obscure." But today we find modern
science almost repeating Heraclitus' dictum when it says: "*All things
are in motion.*" Like all dicta which briefly resume wide truths, this
dictum of modern science requires expanding and explaining if it is
not to be misinterpreted. By the words "All things are in motion"
we are to understand that, step by step, science has found it possible to describe our experience of perceptual changes by types of
relative motion: this motion being that of the ideal points, the ideal
rigid bodies, or the ideal strainable media which stand for us as the
signs or symbols of the real world of sense-impressions. We interpret, describe, and resume the sequences of this real world of sense-
impressions by discussing the relative positions, velocities, accelera-
tions, rotations, spins, and strains of an ideal geometrical world
which stands for us as a conceptual representation of the perceptual

[6] From Karl Pearson, *The Grammar of Science* (Everyman ed.), pp. 203-20.
Copyright, 1937, by E. P. Dutton and Co., Inc.

world. In our Chapter V we saw that space and time did not themselves correspond to actual perceptions, but were *modes* under
which we perceived, and by which we discriminated, groups of
sense-impressions. So motion as the combination of space with time
is essentially a *mode* of perception and not in itself a perception.
The more clearly this is realised the better able the reader will be
to appreciate that the "motion of bodies" is not a reality of perception, but is the conceptual manner in which we represent this mode
of perception and by aid of which we describe changes in groups
of sense-impression; the perceptual reality is the complexity and
variety of the sense-impressions which crowd into the telephonic
brain-exchange. That the results which flow from the conceptual
world of geometrical motions agree so closely with our perceptual
experience of the outside world of phenomena is a phase of that
accordance between the perceptive and reasoning faculties upon
which I have laid stress in an earlier part of this volume.

Wherein lies the advance from Heraclitus to the modern scientist?
Why was the dictum of one not unjustly termed obscure, while
the other claims—and rightly claims—to find in the development of
his dictum the sole basis for our knowledge of the physical universe?
The difference lies in this: Heraclitus left his flow undescribed and
unmeasured, while modern science devotes its best energies to the
accurate investigation and analysis of each and every type of motion which can possibly be used as a means of describing and resuming any sequence of sense-impressions. The whole object of
physical science is the discovery of ideal elementary motions which
will enable us to describe in the simplest language the widest ranges
of phenomena; it lies in the symbolisation of the physical universe
by aid of the geometrical motions of a group of geometrical forms.
To do this is to construct the world mechanically; but this mechanism, be it noted, is a product of conception, and does not lie in
our perceptions themselves. Startling as it may, when first stated,
appear to the reader, it is nevertheless true that the mind struggles
in vain to clearly realise the motion of anything which is neither a
geometrical point nor a body bounded by continuous surfaces; the
mind absolutely rebels against the notion of anything moving but
these conceptual creations, which are limits, unrealisable, as we have
seen, in the field of perception. If the world of phenomena be, as
the materialists would have us to believe, a world of moving bodies
like the conceptual world by which science symbolises it, if we are
to assert the perceptual existence of atom and ether, then in both
cases we are incapable of considering the ultimate element which
moves as anything but a perceptual realisation of geometrical ideals.

Yet, so far as our *sensible* experience goes, these geometrical ideals have no phenomenal existence! We have clearly, then, no right to infer as a basis of perception things which our whole experience up to the present shows us exist solely in the field of conception. It is absolutely illogical to fill up a void in our perceptual experience by projecting into it a load of conceptions utterly unlike the adjacent perceptual strata. It is "a profound psychological mistake," says George Henry Lewes, "to assert that whenever we can form clear ideas, not in themselves contradictory, these ideas must of necessity represent truths of nature." The reader will, we feel certain, find it impossible to conceive anything other than geometrical ideals as the moving element at the basis of phenomena. The attempt, however, to conceive something else is worth the making for it inevitably leads us to the conclusion that the term "moving body" is not scientific when applied to perceptual experience. In external perception we have sense-impressions and more or less permanent groupings of sense-impressions. These sense-impressions vary, dissolve, form new groups—that is, they *change.* Of the universe as contained in messages received at the brain telephonic exchange, or of groups of sense-impressions, we cannot assert motion—objects appear, disappear, and reappear; sense-impressions alter and modify their grouping. Change is the right word to apply to them rather than motion. It is in the field of conception solely that we can properly talk of the motion of bodies; it is there, and there only, that geometrical forms change their position in absolute time—that is, *move.* In the field of perception motion is but a popular expression to describe the mixed mode in which we discriminate and distinguish groups of sense-impressions.

THE THREE PROBLEMS

That we speak of the motion of bodies as a fact of perceptual experience is largely due to the constructive elements associated with immediate sense-impression. These constructive elements are drawn from our conceptual notions of change, which again flow very naturally from a limited perception; a deeper perceptual experience is required to demonstrate their purely ideal character. But the reader will, perhaps, hardly be prepared to accept the conclusion that change is perceptual, motion conceptual, without closer analysis. This analysis may be summed up in the three questions: *What is it that moves? Why does it move? How does it move?*

In the first place we must settle whether we are asking these questions of the conceptual or of the perceptual sphere. If it be of the former, the world of symbolic motions by aid of which science describes the sequences of our sense-impressions, then these questions are easy to answer. The things which move are points, rigid bodies and strainable media, geometrical concepts one and all. To ask why they move is to ask why we form conceptions at all, and ultimately to question why science exists. Finally, the manner in which they move is that which enables us most effectually to describe the results of our perceptual experience.

If we turn to the perceptual sphere and ask what it is that moves and why it moves, we are compelled to confess ourselves utterly incapable of finding any answers whatever. *Ignorabimus,* we shall always be ignorant say some scientists. That we are really ignorant will be the theme of the present chapter, but I believe that this ignorance does not arise from the limitation of our perceptive or reasoning faculties. It is rather due to our having asked unanswerable questions. We may legitimately ask why the complex of our sense-impressions changes, but, according to the views expressed above, motion is not a reality of perception, and it is therefore, for the sphere of perception, idle to ask what moves and why it moves. With the growth of more accurate insight into the conceptual nature of motion these questions will, I believe, be dismissed like the older questions as to the blue milk of the witches and the influence of the stars. With their dismissal, however, physical science will be for ever relieved of the metaphysical difficulties as to matter and force which it has inherited from the old scholastic traditions. *Ignorabimus,* therefore, does not seem the true answer to the first two questions; it may be a true answer to the problem of changes in sense-impression. The third question—How do things move?—also wants restating to be of any real value, and when restated it merges in the same question asked of the conceptual sphere. What, we must ask, are the conceptual types of motion best suited to describe the stages of our perceptual experience? The answer to this question forms the subject-matter of our next chapter.

Some of my readers may feel inclined to consider that in this discussion we are entirely deserting the plane of common sense. What moves? Why, natural bodies move, they will say, is the common-sense answer. But common sense is often a name for intellectual apathy. Being inquisitive, we naturally ask what these bodies consist in, and probably shall be told that they are quantities of *matter.* Still persisting with our questions we ask: What, then, is matter? It will not do to put us off with the reply that matter is that which moves. All we should, then, have done would be to give a name to the moving thing, but in doing so we should not have succeeded in defining or describing it. The reader may, perhaps, imagine that insight into the nature of matter will be gained by consulting the accepted text-books of science. Let us accordingly examine the statements of one or two.

How the Physicists define Matter

A first writer says: *"Matter is a primary conception of the human mind,"* and more than one elementary text-book provides us with practically the same definition. Now the obscurity and paralogism of this statement can only be equalled by the perversities of the metaphysicians. Matter, we are told, is what moves in the phenomenal world, and if it were asserted that matter is a primary *perception* of the human mind we might be no wiser, but at any rate the statement would not be without sense. But perhaps the phrase is not to be taken literally as signifying that a primary conception actually moves among perceptions, but only that we can form intuitively a conception of what moves perceptually—that the perceptual actually corresponds to the conceptual. In this case we are again thrown back on the fact that conceptual motion is a motion of geometrical ideals, and that these correspond in no accurate sense to our perceptions. Indeed, if matter be a conception at all, like the conception of a circle it ought to be a clear and definite idea, whereas the reader who will honestly ask himself what he *conceives* by matter will find that an answer is impossible, or that in attempting one he is sinking deeper and deeper into the metaphysical quagmire.

Proceeding further, we naturally turn to the little work termed *Matter and Motion*, by Clerk-Maxwell, one of the greatest British physicists of our generation. This is what he writes of matter:—

We are acquainted with matter only as that which may have energy communicated to it from other matter, and which may in its turn communicate energy to other matter.

Now this appears something definite; the only way in which we can understand matter is through the energy which it transfers. What, then, is energy? Here is Clerk-Maxwell's answer:—

Energy, on the other hand, we know only as that which in all natural phenomena is continually passing from one portion of matter to another.

All our hopes are shattered! The only way to understand energy is through matter. Matter has been defined in terms of energy, and energy again in terms of matter. Now Clerk-Maxwell's statements are extremely valuable as expressing concisely the nature of certain conceptual processes, by aid of which we describe certain phases of our perceptual experience, but as defining matter they carry us no further than the statement that matter is that which moves.

We will now turn to the famous *Treatise on Natural Philosophy* of Sir William Thomson (now Lord Kelvin) and Professor Tait—the standard work in the English language on its own branches of physical science. These writers tell us:—

> We cannot, of course, give a definition of *matter* which will satisfy the metaphysician, but the naturalist may be content to know matter as *that which can be perceived by the senses*, or as *that which can be acted upon by*, or *can exert, force*. The latter, and indeed the former also, of these definitions involves the idea of *force*, which, in point of fact, is a direct object of sense; probably of all our senses, and certainly of the "muscular sense." To our chapter on "Properties of Matter" we must refer for further discussion of the question, *What is matter?*

That the naturalist nowadays is not bound to satisfy the metaphysician—any more than he is bound to satisfy the theologian—will be admitted at once by the sympathetic reader of my own volume. But the naturalist is bound in the spirit of science to probe and question every statement, however high the authority on which it is made; and he is further bound to inquire whether a statement as to a physical fact is also in accord with his psychological experience. Science cannot be separated into compartments which have no mutual relationship, no mutual dependence, and no inter-communication. Science and its method form a whole, and if a physical definition be not psychologically true, it is not physically true. Now we have seen that the contents of perception are sense-impressions and stored sense-impressions, and that which can be perceived by the senses are these and these only. Do our authors mean to define all sense-impressions as matter? Would they call colour, hardness, pain, matter? We think this is hardly likely; they would probably tell us that the *source* of certain groups of sense-impressions is what they term matter; but this is not what they say. Had they said it they must themselves have recognised that they were passing beyond the veil of sense-impression and postulating a "thing-in-itself" behind the world of phenomena. They would then have seen that they were unconsciously endeavouring to satisfy the metaphysician, whom they had so properly disowned. This unconscious attempt to satisfy the "metaphysician within themselves" is further evidenced by their second statement, which throws back matter upon *force*. But *force* for these authors is the cause of motion not in the import of an antecedent or accompanying sense-impression—as, for example, relative position as cause—but in the metaphysical sense of a moving agent. They do not, indeed, place this moving agent behind sense-impression; they even describe it as a "direct object of sense," but from the psychological standpoint force must either be a sense-impression or a group of sense-impressions, for as source or object of sense-impressions it would be purely metaphysical. But as a group of sense-impressions in us, force cannot be that which causes motion in an objective world. As to our muscular appreciation of force, that is a point to which we shall find occasion to return later. We ought not, however, to lay much stress on these authors' remarks as to matter, for they expressly tell us that what matter is will be further discussed in another chapter of their work. Unfortunately, this portion of their great treatise has never been published, although they wrote the above remarks more than twenty-five years ago. Perhaps, had they returned to the subject, they would have recognised that, if the word matter had not appeared more frequently in their text than it does in their index, their volumes would have lost not an iota of their inestimable value to the physicist.

One of the two authors of the *Treatise on Natural Philosophy* has, however, published a separate work, entitled, *The Properties of Matter*. On pp. 12-13 of that work we have no less than nine, and on pp. 287-91 we have no less than twenty-five definitions or descriptions of matter, yet so far from matter being rendered intelligible by all these statements with regard to it, Professor Tait himself writes:

We do not know, and are probably incapable of discovering, what matter is.

And again:

The discovery of the ultimate nature of matter is probably beyond the range of human intelligence.

Now these statements mark a considerable advance on the standpoint of the *Treatise on Natural Philosophy*. They will at least suggest to the reader that it is no mere whim on my part to question the right of matter to appear *at all* in scientific treatises. When one author tells us it is a primary conception of the human mind, and another that it is probably beyond the range of human intelligence, we feel an uncomfortable sense of the metaphysician smiling somewhere round the corner. If our leading scientists either fail to tell us what matter is, or even go as far as to assert that we are probably incapable of knowing, it is surely time to question whether this fetish of the metaphysicians need be preserved in the temple of science.

Does Matter occupy Space?

But to return to Professor Tait; he has called his book *The Properties of Matter*, and this the reader will say means something very definite. Now, for the purposes of classifying our sense-impressions, it is undoubtedly useful to term particular groups of them which have certain distinguishing characteristics "material sense-impressions," and these material sense-impressions are what Professor Tait deals with under the properties of matter. It is Professor Tait, the unconscious metaphysician, who groups this class of sense-impressions together and supposes them to flow as properties from something beyond the sphere of perception, namely, matter. As a working definition of matter, Professor Tait considers that we may say: *"Matter is whatever can occupy space."* Now this definition will lead us to a number of ideas which it is instructive to follow up. In the first place, is it perceptual or conceptual space to which the definition applies? If the latter, then matter must be a geometrical form—a result which we think our author does not intend. We think it more probable that Professor Tait looks upon space as itself objective, although he avoids any definite statement on this really important issue. From the standpoint of our present volume, however, space is the mode by which we distinguish coexisting groups of sense-impressions, and therefore only groups of sense-impressions can be said to "occupy" space. This definition would therefore lead us to identify matter with groups of sense-impressions, and in practical everyday life the things which we term matter are certainly more or less permanent groups of sense-impressions, not unknowable "things-in-themselves" beyond sense-impression. Now there can be no scientific objection to our classifying certain more or less permanent groups of sense-impressions together and terming them matter,—to do so indeed leads us very near to John Stuart Mill's definition of matter as a "permanent possibility of sensation"—but this definition of matter then leads us entirely away from matter as the thing which moves. It can hardly be said that weight, hardness, impenetrability *move;* these are sense-impressions in the brain telephonic exchange; their grouping, their variation and succession may lead us to the *conception* of motion, but a sense-impression in itself cannot be said to move; it is there at the brain terminal or not there. In order to bring motion into the sphere of sense-impression, we are compelled to associate colour, hardness, weight, etc., with geometrical forms, and in making such constructs we pass from the plane of perception to that of conception. I move my hand; my power to realize this motion depends on my conceiving my hand bounded by a continuous surface. If the physicist tells me that my hand is an aggregation of discrete molecules, then my idea of the motion of the hand is thrown back on the motion of the swarm of molecules. But the same difficulty arises about the individual molecule. I may surmount it by supposing the molecule to be in itself a corporation of atoms, but I cannot conceive the atom's motion unless it be bounded by a continuous surface or else be a point. The only other way out of the difficulty is to construct the atom of still smaller atoms—(and there are certain phenomena presented by the spectrum analysis of the gaseous elements that might well induce us to believe that the atom cannot be conceived as the ultimate or "prime element of matter")—but what about these smaller atoms. are they geometrical ideals or are they built up of tinier atoms still, and if so where are we to stop? The process reminds us of the lines of Swift:—

> So naturalists observe, a flea
> Has smaller fleas that on him prey;
> And these have smaller still to bite 'em,
> And so proceed *ad infinitum*.

I am unable to verify Swift's statement as to the fleas, but I feel quite sure that to assert the real existence in the world of phenomena of all the concepts by aid of which we scientifically describe phenomena—molecule, atom, prime-atom—even if it be *ad infinitum*, will not save us from having ultimately to consider the moving thing to be a geometrical ideal, from having to postulate the phenomenal existence of what is contrary to our perceptual experience. This point brings out very clearly what the present writer holds to be a fundamental canon of scientific method, namely: *To no concept, however invaluable it may be as a means of describing the routine of perceptions, ought phenomenal existence to be ascribed until its perceptual equivalent has been actually disclosed.*

Whenever we disregard this canon, when, for example, we assert reality for the mechanisms by aid of which we describe our physical experience, then we are more likely than not to conclude with an *antinomy*, or a conflict of rules. For such mechanisms are constructs largely based on conceptual limits, which are unattainable in the field of perception. When we consider space as objective and matter as that which occupies it, we are forming a construct largely based on the geometrical symbols by aid of which we analyse motion conceptually. We are projecting the form and volume of conception into perception, and so accustomed have we got to this conceptual element in the construct that we confuse it with a reality of perception itself. When we go a stage further in the phenomenalising of conceptions, and postulate the reality of atoms, the antinomy becomes clear. If bodies are made up of swarms of atoms, how can they have a real volume or form? What is the volume or form of a swarm of bees or a cloud of dust? Obviously we can only give them shape and size by enclosing them conceptually in an ideal geometrical surface. Just as in a swarm of bees or a cloud of dust odd members of the community near this imaginary surface are continually passing in and out, so—if we phenomenalise conception—we must assert that at the surface of water or of iron odd molecules or atoms are perpetually leaving or, it may be, re-entering the swarm. Condensation and evaporation go on at the surface of the water and the iron gives a metallic smell. Now if the swarm be in this continual state of flow at the surface we can only speak of it as having volume or form *ideally,* or as a mode of conceptually distinguishing one group of sense-impressions from another. It is the conceptual volume or form which occupies space, and it is this form, and not the sense-impressions, which we conceive to move. If we throw back the occupancy of space on the individual members of the swarm, it is certainly not the volumes or forms of the individuals, which we consider as the volume or form of the material body, for the former we treat as imperceptible and the latter as perceptible. Further, we must then infer that the unknown is ultimately unlike the known, that geometrical ideals can be realised in the imperceptible. This, however, is a distinct breach of the second canon of logical inference.

So far, then, our analysis of the physicist's definitions of matter irresistibly forces upon us the following conclusions: That matter as the unknowable cause of sense-impression is a metaphysical entity as meaningless for science as any other postulating of causation in the beyond of sense-impression; it is as idle as any other *thing-in-itself,* as any other projection into the supersensuous, be it the force of the materialists or the infinite mind of the philosophers. The classification of certain groups of sense-impressions as material groups is, on the other hand, scientifically of value; it throws no light, however, on matter as that which perceptually moves. Conceptually all motion is the motion of geometrical ideals, which are so chosen as best to describe those changes of sense-impression which in ordinary language we term perceptual motion.

THE "COMMON-SENSE" VIEW OF MATTER AS
IMPENETRABLE AND HARD

Now the reader may feel inclined, on the basis of his daily experience, to assert that both the physicists above referred to and the author are really quibbling about words, and that we can sufficiently describe matter by saying that it is *impenetrable* and *hard*. Now these terms describe important classes of sense-impressions, and the sense-impressions of impenetrability and hardness are very frequently factors of what we have called material groups of sense-impressions. But it is very doubtful whether we can consider them as invariably associated with these material groups. At any rate if we do we shall find ourselves again involved in the antinomies which result when we pass incautiously to and fro from the field of perception to that of conception. When we say a thing is impenetrable, we can only mean that something else will not pass through it, or that there are two groups of sense-impressions which, in our perceptual experience, we have always been able to distinguish under the mode space. Impenetrability, therefore, can only be a relative term; one thing is impenetrable for a second. When we say that matter is impenetrable we cannot mean that nothing whatever can pass through it. A bird cannot fly through a sheet of plate glass, but a ray of light does penetrate it perfectly easily. A ray of light cannot pass through a brick wall, but a wave of elastic oscillations can. In order to describe the motion of these luminous and electric waves the physicist conceives ether to penetrate all bodies and to act as a medium for the transit of energy through them. Matter cannot therefore be looked upon as the thing which is *absolutely* impenetrable.

Or, are we missing the point of what is meant, when it is asserted that matter is that which is impenetrable? Are we to postulate the real existence of atoms and then to suppose the individual members of the swarm impenetrable? Here again a difficulty arises. There is much that tends to convince physicists that the atom cannot be conceived as the simplest element of the conceptual analysis of material groups. Just as a bell when struck sets the air in motion and gives a note, so we conceive an atom capable of being struck, and of setting not the air but the ether in motion, of giving, as we might express it, an ether note. These notes produce in us certain optical sense-impressions—for example, the bright lines of the spectrum of an attenuated gas. As without seeing two bells we might, and indeed often do, distinguish them by their notes, so the physicist distinguishes an atom of hydrogen from an atom of oxygen, although he has never seen either, by the different light notes which he conceives to arise from them. But as the bell to give a note must be considered as vibrating—changing its shape or undergoing strain—so the physicist practically finds himself compelled to conceive the atom as undergoing strain, or changing its shape.

This conception forces us to suppose the atom built up of distinct parts capable of changing their relative position. What are these ultimate parts of the atom, by the relative motion of which we describe our sense-impressions of the bright lines in the spectrum? We have as yet formed no conception. Does the ether or anything else penetrate between these ultimate parts of the atom? We cannot say. In the present state of our knowledge it is impossible to tell whether it would or would not simplify things to conceive the atom as penetrable or impenetrable. Hence, even if we go so far as to give the concept atom a phenomenal existence, it will not help us to understand what is meant by the assertion that matter is impenetrable.

INDIVIDUALITY DOES NOT DENOTE SAMENESS IN SUBSTANCE

Shall we, however, be more dogmatic still, and, denying that ether is matter, assert that matter is impenetrable *relative* to matter? In order to give any definite answer to this question we have again to pass from the perceptible material group to its supposed elementary basis, the atom, and to ask whether we have any reason for conceiving atoms as incapable of penetrating each other. In the first place, the physicist, although he has never caught an atom, yet conceives it as something which is incapable of disappearing—*it continues to be*. In the next place, if we conceive it as entering into combination with a second atom, although we have no reason for asserting that the two atoms do not mutually penetrate, we are still compelled, in order to describe by aid of atoms our perceptual experience, to conceive that, out of the combination, two separate atoms can again be obtained with the same individual characteristics as the original two possessed. What right have we to postulate these laws with regard to atoms when atoms are, even if "real," still absolutely imperceptible to us, when we are absolutely unable to observe their mutual actions? We have exactly the same logical right as we have to lay down any scientific law whatever. Namely, we find that these laws as to the action of single atoms, when applied to large groups of atoms, enable us to describe with very great accuracy what occurs in those phenomenal bodies which we scientifically symbolise by groups of atoms; they enable us to construct, without contradiction by perceptual experience, those routines of sense-impression which we term chemical reactions.

The hypotheses that the individual atom is both indestructible and impenetrable suffice to elucidate certain physical and chemical properties of the bodies we construct from atoms. But the con-

tinued existence of atoms under physical changes and the reproduction of their individuality on the dissolution of chemical combination might possibly be deduced from other hypotheses than
those of the indestructibility and impenetrability of the individual
atom. It does not follow of logical necessity that because we experience the same group of sense-impressions at different times and
in different places, or even continuously, that there must be one and
the same thing at the basis of these sense-impressions. An example
will clearly show the reader what I mean and at the same time
demonstrate that however useful as hypotheses the indestructibility
and impenetrability of the atom may be, they are still not absolutely
necessary conceptions; so that even if we do project our atom into
an imperceptible of the phenomenal world, it will not follow that
there must be an unchangeable individual something at all times
and in all positions as the basal element of a permanent group of
sense-impressions. The permanency and sameness of the phenomenal body may lie in the individual grouping of the sense-impressions
and not in the sameness of an imperceptible something projected
from conception into phenomena.

The example we will take is that of a wave on the surface of the
sea. The wave forms for us a group of sense-impressions, and we
look upon it, and speak of it, as if it were an individual thing. But
we are compelled to conceive the wave when it is fifty yards off as
consisting of quite different moving things from what it does when
it reaches our feet—the substratum of the wave has changed. Throw
a cork in; it rises and falls as the wave passes it, but is not carried
along by it. The wave may retain its form and be for us exactly
the same group of sense-impressions in different positions and at
different times, and yet its substratum may be continually changing. We might even push the illustration further: we might send
two waves of different individual shapes along the surface of still
water in opposite directions, or in the same direction if the pursuing
wave had the greater speed. One of these waves would meet or
overtake the other; they would coalesce or combine, producing in
us for a time (which depends entirely on their relative speeds) a
new group of sense-impressions differing totally from either individual group; but they would ultimately pass each other and emerge
with their distinct individualities the same as of old. Throughout
the whole of this sequence the substrata of the two individual waves
are changing and for the time of the combination their substratum
is identical, and yet the waves are able to preserve their individual
characteristics, so far as reappearing with them after combination
is concerned. Thus sameness of sense-impressions before and after

a combination is seen from a perceptual example not to involve of necessity a sameness of substratum.

Now I have cited this example of the wave for two reasons. In the first place, it shows us that it is possible to conceive atoms as penetrable by atoms, and as varying from moment to moment in their substratum, without at the same time denying the possibility of their physical permanency and individual reproduction after chemical combination. To consider an atom as consisting always of the same substratum, and as impenetrable by other atoms, may help us to describe easily certain physical and chemical phenomena; but it is quite conceivable that other hypotheses may equally well account for these phenomena, and this being so we have clearly no right first to project special conceptions into the world of real phenomena, and then to assert on the strength of this that matter, penetrable in itself, is impenetrable in its ultimate element, the atom. Clearly impenetrability is neither in perception nor conception a necessary factor of material groups of sense-impressions. Further, the permanence and sameness of such a group do not necessarily involve the conception of a permanent and the same substratum for the group.

My second reason for citing this wave example lies in the light it throws on the possibilities involved in the statement: *"Matter is that which moves."* The wave consists of a particular form of motion in the substratum which for the time constitutes the wave. This form of motion itself moves along the surface of the water. Hence we see that besides the substratum something else can be conceived as moving, namely, *forms of motion.* What if, after all, matter as the moving thing could be best expressed in conception by a form of motion moving, and this whether the substratum remain the same or not? To this suggestion we shall return later, as it is one extremely fruitful in its results.

Hardness not Characteristic of Matter

It remains for us now to deal with the other characteristic, hardness, which is popularly attributed to matter. There are certain persons who are content, when men's ignorance as to the nature of matter is suggested to them, to remark that one has only to knock one's head against a stone wall in order to have a valid demonstration of the existence and the nature of matter. Now if this statement be of any value, it can only mean that the sense-impression of hardness is the essential test of the presence of matter in these persons' opinion. But none of us doubts the existence of the sense-impression hardness associated with other sense-impressions in certain permanent groups; we have been aware of it from childhood's days, and do not require its existence to be experimentally demonstrated now. It is one of those muscular sense-impressions which we shall see are conceived by science to be describable in terms of the relative acceleration of certain parts of our body and of external bodies. But it is difficult to grasp how the sense-impression of hardness can tell us more of the nature of matter than the sense-impression of softness might be supposed to do. There are clearly many things which are popularly termed matter and are certainly not hard. Further, there are things which satisfy the definitions of matter as that which moves or as that which fills space, but which are very far indeed from producing any sense-impression of the nature of hardness or softness; nor would they even satisfy our definition if we said that matter is that which is heavy, heaviness being certainly a more widely-spread factor of material groups of sense-impressions than hardness. Between the sun and planets, between the atoms of bodies, physicists conceive the ether to exist, a medium whose vibrations constitute the channel by means of which electromagnetic and optical energy is transferred from one body to another. In the first place, the ether is a pure conception by aid of which we correlate in conceptual space various motions. These motions are the symbols by which we briefly describe the sequences and relationships we perceive between various groups of phenomena. The ether is thus a mode of resuming our perceptual experience; but, like a good many other conceptions of which we have no direct perception, physicists project it into the phenomenal world and assert its real existence. There seems to be just as much, or little, logic in this assertion as in the postulate that there is a real substratum, matter, at the back of groups of sense-impressions; both at present are metaphysical statements. Now there is no evidence forthcoming that the ether must be conceived as either hard or heavy, and yet it can be strained or its parts put in relative motion. Further, from Professor Tait's standpoint, it occupies space. Hence those who associate matter with hardness and weight must be prepared to deny that the ether is matter, or be content to call it non-matter. It is worth noting, at the same time, that the metaphysicians—whether they be materialists asserting the phenomenal existence both of space and of a permanent substratum of sense-impression, or "common-sense" philosophers asking us to knock our heads against stone walls—reach hopelessly divergent results when they say that matter is that which moves, that matter occupies space, and that matter is that which is heavy and hard.

• C. D. Broad (1887–   )

The Ideal of Pure Mechanism[7]

C. D. Broad, whom we have already met in the selections for
Chapter I, here tries to explain what is involved in the mechanistic
(materialistic) ideal. He lists briefly the tenets which a mechanical
view of nature entails, and shows how mechanism is really *monistic*
in its consequences; positing one kind of stuff with one property,
and one kind of change with one law of change. And he shows
some of the limitations of pure mechanism from the standpoint of
theory of knowledge.

In this chapter I want to consider some of the characteristic differences which there seem to be among material objects, and to
inquire how far these differences are ultimate and irreducible. On
the face of it the world of material objects is divided pretty sharply
into those which are alive and those which are not. And the latter
seem to be of many different kinds, such as Oxygen, Silver, etc. The
question which is of the greatest importance for our purpose is the
nature of living organisms, since the only minds that we know of
are bound up with them. But the famous controversy between
Mechanists and Vitalists about living organisms is merely a particular case of the general question: Are the apparently different kinds
of material objects irreducibly different?
It is this general question which I want to discuss at present.
I do not expect to be able to give a definite answer to it; and I am
not certain that the quesion can ever be settled conclusively. But
we can at least try to analyse the various alternatives, to state them
clearly, and to see the implications of each. Once this has been
done it is at least possible that people with an adequate knowledge
of the relevant facts may be able to answer the question with a
definite Yes or No; and, until it has been done, all controversy on
the subject is very much in the air. I think one feels that the disputes between Mechanists and Vitalists are unsatisfactory for two

[7] From C. D. Broad, *The Mind and Its Pace in Nature*, pp. 43-52. Copyright,
1952, by the Humanities Press, Inc.

reasons. (i) One is never quite sure what is meant by "Mechanism" and by "Vitalism"; and one suspects that both names cover a multitude of theories which the protagonists have never distinguished and put clearly before themselves. And (ii) one wonders whether the question ought not to have been raised long before the level of life. Certainly living beings behave in a very different way from non-living ones; but it is also true that substances which interact chemically behave in a very different way from those which merely hit each other, like two billiard-balls. The question: Is chemical behaviour ultimately different from dynamical behaviour? seems just as reasonable as the question: Is vital behaviour ultimately different from non-vital behaviour? And we are much more likely to answer the latter question rightly if we see it in relation to similar questions which might be raised about other apparent differences of kind in the material realm.

The Ideal of Pure Mechanism. Let us first ask ourselves what would be the ideal of a mechanical view of the material realm. I think, in the first place, that it would suppose that there is only one fundamental kind of stuff out of which every material object is made. Next, it would suppose that this stuff has only one intrinsic quality, over and above its purely spatio-temporal and causal characteristics. The property ascribed to it might, e.g., be inertial mass or electric charge. Thirdly, it would suppose that there is only one fundamental kind of change, viz., change in the relative positions of the particles of this stuff. Lastly, it would suppose that there is one fundamental law according to which one particle of this stuff affects the changes of another particle. It would suppose that this law connects particles by pairs, and that the action of any two aggregates of particles as wholes on each other is compounded in a simple and uniform way from the actions which the constituent particles taken by pairs would have on each other. Thus the essence of Pure Mechanism is (a) a single kind of stuff, all of whose parts are exactly alike except for differences of position and motion; (b) a single fundamental kind of change, viz., change of position. Imposed on this there may of course be changes of a higher order, e.g., changes of velocity, of acceleration, and so on; (c) a single elementary causal law, according to which particles influence each other by pairs; and (d) a single and simple principle of composition, according to which the behaviour of any aggregate of particles, or the influence of any one aggregate on any other, follows in a uniform way from the mutual influences of the constituent particles taken by pairs.

A set of gravitating particles, on the classical theory of gravitation, is an almost perfect example of the ideal of Pure Mechanism.

The single elementary law is the inverse-square law for any pair of particles. The single and simple principle of composition is the rule that the influence of any set of particles on a single particle is the vector-sum of the influences that each would exert taken by itself. An electronic theory of matter departs to some extent from this ideal. In the first place, it has to assume at present that there are two ultimately different kinds of particle, viz., protons and electrons. Secondly, the laws of electro-magnetics cannot, so far as we know, be reduced to central forces. Thirdly, gravitational phenomena do not at present fall within the scheme; and so it is necessary to ascribe masses as well as charges to the ultimate particles, and to introduce other elementary forces besides those of electro-magnetics.

On a purely mechanical theory all the apparently different kinds of matter would be made of the same stuff. They would differ only in the number, arrangement and movements of their constituent particles. And their apparently different kinds of behaviour would not be ultimately different. For they would all be deducible by a simple principle of composition from the mutual influences of the particles taken by pairs; and these mutual influences would all obey a single law which is quite independent of the configurations and surroundings in which the particles happen to find themselves. The ideal which we have been describing and illustrating may be called "Pure Mechanism."

When a biologist calls himself a "Mechanist" it may fairly be doubted whether he means to assert anything so rigid as this. Probably all that he wishes to assert is that a living body is composed only of bodies, and that its characteristic behaviour is wholly deducible from its structure and components and from the chemical, physical and dynamical laws which these materials would obey if they were isolated or were in non-living combinations. Whether the apparently different kinds of chemical substance are really just so many different configurations of a single kind of particles, and whether the chemical and physical laws are just the compounded results of the action of a number of similar particles obeying a single elementary law and a single principle of composition, he is not compelled as a biologist to decide. I shall later on discuss this milder form of "Mechanism," which is all that is presupposed in the controversies between mechanistic and vitalistic biologist. In the meanwhile I want to consider how far the ideal of Pure Mechanism could possibly be an adequate account of the world as we know it.

Limitations of Pure Mechanism. No one of course pretends that a satisfactory account even of purely physical processes in terms of Pure Mechanism *has* ever been given; but the question for us is:

How far, and in what sense, *could* such a theory be adequate to all
the known facts? On the face of it external objects have plenty of
other characteristics besides mass or electric charge, e.g., colour, temperature, etc. And, on the face of it, many changes take place in
the external world besides changes of position, velocity, etc. Now
of course many different views have been held about the nature
and status of such characteristics as colour; but the one thing which
no adequate theory of the external world can do is to ignore them
altogether. I will state here very roughly the alternative types of
theory, and show that none of them is compatible with Pure Mechanism as a complete account of the facts. (1) There is the naive
view that we are in immediate cognitive contact with parts of the
surfaces of external objects, and that the colours and temperatures
which we perceive quite literally inhere in those surfaces independently of our minds and of our bodies. On this view Pure Mechanism breaks down at the first move, for certain parts of the external
world would have various properties different from and irreducible
to the one fundamental property which Pure Mechanism assumes.
This would not mean that what scientists have discovered about the
connexion between heat and molecular motion, or light and periodic
motion of electrons would be wrong. It might be perfectly true, so
far as it went; but it would certainly not be the whole truth about
the external world. We should have to begin by distinguishing between "macroscopic" and "microscopic" properties, to use two very
convenient terms adopted by Lorentz. Colours, temperatures, etc.,
would be macroscopic properties, i.e., they would need a certain
minimum area or volume (and perhaps, as Dr. Whitehead has suggested, a certain minimum duration) to inhere in. Other properties, such as mass or electric charge, might be able to inhere in volumes smaller than these minima and even in volumes and durations
of any degree of smallness. Molecular and electronic theories of
heat and light would then assert that a certain volume is pervaded
by such a colour if and only if it contains certain arrangements of
particles moving in certain ways. What we should have would be
laws connecting the macroscopic qualities which inhere in a volume
with the number, arrangement, and motion of the microscopic particles which are contained in this volume.

On such a view how much would be left of Pure Mechanism?
(i) It would of course not be true of macroscopic properties. (ii) It
might still be true of the microscopic properties in their interactions
with each other. It might be that there is ultimately only one kind
of particle, that it has only one non-spatio-temporal quality, that
these particles affect each other by pairs according to a single law,

and that their effects are compounded according to a single law. (iii) But, even if this were true of the microscopic particles in their relations *with each other*, it plainly could not be the *whole truth* about them. For there will also be laws connecting the presence of such and such a configuration of particles, moving in such and such ways, in a certain region, with the pervasion of this region by such and such a determinate value of a certain macroscopic quality, e.g., a certain shade of red or a temperature of 57° C. These will be just as much laws of the external world as are the laws which connect the motions of one particle with those of another. And it is perfectly clear that the one kind of law cannot possibly be reduced to the other; since colour and temperature are irreducibly different characteristics from figure and motion, however close may be the causal connexion between the occurrence of the one kind of characteristic and that of the other. Moreover, there will have to be a number of different and irreducible laws connecting microscopic with macroscopic characteristics; for there are many different and irreducible determinable macroscopic characteristics, e.g., colour, temperature, sound, etc. And each will need its own peculiar law.

(2) A second conceivable view would be that in perception we are in direct cognitive contact with parts of the surfaces of external objects, and that, so long as we are looking at them or feeling them, they do have the colours or temperatures which they then seem to us to have. But that the inherence of colours and temperatures in external bodies is dependent upon the presence of a suitable bodily organism, or a suitable mind, or of both, in a suitable relation to the external object.

On such a view it is plain that Pure Mechanism cannot be an adequate theory of the external world of matter. For colours and temperatures would belong to external objects on this view, though they would characterise an external object only when very special conditions are fulfilled. And evidently the laws according to which, e.g., a certain shade of colour inheres in a certain external region when a suitable organism or mind is in suitable relations to that region cannot be of the mechanical type.

(3) A third conceivable view is that physical objects can seem to have qualities which do not really belong to any physical object, e.g., that a pillar-box can seem to have a certain shade of red although really no physical object has any colour at all. This type of theory divides into two forms. (a) It might be held that, when a physical object seems to have a certain shade of red, there really is *something* in the world which has this shade of red, although this something cannot be a physical object or literally a part of one.

Some would say that there is a red mental state—a "sensation"—; others that the red colour belongs to something which is neither mental nor physical. On either of these alternatives it would be conceivable that Pure Mechanism was the whole truth about matter considered in its relations with matter. But it would be certain that it is not the whole truth about matter when this limitation is removed. Granted that bits of matter only *seem* to be red or to be hot, we still claim to know a good deal about the conditions under which one bit of matter will seem to be red and another to be blue and about the conditions under which one bit of matter will seem to be hot and another to be cold. This knowledge belongs partly to physics and partly to the physiology and anatomy of the brain and nervous system. We know little or nothing about the mental conditions which have to be fulfilled if an external object is to seem red or hot to a percipient; but we can say that this depends on an unknown mental factor x and on certain physical conditions a, b, c, etc., partly within and partly outside the percipient's body, about which we know a good deal. It is plain then that, on the present theory, physical events and objects do not merely interact mechanically with each other; they also play their part, along with a mental factor, in causing such and such an external object to seem to such and such an observer to have a certain quality which really no physical object has. In fact, for the present purpose, the difference between theories (2) and (3) is simply the following. On theory (2) certain events in the external object, in the observer's body, and possibly in his mind, cause a certain quality to inhere in the external object so long as they are going on. On theory (3) they cause the same quality to *seem* to inhere in the same object, so long as they are going on, though *actually* it does not inhere in any physical object. Theory (1), for the present purpose, differs from theory (2) only in taking the naive view that the body and mind of the observer are irrelevant to the *occurrence* of the sensible quality in the external object, though of course it would admit that these factors are relevant to the *perception* of this quality by the observer. This last point is presumably common to all three theories.

I will now sum up the argument. The plain fact is that the external world, as perceived by us, seems not to have the homogeneity demanded by Pure Mechanism. If it *really* has the various irreducibly different sensible qualities which it *seems* to have, Pure Mechanism cannot be true of the whole of the external world and cannot be the whole truth about any part of it. The best that we can do for Pure Mechanism on this theory is to divide up the external world first on a macroscopic and then on a microscopic scale; to suppose that the macroscopic qualities which pervade any region are causally determined by the microscopic events and objects which exist within it; and to hope that the latter, in their interactions with *each other* at any rate, fulfil the conditions of Pure Mechanism. This result may remind the reader of the carefully qualified compliment which Mr. Gibbon pays to the morality of the Negroes in a foot-note which I forbear from quoting. We must remember, moreover, that there is no *a priori* reason why microscopic events and objects should answer the demands of Pure Mechanism even in their interactions with each other; that, so far as science can tell us at present, they do not; and that, in any case, the laws connecting them with the occurrence of macroscopic qualities *cannot* be mechanical in the sense defined.

If, on the other hand, we deny that physical objects have the various sensible qualities which they seem to us to have, we are still left with the fact that some things *seem* to be red, others to be blue, others to be hot, and so on. And a complete account of the world must include some explanation of such events as "seeming red to me," "seeming blue to you," etc. We can admit that the ultimate physical objects may all be exactly alike, may all have only one non-spatio-temporal and non-causal property, and may interact with each other in the way which Pure Mechanism requires. But we must admit that they are also cause-factors in determining the *appearance*, if not the *occurrence*, of the various sensible qualities at such and such places and times. And, in these transactions, the laws which they obey *cannot* be mechanical.

We may put the whole matter in a nutshell by saying that the appearance of a plurality of irreducible sensible qualities forces us, no matter what theory we adopt about their status, to distinguish two different kinds of law. One may be called "intro-physical" and the other "trans-physical." The intro-physical laws may be, though there seems no positive reason to suppose that they are, of the kind required by Pure Mechanism. If so, there is just one ultimate principle of composition for intra-physical transactions. But the trans-physical laws cannot satisfy the demands of Pure Mechanism; and, so far as I can see, there must be at least as many irreducible trans-physical laws as there are irreducible determinable sense-qualities. The nature of the trans-physical laws will of course depend on the view that we take about the status of sensible qualities. It will be somewhat different for each of the three alternative types of theory which I have mentioned, and it will differ according to which form of the third theory we adopt. But it is not necessary for our present purpose to go into further detail on this point.

• Morris R. Cohen (1880–1947)

Law and Purpose in Biology[8]

Morris Raphael Cohen taught at the College of the City of New York for thirty-six years; first mathematics and later philosophy. Interested in a wide variety of fields including natural science, law, and history, he is famed not as a builder of systems, but as one of the finest critical minds of the past fifty years. Primarily a logician and a philosopher of scientific method, Cohen's great work is *Reason and Nature* (1931) from which the following selection is taken. Here Cohen deals with certain problems of method which arise in comparing physics and biology, chiefly the issue between mechanists and vitalists in the latter science. And finally, he deals with the doctrine of biological evolution, showing its relation to arguments for the purposive nature of the universe. Cohen is partisan only for reason and science. His criticism of mechanists and vitalists alike places the controversy in a richer and more complex perspective.

The Independence of Biologic Method

(1) The Individuality of the Organism. One who has studied physics for any length of time and has become familiar with its usual abstract language is likely to feel that he is in a new intellectual atmosphere when he turns to a book on biology. Treatises like those in the Cambridge Natural History do not seem to utilize methods different from those followed by good historians in describing ancient peoples or by intelligent travellers dealing with modern primitive tribes. This is true even if we should take books like Darwin's *Descent of Man* or *Domestication of Animals*. While in the latter we have an attempt to establish general laws, the method of reasoning seems less like that of mathematical physics and much more like that of history or those which a conscientious referee or judge follows in a court of law. This situation lends

[8] From Morris R. Cohen, *Reason and Nature* (New York, 1931), pp. 276-92. Copyright, 1950, by The Free Press.

colour to the view that biology, like history, is a more concrete science than physics and nearer to reality. Some followers of Bergson like the present Master of Balliol have tried to use this to prove that biology and history, though empirical, give us absolute knowledge of things in themselves, not subject to those limitations of phenomenal and mathematical knowledge that were pointed out by Kant.

Apart from the dubious character of the metaphysical arguments that the abstract is unreal and that mathematical physics eliminates real time, it ought to be clear that this attempt to vindicate for biology a superior type of knowledge different from that of physics, is based on a flagrant neglect of some elementary facts in the case.

One of these is that physics and chemistry, like biology, *begin* with what might be called the natural history stage, i.e. with mere description. But as our knowledge increases, we are able to introduce analytic and experimental methods, and to formulate the relations between phenomena in ever wider laws. Thus the descriptive study of the motion of individual planets gives rise in the course of time to the mathematical theory of astronomy, and so the study of the strength of different materials gives rise to the theory of elasticity, the study of the shape of crystals to mathematical crystallography, etc. So likewise the descriptive stage in the study of atomic weights if followed by Moseley's law in which they are all united by mathematical relations. Is biology an exception to this rule? Not at all. The branches of biology which have made most progress, e.g. biochemistry and genetics, are assuming more and more an experimental and mathematical character like that of other branches of physics. That as we thus progress in the fullness and accuracy of our knowledge we fall behind in the knowledge of reality, is an amazing claim. We can understand its seeming plausibility only if we remember that as our description becomes more scientific, it becomes more removed from the familiar level of common sense. Obviously to the extent that habitual and familiar descriptions seem more "real" to us, all progress in science is at first away from reality. But it is to be observed that the common sense level is not one of primitive metaphysical innocence. The language of common sense is full of animistic, ancient, and scholastic metaphysics; and theoretic science arises not only to satisfy practical needs, but also as a way out of intellectual dissatisfaction aroused by the perplexing contradictions which infest the realm of common sense.

In the second place no test of individuality has ever been proposed that does not accord some individuality to planets, crystals, or electrons, or that will apply without any difficulty throughout the organic realm. Bergson himself is aware of these difficulties and mentions some, e.g. the difficulty of distinguishing between a member of a colony and what is merely a part of an organism. Is the germ cell a separate individual or a part of the body? Bergson tries to avoid these difficulties by assuming only one true individuality, the whole of life, of which all existing individuals are branches. But whatever interest or value may inhere in such a revival of the ancient idea of a cosmic life or a world-soul, Bergson is certainly unfortunate when he tries to use such a metaphysical concept as the whole of life to explain empirical biologic facts such as the supposed resemblance between the eye of a scallop and the vertebrate eye. Apart from the unfortunate circumstance that he is mistaken as to the fact, Bergson's logic in the case will certainly not stand scrutiny. Granted the fact of resemblance, it will not follow that physico-chemical explanations of such resemblance are impossible. Why cannot similar circumstances in different groups of animals produce somewhat similar results? Even if all mechanical explanations were proved impossible, the idea of the whole of life acting on both molluscs and chordates to produce a resemblance is a myth or a metaphor, not a biologic explanation of how or why anything happens. A scientific explanation of such facts of convergent evolution can be stated only, as Willy has done, in verifiable elements according to a method not substantially different from those of physics and chemistry.

(2) THE INFLUENCE OF THE ORGANISM AS A WHOLE. Admittedly biology must always consider the influence of the organism as a whole. This has seemed to some an admission that thereby biology differs in method from the physical sciences that proceed by the summation of the influence of the various parts. As a rough characterization of an outstanding difference, this seems unobjectionable. The attempt, however, to find here an absolute difference between the organic sciences which proceed from the whole to the parts, and the mechanical sciences which proceed from the parts to the whole, does not agree with the facts in the case. In the first place, it is not true that all physical science operates on homogeneous systems only. The Phase Rule for instance is a very important scientific law which deals explicitly with heterogeneous systems. In such systems no part of the effect is fully explained without taking account of the total state of the systems. This becomes obvious when chemical action takes place between the parts or elements of a system. But in the second place even in what may be called a homogeneous system, e.g. the masses of the sun and the planets, the influence of the total whole is necessary to explain the movement

of any actual part. It is only because the influence of the sun figures so predominantly in the bulk of the effect that we forget that no part of the system is simply passive. The physical law of action and reaction means therefore that every part of a mechanical system is also reciprocally cause and effect just as in an organism. There is doubtless such an enormous difference in degree of complexity here that it seems vain to expect that the mathematical methods of homogeneous continuous quantity will ever be applied to biology. But the mathematics of discontinuity has a place in physics as well as in the more developed portions of biology.

(3) THE BIOLOGIC LEVEL OF ANALYSIS. A seemingly promising compromise between mechanism and vitalism as to method is the suggestion that as science studies the relational structure of things, it may analyze different entities in the same way, and the same method may prevail in biology as in physics, though the subject matters are on different levels. While the units of electricity are electrons, of chemistry, atoms, of mechanics, molecules, why may not the units of biology be living cells? Will not this grant the irreducibility of life and yet the applicability of mechanistic methods? Do we not in fact speak of the mechanism of life?

The difficulty with this compromise is that biologic phenomena cannot all be adequately explained in terms of cells as units; and even if such explanation were possible, most vitalists would still be dissatisfied with the compromise. For at bottom, vitalists are opposed to the determinism which is characteristic of scientific methods in physics.

(4) THE SPONTANEITY OF LIFE. No one can well deny that organisms have a greater observable complexity and variability of motion than inanimate systems. If this variability is called spontaneity and spontaneity is identified with indeterminism, then the behaviour of organisms is indeterminate within the limits of our observation. This is a conclusion which vitalists from Bichat to Driesch and Bergson do and must accept. Bergson, more interested in introspective psychology than in biology, is radical in his indeterminism; but even Driesch allows his non-physical entelechies and psychoids to suspend (to what degree?) the operation of physical laws. This fits in very well with the common impression summed up by Bichat that while physical motions are constrained and thus subject to law completely, biologic phenomena involve an element of freedom, and therefore depart more or less from law.

This view is generally rejected by biologists as incompatible with

the character of their method. It is the very business of science to
bring apparently anomalous phenomena under the rubric of universal law; and it cannot accept any a priori limit as to what natural
happenings it may not hope to describe in terms of law. When we
look at the facts closely, we see that the greater complexity and
observable spontaneity of the organic realm is no new type of obstacle in the presence of which scientific method should disarm
itself. Men have been impressed with the fact that the wind blow-
eth where it listeth, and the weather is proverbially uncertain. Yet
we have little faith in the dogma that it is hopeless to seek for explanations here in terms of physical law. What can be more erratic
than the seemingly irregular movements of the bodies called planets
(i.e. wanderers)? Yet by persistent study their motions have been
reduced to law with a degree of accuracy that is far beyond the
power of the ordinary imagination to realize. There seems little
reason to doubt that a good deal of the popular resistance to determinism in biology is grounded in the anthropomorphic idea that
invariable uniformity means inability to resist the compulsion of external law. But to the scientific observer, the motions of a physical
system are not imposed upon it by any observable agency external
to it; and the "laws" of motion do not express any compulsion at all.
They are rather the forms of abstract mathematical description.
Why, then, should not that method of description be extended to
biologic phenomena?

The pretended proofs of an essential inapplicability of deterministic physical method to biology can be dismissed as sheer logical
fallacies. One may describe biologic phenomena in terms analogous
to those of human purpose, but one has no right to turn around
and use the possibility of such description as an argument against
the possibility of a mathematical-physical type of description. So
also we can characterize as fallacious all of Driesch's arguments to
the effect that an organism, unlike anything physical, can respond
differently to the same stimulus and in the same way to different
stimuli. These arguments depend upon taking "same" and "different" in an arbitrary absolutistic sense, not warranted by the character of phenomenal inquiry. Following his analysis, we could also
say that the same bar of iron will act differently to the same objects
(e.g. according to whether they are magnetized or not) and in the
same way (e.g. in the way of attraction) to a number of different
objects. In the absence of knowledge of magnetism, Dreisch's argument would prove that these phenomena are inherently beyond the
possibility of physical explanation.

But while the methodologic determinism of physical science is an irrefutable postulate necessary for the undertaking of experimental tests, it is after all only an ideal and there is no logically conclusive proof that this ideal is always attainable. Nature may not be constructed altogether for the convenience of the experimental scientist. Actually we do observe a higher degree of variability in biology than in physics; and the observed regularities may be likened to the regularity with which very large numbers of men learn the language of their parents, earn their living, marry, honour the dead, etc. If a fundamental physical principle such as the law of the conservation of energy has not been experimentally demonstrated with absolute accuracy, why insist that some departures from it are impossible in biology? The positive reasons for rejecting this suggestion are in the end based on faith in the future progress of science.

This faith need not be in the least blind. We may grant that physics and chemistry have not explained and may never fully explain the behaviour of organisms. But this shortcoming of our knowledge is not cured by adding unverifiable imaginary entities. Vitalism may help us to dramatize nature and give it an anthropomorphic familiarity. But while a traveller through a dark forest may manage to keep up his courage by filling the darkness with guardian angels, he cannot thereby change the nature and direction of the right road through the woods. Vitalism can no more increase the corpus of our knowledge than imaginary delicacies can provide sustaining food for our actual bodies.

(5) CONCLUSION. We conclude, then, that while neither mechanism nor vitalism is free from undue dogmatism, their merits and vices are by no means equal. Vitalism clings to the primitive sense of the mystery of things. It prevents us from sinking into mechanistic dogmatism, and it keeps a window open into the abysmal darkness outside of our little metaphysical kennels. But vitalism cares so much for the sense of mystery that it dogmatically blocks the path of rational physical research and keeps its door open to arbitrary and wilful dreams. Like other attempts to cling to our primitive feelings, it is delightful but childish and barren. The vice of mechanism in practice is at bottom similar to that of vitalism— it will not open its imagination to the possibility of physically determining factors quite other than those already known. It is a vice of economy which becomes deadly to all intellectual life if it rules out everything except sensible qualities. In the end, however, despite the association of vitalism with a hazy idealism (which is really subjectivism and nominalism) mechanism is much more in harmony

with true objective idealism (which insists on the reality of universal ideas). It keeps the essential faith in the rational concatenation of things according to universal law. Not the nominalistic Berkeley but the neo-platonic Newton is the true idealist.

In What Sense is Evolution a Biologic Law?

So closely is the word *evolution* identified in popular thought with the very essence of biology and so many varied and ambitious metaphysical doctrines have recently been erected on the foundation of this vague word, that a closer examination of the question at the head of this section is one of the intellectual necessities of our age. I can only give a succinct summary and refer the reader to the technical works on biology for the supporting evidence.

Evolution and the Unfolding of the Preformed

In its original and still popular meaning, the word *evolution* denotes the unfolding of what is involved in the organism from the beginning. The oak is simply the acorn unfolded, and the great diversity of life is but the unfolding of what was implicit in the original germs of life. Scientific biologists have abandoned this view since the days of C. F. Wolff in the middle of the eighteenth century. But popular philosophy clings to it partly because it makes the creation of the world picturable like the winding of a clock, and partly because it saves us the trouble of actual study as to why any particular form of life succeeds any other determinate form. This in large measure accounts for the popularity of such schemes of cosmic evolution as those of Spencer and Bergson. Having begged omnipotence in the initial assumption—whether in the form of an *elan vital* or universal differentiation and integration—everything else follows without further trouble of thought.

Evolution and Transformism

As currently used by English-speaking biologists, evolution denotes the rejection of the idea that "species" or organic forms have remained constant since creation. This denial is based on two different considerations: (1) empirical evidence such as the facts of paleontology, and (2) the general a priori bias in favour of change as a universal trait of nature.

(1) Few who know the facts are inclined to dispute that the an-

cestors of many of our existing plants and animals were markedly different from their present descendants. There seems little ground for doubting, for instance, that vertebrate animals have arisen in the course of time through modification of older forms. This, however, is not true of all forms of life. There is little, if any, factual evidence to show that our unicellular organisms have changed their form at all; and even some multicellular invertebrates seem to have maintained themselves without substantial change throughout the ages. Darwin and Huxley recognized this and explained it on the ground that those forms that are adapted to their environment need not change at all. This throws an interesting light on the meaning of *adaptation:* a form of life which does not change at all throughout the revolutions of geologic time is best adapted to maintain itself. But passing over this parenthetic observation, we must agree with Huxley that "facts of this kind are undoubtedly fatal to any form of the doctrine of evolution which postulates . . . an intrinsic necessity, on the part of animal forms which have once come into existence, to undergo continual modification."

(2) In the light of these considerations we need not pay much attention to a priori proofs that the transformation of species is not merely an observed process but a necessary consequence of the very organization of life. Spencer's attempted proof of this in terms of dissipation of force and integration of matter can be dismissed as a jumble of inadequate and undigested physical ideas. Moreover, if one of the proofs of evolution, viz. the parallelism between ontogeny and phylogeny, is taken seriously, the constancy of unicellular forms throughout the history of life is thereby already assumed. In general, a priori arguments as to the universality of change must assume that there is also something constant, and they cannot decide what empirical parts or aspects of nature have undergone the actual changes.

Evolution and Orthogenesis or Progress

Certain biologists, by no means all, are unwilling to limit themselves to the doctrine that (some) animal and plant forms have changed in time. They maintain that these changes must be in a definite direction, generally from the simple to the complex (Spencer). For this, also, an overwhelming mass of illustrative and confirmatory material can be gathered. But our test as to what is simple and what is complex must necessarily be somewhat vague, unless we adopt the popular anthropomorphic idea of life as a unilateral development from the amoeba to man—expressed by Emerson in the lines:

> And striving to be man, the worm
> Mounts through all the spires of form.

While this idea of man as the head of the line of evolution is too flattering to human vanity to be ever completely eliminated, it is no part of the science of biology. From a purely scientific point of view every existing form is the end of its line of evolution. If, however, we abandon resemblance to man as the text of simplicity or complexity, shall we say that the evolution of the horse's hoof from four toes is a development from the simple to the complex? Whatever test of simplicity we set up we shall have to admit that many animals lose complicated organs in the course of time. You may, if you like, call these changes degeneration. But by whatever name you call them, so long as they are facts it is not true that all changes or organic form are from the simple to the complex.

In general it may be true that knowing two or three points in the development of an organic form we may often venture to interpolate the form that must have existed in an intermediate stage of time. But the general history of life has not yet shown us any one formula for evolution which will enable us to predict the future forms of life with any greater certainty than we predict the future of political or ecclesiastical organizations.

Evolution and Common Descent

The doctrine of evolution is generally (though not by all biologists) identified with the view that all living forms have a common ancestry. If this ancestry is identified with the relatively simple unicellular organisms, there seems no difference between this and the doctrine that all development is from the simple to the complex. Logically, however, there is the possibility that it is only the limitations of our knowledge or means of exploration that makes us think of all unicellular organisms as alike in their simplicity. If this absolute simplicity or homogeneity is questioned, the assumption of a common ancestry for all forms of life becomes questionable even if we grant that all multicellular organisms are descended from unicellular ones. All sorts of possibilities are then opened. There may then be a certain rough parallel in the way different complex organisms have developed from *similar* beginnings but no common ancestry. There is also the possibility of different earlier forms becoming more alike through the mixing of germ plasm by interbreeding. In any case the facts of convergent evolution—of increasing resemblance between different forms—throws some doubt on the a priori argument that all resemblance must be due to a common ancestry. It has recently become a sort of habit to regard all diversity as having arisen in the course of time out of a common simple source. But to deduce all history from this convenient modern habit is not in the spirit of sober science. There is a good deal of evidence that many species, genera, orders and phyla do have a common ancestry. But that is not enough to establish the universal rule.

Experimental Evolution and Genetics

The facts of variations and heredity, the way offspring differ and yet resemble their parents, form today the subject matter of the rapidly developing science of genetics. With a fine loyalty to the earlier generation of biologists, this science is generally called experimental evolution. But it is well to note that the present study of the laws of genetics under experimental conditions and in the light of mathematical ideas, actually has little to do with Spencerian evolution or even with the more or less speculative ideas of Darwin. Modern genetics originates in the work of De Vries, and more especially Mendel, combined with the careful microscopic study of the cell begun by Schleiden and Schwann. So long as the explanatory ideas of Darwin were the biologist's interest, Mendel's work was unknown. But with the growth of experimental work Mendel's ideas have come to the foreground because they open up methods of research rather than mere explanations of facts already known. Mendel's law, however, is hardly likely to become popular among those who use biologic doctrines to bolster up what are called "organic" philosophies. For Mendel treats the organism as a bundle of more or less independent elements which should be studied separately (as far as possible); and this will not help sweeping assertions about the whole of reality.

Evolution and Natural Selection

As various ideas of Darwin on the causes of the "origin of species," e.g. sexual selection and pangenesis, have been abandoned by modern biology, the principle of natural selection has become the object of heated controversy. Curiously enough this controversy went on for many years before it occurred to some students of biology to undertake experimental investigations to determine whether any such process as natural selection actually prevails. I think it fair to conclude from these recent studies that natural selection is a factor, though not the principal—certainly not the only—factor, in the change or "evolution" of species. But "natural selection" is only a name for a whole group of factors which lead to the elimination of certain organisms embodying certain variations. It does not explain the causes of varaition, nor does it at all prove that every trait of an existing organism makes it adapted to its environment. Many traits are indifferent to survival-value and many that are injurious nevertheless persist. This supports the contention of Huxley that natural selection does not mean the survival of the fittest in any moral sense of the word. It should also warn us against the Spencerian assumption that because thought has been evolved in the struggle for existence it must necessarily serve some use or survival-value. Above all it lends no support to the view that the latest product of "evolution" is necessarily the best for human life, or that carnage and brutality will promote any specific human or moral values. Those who use natural selection as a substitute for a benevolent Providence can find no genuine support in the facts of scientific biology.

Biology and the Argument from Design

From time immemorial men have been profoundly impressed by the wonderful adaptation within organisms and between organisms and their environment. The view, therefore, that animate nature cannot but be the creation of an intelligent and benevolent cause has appealed powerfully to all generations. Is it conceivable that all these marvellous adjustments are the results of blind mechanical forces? Of course in a literal or logical sense the question can readily be answered in the affirmative since there is no logically conclusive proof of any logical contradiction in the idea (which has actually been held, e.g. by Epicureans) that the complicated vital adjustments do arise out of purely physical forces. But as the creation of life by exclusively nonliving forces is unknown in human experience, the positive analogy of the way human beings create purposive arrangements naturally appeals to the popular mind as the most plausible account of the origin of life. If you see a watch, you conclude that some intelligence created it; and if you see the even more complicated and delicate adjustments in living creatures, should you not conclude that a much greater intelligence is back of them?

It is generally believed that the theory of natural selection has broken the force of this argument. But there are enough occasional but vigorous denials of this to make worth while a reconsideration of this vital issue.

Let us note at the outset that even before the advent of Darwinian natural selection, the weakness of the argument from design had been recognized by philosophers from the ancient Greeks to Kant.

In the first place, while arguments which conceive an unknown cosmic creation on the analogy of human activity are psychologically vivid, they are analogies of little logical cogency. Human activity is such a negligibly infinitesimal part of the natural world that there is no reason to suppose that the latter only repeats the human pattern. Let us take a concrete example. It doubtless sounds very unreasonable to suppose that mechanical molecules can of themselves combine to form a watch. It is inconceivable because all the watches we know of are made by men and we have never observed them as natural formations. Let us, however, take another illustration. What is the probability of a sample of uric acid being an artificially manufactured product? A century ago no one would have hesitated to answer: None at all. Uric acid is an organic product and it is impossible for chemists to make it. We now realize the limitations of our previous experience. Yet nothing can be more certain than that our present experience also is limited, and that it is therefore most hazardous to base on it arguments as to what is cosmically impossible.

In the second place the popular idea of creation involves us in such insuperable difficulties that no philosophers—except as they have been subject to theologic influence—have maintained it. The scientific study of nature since the Greeks has always analyzed natural production as a transformation which requires previously existing material. Creation *ex nihilo* has no support in such study. Nor does it really explain anything to say that the animate or inanimate world began by an avowedly incomprehensible and supernatural act. If you need a creator in time to answer the question who made the world, you are bound to face the question who made the creator, and on ad infinitum. It seems therefore intellectually safer to limit ourselves (as regards production) to the infinite chain of natural events and to the relations which we can discover in it.

Despite these considerations, however, the argument from design, based largely on biologic adaptations, continued to figure largely in popular thought and in Anglo-American academic education up to the triumph of Darwinism. Nor need we be surprised at this if we remember that though Kant recognized the inadequacy of the physico-theologic argument, he still characterized as absurd the idea that an organic phenomenon like the growing of a blade of grass could ever be explained on purely physical principles. This concession is, strictly, of no aid to theology, since if the formation of the organic from the inorganic is unthinkable, we shall no more be able to think or understand God's creating life out of previous inorganic matter than *ex nihilo*. But this is perhaps too subtle for popular theology.

The doctrine of natural selection did not directly face the question as to the cause of adaptations. But it effectively weakened the case for an omniscient, omnipotent, and benevolent cause of these adaptations by calling attention to the frightful wastage of life. A creator who has to make so many imperfect or maladapted specimens to achieve the relatively few that survive for any length of time, seems either devoid of love for the imperfect or lacking in power. It is of course open to the adherents of the old theology to say that the misery and suffering of the imperfect is, in some mysterious way hidden to an imperfect intelligence, for the good even of those ill-adapted creatures. But this really abandons the case. One can similarly argue that a great deal of apparent good may turn out to be evil. The undeniable fact is that nature is full of maladaptations, though the observable number of them is rendered small by the fact that the creatures thus affected are so rapidly and extensively eliminated. When, therefore, you find a creature that seems for a time adapted to its environment, you may think of the countless others that were eliminated, and take the adaptation of the present specimen for granted. You may even argue that it could not be here if it were not in some way adapted to maintain itself. But the latter assertion is hardly more than a tautology. If the present seeds of future destruction are maladaptations, the latter are universal.

Yet the causes of adaptations are not thereby explained; and so long as this is true, revival of the physico-theologic argument from design are bound to recur. Especially is this true if we ignore—and we have plenty of emotional motives for ignoring—the fact of death and the inherent unlikelihood of an infinite duration of life on earth. An interesting current example of such revival of the argument from design is the reversal of the position of Paley and the Bridgewater treatises. Instead of arguing from the fitness of the organism, it argues from the fitness of the environment.

Consider the many seemingly exceptional physico-chemical conditions necessary to make life possible. The odds against such a combination occurring by chance are enormous. Hence, it is concluded, some designing agency is more probable. This argument, however, is extremely unfortunate. For even if we were to grant the validity of its mathematical reasoning, the latter could prove nothing more than that in a chance universe spread through time and space, the occurrence of life should be extremely rare. That, however, is precisely the actual case. Life as we know it is a relatively recent episode in an infinitesimal part of space. Even on our tiny globe it occupies a minor part. We do not find it a few miles below the surface of the earth and it disappears a few miles above it.

Nor is the argument for design improved if we rely on empirical evidence. A favourite example of evidence for design is the fact that water unlike most substances expands before reaching the freezing point. This prevents the ocean and the rivers from freezing to the bottom and thus makes it possible for fish and other organisms to continue active life. Here, however, it is only the apparent exception to what we expect to be a law of nature that lends colour to the view of a special intervention to make life possible where otherwise it could not be—just as a man who reaches his destination just before the downpour begins is tempted to think that Providence has held back the rain for his sake. When, however, we are caught in the rain, we do not generally think this has any connection with Providence. Suppose that we lived in a world in which marine life were not possible, on account of water continuing to contract below 39° F. Would it have been legitimate to use this as an argument against design? Actually we do live in a world where life is impossible above certain temperatures. Is this a legitimate argument against design? All we can say with certainty is that life is possible under certain conditions and not under others. Naturally those conditions under which life is possible can be called favourable to life. But this is an analytic proposition and can hardly support a proof that life is the result of design.

The belief or hypothesis that the total universe is the expression of a purpose—even of a definite purpose revealed to us—cannot be disproved. One who holds to that faith can always appeal to the remote future for verification. But neither can we disprove the assertion that the total cosmic process shows no purpose with reference to human life. Theoretically it seems reasonable to suppose that since the category of purpose arises in human affairs, it ought not without adequate justification be stretched to cover the entire universe of non-human relations. It is a common experience that categories applicable in a given realm cause confusion when stretched beyond that realm. But the emotional pull of rival hypotheses does not generally permit of even intellectual neutrality. A universe that is not alive to its core strikes us as cold and bleak and fills us with the almost instinctive fear of the unknown; while the idea that human or quasi-human forces are cosmically dominant produces a satisfaction similar to that of returning home from a lonely trip in a desert.

For the purposes of currently prevailing religion, it is not enough that the world should be merely purposive. It must be purposive in the interests of humanity and in accordance with a definite scheme as to what our best interests are. A purposive world in which the fate of humanity is a mere incident, in which this whole earth of ours plays no greater part than a stray chip from a statue which an artist is perfecting, offers little more support to current religion than a dogmatic materialism. Yet so ingrained is the fear of empty spaces and so strong the human desire for a conscious spectator of our intense but often incommunicable inner strivings, that millions have preferred to believe in a demoniac world, designed to torture all but a few of the elect rather than in a world that indifferently pours its beneficent and destructive rains on the just and the unjust.

• A. N. Whitehead (1861–1947)

Nature and Life[9]

Alfred North Whitehead is the greatest speculative mind which the English-speaking peoples have produced in modern times. After a brilliant career in mathematics at Cambridge and the University of London, Whitehead in 1924 at the age of sixty-three accepted a chair in philosophy at Harvard where he taught for thirteen more years and produced works which made him world famous. The most important of these are *Science and the Modern World, Process and Reality,* and *Adventures of Ideas. Nature and Life* from which the following selection is taken is two lectures given at the University of Chicago in 1934. Asserting that the problem of the status of "life" in "nature" is one of the chief problems of philosophy and science, Whitehead goes on to state his conviction that nature is not static, that different forms of natural existence shade off into one another, and that the separation between body and mind, life and nature, is untenable.

[9] From A. N. Whitehead, *Nature and Life* (1934), pp. 23-24. Copyright, 1938, by The Macmillan Co.

The status of life in Nature is the standing problem of philosophy and of science. Indeed, it is the central meeting point of all the strains of systematic thought, humanistic, naturalistic, philosophic. The very meaning of life is in doubt. When we understand it, we shall also understand its status in the world. But its essence and its status are alike baffling.

After all, this conclusion is not very different from our conclusion respecting Nature, considered in abstraction from the notion of life. We were left with the notion of an activity in which nothing is effected. Also this activity, thus considered, discloses no ground for its own coherence. There is merely a formula for succession. But there is an absence of understandable causation to give a reason for that formula for that succession. Of course, it is always possible to work one's self into a state of complete contentment with an ultimate irrationality. The popular positivistic philosophy adopts this attitude.

The weakness of this positivism is the way in which we all welcome the detached fragments of explanation attained in our present stage of civilization. Suppose that a hundred thousand years ago our ancestors had been wise positivists. They sought for no reasons. What they had observed was sheer matter of fact. It was the development of no necessity. They would have searched for no reasons underlying facts immediately observed. Civilization would never have developed. Our varied powers of detailed observation of the world would have remained dormant. For the peculiarity of a reason is that the intellectual development of its consequences suggests consequences beyond the topics already observed. The extension of observation waits upon some dim apprehension of reasonable connection. For example, the observation of insects on flowers dimly suggests some congruity between the natures of insects and of flowers, and thus leads to a wealth of observation from which whole branches of science have developed. But a consistent positivist should be content with the observed facts—namely, insects visiting flowers. It is a fact of charming simplicity. There is nothing further to be said upon the matter, according to the doctrine of a positivist. At present the scientific world is suffering from a bad attack of muddle-headed positivism, which arbitrarily applies its doctrine and arbitrarily escapes from it. The whole doctrine of life in Nature has suffered from this positivist taint. We are told that there is the routine described in physical and chemical formulae, and that in the process of Nature there is nothing else.

The origin of this persuasion is the dualism which gradually developed in European thought in respect to mind and Nature. At the beginning of the modern period Descartes expresses this dualism with utmost distinctness. For him, there are material substances with spatial relations, and mental substances. The mental substances are external to the material substances. Neither type requires the other type for the completion of its essence. Their unexplained interrelations are unnecessary for their respective existences. In truth, this formation of the problem in terms of minds and matter is unfortunate. It omits the lower forms of life, such as vegetation and the lower animal types. These forms touch upon human mentality at their highest, and upon inorganic Nature at their lowest.

The effect of this sharp division between Nature and life has poisoned all subsequent philosophy. Even when the co-ordinate existence of the two types of actualities is abandoned, there is no proper fusion of the two in most modern schools of thought. For some, Nature is mere appearance and mind is the sole reality. For others, physical Nature is the sole reality and mind is an epiphenomenon. Here the phrases "mere appearance" and "epiphenomenon" obviously carry the implication of slight importance for the understanding of the final nature of things.

The doctrine that I am maintaining is that neither physical Nature nor life can be understood unless we fuse them together as essential factors in the composition of "really real" things whose interconnections and individual characters constitute the universe.

The first step in the argument must be to form some concept of what life can mean. Also, we require that the deficiencies in our concept of physical Nature should be supplied by its fusion with life. And we require that, on the other hand, the notion of life should involve the notion of physical Nature.

Now as a first approximation the notion of life implies a certain absoluteness of self-enjoyment. This must mean a certain immediate individuality, which is a complex process of appropriating into a unity of existence the many data presented as relevant by the physical processes of nature. Life implies the absolute, individual self-enjoyment arising out of this process of appropriation. I have, in my recent writings, used the word "prehension" to express this process of appropriation. Also, I have termed each individual act of immediate self-enjoyment an "occasion of experience." I hold that these unities of existence, these occasions of experience, are the really real things which in their collective unity compose the evolving universe, ever plunging into the creative advance.

But these are forward references to the issue of the argument. At first approximation we have conceived life as implying absolute, individual self-enjoyment of a process of appropriation. The data appropriated are provided by the antecedent functioning of the universe. Thus, the occasion of experience is absolute in respect to its immediate self-enjoyment. How it deals with its data is to be understood without reference to any other concurrent occasions. Thus, the occasion, in reference to its internal process, requires no contemporary process in order to exist. In fact this mutual independence in the internal process of self-adjustment is the definition of contemporaneousness.

This concept of self-enjoyment does not exhaust that aspect of process here termed "life." Process for its intelligibility involves the notion of a creative activity belonging to the very essence of each occasion. It is the process of eliciting into actual being factors in the universe which antecedently to that process exist only in the mode of unrealized potentialities. The process of self-creation is the transformation of the potential into the actual, and the fact of such transformation includes the immediacy of self-enjoyment.

Thus, in conceiving the function of life in an occasion of experience, we must discriminate the actualized data presented by the antecedent world, the non-actualized potentialities which lie ready to promote their fusion into a new unity of experience, and the immediacy of self-enjoyment which belongs to the creative fusion of those data with those potentialities. This is the doctrine of the creative advance whereby it belongs to the essence of the universe, that it passes into a future. It is nonsense to conceive of Nature as a static fact, even for an instant devoid of duration. There is no Nature apart from transition, and there is no transition apart from temporal duration. This is the reason why the notion of an instant of time, conceived as a primary simple fact, is nonsense.

But even yet we have not exhausted the notion of creation which is essential to the understanding of Nature. We must add yet another character to our description of life. This missing characteristic is "aim." By this term "aim" is meant the exclusion of the boundless wealth of alternative potentiality, and the inclusion of that definite factor of novelty which constitutes the selected way of entertaining those data in that process of unification. The aim is at that complex of feeling which is the enjoyment of those data in that way. "That way of enjoyment" is selected from the boundless wealth of alternatives. It has been aimed at for actualization in that process.

Thus, the characteristics of life are absolute self-enjoyment, creative activity, aim. Here "aim" evidently involves the entertainment of the purely ideal so as to be directive of the creative process.

Also, the enjoyment belongs to the process and is not a characteristic of any static result. The aim is at the enjoyment belonging to the process.

The question at once arises as to whether this factor of life in Nature, as thus interpreted, corresponds to anything that we observe in Nature. All philosophy is an endeavor to obtain a self-consistent understanding of things observed. Thus, its development is guided in two ways—one is the demand for a coherent self-consistency, and the other is the elucidation of things observed. It is, therefore, our first task to compare the foregoing doctrine of life in Nature with our direct observations.

Without doubt the sort of observations most prominent in our conscious experience are the sense-perceptions. Sight, hearing, taste, smell, touch constitute a rough list of our major modes of perception through the senses. But there are an indefinite set of obscure bodily feelings which form a background of feeling with items occasionally flashing into prominence. The peculiarity of sense-perception is its dual character, partly irrelevant to the body and partly referent to the body. In the case of sight, the irrelevance to the body is at its maximum. We look at the scenery, at a picture, or at an approaching car on the road, as an external presentation given for our mental entertainment or mental anxiety. There it is, exposed to view. But, on reflection, we elicit the underlying experience that we were seeing with our eyes. Usually this fact is not in explicit consciousness at the moment of perception. The bodily reference is recessive, the visible presentation is dominant. In the other modes of sensation the body is more prominent. There is great variation in this respect between the different modes. In any doctrine as to the information derived from sense-perception this dual reference—external reference and bodily reference—should be kept in mind. The current philosophic doctrines, mostly derived from Hume, are defective by reason of their neglect of bodily reference. Their vice is the deduction of a sharp-cut doctrine from an assumed sharp-cut mode of perception. The truth is that our sense-perceptions are extraordinarily vague and confused modes of experience. Also, there is every evidence that their prominent side of external reference is very superficial in its disclosure of the universe. It is important. For example, pragmatically a paving stone is a hard, solid, static, irremovable fact. This is what sense-perception, on its sharp-cut side, discloses. But if physical science can be correct, this is a very superficial account of that portion of the universe which we call the paving stone. Modern physical science is the issue of a co-ordinated effort, sustained for more than three centuries, to understand those activities of Nature by reason of which the transitions of sense-perception occur.

Two conclusions are now abundantly clear. One is that sense-perception omits any discrimination of the fundamental activities within Nature. For example, consider the difference between the paving stone as perceived visually, or by falling upon it, and the molecular activities of the paving stone as described by the physicist. The second conclusion is the failure of science to endow its formulae for activity with any meaning. The divergence of the formulae about Nature from the appearance of Nature has robbed the formulae of any explanatory character. It has even robbed us of reason for believing that the past gives any ground for expectation of the future. In fact, science conceived as resting on mere sense-perception, with no other source of observation, is bankrupt, so far as concerns its claim to self-sufficiency.

Science can find no individual enjoyment in Nature; science can find no aim in Nature; science can find no creativity in Nature; it finds mere rules of succession. These negations are true of natural science. They are inherent in its methodology. The reason for this blindness of physical science lies in the fact that such science only deals with half the evidence provided by human experience. It divides the seamless coat—or, to change the metaphor into a happier form, it examines the coat, which is superficial, and neglects the body which is fundamental.

The disastrous separation of body and mind which has been fixed on European thought by Descartes is responsible for this blindness of science. In one sense the abstraction has been a happy one, in that it has allowed the simplest things to be considered first, for about ten generations. Now these simplest things are those widespread habits of Nature that dominate the whole stretch of the universe within our remotest, vaguest observation. None of these laws of Nature gives the slightest evidence of necessity. They are the modes of procedure which within the scale of our observations do in fact prevail. I mean the fact that the extensiveness of the universe is dimensional, the fact that the number of spatial dimensions is three, the spatial laws of geometry, the ultimate formulae for physical occurrences. There is no necessity in any of these ways of behavior. They exist as average, regulative conditions because the majority of actualities are swaying each other to modes of interconnection exemplifying those laws. New modes of self-expression may be gaining ground. We cannot tell. But, to judge by all analogy, after a sufficient span of existence our present laws will fade into unimportance. New interests will dominate. In our present sense of the term, our spatio-physical epoch will pass into that background of the past, which conditions all things dimly and without evident effect on the decision of prominent relations.

These massive laws, at present prevailing, are the general physical laws of inorganic nature. At a certain scale of observation they are prevalent without hint of interference. The formation of suns, the motions of planets, the geologic changes on the earth, seem to proceed with a massive impetus which excludes any hint of modification by other agencies. To this extent sense-perception on which science relies discloses no aim in Nature.

Yet it is untrue to state that the general observation of mankind, in which sense-perception is only one factor, discloses no aim. The exact contrary is the case. All explanations of the sociological functionings of mankind include "aim" as an essential factor in explanation. For example, in a criminal trial where the evidence is circumstantial the demonstration of motive is one chief reliance of the prosecution. In such a trial would the defense plead the doctrine that purpose could not direct the motions of the body, and that to indict the thief for stealing was analogous to indicting the sun for rising? Again no statesman can conduct international relations without some estimate—implicit or explicit in his consciousness—of the types of patriotism respectively prevalent in various nations and in the statesmen of these nations. A lost dog can be seen trying to find his master to trying to find his way home. In fact we are *directly* conscious of our purposes as *directive* of our actions. Apart from such direction no doctrine could in any sense be acted upon. The notions entertained mentally would have no effect upon bodily actions. Thus, what happens would happen in complete indifference to the entertainment of such notions.

Scientific reasoning is completely dominated by the presupposition that mental functionings are not properly part of Nature. Accordingly it disregards all those mental antecedents which mankind habitually presuppose as effective in guiding cosmological functions. As a method this procedure is entirely justifiable, provided that we recognize the limitations involved. These limitations are both obvious and undefined. The gradual eliciting of their definition is the hope of philosophy.

The points that I would emphasize are: First, that this sharp division between mentality and Nature has no ground in our fundamental observation. We find ourselves living within Nature. Second, I conclude that we should conceive mental operations as among the factors which make up the constitution of Nature. Third, that we should reject the notion of idle wheels in the process of Nature. Every factor which emerges makes a difference, and that difference can only be expressed in terms of the individual character of that factor. Fourth, that we have now the task of defining natural facts, so as to understand how mental occurrences are operative in conditioning the subsequent course of Nature.

A rough division can be made of six types of occurrences in Nature. The first type is human existence, body and mind. The second type includes all sorts of animal life, insects, the vertebrates, and other genera. In fact all the various types of animal life other than human. The third type includes all vegetable life. The fourth type consists of the single living cells. The fifth type consists of all large-scale inorganic aggregates, on a scale comparable to the size of animal bodies, or larger. The sixth type is composed of the happenings on an infinitesimal scale, disclosed by the minute analysis of modern physics.

Now all these functionings of Nature influence each other, require each other, and lead on to each other. The list has purposely been made roughly, without any scientific pretension. The sharp-cut scientific classifications are essential for scientific method, but they are dangerous for philosophy. Such classification hides the truth that the different modes of natural existence shade off into each other. There is the animal life with its central direction of a society of cells, there is the vegetable life with its organized republic of cells, there is the cell life with its organized republic of molecules, there is the large-scale inorganic society of molecules with its passive acceptance of necessities derived from spatial relations, there is the inframolecular activity which has lost all trace of the passivity of inorganic Nature on a larger scale.

In this survey some main conclusions stand out. One conclusion is the diverse modes of functioning which are produced by diverse modes of organization. The second conclusion is the aspect of continuity between these different modes. There are border-line cases, which bridge the gaps. Often the border-line cases are unstable, and pass quickly. But span of existence is merely relative to our habits of human life. For infra-molecular occurrences, a second is a vast period of time. A third conclusion is the difference in the aspects of Nature according as we change the scale of observation. Each scale of observation presents us with average effects proper to that scale.

Suggested Further Readings

Benjamin, A. C. *An Introduction to the Philosophy of Science.* New York: The Macmillan Co., 1937.

Bergson, Henri. *Creative Evolution.* Translated by Arthur Mitchell. New York: Henry Holt & Co., Inc., 1911.

Collingwood, R. G. *The Idea of Nature.* London and New York: Oxford University Press, 1945.

Eddington, A. S. *The Nature of the Physical World.* New York: The Macmillan Co., 1937.

Elliot, Hugh. *Modern Science and Materialism.* New York: Longmans, Green & Co., Inc., 1919.

Haldane, J. B. S. *The Philosophy of a Biologist.* London: Oxford University Press, 1935.

Joad, C. E. M. *Matter, Life and Value.* New York: Oxford University Press, 1929. Chaps. i, iv.

Loeb, Jacques. *The Mechanistic Conception of Life.* Chicago: University of Chicago Press, 1912.

Margenau, Henry. *The Nature of Physical Reality: A Philosophy of Modern Physics.* New York: McGraw Hill Book Co., Inc., 1950. Chaps. i-iv, ix, xix, xxi.

Morgan, C. Lloyd. *Emergent Evolution.* New York: Henry Holt & Co., Inc., 1926.

Pepper, Stephen C. *World Hypotheses: A Study In Evidence.* Berkeley: University of California Press, 1942. Chap. ix, "Mechanism."

Whitehead, A. N. *Science and the Modern World.* Chaps. ii, iii.

———. *Adventures of Ideas.* New York: The Macmillan Co., 1933. Chap. vii.

CHAPTER 4

Mind and the Cosmos

THE MIND AND ITS BODY

The point of view which sees the world of nature as a series of emergent properties or types of existence begins with matter, passes on to life, and ends with mind. And this way of looking at the world is a challenge to the standpoint of materialism not from biology but from philosophy itself. In its most extreme form, as a doctrine about the nature of ultimate reality, it becomes the theory of philosophical idealism. But this is its end point, and before it becomes a theory of reality, it originates in certain views which, however mistaken they may perhaps be, seem to spring from the evidence and the experiences of common sense.

These views are as follows. All normal human individuals possess *bodies* and they possess *minds*. These are completely different in their natures and in the way in which we experience them, but they are nonetheless joined or bound together throughout our lifetime. After death the body disintegrates, but there may be some sense in which the mind "lives on." Bodies are examples of that "matter" upon which the materialist builds his picture of the world, and they are therefore subject to all those mechanical and rigidly determined laws of nature which hold for matter. Bodies exist in space and time, are observable by all the usual methods of observation, and have, therefore, a public character.

But minds are very different. They exist in time, but it is a very personal and private time to which only the individual himself has access. They do not exist in space, nor do they seem to be subject to the mechanical laws of outward nature. Imagine for a moment the Eiffel Tower. How large is this image? An inch? Smaller? Where is it? In the imagination? But where is the imagination? In the brain? How much space does the imagination take up in the brain? And so how much space does the image of the Eiffel Tower take up in the brain? The foolishness of these questions

147

shows the perplexities which would arise by considering "the mind" as being in space. Also the direct workings of my mind are not open to the inspection of others, nor do I have direct access to theirs. All knowledge of other minds (short of telepathy—an undemonstrated phenomenon) comes not directly but by inference, through listening to their words and observing their bodily behavior.

This view of the fundamental separateness of mind and matter, or of mind and body was classically formulated by Descartes in the seventeenth century. It assumes that we live two lives; one the life of our bodies, which is public; the other the life of our minds, which is private, and that these two lives are lived in two different worlds. There is an inner world where occur my feelings of pleasure and pain, my perceptions of form and color, my deliberations, and my desires. And there is an outer world where my body moves, acts, collides with other bodies, and in general expresses its normal patterns of behavior.

Now, the distinction between the fundamental separateness of mind and body—this *dualism* as it is usually called—is more a distinction between two kinds of existence than between two modes of experience which have nothing to do with one another, and which, like parallel lines, never meet. For it is also a matter of common sense that there is a real *interaction* here. The *mind acts upon* and brings about changes in the body. And alternately the *body acts upon* and brings about changes in the mind. A man decides to leave his house and his arms perform certain acts, his legs move, his body changes its position in space. A tumor appears in the brain of a woman and her memory fades, her thoughts become hazy, and her perceptions grow disconnected. Moreover, the causal process alternates. Bodily symptoms may cause anxiety, anxiety may increase the amount of stomach acidity, increase of stomach acidity may produce an ulcer, an ulcer may produce pain, pain may induce deliberation, deliberation may result in a visit to a physician, a visit to a physician may reduce bodily symptoms. So the interactive cycle appears to the eye of common sense.

This is simple enough until one asks: But how is interaction possible? How can two forms of existence so incommensurable as bodies in space and minds not in space act upon one another? There is no difficulty in answering this question so long as we give "mind" a bodily interpretation; that is, identify it with the physical brain. That an impulse (electric charge?) in the nervous system can cause a muscle to move is easy to comprehend. But how can a *feeling* of fear cause a muscle to move? Naturally, if one reduces mind to matter, as the materialist insists upon doing, the difficulty vanishes.

A pain becomes merely a type of nerve stimulation. A feeling of fear is merely an electro-chemical impulse in the central nervous system. But it seems clear that this type of reduction is ill-advised. States of consciousness may be correlated with states of the brain but they are *not identical* with them. It is even probable that states of consciousness never exist in the absence of brain states and are dependent upon them. But to say that consciousness *depends on* the brain is not to say that it *is* the brain. So the root difficulty with the theory of interaction remains.

Two other theories of the relation of mind and body have arisen as alternatives to the theory of interaction, both also in the seventeenth century. For Descartes and his doctrine of dualistic interaction was immediately followed, on the one hand, by Leibniz and his *parallelism* and, on the other, by Spinoza and his *double-aspect theory*.

Parallelism starts with the same assumption as Cartesian dualism; namely that there is a basic difference between mind and body. But it denies the simple assumptions of common sense that there is a *causal relation* between them. It says only that they behave in a parallel fashion. They are like two lines which never meet but run on side by side to infinity. Mental events can only cause mental events, and physical events can only cause other physical events, but, whenever a mental event occurs, there is a corresponding physical event which accompanies it. Parallelism only denies that the two can cause one another if one means by cause "an active production" of one thing by another. But it does assert a constant conjunction of mental and physical events (the headache and the over-stimulated optic nerve for example) in that the two occur simultaneously.

The chief difficulty with the parallel theory is that it seems to cut the universe in two. It says: mind is mind and body is body and never the twain shall meet. But this only raises a further question. Why should there always be a one-to-one correlation between the series of mental and the series of physical events? Leibniz answered the question simply: "The soul follows its own laws, and the body likewise follows its own laws; and they agree with each other in virtue of the pre-established harmony between all substances, since they are all representations of one and the same universe." [1] But if one asks where the pre-established harmony itself comes from, Leibniz further answers: from God the author of the universe. Beyond this one cannot go, and it is not therefore surprising that a theory of the relation of body and mind which depends upon the

[1] Leibniz, *The Mondology*, trans. Latta (Oxford, 1925), pp. 262 f.

assumption of the existence of God should not in the modern world have won great scientific favor.

If the chief difficulty of the parallel theory is that it seems to cut the universe in two, the chief virtue of the double-aspect theory of Spinoza is that it restores the unity of the world. Spinoza thought that the universe (which he called "substance") could not be known directly, but that it always appeared under two "modes" or "aspects"; mind and body. Mind and body are not therefore two separate things, but aspects or forms of appearing of the same underlying but unknown substance. Mind and body are two sides of the same coin; wherever one appears, the other is bound to be also. This is an ingenious theory. Its chief difficulty lies in supposing that there is a single substance underlying both mind and body and that it can never be directly known. For common sense will always ask: What right have we to assume something which we cannot immediately experience?

The most adventuresome side of the double-aspect theory is its assertion that wherever body (matter) is to be found, there mind in some sense is to be found also. This means that little as we are accustomed to think so, there is "mind" in crystals, metals, and rocks; in short, in the realm of "inorganic nature" as well as the realm of living things. Naturally this does not mean that metals have ideas or that rocks deliberate. These higher manifestations of mind are only to be found in higher and more complex manifestations of body. But why should it not be the case that low grade bodies like stones also have low grade minds? The consequence of the double-aspect theory is that it finds mind to be everywhere in nature, and, unaccustomed as the ordinary man is to this type of metaphysical speculation, some very great philosophers, notably Spinoza, Schopenhaur (see p. 216), and Whitehead (see p. 138) have asserted it seriously. This is perhaps the extreme form of philosophical idealism.

The theories of interaction, parallelism, double-aspect, all stem from or are an answer to the dualism of Descartes and to the common-sense point of view which finds a fundamental separateness of mind and body. This way of looking at the matter is as old as Plato. And because Christianity has always emphasized the superiority of spirit to body, and because it believes in the immortality of the soul, it has perpetuated the separation asserted by both Plato and Descartes. Thus the dominant religion has supported the pronouncements of common sense.

But the separation of mind and body, as envisaged by Descartes, does violence, it has been asserted, to the real relation between them. And this is because it rests upon the assumption that body is a "thing" and that mind is equally a "thing" and that of course the two "things" are separate. Naturally they are not the same kind of thing; body is material and mind is spiritual. But this leads to the image that body is a machine composed of matter and that it is inhabited by a ghost which is spiritual, and that when the machine falls apart, the ghost leaves it to take up its abode elsewhere.[2] Obviously the language is ironic, but it points to a real difficulty, perhaps even a real error—the error of believing that the mind like the body is a "thing."

But there is another tradition in philosophy which goes back to Aristotle and whose best modern representative is John Dewey. This tradition views mind not as a thing but as a *process*, not as a substance but as a *function*. And as soon as this is asserted, the old separateness of body and mind breaks down. Mind and body together form an organic unity. The mind (or *psyche*), as Aristotle said, is simply the form or actual organizing principle of the animal body; together they make one organism. Dewey uses different language but what he says is much the same. Mind is connected with body because both grow up in the environment of nature, and the evolving needs of an organism in nature are productive of its mind. Mind and body emerge together within nature.

THE MIND AND ITS KNOWLEDGE

Some light is cast on the question of the place and importance of "mind" in the universe by considering the relation of the mind to its body. But even more illumination is to be gained by raising the question of the relation of the knowing mind to the world which it knows. This is the question of appearance and reality. Is there a real, existent world "out there" of which our mind gives us information? Does this world keep its existence and character whether any mind perceives it or not? To what extent is the world merely "our idea" of it? Does all knowledge depend on "the point of view" or are some things fixed, certain, and objective no matter what the point of view? How much of what we perceive is *discovered in* the world? And how much is *created by* the mind itself in the knowing process? These are some of the questions which arise when we consider the mind and its knowledge.

To these questions philosophers have given a wide variety of answers. Some of them seem like the pronouncements of common

[2] The image is taken from Gilbert Ryle, *The Concept of Mind* (New York: Barnes & Noble, Inc., 1950), pp. 15 ff.

sense. Some are quite subtle and even technical. But we may distinguish five of them here.

1. *Common-sense Realism:* Things exist in the world just as they are and independent of being known, and they are not changed by being known.

2. *Dualism:* There are two things—internal states of mind and the external objects which cause them. When our ideas are like things we can trust them. But ideas can be mistaken.

3. *Subjectivism:* The world which we perceive by our senses does not exist independently of our consciousness of it.

4. *Phenomenalism:* There is a real world and there is the way this real world appears. We can never know things in themselves but only how they appear, and these appearances are subject to laws which the mind itself imposes.

5. *Reflective Realism:* There is a world independent of thought existing in an objective space and time, and this world continues to exist whether observed or not.

(1) is a position which has been held in all ages. (5) was common among the Greeks and has been worked out in modern fashion since 1900. (2), (3), and (4) found classic expression respectively in John Locke, George Berkeley, and Immanuel Kant, during what was the golden age of modern theory of knowledge, namely the hundred years between Lock's *Essay Concerning Human Understanding* (1689) and Kant's *Critique of Pure Reason* (1781).

Common-sense realism, which holds that things exist in the world just as they are and independent of being known, is difficult to maintain after reflecting about the world of our experience. For it soon appears that there are types of perception to which we hesitate to give the status of knowledge. The objects in our dreams seem at the time to have an actuality however strange and distorted, but we cannot call our dreams perception in the same sense that our waking experience of objects is perception. Also there are optical illusions like the oar "bent" by the water, or the pool in the desert that is not there when we come to it although we "saw it there" when we were a mile away. Dreams and illusions destroy our confidence in the "existence" of all that we perceive. They suggest to us that some of our ideas are wild and some are in error. They lead to the more reflective position of dualism.

Dualism is the position associated with John Locke. It has some elements in common with common-sense realism and at the same time with a reasonably scientific view of the world. It seems to arise as an explanation of the errors of our perception and as a doctrine telling us where confidence in our perceptions is to be justified.

It will be noticed that there is a certain similarity between this doctrine of Locke and Descartes' dualism of mind and body. Locke says that there is an external world of things which the mind may know, but it always knows them indirectly through the ideas which it has of them. This means that we must always distinguish between two separate orders of things: the sensations (as of the hardness of a rock or the fragrance of a flower) which are immediately presented to our consciousness, and the outward "things" (the rock or the rose itself) which we can assume because of our sensations of them. Of course we always view objects from a certain point in space and from a certain angle, and this gives us our perspective toward them. The things themselves are known through their appearance, and our *ideas* of things represent the things themselves.

But if we reflect upon the two sensations above, the "hardness" of the rock and the "fragrance" of the flower, we shall see that they are quite different. And Locke distinguished sharply between them. He called perceptions like the hardness of the rock *primary qualities* and those like the fragrance of the rose *secondary qualities*. Primary qualities like shape, solidity, motion, and extension are qualities possessed by objects themselves, but secondary qualities like color, odor, taste, and sound are simply in us—they are the sensations which bodies excite in us without having any such characteristics themselves. Primary qualities are "real," for they belong to objects even when no mind is perceiving them. Secondary qualities only exist at the moment when a mind is experiencing them.

It should be apparent that there is much in the dualistic position which fits in with science and common sense. In the first place it informs us that ideas may be mistaken, and that they are to be trusted when they represent, or are in agreement with, or mirror, the nature of things. The world outside is the test of the validity of our ideas. And in the second place this view attributes chief reality to the primary qualities, which are just those in which physical science has the greatest interest because they are most susceptible to measurement. But it should also be clear that the dualistic position does not give mind a pre-eminent status in the universe. The activity of the mind may be responsible for error, but it is not responsible for truth. Truth comes from the real world outside the mind, and the mind can best learn the truth as a passive instrument, as a blank tablet upon which the ideas from outside may be impressed.

It was inevitable that the dualism of Locke should be followed

by the *subjectivism* of Berkeley. Locke's belief in the independent
existence of the external world stems largely from his belief that
the primary qualities are really qualities of things and do not depend on the mind. But what if primary qualities like shape, extension, and solidity are as much dependent upon the mind as the secondary qualities of color, smell, and taste? This is exactly what
Berkeley set out to prove (see the first selection at end of this chapter). It is impossible, he said, to conceive of a body which has extension but no color. And it is impossible for a color not to appear
as a patch which is extended. Therefore primary and secondary
qualities cannot be separated in experience, and the former are as
much a product of the mind as the latter. Moreover, our perceptions of the sizes, shapes, and distances of objects are relative and
depend mainly upon the conditions of the perceiving self. And if
all qualities of bodies are dependent upon being perceived by minds,
we have no longer strict proof of the independent existence of the
material world. It would seem, then, that minds and their ideas
are all that we can surely assert to exist. Objects exist only as they
are perceived. Berkeley's theory turns the doctrine of Locke and
of common sense upside down. It does not support the view that objects exist independently of consciousness. It holds rather that
objects exist only insofar as we are conscious of them. And this to
a large extent emphasizes the role of the mind in nature. For it
almost says: the world is my idea!

The *phenomenalism* of Kant is at once more radical and more
conservative than the subjectivism of Berkeley. It is more conservative because it does admit, with Locke, an external world, and it
agrees with Locke also that *the external world is not directly know-
able.* Kant distinguishes between a universe of *things-in-themselves*
which we can never know and a world of *phenomena* or appearances or ordered perceptions which is what we do know. But concerning these appearances (what Locke and Berkeley both would
have called "ideas") Kant is more radical than Berkeley. Berkeley
thought that the ideas or elements of our world are subjective, but
he never doubted that *the order in which they appeared in the mind*
was due to something outside the mind. But Kant said that not
only the elements of our knowledge are subjective, but even the
forms and relations under which they appear. For example space
and time. We ordinarily think of space and time as outside us.
Space is the dimensions of the outside world where things are.
Time is the order of external events according to which they happen. But Kant said that space and time are not characteristics of
the outside world; they are forms or molds of the mind itself—forms

which *the mind imposes* on all its experience. It is like seeing the world through a pair of green-colored glasses which one could never remove. If the world is green, it is not because it is really so, but because the light filters through a form in which greenness is a given. This way of looking at the world explains much. If the physicist marvels at the way in which mathematics can be applied to the world, he has discovered less about nature than the human mind. Thus Kantian phenomenalism gives a bold new place to mind in the universe. Instead of holding that mind abstracts laws from nature, it says that mind imposes laws upon nature. More dignity and power the mind could scarcely have!

THE MIND AND ITS FREEDOM

A third area in which the question of the status of mind in the universe arises is that of will, decision, and self-determination. And here again the issues are closely related to the problem of materialism and to the dualistic position which is a commonplace of Western thought. The separation of body and mind, which was asserted by Descartes, assumes an inner world of feeling and perceptions and an outer world where the body acts as any other material object in nature. The separation of the mind from the external world which it knows indirectly through its sensations and ideas, which was asserted by Locke, makes mind dependent upon its objects. What is the situation of the self and its powers of will? Is the human mind free to think, to will, and to act? Or is it simply a part of nature, moving in tune with the other parts of nature, and like them compelled to act according to those iron-clad laws of behavior which seem to be universally applicable? This is the somewhat loose way in which the issue is frequently stated.

It is probably not difficult to account for this way of putting it. The standpoint of materialism (which views the universe as a machine whose parts are geared together and which operates according to laws uniformly applicable) is somehow offensive to the human view of its own nature. We feel ourselves to be free, to act (within limits) as we wish, to be more than *mere things* which are bits of matter in motion, in short, to be *responsible persons*. But with all due respect for this feeling, it is not clear that it is logically incompatible with the principle that uniform rules of causation apply throughout nature, in short, that every effect has a cause. Let us consider for a moment what the principle of causation means.

Common sense recognizes in loose but simple terms that events occur with some regularity, that acts have consequences, that objects affect one another. So we know that there is a relation between fire and burnt fingers, potassium cyanide and dead bodies, heat and boiling water. It is interesting that common sense formulates these relations in two quite different ways. We say: "Fire burns," "Potassium cyanide kills," "Heat boils water." This way of putting it emphasizes causes as active agencies, as *forces which produce their effects* through their own natural powers. But sometimes we put it a little differently. We say: "If you put your finger in the fire, it will certainly be burnt," or "If you swallow three ounces of potassium cyanide you will inevitably die," or "If water is heated to a temperature of 212° F. it will surely boil." And this second way of putting it suggests that between cause and effect there is some kind of inevitable or *necessary connection*. These are the two characteristics of the causal relation according to a long tradition going back at least as far as Aristotle: (1) that the cause always produces the effect and (2) that between cause and effect there is a necessary connection.

Both of these supposed characteristics were treated to a devastating analysis by the British philosopher David Hume in the eighteenth century (see p. 187). Hume held that all our knowledge about causes and their effects comes from observation and experience, and that when we examine or experience cause and effect, we can in no wise observe a necessary relation between them. Nor, indeed, can we see the cause *produce* the effect. We only see first the cause, then we see it followed by what we call the effect, but the joining of the two together, "that unknown glue" as Hume puts it, is nowhere discoverable in our experience. Hume's theory of causation admits that effects follow causes in time, and that this occurs with the regularity of repeatable sequence. But he insists that the law of cause and effect is merely a *description* of a causal sequence; it merely points to a *constant conjunction* of elements in our experience.

Modern science has learned much from Hume. It agrees that causation may be considered as a constant conjunction in which the cause is taken to be the *sufficient condition* for the occurrence of the effect. If potassium cyanide is sufficient to cause death, then it may be taken as the cause of which death is the effect. But science is not only interested in describing the past, it is also interested in that kind of generalization by means of which the future may be predicted. Science is, of course, deterministic. It believes in universal causation which it formulates in this way: "For any class of events (X), there is a class of conditions (Y), such that whenever an instance of (Y) occurs, an instance of (X) occurs also." And it may state this in the form of a prediction: "If in the future an instance of (Y) occurs, then an instance of (X) will occur likewise."

From the foregoing it will be seen that there is not one, but at least three, possible accounts of causality, and that they depend on quite different general concepts—the idea of necessity, the idea of regularity, and the idea of predictability. They may be summarized as follows:

1. *Casuality as production:* Any cause (A) produces its effect (B) and the relation between them is a *necessary connection*.

2. *Causality as description:* Any cause (A) is simply observed to regularly precede its effect (B), and the relation between them is one of *constant conjunction*. (The theory of Hume.)

3. *Causality as prediction:* Any appearance of cause (A) in the future will always be followed by its effect (B) and the relation between them is simply one of *predictability*.

The traditional problem of free will versus determinism is ancient, continuous, and full of confusions. It is surely related to the question as to whether and in what manner the principle of causality may be said to apply to the behavior of human beings. But, since the principle of causality is (as we have just shown) susceptible of different interpretations, it is not always clear just what question is being asked. Philosophical discussions about the freedom of the will generally bring in and sometimes confuse the following issues: (1) whether there is genuine chance, novelty, and spontaneity in the world, (2) whether the law of causality as constant conjunction applies to human acts, (3) whether human behavior is always compelled by outside forces, (4) whether the decisions made by human will are illusory, (5) whether there is regularity in human behavior, (6) whether man is only a cog in Nature's machine, and (7) whether human acts are predictable. The question of free will versus determinism involves separate issues of chance, compulsion, causality, and predictability.

The issue is generally stated as freedom versus determinism, but this is an inaccurate use of terms. *Determinism* (the doctrine that all events have causes) should be opposed to *indeterminism* (the doctrine that some events really do not have causes). *Freedom* (the doctrine that the human will has real power to make decisions) should be opposed to *compulsion* (the doctrine that we are always compelled by forces outside our will and our control). *Chance* (the doctrine that there are real possibilities of novelty and spontaneity in the future) should be opposed to *necessity* (the doctrine that the past decrees completely what the future is to be). *Fatalism* (the resignation which comes of the belief that what will happen, will happen regardless of what we try to do) should be opposed to *self-determination* (the confidence that our wills have power to make and to carry out decisions). *Predictability* (the doctrine that human acts can be predicted in advance according to the principles of probability) should be opposed to *unpredictability* (the doctrine that human acts cannot be predicted in advance). It seems clear that we have here not one but five different issues:

1. Indeterminism versus determinism
2. Freedom versus compulsion
3. Chance versus necessity
4. Self-determination versus fatalism
5. Predictability versus unpredictability

Of course there are relations between these five oppositions. Freedom is related to self-determination. Determinism is related to predictability. Chance is probably related to self-determination. But there is no reason to believe that determinism is incompatible with self-determination. And on the other hand, indeterminism is related to unpredictability, fatalism may be inferred from necessity, but there is no reason to believe that indeterminism is related to freedom. Each of these oppositions is a philosophical problem in its own right. Freedom versus compulsion is one of the fundamental problems of ethics (it is discussed by Aristotle in the first selection at the end of the next chapter). Predictability versus unpredictability is one of the major issues in the theory of method of the social sciences. Chance versus necessity and self-determination versus fatalism are related questions which are considered by William James (in the third selection at the conclusion of this chapter).

It is not possible to discuss each of the above five issues in detail nor with the completeness with which they have been treated throughout the history of philosophy. But a preliminary approach may be made (simply for purposes of discussion) through a few crucial questions and tentative answers to them presented here with a brevity which may wear the mask of dogmatism.

Do our acts have causes? (The question of determinism.) Yes. Human acts like all other events are natural events. They have causes and they have consequences of which they are, in turn, the causes. This is in no sense a denial of human freedom; it states the way in which freedom is possible. Without such moral causality there would be no meaning to deliberation, moral education, rewards and punishments.

Do our acts have causes which come completely and exclusively from outside our will? (The question of compulsion.) Sometimes this is the case but certainly not always. Freedom is perhaps not an absolute matter. We are always more or less free according to "the rate of opportunity" we enjoy. And our health, strength, early history, family background, and economic status impose certain limitations. But often these are not so much the limitations of our will as the very materials which have gone into its making. We are never the victims of pure compulsion.

Does the human will itself have power to make decisions? (The question of self-determination.) Certainly it does, and in this sense the will is free. Our self is a unity, and our ego is a repository of much of the primal force of the universe. Authentic self-determination is possible. We face real alternatives of conduct and we may freely choose between them.

Is all human action really beyond human control in that what is fated to happen will happen? (The question of fatalism.) This question is answered in the negative by the answer to the previous question. We are not puppets in the universe but minded creatures whose wills "make a difference."

When we choose to act in a certain way, that is, choose one alternative rather than another, is it the case that we could have chosen otherwise? (The question of avoidability.) This question is too full of verbal difficulties to be simply answered—difficulties growing out of the various meanings of "could" and "would" and the difficulties due to the confounding of different roles and perspectives in time.

Can our acts be predicted in advance? By ourselves? By others? With absolute certainty? With a fair degree of probability? (The question of predictability.) The act of predicting is engaged in not by a participant, but by a spectator who views from outside. Probably, therefore, no individual ever tries "to predict" his own behavior in advance. Also, from the inside our future seems unknown and full of diverse possibilities. But outsiders, viewing us in terms of our "case history" or life span, can make predictions about our future courses of action. These predictions can never be certain, but as psychology and the social sciences grow in precision, they can be expected to gain in degree of probability. When, as spectators, we view our own past, the course of our life may seem to have a certain inevitability. But when we speculate on our own future, it generally seems mysterious and remote. It is like reading a novel by Dostoevski. As we read, we do not really have any idea of how exactly it will end. But when we come to the last page, everything seems to have occurred through the strictest causality.

The freedom of the human mind in nature is often treated as an absolute, as if there were only freedom or compulsion. But it may be that freedom itself is a matter of degree, and that this freedom increases as we pass from stones to plants, to animals, to men. The higher freedom is a function of consciousness. Self-consciousness precedes self-determination. And our acts of free choice depend upon the cooperation of a reasonable mind and a strong will. Responsible moral acts are perhaps the culmination of the power of mind in nature.

NATURE AS A COSMOS

As we have seen, the realm of nature is one of the great areas of attention, which takes its place beside the area of the human and the area of the divine, within the map of our total experience. And the sustained human interest in nature has produced the body of the natural sciences and that reflection upon them which has created the philosophy of nature and metaphysics. It is our interest in nature which produces theories about matter in motion, about the domain of living things, about mind and its relation to the body in which it lodges, about the external world which it knows, and about the freedom which it enjoys. But if matter, life, and mind are all somehow to be found within nature, still it is not quite clear what their relationship is to one another or, indeed, just how they individually contribute to that nature of which they are a part.

Here again there is room for a legitimate difference of opinion. We have already seen that the philosophic impulse tends on the one hand to relate the items of our experience in a fashion which will express the sense of wholeness and connectedness, and on the other to refine meanings toward greater clarity and to analyze things into their smallest constituent parts. These two impulses spring perhaps ultimately from two irreducible tendencies within the knowing process—the ability to discover likenesses amidst difference, and the ability to discriminate between different things—and have their consequences for a philosophy of nature and for metaphysics. The second causes men to see nature as a collection, as a mere aggregate of specific substances or events. The first causes men to see nature as a system of related parts, as a unity, as a *cosmos*.

It was the Greeks who first conceived of the universe as a system of order (or an ordering together, which is what a cosmos means in Greek), and subsequent ages have repeated, each in its own way, their sense of how "mere nature" constitutes a universe. Thus Alexander Pope in the eighteenth century:

> What if the foot, ordained the dust to tread,
> Or hand, to toil, aspired to be the head?
> What if the head, the eye, or ear repined
> To serve mere engines to the ruling Mind?
> Just as absurd for any part to claim
> To be another, in this general frame:
> Just as absurd, to mourn the tasks or pains,
> The great directing Mind of All ordains.
> All are but parts of one stupendous whole,
> Whose body Nature is, and God the soul;

Pope's conception of "the ruling Mind" is very Greek, very Platonic, and his metaphor of nature as the body of God is a type of pantheism which Spinoza would have understood, although it would be an offense to the more conservative Christian tradition. Christianity is more at home with the type of cosmology held by Sir Isaac Newton.

Newton, after presenting in his great work an account of the principles governing the movement of all natural bodies, took five pages at its very end (General Scholium to Book III) to relate the world of nature, whose secrets he had just unfolded, to the God in whose existence he profoundly believed. "This most beautiful system of the sun, planets, and comets could" he said "only proceed from the counsel and domination of an intelligent and powerful being." And he continues "This Being governs all things not as the soul of the world, but as Lord over all . . ." But of course, to see nature as a cosmos does not require either that one believe in God, or that one find nature's orderliness to be friendly or comfortable to man. Schopenhauer also viewed nature as a cosmos (see the fourth selection at end of this chapter), but though he thought of every force in nature as a manifestation of a cosmic "will," this will was a blind striving, meaningless and purposeless from the point of view of human values, and uncreated by the hand of God.

Plato and Aristotle in the ancient world, Newton and Spinoza in the seventeenth century, Schopenhauer and Schelling in the nineteenth, Samuel Alexander and Alfred North Whitehead in our own time have been great cosmologists—men who have tried in their philosophy to give some account of the interrelations of the parts of the universe, to show that nature is best conceived as a unified field of experience showing multiple but related traits. Of course, each age has its own picture of how nature as a whole is to be conceived, its own perspective upon the way in which scientific knowledge may be unified. For the Greeks, nature is conceived according to the analogy of the living organism. To Plato the world was "a living creature truly endowed with soul and intelligence by the providence of God." During the Renaissance the dualistic view reigned supreme; mind existed not inside but outside of nature, in the intelligence of a transcendent God who had set the world-machine in operation. The nineteenth century returned to the Greek idea, but it interpreted "mind" not in terms of a faculty of reason but as the expression of will and feeling. Therefore the cosmology of Schelling and Schopenhauer builds these nonrational elements into a cosmic principle. And finally, modern cosmology, having been influenced by theories of evolution and development, sees nature as a world of *process* where substances are turned into functions, things become events, and where *what things are* is defind *by what they do*. This last perspective emphasizes not the static quality of "objects," but the active operation of "happenings." In the account which it favors, our usual dependence upon nouns and adjectives (things and their qualities) is replaced by a dependence upon verbs (actions). Certain advances in modern physics have suggested this new point of view. And this shows that the cosmology of an age and its science are inseparably joined. The cosmology of the Greeks, of the seventeenth century, and of the modern world are, in the end, the products of their scientific imagination.

The following selections—"Things and Ideas" by George Berkeley, "The Understanding and the Will" by David Hume, "The Dilemma of Determinism" by William James, and "The World as Will" by Arthur Schopenhauer—are all concerned with the mind, its knowledge, its freedom, and its status in the universe. Berkeley and Hume wrote during the eighteenth century, James and Schopenhauer during the nineteenth.

The selection from Berkeley has been included to show one typical position (subjectivism) concerning the mind and its knowledge. The selection from Hume illustrates an important aspect of the problem of causality and its relation to the will, while that from William James is an eloquent defense of chance and self-determination. The selection from Schopenhauer has been included as an example of cosmological thinking which sees mind in one of its aspects (will) as the clue to nature and to her inmost operations.

• George Berkeley (1685–1753)

Things and Ideas [3]

George Berkeley was born in Ireland, studied at Trinity College in Dublin, and later become Bishop of Cloyne. Among his chief works are *An Essay Toward A New Theory of Vision, A Treatise Concerning the Principles of Human Knowledge*, and *Three Dialogues between Hylas and Philonous* from which the following selection is taken. Berkeley's chief purpose is religious—to refute materialism and atheism—but he attempts this in true philosophic fashion. He builds on the empiricism of his predecessor John Locke but tries to show that Locke's dualism is untenable and that, in the end, all that exists are spirits (minds) and ideas—the position of subjectivism. Berkeley's effort to show that there is no such thing as material substance depends upon his proof that the primary qualities, which Locke thought really belonged to objects, are just as relative to a perceiver and just as subjective as the secondary qualities, which even Locke had admitted did not belong to bodies in the external world.

Phil. Can any doctrine be true that necessarily leads a man into an absurdity?

Hyl. Without doubt it cannot.

Phil. Is it not an absurdity to think that the same thing should be at the same time both cold and warm?

Hyl. It is.

Phil. Suppose now one of your hands hot, and the other cold, and that they are both at once put into the same vessel of water, in an intermediate state; will not the water seem cold to one hand, and warm to the other?

Hyl. It will.

Phil. Ought we not therefore, by our principles, to conclude it is really both cold and warm at the same time, that is, according to your own concession, to believe an absurdity?

Hyl. I confess it seems so.

Phil. Consequently, the principles themselves are false, since you have granted that no true principle leads to an absurdity.

[3] From George Berkeley, *Three Dialogues between Hylas and Philonous*, First Dialogue.

Hyl. But, after all, can anything be more absurd than to say *there is no heat in the fire?*

Phil. To make the point still clearer; tell me whether, in two cases exactly alike, we ought not to make the same judgment?

Hyl. We ought.

Phil. When a pin pricks your finger, doth it not rend and divide the fibres of your flesh?

Hyl. It doth.

Phil. And when a coal burns your finger, doth it any more?

Hyl. It doth not.

Phil. Since, therefore, you neither judge the sensation itself occasioned by the pin, nor anything like it to be in the pin; you should not, conformably to what you have now granted, judge the sensation occasioned by the fire, or anything like it, to be in the fire.

Hyl. Well, since it must be so, I am content to yield this point, and acknowledge that heat and cold are only sensations existing in our minds. But there still remain qualities enough to secure the reality of external things.

Phil. But what will you say, Hylas, if it shall appear that the case is the same with regard to all other sensible qualities, and that they can no more be supposed to exist without the mind, than heat and cold?

Hyl. Then indeed you will have done something to the purpose; but that is what I despair of seeing proved.

．　　．　　．　　．　　．

Phil. Then as to *sounds,* what must we think of them: are they accidents really inherent in external bodies, or not?

Hyl. That they inhere not in the sonorous bodies is plain from hence; because a bell struck in the exhausted receiver of an air-pump sends forth no sound. The air, therefore, must be thought the subject of sound.

Phil. What reason is there for that, Hylas?

Hyl. Because, when any motion is raised in the air, we perceive a sound greater or lesser, according to the air's motion; but without some motion in the air, we never hear any sound at all.

Phil. And granting that we never hear a sound but when some motion is produced in the air, yet I do not see how you can infer from thence, that the sound itself is in the air.

Hyl. It is this very motion in the external air that produces in the mind the sensation of *sound.* For, striking on the drum of the ear, it causeth a vibration, which by the auditory nerves being communicated to the brain, the soul is thereupon affected with the sensation called *sound*.

Phil. What! is sound then a sensation?

Hyl. I tell you, as perceived by us, it is a particular sensation in the mind.

Phil. And can any sensation exist without the mind?

Hyl. No, certainly.

Phil. How then can sound, being a sensation, exist in the air, if by the *air* you mean a senseless substance existing without the mind?

Hyl. You must distinguish, Philonous, between sound as it is perceived by us, and as it is in itself; or (which is the same thing) between the sound we immediately perceive, and that which exists without us. The former, indeed, is a particular kind of sensation, but the latter is merely a vibrative or undulatory motion in the air.

Phil. I thought I had already obviated that distinction, by the answer I gave when you were applying it in a like case before. But, to say no more of that, are you sure then that sound is really nothing but motion?

Hyl. I am.

Phil. Whatever therefore agrees to real sound, may with truth be attributed to motion?

Hyl. It may.

Phil. It is then good sense to speak of *motion* as of a thing that is *loud, sweet, acute,* or *grave.*

Hyl. I see you are resolved not to understand me. Is it not evident those accidents or modes belong only to sensible sound, or *sound* in the real and philosophic sense; which, as I just now told you, is nothing but a certain motion of the air?

Phil. It seems then there are two sorts of sound—the one vulgar, or that which is heard, the other philosophical and real?

Hyl. Even so.

Phil. And the latter consists in motion?

Hyl. I told you so before.

Phil. Tell me, Hylas, to which of the senses, think you, the idea of motion belongs? to the hearing?

Hyl. No, certainly; but to the sight and touch.

Phil. It should follow then, that, according to you, real sounds may possibly be *seen* or *felt*, but never *heard*.

Hyl. Look you, Philonous, you may, if you please, make a jest of my opinion, but that will not alter the truth of things. I own, indeed, the inferences you draw into me, sound something oddly; but common language, you know, is framed by, and for the use of the vulgar; we must not therefore wonder, if expressions adapted to exact philosophic notions seem uncouth and out of the way.

Phil. Is it come to that? I assure you, I imagine myself to have gained no small point, since you make so light of departing from common phrases and opinions; it being a main part of our inquiry, to examine whose notions are widest of the common road, and most repugnant to the general sense of the world. But, can you think it no more than a philosophical paradox, to say that *real sounds are never heard,* and that the idea of them is obtained by some other sense? And is there nothing in this contrary to nature and the truth of things?

Hyl. To deal ingenuously, I do not like it. And, after the concessions already made, I had as well grant that sounds too have no real being without the mind.

Phil. And I hope you will make no difficulty to acknowledge the same of *colours.*

Hyl. Pardon me: the case of colours is very different. Can anything be plainer than that we see them on the objects?

Phil. The objects you speak of are, I suppose, corporeal Substances existing without the mind?

Hyl. They are.

Phil. And have true and real colours inhering in them?

Hyl. Each visible object hath that colour which we see in it.

Phil. How! is there anything visible but what we perceive by sight?

Hyl. There is not.

Phil. And, do we perceive anything by sense which we do not perceive immediately?

Hyl. How often must I be obliged to repeat the same thing? I tell you, we do not.

Phil. Have patience, good Hylas; and tell me once more, whether there is anything immediately perceived by the senses, except sensible qualities. I know you asserted there was not; but I would now be informed, whether you still persist in the same opinion.

Hyl. I do.

Phil. Pray, is your corporeal substance either a sensible quality, or made up of sensible qualities?

Hyl. What a question that is! who ever thought it was?

Phil. My reason for asking was, because in saying, *each visible object hath that colour which we see in it,* you make visible objects to be corporeal substances: which implies either that corporeal substances are sensible qualities, or else that there is something beside sensible qualities perceived by sight: but, as this point was formerly agreed between us, and is still maintained by you, it is a clear consequence, that your corporeal substance is nothing distinct from sensible qualities.

Hyl. You may draw as many absurd consequences as you please, and endeavor to perplex the plainest things; but you shall never persuade me out of my senses. I clearly understand my own meaning.

Phil. I wish you would make me understand it too. But, since you are unwilling to have your notion of corporeal substance examined, I shall urge that point no farther. Only be pleased to let me know whether the same colours which we see exist in external bodies, or some other.

Hyl. The very same.

Phil. What! are then the beautiful red and purple we see on yonder clouds really in them? Or do you imagine they have in themselves any other form than that of a dark mist or vapour?

Hyl. I must own, Philonous, those colours are not really in the clouds as they seem to be at this distance. They are only apparent colours.

Phil. *Apparent* call you them? how shall we distinguish these apparent colours from real?

Hyl. Very easily. Those are to be thought apparent which, appearing only at a distance, vanish upon a nearer approach.

Phil. And those, I suppose, are to be thought real which are discovered by the most near and exact survey.

Hyl. Right.

Phil. Is the nearest and exactest survey made by the help of a microscope, or by the naked eye?

Hyl. By a microscope, doubtless.

Phil. But a microscope often discovers colours in an object different from those perceived by the unassisted sight. And, in case we had microscopes magnifying to any assigned degree, it is certain that no object whatsoever, viewed through them, would appear in the same colour which it exhibits to the naked eye.

Hyl. And what will you conclude from all this? You cannot argue that there are really and naturally no colours on objects: because by artificial managements they may be altered, or made to vanish.

Phil. I think it may evidently be concluded from your own concessions, that all the colours we see with our naked eyes are only apparent as those on the clouds, since they vanish upon a more close and accurate inspection which is afforded us by a microscope. Then, as to what you say by way of prevention: I ask you whether the real and natural state of an object is better discovered by a very sharp and piercing sight, or by one which is less sharp?

Hyl. By the former without doubt.

Phil. Is it not plain from *Dioptrics* that microscopes make the sight more penetrating, and represent objects as they would appear to the eye in case it were naturally endowed with a most exquisite sharpness?

Hyl. It is.

Phil. Consequently the microscopical representation is to be thought that which best sets forth the real nature of the thing, or what it is in itself. The colours, therefore, by it perceived are more genuine and real than those perceived otherwise.

Hyl. I confess there is something in what you say.

Phil. Besides, it is not only possible but manifest, that there actually are animals whose eyes are by nature framed to perceive those things which by reason of their minuteness escape our sight. What think you of those inconceivably small animals perceived by glasses? must we suppose they are all stark blind? Or, in case they see, can it be imagined their sight hath not the same use in preserving their bodies from injuries, which appears in that of all other animals? And if it hath, is it not evident they must see particles less than their own bodies, which will present them with a far different view in each object from that which strikes our senses? Even our own eyes do not always represent objects to us after the same manner. In the *jaundice* every one knows that all things seem yellow. Is it not therefore highly probable those animals in whose eyes we discern a very different texture from that of ours, and whose bodies abound with different humours, do not see the same colours in every object that we do? From all which, should it not seem to follow that all colours are equally apparent, and that none of those which we perceive are really inherent in any outward object?

Hyl. It should.

Phil. The point will be past all doubt, if you consider that, in case colours were real properties or affections inherent in external bodies, they could admit of no alteration without some change wrought in the very bodies themselves: but, is it not evident from what hath been said that, upon the use of microscopes, upon a change happening in the humours of the eye, or a variation of distance, without any manner of real alteration in the thing itself, the colours of any object are either changed, or totally disappear? Nay, all other circumstances remaining the same, change but the situation of some objects, and they shall present different colours to the eye. The same thing happens upon viewing an object in various degrees of light. And what is more known than that the same bodies appear differently coloured by candlelight from what they do in the open day? Add to these the experiment of a prism which, separating the heterogeneous rays of light, alters the colour of any object, and will cause the whitest to appear of a deep blue or red to the naked eye. And now tell me whether you are still of opinion that every body hath its true real colour inhering in it: and, if you think it hath, I would fain know farther from you, what certain distance and position of the object, what peculiar texture and formation of the eye, what degree or kind of light is necessary for ascertaining that true colour, and distinguishing it from apparent ones.

Hyl. I own myself entirely satisfied, that they are equally apparent, and that there is no such thing as colour really inhering in external bodies, but that it is altogether in the light. And what confirms me in this opinion is that in proportion to the light colours are still more or less vivid; and if there be no light, then are there no colours perceived. Besides, allowing there are colours on external objects, yet, how is it possible for us to perceive them? For no external body affects the mind, unless it acts first on our organs of sense. But the only action of bodies is motion; and motion cannot be communicated otherwise than by impulse. A distant object therefore cannot act on the eye, nor consequently make itself or its properties perceivable to the soul. Whence it plainly follows that it is immediately some contiguous substance, which, operating on the eye, occasions a perception of colours: and such is light.

Phil. How! is light then a substance?

Hyl. I tell you, Philonous, external light is nothing but a thin fluid substance, whose minute particles being agitated with a brisk motion, and in various manners reflected from the different surfaces of outward objects to the eyes, communicate different motions to the optic nerves; which, being propagated to the brain, cause therein various impressions; and these are attended with the sensations of red, blue, yellow, &c.

Phil. It seems then the light doth no more than shake the optic nerves.

Hyl. Nothing else.

Phil. And, consequent to each particular motion of the nerves, the mind is affected with a sensation, which is some particular colour.

Hyl. Right.

Phil. And these sensations have no existence without the mind.

Hyl. They have not.

Phil. How then do you affirm that colours are in the light; since by *light* you understand a corporeal substance external to the mind?

Hyl. Light and colours, as immediately perceived by us, I grant cannot exist without the mind. But, in themselves they are only the motions and configurations of certain insensible particles of matter.

Phil. Colours, then, in the vulgar sense, or taken for the immediate objects of sight, cannot agree to any but a perceiving substance.

Hyl. That is what I say.

Phil. Well then, since you give up the point as to those sensible qualities which are alone thought colours by all mankind beside, you may hold what you please with regard to those invisible ones of the philosophers. It is not my business to dispute about them; only I would advise you to bethink yourself, whether, considering the inquiry we are upon, it be prudent for you to affirm—*the red and blue which we see are not real colours, but certain unknown motions and figures, which no man ever did or can see, are truly so.* Are not these shocking notions, and are not they subject to as many ridiculous inferences, as those you were obliged to renounce before in the case of sounds?

Hyl. I frankly own, Philonous, that it is in vain to stand out any longer. Colours, sounds, tastes, in a word all those termed *secondary qualities,* have certainly no existence without the mind. But, by this acknowledgment I must not be supposed to derogate anything from the reality of Matter or external subjects; seeing it is no more than several philosophers maintain, who nevertheless are the farthest imaginable from denying Matter. For the clearer understanding of this, you must know sensible qualities are by philosophers divided into *primary* and *secondary*. The former are Extension, Figure, Solidity, Gravity, Motion, and Rest. And these they hold exist really in bodies. The latter are those above enumerated; or, briefly, all sensible qualities beside the Primary, which they assert are only so many sensations or ideas existing nowhere but in the mind. But all this, I doubt not, you are apprised of. For my part, I have been a long time sensible there was such an opinion current among philosophers, but was never thoroughly convinced of its truth until now.

Phil. You are still then of opinion that *extension* and *figures* are inherent in external unthinking substances?

Hyl. I am.

Phil. But what if the same arguments which are brought against Secondary Qualities will hold good against these also?

Hyl. Why then I shall be obliged to think, they too exist only in the mind.

Phil. Is it your opinion the very figure and extension which you perceive by sense exist in the outward object or material substance?

Hyl. It is.

Phil. Have all other animals as good grounds to think the same of the figure and extension which they see and feel?

Hyl. Without doubt, if they have any thought at all.

Phil. Answer me, Hylas. Think you the senses were bestowed upon all animals for their preservation and well-being in life; or were they given to men alone for this end?

Hyl. I make no question but they have the same use in all other animals.

Phil. If so, is it not necessary they should be enabled by them to perceive their own limbs, and those bodies which are capable of harming them?

Hyl. Certainly.

Phil. A mite therefore must be supposed to see his own foot, and things equal or even less than it, as bodies of some considerable dimension; though at the same time they appear to you scarce discernible, or at best as so many visible points?

Hyl. I cannot deny it.

Phil. And to creatures less than the mite they will seem yet larger?

Hyl. They will.

Phil. Insomuch that what you can hardly discern will to another extremely minute animal appear as some huge mountain?

Hyl. All this I grant.

Phil. Can one and the same thing be at the same time in itself of different dimensions?

Hyl. They were absurd to imagine.

Phil. But, from what you have laid down it follows that both the extension by you perceived, and that perceived by the mite itself, as likewise all those perceived by lesser animals, are each of them the true extension of the mite's foot; that is to say, by your own principles you are led into an absurdity.

Hyl. There seems to be some difficulty in the point.

Phil. Again, have you not acknowledged that no real inherent property of any object can be changed without some change in the thing itself?

Hyl. I have.

Phil. But, as we approach to or recede from an object, the visible extension varies, being at one distance ten or a hundred times greater than at another. Doth it not therefore follow from hence likewise that it is not really inherent in the object?

Hyl. I own I am at a loss what to think.

Phil. Your judgment will soon be determined, if you will venture to think as freely concerning this quality as you have done concerning the rest. Was it not admitted as a good argument, that neither heat nor cold was in the water, because it seemed warm to one hand and cold to the other?

Hyl. It was.

Phil. Is it not the very same reasoning to conclude there is no extension or figure in an object, because to no one eye it shall seem little, smooth, and round when at the same time it appears to the other, great, uneven, and angular?

Hyl. The very same. But does this latter fact ever happen?

Phil. You may at any time make the experiment, by looking with one eye bare, and with the other through a microscope.

Hyl. I know not how to maintain it, and yet I am loath to give up *extension,* I see so many odd consequences following upon such a concession.

Phil. Odd, say you? After the concessions already made, I hope you will stick at nothing for its oddness. But, on the other hand, should it not seem very odd, if the general reasoning which includes all other sensible qualities did not also include extension? If it be allowed that no idea nor anything like an idea can exist in an unperceiving substance, then surely it follows that no figure or mode of extension, which we can either perceive or imagine, or have any idea of, can be really inherent in Matter; not to mention the peculiar difficulty there must be in conceiving a material substance, prior to and distinct from extension, to be the *substratum* of extension. Be the sensible quality what it will—figure, or sound, or colour; it seems alike impossible it should subsist in that which doth not perceive it.

Hyl. I give up the point for the present, reserving still a right to retract my opinion, in case I shall hereafter discover any false step in my progress to it.

Phil. That is a right you cannot be denied. Figures and extension being despatched, we proceed next to *motion*. Can a real motion in any external body be at the same time both very swift and very slow?

Hyl. It cannot.

Phil. Is not the motion of a body swift in a reciprocal proportion to the time it takes up in describing any given space? Thus a body that describes a mile in an hour moves three times faster than it would in case it described only a mile in three hours.

Hyl. I agree with you.

Phil. And is not time measured by the succession of ideas in our minds?

Hyl. It is.

Phil. And is it not possible ideas should succeed one another twice as fast in your mind as they do in mine, or in that of some spirit of another kind?

Hyl. I own it.

Phil. Consequently, the same body may to another seem to perform its motion over any space in half the time that it doth to you. And the same reasoning will hold as to any other proportion: that is to say, according to your principles (since the motions perceived are both really in the object) it is possible one and the same body shall be really moved the same way at once, both very swift and very slow. How is this consistent either with common sense, or with what you just now granted?

Hyl. I have nothing to say to it.

Phil. Then as for *solidity*; either you do not mean any sensible quality by that word, and so it is beside our inquiry: or if you do, it must be either hardness or resistance. But both the one and the other are plainly relative to our senses: it being evident that what seems hard to one animal may appear soft to another, who hath greater force and firmness of limbs. Nor is it less plain that the resistance I feel is not in the body.

Hyl. I own the very sensation of resistance, which is all you immediately perceive, is not in the *body*, but the cause of that sensation is.

Phil. But the causes of our sensations are not things immediately perceived, and therefore not sensible. This point I thought had been already determined.

Hyl. I own it was; but you will pardon me if I seem a little embarrassed: I know not how to quit my old notions.

Phil. To help you out, do but consider that if *extension* be once acknowledged to have no existence without the mind, the same must necessarily be granted of motion, solidity, and gravity— since they all evidently suppose extension. It is therefore superfluous to inquire particularly concerning each of them. In denying extension, you have denied them all to have any real existence.

Hyl. I wonder, Philonous, if what you say be true, why those philosophers who deny the Secondary Qualities any real existence, should yet attribute it to the Primary. If there is no difference between them, how can this be accounted for?

Phil. It is not my business to account for every opinion of the philosophers. But, among other reasons which may be assigned for this, it seems probable that pleasure and pain being rather annexed to the former than the latter may be one. Heat and cold, tastes and smells, have something more vividly pleasing or disagreeable than the ideas of extension, figure, and motion affect us with. And, it being too visibly absurd to hold that pain or pleasure can be in an unperceiving Substance, men are more easily weaned from believing the external existence of the Secondary than the Primary Qualities. You will be satisfied there is something in this, if you recollect the difference you made between an intense and more moderate degree of heat; allowing the one a real existence, while you denied it to the other. But, after all, there is no rational ground for that distinction; for, surely an indifferent sensation is as truly *a sensation* as one more pleasing or painful; and consequently should not any more than they be supposed to exist in an unthinking subject.

Hyl. It is just come into my head, Philonous, that I have somewhere heard of a distinction between absolute and sensible extension. Now, though it be acknowledged that *great* and *small*, consisting merely in the relation which other extended beings have to the parts of our own bodies, do not easily inhere in the Substances themselves; yet nothing obliges us to hold the same with regard to *absolute extension*, which is something abstracted from *great* and *small,* from this or that particular magnitude or figure. So likewise as to motion; *swift* and *slow* are altogether relative to the succession of ideas in our own minds. But, it doth not follow, because those modifications of motion exist not without the mind, that therefore absolute motion abstracted from them doth not.

Phil. Pray what is it that distinguishes one motion, or one part of extension, from another? It is not something sensible, as some degree of swiftness or slowness, some certain magnitude or figure peculiar to each?

Hyl. I think so.

Phil. These qualities, therefore, stripped of all sensible properties, are without all specific and numerical differences, as the schools call them.

Hyl. They are.

Phil. That is to say, they are extension in general, and motion in general.

Hyl. Let it be so.

Phil. But it is a universally received maxim that *Everything which exists is particular.* How then can motion in general, or extension in general, exist in any corporeal Substance?

Hyl. I will take time to solve your difficulty.

Phil. But I think the point may be speedily decided. Without doubt you can tell whether you are able to frame this or that idea. Now I am content to put our dispute on this issue. If you can frame in your thoughts a distinct abstract idea of motion or extension; divested of all those sensible modes, as swift and slow, great and small, round and square, and the like, which are acknowledged to exist only in the mind, I will then yield the point you contend for. But, if you cannot, it will be unreasonable on your side to insist any longer upon what you have no notion of.

Hyl. To confess ingenuously, I cannot.

Phil. Can you even separate the ideas of extension and motion from the ideas of all those qualities which they who make the distinction term *secondary?*

Hyl. What! is it not an easy matter to consider extension and motion by themselves, abstracted from all other sensible qualities? Pray how do the mathematicians treat of them?

Phil. I acknowledge, Hylas, it is not difficult to form general propositions and reasonings about those qualities, without mentioning any other; and, in this sense, to consider or treat of them abstractedly. But, how doth it follow that, because I can pronounce the word *motion* by itself, I can form the idea of it in my mind exclusive of body? Or, because theorems may be made of extension and figures, without any mention of *great* or *small*, or any other sensible mode or quality, that therefore it is possible such an abstract idea of extension, without any particular size or figure, or sensible quality, should be distinctly formed, and apprehended by the mind? Mathematicians treat of quality, without regarding what other sensible qualities it is attended with, as being altogether indifferent to their demonstrations. But when laying aside the words, they contemplate the bare ideas, I believe you will find, they are not the pure abstracted ideas of extension.

Hyl. But what say you to *pure intellect?* May not abstracted idea be framed by that faculty?

Phil. Since I cannot frame abstract ideas at all, it is plain I cannot frame them by the help of *pure intellect;* whatsoever faculty you understand by those words. Besides, not to inquire into the nature of pure intellect and its spiritual objects, as *virtue, reason, God,* or the like, thus much seems manifest, that sensible things are only to be perceived by sense, or represented by the imagination. Figures, therefore, and extension, being originally perceived by sense, do not belong to pure intellect: but, for your farther satisfaction, try if you can frame the idea of any figure, abstracted from all particularities of size, or even from other sensible qualities.

Hyl. Let me think a little——I do not find that I can.

Phil. And can you think it possible that should really exist in nature which implies a repugnancy in its conception?

Hyl. By no means.

Phil. Since therefore it is impossible even for the mind to disunite the ideas of extension and motion from all other sensible qualities, doth it not follow, that where the one exist there necessarily the other exist likewise?

Hyl. It should seem so.

Phil. Consequently, the very same arguments which you admitted as conclusive against the Secondary Qualities are, without any farther application of force, against the Primary too. Besides, if you will trust your senses, is it not plain all sensible qualities coexist, or to them appear as being in the same place? Do they ever represent a motion, or figure, as being divested of all other visible and tangible qualities?

Hyl. You need say no more on this head. I am free to own, if there be no secret error or oversight in our proceedings hitherto, that all sensible qualities are alike to be denied existence without the mind. But, my fear is that I have been too liberal in my former concessions, or overlooked some fallacy or other. In short, I did not take time to think.

Phil. For that matter, Hylas, you may take what time you please in reviewing the progress of our inquiry. You are at liberty to recover any slips you might have made, or offer whatever you have omitted which makes for your first opinion.

Hyl. One great oversight I take to be this—that I did not sufficiently distinguish the *object* from the *sensation*. Now, though this latter may not exist without the mind, yet it will not thence follow that the former cannot.

Phil. What object do you mean? The object of the senses?

Hyl. The same.

Phil. It is then immediately perceived?

Hyl. Right.

Phil. Make me to understand the difference between what is immediately perceived, and a sensation.

Hyl. The sensation I take to be an act of the mind perceiving; besides which, there is something perceived; and this I call the *object*. For example, there is red and yellow on that tulip. But then the act of perceiving those colours is in me only, and not in the tulip.

Phil. What tulip do you speak of? Is it that which you see?

Hyl. The same.

Phil. And what do you see beside colour, figure, and extension?

Hyl. Nothing.

Phil. What you would say then is that the red and yellow are coexistent with the extension; is it not?

Hyl. That is not all; I would say they have a real existence without the mind, in some unthinking substance.

Phil. That the colours are really in the tulip which I see is manifest. Neither can it be denied that this tulip may exist independent of your mind or mine; but, that any immediate object of the senses—that is, any idea, or combination of ideas—should exist in an unthinking substance, or exterior to all minds, is in itself an evident contradiction. Nor can I imagine how this follows from what you said just now, to wit, that the red and yellow were on the tulip *you saw*, since you do not pretend to *see* that unthinking substance.

Hyl. You have an artful way, Philonous, of diverting our inquiry from the subject.

Phil. I see you have no mind to be pressed that way. To return then to your distinction between *sensation* and *object;* if I take you right, you distinguish in every perception two things, the one an action of the mind, the other not.

Hyl. True.

Phil. And this action cannot exist in, or belong to, any unthinking thing; but, whatever beside is implied in a perception may?

Hyl. That is my meaning.

Phil. So that if there was a perception without any act of the mind, it were possible such a perception should exist in an unthinking substance?

Hyl. I grant it. But it is impossible there should be such a perception.

Phil. When is the mind said to be active?

Hyl. When it produces, puts an end to, or changes, anything.

Phil. Can the mind produce, discontinue, or change anything, but by an act of the will?

Hyl. It cannot.

Phil. The mind therefore is to be accounted *active* in its perceptions so far forth as *volition* is included in them?

Hyl. It is.

Phil. In plucking this flower I am active; because I do it by the motion of my hand, which was consequent upon my volition; so likewise in applying it to my nose. But is either of these smelling?

Hyl. No.

Phil. I act too in drawing the air through my nose; because my breathing so rather than otherwise is the effect of my volition. But neither can this be called *smelling:* for, if it were, I should smell every time I breathed in that manner?

Hyl. True.

Phil. Smelling then is somewhat consequent to all this?

Hyl. It is.

Phil. But I do not find my will concerned any farther. Whatever more there is—as that I perceive such a particular smell, or any smell at all—this is independent of my will, and therein I am altogether passive. Do you find it otherwise with you, Hylas?

Hyl. No, the very same.

Phil. Then, as to seeing, is it not in your power to open your eyes, or keep them shut; to turn them this or that way?

Hyl. Without doubt.

Phil. But, doth it in like manner depend on your will that in looking on this flower you perceive *white* rather than any other colour? Or, directing your open eyes towards yonder part of the heaven, can you avoid seeing the sun? Or is light or darkness the effect of your volition?

Hyl. No certainly.

Phil. You are then in these respects altogether passive?

Hyl. I am.

Phil. Tell me now, whether *seeing* consists in perceiving light and colours, or in opening and turning the eyes?

Hyl. Without doubt, in the former.

Phil. Since therefore you are in the very perception of light and colours altogether passive, what is become of that action you were speaking of as an ingredient in every sensation? And, doth it not follow from your own concessions, that the perception of light and colours, including no action in it, may exist in an unperceiving substance? And is not this a plain contradiction?

Hyl. I know not what to think of it.

Phil. Besides, since you distinguish the *active* and *passive* in every perception, you must do it in that of pain. But how is it possible that pain, be it as little active as you please, should exist in an unperceiving substance? In short, do but consider the point, and then confess ingenuously, whether light and colours, tastes, sounds, &c., are not all equally passions or sensations in the soul. You may indeed call them *external objects*, and give them in words what subsistence you please. But, examine your own thoughts, and then tell me whether it be not as I say?

Hyl. I acknowledge, Philonous, that, upon a fair observation of what passes in my mind, I can discover nothing else but that I am a thinking being, affected with variety of sensations; neither is it possible to conceive how a sensation should exist in an unperceiving substance. But then, on the other hand, when I look on sensible things in a different view, considering them as so many modes and qualities, I find it necessary to suppose a material *substratum*, without which they cannot be conceived to exist.

Phil. *Material substratum* call you it? Pray, by which of your senses came you acquainted with that being?

Hyl. It is not itself sensible; its modes and qualities only being perceived by the senses.

Phil. I presume then it was by reflection and reason you obtained the idea of it?

Hyl. I do not pretend to any proper positive idea of it. However, I conclude it exists, because qualities cannot be conceived to exist without a support.

Phil. It seems then you have only a relative notion of it, or that you conceive it not otherwise than by conceiving the relation it bears to sensible qualities?

Hyl. Right.

Phil. Be pleased therefore to let me know wherein that relation consists.

Hyl. It is not sufficiently expressed in the term *substratum* or *substance?*

Phil. If so, the word *substratum* should import that it is spread under the sensible qualities or accidents?

Hyl. True.

Phil. And consequently under extension?

Hyl. I own it.

Phil. It is therefore somewhat in its own nature entirely distinct from extension?

Hyl. I tell you, extension is only a mode, and Matter is something that supports modes. And is it not evident the thing supported is different from the thing supporting?

Phil. So that something distinct from, and exclusive of, extension is supposed to be the *substratum* of extension?

Hyl. Just so.

Phil. Answer me, Hylas. Can a thing be spread without extension? or is not the idea of extension necessarily included in *spreading?*

Hyl. It is.

Phil. Whatsoever therefore you suppose spread under anything must have in itself an extension distinct from the extension of that thing under which it is spread?

Hyl. It must.

Phil. Consequently, every corporeal substance being the *substratum* of extension must have in itself another extension, by which it is qualified to be a *substratum* and so on to infinity? And I ask whether this be not absurd in itself, and repugnant to what you granted just now, to wit, that the *substratum* was something distinct from and exclusive of extension?

Hyl. Aye, but, Philonous, you take me wrong. I do not mean that Matter is *spread* in a gross literal sense under extension. The word *substratum* is used only to express in general the same thing with *substance.*

Phil. Well then, let us examine the relation implied in the term *substance.* Is it not that it stands under accidents?

Hyl. The very same.

Phil. But, that one thing may stand under or support another, must it not be extended?

Hyl. It must.

Phil. Is not therefore this supposition liable to the same absurdity with the former?

Hyl. You still take things in a strict literal sense; that is not fair, Philonous.

Phil. I am not for imposing any sense on your words: you are at liberty to explain them as you please. Only, I beseech you, make me understand something by them. You tell me Matter supports or stands under accidents. How! is it as your legs support your body?

Hyl. No; that is the literal sense.

Phil. Pray let me know any sense, literal or not literal, that you understand it in. . . . How long must I wait for an answer, Hylas?

Hyl. I declare I know not what to say. I once thought I understood well enough what was meant by Matter's supporting accidents. But now, the more I think on it the less can I comprehend it; in short I find that I know nothing of it.

Phil. It seems then you have no idea at all, neither relative nor positive, of Matter; you know neither what it is in itself, nor what relation it bears to accidents?

Hyl. I acknowledge it.

Phil. And yet you asserted that you could not conceive how qualities or accidents should really exist, without conceiving at the same time a material support of them?

Hyl. I did.

Phil. That is to say, when you conceive the real existence of qualities, you do withal conceive something which you cannot conceive?

Hyl. I was wrong I own. But still I fear there is some fallacy or other. Pray what think you of this? It is just come into my head that the ground of all our mistake lies in your treating of each quality by itself. Now, I grant that each quality cannot singly subsist without the mind. Colour cannot without extension, neither can figure without some other sensible quality. But, as the several qualities united or blended together form entire sensible things, nothing hinders why such things may not be supposed to exist without the mind.

Phil. Either, Hylas, you are jesting, or have a very bad memory. Though indeed we went through all the qualities by name one after another; yet my arguments, or rather your concessions, nowhere tended to prove that the Secondary Qualities did not subsist each alone by itself; but, that they were not *at all* without the mind. Indeed, in treating of figure and motion we concluded they could not exist without the mind, because it was impossible even in thought to separate them from all secondary qualities, so as to conceive them existing by themselves. But then this was not the only argument made use of upon that occasion. But (to pass by all that hath been hitherto said, and reckon it for nothing, if you will have it so) I am content to put the whole upon this issue. If you can conceive it possible for any mixture or combination of qualities, or any sensible object whatever, to exist without the mind, then I will grant it actually to be so.

Hyl. If it comes to that the point will soon be decided. What more easy than to conceive a tree or house existing by itself, independent of, and unperceived by, any mind whatsoever? I do at this present time conceive them existing after that manner.

Phil. How say you, Hylas, can you see a thing which is at the same time unseen?

Hyl. No, that were a contradiction.

Phil. It is not as great a contradiction to talk of *conceiving* a thing which is *unconceived?*

Hyl. It is.

Phil. The tree or house therefore which you think of is conceived by you?

Hyl. How should it be otherwise?

Phil. And what is conceived is surely in the mind?

Hyl. Without question, that which is conceived is in the mind.

Phil. How then came you to say, you conceived a house or tree existing independent and out of all minds whatsoever?

Hyl. That was I own an oversight; but stay, let me consider what led me into it—It is a pleasant mistake enough. As I was thinking of a tree in a solitary place where no one was present to see it, methought that was to conceive a tree as existing unperceived or unthought of—not considering that I myself conceived it all the while. But now I plainly see that all I can do is to frame ideas in my own mind. I may indeed conceive in my own thoughts the idea of a tree, or a house, or a mountain, but that is all. And this is far from proving that I can conceive them *existing out of the minds of all Spirits.*

Phil. You acknowledge then that you cannot possibly conceive how any one corporeal sensible thing should exist otherwise than in a mind?

Hyl. I do.

Phil. And yet you will earnestly contend for the truth of that which you cannot so much as conceive?

· · · · ·

Hyl. To speak the truth, Philonous, I think there are two kinds of objects:—the one perceived immediately, which are likewise called ideas; the other are real things or external objects, perceived by the mediation of ideas, which are their images and representations. Now, I own ideas do not exist without the mind; but the latter sort of objects do. I am sorry I did not think of this distinction sooner; it would probably have cut short your discourse.

Phil. Are those external objects perceived by sense, or by some other faculty?

Hyl. They are perceived by sense.

Phil. How! is there anything perceived by sense which is not immediately perceived?

Hyl. Yes, Philonous, in some sort there is. For example, when I look on a picture or statue of Julius Caesar, I may be said after a manner to perceive him (though not immediately) by my senses.

Phil. It seems then you will have our ideas, which alone are immediately perceived, to be pictures of external things: and that these also are perceived by sense, inasmuch as they have a conformity or resemblance to our ideas?

Hyl. That is my meaning.

Phil. And, in the same way that Julius Caesar, in himself invisible, is nevertheless perceived by sight; real things, in themselves imperceptible, are perceived by sense.

Hyl. In the very same.

Phil. Tell me, Hylas, when you behold the picture of Julius Caesar, do you see with your eyes any more than some colours and figures, with a certain symmetry and composition of the whole?

Hyl. Nothing else.

Phil. And would not a man who had never known anything of Julius Caesar see as much?

Hyl. He would.

Phil. Consequently he hath his sight, and the use of it, in as perfect a degree as you?

Hyl. I agree with you.

Phil. Whence comes it then that your thoughts are directed to the Roman emperor, and his are not? This cannot proceed from the sensations or ideas of sense by you then perceived; since you acknowledge you have no advantage over him in that respect. It should seem therefore to proceed from reason and memory: should it not?

Hyl. It should.

Phil. Consequently, it will not follow from that instance that anything is perceived by sense which is not immediately perceived. Though I grant we may, in one acceptation, be said to perceive sensible things mediately by sense—that is, when, from a frequently perceived connexion, the immediate perception of ideas by one sense suggest to the mind others, perhaps belonging to another sense, which are wont to be connected with them. For instance, when I hear a coach drive along the streets, immediately I perceive only the sound; but, from the experience I have had that such a sound is connected with a coach, I am said to hear the coach. It is neverthless evident that, in truth and strictness, nothing can be *heard* but *sound;* and the coach is not then properly perceived by sense, but suggested from experience. So likewise when we are said to see a red-hot bar of iron; the solidity and heat of the iron are not the objects of sight, but suggested to the imagination by the colour and figure which are properly perceived by that sense. In short, those things alone are actually and strictly perceived by any sense, which would have been perceived in case that same sense had then been first conferred on us. As for other things, it is plain they are only suggested to the mind by experience, grounded on former perceptions. But, to return to your comparison of Caesar's picture, it is plain, if you keep to that, you must hold the real things or achetypes of our ideas are not perceived by sense, but by some internal faculty of the soul, as reason or memory. I would therefore fain know what arguments you can draw from reason for the existence of what you call *real things* or *material objects.* Or, whether you remember to have seen them formerly as they are in themselves; or, if you have heard or read of any one that did.

Hyl. I see, Philonous, you are disposed to raillery; but that will never convince me.

Phil. My aim is only to learn from you the way to come at the knowledge of *material beings.* Whatever we perceive is perceived immediately or mediately: by sense; or by reason and reflection. But, as you have excluded sense, pray show me what reason you have to believe their existence; or what *medium* you can possibly make use of to prove it, either to mine or your own understanding.

Hyl. To deal ingenuously, Philonous, now I consider the point, I do not find I can give you any good reason for it. But, thus much seems pretty plain, that it is at least possible such things may really exist. And, as long as there is no absurdity in supposing them, I am resolved to believe as I did, till you bring good reasons to the contrary.

Phil. What! is it come to this, that you only believe the existence of material objects, and that your belief is founded barely on the possibility of its being true? Then you will have me bring reasons against it: though another would think it reasonable the proof should lie on him who holds the affirmative. And, after all, this very point which you are now resolved to maintain, without any reason, is in effect what you have more than once during this discourse seen good reason to give up. But, to pass over all this; if I understand you rightly, you say our ideas do not exist without the mind; but that they are copies, images, or representations, of certain originals that do?

Hyl. You take me right.

Phil. They are then like external things?

Hyl. They are.

Phil. Have those things a stable and permanent nature, independent of our senses; or are they in a perpetual change, upon our producing any motions in our bodies, suspending, exerting, or altering, our faculties or organs of sense?

Hyl. Real things, it is plain, have a fixed and real nature, which remains the same notwithstanding any change in our senses, or in the posture and motion of our bodies; which indeed may affect the ideas in our minds, but it were absurd to think they had the same effect on things existing without the mind.

Phil. How then is it possible that things perpetually fleeting and variable as our ideas should be copies or images of anything fixed and constant? Or, in other words, since all sensible qualities, as size, figure, colour, &c., that is, our ideas, are continually changing upon every alteration in the distance, medium, or instruments of sensation; how can any determinate material objects be properly represented or painted forth by several distinct things, each of which is so different from and unlike the rest? Or, if you say it resembles some one only of our ideas, how shall we be able to distinguish the true copy from all the false ones?

Hyl. I profess, Philonous, I am at a loss. I know not what to say to this.

Phil. But neither is this all. Which are material objects in them-selves—perceptible or imperceptible?

Hyl. Properly and immediately nothing can be perceived but ideas. All material things, therefore, are in themselves insensible, and to be perceived only by our ideas.

Phil. Ideas then are sensible, and their archetypes or originals in-sensible?

Hyl. Right.

Phil. But how can that which is sensible be like that which is in-sensible? Can a real thing, in itself *invisible*, be like a *colour;* or a real thing, which is not *audible,* be like a *sound?* In a word, can anything be like a sensation or idea, but another sensation or idea?

Hyl. I must own, I think not.

Phil. Is it possible there should be any doubt on the point? Do you not perfectly know your own ideas?

Hyl. I know them perfectly; since what I do not perceive or know can be no part of my idea.

Phil. Consider, therefore, and examine them, and then tell me if there be anything in them which can exist without the mind? or if you can conceive anything like them existing without the mind?

Hyl. Upon inquiry, I find it is impossible for me to conceive or un-derstand how anything but an idea can be like an idea. And it is most evident that *no idea can exist without the mind.*

Phil. You are therefore, by our principles, forced to deny the reality of sensible things; since you made it to consist in an absolute existence exterior to the mind. That is to say, you are a down-right sceptic. So I have gained my point, which was to shew your principles led to Scepticism.

Hyl. For the present I am, if not entirely convinced, at least si-lenced.

• David Hume (1711–76)

The Understanding and the Will[4]

David Hume was born in Edinburgh, studied law there, and later held public office. He was known during his lifetime as an essayist and historian. His greatest philosophical work, *A Treatise on Human Nature*, was written during a stay in France when he was only twenty-six. He afterwards wrote parts of this work again for a more popular audience. One of these was *An Enquiry Concerning Human Understanding*, from which the following selection is taken. Hume shows here that all knowledge is either of relations of ideas or of matters of fact, and that all our knowledge of matters of fact comes from experience and is founded on the idea of cause and effect. He then analyzes this idea showing that it means the constant conjunction of events in experience and that our prediction of future events is really based on habit. The last few pages is devoted to an analysis of how the human will operates on the mind and on the body.

Part I

All the objects of human reason or enquiry may naturally be divided into two kinds, to wit, *Relations of Ideas,* and *Matters of Fact.* Of the first kind are the sciences of Geometry, Algebra, and Arithmetic; and in short, every affirmation which is either intuitively or demonstratively certain. *That the square of the hypothenuse is equal to the squares of the two sides,* is a proposition which expresses a relation between these figures. *That three times five is equal to the half of thirty,* expresses a relation between these numbers. Propositions of this kind are discoverable by the mere operation of thought, without dependence on what is anywhere existent in the universe. Though there never were a circle or triangle in nature, the truths demonstrated by Euclid would for ever retain their certainty and evidence.

Matters of fact, which are the second objects of human reason,

---

4 From David Hume, *An Enquiry Concerning Human Understanding,* the major portion of Sec. iv and Sec. vii, Pt. I.

are not ascertained in the same manner; nor is our evidence of their truth, however great, of a like nature with the foregoing. The contrary of every matter of fact is still possible; because it can never imply a contradiction, and is conceived by the mind with the same facility and distinctness, as if ever so conformable to reality. *That the sun will not rise to-morrow* is no less intelligible a proposition, and implies no more contradiction than the affirmation, *that it will rise.* We should in vain, therefore, attempt to demonstrate its falsehood. Were it demonstratively false, it would imply a contradiction, and could never be distinctly conceived by the mind.

It may, therefore, be a subject worthy of curiosity, to enquire what is the nature of that evidence which assures us of any real existence and matter of fact, beyond the present testimony of our senses, or the records of our memory. This part of philosophy, it is observable, has been little cultivated, either by the ancients or moderns; and therefore our doubts and errors, in the prosecution of so important an enquiry, may be the more excusable; while we march through such difficult paths without any guide or direction. They may even prove useful, by exciting curiosity, and destroying that implicit faith and security, which is the bane of all reasoning and free enquiry. The discovery of defects in the common philosophy, if any such there be, will not, I presume, be a discouragement, but rather an incitement, as is usual, to attempt something more full and satisfactory than has yet been proposed to the public.

All reasonings concerning matter of fact seem to be founded on the relation of *Cause and Effect.* By means of that relation alone we can go beyond the evidence of our memory and senses. If you were to ask a man, why he believes any matter of fact, which is absent; for instance, that his friend is in the country, or in France; he would give you a reason; and this reason would be some other fact; as a letter received from him, or the knowledge of his former resolutions and promises. A man finding a watch or any other machine in a desert island, would conclude that there had once been men in that island. All our reasonings concerning fact are of the same nature. And here it is constantly supposed that there is a connexion between the present fact and that which is inferred from it. Were there nothing to bind them together, the inference would be entirely precarious. The hearing of an articulate voice and rational discourse in the dark assures us of the presence of some person: Why? because these are the effects of the human make and fabric, and closely connected with it. If we anatomize all the other reasonings of this nature, we shall find that they are founded on the relation of cause and effect, and that this relation is either near or remote, direct or collateral. Heat and light are collateral effects of fire, and the one effect may justly be inferred from the other.

If we would satisfy ourselves, therefore, concerning the nature of that evidence, which assures us of matters of fact, we must enquire how we arrive at the knowledge of cause and effect.

I shall venture to affirm, as a general proposition which admits of no exception, that the knowledge of this relation is not, in any instance, attained by reasonings a priori; but arises entirely from experience, when we find that any particular objects are constantly conjoined with each other. Let an object be presented to a man of ever so strong natural reason and abilities; if that object be entirely new to him, he will not be able, by the most accurate examination of its sensible qualities, to discover any of its causes or effects. Adam, though his rational faculties be supposed, at the very first, entirely perfect, could not have inferred from the fluidity and transparency of water that it would suffocate him, or from the light and warmth of fire that it would consume him. No object ever discovers, by the qualities which appear to the senses, either the causes which produced it, or the effects which will arise from it; nor can our reason, unassisted by experience, ever draw any inference concerning real existence and matter of fact.

This proposition, that causes and effects are discoverable, not by reason but by experience, will readily be admitted with regard to such objects, as we remember to have once been altogether unknown to us; since we must be conscious of the utter inability, which we then lay under, of foretelling what would arise from them. Present two smooth pieces of marble to a man who has no tincture of natural philosophy; he will never discover that they will adhere together in such a manner as to require great force to separate them in a direct line, while they make so small a resistance to a lateral pressure. Such events, as bear little analogy to the common course of nature, are also readily confessed to be known only by experience; nor does any man imagine that the explosion of gunpowder, or the attraction of a loadstone, could ever be discovered by arguments a priori. In like manner, when an effect is supposed to depend upon an intricate machinery or secret structure of parts, we make no difficulty in attributing all our knowledge of it to experience. Who will assert that he can give the ultimate reason, why milk or bread is proper nourishment for a man, not for a lion or a tiger?

But the same truth may not appear, at first sight, to have the same evidence with regard to events, which have become familiar to us from our first appearance in the world, which bear a close analogy to the whole course of nature, and which are supposed to depend on the simple qualities of objects, without any secret structure of parts. We are apt to imagine that we could discover these effects by the mere operation of our reason, without experience. We fancy, that were we brought on a sudden into this world, we could at first have inferred that one Billiard-ball would communicate motion to another upon impulse; and that we needed not to have waited for the event, in order to pronounce with certainty concerning it. Such is the influence of custom, that, where it is strongest, it not only covers our natural ignorance, but even conceals itself, and seems not to take place, merely because it is found in the highest degree.

But to convince us that all the laws of nature, and all the operations of bodies without exception, are known only by experience, the following reflections may, perhaps, suffice. Were any object presented to us, and were we required to pronounce concerning the effect, which will result from it, without consulting past observation; after what manner, I beseech you, must the mind proceed in this operation? It must invent or imagine some event, which it ascribes to the object as its effect; and it is plain that this invention must be entirely arbitrary. The mind can never possibly find the effect in the supposed cause, by the most accurate scrutiny and examination. For the effect is totally different from the cause, and consequently can never be discovered in it. Motion in the second Billiard-ball is a quite distinct event from motion in the first: nor is there anything in the one to suggest the smallest hint of the other. A stone or piece of metal raised into the air, and left without any support, immediately falls, but to consider the matter *a priori*, is there anything we discover in this situation which can beget the idea of a downward, rather than an upward, or any other motion, in the stone or metal?

And as the first imagination or invention of a particular effect, in all natural operations, is arbitrary, where we consult not experience; so must we also esteem the supposed tie or connexion between the cause and effect, which binds them together, and renders it impossible that any other effect could result from the operation of that cause. When I see, for instance, a Billiard-ball moving in a straight line towards another; even suppose motion in the second ball should by accident be suggested to me, as the result of their contact or impulse; may I not conceive, that a hundred different events might as well follow from that cause? May not both these balls remain at absolute rest? May not the first ball return in a straight line, or leap off from the second in any line or direction?

All these suppositions are consistent and conceivable. Why then should we give the preference to one, which is no more consistent or conceivable than the rest? All our reasonings *a priori* will never be able to show us any foundation for this preference.

In a word, then, every effect is a distinct event from its cause. It could not, therefore, be discovered in the cause, and the first invention or conception of it, *a priori*, must be entirely arbitrary. And even after it is suggested, the conjunction of it with the cause must appear equally arbitrary; since there are always many other effects, which, to reason, must seem fully as consistent and natural. In vain, therefore, should we pretend to determine any single event, or infer any cause or effect, without the assistance of observation and experience.

Hence we may discover the reason why no philosopher, who is rational and modest, has ever pretended to assign the ultimate cause of any natural operation, or to show distinctly the action of that power, which produces any single effect in the universe. It is confessed that the utmost effort of human reason is to reduce the principles, productive of natural phenomena, to a greater simplicity, and to resolve the many particular effects into a few general causes, by means of reasonings from analogy, experience, and observation. But as to the causes of these general causes, we should in vain attempt their discovery; nor shall we ever be able to satisfy ourselves, by any particular explication of them. These ultimate springs and principles are totally shut up from human curiosity and enquiry. Elasticity, gravity, cohesion of parts, communication of motion by impulse; these are probably the ultimate causes and principles which we ever discover in nature; and we may esteem ourselves sufficiently happy, if, by accurate enquiry and reasoning, we can trace up the particular phenomena to, or near to, these general principles. The most perfect philosophy of the natural kind only staves off our ignorance a little longer: as perhaps the most perfect philosophy of the moral or metaphysical kind serves only to discover larger portions of it. Thus the observation of human blindness and weakness is the result of all philosophy, and meets us at every turn, in spite of our endeavours to elude or avoid it.

Nor is geometry, when taken into the assistance of natural philosophy, ever able to remedy this defect, or lead us into the knowledge of ultimate causes, by all that accuracy of reasoning for which it is so justly celebrated. Every part of mixed mathematics proceeds upon the supposition that certain laws are established by nature in her operations; and abstract reasonings are employed, either to assist experience in the discovery of these laws, or to determine their influence in particular instances, where it depends upon any precise degree of distance and quantity. Thus, it is a law of motion, discovered by experience, that the moment or force of any body in motion is in the compound ratio or proportion of its solid contents and its velocity; and consequently, that a small force may remove the greatest obstacle or raise the greatest weight, if, by any contrivance or machinery, we can increase the velocity of that force, so as to make it an overmatch for its antagonist. Geometry assists us in the application of this law, by giving us the just dimensions of all the parts and figures which can enter into any species of machine; but still the discovery of the law itself is owing merely to experience, and all the abstract reasonings in the world could never lead us one step towards the knowledge of it. When we reason *a priori*, and consider merely any object or cause, as it appears to the mind, independent of all observation, it never could suggest to us the notion of any distinct object, such as its effect; much less, show us the inseparable and inviolable connexion between them. A man must be very sagacious who could discover by reasoning that crystal is the effect of heat, and ice of cold, without being previously acquainted with the operation of these qualities.

Part II

But we have not yet attained any tolerable satisfaction with regard to the question first proposed. Each solution still gives rise to a new question as difficult as the foregoing, and leads us on to farther enquiries. When it is asked, *What is the nature of all our reasonings concerning matter of fact?* the proper answer seems to be, that they are founded on the relation of cause and effect. When again it is asked, *What is the foundation of all our reasonings and conclusions concerning that relation?* it may be replied in one word, Experience. But when we still carry on our sifting humour, and ask, *What is the foundation of all conclusions from experience?* this implies a new question, which may be of more difficult solution and explication. Philosophers, that give themselves airs of superior wisdom and sufficiency, have a hard task when they encounter persons of inquisitive dispositions, who push them from every corner to which they retreat, and who are sure at last to bring them to some dangerous dilemma. The best expedient to prevent this confusion, is to be modest in our pretensions; and even to discover the difficulty ourselves before it is objected to us. By this means, we may make a kind of merit of our very ignorance.

I shall content myself, in this section, with an easy task, and shall pretend only to give a negative answer to the question here proposed. I say then, that, even after we have experience of the operations of cause and effect, our conclusions from that experience are *not* founded on reasoning, or any process of the understanding. This answer we must endeavour both to explain and to defend.

It must certainly be allowed, that nature has kept us at a great distance from all her secrets, and has afforded us only the knowledge of a few superficial qualities of objects; while she conceals from us those powers and principles on which the influence of those objects entirely depends. Our senses inform us of the colour, weight, and consistence of bread; but neither sense nor reason can ever inform us of those qualities which fit it for the nourishment and support of a human body. Sight or feeling conveys an idea of the actual motion of bodies; but as to that wonderful force or power, which would carry on a moving body for ever in a continued change of place, and which bodies never lose but by communicating it to others; of this we cannot form the most distant conception. But notwithstanding this ignorance of natural powers and principles, we always presume, when we see like sensible qualities, that they have like secret powers, and expect that effects, similar to those which we have experienced, will follow from them. If a body of like colour and consistence with that bread, which we have formerly eat, be presented to us, we make no scruple of repeating the experiment, and foresee, with certainty, like nourishment and support. Now this is a process of the mind or thought, of which I would willingly know the foundation. It is allowed on all hands that there is no known connexion between the sensible qualities and the secret powers; and consequently, that the mind is not led to form such a conclusion concerning their constant and regular conjunction, by anything which it knows of their nature. As to past *Experience,* it can be allowed to give *direct* and *certain* information of those precise objects only, and that precise period of time, which fell under its cognizance: but why this experience should be extended to future times, and to other objects, which, for aught we know, may be only in appearance similar; this is the main question of which I would insist. The bread, which I formerly eat, nourished me; that is, a body of such sensible qualities was, at that time, endued with such secret powers: but does it follow, that other bread must also nourish me at another time, and that like sensible qualities must always be attended with like secret powers? The consequence seems nowise necessary. At least, it must be acknowledged that there is here a consequence drawn by the mind; that there is a certain step taken; a process of thought, and an inference, which wants to be explained. These two propositions are far from being the same, *I have found that such an object has always been attended with such an effect, and I foresee, that other objects, which are, in appearance, similar, will be attended with similar effects.* I shall allow, if you please, that the one proposition may justly be inferred from the other; I know, in fact, that it always is inferred. But if you insist that the inference is made by a chain of reasoning, I desire you to produce that reasoning. The connexion between these propositions is not intuitive. There is required a medium, which may enable the mind to draw such an inference, if indeed it be drawn by reasoning and argument. What that medium is, I must confess, passes my comprehension; and it is incumbent on those to produce it, who assert that it really exists, and is the origin of all our conclusions concerning matter of fact.

This negative argument must certainly, in process of time, become altogether convincing, if many penetrating and able philosophers shall turn their enquiries this way and no one be ever able to discover any connecting proposition or intermediate step, which supports the understanding in this conclusion. But as the question is yet new, every reader may not trust so far to his own penetration, as to conclude, because an argument escapes his enquiry, that therefore it does not really exist. For this reason it may be requisite to venture upon a more difficult task; and enumerating all the branches of human knowledge, endeavour to show that none of them can afford such an argument.

All reasonings may be divided into two kinds, namely, demonstrative reasoning, or that concerning relations of ideas, and moral reasoning, or that concerning matter of fact and existence. That there are no demonstrative arguments in the case seems evident; since it implies no contradiction that the course of nature may change, and that an object, seemingly like those which we have experienced, may be attended with different or contrary effects. May I not clearly and distinctly conceive that a body, falling from the clouds, and which, in all other respects, resembles snow, has yet the taste of salt or feeling of fire? Is there any more intelligible proposition than to affirm, that all the trees will flourish in December and January, and decay in May and June? Now whatever is intelligible, and can be distinctly conceived, implies no contradiction, and can never be proved false by any demonstrative argument or abstract reasoning *a priori.*

If we be, therefore, engaged by arguments to put trust in past experience, and make it the standard of our future judgement, these arguments must be probable only, or such as regard matter of fact and real existence, according to the division above mentioned. But that there is no argument of this kind, must appear, if our explication of that species of reasoning be admitted as solid and satisfactory. We have said that all arguments concerning existence are founded on the relation of cause and effect; that our knowledge of that relation is derived entirely from experience; and that all our experimental conclusions proceed upon the supposition that the future will be conformable to the past. To endeavour, therefore, the proof of this last supposition by probable arguments, or arguments regarding existence, must be evidently going in a circle, and taking that for granted, which is the very point in question.

In reality, all arguments from experience are founded on the similarity which we discover among natural objects, and by which we are induced to expect effects similar to those which we have found to follow from such objects. And though none but a fool or madman will ever pretend to dispute the authority of experience, or to reject that great guide of human life, it may surely be allowed a philosopher to have so much curiosity at least as to examine the principle of human nature, which gives this mighty authority to experience, and makes us draw advantage from that similarity which nature has placed among different objects. From causes which appear *similar* we expect similar effects. This is the sum of all our experimental conclusions. Now it seems evident that, if this conclusion were formed by reason, it would be as perfect at first, and upon one instance, as after ever so long a course of experience. But the case is far otherwise. Nothing so like as eggs; yet no one, on account of this appearing similarity, expects the same taste and relish in all of them. It is only after a long course of uniform experiments in any kind, that we attain a firm reliance and security with regard to a particular event. Now where is that process of reasoning which, from one instance, draws a conclusion, so different from that which it infers from a hundred instances that are nowise different from that single one? This question I propose as much for the sake of information, as with an intention of raising difficulties. I cannot find, I cannot imagine any such reasoning. But I keep my mind still open to instruction, if any one will vouchsafe to bestow it on me.

Should it be said that, from a number of uniform experiments, we *infer* a connexion between the sensible qualities and the secret powers; this, I must confess, seems the same difficulty, couched in different terms. The question still recurs, on what process of argument this *inference* is founded? Where is the medium, the inter-posing ideas, which join propositions so very wide of each other? It is confessed that the colour, consistence, and other sensible qual-ities of bread appear not, of themselves, to have any connexion with the secret powers of nourishment and support. For otherwise we could infer these secret powers from the first appearance of these sensible qualities, without the aid of experience; contrary to the sentiment of all philosophers, and contrary to plain matter of fact. Here, then, is our natural state of ignorance with regard to the powers and influence of all objects. How is this remedied by experience? It only shows us a number of uniform effects, result-ing from certain objects, and teaches us that those particular objects, at that particular time, were endowed with similar sensible qualities, is produced, we expect similar powers and forces, and look for a like effect. From a body of like colour and consistence with bread we expect like nourishment and support. But this surely is a step or progress of the mind, which wants to be explained. When a man says, *I have found, in all past instances, such sensible qualities con-joined with such secret powers:* and when he says, *Similar sensible qualities will always be conjoined with similar secret powers,* he is not guilty of a tautology, nor are those propositions in any respect the same. You say that the one proposition is an inference from the other. But you must confess that the inference is not intuitive; neither is it demonstrative: Of what nature is it, then? To say it is experimental, is begging the question. For all inferences from experiences from experience suppose, as their foundation, that the future will resemble the past, and that similar powers will be conjoined with similar sensible qualities. If there be any suspicion that the course of nature may change, and that the past may be no rule for the future, all experience becomes useless, and can give rise to no inference or conclusion. It is impossible, therefore, that any arguments from experience can prove this resemblance of the past to the future; since all these arguments are founded on the supposition of that resemblance. Let the course of things be al-lowed hitherto ever so regular; that alone, without some new argu-ment or inference, proves not that, for the future, it will continue so. In vain do you pretend to have learned the nature of bodies from your past experience. Their secret nature, and consequently all their effects and influence, may change, without any change in their sensible qualities. This happens sometimes, and with regard to some objects: Why may it happen always, and with regard to all objects? What logic, what process of argument secures you against this supposition? My practice, you say, refutes my doubts. But you mistake the purport of my question. As an agent, I am quite satisfied in the point; but as a philosopher, who has some share of curiosity, I will not say scepticism, I want to learn the foundation of this inference. No reading, no enquiry has yet been able to remove my difficulty, or give me satisfaction in a matter of such importance. Can I do better than propose the difficulty to the public, even though, perhaps, I have small hopes of obtaining a solution? We shall, at least, by this means, be sensible of our ignorance, if we do not augment our knowledge.

· · · · ·

There are no ideas, which occur in metaphysics more obscure and uncertain, than those of *power, force, energy* or *necessary connexion,* of which it is every moment necessary for us to treat in all our disquisitions. We shall, therefore, endeavour, in this section, to fix, if possible, the precise meaning of these terms, and thereby remove some part of that obscurity, which is so much complained of in this species of philosophy.

It seems a proposition, which will not admit of much dispute, that all our ideas are nothing but copies of our impressions, or, in other words, that it is impossible for us to *think* of anything, which we have not antecedently *felt*, either by our external or internal senses. I have endeavoured to explain and prove this proposition, and have expressed my hopes, that, by a proper application of it, men may reach a greater clearness and precision in philosophical reasonings, than what they have hitherto been able to attain. Complex ideas may, perhaps, be well known by definition, which is nothing but an enumeration of those parts or simple ideas, that compose them. But when we have pushed up definitions to the most simple ideas, and find still some ambiguity and obscurity; what resource are we then possessed of? By what invention can we throw light upon these ideas, and render them altogether precise and determinate to our intellectual view? Produce the impressions or original sentiments, from which the ideas are copied. These impressions are all strong and sensible. They admit not of ambiguity. They are not only placed in a full light themselves, but may throw light on their correspondent ideas, which lie in obscurity. And by this means, we may, perhaps, attain a new microscope or species of optics, by which, in the moral sciences, the most minute, and most simple ideas may be so enlarged as to fall readily under our apprehension, and be equally known with the grossest and most sensible ideas, that can be the object of our enquiry.

To be fully acquainted, therefore, with the idea of power or necessary connexion, let us examine its impression; and in order to find the impression with greater certainty, let us search for it in all the sources, from which it may possibly be derived.

When we look about us towards external objects, and consider the operation of causes, we are never able, in a single instance, to discover any power or necessary connexion; any quality, which binds the effect to the cause, and renders the one an infallible consequence of the other. We only find, that the one does actually, in fact, follow the other. The impulse of one billiard-ball is attended with motion in the second. This is the whole that appears to the *outward* senses. The mind feels no sentiment or *inward* impression from this succession of objects: Consequently there is not, in any single, particular instance of cause and effect, any thing which can suggest the idea of power or necessary connexion.

From the first appearance of an object, we never can conjecture what effect will result from it. But were the power or energy of any cause discoverable by the mind, we could foresee the effect, even without experience; and might, at first, pronounce with certainty concerning it, by mere dint of thought and reasoning.

In reality, there is no part of matter, that does ever, by its sensible qualities, discover any power or energy, or give us ground to imagine, that it could produce any thing, or be followed by any other object, which we could denominate its effect. Solidity, extension, motion; these qualities are all complete in themselves, and never point out any other event which may result from them. The scenes of the universe are continually shifting, and one object follows another in an uninterrupted succession; but the power of force, which actuates the whole machine, is entirely concealed from us, and never discovers itself in any of the sensible qualities of body. We know, that, in fact, heat is a constant attendant of flame; but what is the connexion between them, we have no room so much as to conjecture or imagine. It is impossible, therefore, that the idea of power can be derived from the contemplation of bodies, in single instances of their operation; because no bodies ever discover any power, which can be the original of this idea.

Since, therefore, external objects as they appear to the senses, give us no idea of power or necessary connexion, by their operation in particular instances, let us see, whether this idea be derived from reflexion on the operations of our own minds, and be copied from any internal impression. It may be said, that we are every moment conscious of internal power; while we feel, that, by the simple command of our will, we can move the organs of our body, or direct the faculties of our mind. An act of volition produces motion in our limbs, or raises a new idea in our imagination. This influence of the will we know by consciousness. Hence we acquire the idea of power or energy; and are certain, that we ourselves and all other intelligent beings are possessed of power. This idea, then, is an idea of reflection, since it arises from reflecting on the operations of our own mind, and on the command which is exercised by will, both over the organs of the body and the faculties of the soul.

We shall proceed to examine this pretension; and first with regard to the influence of volition over the organs of the body. This influence, we may observe, is a fact, which, like all other natural events, can be known only by experience, and can never be foreseen from any apparent energy or power in the cause, which connects it with the effect, and renders the one an infallible consequence of the other. The motion of our body follows upon the command of our will. Of this we are every moment conscious. But the means, by which this is effected; the energy, by which the will performs so extraordinary an operation; of this we are so far from being immediately conscious, that it must for ever escape our most diligent enquiry.

For *first;* is there any principle in all nature more mysterious than the union of soul with body; by which a supposed spiritual substance acquires such an influence over a material one, that the most refined thought is able to actuate the grossest matter? Were we empowered, by a secret wish, to remove mountains, or control the planets in their orbit; this extensive authority would not be more extraordinary, nor more beyond our comprehension. But if by consciousness we perceived any power or energy in the will, we must know this power; we must know its connexion with the effect; we must know the secret union of soul and body, and the nature of both these substances; by which the one is able to operate, in so many instances, upon the other.

Secondly, We are not able to move all the organs of the body with a like authority; though we cannot assign any reason besides experience, for so remarkable a difference between one and the other. Why has the will an influence over the tongue and fingers, not over the heart and liver? This question would never embarrass us, were we conscious of a power in the former case, not in the latter. We should then perceive, independent of experience, why the authority of will over the organs of the body is circumscribed within such particular limits. Being in that case fully acquainted with the power or force, by which it operates, we should also know, why its influence reaches precisely to such boundaries, and no farther.

A man, suddenly struck with palsy in the leg or arm, or who had newly lost those members, frequently endeavours, at first to move them, and employ them in their usual offices. Here he is as much conscious of power to command such limbs, as a man in perfect health is conscious of power to actuate any member which remains in its natural state and condition. But consciousness never deceives. Consequently, neither in the one case nor in the other, are we ever conscious of any power. We learn the influence of our will from experience alone. And experience only teaches us, how one event constantly follows another; without instructing us in the secret connexion, which binds them together, and renders them inseparable.

Thirdly, We learn from anatomy, that the immediate object of power in voluntary motion, is not the member itself which is moved, but certain muscles, and nerves, and animal spirits, and, perhaps, something still more minute and more unknown, through which the motion is successfully propagated, ere it reach the member itself whose motion is the immediate object of volition. Can there be a more certain proof that the power, by which this whole operation is performed, so far from being directly and fully known by an inward sentiment or consciousness, is, to the last degree, mysterious and unintelligible? Here the mind wills a certain event: Immediately another event, unknown to ourselves, and totally different from the one intended, is produced: This produces another, equally unknown: Till at last, through a long succession, the desired event is produced. But if the original power were felt, it must be known: Were it known, its effect also must be known; since all power is relative to its effect. And *vice versa,* if the effect be not known, the power cannot be known nor felt. How indeed can we be conscious of a power to move our limbs, when we have no such power; but only that to move certain animal spirits, which, though they produce at last the motion of our limbs, yet operate in such a manner as is wholly beyond our comprehension?

We may, therefore, conclude from the whole, I hope, without any temerity, though with assurance; that our idea of power is not copied from any sentiment or consciousness of power within ourselves, when we give rise to animal motion, or apply our limbs, to their proper use and office. That their motion follows the command of the will is a matter of common experience, like other natural events: But the power or energy by which this is effected, like that in other natural events, is unknown and inconceivable.

Shall we then assert, that we are conscious of a power or energy in our own minds, when, by an act or command of our will, we raise up a new idea, fix the mind to the contemplation of it, turn it on all sides, and at last dismiss it for some other idea, when we think that we have surveyed it with sufficient accuracy? I believe the same arguments will prove, that even this command of the will gives us no real idea of force or energy.

First, It must be allowed, that, when we know a power, we know that very circumstance in the cause, by which it is enabled to produce the effect: For these are supposed to be synonymous. We must, therefore, know both the cause and effect, and the relation between them. But do we pretend to be acquainted with the nature of the human soul and the nature of an idea, or the aptitude of the one to produce the other? This is a real creation; a production of something out of nothing: Which implies a power so great, that it may seem at first sight, beyond the reach of any being, less than infinite. At least it must be owned, that such a power is not felt, nor known, nor even conceivable by the mind. We only feel the event, namely the existence of an idea, consequent to a command of the will: But the manner, in which this operation is performed, the power by which it is produced, is entirely beyond our comprehension.

Secondly, The command of the mind over itself is limited, as well as its command over the body; and these limits are not known by reason, or any acquaintance with the nature of cause and effect, but only by experience and observation, as in all other natural events and in the operation of external objects. Our authority over our sentiments and passions is much weaker than that over our ideas; and even the latter authority is circumscribed within very narrow boundaries. Will any one pretend to assign the ultimate reason of these boundaries, or show why the power is deficient in one case, not in another.

Thirdly, This self-command is very different at different times. A man in health possesses more of it than one languishing with sickness. We are more master of our thoughts in the morning than in the evening: Fasting, than after a full meal. Can we give any reason for these variations, except experience? Where then is the power, of which we pretend to be conscious? Is there not here, either in a spiritual or material substance, or both, some secret mechanism or structure of parts, upon which the effect depends, and which, being entirely unknown to us, renders the power or energy of the will equally unknown and incomprehensible?

Volition is surely an act of the mind, with which we are sufficiently acquainted. Reflect upon it. Consider it on all sides. Do you find anything in it like this creative power, by which it raises from nothing a new idea, and with a kind of *Fiat* imitates the omnipotence of its Maker, if I may be allowed so to speak, who called forth into existence all the various scenes of nature? So far from being conscious of this energy in the will, it requires as certain experience as that of which we are possessed, to convince us that such extraordinary effects do ever result from a simple act of volition.

• William James (1842–1910)

The Dilemma of Determinism[5]

William James, an example of whose work appeared in Chapter I, here discusses the problem of the freedom of the will. There is a slight discrepancy between James and the text in the matter of terminology. The position which James calls determinism (which holds that the parts of the universe, now absolutely fixed, decree what the future will be) is what we have already called necessity, and the second aspect of his determinism, its psychological consequences, we have already called fatalism. Needless to say, James is opposed to both necessity and fatalism, holding with his usual enthusiasm that the world is full of possibilities, and that, although it is strictly impossible to prove free will, it is important to assume the will is free in order to act with freedom.

A common opinion prevails that the juice has ages ago been pressed out of the free-will controversy, and that no new champion can do more than warm up stale arguments which every one has heard. This is a radical mistake. I know of no subject less worn out, or in which inventive genius has a better chance of breaking open new ground—not, perhaps, of forcing a conclusion or of coercing assent, but of deepening our sense of what the issue between the two parties really is, of what the ideas of fate and of free will imply. . . . I cannot pretend to vie in originality with any of the

[5] From William James, "An Address to Harvard Divinity Students," later published in the *Unitarian Review*, 1884.

masters I have named, and my ambition limits itself to just one little point. If I can make two of the necessarily implied corollaries of determinism clearer to you than they have been made before, I shall have made it possible for you to decide for or against that doctrine with a better understanding of what you are about. And if you prefer not to decide at all, but to remain doubters, you will at least see more plainly what the subject of your hesitation is. I thus disclaim openly on the threshold all pretension to prove to you that the freedom of the will is true. The most I hope is to induce some of you to follow my own example in assuming it true and acting as if it were true. If it be true, it seems to me that this is involved in the strict logic of the case. Its truth ought not to be forced willy-nilly down our indifferent throats. It ought to be freely espoused by men who can equally well turn their backs upon it. In other words, our first act of freedom, if we are free, ought in all inward propriety to be to affirm that we are free. This should exclude, it seems to me, from the free-will side of the question all hope of a coercive demonstration—a demonstration which I, for one, am perfectly contented to go without.

With thus much understood at the outset, we can advance. But not without one more point understood as well. The arguments I am about to urge all proceed on two suppositions: first, when we make theories about the world and discuss them with one another, we do so in order to attain a conception of things which shall give us subjective satisfaction; and second, if there be two conceptions, and the one seems to us, on the whole, more rational than the other, we are entitled to suppose that the more rational one is the truer of the two. I hope that you are all willing to make these suppositions with me; for I am afraid that if there be any of you here who are not, they will find little edification in the rest of what I have to say. I cannot stop to argue the point; but I myself believe that all the magnificent achievements of mathematical and physical science—our doctrines of evolution, of uniformity of law, and the rest—proceed from our indomitable desire to cast the world into a more rational shape in our minds than the shape into which it is thrown there by the crude order of our experience. The world has shown itself, to a great extent, plastic to this demand of ours for rationality. How much farther it will show itself plastic no one can say. Our only means of finding out is to try; and I, for one, feel as free to try conceptions of moral as of mechanical or of logical rationality. If a certain formula for expressing the nature of the world violates my moral demand, I shall feel as free to throw it overboard, or at least to doubt it, as if it disappointed my demand for uniformity of sequence, for example; the one demand being, so far as I can see, quite as subjective and emotional as the other is. The principle of causality, for example—what is it but a postulate, an empty name covering simply a demand that the sequence of events shall some day manifest a deeper kind of belonging of one thing with another than the mere arbitrary juxtaposition which now phenomenally appears? It is as much an altar to an unknown god as the one that Saint Paul found at Athens. All our scientific and philosophic ideals are altars to unknown gods. Uniformity is as much so as is free will. If this be admitted, we can debate on even terms. But if any one pretends that while freedom and variety are, in the first instance, subjective demands, necessity and uniformity are something altogether different, I do not see how we can debate at all.

· · · · ·

Fortunately, no ambiguities hang about this word [determinism] or about its opposite, indeterminism. Both designate an outward way in which things may happen, and their cold and mathematical sound has no sentimental associations that can bribe our partiality either way in advance. Now, evidence of an external kind to decide between determinism and indeterminism is, as I intimated a while back, strictly impossible to find. Let us look at the difference between them and see for ourselves. What does determinism profess?

It professes that those parts of the universe already laid down absolutely appoint and decree what the other parts shall be. The future has no ambiguous possibilities hidden in its womb: the part we call the present is compatible with only one totality. Any other future complement than the one fixed from eternity is impossible. The whole is in each and every part, and welds it with the rest into an absolute unity, an iron block, in which there can be no equivocation or shadow of turning.

> With earth's first clay they did the last man knead,
> And there of the last harvest sowed the seed.
> And the first morning of creation wrote
> What the last dawn of reckoning shall read.

Indeterminism, on the contrary, says that the parts have a certain amount of loose play on one another, so that the laying down of one of them does not necessarily determine what the others shall be. It admits that possibilities may be in excess of actualities, and that things not yet revealed to our knowledge may really in themselves be ambiguous. Of two alternative futures which we conceive, both may now be really possible; and the one become impossible only at the very moment when the other excludes it by becoming real itself. Indeterminism thus denies the world to be one unbending unit of fact. It says there is a certain ultimate pluralism in it; and, so saying, it corroborates our ordinary unsophisticated view of things. To that view, actualities seem to float in a wider sea of possibilities from out of which they are chosen; and, *somewhere*, indeterminism says, such possibilities exist, and form a part of truth.

Determinism, on the contrary, says they exist *nowhere*, and that necessity on the one hand and impossibility on the other are the sole categories of the real. Possibilities that fail to get realized are, for determinism, pure illusions: they never were possibilities at all. There is nothing inchoate, it says, about this universe of ours, all that was or is or shall be actual in it having been from eternity virtually there. The cloud of alternatives our minds escort this mass of actuality withal is a cloud of sheer deceptions, to which "impossibilities" is the only name that rightfully belongs.

The issue, it will be seen, is a perfectly sharp one, which no eulogistic terminology can smear over or wipe out. The truth *must* lie with one side or the other, and its lying with one side makes the other false.

• • • • •

The stronghold of the deterministic sentiment is the antipathy to the idea of chance. As soon as we begin to talk indeterminism to our friends, we find a number of them shaking their heads. This notion of alternative possibility, they say, this admission that any one of several things may come to pass, is, after all, only a round-about name for chance; and chance is something the notion of which no sane mind can for an instant tolerate in the world. What is it, they ask, but barefaced crazy unreason, the negation of intelligibility and law? And if the slightest particle of it exist anywhere, what is to prevent the whole fabric from falling together, the stars from going out, and chaos from recommencing her topsy-turvy reign?

• • • • •

The sting of the word "chance" seems to lie in the assumption that it means something positive, and that if anything happens by chance, it must needs be something of an intrinsically irrational and preposterous sort. Now, chance means nothing of the kind.

It is a purely negative and relative term, giving us no information about that of which it is predicated, except that it happens to be disconnected with something else—not controlled, secured, or necessitated by other things in advance of its own actual presence. As this point is the most subtle one of the whole lecture, and at the same time the point on which all the rest hinges, I beg you to pay particular attention to it. What I say is that it tells us nothing about what a thing may be in itself to call it "chance." It may be a bad thing, it may be a good thing. It may be lucidity, transparency, fitness incarnate, matching the whole system of other things, when it has once befallen, in an unimaginably perfect way. All you mean by calling it "chance" is that this is not guaranteed, that it may also fall out otherwise. For the system of other things has no positive hold on the chance-thing. Its origin is in a certain fashion negative: it escapes, and says, Hands off! coming, when it comes, as a free gift, or not at all.

· · · · ·

What is meant by saying that my choice of which way to walk home after the lecture is ambiguous and matter of chance as far as the present moment is concerned? It means that both Divinity Avenue and Oxford Street are called; but that only one, and that one *either* one, shall be chosen. Now, I ask you seriously to suppose that this ambiguity of my choice is real; and then to make the impossible hypothesis that the choice is made twice over, and each time falls on a different street. In other words, imagine that I first walk through Divinity Avenue, and then imagine that the powers governing the universe annihilate ten minutes of time with all that it contained, and set me back at the door of this hall just as I was before the choice was made. Imagine then that, everything else being the same, I now make a different choice and traverse Oxford Street. You, as passive spectators, look on and see the two alternative universes—one of them with me walking through Divinity Avenue in it, the other with the same me walking through Oxford Street. Now, if you are determinists you believe one of these universes to have been from eternity impossible: you believe it to have been impossible because of the intrinsic irrationality or accidentality somewhere involved in it. But looking outwardly at these universes, can you say which is the impossible and accidental one, and which the rational and necessary one? I doubt if the most iron-clad determinist among you could have the slightest glimmer of light on this point. In other words, either universe *after the fact* and once there would, to our means of observation and understanding, appear just as rational as the other. There would be absolutely no criterion by which we might judge one necessary and the other matter of chance. Suppose now we relieve the gods of their hypothetical task and assume my choice, once made, to be made forever. I go through Divinity Avenue for good and all. If, as good determinists, you now begin to affirm, what all good determinists punctually do affirm, that in the nature of things I *couldn't* have gone through Oxford Street—had I done so it would have been chance, irrationality, insanity, a horrid gap in nature—I simply call your attention to this, that your affirmation is what the Germans call a *Machtspruch*, a mere conception fulminated as a dogma and based on no insight into details. Before my choice, either street seemed as natural to you as to me. Had I happened to take Oxford Street, Divinity Avenue would have figured in your philosophy as the gap in nature; and you would have so proclaimed it with the best deterministic conscience in the world.

But what a hollow outcry, then, is this against a chance which, if it were present to us, we could by no character whatever distinguish from a rational necessity! I have taken the most trivial of examples, but no possible example could lead to any different result. For what are the alternatives which, in point of fact, offer themselves to human volition? What are those futures that now seem matters of chance? Are they not one and all like the Divinity Avenue and Oxford Street of our example? Are they not all of them *kinds* of things already here and based in the existing frame of nature? Is any one ever tempted to produce an *absolute* accident, something utterly irrelevant to the rest of the world? Do not all the motives that assail us, all the futures that offer themselves to our choice, spring equally from the soil of the past; and would not either one of them, whether realized through chance or through necessity, the moment it was realized, seem to us to fit that past, and in the completest and most continuous manner to interdigitate with the phenomena already there?

The more one thinks of the matter, the more one wonders that so empty and gratuitous a hubbub as this outcry against chance should have found so great an echo in the hearts of men. It is a word that tells us absolutely nothing about what chances, or about the *modus operandi* of the chancing; and the use of it as a war cry shows only a temper of intellectual absolutism, a demand that the world shall be a solid block, subject to one control—which temper, which demand, the world may not be bound to gratify at all. In every outwardly verifiable and practical respect, a world in which the alternatives that now actually distract *your* choice were decided by pure chance would be by *me* absolutely undistinguished from the world in which I now live. I am, therefore, entirely willing to call it, so far as your choices go, a world of chance for me. To *yourselves*, it is true, those very acts of choice, which to me are so blind, opaque, and external, are the opposites of this, for you are within them and effect them. To you they appear as decisions; and decisions, for him who makes them, are altogether peculiar psychic facts. Self-luminous and self-justifying at the living moment at which they occur, they appeal to no outside moment to put its stamp upon them or make them continuous with the rest of nature. Themselves it is rather who seem to make nature continuous; and in their strange and intense function of granting consent to one possibility and withholding it from another, to transform an equivocal and double future into an inalterable and simple past.

· · · · ·

I wish first of all to show you just what the notion that this is a deterministic world implies. The implications I call your attention to are all bound up with the fact that it is a world in which we constantly have to make what I shall, with your permission, call judgments of regret. Hardly an hour passes in which we do not wish that something might be otherwise; and happy indeed are those of us whose hearts have never echoed the wish of Omar Khayam—

> That we might clasp, ere closed, the book of fate,
>   And make the writer on a fairer leaf
> Inscribe our names, or quite obliterate.

> Ah! Love, could you and I with fate conspire
> To mend this sorry scheme of things entire,
>   Would we not shatter it to bits, and then
> Remould it nearer to the heart's desire?

Now, it is undeniable that most of these regrets are foolish, and quite on a par in point of philosophic value with the criticisms on the universe of that friend of our infancy, the hero of the fable "The Atheist and the Acorn"—

> Fool! had that bough a pumpkin bore,
> Thy whimsies would have worked no more, etc.

Even from the point of view of our own ends, we should probably make a botch of remodelling the universe. How much more then from the point of view of ends we cannot see! Wise men therefore regret as little as they can. But still some regrets are pretty obstinate and hard to stifle—regrets for acts of wanton cruelty or treachery, for example, whether performed by others or by ourselves. Hardly any one can remain *entirely* optimistic after reading the confession of the murderer at Brockton the other day; how, to get rid of the wife whose continued existence bored him, he inveigled her into a desert spot, shot her four times, and then, as she lay on the ground and said to him, "You didn't do it on purpose, did you, dear?" replied, "No, I didn't do it on purpose," as he raised a rock and smashed her skull. Such an occurrence, with the mind sentence and self-satisfaction of the prisoner, is a field for a crop of regrets, which one need not take up in detail. We feel that, although a perfect mechanical fit to the rest of the universe, it is a bad moral fit, and that something else would really have been better in its place.

But for the deterministic philosophy the murder, the sentence, and the prisoner's optimism were all necessary from eternity; and nothing else for a moment had a ghost of a chance of being put into their place. To admit such a chance, the determinists tell us, would be to make a suicide of reason; so we must steel our hearts against the thought. And here our plot thickens, for we see the first of those difficult implications of determinism and monism which it is my purpose to make you feel. If this Brockton murder was called for by the rest of the universe, if it had to come at its preappointed hour, and if nothing else would have been consistent with the sense of the whole, what are we to think of the universe? Are we stubbornly to stick to our judgment of regret, and say, though it *couldn't* be, yet it *would* have been a better universe with something different from this Brockton murder in it? That, of course, seems the natural and spontaneous thing for us to do; and yet it is nothing short of deliberately espousing a kind of pessimism. The judgment of regret calls the murder bad. Calling a thing bad means, if it mean anything at all, that the thing ought not to be, that something else ought to be in its stead. Determinism, in denying that anything else can be in its stead, virtually defines the universe as a place in which what ought to be is impossible—in other words, as an organism whose constitution is afflicted with an incurable taint, an irremediable flaw.

The only deterministic escape from pessimism is everywhere to abandon the judgment of regret. That this can be done, history shows to be not impossible. The devil, *quoad existentiam*, may be good. That is, although he be a *principle* of evil, yet the universe, with such a principle in it, may practically be a better universe than it could have been without. On every hand, in a small way, we find that a certain amount of evil is a condition by which a higher form of good is brought. There is nothing to prevent anybody from generalizing this view, and trusting that if we could but see things in the largest of all ways, even such matters as this Brockton murder would appear to be paid for by the uses that follow in their train. An optimism *quand même,* a systematic and infatuated optimism like that ridiculed by Voltaire in his *Candide,* is one of the possible ideal ways in which a man may train himself to look on life. Bereft of dogmatic hardness and lit up with the expression of a tender and pathetic hope, such an optimism has been the grace of some of the most religious characters that ever lived.

> Throb thine with Nature's throbbing breast,
> And all is clear from east to west.

Even cruelty and treachery may be among the absolutely blessed fruits of time, and to quarrel with any of their details may be blasphemy. The only real blasphemy, in short, may be that pessimistic temper of the soul which lets it give way to such things as regrets, remorse, and grief.

Thus, our deterministic pessimism may become a deterministic optimism at the price of extinguishing our judgments of regret.

But does not this immediately bring us into a curious logical predicament? Our determinism leads us to call our judgments of regret wrong, because they are pessimistic in implying that what is impossible yet ought to be. But how then about the judgments of regret themselves? If they are wrong, other judgments, judgments of approval presumably, ought to be in their place. But as they are necessitated, nothing else *can* be in their place; and the universe is just what it was before—namely, a place in which what ought to be appears impossible. We have got one foot out of the pessimistic bog, but the other one sinks all the deeper. We have rescued our actions from the bonds of evil, but our judgments are now held fast. When murders and treacheries cease to be sins, regrets are theoretic absurdities and errors. The theoretic and the active life thus play a kind of see-saw with each other on the ground of evil. The rise of either sends the other down. Murder and treachery cannot be good without regret being bad: regret cannot be good without treachery and murder being bad. Both, however, are supposed to have been foredoomed; so something must be fatally unreasonable, absurd, and wrong in the world. It must be a place of which either sin or error forms a necessary part. From this dilemma there seems at first sight no escape. Are we then so soon to fall back into the pessimism from which we thought we had emerged? And is there no possible way by which we may, with good intellectual consciences, call the cruelties and the treacheries, the reluctances and the regrets, *all* good together?

. . . . .

We have thus clearly revealed to our view what may be called the dilemma of determinism, so far as determinism pretends to think things out at all. A merely mechanical determinism, it is true, rather rejoices in not thinking them out. It is very sure that the universe must satisfy its postulate of a physical continuity and coherence, but it smiles at any one who comes forward with a postulate of moral coherence as well. I may suppose, however, that the number of purely mechanical or hard determinists among you this evening is small. The determinism to whose seductions you are most exposed is what I have called soft determinism—the determinism which allows considerations of good and bad to mingle with those of cause and effect in deciding what sort of a universe this may rationally be held to be. The dilemma of this determinism is one whose left horn is pessimism and whose right horn is subjectivism. In other words, if determinism is to escape pessimism, it must leave off looking at the goods and ills of life in a simple objective way, and regard them as materials, indifferent in themselves, for the production of consciousness, scientific and ethical, in us.

To escape pessimism is, as we all know, no easy task. Your own studies have sufficiently shown you the almost desperate difficulty of making the notion that there is a single principle of things, and that principle absolute perfection, rhyme together with our daily vision of the facts of life. If perfection be the principle, how comes there any imperfection here? If God be good, how came he to create—or, if he did not create, how comes he to permit—the devil? The evil facts must be explained as seeming: the devil must be whitewashed, the universe must be disinfected, if neither God's goodness nor his unity and power are to remain impugned. And of all the various ways of operating the disinfection, and making bad seem less bad, the way of subjectivism appears by far the best.

For, after all, is there not something rather absurd in our ordinary notion of external things being good or bad in themselves? Can murders and treacheries, considered as mere outward happenings, or motions of matter, be bad without any one to feel their badness? And could paradise properly be good in the absence of a sentient principle by which the goodness was perceived? Outward goods and evils seem practically indistinguishable except in so far as they result in getting moral judgments made about them. But then the moral judgments seem the main thing, and the outward facts mere perishing instruments for their production. This is subjectivism.

. . . . .

No one, I hope, will accuse me, after I have said all this, of underrating the reason in favor of subjectivism. And now that I proceed to say why those reasons, strong as they are, fail to convince my own mind, I trust the presumption may be that my objections are stronger still.

I frankly confess that they are of a practical order. If we practically take up subjectivism in a sincere and radical manner and follow its consequences, we meet with some that make us pause. Let a subjectivism begin in never so severe and intellectual a way, it is forced by the law of its nature to develop another side of itself and end with the corruptest curiosity. Once dismiss the notion that certain duties are good in themselves, and that we are here to do them, no matter how we feel about them; once consecrate the opposite notion that our performances and our violations of duty are for a common purpose, the attainment of subjective knowledge and feeling, and that the deepening of these is the chief end of our lives—and at what point on the downward slope are we to stop? In theology, subjectivism develops as its "left wing" antinomianism. In literature, its left wing is romanticism. And in practical life it is either a nerveless sentimentality or a sensualism without bounds.

Everywhere it fosters the fatalistic mood of mind. It makes those who are already too inert more passive still; it renders wholly reckless those whose energy is already in excess. All through history we find how subjectivism, as soon as it has a free career, exhausts itself in every sort of spiritual, moral, and practical license. Its optimism turns to an ethical indifference, which infallibly brings dissolution in its train.

. . . . .

The only escape is by the practical way. And since I have mentioned the nowadays much-reviled name of Carlyle, let me mention it once more, and say it is the way of his teaching. No matter for Carlyle's life, no matter for a great deal of his writing. What was the most important thing he said to us? He said: "Hang your sensibilities! Stop your sniveling complaints, and your equally sniveling raptures! Leave off your general emotional tomfoolery, and get to work like men!" But this means a complete rupture with the subjectivist philosophy of things. It says conduct, and not sensibility, is the ultimate fact for our recognition. With the vision of certain works to be done, of certain outward changes to be wrought or resisted, it says our intellectual horizon terminates. No matter how we succeed in doing these outward duties, whether gladly and spontaneously, or heavily and unwillingly, do them we somehow must; for the leaving of them undone is perdition. No matter how we feel; if we are only faithful in the outward act and refuse to do wrong, the world will in so far be safe, and we quit of our debt toward it. Take, then, the yoke upon our shoulders; bend our neck beneath the heavy legality of its weight; regard something else than our feeling as our limit, our master, and our law; be willing to live and die in its service—and, at a stroke, we have passed from the subjective into the objective philosophy of things, much as one awakens from some feverish dream, full of bad lights and noises, to find one's self bathed in the sacred coolness and quiet of the air of the night.

But what is the essence of this philosophy of objective conduct, so old-fashioned and finite, but so chaste and sane and strong, when compared with its romantic rival? It is the recognition of limits, foreign and opaque to our understanding. It is the willingness, after bringing about some external good, to feel at peace; for our responsibility ends with the performance of that duty, and the burden of the rest we may lay on higher powers.

> Look to thyself, O Universe,
> Thou art better and not worse—

we may say in that philosophy, the moment we have done our stroke of conduct, however small. For in the view of that philosophy the universe belongs to a plurality of semi-independent forces, each one of which may help or hinder, and be helped or hindered by, the operations of the rest.

But this brings us right back, after such a long detour, to the question of indeterminism and to the conclusion of all I came here to say tonight. For the only consistent way of representing a pluralism and a world whose parts may affect one another through their conduct being either good or bad is the indeterministic way. What interest, zest, or excitement can there be in achieving the right way, unless we are enabled to feel that the wrong way is also a possible and a natural way—nay, more, a menacing and an imminent way? And what sense can there be in condemning ourselves for taking the wrong way, unless we need have done nothing of the sort, unless the right way was open to us as well? I cannot understand the willingness to act, no matter how we feel, without the belief that acts are really good and bad. I cannot understand the belief that an act is bad, without regret at its happening. I cannot understand regret without the admission of real, genuine possibilities in the world. Only *then* is it other than a mockery to feel, after we have failed to do our best, that an irreparable opportunity is gone from the universe, the loss of which it must forever after mourn.

If you insist that this is all superstition, that possibility is in the eye of science and reason impossibility, and that if I act badly 'tis that the universe was foredoomed to suffer this defect, you fall right back into the dilemma, the labyrinth, of pessimism and subjectivism, from out of whose toils we have just wound our way.

Now, we are of course free to fall back, if we please. For my own part, though, whatever difficulties may beset the philosophy of determinism, with its alternative of pessimism or romanticism, contains difficulties that are greater still. But you will remember that I expressly repudiated awhile ago the pretension to offer any arguments which could be coercive in a so-called scientific fashion in this matter. And I consequently find myself, at the end of this long talk, obliged to state my conclusions in an altogether personal way. This personal method of appeal seems to be among the very conditions of the problem; and the most any one can do is to confess as candidly as he can the grounds for the faith that is in him, and leave his example to work on others as it may.

Let me, then, without circumlocution say just this. The world is enigmatical enough in all conscience, whatever theory we may take up toward it. The indeterminism I defend, the free-will theory of popular sense based on the judgment of regret, represents that world as vulnerable, and liable to be injured by certain of its parts if they act wrong. And it represents their acting wrong as a matter of possibility or accident, neither inevitable nor yet to be infallibly warded off. In all this, it is a theory devoid either of transparency or of stability. It gives us a pluralistic, restless universe, in which no single point of view can ever take in the whole scene; and to a mind possessed of the love of unity at any cost, it will, no doubt, remain forever inacceptable. A friend with such a mind once told me that the thought of my universe made him sick, like the sight of the horrible motion of a mass of maggots in their carrion bed.

But while I freely admit that the pluralism and the restlessness are repugnant and irrational in a certain way, I find that every alternative to them is irrational in a deeper way. The indeterminism with its maggots, if you please to speak so about it, offends only the native absolutism of my intellect—an absolutism which, after all, perhaps, deserves to be snubbed and kept in check. But the determinism with its necessary carrion, to continue the figure of speech, and with no possible maggots to eat the latter up, violates my sense of moral reality through and through. When, for example, I imagine such carrion as the Brockton murder, I cannot conceive it as an act by which the universe, as a whole, logically and necessarily expresses its nature without shrinking from complicity with such a whole. And I deliberately refuse to keep on terms of loyalty with the universe by saying blankly that the murder, since it does flow from the nature of the whole, is not carrion. There are *some* instinctive reactions which I, for one, will not tamper with. The only remaining alternative, the attitude of gnostical romanticism, wrenches my personal instincts in quite as violent a way. It falsifies the simple objectivity of their deliverance. It makes the goose-flesh the murder excites in me a sufficient reason for the perpetration of the crime. It transforms life from a tragic reality into an insincere melodramatic exhibition, as foul or as tawdry as any one's diseased curiosity pleases to carry it out. And with its consecration of the *roman naturaliste* state of mind, and its enthronement of the baser crew of Parisian *litterateurs* among the eternally indispensable organs by which the infinite spirit of things attains to that subjective illumination which is the task of its life, it leaves me in presence of a sort of subjective carrion considerably more noisome than the objective carrion I called it in to take away.

No! better a thousand times, than such systematic corruption of our moral sanity, the plainest pesimism, so that it be straightforward; but better far than that the world of chance. Make as great an uproar about chance as you please, I know that chance means pluralism and nothing more. If some of the members of pluralism are bad, the philosophy of pluralism, whatever broad views it may deny me, permits me, at least, to turn to the other members with a clean breast of affection and an unsophisticated moral sense. And if I still wish to think of the world as a totality, it lets me feel that a world with a *chance* in it of being altogether good, even if the chance never come to pass, is better than a world with no chance at all. That "chance" whose very notion I am exhorted and conjured to banish from my view of the future as the suicide of reason concerning it, that "chance" is—what? Just this—the chance that in moral respects the future may be other and better than the past has been. This is the only chance we have any motive for supposing to exist. Shame, rather, on its repudiation and its denial! For its presence is the vital air which lets the world live, the salt which keeps it sweet.

• Arthur Schopenhauer (1788–1860)

The World as Will [6]

Arthur Schopenhauer was born in Danzig and educated at Berlin and Gottingen. After a brief and disappointing teaching career, he retired to devote his time to philosophy and writing. He won fame for his style and for his pessimistic point of view. His chief works are *The Four-fold Root of the Principle of Sufficient Reason, The Basis of Morality,* and his masterpiece *The World as Will and Idea,* from which the following selection is taken. In it Schopenhauer presents his cosmological doctrines—that "will" is the real inner character of all nature, the kernel of every particular thing, of matter in motion, and of man. He of course means by "will" something more general, more metaphysical, than the usual psychological usage of the term implies.

Whoever has now gained from all these expositions a knowledge *in abstracto,* and therefore clear and certain, of what every one knows directly *in concreto, i.e.,* as feeling, a knowledge that his will is the real inner nature of his phenomenal being, which manifests itself to him as idea, both in his actions and in their permanent substratum, his body, and that his will is that which is most immediate in his consciousness, though it has not as such completely passed into the form of idea in which object and subject stand over against each other, but makes itself known to him in a direct manner, in which he does not quite clearly distinguish subject and object, yet is not known as a whole to the individual himself, but only in its particular acts,—whoever, I say, has with me gained this conviction will find that of itself it affords him the key to the knowledge of the inmost being of the whole nature; for he now transfers it to all those phenomena which are not given to him, like his own phenomenal existence, both in direct and indirect knowledge, but only in the latter, thus merely one-sidedly as *idea* alone. He will recognize this will of which we are speaking not only in those

[6] From Arthur Schopenhauer, *The Word as Will and Idea,* trans. Haldane and Kemp (1883-86), Bk. II, Secs. xxi-xxiii.

phenomenal existences which exactly resemble his own, in men and animals as their inmost nature, but the course of reflection will lead him to recognize the force which germinates and vegetates in the plant, and indeed the force through which the crystal is formed, that by which the magnet turns to the north pole, the force whose shock he experiences from the contact of two different kinds of metals, the force which appears in the elective affinities of matter as repulsion and attraction, decomposition and combination, and, lastly, even gravitation, which acts so powerfully throughout matter, draws the stone to the earth and the earth to the sun,—all these, I say, he will recognise as different only in their phenomenal existence, but in their inner nature as identical, as that which is directly known to him so intimately and so much better than anything else, and which in its most distinct manifestation is called *will*. It is this application of reflection alone that prevents us from remaining any longer at the phenomenon, and leads us to the *thing-in-itself*. Phenomenal existence is idea and nothing more. All idea, of whatever kind it may be, all *object*, is *phenomenal* existence, but the *will* alone is a *thing-in-itself*. As such, it is throughout not idea, but *toto genere* different from it; it is that of which all idea, all object, is the phenomenal appearance, the visibility, the objectification. It is the inmost nature, the kernel, of every particular thing, and also of the whole. It appears in every blind force of nature and also in the preconsidered action of man; and the great difference between these two is merely in the degree of the manifestation, not in the nature of what manifests itself.

Now, if we are to think as an object this thing-in-itself (we wish to retain the Kantian expression as a standing formula), which, as such, is never object, because all object is its mere manifestation, and therefore cannot be it itself, we must borrow for it the name and concept of an object, of something in some way objectively given, consequently of one of its own manifestations. But in order to serve as a clue for the understanding, this can be no other than the most complete of all its manifestations, i.e., the most distinct, the most developed, and directly enlightened by knowledge. Now this is the human will. It is, however, well to observe that here, at any rate, we only make use of a *denominatio a potiori*, through which, therefore, the concept of will receives a greater extension than it has hitherto had. Knowledge of the identical in different phenomena, and of difference in similar phenomena, is, as Plato so often remarks, a *sine qua non* of philosophy. But hitherto it was not recognised that every kind of active and operating force in nature is essentially identical with will, and therefore the multifarious kinds of phenomena were not seen to be merely different species of the same genus, but treated as heterogeneous. Consequently there could be no word to denote the concept of this genus. I therefore name the genus after its most important species, the direct knowledge of which lies nearer to us and guides us to the indirect knowledge of all other species. But whoever is incapable of carrying out the required extension of the concept will remain involved in a permanent misunderstanding. For by the word *will* he understands only that species of it which has hitherto been exclusively denoted by it, the will which is guided by knowledge, and whose manifestation follows only upon motives, and indeed merely abstract motives, and thus takes place under the guidance of the reason. This, we have said, is only the most prominent example of the manifestation of will. We must now distinctly separate in thought the inmost essence of this manifestation which is known to us directly, and then transfer it to all the weaker, less distinct manifestations of the same nature, and thus we shall accomplish the desired extension of the concept of will. From another point of view I should be equally misunderstood by any one who should think that it is all the same in the end whether we denote this inner nature of all phenomena by the word *will* or by any other. This would be the case if the thing-in-itself were something whose existence we merely *inferred,* and thus knew indirectly and only in the abstract. Then, indeed, we might call it what we pleased; the name would stand merely as the symbol of an unknown quantity. But the word *will,* which like a magic spell, discloses to us the inmost being of everything in nature, is by no means an unknown quantity, something arrived at only by inference, but is fully and immediately comprehended, and is so familiar to us that we know and understand what will is far better than anything else whatever. The concept of will has hitherto commonly been subordinated to that of force, but I reverse the matter entirely, and desire that every force in nature should be thought as will. It must not be supposed that this is mere verbal quibbling or of no consequence; rather, it is of the greatest significance and importance. For at the foundation of the concept of force, as of all other concepts, there ultimately lies the knowledge in sense-perception of the objective world, that is to say, the phenomenon, the idea; and the concept is constructed out of this. It is an abstraction from the province in which cause and effect reign, i.e., from ideas of perception, and means just the causal nature of causes at the point at which this causal nature is no further etiologically explicable, but is the necessary presupposition of all etiological explanation. The concept will, on the other hand, is of all possible concepts the only one which has its source *not* in the phenomenal, *not* in the mere idea of perception, but comes from within, and proceeds from the most immediate consciousness of each of us, in which each of us knows his own individuality, according to its nature, immediately, apart from all form, even that of subject and object, and which at the same time is this individuality, for here the subject and the object of knowledge are one. If, therefore, we refer the concept of *force* to that of *will*, we have in fact referred the less known to what is infinitely better known; indeed, to the one thing that is really immediately and fully known to us, and have very greatly extended our knowledge. If, on the contrary, we subsume the concept of will under that of force, as has hitherto always been done, we renounce the only immediate knowledge which we have of the inner nature of the world, from the phenomenal, and with which we can therefore never go beyond the phenomenal.

The *will* as a thing-in-itself is quite different from its phenomenal appearance, and entirely free from all the forms of the phenomenal, into which it first passes when it manifests itself, and which therefore only concern its *objectivity*, and are foreign to the will itself. Even the most universal form of all idea, that of being object for a subject, does not concern it; still less the forms which are subordinate to this and which collectively have their common expression in the principle of sufficient reason, to which we know that time and space belong, and consequently multiplicity also, which exists and is possible only through these. In this last regard I shall call time and space the *principium individuationis*, borrowing an expression from the old schoolmen, and I beg to draw attention to this, once for all. For it is only through the medium of time and space that what is one and the same, both according to its nature and to its concept, yet appears as different, as a multiplicity of co-existent and successive phenomena. Thus time and space are the *principium individuationis*, the subject of so many subtleties and disputes among the schoolmen. According to what has been said, the will as a thing-in-itself lies outside the province of the principle of sufficient reason in all its forms, and is consequently completely groundless, although all its manifestations are entirely subordinated to the principle of sufficient reason. Further, it is free from all *multiplicity*, although its manifestations in time and space are innumerable. It is itself one, though not in the sense in which an object is one, for the unity of an object can only be known in opposition to a possible multiplicity; nor yet in the sense in which a concept is one, for the unity of a concept originates only in abstraction from a multiplicity; but it is one as that which lies outside time and space, the *principium individuationis,* i.e., the possibility of multiplicity. Only when all this has become quite clear to us through the subsequent examination of the phenomena and different manifestations of the will, shall we fully understand the meaning of the Kantian doctrine that time, space and causality do not belong to the thing-in-itself, but are only forms of knowing.

The uncaused nature of will has been actually recognised, where it manifests itself most distinctly, as the will of man, and this has been called free, independent. But on account of the uncaused nature of the will itself, the necessity to which its manifestation is everywhere subjected has been overlooked and actions are treated as free, which they are not. For every individual action follows with strict necessity from the effect of the motive upon the character. All necessity is, as we have already said, the relation of the consequent to the reason, and nothing more. The principle of sufficient reason is the universal form of all phenomena, and man in his action must be subordinated to it like every other phenomenon. But because in self-consciousness the will is known directly and in itself, in this consciousness lies also the consciousness of freedom. The fact is, however, overlooked that the individual, the person, is not will as a thing-in-itself, but is a *phenomenon* of will, is already determined as such, and has come under the form of the phenomenal, the principle of sufficient reason. Hence arises the strange fact that every one believes himself *a priori* to be perfectly free, even in his individual actions, and thinks that at every moment he can commence another manner of life, which just means that he can become another person. But *a posteriori,* through experience, he finds to his astonishment that he is not free, but subjected to necessity; that in spite of all his resolutions and beginning of his life to the end of it, he must carry out the very character which he himself condemns, and as it were play the part he has undertaken to the end. I cannot pursue this subject further at present, for it belongs, as ethical, to another part of this work. In the meantime, I only wish to point out here that the *phenomenon* of the will which in itself is uncaused, is yet as such subordinated to the law of necessity, that is, the principle of sufficient reason, so that in the necessity with which the phenomena of nature follow each other, we may find nothing to hinder us from recognising in them the manifestations of will.

Only those changes which have no other ground than a motive, i.e., an idea, have hitherto been regarded as manifestations of will. Therefore in nature a will has only been attributed to man, or at the most to animals; for knowledge, the idea is, of course, as I have said elsewhere, the true and exclusive characteristic of animal life. But that the will is also active where no knowledge guides it, we see at once in the instinct and the mechanical skill of animals. That they have ideas and knowledge is here not to the point, for the end towards which they strive as definitely as if it were a known motive, is yet entirely unknown to them. Therefore in such cases their action takes place without motive, is not guided by the idea, and shows us first and most distinctly how the will may be active entirely without knowledge. The bird of a year old has no idea of the eggs for which it builds a nest; the young spider has no idea of the prey for which it spins a web; nor has the ant-lion any idea of the ants for which he digs a trench for the first time. The larva of the stag-beetle makes the hole in the wood, in which it is to await its metamorphosis, twice as big if it is going to be a male beetle as if it is going to be a female, so that if it is a male there may be room for the horns, of which, however, it has no idea. In such actions of these creatures the will is clearly operative as in their other actions, but it is in blind activity, which is indeed accompanied by knowledge but not guided by it. If now we have once gained insight into the fact, that idea as motive is not a necessary and essential condition of the activity of the will, we shall more easily recognise the activity of will where it is less apparent. For example, we shall see that the house of the snail is no more made by a will which is foreign to the snail itself, than the house which we build is produced through another will than our own; but we shall recognise in both houses the work of a will which objectifies itself in both the phenomena—a will which works in us according to motives, but in the snail still blindly as formative impulse directed outwards. In us also the same will is in many ways only blindly active: in all the functions of our body which are not guided by knowledge, in all its vital and vegetative processes, digestion, circulation, secretion, growth, reproduction. Not only the actions of the body, but the whole body itself is, as we have shown above, phenomenon of the will, objectified will, concrete will. All that goes on in it must therefore proceed through will, although here this will is not guided by knowledge, but acts blindly according to causes, which in this case are called *stimuli*.

I call a *cause*, in the narrowest sense of the word, that state of matter, which, while it introduces another state with necessity, yet suffers just as great a change itself as that which it causes; which is expressed in the rule, "action and reaction are equal." Further, in the case of what is properly speaking a cause, the effect increases directly in proportion to the cause, and therefore also the reaction.

So that, if once the mode of operation be known, the degree of the effect may be measured and calculated from the degree of the intensity of the cause; and conversely the degree of the intensity of the cause may be calculated from the degree of the effect. Such causes, properly so called, operate in all the phenomena of mechanics, chemistry, and so forth; in short, in all the changes of unorganized bodies. On the other hand, I call a *stimulus,* such a cause as sustains no reaction proportional to its effect, and the intensity of which does not vary directly in proportion to the intensity of its effect, so that the effect cannot be measured by it. On the contrary, a small increase of the stimulus may cause a very great increase of the effect, or conversely, it may eliminate the previous effect altogether, and so forth. All effects upon organised bodies as such are of this kind. All properly organic and vegetative changes of the animal body must therefore be referred to stimuli, not to mere causes. But the stimulus, like every cause and motive generally, never determines more than the point of time and space at which the manifestation of every force is to take place, and does not determine the inner nature of the force itself which is manifested. This inner nature we know, from our previous investigation, is will, to which therefore we ascribe both the unconscious and the conscious changes of the body. The stimulus holds the mean, forms the transition between the motive, which is causality accompanied throughout by knowledge, and the cause in the narrowest sense. In particular cases, it is sometimes nearer a motive, sometimes nearer a cause, but yet it can always be distinguished from both. Thus, for example, the rising of the sap in a plant follows upon stimuli, and cannot be explained from mere causes, according to the laws of hydraulics or capillary attraction; yet it is certainly assisted by these, and altogether approaches very near to a purely causal change. On the other hand, the movements of the *Hedysarum gyrans* and the *Mimosa pudica,* although still following upon mere stimuli, are yet very like movements which follow upon motives, and seem almost to wish to make the transition. The contraction of the pupils of the eyes as the light is increased is due to stimuli, but it passes into movement which is due to motive; for it takes place, because too strong lights would affect the retina painfully, and to avoid this we contract the pupils. The occasion of an erection is a motive, because it is an idea, yet it operates with the necessity of a stimulus, i.e., it cannot be resisted, but we must put the idea away in order to make it cease to affect us. This is also the case with disgusting things, which excite the desire to vomit. Thus we have treated the instinct of animals as an actual link, of quite a distinct kind, between movement following upon stimuli and action following upon a known motive. Now we might be asked to regard breathing as another link of this kind. It has been disputed whether it belongs to the voluntary or the involuntary movements, that is to say, whether it follows upon motive or stimulus, and perhaps it may be explained as something which is between the two. Marshall Hall ("The Diseases of the Nervous System," 293 sq.) explains it as a mixed function, for it is partly under the influence of the cerebral (voluntary) and partly under that of the spinal (non-voluntary) nerves. However, we are finally obliged to number it with the expressions of will which result from motives. For other motives, i.e., mere ideas, can determine the will to check it or accelerate it, and, as is the case with every other voluntary action, it seems to us that we could give up breathing altogether and voluntarily suffocate. And in fact we could do so if any other motive influenced the will sufficiently strong to overcome the pressing desire for air. According to some accounts Diogenes actually put an end to his life in this way. Certain negroes also are said to have done this. If this be true, it affords us a good example of the influence of abstract motives, i.e., of the victory of distinctively rational over merely animal will. For, that breathing is at least partially conditioned by cerebral activity is shown by the fact that the primary cause of death from prussic acid is that it paralyses the brain, and so, indirectly, restricts the breathing; but if the breathing be artificially maintained till the stupefaction of the brain has passed away, death will not ensue. We may also observe in passing that breathing affords us the most obvious example of the fact that motives act with just as much necessity as stimuli, or as causes in the narrowest sense of the word, and their operation can only be neutralised by antagonistic motives, as action is neutralised by reaction. For, in the case of breathing, the illusion that we can stop when we like is much weaker than in the case of other movements which follow upon motives; because in breathing the motive is very powerful, very near to us, and its satisfaction is very easy, for the muscles which accomplish it are never tired, nothing, as a rule, obstructs it, and the whole process is supported by the most inveterate habit of the individual. And yet all motives act with the same necessity. The knowledge that necessity is common to movements following upon motives, and those following upon stimuli, makes it easier for us to understand that that also which takes place in our bodily organism in accordance with stimuli and in obedience to law, is yet, according to its inner nature—will, which in all its manifestations, though never in itself, is subordinated to the principle of sufficient reason, that is, to necessity. Accordingly, we shall not rest contented with recognising that animals, both in their actions and also in their whole existence, bodily structure and organisation, are manifestations of will; but we shall extend to plants also this immediate knowledge of the essential nature of things which is given to us alone. Now all the movements of plants follow upon stimuli; for the absence of knowledge, and the movement following upon motives which is conditioned by knowledge, constitutes the only essential difference between animals and plants. Therefore, what appears for the idea as plant life, as mere vegetation, as blindly impelling force, we shall claim, according to its inner nature for will, and recognise it as just that which constitutes the basis of our own phenomenal being, as it expresses itself in our actions, and also in the whole existence of our body itself.

It only remains for us to take the final step, the extension of our way of looking at things to all those forces which act in nature in accordance with universal, unchangeable laws, in conformity with which the movements of all those bodies take place, which are wholly without organs, and have therefore no susceptibility for stimuli, and have no knowledge, which is the necessary condition of motives. Thus we must also apply the key to the understanding of the inner nature of things, which the immediate knowledge of our own existence alone can give us, to those phenomena of the unorganised world which are most remote from us. And if we consider them attentively, if we observe the strong and unceasing impulse with which the waters hurry to the ocean, the persistency with which the magnet turns ever to the north pole, the readiness with which iron flies to the magnet, the eagerness with which the electric poles seek to be reunited, and which, just like human desire, is increased by obstacles; if we see the crystal quickly and suddenly take form with such wonderful regularity of construction, which is clearly only a perfectly definite and accurately determined impulse in different directions, seized and retained by crystallisation; if we observe the choice with which bodies repel and attract each other, combined and separate, when they are set free in a fluid state, and emancipated from the bonds of rigidity; lastly, if we feel directly how a burden unceasingly presses and strains upon it in pursuit of its one tendency; if we observe all this, I say, it will require no great effort of the imagination to recognise, even at so great a distance, our own nature. That which in us pursues its ends by the light of knowledge; but here, in the weakest of its manifestations, only strives blindly and dumbly in a one-sided and unchangeable manner, must yet in both cases come under the name of will, as it is everywhere one and the same—just as the first dim light of dawn must share the name of sunlight with the rays of the full mid-day. For the name *will* denotes that which is the inner nature of everything in the world, and the one kernel of every phenomenon. Yet the remoteness, and indeed the appearance of absolute difference between the phenomena of unorganised nature and the will which we know as the inner reality of our own being arises chiefly from the contrast between the completely determined conformity to law of the one species of phenomena, and the apparently unfettered freedom of the other. For in man, individuality makes itself powerfully felt. Every one has a character of his own; and therefore the same motive has not the same influence over all, and a thousand circumstances which exist in the wide sphere of the knowledge of the individual, but are unknown to others, modify its effect. Therefore action cannot be predetermined from the motive alone, for the other factor is wanting, the accurate acquaintance with the individual character, and with the knowledge which accompanies it. On the other hand, the phenomena of the forces of nature illustrate the opposite extreme. They act according to universal laws, without variation, without individuality in accordance with openly manifest circumstances, subject to the most exact predetermination; and the same force of nature appears in its million phenomena in precisely the same way. In order to explain this point and prove the identity of the *one* indivisible will in all its different phenomena, in the weakest as in the strongest, we must first of all consider the relation of the will as thing-in-itself to its phenomena, that is, the relation of the world as will to the world as idea; for this will open to us the best way to a more thorough investigation of the whole subject we are considering in this second book.

SUGGESTED FURTHER READINGS

ALEXANDER, S. *Space, Time and Deity.* 2 vols. London: Macmillan & Co., Ltd., 1927.

ARISTOTLE. *De Anima.* London: Oxford University Press, 1927. Bks. II, III.

BERGSON, HENRI. *Matter and Memory.* London: Macmillan & Co., Ltd., 1929. Chaps. i, iv.

BERKELEY, GEORGE. *The Principles of Human Knowledge.* New York: Charles Scribner's Sons, 1929.

BROAD, C. D. *The Mind and Its Place In Nature.* New York: Humanities Press, Inc., 1952. Chaps. iii, vii, xiii.

COLLINGWOOD, R. G. *The Idea of Nature.* London and New York: Oxford University Press, 1945.

COMPTON, ARTHUR H. *The Idea of Nature.* New Haven: Yale University Press, 1935.

DEWEY, JOHN. *Experience and Nature.* New York: W. W. Norton & Co., Inc., 1935. Chap. vi, "Nature, Mind and the Subject" and Chap. vii, "Nature, Life and Body-Mind."

KANT, IMMANUEL. *Prolegomena to Any Future Metaphysic.* New York: Liberal Arts Press, 1951.

LOCKE, JOHN. *Essay Concerning Human Understanding.* London: Oxford University Press, 1924.

MORRIS, CHARLES W. *Six Theories of Mind.* Chicago: University of Chicago Press, 1932.

PLATO. *Timaeus.* New York: Liberal Arts Press, 1954.

RYLE, GILBERT. *The Concept of Mind.* New York: Barnes & Noble, Inc., 1950. Chaps. i, ii, vi, ix.

WEISS, PAUL. *Man's Freedom.* New Haven: Yale University Press, 1950.

WHITEHEAD, A. N. *Adventures of Ideas.* New York: The Macmillan Co., 1933. Chaps. viii, ix, x.

CHAPTER 5

Individual Decision

THE MORAL SITUATION

In passing from the world of nature to the world of human experience, the philosopher is forced of necessity to shift his ground. When we reflect upon matter and life, there is a certain distance, a certain objectivity in our point of view. And even when we reflect upon the nature of mind and its place in the cosmos, although we are considering a human attribute, we are still forced to assume a certain humility. The universe is large; the human animal occupies but a fraction of its space, and this causes us to think of the human position with a certain detachment. Thus, in philosophizing about nature, the philosopher (even though he is no scientist and although philosophy is not scientific) to a large extent assumes the scientific attitude. He reflects upon nature more as a bystander than as a participant. He looks upon his place in nature more as a neutral than as a partisan.

But in philosophizing about specifically human experience, the case is different. Whether we are pondering the nature of individual decision, the problems of social living, the characteristics of the arts, or the "laws" of history, the human individual and the things he does and the things he makes are in the center of the picture. Man in this case is not only *the subject* who philosophizes and reflects; he is at the same time *the object* upon which the reflection and the philosophizing takes place. And this situation where man is at once the subject and the object has unusual consequences.

When we speculate and reflect about nature, we do not expect that our speculations will change or transform nature itself. When we observe matter and life, they are not usually changed by our observation. When we "ask questions of nature" it is only in a metaphorical sense that nature can be said to answer us. And, of course, no book about plants and animals can be read by plants and animals with indignation or delight.

But when we speculate and reflect upon human experience, we speak our thoughts or write them in words, and our language is heard or read by others who nod or frown and answer back and whose actions may even be *changed* by the words which are spoken or written. To philosophize about human experience may change human experience. What we believe about individual decision may affect our own individual decisions. Our philosophy of social living may determine our social life. Our theory of the arts may control our response to the arts. Our reading of the course of history may contribute to the making of future history.

The philosophizing which concerns human experience is thus concrete and practical in a very special sense. And it also has another characteristic; it is unashamedly centered in those things which human beings seek and prize—the things which the philosopher calls *values*. There are several theories about what values are. Some philosophers insist that values are qualities of things. They say that the beauty lies in the sunset, that the goodness lies in the act of human generosity. These values are there and we simply discover them. Others believe that values exist only in the perceiving mind, in the eye that sees and the mind that judges the sunset beautiful, or in the moral sense which ascribes goodness and generosity to the act of sharing. To these philosophers, values are as much created by men as discovered by them. And there is still a third view of value which sees it as neither thing nor mental product, but a relation between the two, a cooperation between the knowing mind and the nature of things.

Nor is there agreement as to the definition of what *value* means. Some say that a value is anything agreeable in our experience. Others say that it is what satisfies our desires. Still others say it is anything which arouses our interest. And another school says it is the worth of objects, the quality of things which makes them worthy of existing by themselves. But however they differ in detail, all schools seem to agree on one central point, *values are the things for which we strive and they are central in human experience.* Therefore, philosophizing about human experience is inherently philosophizing about values, and this includes the values expressed in history, the values of the arts, the values of social living, and the moral values which are to be found in our acts of individual decision.

The *moral situation* is perhaps that which defines the characteristic of human individuals. Bits of matter move in space. Living things do more; they interact with their environment. But only human persons exist in a situation where they *are faced with choices,* where, to the many possible alternatives, they must respond with an act of will, where they are called upon *to make a decision.* The human body, like other material objects, moves in space. The human animal, like other animals, reacts to its natural environment. But any account which reduces human behavior to merely physical action or organic interaction leaves out that which is distinctively human, a preoccupation with the problems of moral choice. Human persons are perpetually deciding between alternatives which they call good and bad, right and wrong, admirable and unjust. And they also constantly express reflective judgments upon the morality of their own conduct and that of their fellows. How are these judgments arrived at? What do they mean? And how in turn do these estimates of right and wrong influence the moral decisions of the individual? Perhaps the best approach to these questions is to attempt to understand what is involved in a *moral situation.*

The elements of physical movement are matter, space, and force; and so we say that the formal relation between these elements is the structure of motion. The elements of animal behavior are the needs of the organism and the nature of its environment, and we say that the formal relation between these is the structure of animal behavior. Is it similarly possible to distinguish the elements, and so to describe the structure, of the situation of moral choice?

There are three elements which enter into every case of individual decision and therefore into every situation of moral choice: (1) the individual self which must make the choice; (2) the social situation (the society within which he lives and the the moral tradition of the group which makes a claim upon him); and (3) the standards of value which lie back of society's demands and which spring from the character of the individual, and to which, therefore, the individual ultimately appeals when he chooses. *Selves, social environment, standards of value* are the elements of every moral situation.

When we speak about individual selves, we refer on the one hand to *centers of decision* and on the other to *moral organisms which have achieved a certain stage of growth.* The self (for all of its possibility of spontaneous and original action) is also a collection of habits and previous experiences, and these give it its nature. The abiding elements of the self (although even these are not mechanically fixed and may change) are precisely what we call the *character* of the individual. And this is one of the determinants of moral choice.

No individual decision is made in a social vacuum. We live our lives in the presence of our families, our neighbors, our countrymen (perhaps even our international neighbors), and our choices are bound to be affected by their natures, their needs, and their approval and disapproval. They contribute, not only most of the occasions for our moral deliberation, but even the standards which we recognize to be relevant to the act of moral choice.

Standards of value are that to which we appeal when we try to justify our decisions, and this may be before our decisions have actually been made and when we are still in the process of deliberation, or after they have been made and we try to explain them to ourselves or others. A cause of a belief is whatever is responsible for the belief. A reason for a belief is the evidence that the belief is true. A reason for an act is the evidence that the act is right, its conformity with a right standard of value. Standards of value are not always the *causes* of moral behavior, but they are inevitably the *reason* for such behavior.

To distinguish the elements of the moral situation as individual selves, social contexts, and standards of value is only the first step. For the structure of any moral situation is complicated and requires that we relate these elements to one another and add others which grow out of them. Perhaps the best way to relate these elements and, at the same time, reduce the complication as much as possible is to consider the following statements, which we may call *the six postulates of moral experience.*

1. *Moral conduct is voluntary.* Our moral choices are the consequence of our individual decisions. And this means that we may be held responsible for our acts. Involuntary behavior (where the causes of acts are external to the doer of the acts) may be compulsory or ignorant and then can neither be the object of moral judgment nor worthy of being called moral conduct. Morality presupposes freedom and self-determination.

2. *Persons have motives.* This does not mean that there are simply causes for their acts, like desires or preferences. Desires and preferences are natural facts. But the motives of persons which we judge morally good or bad are *their intentions.* We sometimes find that two individuals have performed the same act (say, giving money to charity), but one with a good, the other with an ignoble motive. In judging intentions we bring in considerations like "good character" and a righteous will.

3. *Acts are performed by selves which endure.* This postulate is only an elaboration of the first element in the moral situation. It repeats the insistence that the moral person is the

acting subject of moral behavior, but adds that selves have a certain permanence and that moral acts are not free-floating occurrences, but products of selves.

4. *Acts have consequences.* This is perhaps the most obvious of the postulates. Moral acts make a difference in the state of affairs. The world is different after a moral act—different in feeling, attitude, quality. Acts affect the state of those who perform them and of others who are affected by them. Moral acts have consequences in pleasure and pain, happiness and unhappiness, approval and disapproval.

5. *Deliberation is relevant.* As Aristotle pointed out (see the first selection at end of this chapter), we make purposive choices and these choices are confined to the things which lie within our power, they are not guided by passion, and they demand deliberation. Of course, he added, we do not deliberate about ultimate ends, but about what means are best adapted to bring about the ends we have in view. Still, we weigh alternatives and consider carefully (sometimes even painfully) according to the gravity of the problem which we face. Thus, there is some sort of calculation (or, as Bentham called it, "moral arithmetic") which enters into our final serious choices.

6. *Conduct can be reasonable.* This is closely related to the previous postulate. There is one theory which holds that all our acts are the product of passion, desire, or unconscious motivation and that reason is only a mask which the self wears to hide the real arbitrariness and irrationality of its acts. But, for moral experience to have meaning, one must assume that there can be *a good reason for an act,* and that such good reasons *may* have the power of ethical persuasion. This is not to say that conduct always is reasonable, merely that there exists the possibility that it may be so.

The postulates of moral experience are hardly capable of demonstration. We appeal to them as we do to principles of logic, as those ideas which are to be presupposed if the human reasoning process is to make sense. Unless conduct is voluntary, persons have motives and acts are performed by selves and have consequences; unless deliberation is relevant and conduct can be reasonable, our experiences of moral indignation and moral approbation simply do not make sense.

THE NECESSITY FOR MORAL JUDGMENTS

Persons act and their acts have moral consequences. Prior to acting they deliberate about the moral quality of the alternatives before them and about the probable consequences which these alternatives may have. And this situation terminates with a moral judgment. The moral situation begins with a problem of choosing between competing alternatives. It ends (at least in its first phase) when the individual acts decisively. But between the presentation of the moral problem (What ought I to do?) and the decisive act, comes the period of deliberation. And the period of deliberation ends with the formulation of a moral judgment (I ought to do X).

Of course, moral judgments are made at other times too. Long after we have committed an act we may retrospectively consider it and say: "That act was wrong; it surely has had unfortunate consequences." Or we may say of someone we know: "He is basically a good man." Whenever such terms as right and wrong or good and bad enter into discussion, we are probably in the presence of moral discourse and a moral judgment. There is a difference in the way we use these two pairs of terms. Right and wrong always refer to *the moral quality of acts*. On the other hand, good and bad refer either to *the consequences of acts* or to *the persons who act, their characters, motives, intentions*. But although whenever these terms appear, morality is implied, one ought to distinguish between *the primary moral judgment* made by a self during the process of deliberation, and the secondary moral judgments made later by the same self or by others after the decision has been made. For, between the moral judgment of the participant and the moral judgment of the spectator there is a most important situational difference.

Primary moral judgments are the important ones and, therefore, before turning to the question of the specific interpretation of any moral judgment whatsoever, a word should be said about primary moral judgments in the process of deliberation. One of the elements of the moral situation previously mentioned was the society within which one lives and the moral tradition of the groups to which the individual belongs. Such tradition always performs an important function for the individual; it provides him with a system of customary morality upon which he may depend. Ordinarily we follow almost automatically the rules of conduct and the maxims of prudence of our parents, our coreligionists, and our countrymen. The individual's standards of honesty, sexual morality, and social behavior are the product of parental training, religious instruction, public education. And it is fortunate that it is so. No individual could produce a total system of conduct, nor would he have time to deliberate about every choice with which he was ever faced. But there are times when the clarity of the prescriptions of custom become obscured, or moments when we become aware that authorities conflict. The standards of rigid honesty demanded by religion come into conflict with the more easygoing and opportunistic morality of business. We have duties to revere and support our parents which become incompatible with our duties to honor and protect our nation. In these cases (as well as the other grave and momentous crises of our life) custom and authority break down and we are forced to be reflective and self-dependent about our moral activity.

What exactly is the nature of a moral judgment? In the last twenty years philosophers in England and the United States have become more and more perplexed about this question. And the factor most responsible for this new concern is the slow recognition that the language of moral discourse is highly ambiguous, and not nearly so simple as previously believed. And the heart of the matter seems to be that we have for a long time been deceived by *the only apparent similarity* between factual statements and moral judgments. Consider the following statements: (1) "Tables are generally flat" and (2) "Lying is generally wrong." They look much alike. Each is properly qualified. And each asserts a particular quality of a kind of object or a kind of act. But what of the apparent similarity of the two qualities? Is "wrongness" the same kind of thing as "flatness"? Can we prove the two statements in the same way? Is the "wrongness" of acts of lying as observable and demonstrable as the "flatness" of different tables? How exactly do we observe the "wrongness" of a lie? The extreme difficulty of answering these questions seems (at least to some moralists) to prove that the two statements are not alike at all, and that we are deceived if we think them so. What then does the statement "Lying is generally wrong" really say?

In the first place (insist these new critics of moral discourse), it says nothing factual, nothing publicly verifiable, nothing which could be judged to be either true or false. It is more like an exclamation of delight or disgust which tells us little about the world, but a great deal about the attitude or feelings of the person who exclaims. Moral judgments are then first an expression of moral *sentiments* or *emotions,* and the statement "Lying is generally wrong" really means "In general, I feel opposed, disapproving, even outraged about lying."

But there is another aspect as well. For when I say frankly, "I feel quite disapproving about lying," I not only want to express my disapproval, but I want it to have a practical effect on the conduct of others. I want them to disapprove too and I want them (as myself) not to lie. So there is always an imperative aspect to my statement. It expresses how I feel, but it also indicates how I want others to act. Implicitly it orders them to act in a certain fashion. The complete meaning of "Lying is generally wrong" is then "I feel generally disapproving about lying and I want you to feel that way too so that you will not lie." Such a statement is expressive and practical, but it is not scientific. Exclamations and commands are not forms of language which are capable of verification.

This account of moral judgment has much to recommend it. By pointing to the emotional and imperative elements in "statements" about conduct, it serves to bring down to earth the boundless hopes of the nineteenth century that ethics could be made a science like physics or biology or psychology. But it has serious weaknesses too. It works best when we think of moral judgments publicly uttered, of moral disagreements, and of the attempts to influence others in argument. It is less plausible when we consider it from the point of view of the moral situation, of the solitary individual in his private act of moral deliberation trying desperately to decide for himself which alternative before him is right. Here the issues of public persuasion and self-expression fade away, and we are left with the burden of real calculation.

It was Aristotle who first pointed out that, when we deliberate about practical matters lying within our power, we deliberate not about ends but about means. A physician does not ask himself if he wishes to heal his patient. He assumes this end and only deliberates about the best means to bring this about. A businessman does not deliberate about whether he ought to make money; he takes this end as given, and only calculates concerning the way in which this can best be done. In morals too, Aristotle argues, we propose or accept an end or supreme value and then only deliberate about means for its achievement. This casts a new light on moral judgments, for it suggests, not that they are expressions of emotion or imperatives, but that they refer to some ultimate moral value. We call persons good or bad and we call acts right or wrong, not merely because we do or do not feel emotionally well disposed toward them, but rather *according to whether they do or do not conform to some ultimate moral standard.* This, of course, only pushes the problem back one step further. What is the nature of that ultimate moral standard in terms of which all our judgments of the goodness and badness of persons and the rightness and wrongness of acts are to be made?

The Appeal to Moral Standards

It is at this point that we return to the great classical tradition of moral philosophy. For, the chief historical differences between moralists have always been apropos of the nature of the ultimate moral standard. And yet it is both surprising and interesting that there have been but three theories which between them divide the allegiance of practically all moral philosophers. One of these is the theory that acts are right in proportion as they increase the quantity of happiness or pleasurable feeling in the world. Another is the theory that acts are right when they are motivated by the belief that we should rigidly do our duty. And the third is the theory that conduct is right when it promotes the growth and development of an admirable self.

Is there any reason why just these three should be the great traditions of moral theory? In a sense there is. Let us remember that in explaining the structure of the moral situation we appealed to what we called the six postulates of moral experience, to those presuppositions which are to be taken for granted if moral experience is to make sense. And among them appear these three; *Acts have consequences, Persons have motives, Acts are performed by selves which endure.* Now, each of the three great traditions of moral theory seizes upon one of the factors of the moral situation as its great truth. Each takes one feature of the elephant to be the elephant itself. *Hedonism* and *utilitarianism* (the first theory) are based upon the supreme importance of the fact that acts have consequences of pain and pleasure. *Kantianism* or *formalism* (the second theory) is based upon the supreme importance of the fact that persons have motives and that they may be good or bad. *Self-realization* (the third theory) is based upon the supreme importance of the fact that acts are performed by selves which endure and upon the necessity for these selves to grow and develop morally. Let us consider each of these theories in slightly greater detail.

The theory which says that acts are right in proportion as they increase the quantity of happiness or pleasurable feeling in the world has two versions and two great exponents in the modern world; the *hedonism* of Jeremy Bentham in the eighteenth century, and the *utilitarianism* of John Stuart Mill in the nineteenth.

It was Bentham's belief that all mankind was under the power of two great feelings, pleasure and pain, and that in these feelings are to be found both the motives from which we act and the reasons why any act is right or wrong. A right act is that one among all the alternatives which will produce the greatest sum total of pleasurable feeling for mankind. Any alternative to this act is a wrong act. And when we think of pleasure as a quantity, we must see that, like physical volume, it has dimensions. Pleasure has intensity, duration, certainty, and propinquity, and when we try to estimate a sum of future pleasure, we must ask: How intense will it be? How long will it last? How certain is it to be felt? How remote is it? Moral deliberation is then for Bentham a process of calculating future pleasures and choosing the course of action which will produce the greatest quantity. This all sounds simple enough. But there is one difficulty. It is the problem of motive. Bentham asks that we choose the act which will produce the greatest total of pleasure for all mankind. That requires altruism. But on the other hand are we not all incurably selfish? We all want pleasure, but for ourselves. What is to guarantee that in our choices of alternative acts we will not choose our own lesser pleasure rather than the greater pleasure of the rest of mankind? Bentham sensed this problem and he had an answer for it. Psychologically each one does seek his own individual happiness. Morally the ultimate end is the greatest good for the greatest number. But it is just here that the legislator or lawmaker for society comes in. Selfish persons are induced to act morally by a system of "sanctions," that is, by legal rewards and punishments. It is precisely by the coercive force of public law that a coincidence of interest between the individual and society is secured.

The second version of the theory that pleasure is the standard of morality is the utilitarianism of John Stuart Mill (see selection on page 255). Mill differs from Bentham in three important respects. In the first place whereas Bentham asserted that the psylogical motivation of men is absolute egoism, Mill includes altruism also. For, since man conceives of himself as a member of a social whole, he has certain natural social feelings. In the second place, whereas for Bentham pleasures differ from one another only quantitatively (that is, in intensity and duration), for Mill there are differences of quality as well. And finally, while the whole temper of Bentham's moral theory is abstract, consistent, and uncompromising, Mill's doctrines are more concrete, but less internally consistent because of the concessions which he makes to both an ethics of conscience and an ethics of self-realization.

Mill agrees with Bentham that our acts are right as they tend to promote happiness and wrong as they tend to promote the reverse, but he sees that, although pleasure and pain are the only things desirable as ends, some kinds of pleasure are more desirable and more valuable than others. These are the pleasures of the higher faculties of men; not the pleasures of food and drink and bodily comfort (which Mill calls the pleasures of a satisfied pig), but the pleasures of knowledge, of beautiful objects, and of human companionship. If one asks however what is the proof that the so-called "higher" pleasures are more valuable than the so-called "lower," Mill falls back on an old argument which he has borrowed from Plato. The only proof lies in the preference of those who have had experience of both, and that, he thinks, always favors the pleasures of man's higher faculties.

Mill's treatment of the problem of selfishness also exhibits a certain idealism. The multiplication of happiness is of course the aim of life. But in choosing between one's own and another's we are required to be as impartial as a benevolent spectator. Or better, we are to follow the morality of Jesus which bids us hold to the happiness of our neighbor as to our own. And this can best be encouraged, not, as Bentham would have advocated, by the imposition of legal penalties for completely selfish (and hence antisocial) conduct, but through education and public opinion which should establish in the mind of each individual a close association between his own happiness and the happiness of the entire society of which he is a part. For only this would make the impulse to promote the public good one of the habitual motives of individual action. Nor is this use of education artificial or strained. It has a firm foundation upon which to build, a powerful principle in human nature—the social feelings of mankind.

The theory that acts are right when they are performed out of the motive of strict attention to duty is the theory of the great eighteenth-century German philosopher Immanuel Kant. Kant is well aware of both of the postulates of moral experience—that *acts have consequences* and that *persons have motives*. Unlike Bentham and Mill, however, he would have said that the consequences of acts in terms of pleasure and pain are of no *moral* importance. The moral characteristics of human acts are to be found in the motives from which they are done. And the only thing which makes an act right is the fact that it is done from a good will, that is, that our motive in performing it is a recognition of and respect for what our duty is.

The clue to the Kantian system of morality is the word *duty*. It is therefore somewhat stern and uncompromising in its description of what is morally right. We are all well aware of the great dilemma with which we are faced in many of our moral choices: to benefit ourselves or others; to do what we want to do or to do what we know we really ought to do; to follow what reason tells us is our duty or to follow what our desires cry out for. The heart of temptation is the conflict between duty and inclination, and it is Kant's contention that, for an act to be a moral act, it must be done from the motive of duty. This is indeed rigorous, for it says that even where we choose consequences which deny ourselves and are for the happiness and welfare of others, our act does not possess rightness for this reason. It is only if we act out of respect for what we recognize as the moral law that our act is right.

But what is this moral law and where does it come from? In the first place the moral law is a dictate of our reason. It does not come from society, although the laws of society may try to define our civic duties from the outside, nor does Kant say that it comes from God. It comes from pure reason, from our possession of reason (and it is in this sense that what we call our conscience is simply our *practical reason*), from within our own nature. This is what Kant means by saying that we are *autonomous,* that the moral law is that which a man imposes upon himself.

Can the moral law be stated more concretely? Yes, says Kant; at least there are two ways of stating it which each bring out a particular one of its requirements. The moral law is expressed by the words "You ought," and it is a command which reason gives to the will of man. Above all, it is a command beyond which there is no appeal. Kant calls the moral law the *categorical imperative;* this is only another name for *the absolute must.*

The first way of expressing the moral law is this: *Act always in such a fashion that you could at the same time will that it should be a universal law of conduct.* When you choose for yourself, pretend that you are choosing for everybody. Put anybody in your own place, and if you can say, "Yes, this act would be universally right," then the chances are it is your duty. This way of expressing the moral law points to one of the most general sources of immorality —our tendency toward self-indulgence, to make exceptions in our own favor. It is very human to say: "Yes, I know that lying is wrong, but this little one which I can tell to escape the blame, it will really hurt no one. Of course I am not in favor of lying, but this little one, just this once. Where is the harm in that?" But Kant takes us up sternly; "Do you really mean that it is universally permissible to tell lies whenever it will help us? Are you advocating that lying for convenience be made a universal maxim of moral conduct?" And at this point the untenability of the behavior becomes self-evident.

The second way of expressing the moral law is this: *Always act so as to treat humanity whether in the case of yourself or anyone else always as an end and never as merely a means.* This second statement is the Kantian way of calling attention to the dignity and worth of human persons. It both calls upon us not to degrade ourselves nor exploit our fellows in a fashion inconsistent with their humanity, and it is based on the same kind of reasoning which underlies Kant's entire moral system. Personality is to be respected not because it can feel pleasure and pain, nor even because it is the creation of God. It is to be respected because it is rational, because it possesses free will, and because it shares a common moral nature.

The theory that acts are right when they promote the growth and development of an admirable self is the legacy which Greece bequeathed to the modern world. This doctrine has been enriched by Christian teaching, and it appears in modern philosophy in the writings of the great British idealists of the nineteenth century, T. H. Green, Bernard Bosanquet, and F. H. Bradley (see selection on page 278), but its great propounders are Plato and Aristotle.

Plato it is who, in the *Republic*, first states clearly the Greek ideal of the moral life. Everything in the world has its proper function, and when this function is well performed we say of the thing that it has an excellence which is its proper virtue. The function of a knife is to cut, its excellence is its cutting well, and its sharpness is its proper virtue. Can the same be true of the human self or "soul"? Yes, says Plato, the self too has its proper function; when it functions well it is excellent, and justice is its proper virtue.

For Plato the self is a threefold organism. One of its parts is appetite or desire. Another is emotion or feeling. The third and highest is reason, the ruling aspect of personality. The self is healthy and realizes the best which is in it when reason is the guide of life, and when it allots the proper place to desire and emotion. Reason gives each claim of desire or emotion its judicial consideration and harmonizes demands which, should they get beyond reason's control, would produce a discordant and inharmonious self.

Aristotle too sees the good for man as the harmony recognized by Plato. But to this he adds his famous insight that virtue consists in being moderate, in always acting somewhere between imprudent extremes. To be courageous is to be something between cowardly on the one hand and foolhardy on the other. To be friendly is to be something between obsequious on the one hand and surly on the other. To be moderate in expenditure is to be something between stingy on the one hand and extravagant on the other.

The Greek view of life both stresses the importance of reason as the distinctive human characteristic and sees in reason's functioning the impulse to harmony and proportion. Aristotle's principle of the golden mean in conduct reminds one irresistibly of the principle of proportionality in the work of art. And it is true that the Greek view of the self sometimes suggests that it too is a work of art, good in its justice, beautiful in its harmony, the noblest object which it is in the power of man himself to make. Naturally, in the work of art, one judges the part according as it functions in and contributes to the whole. Naturally also in morality, one judges the individual moral act as it reflects and contributes to the complete and enduring moral self. This is the chief insight of the moral standard of self-realization.

We have now examined briefly the three moral standards which traditional ethics has put forward for the judgment of the rightness or wrongness of acts; the standard of pleasure or pain in consequences, the standard of duty as motive, and the standard of the relation to the perfecting of the human self. Are these really mutually exclusive alternatives? Certainly their partisans seem to think so. In the selections from Kant, Mill, and Bradley at the end of this chapter, you will find some evidence for this belief. You will find Kant criticizing the theory that pleasurable consequences make an act good. You will find Mill denying that the motive of an agent has anything to do with the morality of an action. And you will find Bradley in turn arguing that the claim of pleasure to be the ultimate end is in direct conflict with our moral consciousness.

But even if utilitarianism, Kantianism, and self-realization cannot all be true to the extent of the extreme claims which each makes to be the *sole moral standard*, it may be that, more modestly conceived, each one presents a truth of the valuational consciousness which a moralist dare neglect only at his peril.

Behind the morality of utilitarianism lies a stubborn insight which we might call the principle of quantity. It says *values ought always to be maximized*. Behind the morality of Kant lies an equally stubborn insight which we might call the principle of universality. It says *values ought always to be judged according to universal considerations*. Behind the morality of self-realization lies another stubborn insight which we might call the principle of harmony. It says *values ought to be harmonized so as to include as many diverse goods as possible*. We have already presented what we have called the six postulates of moral experience. Perhaps these three which we have just mentioned—the principle of quantity, the principle of universality, and the principle of harmony—could be called the three axioms of moral value.

THE SEARCH FOR MORAL WISDOM

Of course, to speak of "axioms" and "postulates" of the moral life is misleading. For it suggests the comparison with Euclid's geometry which is exact, scientific, demonstrative. Moral philosophy by its very nature can never in the same sense be either exact or scientific. The propositions, "Water boils at 212° F.," or "If two straight lines intersect, the opposite angles are equal," are scientific, not merely because they gain universal assent, but because that assent is itself based upon demonstration or experiment publicly verifiable. But the proposition, "An act is morally right if and only if it is performed out of respect for the moral law," has not gained universal assent nor does it appear that there is any way to prove it. And it is the fact of moral disagreement which has in part thrown moral philosophy into disrepute and indicated its unscientific character.

But an important question remains. Even if moral philosophy is truly unscientific, does that outlaw its usefulness? And the answer to this question is, I am persuaded, "no." And, to think that it might be "yes," is not to understand the double aspect of the impulse which leads the moral philosopher to his vocation. One may write a moral treatise in the fashion of Newton's *Optics* or Darwin's *Origin of Species*—to contemplate and understand a certain type of experience and to explore it systematically in scientific terms. On the other hand a moral treatise may be written as the responsible assertion of a human ideal; as a personally grounded communication of the wisdom of life. Ethics may be written from the outside or from the inside—from the point of view of neutral spectator or of active participant. Ethics can therefore tend either toward neutral description or moral revelation.

Whether ethics is scientific or not, it will always express the search for moral wisdom. In some sense a moral philosopher always tries to state the insights derivable from his own moral experience. And others will be interested in it for this reason. Plato's *Republic* begins when the middle-aged Socrates meets again his acquaintance, the very old Cephalus, and asks him about the condition of old age. "For," says Socrates, "I enjoy talking with the very old. We have to learn of them as from travellers who have preceded us on a road in which we too must one day travel." So also must we learn from the sages of the moral life, and when we read Aristotle and

Kant, Schopenhauer or Spinoza, it is as much to share their insights as to admire their "facts." Aristotle has given us in his *Nicomachean Ethics* almost scientific accounts of justice, pleasure, and moral responsibility. But he has also shown in some detail the virtues of moderate activity, the wisdom of "nothing to excess." Kant has provided a carefully systematized picture of the function of reason in morality, but he will probably be remembered best for his earnest (because it grew out of deep personal conviction) insistence that always and under every circumstance we must do our duty. Spinoza's *Ethics* is cast in the forbidding form of a geometrical demonstration, but between the lines can be discerned the gentle patience of a man who counsels resignation in the face of nature's unalterable laws. The ages have demonstrated that there are certain paths of life, certain permanent possibilities of moral experience, which each age repeats in its own fashion. The pessimistic wisdom of Stoic ethics which says: Adapt the self to the world; want what you get, renounce what is beyond your powers, and the optimistic wisdom of a dynamic ethics which says: Adapt the world to yourself, get what you want, strive even beyond your powers, are each reformulated in every epoch. The analytical and factual consideration of the moral situation and the problems of individual decision properly end, not in intellectual play, but in a communication of the wisdom of life.

The selections "Moral Responsibility" by Aristotle, "The Principle of Utility" by John Stuart Mill, "The Nature of Duty" by Immanuel Kant, "Why Should I Be Moral?" by F. H. Bradley, and "The True and Final Good" by Spinoza are all concerned with the conditions or consequences of individual decision. They cover a period of twenty-two centuries of moral speculation. The selection from Aristotle has been included because, despite its antiquity, it defines the moral situation. The selections from Mill, Kant, and Bradley are each appeals to a different moral standard, and hence represent the three great traditions of moral theory. The brief selection from Spinoza has been included, less for its systematic quality, than because its candor and simplicity show one of the possible outcomes of the search for moral wisdom.

• Aristotle (384–322 B.C.)

Moral Responsibility [1]

Aristotle, who died three hundred years before the birth of Christ, is, together with Plato, one of the greatest philosophers of the ancient world. Scientifically minded and a great biologist, he wrote on almost every philosophical subject and gave to the western world a formulation for its basic problems which live even today. He is the founder of logic and a psychologist, physicist, metaphysician, moralist, and literary critic into the bargain. The following selection, taken from his *Nicomachean Ethics*, treats of the conditions of moral action, distinguishes between voluntary and involuntary conduct, and in general describes the nature of moral purpose, deliberation, and moral choice.

As virtue is concerned with emotions and actions, and such emotions and actions as are voluntary are the subjects of praise and blame, while such as are involuntary are the subjects of pardon and sometimes even of pity, it is necessary, I think, in an investigation of virtue to distinguish what is voluntary from what is involuntary. It will also be useful in legislation as bearing upon the honours and punishments which the legislator assigns.

It is generally admitted that acts done under compulsion, or from ignorance, are involuntary. But an act is compulsory, if its origin is external to the agent or patient, i.e., if it is one in which the agent or the patient contributes nothing, as e.g. if the wind, or people who have us in their power, were to carry us in a certain direction. But if an action is done from fear of greater evils or for some noble end, e.g. if a tyrant, who had our parents and children in his power, were to order us to do some shameful act, on condition that, if we did it, their lives should be spared, and, if not, they should be put to death, it is a question whether such action is voluntary or involuntary. The case of throwing goods overboard during a storm at sea is similar; for although nobody would volun-

[1] From Aristotle, *Nicomachean Ethics,* trans. J. E. C. Welldon (1892), Bk. III, chaps. i-viii.

tarily make such a sacrifice in the abstract, yet every sensible person will make it for his own safety and the safety of his fellow passengers. Actions like this, although they are of a mixed character, are more like voluntary than involuntary actions, as they are chosen at the time of performing them, and the end or character of an action depends upon the choice made at the moment of performing it. When we speak then of an action as voluntary or involuntary, we must have regard to the time at which a person peforms it. The person whose actions we are considering acts voluntarily; for in actions like his the original power which sets the instrumentality of his limbs in motion lies in himself, and when the origin of a thing lies in a person himself, it is in his power either to do it or not to do it. Such actions then are practically voluntary, although in the abstract they may be said perhaps to be involuntary, as nobody would choose any such action in itself.

Such actions are at times subjects of praise, when people submit to something that is shameful or painful for the sake of gaining what is great and noble; or in the contrary case they are the subjects of censure, as it is only a bad man who would submit to what is utterly shameful, if his object were not noble at all, or were indifferent. There are also some actions which are pardonable, although not laudable, as when a person is induced to do what is wrong by such causes as are too strong for human nature and do not admit of resistance. Yet it is probable that there are some actions where compulsion is an impossibility; a person would rather suffer the most dreadful form of death than do them. Thus the reasons which constrained Alcmaeon in Euripides to murder his mother are clearly ridiculous.

It is sometimes difficult to determine what ought to be chosen or endured for the sake of obtaining or avoiding a certain result. But it is still more difficult to abide by our decisions; for it generally happens that, while the consequence which we expect is painful, the act which we are constrained to do is shameful, and therefore we receive censure or praise according as we yield or do not yield to the constraint.

What class of actions then is it that may be rightly called compulsory? Actions it may be said are compulsory in the abstract, whenever the cause is external to the agent and he contributes nothing to it. But if an action, although involuntary in itself, is chosen at a particular time and for a particular end, and if its original cause lies in the agent himself, then, although such an action is involuntary in itself, it is voluntary at that time and for that end. Such an action however is more like a voluntary than an involuntary action; for actions fall under the category of particulars, and in the supposed case the particular action is voluntary.

It is not easy to state what kind of actions are to be chosen for certain ends, as particular cases admit of many differences. It might be argued that whatever is pleasant or noble is compulsory, as pleasure and nobleness are external to ourselves and exercise a constraint upon us; but if that were so, every action would be compulsory, as these are the motives of all actions in us all. Again, if a person acts under compulsion and involuntarily, his action is painful to him; but if the motives of his action are pleasure and nobleness, it is pleasant. It is ridiculous to lay the blame of our wrong actions upon external causes, rather than upon the facility with which we ourselves are caught by such causes, and, while we take the credit of our noble actions to ourselves, to lay the blame of our shameful actions upon pleasure. It seems then that an action is compulsory if its origin is external to the agent, i.e. if the person who is the subject of compulsion is in no sense contributory to the action.

An action which is due to ignorance is always non-voluntary; but it is not involuntary, unless it is followed by pain and excites a feeling of regret. For if a person has performed an action, whatever it may be, from ignorance, and yet feels no distress at his action, it is true that he has not acted voluntarily, as he was not aware of what he was doing, but on the other hand, he has not acted involuntarily, so long as he feels no pain.

If a person who has acted from ignorance regrets what he has done, it may be said that he is an involuntary agent; but, if he does not regret it, his case is different, and he may be called a non-voluntary agent, for, as there is this difference, it is better that he should have a special name.

It would seem, too, that there is a difference between acting from ignorance and doing a thing in ignorance. Thus, if a person is intoxicated or infuriated, he is not regarded as acting from ignorance, but as acting from intoxication or fury; yet he does not act consciously but in ignorance.

It must be admitted then that every vicious person is ignorant of what he ought to do, and what he ought to abstain from doing, and that ignorance is the error which makes people unjust and generally wicked. But when we speak of an action as involuntary, we do not mean merely that a person is ignorant of his true interest. The ignorance which is the cause of involuntary action, as distinguished from that which is the cause of vice, is not such ignorance as affects the moral purpose, nor again is it ignorance of the universal; for this is censurable. It is rather ignorance of particulars, i.e. ignorance of the particular circumstances and occasion of the action. Where this ignorance exists, there is room for pity and forgiveness, as one who is ignorant of any such particular is an involuntary agent.

It will perhaps be as well then to define the nature and number of these particular. They are

1. the agent,
2. the act,
3. the occasion or circumstances of the act.

Sometimes also

4. the instrument, e.g. a tool,
5. the object, e.g. safety, and
6. the manner of doing an act, e.g. gently or violently.

Nobody but a madman can be ignorant of all these particulars. It is clear that nobody can be ignorant of the agent; for how can a person be ignorant of himself? But a person may be ignorant of what he is doing, as when people say that a word escaped them unawares or that they did not know a subject was forbidden, like Aeschylus when he revealed the mysteries, or that he only meant to show the working of a weapon when he discharged it, like the man who discharged the catapult. Again, a person may take his son for an enemy like Merope, or a pointed foil for a foil that has its button on, or a solid stone for a pumice stone, or he may kill somebody by a blow that was meant to save him, or he may deal a fatal blow while only intending, as in a sparring match, to give a lesson in the art of dealing a blow. As there may be ignorance in regard to all these particular circumstances of an action, it may be said that a person has acted involuntarily, if he was ignorant of any one of them, and especially of such particulars as seem to be most important, i.e. of the circumstances of the action, and of its natural result. But if an action is to be called involuntary in respect of such ignorance, it is necessary that it should be painful to the agent and should excite in him a feeling of regret.

As an action is involuntary if done under compulsion or from ignorance, it would seem to follow that it is voluntary if the agent originates it with a knowledge of the particular circumstances of the action. For it is perhaps wrong to say that actions which are due to passion or desire are involuntary. For in the first place upon that hypothesis none of the lower animals can any more be said to act involuntarily, nor can children; and secondly is it to be argued that nothing which we do from desire or passion is voluntary? or are our noble actions done voluntarily, and our shameful actions involuntarily? Surely the latter view is ridiculous, if one and the same person is the author of both kinds of action. But it would seem irrational to assert that such things as ought to be the objects of desire are desired involuntarily; and there are certain things which ought to be the occasions of anger, and certain things such as health and learning, which ought to be the objects of desire. Again, it seems that what is involuntary is painful, but what is done from desire is pleasant. Again, what difference is there, in respect of involuntariness, between errors of reason and errors of passion? It is our duty to avoid both; but the irrational emotions seem to be as truly human as the reason itself and therefore we are as truly responsible for our emotions as for our reasoning. Such actions then as proceed from passion and desire are not less the actions of the man than rational actions; it is absurd therefore to regard these as involuntary.

Having thus distinguished voluntary from involuntary action, we naturally proceed to discuss moral purpose. For it would seem that the moral purpose is most closely related to virtue, and is a better criterion of character than actions themselves are.

It is clear that moral purpose is something voluntary. Still moral purpose and volition are not identical; volition is a term of wider range. For while children and the lower animals participate in volition, they do not participate in moral purpose. Also we speak of actions done on the spur of the moment as being voluntary, but not as being done with moral purpose.

It would appear then that the definition of moral purpose as desire, or passion, or wish, or opinion of some sort is a mistake. For moral purpose is not like desire and passion common to irrational creatures as well as to Man. Again, an incontinent person acts from desire but not from moral purpose. On the other hand a continent person acts from moral purpose but not from desire. Again, desire is contrary to moral purpose, but one desire is not contrary to another. Desire, too, is, but moral purpose is not, directed to pleasures and pains. Still less can moral purpose be the same thing as passion; for there are no actions which seem to be so little directed by moral purpose as those which are due to angry passion. Now again is moral purpose the same thing as wish, although it is clear that it is nearly allied to it. For moral purpose does not apply to impossibilities, and anybody who should say that he had a purpose of achieving what is impossible would be thought a fool. But there is such a thing as wishing for the impossible, as e.g. for immortality. Again, while we may wish for things which could not possibly be affected by our own action, as e.g. for the victory of a certain actor or athlete, it can never be said that we purpose such things; we only purpose what may, as we think, be possibly effected by our own action. Again, the wish is directed rather to the end, but the moral purpose to the means. Thus we wish to be in good health, but we purpose or choose the means of being in good health. Or again we wish to be happy and admit the wish; but we cannot appropriately say that we purpose or choose to be happy. For it seems to be a general law that our moral purpose is confined to such things as lie within our own power. Nor again can moral purpose be opinion, for it seems that the sphere of opinion is universal; it embraces things which are eternal or impossible as much as things which lie within our own power. Opinion too, unlike moral purpose, is distinguished by being true or false, not by being good or evil. Perhaps there is nobody who maintains that moral purpose is identical with opinion of a particular kind. For it is according as we purpose or choose what is good or evil, and not according as we hold particular opinions, that we possess a certain character. Again, we choose to accept or avoid a thing and so on, but we opine what a thing is, or for whom or in what way it is beneficial. We do not opine at all to accept or avoid a thing. Again, whereas moral purpose is praised rather as being directed to a proper end than as being correct, opinion is praised as being true. Again, we purpose or choose such things as we best know to be good; but we form an opinion of things of which we have no knowledge. Again, it is apparently not the same people who make the best choice and who form the best opinions. There are some people who form a better opinion than others, but are prevented by vice from making the right choice. It is possible that opinion may precede moral purpose or follow it, but that is not the point; for the question which we are considering is simply this, whether moral purpose is identical with opinion of a particular kind.

What then is the nature and character of moral purpose, since it is none of the things which have been mentioned? It is clearly voluntary, but there are things which are voluntary and yet are not chosen or purposed. It may be said, I think, that a thing is voluntary, if it is the result of previous deliberation, for moral purpose implies reason and thought. The very name (*proairesis*) seems to indicate previous deliberation, as it denotes something chosen in preference to other things.

The quesion is, Do we deliberate upon everything? Is everything a matter for deliberation, or are there some things which are not subjects of deliberation?

We must presumably understand by "a matter of deliberation" not that about which a fool or a madman, but that about which a sensible person, would deliberate.

Nobody deliberates about things which are eternal, i.e. immutable, as e.g. the universe or the incommensurability of the diagonal and the side of a square; or about things which are in motion but always follow the same course, whether of necessity or by nature or for some other cause, as e.g. the solstices and sunrisings; or about things which are wholly irregular like droughts and showers; or about mere matters of chance such as the finding of a treasure. Nor again are all human affairs matters of deliberation; thus no Lacedaemonian will deliberate upon the best constitution for the Scythians. The reason why we do not deliberate about these things is that none of them can be effected by our action. The matters about which we deliberate are practical matters lying within our power. There is in fact no other class of matters left; for it would seem that the causes of things are nature, necessity, chance, and besides these only intelligence, and human agency in its various forms. But different classes of people deliberate about such practical matters as depend upon their several actions. Further, those sciences, which are exact and complete in themselves, do not admit of deliberation, as e.g. writing; for we are in no doubt as to the proper way of writing. But if a thing depends upon our own action and is not invariable, it is a matter of deliberation, as e.g. questions of medicine, of finance, or of navigation rather than of gymnastic, as being less exactly systematized, and similarly all other arts, and again, the arts more than the sciences, as we are more in doubt about them.

Deliberation occurs in cases which fall under a general rule, if it is uncertain what the issue will be, and in cases which do not admit of an absolute decision. We invite the help of other people in our deliberations upon matters of importance, when we distrust our own ability to decide them.

Again, we deliberate not about ends but about the means to ends. Thus a doctor does not deliberate whether he shall cure his patients, nor an orator whether he shall persuade his audience, nor a statesman whether he shall produce law and order, nor does any one else deliberate about his end. They all propose to themselves a certain end and then consider how and by what means it can be attained, and if it appears capable of attainment by several means, they consider what will be the easiest and best means of attaining it, and if there is only one means of attaining it, how it may be attained by this means, and by what means this means itself can be attained, until they come to the first cause, which in the order of discovery is last. For it seems that deliberation is a process of investigation and analysis such as this: it is like the analysis of a geometrical figure. It appears however that, while investigation is not always deliberation, mathematical investigations, e.g. not being so, deliberation is always investigation, and that that which is last in the order of analysis is first in the order of production.

If in a deliberation we come upon an impossibility, we abandon our task, as e.g. if money is required and it is impossible to provide the money; but if it appears to be possible, we set about doing it. By possibilities I mean such things as may be effected by our own actions; for what is done by our friends may be said to be done by ourselves, as the origin of it lies in ourselves. The question is sometimes what instruments are necessary, and at other times how they are to be used. Similarly in all other cases it is sometimes the means of doing a certain thing and at other times the manner or the agency that is in question.

It seems, as has been said, that a man originates his own actions. Deliberation touches such things as may be done by a man himself, and actions are done for the sake of something which lies beyond themselves. Accordingly it is not the end, but the means to the end, that will be matter of deliberation. Nor again will particular questions be matters of deliberation, as e.g. the question whether a particular thing is a loaf or has been properly baked; that is rather a matter of perception, and, if we go on deliberating for ever, we shall never come to an end.

The objects of deliberation and of moral purpose are the same, except that the object of moral purpose is already determined; for it is that which is preferred after deliberation. For everybody gives up inquiring how he shall act when he has traced back the origin of his action to himself and to the dominant part of himself, i.e. to the part which exercises moral choice or purpose. There is an illustration of this principle in the ancient polities which Homer represented, for in them the kings promulgated their purpose, whatever it might be, to the people.

But if the object of our moral purpose is that which, being in our power, is after deliberation the object of our desire, it follows that the moral purpose is a deliberative desire of something which is in our power; for we first deliberate upon a thing and, after passing judgment upon it, we desire it in accordance with our deliberation.

Let us now leave this rough sketch of the moral purpose. We

have shown what are the matters with which it deals, and that it is directed to the means rather than to the ends.

We have said that the wish is directed to the end; but there are some people who hold that the end is the good, and others that it is what appears to be good. If it is said that the object of wish is the good, it follows that where a person's moral purpose or choice is wrong that which he wishes is not in the proper sense an object of wish; for if it is an object of wish it will also be a good, but it was perhaps an evil. If on the other hand, it is said that it is what appears to be good which is the object of wish, it follows that there is no such thing as a natural object of wish, but that it is in every man's case that which seems good to him. But different, and it may be even opposite things, seem good to different people.

If these conclusions are not satisfactory, it will perhaps be best to say that in an absolute or true sense it is the good which is the object of wish, but that in reference to the individual it is that which appears to be good. Hence it is the true good which is good relatively to the virtuous man, and something that need not be defined which is good relatively to the vicious man. The case is much the same as in the body; when people are in a good state of health it is things which are truly wholesome that are wholesome to them, but when they are in a bad state of health it is other things, and so with things that are bitter, sweet, hot, heavy, and the rest. For the virtuous man forms a right judgment of particular cases, and in every case that which is true appears true to him. For every moral state has its own honours and pleasures, nor is there any point perhaps so distinctive of the virtuous man as his power of seeing the truth in all cases, because he is, as it were, the standard and measure of things. It seems to be pleasure which most frequently deceives people, for pleasure appears to be good, although it is not, and the result is that they choose what is pleasant as if it were good, and avoid pain as if it were evil.

As it is the end which is the object of wish, and the means to the end which are the objects of deliberation and moral purpose, it follows that such actions as are concerned with the means will be determined by moral purpose and will be voluntary. But it is with the means that the activities of the virtues are concerned.

Virtue and vice are both alike in our own power; for where it is in our power to act, it is also in our power to refrain from acting, and where it is in our power to refrain from acting, it is also in our power to act. Hence if it is in our power to act when action is noble, it will also be in our power to refrain from acting when inaction is shameful, and if it is in our power to refrain from acting when inaction is noble, it will also be in our power to act when action is shameful. But if it is in our power to do, and likewise not to do, what is noble and shameful, and if so to act or not to act is as we have seen to be good or bad, it follows that it is in our power to be virtuous or vicious. The saying

> None would be wicked, none would not be blessed,

seems to be partly false and partly true; for while nobody is blessed against his will, vice is voluntary.

If this is not the case, it is necessary to dispute the statements which have just been made and to say that a man is not the author or father of his actions in the same sense as he is of his family. But if these statements appear to be true and we cannot refer our actions to any other original sources than such as lie in our own power, then whatever it is that has its sources in us must itself be in our own power and must be voluntary. This view seems to be supported by the testimony both of private individuals and of legislators themselves; for legislators punish and chastise evil-doers, unless the evil be done under compulsion or from ignorance for which its authors are not responsible; but they pay honour to people who perform noble actions, their object being to discourage the one class of actions and to stimulate the others. Yet nobody stimulates us to do such things are are not in our own power or voluntary. It would be useless, e.g., to persuade us not to get hot, or to feel pain or hunger, or anything of the kind, as we should experience these sensations all the same. I say "ignorance for which a person is not responsible," as we punish a person for mere ignorance, if it seems that he is responsible for it. Thus the punishments inflicted on drunken people who commit a crime are double, as the origin of the crime lies in the person himself, for it was in his power not to get drunk, and the drunkenness was the cause of his ignorance.

Again, we punish people who are ignorant of any legal point, if they ought to know it, and could easily know it. Similarly in other cases we punish people, whenever it seems that their ignorance was due to carelessness; for they had it in their power not to be ignorant, as they might have taken the trouble to inform themselves. It will perhaps be argued that a person is of such a character that he cannot take the trouble; but the answer is that people are themselves responsible for having acquired such a character by their dissolute life, and for being unjust or licentious, as their injustice is the consequence of doing wrong, and their licentiousness of spending their time in drinking and other such things. For a person's character depends upon the way in which he exercises his powers. The case of people who practice with a view to any competition or action is a proof of this law; for they are never weary of exercising.

Now a person must be utterly senseless, if he does not know that moral states are formed by the exercise of the powers in one way or another. Again, it is irrational to assert that one who acts licentiously does not wish to be licentious. If a person, not acting in ignorance, commits such actions as will make him unjust, he will be voluntarily unjust. But it does not follow that, if he wishes, he will cease to be unjust and will be just, any more than it follows that a sick man, if he wishes, will be well. It may happen that he is voluntarily ill through living an incontinent life, and disobeying his doctors. If so, it was once in his power not to be ill; but, as he has thrown the opportunity away, it is no longer in his power. Similarly, when a man has thrown a stone, it is no longer possible for him to recall it; still for all that it was in his power to throw or fling it, as the original act was in his power. So too the unjust or licentious person had it in his power in the first instance not to become such, and therefore he is voluntarily unjust or licentious; but when he has become such, it is no longer in his power not to be unjust or licentious.

But not only are the vices of the soul voluntary, the vices of the body are also voluntary in some cases, and in these cases are censured. For while nobody censures people who are born ugly, we censure people whose ugliness arises from negligence and want of exercise. It is the same with bodily infirmities and defects; nobody would find fault with a person who is born blind or whose blindness is the result of illness or of a blow; he would rather be an object of pity; but if his blindness were the result of intemperance or licentiousness of any kind, he would be universally censured.

Such bodily vices then as depend on ourselves are subjects of censure, and such as do not depend on ourselves are not. But if so, it follows that other than bodily vices, if they are objects of censure, must depend on ourselves.

It may be said however that we all aspire after what appears to be good, only we are not masters of the appearance. But the appearance which the end takes in the eyes of each of us depends upon his character. If each of us then is in a certain sense responsible for his moral state, he will be himself in a certain sense responsible for the appearance; but, if not, nobody will be responsible for his own evil doing, everybody will act as he does from ignorance cf the end and under the impression that this will be the means of gaining the supreme good, the aspiration after the true end will not be a matter of our own choice, and it will be necessary for a man to be born with a sort of moral vision, enabling him to form a noble judgment and to choose that which is truly good. He who naturally possesses this noble judgment will be Nature's noble; for he will possess the greatest and noblest of all gifts, the gift which can never be received or learnt from anybody else, but must always be kept as Nature herself gave it, and to possess this natural gift in virtue and honour is to have a perfect and sincere nobility of nature.

If these considerations are true, why should virtue be voluntary rather than vice? For both alike, for the good and for the evil, the end is apparent and ordained by Nature, or in whatever way it may be, and it is to the end that men refer all their actions, however they may act. Whether the end then, whatever it be which any individual regards as the end, does not so appear to him by nature but depends in part on himself, or whether the end is naturally ordained, but virtue is voluntary, as the virtuous man does voluntarily all that he does to gain the end, in either case vice will be voluntary as much as virtue; for the personality of the bad man is as potent an influence as that of the good man in his actions, if not in his conception of the end.

If then, as is generally allowed, the virtues are voluntary (for we are ourselves, in a sense, partly responsible for our moral states, and it is because we possess a certain character that the end which we set before ourselves is of a certain kind), it follows that our vices too must be voluntary, as what is true of one is equally true of the other.

We have now described in outline the nature of the virtues generally. We have shown that they are means between two vices and that they are moral states. We have explained what are the causes producing them and that they naturally issue in the performance of the actions by which they are produced, that they are in our own power and voluntary, and that they are determined by the rule of right reason. But actions and moral states are not voluntary in the same sense. For while we are masters of our actions from beginning to end, inasmuch as we know the particulars, we are masters only of the beginning of our moral states; we do not perceive the particular steps in diseases. But as it was in our power to act in one way or another, our moral states are voluntary.

• John Stuart Mill (1806–73)

The Principle of Utility [2]

John Stuart Mill is perhaps the greatest British philosopher of
the nineteenth century. Strictly educated by his father, James Mill,
to be a philosopher and social reformer, he wrote on logic, political
economy, and moral theory. His essay *Utilitarianism,* from which
the following selection is taken, is an attempt to explain and defend
the doctrine of that name. Mill shows that utilitarianism is a theory
which takes the moral aim to be the maximization of happiness for
society, defends it against the charge that this is a "materialistic"
point of view, and gives it an extremely flexible and idealistic
character.

A passing remark is all that needs be given to the ignorant blunder of supposing that those who stand up for utility as the test of
right and wrong, use the term in that restricted and merely col-
loquial sense in which utility is opposed to pleasure. An apology is
due to the philosophical opponents of utilitarianism, for even the
momentary appearance of confounding them with any one capable
of so absurd a misconception; which is the more extraordinary, inasmuch as the contrary accusation, of referring everything to pleasure, and that too in its grossest form, is another of the common
charges against utilitarianism: and, as has been pointedly remarked
by an able writer, the same sort of persons, and often the very same
persons, denounce the theory "as impracticably dry when the word
utility precedes the word pleasure, and as too practicably voluptuous
when the word pleasure precedes the word utility." Those who
know anything about the matter are aware that every writer, from
Epicurus to Bentham, who maintained the theory of utility, meant
by it, not something to be contradistinguished from pleasure, but
pleasure itself, together with exemption from pain; and instead of
opposing the useful to the agreeable or the ornamental, have always
declared that the useful means these, among other things. Yet the

[2] From J. S. Mill, *Utilitarianism,* chap. ii, originally published in *Fraser's Maga-
zine,* 1863.

common herd, including the herd of writers, not only in newspapers and periodicals, but in books of weight and pretension, are perpetually falling into this shallow mistake. Having caught up the word utilitarian, while knowing nothing whatever about it but its sound, they habitually express by it the rejection, or the neglect, of pleasure in some of its forms; of beauty, of ornament, or of amusement. Nor is the term thus ignorantly misapplied solely in disparagement, but occasionally in compliment; as though it implied superiority to frivolity and the mere pleasures of the moment. And this perverted use is the only one in which the word is popularly known, and the one from which the new generation are acquiring their sole notion of its meaning. Those who introduced the word, but who had for many years discontinued it as a distinctive appellation, may well feel themselves called upon to resume it, if by doing so they can hope to contribute anything towards rescuing it from this utter degradation.

The creed which accepts as the foundation of morals, Utility, or the Greatest Happiness Principle, holds that actions are right in proportion as they tend to promote happiness, wrong as they tend to produce the reverse of happiness. By happiness is intended pleasure, and the absence of pain; by unhappiness, pain, and the privation of pleasure. To give a clear view of the moral standard set up by the theory, much more requires to be said; in particular, what things it includes in the ideas of pain and pleasure; and to what extent this is left an open question. But these supplementary explanations do not affect the theory of life on which this theory of morality is grounded—namely, that pleasure, and freedom from pain, are the only things desirable as ends; and that all desirable things (which are as numerous in the utilitarian as in any other scheme) are desirable either for the pleasure inherent in themselves, or as means to the promotion of pleasure and the prevention of pain.

Now, such a theory of life excites in many minds, and among them in some of the most estimable in feeling and purpose, inveterate dislike. To suppose that life has (as they express it) no higher end than pleasure—no better and nobler object of desire and pursuit —they designate as utterly mean and grovelling; as a doctrine worthy only of swine, to whom the followers of Epicurus were, at a very early period, contemptuously likened; and modern holders of the doctrine are occasionally made the subject of equally polite comparisons by its German, French, and English assailants.

When thus attacked, the Epicureans have always answered, that it is not they, but their accusers, who represent human nature in a degrading light; since the accusation supposes human beings to be capable of no pleasures except those of which swine are capable. If this supposition were true, the charge could not be gainsaid, but would then be no longer an imputation; for if the sources of pleasure were precisely the same to human beings and to swine, the rule of life which is good enough for the one would be good enough for the other. The comparison of the Epicurean life to that of beasts is felt as degrading, precisely because a beast's pleasures do not satisfy a human being's conceptions of happiness. Human beings have faculties more elevated than the animal appetites, and when once made conscious of them, do not regard anything as happiness which does not include their gratification. I do not, indeed, consider the Epicureans to have been by any means faultless in drawing out their scheme of consequences from the utilitarian principle. To do this in any sufficient manner, many Stoic, as well as Christian elements require to be included. But there is no known Epicurean theory of life which does not assign to the pleasures of the intellect, of the feelings and imagination, and of the moral sentiments, a much higher value as pleasures than to those of mere sensation. It must be admitted, however, that utilitarian writers in general have placed the superiority of mental over bodily pleasures chiefly in the greater permanency, safety, uncostliness, etc., of the former—that is, in their circumstantial advantages rather than in their intrinsic nature. And on all these points utilitarians have fully proved their case; but they might have taken the other, and, as it may be called, higher ground, with entire consistency. It is quite compatible with the principle of utility to recognise the fact, that some kinds of pleasure are more desirable and more valuable than others. It would be absurd that while, in estimating all other things, quality is considered as well as quantity, the estimation of pleasures should be supposed to depend on quantity alone.

If I am asked, what I mean by difference of quality in pleasures, or what makes one pleasure more valuable than another, merely as a pleasure, except its being greater in amount, there is but one possible answer. Of two pleasures, if there be one to which all or almost all who have experience of both give a decided preference, irrespective of any feeling of moral obligation to prefer it, that is the more desirable pleasure. If one of the two is, by those who are competently acquainted with both, placed so far above the other that they prefer it, even though knowing it to be attended with a greater amount of discontent, and would not resign it for any quantity of the other pleasure which their nature is capable of, we are justified in ascribing to the preferred enjoyment a superiority in quality, so far outweighing quantity as to render it, in comparison, of small account.

Now it is an unquestionable fact that those who are equally acquainted with, and equally capable of appreciating and enjoying, both, do give a most marked preference to the manner of existence which employs their higher faculties. Few human creatures would consent to be changed into any of the lower animals, for a promise of the fullest allowance of a beast's pleasures; no intelligent human being would consent to be a fool, no instructed person would be an ignoramus, no person of feeling and conscience would be selfish and base, even though they should be persuaded that the fool, the dunce, or the rascal is better satisfied with his lot than they are with theirs. They would not resign what they possess more than he for the most complete satisfaction of all the desires which they have in common with him. If they ever fancy they would, it is only in cases of unhappiness so extreme, that to escape from it they would exchange their lot for almost any other, however undesirable in their own eyes. A being of higher faculties requires more to make him happy, is capable probably of more acute suffering, and certainly accessible to it at more points, than one of an inferior type; but in spite of these liabilities, he can never really wish to sink into what he feels to be a lower grade of existence. We may give what explanation we please of this unwillingness; we may attribute it to pride, a name which is given indiscriminately to some of the most and to some of the least estimable feelings of which mankind are capable: we may refer it to the love of liberty and personal independence, an appeal to which was with the Stoics one of the most effective means for the inculcation of it; to the love of power, or to the love of excitement, both of which do really enter into and contribute to it: but its most appropriate appellation is a sense of dignity, which all human beings possess in one form or other, and in some, though by no means in exact, proportion to their higher faculties, and which is so essential a part of the happiness of those in whom it is strong, that nothing which conflicts with it could be, otherwise than momentarily, an object of desire to them. Whoever supposes that this preference takes place at a sacrifice of happiness—that the superior being, in anything like equal circumstances, is not happier than the inferior—confounds the two very different ideas, of happiness, and content. It is indisputable that the being whose capacities of enjoyment are low, has the greatest chance of having them fully satisfied; and a highly endowed being will always feel that any happiness which he can look for, as the world is constituted, is imperfect.

But he can learn to bear its imperfections, if they are at all bearable; and they will not make him envy the being who is indeed unconscious of the imperfections, but only because he feels not at all the good which those imperfections qualify. It is better to be a human being dissatisfied than a pig satisfied; better to be Socrates dissatisfied than a fool satisfied. And if the fool, or the pig, are of a different opinion, it is because they only know their side of the question. The other party to the comparison knows both sides.

It may be objected, that many who are capable of the higher pleasures, occasionally, under the influence of temptation, postpone them to the lower. But this is quite compatible with a full appreciation of the intrinsic superiority of the higher. Men often, from infirmity of character, make their election for the nearer good, though they know it to be the less valuable; and this no less when the choice is between two bodily pleasures, than when it is between bodily and mental. They pursue sensual indulgences to the injury of health, though perfectly aware that health is the greater good. It may be further objected, that many who begin with youthful enthusiasm for everything noble, as they advance in years sink into indolence and selfishness. But I do not believe that those who undergo this very common change, voluntarily choose the lower description of pleasures in preference to the higher. I believe that before they devote themselves exclusively to the one, they have already become incapable of the other. Capacity for the nobler feelings is in most natures a very tender plant, easily killed, not only by hostile influences, but by mere want of sustenance; and in the majority of young persons it speedily dies away if the occupations to which their position in life has devoted them, and the society into which it has thrown them, are not favourable to keeping that higher capacity in exercise. Men lose their high aspirations as they lose their intellectual tastes, because they have not time or opportunity for indulging them; and they addict themselves to inferior pleasures, not because they deliberately prefer them, but because they are either the only ones to which they have access, or the only ones which they are any longer capable of enjoying. It may be questioned whether any one who has remained equally susceptible to both classes of pleasures, ever knowingly and calmly preferred the lower; though many, in all ages, have broken down in an ineffectual attempt to combine both.

From this verdict of the only competent judges, I apprehend there can be no appeal. On a question which is the best worth having of two pleasures, or which of two modes of existence is the most grateful to the feelings, apart from its moral attributes and from its consequences, the judgment of those who are qualified by knowledge of both, or, if they differ, that of the majority among them, must be admitted as final. And there needs be the less hesitation to accept this judgment respecting the quality of pleasures, since there is no other tribunal to be referred to even on the question of quantity. What means are there of determining which is the acutest of two pains, or the intensest of two pleasurable sensations, except the general suffrage of those who are familiar with both? Neither pains nor pleasures are homogeneous, and pain is always heterogeneous with pleasure. What is there to decide whether a particular pleasure is worth purchasing at the cost of a particular pain, except the feelings and judgment of the experienced? When, therefore, those feelings and judgment declare the pleasures derived from the higher faculties to be preferable in kind, apart from the question of intensity, to those of which the animal nature, disjoined from the higher faculties, is suspectible, they are entitled on this subject to the same regard.

I have dwelt on this point, as being a necessary part of a perfectly just conception of Utility or Happiness, considered as the directive rule of human conduct. But it is by no means an indispensable condition to the acceptance of the utilitarian standard; for that standard is not the agent's own greatest happiness, but the greatest amount of happiness altogether; and if it may possibly be doubted whether a noble character is always the happier for its nobleness, there can be no doubt that it makes other people happier, and that the world in general is immensely a gainer by it. Utilitarianism, therefore, could only attain its end by the general cultivation of nobleness of character, even if each individual were only benefited by the nobleness of others, and his own, so far as happiness is concerned, were a sheer deduction from the benefit. But the bare enunciation of such an absurdity as this last, renders refutation superfluous.

According to the Greatest Happiness Principle, as above explained, the ultimate end, with reference to and for the sake of which all other things are desirable (whether we are considering our own good or that of other people), is an existence exempt as far as possible from pain, and as rich as possible in enjoyments, both in point of quantity and quality; the test of quality, and the rule for measuring it against quantity, being the preference felt by those who in their opportunities of experience, to which must be added their habits of self-consciousness and self-observation, are best furnished with the means of comparison. This, being, according to the utilitarian opinion, the end of human action, is necessarily also the standard of morality; which may accordingly be defined, the rules and precepts for human conduct, by the observance of which an existence such as has been described might be, to the greatest extent possible, secured to all mankind; and not to them only, but, so far as the nature of things admits, to the whole sentient creation.

Against this doctrine, however, arises another class of objectors, who say that happiness, in any form, cannot be the rational purpose of human life and action; because, in the first place, it is unattainable: and they contemptuously ask, what right hast thou to be happy? a question which Mr. Carlyle clenches by the addition, What right, a short time ago, hadst thou even to be? Next, they say, that men can do without happiness; that all noble human beings have felt this, and could not have become noble but by learning the lesson of Entsagen, or renunciation; which lesson, thoroughly learnt and submitted to, they affirm to be the beginning and necessary condition of all virtue.

The first of these objections would go the root of the matter were it well founded; for if no happiness is to be had at all by human beings, the attainment of it cannot be the end of morality, or of any rational conduct. Though, even in that case, something might still be said for the utilitarian theory; since utility includes not solely the pursuit of happiness, but the prevention or mitigation of unhappiness; and if the former aim be chimerical, there will be all the greater scope and more imperative need for the latter, so long at least as mankind think fit to live, and do not take refuge in the simultaneous act of suicide recommended under certain conditions by Novalis. When, however, it is thus positively asserted to be impossible that human life should be happy, the assertion, if not something like a verbal quibble, is at least an exaggeration. If by happiness be meant a continuity of highly pleasurable excitement, it is evident enough that this is impossible. A state of exalted pleasure lasts only moments, or in some cases, and with some intermissions, hours or days, and is the occasional brilliant flash of enjoyment, not its permanent and steady flame. Of this the philosophers who have taught that happiness is the end of life were as fully aware as those who taunt them. The happiness which they meant was not a life of rapture; but moments of such, in an existence made up of few and transitory pains, many and various pleasures, with a decided predominance of the active over the passive, and having as the foundation of the whole, not to expect more from life than it is capable of bestowing. A life thus composed, to those who have been fortunate enough to obtain it, has always appeared worthy of the name of happiness. And such an existence is even now the lot of many, during some considerable portion of their lives. The present wretched education, and wretched social arrangements, are the only real hindrance to its being attainable by almost all.

The objectors perhaps may doubt whether human beings, if taught to consider happiness as the end of life, would be satisfied with such a moderate share of it. But great numbers of mankind have been satisfied with much less. The main constituents of a satisfied life appear to be two, either of which by itself is often found sufficient for the purpose: with much excitement, many can reconcile themselves to a considerable quantity of pain. There is assuredly no inherent impossibility in enabling even the mass of mankind to unite both; since the two are so far from being incompatible that they are in natural alliance, the prolongation of either being a preparation for, and exciting a wish for, the other. It is only those in whom indolence amounts to a vice, that do not desire excitement after an interval of repose: it is only those in whom the need of excitement is a disease that feel the tranquillity which follows excitement dull and insipid, instead of pleasurable in direct proportion to the excitement which preceded it. When people who are tolerably fortunate in their outward lot do not find in life sufficient enjoyment to make it valuable to them, the cause generally is, caring for nobody but themselves. To those who have neither public nor private affections, the excitements of life are much curtailed, and in any case dwindle in value as the time approaches when all selfish interests must be terminated by death: while those who leave after them objects of personal affection, and especially those who have also cultivated a fellow-feeling with the collective interests of mankind, retain as lively an interest in life on the eve of death as in the vigour of youth and health. Next to selfishness, the principle cause which makes life unsatisfactory is want of mental cultivation. A cultivated mind—I do not mean that of a philosopher, but any mind to which the fountains of knowledge have been opened, and which has been taught, in any tolerable degree, to exercise its faculties—finds sources of inexhaustible interest in all that surrounds it; in the objects of nature, the achievements of art, the imaginations of poetry, the incidents of history, the ways of mankind, past and present, and their prospects in the future. It is possible, indeed, to become indifferent to all this, and that too without having exhausted a thousandth part of it; but only when one has had from the beginning no moral or human interest in these things, and has sought in them only the gratification of curiosity.

Now there is absolutely no reason in the nature of things why an amount of mental culture sufficient to give an intelligent inter-

est in these objects of contemplation, should not be the inheritance
of every one born in a civilised country. As little is there an inherent necessity that any human being should be a selfish egotist,
devoid of every feeling or care but those which centre in his own
miserable individuality. Something far superior to this is sufficiently
common even now, to give ample earnest of what the human species
may be made. Genuine private affections, and a sincere interest
in the public good, are possible, though in unequal degrees, to every
rightly brought up human being. In a world in which there is so
much to interest, so much to enjoy, and so much also to correct and
improve, every one who has this moderate amount of moral and intellectual requisites is capable of an existence which may be called
enviable; and unless such a person, through bad laws, or subjection
to the will of others, is denied the liberty to use the sources of happiness within his reach, he will not fail to find this enviable existence, if he escape the positive evils of life, the great sources of
physical and mental suffering—such as indigence, disease, and the
unkindness, worthlessness, or premature loss of objects of affection.
The main stress of the problem lies, therefore, in the contest with
these calamities, from which it is a rare good fortune entirely to
escape; which, as things now are, cannot be obviated, and often
cannot be in any material degree mitigated. Yet no one whose opinion deserves a moment's consideration can doubt that most of the
great positive evils of the world are in themselves removable, and
will, if human affairs continue to improve, be in the end reduced
within narrow limits. Poverty, in any sense implying suffering, may
be completely extinguished by the wisdom of society, combined with
the good sense and providence of individuals. Even that most in-
tractable of enemies, disease, may be indefinitely reduced in dimensions by good physical and moral education, and proper control of
noxious influences; while the progress of science holds out a promise for the future of still more direct conquests over this detestable
foe. And every advance in that direction relieves us from some, not
only of the chances which cut short our own lives, but, what
concerns us still more, which deprive us of those in whom our happiness is wrapt up. As for vicissitudes of fortune, and other disappointments connected with worldly circumstances, these are principally the effect either of gross imprudence, of ill-regulated desires,
or of bad or imperfect social institutions. All the grand sources, in
short, of human suffering are in a great degree, many of them almost
entirely, conquerable by human care and effort; and though their
removal is grievously slow—though a long succession of generations
will perish in the breach before the conquest is completed, and this

world becomes all that, if will and knowledge were not wanting, it might easily be made—yet every mind sufficiently intelligent and generous to bear a part, however small and unconspicuous, in the endeavour, will draw a noble enjoyment from the contest itself, which he would not for any bribe in the form of selfish indulgence consent to be without.

And this leads to the true estimation of what is said by the objectors concerning the possibility, and the obligation, of learning to do without happiness. Unquestionably it is possible to do without happiness; it is done involuntarily by nineteen-twentieths of mankind, even in those parts of our present world which are least deep in barbarism; and it often has to be done voluntarily by the hero or the martyr, for the sake of something which he prizes more than his individual happiness. But this something, what is it, unless the happiness of others, or some of the requisites of happiness? It is noble to be capable of resigning entirely one's own portion of happiness, or chances of it: but, after all, this self-sacrifice must be for some end; it is not its own end; and if we are told that its end is not happiness, but virtue, which is better than happiness, I ask, would the sacrifice be made if the hero or martyr did not believe that it would earn for others immunity from similar sacrifices? Would it be made if he thought that his renunciation of happiness for himself would produce no fruit for any of his fellow creatures, but to make their lot like his, and place them also in the condition of persons who have renounced happiness? All honour to those who can abnegate for themselves the personal enjoyment of life, when by such renunciation they contribute worthily to increase the amount of happiness in the world; but he who does it, or professes to do it, for any other purpose, is no more deserving of admiration than the ascetic mounted on his pillar. He may be an inspiring proof of what men *can* do, but assuredly not an example of what they *should*.

Though it is only in a very imperfect state of the world's arrangements that any one can best serve the happiness of others by the absolute sacrifice of his own, yet so long as the world is in that imperfect state, I fully acknowledge that the readiness to make such a sacrifice is the highest virtue which can be found in man. I will add, that in this condition of the world, paradoxical as the assertion may be, the conscious ability to do without happiness gives the best prospect of realising such happiness as is attainable. For nothing except that consciousness can raise a person above the chances of life, by making him feel that, let fate and fortune do their worst, they have not power to subdue him: which, once felt, frees him from excess of anxiety concerning the evils of life, and enables him, like many a Stoic in the worst times of the Roman Empire, to cultivate in tranquillity the sources of satisfaction accessible to him, without concerning himself about the uncertainty of their duration, any more than about their inevitable end.

Meanwhile, let utilitarians never cease to claim the morality of self devotion as a possession which belongs by as good a right to them, as either to the Stoic or to the Transcendentalist. The utilitarian morality does recognise in human beings the power of sacrificing their own greatest good for the good of others. It only refuses to admit that the sacrifice is itself a good. A sacrifice which does not increase, or tend to increase, the sum total of happiness, it considers as wasted. The only self-renunciation which it applauds, is devotion to the happiness, or to some of the means of happiness, of others; either of mankind collectively, or of individuals within the limits imposed by the collective interests of mankind.

I must again repeat, what the assailants of utilitarianism seldom have the justice to acknowledge, that the happiness which forms the utilitarian standard of what is right in conduct, is not the agent's own happiness, but that of all concerned. As between his own happiness and that of others, utilitarianism requires him to be as strictly impartial as a disinterested and benevolent spectator. In the golden rule of Jesus of Nazareth, we read the complete spirit of the ethics of utility. To do as you would be done by, and to love your neighbor as yourself, constitute the ideal perfection of utilitarian morality. As the means of making the nearest approach to this ideal, utility would enjoin, first, that laws and social arrangements should place the happiness, or (as speaking practically it may be called) the interest, of every individual, as nearly as possible in harmony with the interest of the whole; and secondly, that education and opinion, which have so vast a power over human character, should so use that power as to establish in the mind of every individual an indissoluble association between his own happiness and the good of the whole; especially between his own happiness and the practice of such modes of conduct, negative and positive, as regard for the universal happiness prescribes; so that not only he may be unable to conceive the possibility of happiness to himself, consistently with conduct opposed to the general good, but also that a direct impulse to promote the general good may be in every individual one of the habitual motives of action, and the sentiments connected therewith may fill a large and prominent place in every human being's sentient existence. If the impugners of the utilitarian morality represented it to their own minds in this its true character, I know not what recommendation possessed by any other morality they could possibly affirm to be wanting to it; what more beautiful or more exalted developments of human nature any other ethical system can be supposed to foster, or what springs of action, not accessible to the utilitarian, such systems rely on for giving effect to their mandates.

The objectors to utilitarianism cannot always be charged with representing it in a discreditable light. On the contrary, those among them who entertain anything like a just idea of its disinterested character, sometimes find fault with its standard as being too high for humanity. They say it is exacting too much to require that people shall always act from the inducement of promoting the general interests of society. But this is to mistake the very meaning of a standard of morals, and confound the rule of action with the motive of it. It is the business of ethics to tell us what are our duties, or by what test we may know them; but no system of ethics requires that the sole motive of all we do shall be a feeling of duty; on the contrary, ninety-nine hundredths of all our actions are done from other motives, and rightly so done, if the rule of duty does not condemn them. It is the more unjust to utilitarianism that this particular misapprehension should be made a ground of objection to it, inasmuch as utilitarian moralists have gone beyond almost all others in affirming that the motive has nothing to do with the morality of the action, though much with the worth of the agent. He who saves a fellow creature from drowning does what is morally right, whether his motive be duty, or the hope of being paid for his trouble; he who betrays the friend that trusts him, is guilty of a crime, even if his object be to serve another friend to whom he is under greater obligations. But to speak only of actions done from the motive of duty, and in direct obedience to principle: it is a misapprehension of the utilitarian mode of thought, to conceive it as implying that people should fix their minds upon so wide a generality as the world, or society at large. The great majority of good actions are intended not for the benefit of the world, but for that of individuals, of which the good of the world is made up; and the thoughts of the most virtuous man need not on these occasions travel beyond the particular persons concerned, except so far as is necessary to assure himself that in benefitting them he is not violating the rights, that is, the legitimate and authorised expectations, of any one else. The multiplication of happiness is, according to the utilitarian ethics, the object of virtue; the occasions on which any person (except one in a thousand) has it in his power to do this on an extended scale, in other words to be a public benefactor, are but exceptional; and on these occasions alone is he called on to consider public utility; in every other case, private utility, the interest or happiness of some few persons, is all he has to attend to. Those alone the influence of whose actions extends to society in general, need concern themselves habitually about so large an object. In the case of abstinences indeed—of things which people forbear to do from moral considerations, though the consequences in the particular case might be beneficial—it would be unworthy of an intelligent agent not to be consciously aware that the action is of a class which, if practised generally, would be generally injurious, and that this is the ground of the obligation to abstain from it. The amount of regard for the public interest implied in this recognition, is no greater than is demanded by every system of morals, for they all enjoin to abstain from whatever is manifestly pernicious to society.

• Immanuel Kant (1724–1804)

The Nature of Duty[3]

Immanuel Kant, who taught most of his life in the eighteenth century at Koenigsburg in East Prussia, lived quietly, but he provided a revolution in philosophic thought. His *Critique of Pure Reason* (1781) is the greatest treatise of the age on the theory of knowledge, but Kant was interested no less in problems of morality and religion. His brief work, *The Metaphysics of Ethics,* from which the following selection is taken, shows Kant's moral system in all its purity and rigor. It presents his belief that the good will makes acts good, that to be moral an act must be done out of respect for the moral law and not from desire or inclination. Finally, he shows that in the idea of law itself is the principle of universality which is crucial for ethics.

Nothing can possibly be conceived in the world, or even out of it, which can be called good without qualification, except a Good Will. Intelligence, wit, judgment, and the other *talents* of the mind, however they may be named, or courage, resolution, perseverance, as qualities of temperament, are undoubtedly good and desirable in many respects; but these gifts of nature may also become extremely

[3] From Immanuel Kant, *The Metaphysics of Ethics* (1787), trans. T. K. Abbott (1873), Sec. i.

bad and mischievous if the will which is to make use of them, and which, therefore, constitutes what is called *character*, is not good. It is the same with the *gifts of fortune*. Power, riches, honour, even health, and the general well-being and contentment with one's condition which is called *happiness*, inspire pride, and often presumption, if there is not a good will to correct the influence of these on the mind, and with this also to rectify the whole principle of acting, and adapt it to its end. The sight of a being who is not adorned with a single feature of a pure and good will, enjoying unbroken prosperity, can never give pleasure to an impartial rational spectator. Thus a good will appears to constitute the indispensable condition even of being worthy of happiness.

There are even some qualities which are of service to this good will itself, and may facilitate its action, yet which have no intrinsic unconditional value, but always presuppose a good will, and this qualifies the esteem that we justly have for them, and does not permit us to regard them as absolutely good. Moderation in the affections and passions, self-control and calm deliberation are not only good in many respects, but even seem to constitute part of the intrinsic worth of the person; but they are far from deserving to be called good without qualification, although they have been so unconditionally praised by the ancients. For without the principles of a good will, they may become extremely bad, and the coolness of a villain not only makes him far more dangerous, but also directly makes him more abominable in our eyes than he would have been without it.

A good will is good not because of what it performs or effects, not by its aptness for the attainment of some proposed end, but simply by virtue of the volition, that is it is good in itself, and considered by itself is to be esteemed much higher than all that can be brought about by it in favour of any inclination, nay even of the sum total of all inclinations. Even if it should happen that, owing to special disfavour of fortune, or the niggardly provision of a stepmotherly nature, this will should wholly lack power to accomplish its purpose, if with its greatest efforts it should yet achieve nothing, and there should remain only the good will (not, to be sure, a mere wish, but the summoning of all means in our power), then, like a jewel, it would still shine by its own light, as a thing which has its whole value in itself. Its usefulness or fruitlessness can neither add nor take away anything from this value. It would be, as it were, only the setting to enable us to handle it the more conveniently in common commerce, or to attract to it the attention of those who are not yet connoisseurs, but not to recommend it to true connoisseurs, or to determine its value.

There is, however, something so strange in this idea of the absolute value of the mere will, in which no account is taken of its utility, that notwithstanding the thorough assent of even common reason to the idea, yet a suspicion must arise that it may perhaps really be the product of mere high-flown fancy, and that we may have misunderstood the purpose of nature in assigning reason as the governor of our will. Therefore we will examine this idea from this point of view.

In the physical constitution of an organized being, that is, a being adapted suitably to the purposes of life, we assume it as a fundamental principle that no organ for any purpose will be found but what is also the fittest and best adapted for that purpose. Now in a being which has reason and a will, if the proper object of nature were its *conservation*, its *welfare*, in a word, its *happiness*, then nature would have hit upon a very bad arrangement in selecting the reason of the creature to carry out this purpose. For all the actions which the creature has to perform with a view to this purpose, and the whole rule of its conduct, would be far more surely prescribed to it by instinct, and that end would have been attained thereby much more certainly than it ever can be by reason. Should reason have been communicated to this favoured creature over and above, it must only have served it to contemplate the happy constitution of its nature, to admire it, to congratulate itself thereon, and to feel thankful for it to the beneficent cause, but not that it should subject its desires to that weak and delusive guidance, and meddle bunglingly with the purpose of nature. In a word, nature would have taken care that reason should not break forth into *practical exercise*, nor have the presumption, with its weak insight, to think out for itself the plan of happiness, and of the means of attaining it. Nature would not only have taken on herself the choice of the ends, but also of the means, and with wise foresight would have entrusted both to instinct.

And, in fact, we find that the more cultivated reason applies itself with deliberate purpose to the enjoyment of life and happiness, so much the more does the man fail of true satisfaction. And from this circumstance there arises in many, if they are candid enough to confess it, a certain degree of *misology*, that is, hatred of reason, especially in the case of those who are most experienced in the use of it, because after calculating all the advantages they derive, I do not say from the invention of all the arts of common luxury, but even from the sciences (which seem to them to be after all only a luxury of the understanding), they find that they have, in fact, only brought more trouble on their shoulders, rather than gained in happiness; and they end by envying, rather than despising, the more common stamp of men who keep closer to the guidance of mere instinct, and do not allow their reason much influence on their conduct. And this we must admit, that the judgment of those who would very much lower the lofty eulogies of the advantages which reason gives us in regard to the happiness and satisfaction of life, or who would even reduce them to nothing, is by no means morose or ungrateful to the goodness with which the world is governed, but that there lies at the root of these judgments the idea that our existence has a different and far nobler end, for which, and not for happiness, reason is properly intended, and which must, therefore, be regarded as the supreme condition to which the private ends of man must, for the most part, be postponed.

For as reason is not competent to guide the will with certainty in regard to its objects and the satisfaction of all our wants (which it to some extent even multiplies), this being an end to which an implanted instinct would have led with much greater certainty; and since, nevertheless, reason is imparted to us as a practical faculty, i.e., as one which is to have influence on the *will*, therefore, admitting that nature generally in the distribution of her capacities has adapted the means to the end, its true destination must be to produce a *will*, not merely good as a *means* to something else, but *good in itself*, for which reason was absolutely necessary. This will then, though not indeed the sole and complete good, must be the supreme good and the condition of every other, even of the desire of happiness. Under these circumstances, there is nothing inconsistent with the wisdom of nature in the fact that the cultivation of the reason, which is requisite for the first and unconditional purpose, does in many ways interfere, at least in this life, with the attainment of the second, which is always conditional, namely, happiness. Nay, it may even reduce it to nothing, without nature thereby failing of her purpose. For reason recognises the establishment of a good will as its highest practical destination, and in attaining this purpose is capable only of a satisfaction of its own proper kind, namely, that from the attainment of an end, which end again is determined by reason only, notwithstanding that this may involve many a disappointment to the ends of inclination.

We have then to develop the notion of a will which deserves to be highly esteemed for itself, and is good without a view to anything further, a notion which exists already in the sound natural understanding, requiring rather to be cleared up than to be taught, and which in estimating the value of our actions always takes the first place, and constitutes the condition of all the rest. In order to do this we will take the notion of duty, which includes that of a good will, although implying certain subjective restrictions and hindrances. These, however, far from concealing it, or rendering it unrecognisable, rather bring it out by contrast, and make it shine forth so much the brighter.

I omit here all actions which are already recognised as inconsistent with duty, although they may be useful for this or that purpose, for with these the question whether they are done *from duty* cannot arise at all, since they even conflict with it. I also set aside those actions which really conform to duty, but to which men have *no* direct *inclination*, performing them because they are impelled thereto by some other inclination. For in this case we can readily distinguish whether the action which agrees with duty is done *from duty*, or from a selfish view. It is much harder to make this distinction when the action accords with duty, and the subject has besides a *direct* inclination to it. For example, it is always a matter of duty that a dealer should not overcharge an inexperienced purchaser, and wherever there is much commerce the prudent tradesman does not overcharge, but keeps a fixed price for every one, so that a child buys of him as well as any other. Men are thus *honestly* served; but this is not enough to make us believe that the tradesman has so acted from duty and from principles of honesty: his own advantage required it; it is out of the question in this case to suppose that he might besides have a direct inclination in favour of the buyers, so that, as it were, from love he should give no advantage to one another. Accordingly the action was done neither from duty nor from direct inclination, but merely with a selfish view.

On the other hand, it is a duty to maintain one's life; and, in addition, every one has also a direct inclination to do so. But on this account the often anxious care which most men take for it has no intrinsic worth, and their maxim has no moral import. They preserve their life *as duty requires*, no doubt, but not *because duty requires*. On the other hand, if adversity and hopeless sorrow have completely taken away the relish for life; if the unfortunate one, strong in mind, indignant at his fate rather than desponding or dejected, wishes for death, and yet preserves his life without loving it—not from inclination or fear, but from duty—then his maxim has a moral worth.

To be beneficent when we can is a duty; and besides this, there are many minds so sympathetically constituted that, without any other motive of vanity or self-interest, they find a pleasure in spreading joy around them, and can take delight in the satisfaction of others so far as it is their own work. But I maintain that in such a case an action of this kind, however proper, however amiable it may be, has nevertheless no true moral worth, but is on a level with other inclinations, e. g., the inclination to honour, which, if it is happily directed to that which is in fact of public utility and accordant with duty, and consequently honourable, deserves praise and encouragement, but not esteem. For the maxim lacks the moral import, namely, that such actions be done *from duty*, not from inclination. Put the case that the mind of that philanthropist were clouded by sorrow of his own, extinguishing all sympathy with the lot of others, and that while he still has the power to benefit others in distress, he is not touched by their trouble because he is absorbed with his own; and now suppose that he tears himself out of this dead insensibility, and performs the action without any inclination to it, but simply from duty, then first has his action its genuine moral worth. Further still; if nature has put little sympathy in the heart of this or that man; if he, supposed to be an upright man, is by temperament cold and indifferent to the sufferings of others, perhaps because in respect of his own he is provided with the special gift of patience and fortitude, and supposes, or even requires, that others should have the same—and such a man would certainly not be the meanest product of nature—but if nature had not specially framed him for a philanthropist, would he not still find in himself a source from whence to give himself a far higher worth than that of a good-natured temperament could be? Unquestionably. It is just in this that the moral worth of the character is brought out which is incomparably the highest of all, namely, that he is beneficent, not from inclination, but from duty.

To secure one's own happiness is a duty, at least indirectly; for discontent with one's condition, under a pressure of many anxieties and amidst unsatisfied wants, might easily become a great *temptation to transgression of duty*. But here again, without looking to duty, all men have already the strongest and most intimate inclination to happiness, because it is just in this idea that all inclinations are combined in one total. But the precept of happiness is often of such a sort that it greatly interferes with some inclinations, and yet a man cannot form any definite and certain conception of the sum of satisfaction of all of them which is called happiness. It is not then to be wondered at that a single inclination, definite both as to what it promises and as to the time within which it can be gratified, is often able to overcome such a fluctuating idea, and that a gouty patient, for instance, can choose to enjoy what he likes, and to suffer what he may, since, according to his calculation, on this occasion at least, he has (only) not sacrificed the enjoyment of the present moment to a possibly mistaken expectation of a happiness which is supposed to be found in health. But even in this case, if the general desire for happiness did not influence his will, and supposing that in his particular case health was not a necessary element in this calculation, there yet remains in this, as in all other cases, this law, namely, that he should promote his happiness not from inclination but from duty, and by this would his conduct first acquire true moral worth.

It is in this manner, undoubtedly, that we are to understand those passages of Scripture also in which we are commanded to love our neighbor, even our enemy. For love, as an affection, cannot be commanded, but beneficence for duty's sake may; even though we are not impelled to it by any inclination—nay, are even repelled by a natural and unconquerable aversion. This is *practical* love, and not *pathological*—a love which is seated in the will, and not in the propensions of sense—in principles of action and not of tender sympathy; and it is this love alone which can be commanded.

The second proposition is: That an action done from duty derives its moral worth, *not from the purpose* which is to be attained by it, but from the maxim by which it is determined, and therefore does not depend on the realization of the object of the action, but merely on the *principle of volition* by which the action has taken place, without regard to any object of desire. It is clear from what precedes that the purposes which we may have in view in our actions, or their effects regarded as ends and springs of the will, cannot give to actions any unconditional or moral worth. In what, then, can their worth lie, if it is not to consist in the will and in reference to its expected effect? It cannot lie anywhere but in the *principle of the will* without regard to the ends which can be attained by the action. For the will stands between its *a priori* principle, which is formal, and its *a posteriori* spring, which is material, as between two roads, and as it must be determined by something, it follows that it must be determined by the formal principle of volition when an action is done from duty, in which case every material principle has been withdrawn from it.

The third proposition, which is a consequence of the two preceding, I would express thus: *Duty is the necessity of acting from respect for the law.* I may have *inclination* for an object as the effect of my proposed action, but I cannot have *respect* for it, just for this reason, that it is an effect and not an energy of will. Similarly, I cannot have respect for inclination, whether my own or another's; I can at most, if my own, approve it; if another's, sometimes even love it; *i.e.*, look on it as favourable to my own interest. It is only what is connected with my will as a principle, by no means as an effect—what does not subserve my inclination, but overpowers it, or at least in case of choice excludes it from its calculation—in other words, simply the law of itself, which can be an object of respect, and hence a command. Now an action done from duty must wholly exclude the influence of inclination, and with it every object of the will, so that nothing remains which can determine the will except objectively the *law*, and subjectively *pure respect* for this practical law, and consequently the maxim that I should follow this law even to the thwarting of all my inclinations.

Thus the moral worth of an action does not lie in the effect expected from it, nor in any principle of action which requires to borrow its motive from this expected effect. For all these effects—agreeableness of one's condition, and even the promotion of the happiness of others—could have been also brought about by other causes, so that for this there would have been no need of the will of a rational being; whereas it is in this alone that the supreme and unconditional good can be found. The pre-eminent good which we call moral can therefore consist in nothing else than *the conception of law* in itself, *which certainly is only possible in a rational being,* in so far as this conception, and not the expected effect, determines the will. This is a good which is already present in the person who acts accordingly, and we have not to wait for it to appear first in the result.

But what sort of law can that be, the conception of which must determine the will, even without paying any regard to the effect expected from it, in order that this will may be called good absolutely and without qualification? As I have deprived the will of every impulse which could arise to it from obedience to any law, there remains nothing but the universal conformity of its actions to law in general, which alone is to serve the will as a principle, *i.e.*, I am never to act otherwise than so *that I could also will that my maxim should become a universal law.* Here now, it is the simple conformity to law in general, without assuming any particular law applicable to certain actions, that serves the will as its principle, and must so serve it, if duty is not to be a vain delusion and a chimerical notion. The common reason of men in its practical judgments perfectly coincides with this, and always has in view the principle here suggested. Let the question be, for example: May I when in distress make a promise with the intention not to keep it? I readily distinguish here between the two significations which the question may have: Whether it is prudent, or whether it is right, to make a false promise. The former may undoubtedly often be the case. I see clearly indeed that it is not enough to extricate myself from a present difficulty by means of this subterfuge, but it must be well considered whether there may not hereafter spring from this lie much greater inconvenience than that from which I now free myself, and as, with all my supposed *cunning*, the consequences cannot be so easily foreseen but that credit once lost may be much more injurious to me than any mischief which I seek to avoid at present, it should be considered whether it would not be more *prudent* to act herein according to a universal maxim, and to make it a habit to promise nothing except with the intention of keeping it. But it is soon clear to me that such a maxim will still only be based on the fear of consequences. Now it is a wholly different thing to be truthful from duty, and to be so from apprehension of injurious consequences. In the first case, the very notion of the action already implies a law for me; in the second case, I must first look about elsewhere to see what results may be combined with it which would affect myself. For to deviate from the principle of duty is beyond all doubt wicked; but to be unfaithful to my maxim of prudence may often be very advantageous to me, although to abide by it is certainly safer. The shortest way, however, and an unerring one, to discover the answer to this question whether a lying promise is consistent with duty, is to ask myself, Should I be content that my maxim (to extricate myself from difficulty by a false promise) should hold good as a universal law, for myself as well as for others? and should I be able to say to myself, "Every one may make a deceitful promise when he finds himself in a difficulty from which he cannot otherwise extricate himself"? Then I presently become aware that while I can will the lie, I can by no means will that lying should be a universal law. For with such a law there would be no promises at all, since it would be in vain to allege my intention in regard to my future actions to those who would not believe this allegation, or if they over hastily did so would pay me back in my own coin. Hence my maxim, as soon as it should be made a universal law, would necessarily destroy itself.

I do not, therefore, need any far-reaching penetration to discern what I have to do in order that my will may be morally good. Inexperienced in the course of the world, incapable of being prepared for all its contingencies, I only ask myself: Canst thou also will that thy maxim should be a universal law? If not, then it must be rejected, and that not because of a disadvantage accruing from it to myself or even to others, but because it cannot enter as a principle into a possible universal legislation, and reason extorts from me immediate respect for such legislation. I do not indeed as yet *discern* on what this respect is based (this the philosopher may inquire), but at least I understand this, that it is an estimation of the worth which far outweighs all worth of what is recommended by inclination, and that the necessity of acting from *pure* respect for the practical law is what constitutes duty, to which every other motive must give place, because it is the condition of a will being good *in itself*, and the worth of such a will is above everything.

Thus, then, without quitting the moral knowledge of common human reason, we have arrived at its principle. And although, no doubt, common men do not conceive it in such an abstract and universal form, yet they always have it really before their eyes, and use it as the standard of their decision. Here it would be easy to show how, with this compass in hand, men are well able to distinguish, in every case that occurs, what is good, what bad, comformably to duty or inconsistent with it, if, without in the least teaching them anything new, we only, like Socrates, direct their attention to the principle they themselves employ; and that therefore we do not need science and philosophy to know what we should do to be honest and good, yea even wise and virtuous. Indeed we might well have conjectured beforehand that the knowledge of what every man is bound to do, and therefore also to know would be within the reach of every man, even the commonest. Here we cannot forbear admiration when we see how great an advantage the practical judgment has over the theoretical in the common understanding of men. In the latter, if common reason ventures to depart from the laws of experience and from the perceptions of the senses, it falls into mere inconceivabilities and self-contradictions, at least into a chaos of uncertainty, obscurity, and instability. But in the practical sphere it is just when the common understanding excludes all sensible springs from practical laws that its power of judgment begins to show itself to advantage. It then becomes even subtle, whether it be that it chicanes with its own conscience or with other claims respecting what is to be called right, or whether it desires for its own instruction to determine honestly the worth of actions; and, in the latter case, it may even have as good a hope of hitting the mark as any philosopher whatever can promise himself. Nay, it is almost more sure of doing so, because the philosopher cannot have any other principle, while he may easily perplex his judgment by a multitude of considerations foreign to the matter, and so turn aside from the right way. Would it not therefore be wiser in moral concerns to acquiesce in the judgment of common reason, or at most only to call in philosophy for the purpose of rendering the system of morals more complete and intelligible, and its rules more convenient for use (especially for disputation), but not so as to draw off the common understanding from its happy simplicity, or to bring it by means of philosophy into a new path of inquiry and instruction.

Innocence is indeed a glorious thing, only, on the other hand, it is very sad that it cannot well maintain itself, and is easily seduced. On this account even wisdom—which otherwise consists more in conduct than in knowledge—yet has need of science, not in order to learn from it, but to secure for its precepts admission and permanence. Against all the commands of duty which reason represents to man as so deserving of respect, he feels in himself a powerful counterpoise in his wants and inclinations, the entire satisfaction of which he sums up under the name of happiness. Now reason issues its commands unyieldingly, without promising anything to the inclinations, and, as it were, with disregard and contempt for these claims, which are so impetuous, and at the same time so plausible, and which will not allow themselves to be suppressed by any command. Hence there arises a natural *dialectic*, I. E., a disposition to argue against these strict laws of duty and to question their validity, or at least their purity and strictness; and, if possible, to make them more accordant with our wishes and inclinations, that is to say, to corrupt them at their very source, and entirely to destroy their worth—a thing which even common practical reason cannot ultimately call good.

Thus is the *common reason of man* compelled to go out of its sphere, and to take a step into the field of a *practical philosophy*, not to satisfy any speculative want (which never occurs to it as long as it is content to be mere sound reason), but even on practical grounds, in order to attain in it information and clear instruction respecting the source of its principle, and the correct determination of it in opposition to the maxims which are based on wants and inclinations, so that it may escape from the perplexity of opposite claims, and not run the risk of losing all genuine moral principles through the equivocation into which it easily falls. Thus, when practical reason cultivates itself, there insensibly arises in it a dialectic which forces it to seek aid in philosophy, just as happens to it in its theoretic use; and in this case, therefore, as well as in the other, it will find rest nowhere but in a thorough critical examination of our reason.

• F. H. Bradley (1846–1924)

Why Should I Be Moral? [4]

F. H. Bradley, Oxford don and subtle dialectician is perhaps the most analytical of the British idealists of the late nineteenth century. Much influenced by the ideas of Hegel from the continent, his ideas are yet distinctly his own. Bradley represents a reaction against the empiricism of Mill whether expressed in logic, psychology, or ethics. Bradley's best-known works are *Principles of Logic, Appearance and Reality,* and *Ethical Studies,* from which the following selection is taken. In it Bradley shows the absurdity of asking the question: Why should I be moral? and in so doing presents in simple terms the ethical theory of self-realization.

Why should I be moral? The question is natural, and yet seems strange. It appears to be one we ought to ask, and yet we feel, when we ask it, that we are wholly removed from the moral point of view.

To ask the question Why? is rational; for reason teaches us to do nothing blindly, nothing without end or aim. She teaches us that what is good must be food for something, and that what is good for nothing is not good at all. And so we take it as certain that there is an end on one side, means on the other; and that only if the end is good, and the means conduce to it, have we a right to say the means are good. It is rational, then, always to inquire, Why should I do it?

But here the question seems strange. For morality (and she too is reason) teaches us that, if we look on her only as good for something else, we never in that case have seen her at all. She says that she is an end to be desired for her own sake, and not as a means to something beyond. Degrade her, and she disappears; and, to keep her, we must love and not merely use her. And so at the question Why? we are in trouble, for that does assume and does take for granted, that virtue in this sense is unreal, and what

[4] From F. H. Bradley, *Ethical Studies* (1876).

we believe is false. Both virtue and the asking Why? seem rational, and yet incompatible one with the other; and the better course will be, not forthwith to reject virtue in favour of the question, but rather to inquire concerning the nature of the Why?

Why should I be virtuous? Why should I? Could anything be more modest? Could anything be less assuming? It is not a dogma; it is only a question. And yet a question may contain (perhaps must contain) an assumption more or less hidden; or, in other words, a dogma. Let us see what is assumed in the asking of our question.

In "Why should I be moral?" the "Why should I?" was another way of saying, What good is virtue? or rather, For what is it good? and we saw that in asking, Is virtue good as a means, and how so? we do assume that virtue is not good, except as a means. The dogma at the root of the question is hence clearly either (1) the general statement that only means are good, or (2) the particular assertion of this in the case of virtue.

To explain; the question For what? Whereto? is either universally applicable, or not so. It holds everywhere, or we mean it to hold only here. Let us suppose, in the first place, that it is meant to hold everywhere.

Then (1) we are taking for granted that nothing is good in itself; that only the means to something else are good; that "good," in a word, = "good for," and good for something else. Such is the general canon by which virtue would have to be measured.

No one perhaps would explicitly put forward such a canon, and yet it may not be waste of time to examine it.

The good is a means: a means is a means to something else, and this is an end. Is the end good? No; if we hold to our general canon, it is not good as an end: the good was always good for something else, and was a means. To be good, the end must be a means, and so on for ever in a process which has no limit. If we ask now What is good? we must answer, There is nothing which is *not* good, for there is nothing which may not be regarded as conducing to something outside itself. Everything is relative to something else. And the essence of the good is to exist by virtue of something else and something else for ever. Everything is something else, is the result which at last we are brought to, if we insist on pressing our canon as universally applicable.

But the above is not needed perhaps; for those who introduced the question Why? did not think of things in general. The good for them was not an infinite process of idle distinction. Their interest is practical, and they do and must understand by the good (which they call a means) some means to an end in itself; which latter they assumed, and unconsciously fix in whatever is agreeable to themselves. If we said to them, for example, "Virtue is a means, and so is everything besides, and a means to everything else besides. Virtue is a means to pleasure, pain, health, disease, wealth, poverty, and is a good, because a means; and so also with pain, poverty, etc. They are all good, because all means. Is this what you mean by the question Why?" they would answer No. And they would answer No, because something has been taken as an end, and therefore good; and has been assumed dogmatically.

The universal application of the question For what? or Whereto? is, we see, repudiated. The question does not hold good everywhere, and we must now consider, secondly, its particular application to virtue.

(2) Something is here assumed to be the end; and further, this is assumed *not* to be virtue; and thus the question is founded, "Is virtue a means to a given end, which end is the good? Is virtue good? and why i.e. as conducing to what good is to good?" The dogma, A or B or C is a good in itself, justifies the inquiry, Is D a means to A, B, or C? And it is the dogmatic character of the question that we wished to point out. Its rationality, put as if universal, is tacitly assumed to end with a certain province; and our answer must be this: *If* your formula will not (on your own admission) apply to everything, what ground have you for supposing it to apply to virtue? "Be virtuous that you may be happy (i.e. pleased)"; then why be happy, and not rather virtuous? "The pleasure of all is an end." *Why* all? "Mine." *Why* mine? Your reply must be, that you take it to be so, and are prepared to argue on the thesis that something not virtue is the end in itself. And so are we; and we shall try to show that this is erroneous. But even if we fail in that, we have, I hope, made it clear that the question, Why should I be moral? rests on the assertion of an end in itself which is not morality; and a point of this importance must not be taken for granted.

It is quite true that to ask Why should I be moral? is *ipso facto* to take one view of morality, is to assume that virtue is a means to something not itself. But it is a mistake to suppose that the general asking of Why? affords any presumption in favour of, or against, any one theory. If any theory could stand upon the What for? as a rational formula, which must always hold good and be satisfied, then, to that extent, no doubt it would have an advantage. But we have seen that all doctrines alike must reject the What for? and agree in this rejection, if they agree in nothing else; since they all must have an end which is not a mere means. And if so, is it not foolish to suppose that its giving a reason for virtue is any argument in favour of Hedonism, when for its own end it can give no reason at all? Is it not clear that, if you have any Ethics, you must have an end which is above the Why? in the sense of What for?; and that, if this is so, the question is now, as it was two thousand years ago, Granted that there is an end, *what* is this end? And the asking that question, as reason and history both tell us, is not in itself the presupposing of a Hedonistic answer, or any other answer.

The claim of pleasure to be the end we are to discuss in another paper. But what is clear at first sight is, that to take virtue as a mere means to an ulterior end is in direct antagonism to the voice of the moral consciousness.

That consciousness, when unwarped by selfishness and not blinded by sophistry, is convinced that to ask for the Why? is simple immorality; to do good for its own sake is virtue, to do it for some ulterior end or object, not itself good, is never virtue; and never to act but for the sake of an end, other than doing well and right, is the mark of vice. And the theory which sees in virtue, as in money-getting, a means which is mistaken for an end, contradicts the voice which proclaims that virtue not only does seem to be, but is, an end in itself.

Taking our stand then, as we hope, on this common consciousness, what answer can we give when the question Why should I be moral? in the sense of What will it advantage me?, is put to us? Here we shall do well, I think, to avoid all praises of the pleasantness of virtue. We may believe that it transcends all possible delights of vice, but it would be well to remember that we desert a moral point of view, that we degrade and prostitute virtue, when to those who do not love her for herself we bring ourselves to recommend her for the sake of her pleasures. Against the base mechanical "vulgarity" which meets us on all sides, with its "what is the use" of goodness, or beauty, or truth, there is but one fitting answer from the friends of science, or art, or religion and virtue, "We do not know, and we do not care."

As a direct answer to the question we should not say more: but, putting ourselves at our questioner's point of view, we may ask in return, Why should I be immoral? Is it not disadvantageous to be so? We can ask, is your view consistent? Does it satisfy you, and give you what you want? And if you are satisfied, and so far as you are satisfied, do see whether it is not because, and so far as, you are false to your theory; so far as you are living not directly with a view to the pleasant, but with a view to something else, or with no view at all, but, as you would call it, without any "reason." We believe that, in your heart, your end is what ours is, but that about this end you not only are sorely mistaken, but in your heart you feel and know it, or at least would do so, if you would only reflect. And more than this I think we ought not to say.

What more are we to say? If a man asserts total scepticism, you cannot argue with him. You can show that he contradicts himself; but if he says, "I do not care"—there is an end of it. So, too, if a man says, "I shall do what I like, because I happen to like it; and as for ends, I recognize none"—you may indeed show him that his conduct is in fact otherwise; and if he will assert anything as an end, if he will but say, "I have no end but myself," then you may argue with him, and try to prove that he is making a mistake as to the nature of the end he alleges. But if he says, "I care not whether I am moral or rational, nor how much I contradict myself," then argument ceases. We, who have the power, believe that what is rational (if it is not yet) at least is to be real, and decline to recognize anything else. For standing on reason we can give, of course, no further reason; but we push our reason against what seems to oppose it, and soon force all to see that moral obligations do not vanish where they cease to be felt or are denied.

Has the question, Why should I be moral? no sense then, and is no positive answer possible? No, the question has no sense at all; it is simply unmeaning, unless it is equivalent to, *Is* morality an end in itself; and, if so, how and in what way is it an end? Is morality the same as the end for man, so that the two are convertible; or is morality one side, or aspect, or element of some end which is larger than itself? Is it the whole end from all points of view, or is it one view of the whole? Is the artist moral, so far as he is a good artist, or the philosopher moral, so far as he is a good philosopher? Are their art or science, and their virtue, one thing from one and the same point of view, or two different things, or one thing from two points of view?

These are not easy questions to answer, and we can not discuss them yet. We have taken the reader now so far as he need go, before proceeding to the following essays. What remains is to point out the most general expression for the end in itself, the ultimate practical "why"; and that we find in the word *self-realization*. But what follows is an anticipation of the sequel, which we can not promise to make intelligible as yet; and the reader who finds difficulties had better go on at once to Essay III.

How can it be proved that self-realization is the end? There is only one way to do that. This is to know what we mean, when we say "self," and "real," and "realize," and "end"; and to know that is to have something like a system of metaphysic, and to say it would be to exhibit that system. Instead of remarking, then, that we lack space to develop our views, let us frankly confess that, properly speaking, we have no such views to develop, and therefore we can not *prove* our thesis. All that we can do is partially to explain it, and try to render it plausible. It is a formula, which our succeeding Essays will in some way fill up, and which here we shall attempt to recommend to the reader beforehand.

An objection will occur at once. "There surely are ends," it will be said, "which are not myself, which fall outside my activity, and which, nevertheless, I do realize, and think I ought to realize." We must try to show that the objection rests upon a misunderstanding, and, as a statement of fact, brings with it insuperable difficulties.

Let us first go to the moral consciousness, and see what that tells us about its end.

Morality implies an end in itself: we take that for granted. Something is to be done, a good is to be realized. But that result is, by itself, not morality: morality differs from art, in that it can not make the act a *mere* means to the result. Yet there is a means. There is not only something to be done, but something to be done by me—I must do the act, must realize the end. Morality implies both the something to be done, and the doing of it by me; and if you consider them as end and means, you can not separate the end and the means. If you choose to change the position of end and means, and say my doing is the end, and the "to be done" is the means, you would not violate the moral consciousness; for the truth is that means and end are not applicable here. The act for me means my act, and there is no end beyond the act. This we see in the belief that failure may be equivalent morally to success— in the saying, that there is nothing good except a good will. In short, for morality the end implies the act, and the act implies self-realization. This, if it were doubtful, would be shown (we may remark in passing) by the feeling of pleasure which attends the putting forth of the act. For if pleasure be the feeling of self, and accompany the act, this indicates that the putting forth of the act is also the putting forth of the self.

But we must not lay too much stress on the moral consciousness, for we shall be reminded, perhaps, that not only can it be, but, like the miser's consciousness, it frequently has been explained, and that both states of mind are illusions generated on one and the same principle.

Let us then dismiss the moral consciousness, and not trouble ourselves about what we think we ought to do; let us try to show that what we do do, is, perfectly or imperfectly, to realize ourselves, and that we can not possibly do anything else; that all we can realize is (accident apart) our ends, or the objects we desire; and that all we can desire is, in a word, self.

This, we think, will be readily admitted by our main psychological party. What we wish to avoid is that it should be admitted in a form which makes it unmeaning; and of this there is perhaps some danger. We do not want the reader to say, "Oh yes, of course, relativity of knowledge—everything is a state of consciousness," and so dismiss the question. If the reader believes that a steam-engine, after it is made, is nothing but a state of the mind of the person or persons who have made it, or who are looking at it, we do not hold what we feel tempted to call such a silly doctrine; and would point out to those who do hold it that, at all events, the engine is a very different state of mind, after it is made, from what it was before.

Again, we do not want the reader to say, "Certainly, every object or end which I propose to myself is, as such, a mere state of my mind—it is a thought in my head, or a state of me, and so, when it becomes real, I become real"; because, though it is very true that my thought, as my thought, can not exist apart from me thinking it, and therefore my proposed end must, as such, be a state of me; yet this is not what we are driving at. All my ends are my thoughts, but all my thoughts are not my ends; and if what we meant by self-realization was, that I have in my head the idea of any future external event, then I should realize myself practically when I see that the engine is going to run off the line, and it does so.

A desired object (as desired) is a thought, and my thought; but it is something more, and that something more is, in short, that it is desired by me. And we ought by right, before we go further, to exhibit a theory of desire; but, if we could do that, we could not stop to do it. However, we say with confidence that, in desire, what is desired must in all cases be self.

If we could accept the theory that the end or motive is always the idea of a pleasure (or pain) of our own, which is associated with the object presented, and which is that in the object which moves us, and the only thing which does move us, then from such a view it would follow at once that all we can aim at is a state of ourselves.

We can not, however, accept the theory, since we believe it both to ignore and to be contrary to facts (see Essay VII); but, though we do not admit that the motive is always, or in most cases, the idea of a state of our feeling self, yet we think it is clear that nothing moves unless it be desired, and that what is desired is ourself. For all objects or ends have been associated with our satisfaction, or (more correctly) have been felt in and as ourselves, or we have felt ourselves therein; and the only reason why they move us now is that, when they are presented to our minds as motives, we do now feel ourselves asserted or affirmed in them. The essence of desire for an object would thus be the feeling of our affirmation in the idea of something not ourself, felt against the feeling of ourself as, without the object, void and negated; and it is the tension of this relation which produces motion. If so, then nothing is desired except that which is identified with ourselves, and we can aim at nothing, except so far as we aim at ourselves in it.

But passing by the above, which we can not here expound and which we lay no stress on, we think that the reader will probably go with us so far as this, that in desire what we want, so far as we want it, is ourselves in some form, or is some state of ourselves; and that our wanting anything else would be psychologically inexplicable.

Let us take this for granted then; but is this what we mean by self-realization? Is the conclusion that, in trying to realize we try to realize some state of ourself, all that we are driving at? No, the self we try to realize is for us a whole, it is not a mere collection of states.

If we may presuppose in the reader a belief in the doctrine that what is wanted is a state of self, we wish, standing upon that, to urge further that the whole self is present in its states, and that therefore the whole self is the object aimed at; and this is what we mean by self-realization. If a state of self is what is desired, can you, we wish to ask, have states of self which are states of nothing (compare Essay I); can you possibly succeed in regarding the self as a collection, or stream, or train, or series, or aggregate? If you can not think of it as a mere one, can you on the other hand think of it as a mere many, as mere ones; or are you not driven, whether you wish it or not, to regard it as a one in many, or a many in one? Are we not forced to look on the self as a whole, which is not merely the sum of its parts, nor yet some other particular beside them? And must we not say that to realize self is always to realize a whole, and that the question in morals is to find the true whole, realizing which will practically realize the true self?

For the present, turning our attention away from it in this form, and contenting ourselves with the proposition that to realize is to realize self, let us now, apart from questions of psychology or metaphysics, see what ends they are, in fact, which living men do propose to themselves, and whether these do not take the form of a whole.

Upon this point there is no need, I think, to dwell at any length; for it seems clear that, if we ask ourselves what it is we should most wish for, we find some general wish which would include and imply our particular wishes. And, if we turn to life, we see that no man has disconnected particular ends; he looks beyond the moment, beyond this or that circumstance or position; his ends are subordinated to wider ends; each situation is seen (consciously or unconsciously) as part of a broader situation, and in this or that act he is aiming at and realizing some larger whole, which is not real in any particular act as such, and yet is realized in the body of acts which carry it out. We need not stop here, because the existence of larger ends, which embrace smaller ends, can not be doubted; and so far we may say that the self we realize is identified with wholes, or that the ideas of the states of self we realize are associated with ideas that stand for wholes.

But is it also true that these larger wholes are included in one whole? I think that it is. I am not forgetting that we act, as a rule, not *from* principle or with the principle before us, and I wish the reader not to forget that the principle may be there and may be our basis or our goal, without our knowing anything about it. And here, of course, I am not saying that it has occurred to every one to ask himself whether he aims at a whole, and what that is; because considerable reflection is required for this, and the amount need not have been reached. Nor again am I saying that every man's actions are consistent, that he does not wander from his end, and that he has not particular ends which will not come under his main end. Nor further do I assert that the life of every man does form a whole; that in some men there are not co-ordinated ends, which are incompatible and incapable of subordination into a system. What I am saying is that, if the life of the normal man be inspected, and the ends he has in view (as exhibited in his acts) be considered, they will, roughly speaking, be embraced in one main end or whole of ends. It has been said that "every man has a different notion of happiness," but this is scarcely correct, unless mere detail be referred to. Certainly, however, every man has a notion of happiness, and *his* notion, though he may not quite know what it is. Most men have a life which they live, and with which they are tolerably satisfied, and that life, when examined, is seen to be fairly systematic; it is seen to be a sphere including spheres, the lower spheres subordinating to themselves and qualifying particular actions, and themselves subordinated to and qualified by the whole. And most men have more or less of an ideal of life—a notion of perfect happiness, which is never quite attained in real life; and if you take (not of course any one, but) the normal decent and serious man, when he has been long enough in the world to know what he wants, you will find that his notion of perfect happiness, or ideal life, is not something straggling, as it were, and discontinuous, but is brought before the mind as a unity, and, if imagined more in detail, is a system where particulars subserve one whole.

Without further dwelling on this, I will ask the reader to reflect whether the ends, proposed to themselves by ordinary persons, are not wholes, and are not in the end numbers in a larger whole; and, if that be so, whether, since it is so, and since all we can want must (as before stated) be ourselves, we must not now say that we aim not only at the realization of self, but of self as a whole; seeing that there is a general object of desire with which self is identified, or (on another view) with the idea of which the idea of our pleasure is associated.

Up to the present we have been trying to point out that what we aim at is self, and self as a whole; in other words, that self as a whole is, in the end, the content of our wills. It will still further, perhaps, tend to clear the matter, if we refer to the form of the will—not, of course, suggesting that the form is anything real apart from the content.

On this head we are obliged to restrict ourselves to the assertion of what we believe to be fact. We remarked in our last Essay that, in saying "I will this or that," we really mean something. In saying it we do not mean (at least, not as a rule) to distinguish a self that wills from a self that does not will; but what we do mean is to distinguish the self, as will in general, from this or that object of desire, and, at the same time, to identify the two; to say, this or that is willed, or the will has uttered itself in this or that. The will is looked on as a whole, and there are two sides or factors to that whole. Let us consider an act of will, and, that we may see more clearly, let us take a deliberate volitional choice. We have conflicting desires, say A and B; we feel two tensions, two drawings (so to speak), but we can not actually affirm ourselves in both. Action does not follow, and we reflect on the two objects of desire, and we are aware that we are reflecting on them, or (if our language allowed us to say it) over them. But we do not merely stand looking on till, so to speak, we find we are gone in one direction, have closed with A or B. For we are aware besides of ourselves, not simply as something theoretically above A and B, but as something also practically above them, as a concentration which is not one or the other, but which is the possibility of either; which is the inner side indifferently of an act which should realize A, or one which should realize B; and hence, which is neither, and yet is superior to both. In short, we do not simply feel ourselves in A and B, but have distinguished ourselves from both, as what is above both. This is one factor in volition, and it is hard to find any name better for it than that of the universal factor, or side, or moment. We need say much less about the second factor. In order to will, we must will something; the universal side by itself is not will at all. To will we must identify ourselves with this, that, or the other; and here we have the particular side, and the second factor in volition. Thirdly, the volition as a whole (and first, as a whole, is it volition) is the identity of both these factors, and the projection or carrying of it out into external existence; the realization both of the particular side, the this or that to be done, and the realization of the inner side of self in the doing of it, with a realization of self in both, as is proclaimed by the feeling of pleasure. This unity of the two factors we may call the individual whole, or again the concrete universal; and, although we are seldom conscious of the distinct factors, yet every act of will will be seen, when analysed, to be a whole of this kind, and so to realize what is always the nature of the will.

But to what end have we made this statement? Our object has been to draw the attention of the reader to the fact that not only what is willed by men, the end they set before themselves, is a whole, but also that the will itself, looked at apart from any particular object or content, is a similar whole: or, to put it in its proper order, the self is realized in a whole of ends because it is a whole, and because it is not satisfied till it has found itself, till content be adequate to form, and that content be realized; and this is what we mean by practical self-realization.

"Realize yourself," "realize yourself as a whole," is the result of the foregoing. The reader, I fear, may be wearied already by these prefatory remarks, but it will be better in the end if we delay yet longer. All we know at present is that we are to realize self as *a* whole; but as to *what* whole it is, we know nothing, and must further consider.

The end we desire (to repeat it) is the finding and possessing ourselves as a whole. We aim at this both in theory and practice. What we want in theory is to understand the object; we want neither to remove nor alter the world of sensuous fact; but we want to get at the truth of it. The whole of science takes it for granted that the "not-ourself" is really intelligible; it stands and falls with this assumption. So long as our theory strikes on the mind as strange and alien, so long do we say we have not found truth; we feel the impulse to go beyond and beyond, we alter and alter our views, till we see them as a consistent whole. There we rest, because then we have found the nature of our own mind and the truth of facts in one. And in practice again, with a difference, we have the same want. Here our aim is not, leaving the given as it is, to find the truth of it; but here we want to force the sensuous fact to correspond to the truth of ourselves. We say, "My sensuous existence is thus, but I truly am not thus; I am different." On the other hand, as a matter of fact, I and my existing world are discrepant; on the other hand, the instinct of my nature tells me that the world is mine. On that impulse I act, I alter and alter the sensuous facts, till I find in them nothing but myself carried out. Then I possess my world, and I do not possess it until I find my will in it; and I do not find that, until what I have is a harmony or a whole in system.

Both in theory and practice my end is to realize myself as a whole. But is this all? Is a *consistent* view all that we want in theory? Is an *harmonious* life all that we want in practice? Certainly not. A doctrine must not only hold together, but it must hold the facts together as well. We can not rest in it simply because it does not contradict itself. The theory must take in the facts, and an ultimate theory must take in all the facts. So again in practice. It is no human ideal to lead "the life of an oyster." We have no right first to find out just what we happen to be and to have, and then to contract our wants to that limit. We can not do it if we would, and morality calls to us that, if we try to do it, we are false to ourselves. Against the sensuous facts around us and within us, we must for ever attempt to widen our empire; we must at least try to go forward, or we shall certainly be driven back.

So self-realization means more than the mere assertion of the self as a whole. And here we may refer to two principles, which Kant put forward under the names of "Homogeneity" and "Specification." Not troubling ourselves with our relation to Kant, we may say that the ideal is neither to be perfectly homogeneous, nor simply to be specified to the last degree, but rather to combine both these elements. Our true being is not the extreme of unity, nor of diversity, but the perfect identity of both. And "Realize yourself" does not mean merely "Be a whole," but "Be an *infinite* whole."

• Benedict Spinoza (1632–77)

The True and Final Good[5]

Baruch (later signing himself Benedict) Spinoza, contemporary of Descartes (of whose *Meditations* this selection is somehow reminiscent), wrote his *Ethics* to demonstrate mathematically his view of the world. A serene thinker, and a Jew excommunicated from the community of his fellow religionists of Amsterdam, he is an illustration of the thoughtful philosophic temper at its best. This selection shows his belief in the vanity of the usual worldly values and his notion that men should strive for perfection of character and for a love of the eternal.

After experience had taught me that all the usual surroundings of social life are vain and futile; seeing that none of the objects of my fears contained in themselves anything either good or bad, except in so far as the mind is affected by them, I finally resolved to inquire whether there might be some real good having power to communicate itself, which would affect the mind singly, to the exclusion of all else; whether, in fact, there might be anything of which the discovery and attainment would enable me to enjoy continuous, supreme, and unending happiness. I say "I finally resolved," for at first sight it seemed unwise willingly to lose hold on what was sure for the sake of something then uncertain. I could see the benefits which are acquired through fame and riches, and that I should be obliged to abandon the quest of such objects, if I seriously devoted myself to the search for something different and new. I perceived that if true happiness chanced to be placed in the former I should necessarily miss it; while if, on the other hand, it were not so placed, and I gave them my whole attention, I should equally fail.

I therefore debated whether it would not be possible to arrive at the new principle, or at any rate at a certainty concerning its

[5] From Spinoza, *The Improvement of the Understanding* (1677), trans. R. H. M. Elwes (1883).

existence, without changing the conduct and usual plan of my life; with this end in view I made many efforts, but in vain. For the ordinary surroundings of life which are esteemed by men (as their actions testify) to be the highest good, may be classed under the three heads—Riches, Fame, and the Pleasures of Sense: with these three the mind is so absorbed that it has little power to reflect on any different good. By sensual pleasure the mind is enthralled to the extent of quiescence, as if the supreme good were actually attained, so that it is quite incapable of thinking of any other object; when such pleasure has been gratified it is followed by extreme melancholy, whereby the mind, though not enthralled, is disturbed and dulled.

The pursuit of honors and riches is likewise very absorbing, especially if such objects be sought simply for their own sake, inasmuch as they are then supposed to constitute the highest good. In the case of fame the mind is still more absorbed, for fame is conceived as always good for its own sake, and as the ultimate end to which all actions are directed. Further, the attainment of riches and fame is not followed as in the case of sensual pleasures by repentance, but, the more we acquire, the greater is our delight, and, consequently, the more we are incited to increase both the one and the other; on the other hand, if our hopes happen to be frustrated we are plunged into the deepest sadness. Fame has the further drawback that it compels its votaries to order their lives according to the opinions of their fellow-men, shunning what they usually shun, and seeking what they usually seek.

When I saw that all these ordinary objects of desire would be obstacles in the way of a search for something different and new— nay, that they were so opposed thereto, that either they or it would have to be abandoned, I was forced to inquire which would prove the most useful to me: for, as I say, I seemed to be willingly losing hold on a sure good for the sake of something uncertain. However, after I had reflected on the matter, I came in the first place to the conclusion that by abandoning the ordinary objects of pursuit, and betaking myself to a new quest, I should be leaving a good, uncertain by reason of its own nature, as may be gathered from what has been said, for the sake of a good not uncertain in its nature (for I sought for a fixed good), but only in the possibility of its attainment.

Further reflection convinced me, that if I could really get to the root of the matter, I should be leaving certain evils for a certain good. I thus perceived that I was in a state of great peril, and I compelled myself to seek with all my strength for a remedy, however uncertain it might be; as a sick man struggling with a deadly disease, when he sees that death will surely be upon him unless a remedy be found, is compelled to seek such a remedy with all his strength, inasmuch as his whole hope lies therein. All the objects pursued by the multitude, not only bring no remedy that tends to preserve our being, but even act as hindrances, causing the death not seldom of those who possess them, and always of those who are possessed by them. There are many examples of men who have suffered persecution even to death for the sake of their riches, and of men who in pursuit of wealth have exposed themselves to so many dangers, that they have paid away their life as a penalty for their folly. Examples are no less numerous of men, who have endured the utmost wretchedness for the sake of gaining or preserving their reputation. Lastly, there are innumerable cases of men, who have hastened their death through over-indulgence in sensual pleasure. All these evils seem to have arisen from the fact, that happiness or unhappiness is made wholly to depend on the quality of the object which we love. When a thing is not loved, no quarrels will arise concerning it—no sadness will be felt if it perishes—no envy if it is possessed by another—no fear, no hatred, in short no disturbances of the mind. All these arise from the love of what is perishable, such as the objects already mentioned. But love toward a thing eternal and infinite feeds the mind wholly with joy, and is itself unmingled with any sadness, wherefore it is greatly to be desired and sought for with all our strength. Yet it was not at random that I used the words, "If I could go to the root of the matter," for, though what I have urged was perfectly clear to my mind, I could not forthwith lay aside all love of riches, sensual enjoyment, and fame. One thing was evident, namely, that while my mind was employed with these thoughts it turned away from its former objects of desire, and seriously considered the search for a new principle; this state of things was a great comfort to me, for I perceived that the evils were not such as to resist all remedies. Although these intervals were at first rare, and of very short duration, yet afterward, as the true good became more and more discernible to me, they became more frequent and more lasting; especially after I had recognized that the acquisition of wealth, sensual pleasure, or fame, is only a hindrance, so long as they are sought as ends not as means; if they be sought as means they will be under restraint, and, far from being hindrances, will further not a little the end for which they are sought, as I will show in due time.

I will here only briefly state what I mean by true good, and also what is the nature of the highest good. In order that this may be rightly understood, we must bear in mind that the terms good and evil are only applied relatively, so that the same thing may be called both good and bad, according to the relations in view, in the same way as it may be called perfect or imperfect. Nothing regarded in its own nature can be called perfect or imperfect; especially when we are aware that all things which come to pass, come to pass according to the eternal order and fixed laws of nature. However, human weakness cannot attain to this order in its own thoughts, but meanwhile man conceives a human character much more stable than his own, and sees that there is no reason why he should not himself acquire such a character. Thus he is led to seek for means which will bring him to this pitch of perfection, and calls everything which will serve as such means a true good. The chief good is that he should arrive, together with other individuals if possible, at the possession of the aforesaid character. What that character is we shall show in due time, namely, that it is the knowledge of the union existing between the mind and the whole of nature. This, then, is the end for which I strive, to attain to such a character myself, and to endeavor that many should attain to it with me. In other words, it is part of my happiness to lend a helping hand, that many others may understand even as I do, so that their understanding and desire may entirely agree with my own. In order to bring this about, it is necessary to understand as much of nature as will enable us to attain to the aforesaid character, and also to form a social order such as is most conducive to the attainment of this character by the greatest number with the least difficulty and danger. We must seek the assistance of Moral Philosophy and the Theory of Education; further, as health is no insignificant means for attaining our end, we must also include the whole science of Medicine, and, as many difficult things are by contrivance rendered easy, and we can in this way gain much time and convenience, the science of Mechanics must in no way be despised. But, before all things, a means must be devised for improving the understanding and purifying it, as far as may be at the outset, so that it may apprehend things without error, and in the best possible way.

Thus it is apparent to every one that I wish to direct all sciences to one end and aim, so that we may attain to the supreme human perfection which we have named; and, therefore, whatsoever in the sciences does not serve to promote our object will have to be rejected as useless. To sum up the matter in a word, all our actions and thoughts must be directed to this one end. Yet, as it is necessary that while we are endeavoring to attain our purpose, and bring the understanding into the right path, we should carry on our life, we are compelled first of all to lay down certain rules of life as provisionally good, to wit, the following:

I. To speak in a manner intelligible to the multitude, and to comply with every general custom that does not hinder the attainment of our purpose. For we can gain from the multitude no small advantages, provided that we strive to accommodate ourselves to its understanding as far as possible; moreover, we shall in this way gain a friendly audience for the reception of the truth.

II. To indulge ourselves with pleasures only in so far as they are necessary for preserving health.

III. Lastly, to endeavor to obtain only sufficient money or other commodities to enable us to preserve our life and health, and to follow such general customs as are consistent with our purpose.

Having laid down these preliminary rules, I will betake myself to the first and most important task, namely, the amendment of the understanding, and the rendering it capable of understanding things in the manner necessary for attaining our end.

SUGGESTED FURTHER READINGS

ARISTOTLE. *Nicomachean Ethics.* Translated by W. D. Ross. London: Oxford University Press, 1925.

BENTHAM, JEREMY. *Introduction to the Principles of Morals and Legislation.* London: Oxford University Press, 1907.

BRADLEY, F. H. *Ethical Studies.* London: Oxford University Press, 1907.

CICERO. *On the Ends of Good and Evil.* (Loeb classics.) Cambridge, Mass.: Harvard University Press.

DEWEY, JOHN. *Human Nature and Conduct.* New York: Henry Holt & Co., Inc., 1922. Pragmatic view.

EWING, A. C. *The Definition of Good.* New York: The Macmillan Co., 1947. Idealistic view.

HARTMANN, NICOLAI. *Ethics.* Translated by STANTON COIT. 3 vols. New York: The Macmillan Co., 1932. Realistic view.

HUME, DAVID. *An Enquiry Concerning the Principles of Morals.* La Salle, Ill.: The Open Court Pub. Co., 1930.

KANT, IMMANUEL. *The Critique of Practical Reason.* Translated by L. W. BECK. Chicago: The University of Chicago Press, 1949.

MILL, JOHN STUART. *Utilitarianism.* (Everyman ed.) New York: E. P. Dutton & Co., Inc., 1911.

MOORE, G. E. *Principia Ethica.* Cambridge: Cambridge University Press, 1929.

PLATO. *Gorgias, Protagoras, Philebus.* 4th ed. Translated by B. JOWETT. London: Oxford University Press, 1953.

SIDGWICK, HENRY. *The Methods of Ethics.* London: Macmillan & Co., Ltd., 1913.

STACE, W. T. *The Concept of Morals.* New York: The Macmillan Co., 1947.

STEVENSON, C. L. *Ethics and Language.* New Haven: Yale University Press, 1945. Modified positivistic view.

CHAPTER 6

Social Living

THE POLITICAL STATE

It is difficult to separate problems of individual decision from problems of social living. And, therefore, the fields of ethics and of political and social philosophy belong close together. Already we have seen that the elements of the moral situation are the self, its social environment, and standards of value. Ethics tends to deal with the decisions of the individual as though they were primarily a matter of the confrontation of the self with standards of value. Political and social philosophy deals more with the social environment, the standards that it suggests or imposes, and the problems that arise when purely individual values conflict with those of society.

The distinction between the individual and society is basic for this field, however artificial it may seem to be. The concepts are, in fact, correlative. We are all prepared to believe that "society" is no mysterious and anonymous entity, and that it is composed of individuals—the grocer, the clergyman, our friends and neighbors, and those others of whom we know, although not by direct acquaintance. But, on the other hand, we are prepared to believe that individuals are "made" by society and by the family, which is society's delegated representative in this task. It is the duty of our parents, teachers, spiritual advisors to humanize us, Americanize us, or Christianize us as the case may be; to make us fit participants in the traditions into which we are born. Society makes individuals. Individuals make up society. It would seem that conflict between them is impossible. But something goes wrong. Society is not quite so unified and homogeneous as one might think. It is composed of antagonistic groups with conflicting values. Christians, Moslems, and Jews do not entirely agree on the nature of the good life; Republicans and Democrats do not entirely agree on the nature of the good political order; large corporations and labor unions do not entirely agree on the nature of the best economic arrangements in society. So long as the groups with which we are identified are a majority or are powerful in society, we feel no special alienation, but, when we feel powerless or are a member of a minority group, values prevail of which we do not approve, and the consciousness of our incompatibility with society becomes acute.

Of course, our points of contact with social institutions tend to radiate outward like a series of ripples on water into which a stone has been thrown. Most of us live in a series of circles; what is nearest to the center of the circles is most real to us—our closest family, our small group of friends, our particular job. Vaguer and further away are a series of larger entities; our region, our nation, the Western World, humanity at large. But among all these entities, there is one that (whether we are aware of it or not) seems to touch our life at almost every point, that provides the framework of order in which we exist, that has over us even the power of life and death. This entity is the political state.

Some of the associations and groups which compose society exist prior to their individual members and are not chosen by them; others are joined by individuals on a voluntary basis. The family and the elementary school are prior to persons. They are the institutions in which individuality is made and formed. We do not choose them, but we are their products. Clubs, trade associations, labor unions are another matter; these we join on a voluntary basis and leave them when we wish. Somewhere in between these two kinds of groups are the church and the state. For we "belong" to them before we have made any conscious choices in the matter, but we continue to belong to them after we have come of age, and we leave them only by a conscious and deliberate act. The state controls the conditions of our life in a very special way.

What is the state? Throughout the history of political philosophy there have been various answers to this question. Some have defined the state as the organization of classes within society wherein one particular class is in control. Others have defined the state as a legal entity, as the only social institution capable of making laws binding upon all. Still others have defined it as the political organization of the community in its entirety. All the various accounts have one central and recurring problem: Is the state to be defined primarily as an agency of power or an agency of welfare for the social whole?

One tradition (which goes back to the ancient Sophists, although it includes Machiavelli, Thomas Hobbes, and John Austin) sees the state as the sovereign authority in society, with the power to issue commands and the right to back them up with coercive penalties. The laws of any state may (as Kant would have wished) be obeyed out of mere respect for them as laws, but no state need depend merely upon public opinion for law enforcement. It has its own police power for this purpose. This particular perspective views the state as resting ultimately upon the power of coercion. Another way of stating this position is to say *the state is that institution which enjoys a monopoly of legitimate violence.* Violence is "legitimate" only when exercised by the state, and it may be exercised through the agencies of a police force and a standing army, the first to maintain internal order, the second to protect against the threat of external aggression.

But another tradition (which goes back to Aristotle [1] and includes such thinkers as John Locke, Rousseau, and Jeremy Bentham) insists that the exercise of power is a means which the state employs, but is not its essence. The essence of the state is to be discovered in the values that cause men to associate in the first place—not only the desire to live, but the desire to live well. This view considers that the state is not an end in itself, but a means to the good life for the citizens, and it implies that political states may be subjected to moral criticism when they do not fulfill their proper function. If the state is but an instrument of social man, if it can never be perfect, and if it always has limitations as well as potentialities, then it can never be worshipped as the chief glory of social life. It is one of the forms which society takes, and, when it functions best, it provides a system of order and control within which the normal activities of living—worship, education, economic maintenance, social intercourse—may take place.

There have been ages that have fallen under the spell of the magic of the sovereign state, that have thought of it as possessing a majesty and an infallibility beyond question. But if the claim of universal supremacy is denied to the state, then it is clear that the coercive power, which lies within its rights, is the power which any government has as guardian of the constitution and upholder of the laws. But the law itself cannot be more than a general framework of order. Therefore, it may function best when it provides the safety and encouragement for other human associations to flourish, whether they be families, churches, or economic enterprises. Here, then, in a contemporary version of the tradition of Aristotle and Locke, is a definition of the political state: *"The state is an association which, acting through law as promulgated by a government*

[1] See p. 322.

298 VARIETIESVARIETIES OF EXPERIENCE

endowed to this end with coercive power, maintains within a community territorially demarcated the universal external conditions of social order." [2]

The history of the political state is largely a history of acts of personal or collective rebellion against its absolute power. For there is an eternal conflict between a strong sense of individuality and the coercive power which the state may from time to time exercise. And this conflict reaches its height when the basis of the individual protest is a moral principle, when, in short, it rests upon the authority of the individual conscience. This position has never been more clearly stated than in the words of the great American writer Henry David Thoreau in his 1849 pamphlet "Civil Disobedience":

Can there not be a government in which majorities do not virtually decide right and wrong, but conscience?—in which majorities decide only those questions to which the rule of expediency is applicable? Must the citizen ever for a moment, or in the least degree, resign his conscience to the legislator? Why has every man a conscience, then? I think that we should be men first, and subjects afterward. It is not desirable to cultivate a respect for the law, so much as for the right. The only obligation which I have a right to assume is to do at any time what I think right. . . .

The appeal to conscience is even more powerful when it is reinforced by a religious sanction; this is perfectly illustrated by a situation in the *Antigone* of Sophocles. A great battle has been fought at Thebes and many of the invaders have fallen, among them the rebel nephew of Creon, the king. Creon orders that the bodies of the slain enemies, including his nephew, remain unburied where they have fallen as a mark of shame—a procedure against which there was a strong religious taboo among the Greeks. Antigone, the king's niece, knowing of his decree, comes secretly to bury her rebel brother. In the act, she is seized by the guards and taken before the king.

Creon
Speak, girl, with head bent low and downcast eyes,
Dost thou plead guilty or deny the deed?

Antigone
Guilty. I did it. I deny it not.

Creon
Now answer this plain question, yes or no,
Wast thou acquainted with the interdict?

---

[2] R. M. MacIver, *The Modern State* (London: Oxford University Press, 1928), p. 22.

Antigone

I knew, all knew; how should I fail to know?

Creon

And yet wert bold enough to break the law?

Antigone

Yes, for these laws were not ordained of Zeus,
And she who sits enthroned with gods below,
Justice, enacted not these human laws.
Nor did I deem that thou, a mortal man,
Could'st by a breath annul and override
The immutable unwritten laws of Heaven.
They were not born today nor yesterday;
They die not; and none know whence they sprang.
I was not like, who feared no mortal's frown,
To disobey these laws and so provoke
The wrath of Heaven. . . .[3]

Antigone's appeal to "the immutable unwritten laws of Heaven" against the decree of an absolute earthly sovereign is a situation which every conflict between state authority and religious scruple repeats. There is a serious moral issue between the loyalties which are demanded by the political state and the religious assertion of a realm of "the things that are not Caesar's"; Christian Scientists refuse to follow local regulations concerning vaccination in the public schools; members of the sect of Jehovah's Witnesses refuse to salute the American flag; Quakers, on the grounds of conscientious objection, refuse to bear arms in the nation's defense.

What then is the relation of political law to morality? Political law, when it is wise, doubtless tries to reflect moral principle as the legislator sees it, but the margin of error in the generality of even the best laws shows the folly of equating the two. The law is not a prescription of morality, and, so long as there are moral personalities, there will be ethical criticism of specific legal enactments—criticism which in some cases will lead to actual civil disobedience. Of course, this is not the only possible response to obvious injustice on the part of the political state. Another possibility which does not deny the claims of conscience, but which at the same time does not disobey the law is provided by the famous case of Socrates (see p. 310). This martyr to the cause of open discussion and rational persuasion, put to death by the Athenian state twenty-three centuries ago, demonstrated the obligation which man owes to the state even when he has suffered injustice at its hands.

[3] In the Loeb ed., trans. F. Storr.

The Problem of Liberty

No problem in the entire field of political and social living is more perplexing than the problem of freedom. That freedom is one of the greatest of social values is undeniable, but exactly what is implied by freedom is not so clear. Is it freedom to be, to have, or to do? Are we concerned with freedom of movement, freedom of speech, or freedom from government economic regulation? Although most Americans agree that freedom is eminently desirable, they are far from agreed as to its specific meaning. Can this meaning be clarified? As a first approach let us consult the original charter of American freedom, the first ten Amendments to the Constitution, which constitute the Bill of Rights. Consider Article I and Article V.

Article I

Congress shall make no law respecting the establishment of religion, or prohibiting the free exercise thereof; or abridging the freedom of speech, or of the press; or the right of the people peaceably to assemble, and to petition the government for a redress of grievances.

Article V

No person shall . . . be deprived of life, liberty, or property without due process of law; nor shall private property be taken for public use without just compensation.

There is a profound difference between these two articles. Both of them deal with our liberties, but they distinguish sharply between two kinds of liberty, and they say that these two kinds make quite different claims upon our government. The first article deals with the freedoms of *religion, speech, the press, assembly,* and *petition,* and these are so absolute, so crucial in their nature that *congress shall make no law whatsoever* in violation of them. They are rights of which the individual can under no circumstances be deprived. They are *the civil liberties.*

The freedoms of the fifth article are different. They are the freedoms of *life, liberty,* and *property.* They are not inalienable or absolute rights. Any man may be deprived of them (criminals, of life and liberty; ordinary citizens, of property, through taxation or civil suit) so long as it has been through the lawful process of the courts and executive authority. The rights of life and property are dear to every man, but they are not on the same level of value as the civil liberties.[4]

[4] This comparison follows A. Meiklejohn, *What Does America Mean?* chap. vi.

But upon what principles can the absoluteness of the freedoms of religion, speech, the press, assembly, and petition be justified? What philosophical premises support their claim to be more fundamental than any authority which the political state has the right to exercise? Traditionally two quite different answers have been given. The first asserts that our freedom is a natural right. The second asserts that it is a public utility.

The doctrine of natural rights had especial currency in the eighteenth century—precisely at the time, that is, when the American government was founded. And it finds its characteristic expression in the words of Thomas Jefferson in the Declaration of Independence: "We hold these truths to be self-evident; that all men are created equal, that they are endowed by their Creator with certain inalienable rights; that among these are life, liberty . . ." In this frame of reference, liberty is inherent in man's nature, a right implanted and ultimately guaranteed by God. In giving divine support to this human right, Jefferson puts a heavy responsibility upon that government which should dare to deny it. But, on the other hand, he can give no *proof* that it is of divine origin. His contention is that this is a truth which is *self-evident*. But what if there are selves to whom is it far from evident, who claim that inequality and subordination are the law of life and intended by the Creator? Between two conflicting claims of self-evidence there is no adjudication, and, in the end, the claims of self-evidence become too shaky a ground upon which to found the civil liberties.

The nineteenth century took another path. Instead of justifying liberty as the gift of God to the individual, it justified it as the gift of a reasonable society to its members; as the result, not of an inference concerning the will of God, but of society's calculation concerning what would produce the greatest happiness for the greatest number. For liberty as a natural right it substituted liberty as a public utility, and the great spokesman for this point of view is, once again, John Stuart Mill.

Mill begins with the assumption that freedom for the individual is the great value, and that the only grounds on which society is justified in interfering with individual liberty is for self-protection (see page 332). Only when the acts of individuals are a threat to the civilized community can their liberties be curtailed. From this general principle, Mill passes on to the most strategic freedom of all, that of thought and discussion, and it is here that his doctrine of the social usefulness of the civil liberties reaches its climax.

Why should society not silence the expression of opinion, no matter how unpopular, subversive, or blasphemous? First, the opinion which it thinks of suppressing may be true. Of course, the opponents of the belief deny this; but they are not infallible, and to silence discussion on the grounds of its falseness is an assumption of infallibility. It is of the greatest importance to society that there be open the possibility of contradicting and disproving current opinion. Only those beliefs are most reliable which have no artificial safeguards to protect them, but are a standing invitation to the whole world to prove them false.

In the second place, the opinion which society thinks of suppressing may be in error, but at the same time contain a portion of truth. It is rare that moral or social doctrines are totally true or totally false. Mill would argue that even repugnant doctrines like national socialism or fascism or communism, while chiefly false, might contain portions of truth which it would be to the advantage of a representative democracy to discuss. There may be in fascism an urge toward strong united effort and, in communism, a concern for the weak and the lowly. These are worth discussion even if the major principles to which they are attached are false and unworthy.

Finally, even if the opinion which society thinks of suppressing is totally false and completely repugnant, it is socially useful for it to be freely aired and discussed. For, however great a threat it seems to the prevailing opinion, it will yet serve to bring out forcefully the most cogent reasons why the prevailing opinion ought to be held. Even "the right opinions" if they are held out of ignorance and prejudice are dangerous. Free discussion of opposing opinions will serve to show the good reasons why the prevailing opinions should be held. Mankind always has a fatal tendency to stop thinking when there is no longer doubt, and thus to hold even the most crucial beliefs about life and society as dogmas which are routinely accepted. In this way even the most necessary beliefs are enfeebled. A healthy society requires ferment more than quiescence, challenge as well as acceptance, an electorate with active and energetic minds rather than a sodden and apathetic people. The freedom of thought and discussion for "dangerous," "unconventional," even "wicked" doctrines has a valuable consequence for society; it keeps alive the search for truth, it stimulates generosity toward new and strange possibilities, it maintains the flow of life in social institutions all too ready to succumb to hardening of the arteries of thought.

Mill's argument for the freedom of thought and discussion is a brilliant appeal for the liberal point of view, for the obligation to follow an argument wherever it leads, for the tolerance of that diversity of opinion through which all sides of an argument are granted fair play. But as a proof of the grounds upon which the civil liberties rest, it, like the argument from natural rights, omits something of great importance. For, in grounding the civil liberties in the greatest-happiness doctrine, Mill suggests (although he does not specifically say so) that the values of freedom are primarily social values. In the end society is to be the judge. In the end even the truth of a doctrine is part of its "utility." At this point there is missing and needed some of the "absolutism" maintained in the doctrine of natural rights.

The natural rights doctrine hinges upon a theological foundation which cannot be proved to the satisfaction of a secular age. The social utility doctrine gives insufficient attention to the *intrinsic* value of liberty; it makes too much dependent upon conditions of social desirability. Perhaps what is wanted here is neither a natural rights nor a social utility, but a *self-realizational* theory of the civil liberties.

Such a theory might argue in the following way. Those same selves which deliberate about the rightness and wrongness of their own acts, as members of society, also deliberate about questions of social policy. And, just as there must be freedom of self-determination for the inner life, so there must be freedom for public discussion and deliberation about outward acts. For these two realms interpenetrate and no sharp line separates them. Selves are largely formed in the process of interacting with their fellows, and the very making of selves requires that they speak freely, answer the words of others, test, with their budding powers of reason, the alternatives before them. But more than this, selfhood is in value (and therefore logically) prior to society, and society must respect *individuality in its own nature* as the source of all values. In a sense John Stuart Mill recognized this. "The worth of a State," he said, "in the long run is the worth of the individuals composing it." But he did not explicitly state that, even beyond its social utility, the freedom of thought and discussion is the very condition of *the making of persons.* But if all value lies in individual selves, and, if their development and realization depend upon an environment where speech is free and individuality is encouraged, then the absoluteness of the claim of the civil liberties is restored.

THE PROBLEM OF PROPERTY

Moral problems connected with property have been traditionally treated under the two headings of *distributive justice* and *economic equality.* And it is clear that, just as the issue of the civil liberties

requires some anaylsis of the doctrines by which they may be justified, so issues of the ownership of property require some consideration of how the values of justice and equality relate to economic
matters. There are two different problems of social living here,
one more particular, and the other more global in its effects. The
first has to do with the distribution of economic burdens, the second
with the underlying philosophy which any political state holds concerning the ownership of property.

To take the more particular and least important first. It has
been held by the courts with some plausibility that the power to tax
is the power to redistribute property. Upon what ethical principles
should taxation be based? Aristotle wrestled with just such a question of distributive justice and saw that the question hinged on
the meaning which one gives to the term "equality." Is it a matter
of treating economic unequals as equal? Or a matter of giving to
unequals "proportionate" treatment? The various forms of taxation
illustrate very well the appeal to alternative principles. A poll tax
or head tax is the same for all. Rich and poor pay alike. But a
graduated income tax distributes the burden according to "ability
to pay." On another level is the question of the relation of what
one pays to what one pays for. Much of state income tax is used
for the support of the public schools and, obviously, it is paid both
by persons with and those without children. Some, therefore, pay
who do not directly benefit (bachelors, for example). But, on the
other hand, the quite considerable state gasoline tax is used largely
for the construction and maintenance of state highways. Here those
who benefit directly from such highways are the ones who pay for
them. Since these four kinds of taxation are in use (often all in
the same community), it is obvious that there is no single principle
of distributive justice which is universally acknowledged.

The second problem is easier to focus sharply because here the
principles are more clearly opposed, and the areas of partisanship
more absolutely drawn. Individualism versus collectivism, capitalism versus socialism, private property versus public property—these
are the oppositions as they are commonly stated. Of course, there
is a certain inaccuracy in these oppositions if it is thought that individualism, capitalism, and private property all stand for the same
thing and are opposed by collectivism, socialism, and public property. Probably there is no social theory whatsoever that denies
the necessity of *personal property* in the sense of ownership of the
articles necessary for consumer use. Clothing, household utensils,
furniture, books, personal effects are privately owned under every

economic system. The chief question, therefore, concerns what are called public utilities or instruments of production; factories, large tracts of fertile land, transportation systems, financial institutions like holding companies and banks. Should these be privately owned and controlled for private profit, or should they be publicly owned and operated, with profits going to the government or society as a whole? Are there any principles of social philosophy which might be of use in the solution of a crucial economic problem of this kind?

Perhaps the first question to ask is this: What justification can be given for the ownership of property in the first place? One of the classical philosophers who pondered this question was John Locke (see p. 344), and the answer which he gave in the *Second Treatise of Civil Government* (1690) is still instructive. Men have a natural right, says Locke, in their own persons, their work, and in the product of their labor. Before things are owned (land or its produce) they are unclaimed in nature, and man removes them from nature and appropriates them for his own consumptive uses. But *he ought not to take more than he can use.* The bounties of nature were not given by God for man to spoil or destroy. Locke's treatment yields two interesting principles about property: (1) the value of property comes from the labor cost in acquiring it, and (2) the right to property depends on the *labor* which secures it, and the *need* which motivated its appropriation.

It is a curious irony that Locke, who was socially conservative, who believed in private property and its protection, and who transmitted this belief to such founders of the American government as Madison and Hamilton, should provide at the same time valuable weapons in the socialist arsenal. For socialists claim, not to be opposed to private property, but only to property which is not used directly by its owner and is rented out to others for a profit. If, runs the socialist argument, you own your own home and live in it, that is a natural use of property. But if you own many houses and rent them out to others for profit, this use of property is perverted, for it means that you *own* for a living rather than *work* for a living; it means you own beyond your need. In a more primitive economy, ownership, productivity, and use go together. The farmer owns his land, by his labor produces grain upon it, and himself consumes the bread made therefrom. But the division of labor and the creation of exchange outside the family produced a society divided between the owners of the means of production, the operators of these means, and the consumers of the goods produced.

At this point the conflict of interests has engulfed society.

Owners of property try to make as much in rent or dividends as possible; operators and laborers try to make as much in wages, salaries, and profits as possible; the consumer tries to buy as cheaply as possible. Producer competes with producer, the interest of the producer conflicts with that of the consumer, management conflicts with labor. The upshot is that the issue of property, which lies at the bottom of the matter, has developed into an issue about the total economic organization of society. It is here that the quarrel between capitalism and economic individualism, on the one hand, and socialism and collectivism, on the other, grows open and troublesome.

Capitalism sees in the search for private profits and the ownership of private property a condition where certain valuable traits of personality may be fostered; a certain economic adventuresomeness, a kind of personal initiative which comes only in a system of free economic enterprise. And it sees these individual qualities as working for the benefit of society as a whole through the development of cheap products, new processes of manufacture, and the development of new areas of expansion within economic society. It therefore frankly accepts and values "the acquisitive instincts" in man as avenues of progress.

It is precisely these acquisitive instincts which distress socialists. For they see them as evidence of individual selfishness which turns men against one another and, in the end, disrupts society. Their goal is not a social order dominated by the conflict of interest between different groups, but what they call "a cooperative commonwealth." For them, the public ownership and operation of the means of production means social cooperation rather than conflict, and a "reasonable" society based upon centralized social planning performed by government experts.

Beginning with a difference in estimate of the values inherent in private property, capitalism and socialism conflict over the mode of organization which should be employed in economic society, and here the difference shifts to a conflicting estimate of the values of individual enterprise and cooperative public activity. It also shifts to concerns which are as much political as economic; whether the economic powers of the state should be absolute and centralized, or whether economic activity should be so far as possible left in the hands of private corporations and labor organizations. The issues here depend partly on one's philosophy of government and cannot even be clarified apart from a study of the nature of political power.

THE DEMOCRATIC IDEA

Problems of the political state, of liberty, and of property, all, in one way or another, fall under the more general consideration of the democratic idea. For behind this idea is a series of moral principles which serve to define the operation of an ideal state, show how liberty is related to it, and even suggest a democratic rather than an oligarchic notion of property.

The idea of democracy has had a long and a complex history, but in it are at least three important ingredients: (1) Aristotle's conception of a "polity" which is *the rule of the many according to a framework of law;* (2) Rousseau's conception of the general will which is *the unified spirit of the political community discovering itself and expressing itself in action;* (3) James Mill's conception that the problem of democracy is to prevent the abuse of power by the rulers and that, therefore, *a system of representative government secures a coincidence of interest between the rulers and the ruled.*

Aristotle quite simply divided governments according to whether the ruler was one man, a few, or many, and then divided each of these into two, according to whether the rule was lawful or lawless. Democracy (in the modern sense of the term) is what he would have called lawful rule by the many. Rousseau's doctrine is more complicated, but he saw the state as a moral personality with a certain unity, and he conceived of individual citizens striving always for unanimity, for that "General Will" which should take up all conflicts into an ultimate agreement. And certainly such striving for rational agreement is central for a democracy. By the time of James Mill (father of J. S. Mill), democracy could no longer be the direct voice of the citizens as it was in the small Athenian city-state, and people could only speak through their periodically elected representatives. Mill said, therefore, that government could only represent the will of the people if all government officials were held directly responsible to them. Thus, legality, general agreement, and the accountability of leaders are all ingredients in the democratic idea.

The democratic idea has both an idealistic and a realistic component. Rousseau's idea realizes that politics can never be defined as pure power, but must also be granted a moral dimension. Alexander Meiklejohn has stated this in a way that brings Rousseau up to date (see p. 354), by saying that democracy is an enterprise in which all the members have a genuine share, and he holds that this enterprise is not merely a matter of a higher level of living, more labor-saving devices, and a greater income, but is a moral and spiritual enterprise in which sensitivity and intelligence must play a major role. This is the inward and essential side of a democracy, as material prosperity may be its outward and superficial consequence.

But democratic theory is also realistic, for it recognizes (even as Jeremy Bentham did) the selfish and self-seeking element in human nature. This is why it is so convinced of the necessity of "checks and balances" in government, why it is suspicious of any extension of executive power, why it makes legislative representatives so directly accountable to the people through periodic elections. It holds that rulers, unchecked, may act for their own interests and not for the good of the people; unless they are carefully watched, they cannot be trusted. And this is not small-mindedness, but a healthy mistrust based on real experience of human nature. And it is also why in a democracy this same mistrust often extends not only to government officials, but also to officials of large corporations and of big labor associations. For democracy as a principle may extend not only to political, but to economic institutions as well.

Democracy may be defined as the political system where those whose interests are at stake are the ones who make the decisions, or as the kind of political enterprise in which all the members have a genuine share. Or, in terms of political machinery, it may be defined as that system of control which includes the safeguarding of the civil liberties and representative government. But, valuable as all these definitions are, they leave out one of the aspects which really separates democracy from all forms of totalitarianism, whether facsist or communist. And this is an aspect which is less legalistic than psychological because it defines the democratic idea less as something exclusively political than as that which narrowly limits and confines the domain of the political.

In every human being there are two impulses, one introverted, one extroverted, one interested in social life and the sharing of experience with others, one interested in individual privacy and in closing to others the important life which one lives alone. This dualism can be developed to an extreme on either side, and it can express itself in social intercourse, literature, morality. It can also express itself in political theory.

The theory of extreme individualism (anarchism or that held by Theoreau, for example) denies the realm of the political altogether. It says that everything is private, man has no political obligation, the state ought not to exist. Or, as Thoreau put it, "That government is best which governs not at all."

The theory of totalitarianism is the exact opposite. If anarchism is the total denial of politics, totalitarianism is the total assertion of politics. It says that *everything* falls under the political. There is no private life. Religion, the family, education, the relations between parents and children, between priest and congregation, even the relations between lovers is subordinate to and under the authority of the political state.

The democratic conception of politics tries earnestly to avoid these two extremes. It believes in privacy, but not to the extent of denying the political state altogether. It believes in public politics but not to the extent of making all aspects of life either public or political. The Rousseauistic emphasis upon the democratic attempt to express the General Will is valid; Hegel's glorification of the absolute state is not. John Stuart Mill's emphasis upon the private conscience, the private soul, the private intellect is sound; Thoreau's glorification of the absolutely introverted life is not. It is in this sense that the psychological or temperamental climate of democracy must be a middle ground between the two extremes. Its continuing problem is always to recognize with an accurate tolerance the relation between political obligation and the ultimate privacy of the individual.

The following selections, "Political Obligation" by Plato, "Citizen, State, Law" by Aristotle, "Liberty" by John Stuart Mill, "Property" by John Locke, and "The Intention of Democracy" by Alexander Meiklejohn, are all concerned with the problems of the individual and society, of politics and economics, which arise in the course of man's social living. Plato and Aristotle are the greatest philosophers of ancient Greece. Locke and Mill are in the English liberal tradition. Meiklejohn is a contemporary.

The selections from Plato and Meiklejohn have been included to show something of the idealistic side of political theory, its appeal to nobility of character as well as mere shrewdness. The analyses of Aristotle and Locke (who have much in common as to temperament and philosophic standpoint although separated by two thousand years) are examples of sober good sense in the treatment of politics and property. And Mill deals with liberty in a fashion halfway between the idealism (if not the literary skill) of Plato, and the British good sense of a Locke.

• Plato (427–347 B.C.)

Political Obligation[5]

The great Athenian Plato founded the Academy (the first university in Europe) and wrote and lectured there four hundred years before the Christian era. A philosopher, whose *Dialogues* are the foundation of all western philosophy, he was chiefly interested in mathematics and the theory of the state. In his youth Plato had been a pupil of Socrates, and almost all we know about Socrates we know through Plato who made him the chief speaker in his dialogues. Plato's best-known works are the *Republic, Protagoras, Apology, Symposium, Phaede,* and *Crito,* the last of which entire forms the following selection. The dialogue takes place after Socrates has been condemned to death for impiety and corrupting the youth and while he awaits in prison the day of his execution. One of his friends comes to aid him to escape, but his heroic refusal brings out his belief that political obligation is not to be taken lightly and his notion of the implied contract between the state and the individual citizen.

Persons of the Dialogue

SOCRATES   CRITO

Scene: THE PRISON OF SOCRATES

Socrates. Why have you come at this hour, Crito? It must be quite early?

Crito. Yes, certainly.

Soc. What is the exact time?

Cr. The dawn is breaking.

Soc. I wonder that the keeper of the prison would let you in.

Cr. He knows me, because I often come, Socrates; moreover, I have done him a kindness.

Soc. And are you only just come?

Cr. No, I came some time ago.

Soc. Then why did you sit and say nothing, instead of awakening me at once?

[5] From Plato, *Crito,* trans. Benjamin Jowett (1871).

Cr. Why, indeed, Socrates, I myself would rather not have all this sleeplessness and sorrow. But I have been wondering at your peaceful slumbers, and that was the reason why I did not awaken you, because I wanted you to be out of pain. I have always thought you happy in the calmness of your temperament; but never did I see the like of the easy, cheerful way in which you bear this calamity.

Soc. Why, Crito, when a man has reached my age he ought not to be repining at the prospect of death.

Cr. And yet other old men find themselves in similar misfortunes, and age does not prevent them from repining.

Soc. That may be. But you have not told me why you come at this early hour.

Cr. I come to bring you a message which is sad and painful; not, as I believe, to yourself, but to all of us who are your friends, and saddest of all to me.

Soc. What! I suppose that the ship has come from Delos, on the arrival of which I am to die?

Cr. No, the ship has not actually arrived, but she will probably be here today, as persons who have come from Sunium tell me that they left her there; and therefore tomorrow, Socrates, will be the last day of your life.

Soc. Very well, Crito; if such is the will of God, I am willing; but my belief is that there will be a delay of a day.

Cr. Why do you say this?

Soc. I will tell you. I am to die on the day after the arrival of the ship?

Cr. Yes; that is what the authorities say.

Soc. But I do not think that the ship will be here until tomorrow; this I gather from a vision which I had last night, or rather only just now, when you fortunately allowed me to sleep.

Cr. And what was the nature of the vision?

Soc. There came to me the likeness of a woman, fair and comely, clothed in white raiment, who called to me and said: O Socrates, "The third day hence to Phthia shalt thou go."

Cr. What a singular dream, Socrates!

Soc. There can be no doubt about the meaning, Crito, I think.

Cr. Yes; the meaning is only too clear. But, Oh! my beloved Socrates, let me entreat you once more to take my advice and escape. For if you die I shall not only lose a friend who can never be replaced, but there is another evil: people who do not know you and me will believe that I might have saved you if I had been willing to give money, but that I did not care. Now, can there be a worse disgrace than this—that I should be thought to value money more than the life of a friend? For the many will not be persuaded that I wanted you to escape, and that you refused.

Soc. But why, my dear Crito, should we care about the opinion of the many? Good men, and they are the only persons who are worth considering, will think of these things truly as they happened.

Cr. But do you see, Socrates, that the opinion of the many must be regarded, as is evident in your own case, because they can do the very greatest evil to any one who has lost their good opinion.

Soc. I only wish, Crito, that they could; for then they could also do the greatest good, and that would be well. But the truth is, that they can do neither good nor evil: they cannot make a man wise or make him foolish; and whatever they do is the result of chance.

Cr. Well, I will not dispute about that; but please to tell me, Socrates, whether you are not acting out of regard to me and your other friends: are you not afraid that if you escape hence we may get into trouble with the informers for having stolen you away, and lose either the whole or a great part of our property; or that even a worse evil may happen to us? Now, if this is your fear, be at ease; for in order to save you, we ought surely to run this, or even a greater risk; be persuaded, then, and do as I say.

Soc. Yes, Crito, that is one fear which you mention, but by no means the only one.

Cr. Fear not. There are persons who at no great cost are willing to save you and bring you out of prison; and as for the informers, you may observe that they are far from being exorbitant in their demands; a little money will satisfy them. My means, which, as I am sure, are ample, are at your service, and if you have a scruple about spending all mine, here are strangers who will give you the use of theirs; and one of them, Simmias the Theban, has brought a sum of money for this very purpose; and Cebes and many others are willing to spend their money too. I say therefore, do not on that account hesitate about making your escape, and do not say, as you did in the court, that you will have a difficulty in knowing what to do with yourself if you escape. For men will love you in other places to which you may go, and not in Athens only; there are friends of mine in Thessaly, if you like to go to them, who will value and protect you, and no Thessalian will give you any trouble. Nor can I think that you are justified, Socrates, in betraying your own life when you might be saved; this is playing into the hands of your enemies and destroyers; and moreover I should say that you were betraying your children; for you might bring them up and educate them; instead of which you go away and leave them, and they will have to take their chance; and if they do not meet with the usual fate of orphans, there will be small thanks to you. No man should bring children into the world who is unwilling to persevere to the end in their nurture and education. But you are choosing the easier part, as I think, not the better and manlier, which would rather have become one who professes virtue in all his actions, like yourself. And indeed, I am ashamed not only of you, but of us who are your friends, when I reflect that this entire business of yours will be attributed to our want of courage. The trial need never have come on, or might have been brought to another issue; and the end of all, which is the crowning absurdity, will seem to have been permitted by us, through cowardice and baseness, who might have saved you, as you might have saved yourself, if we had been good for anything (for there was no difficulty in escaping); and we did not see how disgraceful, Socrates, and also miserable all this will be to us as well as to you. Make your mind up then, or rather have your mind already made up, for the time of deliberation is over, and there is only one thing to be done, which must be done, if at all, this very night, and which any delay will render all but impossible; I beseech you therefore, Socrates, to be persuaded by me, and to do as I say.

Soc. Dear Crito, your zeal is invaluable, if a right one; but if wrong, the greater the zeal the greater the evil; and therefore we ought to consider whether these things shall be done or not. For I am and always have been one of those natures who must be guided by reason, whatever the reason may be which upon reflection appears to me to be the best; and now that this fortune have come upon me, I cannot put away the reasons which I have before given: the principles which I have hitherto honoured and revered I still honour, and unless we can find other and better principles on the instant, I am certain not to agree with you; no, not even if the power of the multitude could inflict many more imprisonments, confiscations, deaths, frightening us like children with hobgoblin terrors. But what will be the fairest way of considering the question? Shall I return to your old argument about the opinions of men? some of which are to be regarded, and others, as we were saying, are not to be regarded. Now were we right in maintaining this before I was condemned? And has the argument which was once good now proved to be talk for the sake of talking;—in fact an amusement only, and altogether vanity? That is what I want to consider with your help, Crito:—whether, under my present circumstances, the argument appears to be in any way different or not; and is to be allowed by me or disallowed. That argument, which, as I believe, is maintained by many who assume to be authorities, was to the effect, as I was saying, that the opinions of some men are to be regarded, and of other men not to be regarded. Now you, Crito, are a disinterested person who are not going to die tomorrow—at least, there is no human probability of this, and you are therefore not liable to be deceived by the circumstances in which you are placed. Tell me then, whether I am right in saying that some opinions, and the opinions of some men only, are to be valued, and other opinions, and the opinions of other men, are not to be valued. I ask you whether I was right in maintaining this?

Cr. Certainly.

Soc. The good are to be regarded, and not the bad?

Cr. Yes.

Soc. And the opinions of the wise are good, and the opinions of the unwise are evil?

Cr. Certainly.

Soc. And what was said about another matter? Was the disciple in gymnastics supposed to attend to the praise and blame and opinion of every man, or of one man only—his physician or trainer, whoever that was?

Cr. Of one man only.

Soc. And he ought to fear the censure and welcome the praise of that one only, and not of the many?

Cr. That is clear.

Soc. And he ought to live and train, and eat and drink in the way which seems good to his single master who has understanding, rather than according to the opinion of all other men put together?

Cr. True.

Soc. And if he disobeys and disregards the opinion and approval of the one, and regards the opinion of the many who have no understanding, will he not suffer evil?

Cr. Certainly he will.

Soc. And what will the evil be, whither tending and what affecting, in the disobedient person?

Cr. Clearly, affecting the body; that is what is destroyed by the evil.

Soc. Very good; and is not this true, Crito, of other things which we need not separately enumerate? In the matter of just and unjust, fair and foul, good and evil, which are the subjects of our present consultation, ought we to follow the opinion of the many and to fear them; or the opinion of the one man who has understanding, and whom we ought to fear and reverence more than all the rest of the world: and whom deserting we shall destroy and injure that principle in us which may be assumed to be improved by justice and deteriorated by injustice;—is there not such a principle?

Cr. Certainly there is Socrates.

Soc. Take a parallel instance:—if, acting under the advice of men who have no understanding, we destroy that which is improvable by health and deteriorated by disease—when that has been destroyed, I say, would life be worth having? And that is—the body?

Cr. Yes.

Soc. Could we live, having an evil and corrupted body?

Cr. Certainly not.

Soc. And will life be worth having, if that higher part of man be depraved, which is improved by justice and deteriorated by injustice? Do we suppose that principle, whatever it may be in man, which has to do with justice and injustice, to be inferior to the body?

Cr. Certainly not.

Soc. More honoured, then?

Cr. Far more honoured.

Soc. Then, my friend, we must not regard what the many say of us: but what he, the one man who has understanding of just and unjust, will say, and what the truth will say. And therefore you begin in error when you suggest that we should regard the opinion of the many about just and unjust, good and evil, honourable and dishonourable.—Well, some one will say, "but the many can kill us."

Cr. Yes, Socrates; that will clearly be the answer.

Soc. That is true: but still I find with surprise that the old argument is, as I conceive, unshaken as ever. And I should like to know whether I may say the same of another proposition—that not life, but a good life, is to be chiefly valued.

Cr. Yes. that also remains.

Soc. And a good life is equivalent to a just and honourable one —that holds also?

Cr. Yes, that holds.

Soc. From these premisses I proceed to argue the question whether I ought or ought not to try and escape without the consent of the Athenians: and if I am clearly right in escaping, then I will make the attempt; but if not, I will abstain. The other considerations which you mention, of money and loss of character and the duty of educating children, are, as I fear, only the doctrines of the multitude, who would be as ready to call people to life, if they were able, as they are to put them to death—and with as little reason. And now, since the argument has thus far prevailed, the only question which remains to be considered is, whether we shall do rightly either in escaping or in suffering others to aid in our escape and paying them in money and thanks, or whether we shall not do rightly; and if the latter, then death or any other calamity which may ensue on my remaining here must not be allowed to enter into the calculation.

Cr. I think that you are right. Socrates; how then shall we proceed?

Soc. Let us consider the matter together, and do you either refute me if you can, and I will be convinced; or else cease, my dear friend, from repeating to me that I ought to escape against the wishes of the Athenians: for I am extremely desirous to be persuaded by you, but not against my own better judgment. And now please to consider my first position, and do your best to answer me.

Cr. I will do my best.

Soc. Are we to say that we are never intentionally to do wrong, or that in one way we ought and in another way we ought not to do wrong, or is doing wrong always evil and dishonourable, as I was just now saying, and as has been already acknowledged by us? Are all our former admissions which were made within a few days to be thrown away? And have we, at our age, been earnestly discoursing with one another all our life long only to discover that we are no better than children? Or are we to rest assured, in spite of the opinion of the many, and in spite of consequences whether better or worse, of the truth of what was then said, that injustice is always an evil and dishonour to him who acts unjustly? Shall we affirm that?

Cr. Yes.

Soc. Then we must do no wrong?

Cr. Certainly not.

Soc. Nor when injured injure in return, as the many imagine; for we must injure no one at all?

Cr. Clearly not.

Soc. Again, Crito, may we do evil?

Cr. Surely not, Socrates.

Soc. And what of doing evil in return for evil, which is the morality of the many—is that just or not?

Cr. Not just.

Soc. For doing evil to another is the same as injuring him?

Cr. Very true.

Soc. Then we ought not to retaliate or render evil for evil to any one, whatever evil we may have suffered from him. But I would have you consider, Crito, whether you really mean what you are saying. For this opinion has never been held, and never will be held, by any considerable number of persons; and those who are agreed and those who are not agreed upon this point have no common ground, and can only despise one another when they see how widely they differ. Tell me, then, whether you agree with and assent to my first principle, that neither injury nor retaliation nor warding off evil by evil is ever right. And shall that be the premiss of our argument? Or do you decline and dissent from this? For this has been of old and is still my opinion; but, if you are of another opinion, let me hear what you have to say. If, however, you remain of the same mind as formerly, I will proceed to the next step.

Cr. You may proceed, for I have not changed my mind.

Soc. Then I will proceed to the next step, which may be put in the form of a question:—Ought a man to do what he admits to be right, or ought he to betray the right?

Cr. He ought to do what he thinks right.

Soc. But if this is true, what is the application? In leaving the prison against the will of the Athenians, do I wrong any? or rather do I not wrong those whom I ought least to wrong? Do I not desert the principles which were acknowledged by us to be just? What do you say?

Cr. I cannot tell, Socrates, for I do not know.

Soc. Then consider the matter in this way:—Imagine that I am about to play truant (you may call the proceeding by any name which you like), and the laws and the government come and interrogate me: "Tell us, Socrates," they say; "what are you about? are you going by an act of yours to overturn us—the laws and the whole state, as far as in you lies? Do you imagine that a state can subsist and not be overthrown, in which the decisions of law have no power, but are set aside and overthrown by individuals?" What will be our answer, Crito, to these and the like words? Any one, and especially a clever rhetorician, will have a good deal to urge about the evil of setting aside the law which requires a sentence to be carried out; and we might reply, "Yes; but the state has injured us and given an unjust sentence." Suppose I say that?

Cr. Very good, Socrates.

Soc. "And was that our agreement with you?" the law would say; "or were you to abide by the sentence of the state?" And if I were to express astonishment at their saying this, the law would probably add: "Answer, Socrates, instead of opening your eyes: you are in the habit of asking and answering questions. Tell us what complaint you have to make against us which justifies you in attempting to destroy us and the state? In the first place did we not bring you into existence? Your father married your mother by our aid and begat you. Say whether you have any objection to urge against those of us who regulate marriage?" None, I should reply. "Or against those of us who regulate the system of nurture and education of children in which you were trained? Were not the laws, who have the charge of this, right in commanding your father to train you in music and gymnastic?" Right, I should reply. "Well then, since you were brought into the world and nurtured and educated by us, can you deny in the first place that you are our child and slave, as your fathers were before you? And if this is true you are not on equal terms with us; nor can you think that you have a right to do to us what we are doing to you. Would you have any right to strike or revile or do any other evil to a father or to your master, if you had one, when you have been struck or reviled by him, or received some other evil at his hands?—would you not say this? And because we think right to destroy you, do you think that you have any right to destroy us in return, and your country as far as in you lies? And will you, O professor of true virtue, say that you are justified in this? Has a philosopher like you failed to discover that our country is more to be valued and higher and holier far than mother or father or any ancestor, and more to be regarded in the eyes of the gods and of men of understanding? also to be soothed, and gently and reverently entreated when angry, even more than a father, and if not persuaded, obeyed? And when we are punished by her, whether with imprisonment or stripes, the punishment is to be endured in silence; and if she lead us to wounds or death in battle, thither we follow as is right; neither may any one yield or retreat or leave his rank, but whether in battle or in a court of law, or in any other place, he must do what his city and his country order him; or he must change their view of what is just: and if he may do no violence to his father or mother, much less may he do violence to his country." What answer shall we make to this, Crito? Do the laws speak truly, or do they not?

Cr. I think that they do.

Soc. Then the laws will say: "Consider, Socrates, if this is true, that in your present attempt you are going to do us wrong. For, after having brought you into the world, and nurtured and educated you, and given you and every other citizen a share in every good that we had to give, we further proclaim and give the right to every Athenian, that if he does not like us when he has come of age and has seen the ways of the city, and made our acquaintance, he may go where he pleases and take his goods with him; and none of us laws will forbid him or interfere with him. Any of you who does not like us and the city, and who wants to go to a colony or to any other city, may go where he likes, and take his goods with him. But he who has experience of the manner in which we order justice and administer the state, and still remains, has entered into an implied contract that he will do as we command him. And he who disobeys us is, as we maintain, thrice wrong; first, because in disobeying us he is disobeying his parents; secondly, because we are the authors of his education; thirdly, because he has made an agreement with us that he will duly obey our commands; and he neither obeys them nor convinces us that our commands are wrong; and we do not rudely impose them, but give him the alternative of obeying or convincing us;—that is what we offer, and he does neither. These are the sort of accusations to which, as we were saying, you, Socrates, will be exposed if you accomplish your intentions; you, above all other Athenians." Suppose I ask, why is this? they will justly retort upon me that I above all other men have acknowledged the agreement. "There is clear proof," they will say, "Socrates, that we and the city were not displeasing to you. Of all Athenians you have been the most constant resident in the city, which, as you never leave, you may be supposed to love. For you never went out of the city either to see the games, except once when you went to the Isthmus, or to any other place unless when you were on military service; nor did you travel as other men do. Nor had you any curiosity to know other states or their laws: your affections did not go beyond us and our state; we were your special favourites, and you acquiesced in our government of you; and this is the state in which you begat your children, which is a proof of your satisfaction. Moreover, you might, if you had liked, have fixed the penalty at banishment in the course of the trial—the state which refuses to let you go now would have let you go then. But you pretended that you preferred death to exile, and that you were not grieved at death. And now you have forgotten these fine sentiments, and pay no respect to us the laws, of whom you are the destroyer; and are doing what only a miserable slave would do, running away and turning your back upon the compacts and agreements which you made as a citizen. And first of all answer this very question: Are we right in saying that you agreed to be governed according to us in deed, and not in word only? Is that true or not?" How shall we answer that, Crito? Must we not agree?

Cr. There is no help, Socrates.

Soc. Then will they not say: "You, Socrates, are breaking the covenants and agreements which you made with us at your leisure, not in any haste or under any compulsion or deception, but having had seventy years to think of them, during which time you were at liberty to leave the city, if we were not to your mind, or if our covenants appeared to you to be unfair. You had your choice, and might have gone either to Lacedaemon or Crete, which you often praise for their good government, or to some other Hellenic or foreign state. Whereas you, above all other Athenians, seemed to be so fond of the state, or, in other words, of us her laws (for who would like a state that has no laws), that you never stirred out of her; the halt, the blind, the maimed were not more stationary in her than you were. And now you run away and forsake your agreements. Not so, Socrates, if you will take our advice; do not make yourself ridiculous by escaping out of the city.

"For just consider, if you transgress and err in this sort of way, what good will you do either to yourself or to your friends? That your friends will be driven into exile and deprived of citizenship, or will lose their property, is tolerably certain; and you yourself, if you fly to one of the neighbouring cities, as, for example, Thebes or Megara, both of which are well-governed cities, will come to them as an enemy, Socrates, and their government will be against you, and all patriotic citizens will cast an evil eye upon you as a subverter of the laws, and you will confirm in the minds of the judges the justice of their own condemnation of you. For he who is a corruptor of the laws is more than likely to be corruptor of the young and foolish portion of mankind. Will you then flee from well-ordered cities and virtuous men? and is existence worth having on these terms? Or will you go to them without shame, and talk to them, Socrates? And what will you say to them? What you say here about virtue and justice and institutions and laws being the best things among men. Would that be decent of you? Surely not. But if you go away from well-governed states to Crito's friends in Thessaly, where there is great disorder and licence, they will be charmed to have the tale of your escape from prison, set off with ludicrous particulars of the manner in which you were wrapped in a goatskin or some other disguise, and metamorphosed as the fashion of runaways is—that is very likely; but will there be no one to remind you that in your old age you violated the most sacred laws from a miserable desire of a little more life. Perhaps not, if you keep them in a good temper; but if they are out of temper you will hear many degrading things; you will live, but how?—as the flatterer of all men, and the servant of all men; and doing what?—eating and drinking in Thessaly, having gone abroad in order that you may get a dinner. And where will be your fine sentiments about justice and virtue then? Say that you wish to live for the sake of your children, that you may bring them up and educate them—will you take them into Thessaly and deprive them of Athenian citizenship?

Is that the benefit which you would confer upon them? Or are you under the impression that they will be better cared for and educated here if you are still alive, although absent from them; for that your friends will take care of them? Do you fancy that if you are an inhabitant of Thessaly they will take care of them, and if you are an inhabitant of the other world they will not take care of them? Nay; but if they who call themselves friends are truly friends, they surely will.

"Listen, then, Socrates, to us who have brought you up. Think not of life and children first, and of justice afterwards, but of justice first, that you may be justified before the princes of the world below. For neither will you nor any that belong to you be happier or holier or juster in this life, or happier in another, if you do as Crito bids. Now you depart in innocence, a sufferer and not a doer of evil; a victim, not of the laws, but of men. But if you go forth, returning evil for evil, and injury for injury, breaking the covenants and agreements which you have made with us, and wronging those whom you ought least to wrong, that is to say, yourself, your friends, your country, and us, we shall be angry with you while you live, and our brethren, the laws in the world below, will receive you as an enemy; for they will know that you have done your best to destroy us. Listen, then, to us and not to Crito."

This is the voice which I seem to hear murmuring in my ears, like the sound of the flute in the ears of the mystic; that voice, I say, is humming in my ears, and prevents me from hearing any other. And I know that anything more which you may say will be vain. Yet speak, if you have anything to say.

Cr. I have nothing to say, Socrates.

Soc. Then let me follow the intimations of the will of God.

• Aristotle (384–322 B.C.)

The Citizen, the State, the Law [6]

Aristotle here writes as a theorist about the state. The following
selection, taken from the *Politics*, asks with the usual Aristotelian
soberness and common sense: What is a citizen? What different
kinds of state are there? Why do states come into being? What
is law? Aristotle defines the state as possessing a moral aim—not
merely that of living, but of living well. And he gives the most
famous of the early classifications of forms of government.

In any inquiry into the nature and character of particular politics
we may say that the first point to be considered is the nature of the
State. At present there is often a difference of opinion, as one party
asserts that it is the State which has done a certain action, and
another that it is not the State but the Oligarchy or the Tyrant by
whom it was governed. Also it is necessary to settle this point, as
a State is the sphere in which all the activity of a statesman or
legislator is displayed, and the polity itself is nothing more than a
certain order of the inhabitants of the State. But as the State
belongs to the category of compound things, like anything else
which is a whole but composed of many parts, it is clear that we
must first investigate the conception of the citizen; for the State
is composed of a number of citizens. We have to inquire then to
whom the title "citizen" belongs, or, in other words, what is the nature of a citizen. For the conception of the citizen as of the State
is often disputed, nor is the world agreed in recognizing the same
person as a citizen. Thus it often happens that one who is a citizen
in a Democracy is not a citizen in an Oligarchy.

Now putting out of sight persons who acquire the title of citizen
in some exceptional way, e.g., honorary citizens, we may lay it down
that it is not residence which constitutes a citizen, as the qualification of residence belongs equally to aliens settled in the country
and to slaves. Nor again does citizenship consist simply in the participation in legal rights to the extent of being party to an action

[6] From Aristotle, *Politics*, trans. J. E. C. Welldon (1883), Bk. III.

as defendant or plaintiff, for this is a qualification possessed equally by the members of different States who associate on the basis of commercial treaties. (It may be observed that in many places resident aliens are not admitted to the full enjoyment even of these legal rights, but are obliged to put themselves under the protection of a patron. It is only in a certain imperfect sense then that they are members of an association so constituted.) Such persons on the contrary are much in the same position as children who are too young to be entered upon the register of the deme or old men who are exempted from civil duties; for although these classes are to be called citizens in a certain sense, it is not in a sense quite absolute and unlimited, but with some such qualifying words as "immature" or "superannuated" or the like, it does not matter what. Our meaning at least is plain; we want a definition of the citizen in the absolute sense, one to whom no such exception can be taken as makes it necessary to correct our definition. For difficulties of a similar kind may be discussed and settled respecting persons who have been disfranchised or exiled. There is nothing whereby a citizen in the absolute sense is so well defined as by participation in judicial power and public office. But the offices of State are of two kinds. Some are determinate in point of time; thus there are certain offices which may never in any circumstances or may only after certain definite intervals be held a second time by the same person. Other officers again are perpetual, e.g., jurors and members of the public Assembly. It will be objected perhaps that jurors and members of the public Assembly are not officers of State at all and that their functions do not invest them with an official status; although it is ridiculous to deny the title of "officers" to the supreme authorities in the State. But this matter we may regard as unimportant; it is a mere question of name. The fact is that there is no word to express rightly the common function of a juror and a member of the public Assembly. Let us call it for distinction's sake a perpetual office. Citizens then we may define as those who participate in judicial and deliberative office.

This is perhaps the definition of a citizen which is most appropriate to all who are so called. It is to be observed however that, where things included under a general head are specifically different and one is conceived of as first, another as second and another as third, there is either no characteristic whatever common to them all as such, or the common characteristic exists only in a slight degree. But polities, as we see, differ specifically from each other, some are later and others earlier; for the corrupt or perverted forms are necessarily later than the uncorrupted. What we mean by perverted forms will appear hereafter. It follows then that the citizen in each polity must also be different. Accordingly it is principally to the citizen in a Democracy that our definition applies; it is possibly true in the other polities, but not necessarily. For in some there is no democratical element, nor are there any regular public assemblies but only extraordinary ones, and the administration of justice is divided among various boards, as e.g. at Lacedaemon, where different civil cases are decided by different Ephors, cases of homicide by the Senate and no doubt other cases by some other magistracy. It is the same at Carthage, where all suits are tried by certain magistrates. However, we need not give up our definition of a citizen, as it admits of correction. For in all polities except Democracy the right of voting in the Assembly and of acting as jurors belongs not to perpetual officers but to persons whose term of office is strictly defined; as it is either to such officers collectively or to some of them that judicial and deliberative functions, whether upon all or upon certain matters only, are assigned.

Thus we see clearly the nature of the citizen. One who enjoys the privilege of participation in deliberative or judicial office—he and he only is, according to our definiton, a citizen of the State in Question, and a State is in general terms such a number of persons thus qualified as is sufficient for an independent life.

.   .   .   .   .

As a sequel to these remarks, we have now to consider whether the virtue of a good man and of a virtuous citizen is to be regarded as identical or different.

But if we are to investigate this point, we must first ascertain roughly the virtue of a citizen. A citizen then like a sailor may be described as a member of a society. And although the sailors have different faculties, one being an oarsman, another a pilot, a third a "look-out" man, and a fourth having some other similar title, it is evident that, while the most exact definition of the virtue or excellence of each will be exclusively appropriate to the individual, there will at the same time be a common definition applicable to all. For safety in navigation is the object they all have in view; it is this that every sailor strives for. Similarly then in the case of the citizens, although they are different, yet it is the safety of the association or in other words of the polity which is their object; and hence the virtue of the citizen is necessarily relative to the polity.

Assuming then that there are several kinds of polity, we see that the virtuous citizen in all polities cannot have a uniform perfect virtue, whereas it is a uniform perfect virtue which in our theory is characteristic of the good man. It is therefore clearly possible to be a virtuous citizen without possessing the virtue characteristic of a virtuous man. However we may investigate and discuss the same question in a different way by taking the case of the best polity. If we assume the possibility of a State consisting solely of virtuous members, still each of them is bound to perform his own work well, and this is itself a result impyling virtue; but as all the citizens cannot be alike, it follows that in this case as in others the virtue of a good citizen and a good man cannot be one and the same. For the virtue of the virtuous citizen must be possessed by all the citizens of this State, as otherwise it cannot be the best possible; but it is impossible that they should all possess the virtue of the good man, unless the citizens of the virtuous State must all be alike, which is contrary to the conception of a State. Again we may put the matter thus: Since the members of the State are dissimilar, and, as an animal e.g. consists of soul and body, soul of reason and appetite, and a household of husband and wife, master and slave, so too a State consists of all these and of other dissimilar elements besides, it follows that the virtue of all the citizens can no more be one and the same than the virtue of a leader and a subordinate member of a chorus.

·   ·   ·   ·   ·

As to the question whether the virtue characteristic of a good man and a virtuous citizen is to be regarded as identical or different, our remarks have served to prove that there are certain States in which they are combined in the same individual and others in which they are distinct, and that in the former they are not found together in every one but only in the practical statesman who exercises or is capable of exercising, whether individually or conjointly with others, an influence in the conduct of public affairs.

This being determined, we have next to consider whether it is right to assume a single polity or several, and, if several, what is the nature of each, and how many there are, and what are the points of distinction between them. A polity may be defined as an order of the State in respect of its offices generally and especially of the supreme office. For the governing class is everywhere supreme in the State, and the nature of the polity is determined by the governing class. I mean e.g. that it is the commons who are supreme in a Democracy and the Few on the other hand in an

Oligarchy, and accordingly we call their polities distinct. The same remark may be extended to all the rest; if the governing class is different, so is the polity.

We must begin by laying down (1) the object for which a State is framed and (2) the various kinds of rule which may be exercised over man in his social existence.

It has been stated at the very outset of our treatise in the discussion of Domestic Economy and the government of slaves that Man is naturally a political animal, and consequently, even where there is no need of mutual service, men are none the less anxious to live together. Still it cannot be denied that the common advantage of all is also a motive of union, more or less operative according to the degree in which each individual is capable of the higher life. Although to the citizens, both collectively and individually, this higher life is emphatically the end proposed, yet life itself is also an object for which they unite and maintain the corporate political association; for it is probable that some degree of the higher life is necessarily implied in merely living, unless there is a great preponderance of hardship in the life. Certain it is that the majority of men endure much suffering without ceasing to cling to life—a proof that a certain happiness or natural sweetness resides in it.

But to proceed to the second point: it is not difficult to distinguish the forms of rule which are generally recognized; for even in our unscientific discourses we often discuss and determine their character. In the government of slaves, although the interests of natural slave and natural master are really identical, yet the object of the rule is nevertheless the interest of the master and is that of the slave only incidentally, because, if the slave is destroyed, it is impossible that the master's government should be maintained. On the other hand, in the rule of children or a wife or a whole household, which in our terminology is economic rule, the end is either the good of the subjects or some common good of rulers and subjects alike, i.e. it is essentially the good of the subjects, as we see in the other arts such as Medicine and Gymnastic, although it may perhaps incidentally be also the good of the rulers themselves. For there is no reason why the gymnastic trainer should not himself be occasionally one of the gymnasts, as the pilot is invariably one of the crew. And thus while the trainer or pilot has in view not his own interest but the interest of those who are under him, yet in any case where he himself shares their position he enjoys incidentally the same benefit as they do; for the one becomes a sailor and the other one of the gymnasts, although he is a trainer. It is because the object of political rule is the benefit of the subjects that in any State framed on the principle of equality and similarity among the citizens a claim is put forward for an alternation of rule. It was originally claimed, as is natural enough, that all should serve the State in turn, and that, as each citizen during his period of rule or office had already paid regard to the interest of another, so that other should in turn pay regard to his. But nowadays the profits derivable from the public service and an official status create a desire for perpetuity of office; it is as though the officers of State, being invalids, were to enjoy good health during all their term of power, in which case it is probable that they would be equally eager for office.

It is evident then that all such polities as regard the good of the community are really normal according to the principle of abstract justice, while such as regard the private good of the rulers are all corruptions or perversions of the normal polities; for the relations of rulers to the subjects in them are like the relations of a master to his slaves, whereas the State is properly a society of free persons.

Having now settled these points, we have next to consider the number of different polities and their nature. We will begin with the normal polities; for when they are determined the perverted forms will be evident at once.

As in any State the polity and the governing class are virtually the same, i.e., the polity is determined by the governing class, as the governing class is the supreme authority in a State, and as supreme power must be vested either in an individual or in a Few or in the Many, it follows that, when the rule of the individual or the Few or the Many is exercised for the benefit of the community at large, the polities are normal, whereas the polities which subserve the private interest either of the individual or the Few or the masses are perversions; for either the members of the State do not deserve the name of citizens, or they ought to have a share in its advantages. The form of Monarchy in which regard is paid to the interest of the community is commonly known as Kingship, and the government of the Few, although of a number exceeding one, for the good of all, as Aristocracy, whether because the rule is in the hands of the best citizens or because they exercise it for the best interests of the State and all its members; while when it is the masses who direct public affairs for the interest of the community, the government is called by the name which is common to all the polities, viz. a Polity. The result in this case is such as might have been expected. For although it is possible to find an individual or a few persons of eminent virtue, it can hardly be the case that a larger number are perfectly accomplished in every form of virtue; at the best they will be accomplished only in military virtue, as it is the only one of which the masses are capable. The consequence is that in this polity, viz. the Polity proper, the military class is supreme, and all who bear arms enjoy full political privileges.

As perverted forms of the polities just mentioned we have Tyranny by the side of Kingship, Oligarchy of Aristocracy and Democracy of Polity. For Tyranny is monarchical rule for the good of the monarch, Oligarchy the rule of a Few for the good of the wealthy, and Democracy the rule of the Many for the good of the poor; none of them subserves the interest of the community at large.

But we ought to describe at rather greater length the nature of these several polities, as the matter is one which presents certain difficulties, and it is proper that a philosophical inquirer in any subject, who looks at something more than the merely practical side, should not ignore or omit any point but should bring to light the actual truth in all.

Tyranny is, as has been said, a form of Monarchy corresponding in the political association to the rule of a master over his slaves; Oligarchy a government where the supreme power in the polity is vested in the propertied classes; Democracy, on the contrary, a government where it is vested in those who possess no considerable property, i.e. the poor.

. . . . .

It is clear then that the State is not merely a local association or an association existing to prevent mutual injury and to promote commercial exchange. So far is this from being the case that, although these are indispensable conditions, if a State is to exist, yet all these conditions do not necessarily imply a State. A State on the contrary is first realized when there is an association of households and independent existence. (This will not be the case, however, unless the members inhabit one and the same locality and have the practice of intermarriage.) It is for this reason that there were established in the different States matrimonial connections, clanships, common sacrifice and such amusements as promote a common life. But all this is the work of friendship, for the choice of a common life implies no more than friendship. And thus while the end of a State is living well, these are only means to the end. A State on the contrary is the association of families and villages in a complete and independent existence or in other words, according to our definition, in a life of felicity and nobleness. We must assume then that the object of the political association is not merely a common life but noble action. And from this it follows that they who contribute most to the association, as so conceived, possess a larger interest in the State than they who are equal or superior in personal liberty or birth but inferior in political virtue, or than they who have the superiority in wealth but the inferiority in virtue.

It is evident then from our observations that in the controversy respecting the different polities each party is the representative of a certain partial justice. It is difficult however to decide what ought to be the supreme authority in the State. It must be either the masses or the rich or the respectable classes or an individual of preeminent merit or a tyrant. But all these suppositions appear to involve awkward consequences. For suppose the poor, as being a majority, distribute among themselves the property of the rich, is such an action not unjust? No, it may be said, for it was decreed by the supreme authority in the State and therefore justly decreed. What then are we to describe as the height of injustice, if not this? Or again, take the whole body of citizens and suppose that the majority distribute among themselves the property of the minority, it is evident that they thereby destroy the State. But it is certainly not the virtue of anything which destroys its possessor, nor can justice be destructive to a State. It is evident then that such a law as we have supposed cannot be just. Again, the same hypothesis would inevitably justify all the actions of a tyrant, as his oppression depends upon superior strength, like the oppression of the wealthy by the masses. Well, then, is it just that rule should be in the hands of the minority or the propertied class? But on that hypothesis, if the minority adopt the same line of action, if they plunder the masses and despoil them of their possessions, is such action just? If it is, so was the action of the majority in the former case. That all such conduct then is wrong and unjust is indisputable. Ought then the respectable classes to enjoy rule and supreme power? But if so, it is a necessary consequence that all the rest of the citizens are excluded from honours, as they do not enjoy the honour of political office. For we regard the offices of State as public honours; and if they are always in the hands of the same persons, it follows that all others are excluded from honour. Is then the rule of the most virtuous individual to be preferred? It may be objected that this is a system still more oligarchical than the last, as it involves the exclusion of a still larger number from honour.

Perhaps however it will be urged that there is an evil in the supremacy of any human being with his liability to the emotions incident to the soul, and that the law ought rather to be supreme. But on that hypothesis, if the law is oligarchical or democratical, what difference will it make to the difficulties we have raised? The difficulties already described will still meet us.

We may defer for the present the discussion of all these cases except one. But the theory that supreme power should be vested in the masses rather than in a few persons, although they are the best, is one which would seem to be refuted by the remarks we have made; and indeed there is a certain difficulty involved in it, although there is probably also a certain degree of truth. For it is possible that the Many, of whom each individual is not a virtuous man, are still collectively superior to the few best persons, i.e. superior not as individuals but as a body, as picnics are superior to feasts supplied at the expense of a single person. For as the total number is large, it is possible that each has a fractional share of virtue and prudence and that, as the multitude collectively may be compared to an individual with many feet, hands and senses, so the same is true of their character and intelligence. It is thus that the Many are better judges than the Few even of musical and poetical compositions; for some judge one part, some another, and all of them collectively the whole. But the point in which virtuous men are superior to any ordinary persons is the same in which handsome people, it is said, are superior to those who are not handsome and the representations of art to the realities, viz. that the features which in real life are distributed among a number of objects are in the works of art collected into one; for, if we take each feature by itself, the eye of one living person and another part of another are more beautiful than those in the painting. Whether the superiority of the Many to the few virtuous persons is possible, whatever be the character of the commons or the masses, is uncertain, or perhaps in some cases it is plainly impossible. For the same line of argument would be equally applicable to the lower animals. It would be absurd however to pretend that a number of the lower animals are superior to a few men; yet there are human beings who may be described as not appreciably superior to the lower animals. At the same time there do exist masses of people in whose case our theory is open to no objection.

•   •   •   •   •

With this discussion of these points we must be content. But the initial difficulty we mentioned as to the supreme authority in the State brings out nothing so clearly as that it is the laws, if rightly enacted, which should be supreme, and that the officers of State, whether one or many, should have supreme authority only in those matters upon which it is wholly impossible for the laws to pronounce exactly because of the difficulty of providing in a general statement for all cases. What should be the character of the laws if rightly enacted has not yet been ascertained; on the contrary our old difficulty still remains. This only is indisputable, that the laws enacted are necessarily relative to the polity in which they exist. But if this is the case, it is evident that the laws adapted to the normal polities are necessarily just, whereas those adapted to the perverted polities are unjust.

We have seen that in all sciences and arts the end proposed is some Good, that in the supreme of all sciences and arts, i.e. the political faculty, the end is preeminently the highest Good and that justice or in other words the interest of the community is the political Good. We have seen too that justice is universally regarded as a species of equality, and that up to a certain point, if not further, the conclusions of the philosophical arguments, in which ethical questions have been discussed and determined, are accepted on all hands, in so far as it is admitted that the notion of justice implies a thing to be given and persons to receive it, and that equals ought to receive an equal share. We have therefore to ascertain the characteristics which constitute personal equality or inequality —a difficult question which can be settled only by the aid of political philosophy.

• John Stuart Mill (1806–73)

Liberty [7]

John Stuart Mill, who wrote as a moralist in a preceding selection, here deals with the problem of freedom. The selection is the first chapter of his influential work *On Liberty*. Mill raises the question of the limits of the power which society can legitimately exercise over the individual and shows it to be only justified on grounds of self-defense. He then divides up the appropriate regions of individual liberties into those of the inward domain of consciousness, the right to frame our own life plan, and the liberty to combine and associate with our fellows.

The subject of this Essay is not the so-called Liberty of the Will, so unfortunately opposed to the misnamed doctrine of Philosophical Necessity; but Civil, or Social Liberty: the nature and limits of the power which can be legitimately exercised by society over the individual. A question seldom stated, and hardly ever discussed, in general terms, but which profoundly influences the practical controversies of the age by its latent presence, and is likely soon to make itself recognized as the vital question of the future. It is so far from being new, that, in a certain sense, it has divided mankind, almost from the remotest ages; but in the stage of progress into which the more civilised portions of the species have now entered, it presents itself under new conditions, and requires a different and more fundamental treatment.

The struggle between Liberty and Authority is the most conspicuous feature in the portions of history with which we are earliest familiar, particularly in that of Greece, Rome, and England. But in old times this contest was between subjects, or some classes of subjects, and the Government. By liberty, was meant protection against the tyranny of the political rulers. The rulers were conceived (except in some of the popular governments of Greece) as in a necessarily antagonistic position to the people whom they

[7] From J. S. Mill, *On Liberty* (1859), chap. i.

ruled. They consisted of a governing One, or a governing tribe or caste, who derived their authority from inheritance or conquest, who, at all events, did not hold it at the pleasure of the governed, and whose supremacy men did not venture, perhaps did not desire, to contest, whatever precautions might be taken against its oppressive exercise. Their power was regarded as necessary, but also as highly dangerous; as a weapon which they would attempt to use against their subjects, no less than against external enemies. To prevent the weaker members of the community from being preyed upon by innumerable vultures, it was needful that there should be an animal of prey stronger than the rest, commissioned to keep them down. But as the king of the vultures would be no less bent upon preying on the flock than any of the minor harpies, it was indispensable to be in a perpetual attitude of defence against his beak and claws. The aim, therefore, of patriots was to set limits to the power which the ruler should be suffered to exercise over the community; and this limitation was what they meant by liberty. It was attempted in two ways. First, by obtaining a recognition of certain immunities, called political liberties or rights, which it was to be regarded as a breach of duty in the ruler to infringe, and which if he did infringe, specific resistance, or general rebellion, was held to be justifiable. A second, and generally a later expedient, was the establishment of constitutional checks, by which the consent of the community, or of a body of some sort, supposed to represent its interests, was made a necessary condition to some of the more important acts of the governing power. To the first of these modes of limitation, the ruling power, in most European countries, was compelled, more or less, to submit. It was not so with the second; and, to attain this, or when already in some degree possessed, to attain it more completely, became everywhere the principal object of the lovers of liberty. And so long as mankind were content to combat one enemy by another, and to be ruled by a master, on condition of being guaranteed more or less efficaciously against his tyranny, they did not carry their aspirations beyond this point.

A time, however, came in the progress of human affairs, when men ceased to think it a necessity of nature that their governors should be an independent power, opposed in interest to themselves. It appeared to them much better that the various magistrates of the State should be their tenants or delegates, revocable at their pleasure. In that way alone, it seemed, could they have complete security that the powers of government would never be abused to their disadvantage. By degrees this new demand for elective and temporary rulers became the prominent object of the exertions of the popular party, wherever any such party existed; and superseded, to a considerable extent, the previous efforts to limit the power of rulers. As the struggle proceeded for making the ruling power emanate from the periodical choice of the ruled, some persons began to think that too much importance had been attached to the limitation of the power itself. That (it might seem) was a re- source against rulers whose interests were habitually opposed to those of the people. What was now wanted was, that the rulers should be identified with the people; that their interest and will should be the interest and will of the nation. The nation did not need to be protected against its own will. There was no fear of its tyrannising over itself. Let the rulers be effectually responsible to it, promptly removable by it, and it could afford to trust them with power of which it could itself dictate the use to be made. Their power was but the nation's own power, concentrated, and in a form convenient for exercise. This mode of thought, or rather perhaps of feeling, was common among the last generation of Euro- pean liberalism, in the Continental section of which it still appar- ently predominates. Those who admit any limit to what a govern- ment may do, except in the case of such governments as they think ought not to exist, stand out as brilliant exceptions among the political thinkers of the Continent. A similar tone of sentiment might by this time have been prevalent in our own country, if the circumstances which for a time encouraged it, had continued un- altered.

But, in political and philosophical theories, as well as in persons, success discloses faults and infirmities which failure might have concealed from observation. The notion, that the people have no need to limit their power over themselves, might seem axiomatic, when popular government was a thing only dreamed about, or read of as having existed at some distant period of the past. Neither was that notion necessarily disturbed by such temporary aberrations as those of the French Revolution, the worst of which were the work of a usurping few, and which, in any case, belonged, not to the permanent working of popular institutions, but to a sudden and convulsive outbreak against monarchical and aristocratic des- potism. In time, however, a democratic republic came to occupy a large portion of the earth's surface, and made itself felt as one of the most powerful members of the community of nations; and elective and responsible government became subject to the observa- tions and criticisms which wait upon a great existing fact. It was now perceived that such phrases as "self-government," and "the

power of the people over themselves," do not express the true state
of the case. The "people" who exercise the power are not always
the same people with those over whom it is exercised; and the
"self-government" spoken of is not the government of each by himself, but of each by all the rest. The will of the people, moreover,
practically means the will of the most numerous or the most active
part of the people; the majority, or those who succeed in making
themselves accepted as the majority; the people, consequently may
desire to oppress a part of their number; and precautions are as
much needed against this as against any other abuse of power.
The limitation, therefore, of the power of government over individuals loses none of its importance when the holders of power are
regularly accountable to the community, that is, to the strongest
party therein. This view of things, recommending itself equally
to the intelligence of thinkers and to the inclination of those important classes in European society to whose real or supposed interests
democracy is adverse, has had no difficulty in establishing itself;
and in political speculations "the tyranny of the majority" is now
generally included among the evils against which society requires
to be on its guard.

Like other tyrannies, the tyranny of the majority was at first, and
is still vulgarly, held in dread, chiefly as operating through the
acts of the public authorities. But reflecting persons perceived
that when society is itself the tyrant—society collectively over the
separate individuals who compose it—its means of tyrannising are
not restricted to the acts which it may do by the hands of its
political functionaries. Society can and does execute its own mandates: and if it issues wrong mandates instead of right, or any
mandates at all in things with which it ought not to meddle, it
practises a social tyranny more formidable than many kinds of
political oppression, since, though not usually upheld by such extreme penalties, it leaves fewer means of escape, penetrating much
more deeply into the details of life, and enslaving the soul itself.
Protection, therefore, against the tyranny of the magistrate is not
enough: there needs protection also against the tyranny of the prevailing opinion and feeling; against the tendency of society to impose, by other means than civil penalties, its own ideas and practices
as rules of conduct on those who dissent from them; to fetter the
development, and, if possible, prevent the formation, of any individuality not in harmony with its ways, and compels all characters
to fashion themselves upon the model of its own. There is a limit
to the legitimate interference of collective opinion with individual

independence: and to find that limit, and maintain it against en-croachment, is as indispensable to a good condition of human affairs, as protection against political despotism.

But though this proposition is not likely to be contested in gen-eral terms, the practical question, where to place the limit—how to make the fitting adjustment between individual independence and social control—is a subject on which nearly everything remains to be done. All that makes existence valuable to any one, depends on the enforcement of restraints upon the actions of other people. Some rules of conduct, therefore, must be imposed, by law in the first place, and by opinion on many things which are not fit sub-jects for the operation of law. What these rules should be is the principal question in human affairs; but if we except a few of the most obvious cases, it is one of those which least progress has been made in resolving. No two ages, and scarcely any two countries, have decided it alike; and the decision of one age or country is a wonder to another. Yet the people of any given age and country no more suspect any difficulty in it, than if it were a subject on which mankind had always been agreed. The rules which obtain among themselves appear to them self-evident and self-justifying. This all but universal illusion is one of the examples of the magical influence of custom, which is not only, as the proverb says, a sec-ond nature, but is continually mistaken for the first. The effect of custom, in preventing any misgiving respecting the rules of conduct which mankind impose on one another, is all the more complete because the subject is one on which it is not generally considered necessary that reasons should be given, either by one person to others or by each to himself. People are accustomed to believe, and have been encouraged in the belief by some who aspire to the char-acter of philosophers, that their feelings, on subjects of this nature, are better than reasons, and render reasons unnecessary. The prac-tical principle which guides them to their opinions on the regulation of human conduct, is the feeling in each person's mind that every-body should be required to act as he, and those with whom he sym-pathises, would like them to act. No one, indeed, acknowledges to himself that his standard of judgment is his own liking; but an opin-ion on a point of conduct, not supported by reasons, can only count as one person's preference; and if the reasons, when given, are a mere appeal to a similar preference felt by other people, it is still only many people's liking instead of one. To an ordinary man, however, his own preference, thus supported, is not only a perfectly satisfactory reason, but the only one he generally has for any of his notions of morality, taste, or propriety, which are not expressly written in his religious creed; and his chief guide in the interpretation even of that. Men's opinions, accordingly, on what is laudable or blamable, are affected by all the multifarious causes which influence their wishes in regard to the conduct of others, and which are as numerous as those which determine their wishes on any other subject. Sometimes their reason—at other times their prejudices or superstitions: often their social affections, not seldom their antisocial ones, their envy or jealousy, their arrogance or contemptuousness; but most commonly their desires or fears for themselves; their legitimate or illegitimate self-interest. Wherever there is an ascendant class, a large portion of the morality of the country emanates from its class interests, and its feelings of class superiority. The morality between Spartans and Helots, between planters and negroes, between princes and subjects, between nobles and roturiers, between men and women, has been for the most part the creation of these class interests and feelings: and the sentiments thus generated react in turn upon the moral feelings of the members of the ascendant class, in their relations among themselves. Where, on the other hand, a class, formerly ascendant, has lost its ascendancy, or where its ascendancy is unpopular, the prevailing moral sentiments frequently bear the impress of an impatient dislike of superiority. Another grand determining principle of the rules of conduct, both in act and forbearance, which have been enforced by law or opinion, has been the servility of mankind towards the supposed preferences or aversions of their temporal masters or of their gods. This servility, though essentially selfish, is not hypocrisy; it gives rise to perfectly genuine sentiments of abhorrence; it made men burn magicians and heretics. Among so many baser influences, the general and obvious interests of society have of course had a share, and a large one, in the direction of the moral sentiments: less, however, as a matter of reason, and on their own account, than as a consequence of the sympathies and antipathies which grew out of them: and sympathies and antipathies which had little or nothing to do with the interests of society, have made themselves felt in the establishment of moralities with quite as great force.

The likings and dislikings of society, or of some powerful portion of it, are thus the main thing which has practically determined the rules laid down for general observance, under the penalties of law or opinion. And in general, those who have been in advance of society in thought and feeling, have left this condition of things unassailed in principle, however they may have come into conflict with it in some of its details. They have occupied themselves rather in inquiring what things society ought to like or dislike, than in questioning whether its likings or dislikings should be a law to individuals. They preferred endeavouring to alter the feelings of mankind on the particular points on which they were themselves heretical, rather than make common cause in defence of freedom, with heretics generally. The only case in which the higher ground has been taken on principle and maintained with consistency, by any but an individual here and there, is that of religious belief: a case instructive in many ways, and not least so as forming a most striking instance of the fallibility of what is called the moral sense: for the *odium theologicum*, in a sincere bigot, is one of the most unequivocal cases of moral feeling. Those who first broke the yoke of what called itself the Universal Church, were in general as little willing to permit difference of religious opinion as that church itself. But when the heat of the conflict was over, without giving a complete victory to any party, and each church or sect was reduced to limit its hopes to retaining possession of the ground it already occupied; minorities, seeing that they had no chance of becoming majorities, were under the necessity of pleading to those whom they could not convert, for permission to differ. It is accordingly on this battle field, almost solely, that the rights of the individual against society have been asserted on broad grounds of principle, and the claim of society to exercise authority over dissentients openly controverted. The great writers to whom the world owes what religious liberty it possesses, have mostly asserted freedom of conscience as an indefeasible right, and denied absolutely that a human being is accountable to others for his religious belief. Yet so natural to mankind is intolerance in whatever they really care about, that religious freedom has hardly anywhere been practically realised, except where religious indifference, which dislikes to have its peace disturbed by theological quarrels, has added its weight to the scale. In the minds of almost all religious persons, even in the most tolerant countries, the duty of toleration is admitted with tacit reserves. One person will bear with dissent in matters of church government, but not of dogma; another can tolerate everybody, short of a Papist or a Unitarian; another every one who believes in revealed religion; a few extend their charity a little further, but stop at the belief in a God and in a future state. Wherever the sentiment of the majority is still genuine and intense, it is found to have abated little of its claim to be obeyed.

In England, from the peculiar circumstances of our political history, though the yoke of opinion is perhaps heavier, that of law is lighter, than in most other countries of Europe; and there is considerable jealousy of direct interference, by the legislative or the executive power, with private conduct; not so much from any just regard for the independence of the individual, as from the still subsisting habit of looking on the government as representing an opposite interest to the public. The majority have not yet learnt to feel the power of the government their power, or its opinions their opinions. When they do so, individual liberty will probably be as much exposed to invasion from the government, as it already is from public opinion. But, as yet, there is a considerable amount of feeling ready to be called forth against any attempt of the law to control individuals in things in which they have not hitherto been accustomed to be controlled by it; and this with very little discrimination as to whether the matter is, or is not, within the legitimate sphere of legal control; insomuch that the feeling, highly salutary on the whole, is perhaps quite as often misplaced as well grounded in the particular instances of its application. There is, in fact, no recognised principle by which the propriety or impropriety of government interference is customarily tested. People decide according to their personal preferences. Some, whenever they see any good to be done, or evil to be remedied, would willingly instigate the government to undertake the business; while others prefer to bear almost any amount of social evil, rather than add one to the departments of human interests amenable to governmental control. And men range themselves on one or the other side in any particular case, according to this general direction of their sentiments; or according to the degree of interest which they feel in the particular thing which it is proposed that the government should do, or according to the belief they entertain that the government would, or would not, do it in the manner they prefer; but very rarely on account of any opinion to which they consistently adhere, as to what things are fit to be done by a government. And it seems to me that in consequence of this absence of rule or principle, one side is at present as often wrong as the other; the interference of government is, with about equal frequency, improperly invoked and improperly condemned.

The object of this Essay is to assert one very simple principle, as entitled to govern absolutely the dealings of society with the individual in the way of compulsion and control, whether the means used be physical force in the form of legal penalties, or the moral coercion of public opinion. That principle is, that the sole end for which mankind are warranted, individually or collectively, in interfering with the liberty of action of any of their number, is self-protection. That the only purpose for which power can be rightfully exercised over any member of a civilised community, against his will, is to prevent harm to others. His own good, either physical or moral, is not a sufficient warrant. He cannot rightfully be compelled to do or forbear because it will be better for him to do so, because it will make him happier, because, in the opinions of others, to do so would be wise, or even right. These are good reasons for remonstrating with him, or reasoning with him, or persuading him, or entreating him, but not for compelling him, or visiting him with any evil in case he do otherwise. To justify that, the conduct from which it is desired to deter him must be calculated to produce evil to some one else. The only part of the conduct of any one, for which he is amenable to society, is that which concerns others. In the part which merely concerns himself, his independence is, of right, absolute. Over himself, over his own body and mind, the individual is sovereign.

It is, perhaps, hardly necessary to say that this doctrine is meant to apply only to human beings in the maturity of their faculties. We are not speaking of children, or of young persons below the age which the law may fix as that of manhood or womanhood. Those who are still in a state to require being taken care of by others, must be protected against their own actions as well as against external injury. For the same reason, we may leave out of consideration those backward states of society in which the race itself may be considered as in its nonage. The early difficulties in the way of spontaneous progress are so great, that there is seldom any choice of means for overcoming them; and a ruler full of the spirit of improvement is warranted in the use of any expedients that will attain an end, perhaps otherwise unattainable. Despotism is a legitimate mode of government in dealing with barbarians, provided the end be their improvement, and the means justified by actually effecting that end. Liberty, as a principle, has no application to any state of things anterior to the time when mankind have become capable of being improved by free and equal discussion. Until then, there is nothing for them but implicit obedience to an Akbar or a Charlemagne, if they are so fortunate as to find one. But as soon as mankind have attained the capacity of being guided to their own improvement by conviction or persuasion (a period long since reached in all nations with whom we need here concern ourselves), compulsion, either in the direct form or in that of pains and penalties for non-compliance, is no longer admissible as a means to their own good, and justifiable only for the security of others.

It is proper to state that I forego any advantage which could be derived to my argument from the idea of abstract right, as a thing independent of utility. I regard utility as the ultimate appeal on all ethical questions; but it must be utility in the largest sense, grounded on the permanent interests of a man as a progressive being. Those interests, I contend, authorise the subjection of individual spontaneity to external control, only in respect to those actions of each, which concern the interest of other people. If any one does an act hurtful to others, there is a *prima facie* case for punishing him, by law, or, where legal penalties are not safely applicable, by general disapprobation. There are also many positive acts for the benefit of others, which he may rightfully be compelled to perform; such as to give evidence in a court of justice; to bear his share in the common defence, or in any other joint work necessary to the interest of the society of which he enjoys the protection; and to perform certain acts of individual beneficence, such as saving a fellow-creature's life, or interposing to protect the defenceless against ill-usage, things which whenever it is obviously a man's duty to do, he may rightfully be made responsible to society for not doing. A person may cause evil to others not only by his actions but by his inaction, and in either case he is justly accountable to them for the injury. The latter case, it is true, requires a much more cautious exercise of compulsion than the former. To make any one answerable for doing evil to others is the rule; to make him answerable for not preventing evil is, comparatively speaking, the exception. Yet there are many cases clear enough and grave enough to justify that exception. In all things which regard the external relations of the individual, he is de jure amenable to those whose interests are concerned, and, if need be, to society as their protector. There are often good reasons for not holding him to the responsibility; but these reasons must arise from the special expediencies of the case: either because it is a kind of case in which he is on the whole likely to act better, when left to his own discretion, than when controlled in any way in which society have it in their power to control him; or because the attempt to exercise control would produce other evils, greater than those which it would prevent. When such reasons as these preclude the enforcement of responsibility, the conscience of the agent himself should step into the vacant judgment seat, and protect those interests of others which have no external protection; judging himself all the more rigidly, because the case does not admit of his being made accountable to the judgment of his fellow-creatures.

But there is a sphere of action in which society, as distinguished from the individual, has, if any, only an indirect interest; comprehending all that portion of a person's life and conduct which affects only himself, or if it also affects others, only with their free, voluntary, and undeceived consent and participation. When I say only himself, I mean directly, and in the first instance; for whatever affects himself, may affect others through himself; and the objection which may be grounded on this contingency, will receive consideration in the sequel. This, then, is the appropriate region of human liberty. It comprises, first, the inward domain of consciousness; demanding liberty of conscience in the most comprehensive sense; liberty of thought and feeling; absolute freedom of opinion and sentiment on all subjects, practical or speculative, scientific, moral, or theological. The liberty of expressing and publishing opinions may seem to fall under a different principle, since it belongs to that part of the conduct of an individual which concerns other people; but, being almost of as much importance as the liberty of thought itself, and resting in great part on the same reasons, is practically inseparable from it. Secondly, the principle requires liberty of tastes and pursuits; of framing the plan of our life to suit our own character; of doing as we like, subject to such consequences as may follow: without impediment from our fellow-creatures, so long as what we do does not harm them, even though they should think our conduct foolish, perverse, or wrong. Thirdly, from this liberty of each individual, follows the liberty, within the same limits, of combination among individuals; freedom to unite, for any purpose not involving harm to others: the persons combining being supposed to be of full age, and not forced or deceived.

No society in which these liberties are not, on the whole, respected, is free, whatever may be its form of government; and none is completely free in which they do not exist absolute and unqualified. The only freedom which deserves the name, is that of pursuing our own good in our own way, so long as we do not attempt to deprive others of theirs, or impede their efforts to obtain it. Each is the proper guardian of his own health, whether bodily, or mental and spiritual. Mankind are greater gainers by suffering each other to live as seems good to themselves, than by compelling each to live as seems good to the rest.

Though this doctrine is anything but new, and, to some persons, may have the air of a truism, there is no doctrine which stands more directly opposed to the general tendency of existing opinion and practice. Society has expended fully as much effort in the attempt (according to its lights) to compel people to conform to its notions of personal as of social excellence. The ancient commonwealths thought themselves entitled to practise, and the ancient philosophers countenanced, the regulation of every part of private conduct by public authority, on the ground that the State had a deep interest in the whole bodily and mental discipline of every one of its citizens; a mode of thinking which may have been admissible in small republics surrounded by powerful enemies, in constant peril of being subverted by foreign attack or internal commotion, and to which even a short interval of relaxed energy and self-command might so easily be fatal that they could not afford to wait for the salutary permanent effects of freedom. In the modern world, the greater size of political communities, and, above all, the separation between spiritual and temporal authority (which placed the direction of men's consciences in other hands than those which controlled their worldly affairs), prevented so great an interference by law in the details of private life; but the engines of moral repression have been wielded more strenuously against divergence from the reigning opinion in self-regarding, than even in social matters; religion, the most powerful of the elements which have entered into the formation of moral feeling, having almost always been governed either by the ambition of a hierarchy, seeking control over every department of human conduct, or by the spirit of Puritanism. And some of those modern reformers who have placed themselves in strongest opposition to the religions of the past, have been no way behind either churches or sects in their assertion of the right of spiritual domination: M. Comte, in particular, whose social system, as unfolded in his *Systeme de Politique Positive*, aims at establishing (though by moral more than by legal appliances) a despotism of society over the individual, surpassing anything contemplated in the political ideal of the most rigid disciplinarian among the ancient philosophers.

Apart from the peculiar tenets of individual thinkers, there is also in the world at large an increasing inclination to stretch unduly the powers of society over the individual, both by the force of opinion and even by that of legislation; and as the tendency of all the changes taking place in the world is to strengthen society, and diminish the power of the individual, this encroachment is not one of the evils which tend spontaneously to disappear, but, on the contrary, to grow more and more formidable. The disposition of mankind, whether as rulers or as fellow-citizens, to impose their own opinions and inclinations as a rule of conduct on others, is so energetically supported by some of the best and by some of the worst feelings incident to human nature, that it is hardly ever kept under restraint by anything but want of power; and as the power is not declining, but growing, unless a strong barrier of moral conviction can be raised against the mischief, we must expect, in the present circumstances of the world, to see it increase.

• John Locke (1632–1704)

Property[8]

John Locke, British philosopher of the seventeenth century, studied at Oxford and spent most of his life as secretary and tutor in the household of several noble families. Primarily interested in the philosophy of knowlege, his most famous work, *An Essay Concerning Human Understanding*, was the first important work in the English empirical tradition. His interests also extended to political and social subjects as evidenced by the *Second Treatise on Civil Government* (1690) from which the following chapter on property is taken. Appealing to the doctrine of natural rights, Locke bases property upon consumption and states in one of its earliest forms the labor theory of economic value.

Whether we consider natural reason, which tells us that men being once born have a right to their preservation, and consequently to meat and drink and such other things as nature affords for their subsistence; or Revelation, which gives us an account of those grants God made of the world to Adam, and to Noah and his sons, 'tis very clear that God, as King David says, Psalm cxv. 16, "has given the earth to the children of men," given it to mankind in common. But this being supposed, it seems to some a very great difficulty how any one should ever come to have a property in anything. I will not content myself to answer that if it be difficult to make out property upon a supposition that God gave the world to Adam and his posterity in common, it is impossible that any man but one universal monarch should have any property upon a supposition that God gave the world to Adam and his heirs in succession, exclusive of all the rest of his posterity. But I shall endeavour to show how men might come to have a property in several parts of that which God gave to mankind in common, and that without any express compact of all the commoners.

God, who hath given the world to men in common, hath also given them reason to make use of it to the best advantage of life and convenience. The earth and all that is therein is given to men

[8] From John Locke, *Second Treatise On Civil Government* (1690), chap. v.

for the support and comfort of their being. And though all the fruits it naturally produces, and beasts it feeds, belong to mankind in common, as they are produced by the spontaneous hand of nature; and nobody has originally a private dominion exclusive of the rest of mankind in any of them as they are thus in their natural state; yet being given for the use of men, there must of necessity be a means to appropriate them some way or other before they can be of any use or at all beneficial to any particular man. The fruit or venison which nourishes the wild Indian, who knows no enclosure, and is still a tenant in common, must be his, and so his, i.e., a part of him, that another can no longer have any right to it, before it can do any good for the support of his life.

Though the earth and all inferior creatures be common to all men, yet every man has a property in his own person; this nobody has any right to but himself. The labour of his body and the work of his hands we may say are properly his. Whatsoever, then, he removes out of the state that nature hath provided and left it in, he hath mixed his labour with, and joined to it something that is his own, and thereby makes it his property. It being by him removed from the common state nature placed it in, it hath by this labour something annexed to it that excludes the common right of other men. For this labour being the unquestionable property of the labourer, no man but he can have a right to what that is once joined to, at least where there is enough, and as good left in common for others.

He that is nourished by the acorns he picked up under an oak, or the apples he gathered from the trees in the wood, has certainly appropriated them to himself. Nobody can deny but the nourishment is his. I ask, then, When did they begin to be his—when he digested, or when he ate, or when he boiled, or when he brought them home, or when he picked them up? And 'tis plain if the first gathering made them not his, nothing else could. That labour put a distinction between them and common; that added something to them more than Nature, the common mother of all, had done, and so they became his private right. And will any one say he had no right to those acorns or apples he thus appropriated, because he had not the consent of all mankind to make them his? Was it a robbery thus to assume to himself what belonged to all in common? If such a consent as that was necessary, man had starved, notwithstanding the plenty God had given him. We see in commons which remain so by compact that 'tis the taking any part of what is common and removing it out of the state nature leaves it in, which begins the property; without which the common is of no use. And the taking of this or that part does not depend on the express consent of all the commoners. Thus the grass my horse has bit, the turfs my servant has cut, and the ore I have dug in any place where I have a right to them in common with others, become my property without the assignation or consent of anybody. The labour that was mine removing them out of that common state they were in, hath fixed my property in them.

By making an explicit consent of every commoner necessary to any one's appropriating to himself any part of what is given in common, children or servants could not cut the meat which their father or master had provided for them in common without assigning to every one his peculiar part. Though the water running in the fountain be every one's yet who can doubt but that in the pitcher is his only who drew it out? His labour hath taken it out of the hands of Nature, where it was common, and belonged equally to all her children, and hath thereby appropriated it to himself.

Thus the law of reason makes the deer that Indian's who hath killed it; 'tis allowed to be his goods who hath bestowed his labour upon it, though before it was the common right of every one. And amongst those who are counted the civilised part of mankind, who have made and multiplied positive laws to determine property, this original law of nature, for the beginning of property in what was before common, still takes place; and by virtue thereof, what fish any one catches in the ocean, that great and still remaining common of mankind, or what ambergris any one takes up here, is, by the labour that removes it out of that common state nature left it in, made his property who takes that pains about it. And even amongst us, the hare that any one is hunting is thought his who pursues her during the chase. For being a beast that is still looked upon as common, and no man's private possession, whoever has employed so much labour about any of that kind as to find and pursue her has thereby removed her from the state of nature wherein she was common, and hath begun a property.

It will perhaps be objected to this, that if gathering the acorns, or other fruits of the earth, etc., makes a right to them, then any one may engross as much as he will. To which I answer, Not so. The same law of nature that does by this means give us property, does also bound that property too. "God has given us all things richly" (1 Tim. vi. 17), is the voice of reason confirmed by inspiration. But how far has He given it us? To enjoy. As much as any one can make use of to any advantage of life before it spoils, so much he may by his labour fix a property in; whatever is beyond this, is more than his share, and belongs to others. Nothing was made by God for man to spoil or destroy. And thus considering the plenty of natural provisions there was a long time in the world, and the few spenders, and to how small a part of that provision the industry of one man could extend itself, and engross it to the prejudice of others—especially keeping within the bounds, set by reason, of what might serve for his use—there could be then little room for quarrels or contentions about property so established.

But the chief matter of property being now not the fruits of the earth, and the beasts that subsist on it, but the earth itself, as that which takes in and carries with it all the rest, I think it is plain that property in that, too, is acquired as the former. As much land as a man tills, plants, improves, cultivates, and can use the product of, so much is his property. He by his labour does as it were enclose it from the common. Nor will it invalidate his right to say, everybody else has an equal title to it; and therefore he cannot appropriate, he cannot enclose, without the consent of all his fellow-commoners, all mankind. God, when He gave the world in common to all mankind, commanded man also to labour, and the penury of his condition required it of him. God and his reason commanded him to subdue the earth, i.e., improve it for the benefit of life, and therein lay out something upon it that was his own, his labour. He that, in obedience to this command of God, subdued, tilled, and sowed any part of it, thereby annexed to it something that was his property, which another had no title to, nor could without injury take from him.

Nor was this appropriation of any parcel of land, by improving it, any prejudice to any other man, since there was still enough and as good left; and more than the yet unprovided could use. So that in effect there was never the less left for others because of his enclosure for himself. For he that leaves as much as another can make use of, does as good as take nothing at all. Nobody could think himself injured by the drinking of another man, though he took a good draught, who had a whole river of the same water left him to quench his thirst; and the case of land and water, where there is enough of both, is perfectly the same.

God gave the world to men in common; but since He gave it them for their benefit, and the greatest conveniences of life they were capable to draw from it, it cannot be supposed He meant it should always remain common and uncultivated. He gave it to the use of the industrious and rational (and labour was to be his title to it), not to the fancy or covetousness of the quarrelsome and contentious. He that had as good left for his improvement as was already taken up, needed not complain, ought not to meddle with what was already improved by another's labour; if he did, it is plain he desired the benefit of another's pains, which he had no right to, and not the ground which God had given him in common with others to labour on, and whereof there was as good left as that already possessed, and more than he knew what to do with, or his industry could reach to.

It is true, in land that is common in England, or any other country where there is plenty of people under Government, who have money and commerce, no one can enclose or appropriate any part without the consent of all his fellow-commoners: because this is left common by compact, i.e., by the law of the land, which is not to be violated. And though it be common in respect of some men, it is not so to all mankind; but is the joint property of this country, or this parish. Besides, the remainder, after such enclosure, would not be as good to the rest of the commoners as the whole was, when they could all make use of the whole; whereas in the beginning and first peopling of the great common of the world it was quite otherwise. The law man was under was rather for appropriating. God commanded, and his wants forced him, to labour. That was his property, which could not be taken from him wherever he had fixed it. And hence subduing or cultivating the earth, and having dominion, we see are joined together. The one gave title to the other. So that God, by commanding to subdue, gave authority so far to appropriate. And the condition of human life, which requires labour and materials to work on, necessarily introduces private possessions.

The measure of property nature has well set by the extent of men's labour and the convenience of life. No man's labour could subdue or appropriate all; nor could his enjoyment consume more than a small part; so that it was impossible for any man, this way, to intrench upon the right of another, or acquire to himself a property to the prejudice of his neighbour, who would still have room for as good and as large a possession (after the other had taken out his) as before it was appropriated. Which measure did confine every man's possession to a very moderate proportion, and such as he might appropriate to himself without injury to anybody, in the first ages of the world, when men were more in danger to be lost by wandering from their company in the then vast wilderness of the earth than to be straitened for want of room to plant in. And the same measure may be allowed still without prejudice to anybody, as full as the world seems. For supposing a man or family in the state they were at first peopling of the world by the children of Adam or Noah; let him plant in some island vacant places of America, we shall find that the possessions he could make himself, upon the measures we have given, would not be very large, nor, even to this day, prejudice the rest of mankind, or give them reason to complain or think themselves injured by this man's encroachment, though the race of men have now spread themselves to all the corners of the world, and do infinitely exceed the small number that was at the beginning. Nay, the extent of ground is of so little value without labour, that I have heard it affirmed that in Spain itself a man may be permitted to plough, sow, and reap, without being disturbed, upon land he has no other title to but only his making use of it. But on the contrary, the inhabitants think themselves beholden to him who by his industry on neglected and consequently waste land has increased the stock of corn which they wanted. But be this as it will, which I lay no stress on, this I dare boldly affirm—that the same rule of propriety, viz., that every man should have as much as he could make use of, would hold still in the world without straitening anybody, since there is land enough in the world to suffice double the inhabitants, had not the invention of money, and the tacit agreement of men to put a value on it, introduced (by consent) larger possessions and a right to them; which how it has done I shall by-and-bye show more at large.

This is certain, that in the beginning, before the desire of having more than man needed had altered the intrinsic value of things, which depends only on their usefulness to the life of man; or had agreed that a little piece of yellow metal which would keep without wasting or decay should be worth a great piece of flesh or a whole heap of corn, though men had a right to appropriate by their labour, each one to himself, as much of the things of nature as he could use, yet this could not be much, nor to the prejudice of others, where the same plenty was still left to those who would use the same industry.

Before the appropriation of land, he who gathered as much of the wild fruit, killed, caught, or tamed as many of the beasts as he could; he that so employed his pains about any of the spontaneous products of nature as any way to alter them from the state which nature put them in, by placing any of his labour on them, did thereby acquire a propriety in them. But if they perished in his possession without their due use; if the fruits rotted, or the venison putrefied before he could spend it, he offended against the common law of nature, and was liable to be punished; he invaded his neighbour's share, for he had no right further than his use called for any of them and they might serve to afford him conveniences of life.

The same measures governed the possessions of land, too. Whatsoever he tilled and reaped, laid up, and made use of before it spoiled, that was his peculiar right; whatsoever he enclosed and could feed and make use of, the cattle and product was also his. But if either the grass of his enclosure rotted on the ground, or the fruit of his planting perished without gathering and laying up, this part of the earth, notwithstanding his enclosure, was still to be looked on as waste, and might be the possession of any other. Thus, at the beginning, Cain might take as much ground as he could till and make it his own land, and yet leave enough for Abel's sheep to feed on; a few acres would serve for both their possessions. But as families increased, and industry enlarged their stocks, their possessions enlarged with the need of them; but yet it was commonly without any fixed property in the ground they made use of, till they incorporated, settled themselves together, and built cities; and then, by consent, they came in time to set out the bounds of their distinct territories, and agree on limits between them and their neighbours, and, by laws within themselves, settled the properties of those of the same society. For we see that in that part of the world which was first inhabited, and therefore like to be the best people, even as low down as Abraham's time they wandered with their flocks and their herds, which were their substance, freely up and down; and this Abraham did in a country where he was a stranger: whence it is plain that at least a great part of the land lay in common; that the inhabitants valued it or not, nor claimed property in any more than they made use of. But when there was not room enough in the same place for their herds to feed together, they by consent, as Abraham and Lot did (Gen. xiii. 5), separated and enlarged their pasture where it best liked them. And for the same reason Esau went from his father and his brother, and planted in Mount Seir (Gen. xxxvi. 6).

And thus, without supposing any private dominion and property in Adam over all the world, exclusive of all other men, which can no way be proved, nor any one's property be made out from it; but supposing the world given as it was to the children of men in common, we see how labour could make men distinct titles to several parcels of it for their private uses, wherein there could be no doubt of right, no room for quarrel.

Nor is it so strange, as perhaps before consideration it may appear, that the property of labour should be able to overbalance the community of land. For it is labour indeed that puts the difference of value on everything; and let any one consider what the difference is between an acre of land planted with tobacco or sugar, sown with wheat or barley, and an acre of the same land lying in common without any husbandry upon it, and he will find that the improvement of labour makes the far greater part of the value. I think it will be but a very modest computation to say that of the products of the earth useful to the life of man nine-tenths are the effects of labour; nay, if we will rightly estimate things as they come to our use, and cast up the several expenses about them—what in them is purely owing to nature, and what to labour—we shall find that in most of them ninety-nine hundredths are wholly to be put on the account of labour.

There cannot be a clearer demonstration of anything than several nations of the Americans are of this, who are rich in land and poor in all the comforts of life, whom nature having furnished as liberally as any other people with the materials of plenty—i.e., a fruitful soil, apt to produce in abundance what might serve for food, raiment, and delight—yet, for want of improving it by labour, have not one-hundredth part of the conveniences we enjoy. And a king of a large and fruitful territory there, feeds, lodges, and is clad worse than a day-labourer in England.

To make this a little clearer, let us but trace some of the ordinary provisions of life through their several progresses before they come to our use, and see how much they receive of their value from human industry. Bread, wine, and cloth are by compact and agreement, settled the property which labour and industry began—and the leagues that have been made between several states and kingdoms, either expressly or tacitly disowning all claim and right to the land in the other's possession, have, by common consent, given up their pretences to their natural common right, which originally they had to those countries; and so have, by positive agreement, settled a property amongst themselves in distinct parts of the world —yet there are still great tracts of ground to be found which, the inhabitants thereof not having joined with the rest of mankind in the consent of the use of their common money, lie waste, and are more than the people who dwell on it do or can make use of, and so still lie in common; though this can scarce happen amongst that part of mankind that have consented to the use of money.

The greatest part of things really useful to the life of man, and such as the necessity of subsisting made the first commoners of the world look after, as it doth the Americans now, are generally things of short duration, such as, if they are not consumed by use, will decay and perish of themselves: gold, silver, and diamonds are things that fancy or agreement have put the value on more than real use and the necessary support of life. Now, of those good things which nature hath provided in common, every one hath a right, as hath been said, to as much as he could use, and had a property in all he could effect with his labour—all that his industry could extend to, to alter from the state nature had put it in, was his. He that gathered a hundred bushels of acorns or apples had thereby a property in them; they were his goods as soon as gathered. He was only to look that he used them before they spoiled, else he took more than his share, and robbed others; and, indeed, it was a foolish thing, as well as dishonest, to hoard up more than he could make use of. If he gave away a part to anybody else, so that it perished not uselessly in his possession, these he also made use of; and if he also bartered away plums that would have rotted in a week, for nuts that would last good for his eating a whole year, he did no injury; he wasted not the common stock, destroyed no part of the portion of goods that belonged to others, so long as nothing perished uselessly in his hands. Again, if he would give his nuts for a piece of metal, pleased with its colour, or exchange his sheep for shells, or wool for a sparkling pebble or a diamond, and keep those by him all his life, he invaded not the right of others; he might heap up as much of these durable things as he pleased, the exceeding of the bounds of his just property not lying in the largeness of his possessions, but the perishing of anything uselessly in it.

And thus came in the use of money—some lasting thing that men might keep without spoiling, and that, by mutual consent, men would take in exchange for the truly useful but perishable supports of life.

And as different degrees of industry were apt to give men possessions in different proportions, so this invention of money gave them the opportunity to continue and enlarge them; for supposing an island, separate from all possible commerce with the rest of the world, wherein there were but a hundred families—but there were sheep, horses, and cows, with other useful animals, wholesome fruits, and land enough for corn for a hundred thousand times as many, but nothing in the island, either because of its commonness or perishableness, fit to supply the place of money—what reason could any one have there to enlarge his possessions beyond the use of his family and a plentiful supply to its consumption, either in what their own industry produced, or they could barter for like perishable useful commodities with others? Where there is not something both lasting and scarce, and so valuable to be hoarded up, there men will not be apt to enlarge their possessions of land, were it never so rich, never so free for them to take; for I ask, what would a man value ten thousand or a hundred thousand acres of excellent land, ready cultivated, and well stocked too with cattle, in the middle of the inland parts of America, where he had no hopes of commerce with other parts of the world, to draw money to him by the sale of the product? It would not be worth the enclosing, and we should see him give up again to the wild common of nature whatever was more than would supply the conveniences of life to be had there for him and his family.

Thus in the beginning all the world was America, and more so than that is now, for no such thing as money was anywhere known. Find out something that hath the use and value of money amongst his neighbours, you shall see the same man will begin presently to enlarge his possessions.

But since gold and silver, being little useful to the life of man in proportion to food, raiment, and carriage, has its value only from the consent of men, whereof labour yet makes, in great part, the measure, it is plain that the consent of men have agreed to a disproportionate and unequal possession of the earth—I mean out of the bounds of society and compact; for in governments the laws regulate it; they having, by consent, found out and agreed in a way how a man may rightfully and without injury possess more than he himself can make use of by receiving gold and silver, which may continue long in a man's possession, without decaying for the overplus, and agreeing those metals should have a value.

And thus, I think, it is very easy to conceive without any difficulty how labour could at first begin a title of property in the common things of nature, and how the spending it upon our uses bounded it; so that there could then be no reason of quarrelling about title, nor any doubt about the largeness of possession it gave. Right and conveniency went together; for as a man had a right to all he could employ his labour upon, so he had no temptation to labour for more than he could make use of. This left no room for controversy about the title, nor for encroachment on the right of others; what portion a man carved to himself was easily seen, and it was useless, as well as dishonest, to carve himself too much, or take more than he needed.

• Alexander Meiklejohn (1872–   )

The Intention of Democracy[9]

Alexander Meiklejohn, philosopher, educator, follower of Kant, and passionate advocate of civil liberties, is perhaps not a classical philosopher in the same sense as Locke or Mill. But his moving, deeply felt, and idealistic book *What Does America Mean?*, from which the following selection is taken, deserves to be better known than it at present is. Here Meiklejohn argues that democracy is an enterprise in which all have a genuine share, and that it is a spiritual venture, not a mere arrangement of governmental machinery.

It was said, early in this book, that liberty cannot be properly understood unless it is seen as a phase of democratic living. Men can be free, we said, only when their relations are those of equals and brothers. Since that statement was made we have been examining the error which has mistaken independence for liberty. It is now time that we turn to the positive side of our argument, that we try to determine what, in the life of a democracy, liberty really is.

For this purpose, it is evident that we must agree upon the meaning of democracy. We must give to that idea, which is the most fundamental of all our social concepts, a clear and stable meaning.

My own definition of a democracy would be that it is a society which is carrying on an enterprise in which all its members have a genuine share. It implies, first, that the group has something to do. It assumes, also, that the undertaking is such that all people can actively and responsibly partake in the achievement.

Now it is very clear that this definition brings us face to face with a crucial issue which has been running beneath all our argument. Does it mean anything to say that America has a purpose, a commitment? Is there any sense in the statement that a nation has a common spiritual life in which all its people may share or fail to share? If not, I cannot see that either democracy or any

[9] From Alexander Meiklejohn, *What Does America Mean?* (New York: W. W. Norton & Co., Inc., 1935), chap. xii. By permission of the author.

other principle of social living has any significance. Unless in the life of a social group some dominant purpose can be found, in terms of which it can be assessed, in relation to which its manifold activities can be judged as good or bad, then planning for such a group seems to me to be nonsense. Human reason, as the critic and guide of human living, stands or falls with the answer to the question, "What are we, as human beings, trying to do?"

It is at this most crucial point in social theory that I find the central contention of this book most critically true. Here the distinction between inner and outer interpretations of life seems to me essential and decisive. To put the matter very bluntly I would say that if the life of a nation is seen in outer terms it has no single purpose running through it. It is meaningless and chaotic. If, on the other hand, our thinking is inner, if human actions are seen in terms of persons and their ideals, the life of any group may be seen as a single enterprise dominated by a single purpose. A society whose activities are interpreted merely as efforts toward comfort and convenience becomes inevitably for those who so know it a huge welter of desires and interests which, as such, have no principles in common. A social group, on the other hand, in which men are known as seeking, successfully or unsuccessfully, for truth, fairness, justice, gentleness, generosity, runs together into significance. An outer world—or rather, a world known in outer terms—is multifarious. An inner world is, in its very nature, seeking for unity. It has a sense of the direction in which it is trying to go. At every point it succeeds or fails in relation to that single direction.

The issue here raised is so difficult and, at the same time, so decisive that we must, I fear, turn aside for the moment from our attempt to define democracy. We must face first the deeper human problem. Has human living at large a dominant purpose which runs through it from end to end, from limit to limit? Can the life of man be known as having a dominant ideal? If that question is answered with a "No," then all our studies of democracy and liberty are, I think, fruitless. But, if the answer is "Yes," then we have a human principle in terms of which democracy can be defined, in relation to which liberty can have meaning. I must ask the reader, therefore, to take with me a survey of human activities, to see whether or not we can discover within them any dominating purpose.

If I now proceed to list deeds which men have done, which they have succeeded or failed in doing, I have little fear that my catalogue will be taken as intending to be an accurate accounting. All that I ask of it is that, if possible, it shall suggest the general drive which has run through the thousands of years in which men have been making themselves and their societies. To this end I shall quite frankly select those activities which make most vivid appeal to my own imagination, in which the human quality seems to me to come out most clearly. Very frankly, too, I shall be stressing in these notes, not our mistakes and blunders, not our crimes and errors, but rather our achievements and, beyond these, our intentions of achievement. My purpose is to discover, as well as I can, what the minds and wills of men are driving at.

When the question is asked in this form, the record of human life can be seen as a long list of inventions. Men have, throughout the ages, used their bodies, their wills, their wits, in getting things done. But they have also forever tried to improve their modes of action. At his best, man is always dissatisfied with himself. In some fundamental sense he is always struggling away from what he has achieved toward something better which he might do. He is, characteristically, an inventing animal.

What, then, have men invented? In answer to that question I present a very haphazard and miscellaneous list.

First, we have made agriculture. The semi-animal who, long ago, fumbled his way toward digging of the soil with fingers or bits of wood or stone, can now produce a vast and varied supply of human food. With infinite cleverness and skill, he has developed, first, his wants and, second, his devices for satisfying them. More and more, as a master, he has summoned the world of vegetation to feed and please him.

Second, we have invented ways of using physical power. The untutored brute who, ages ago, tugged and pulled to move himself and other things about, has harnessed in his service the forces of the outer world. He made the wheel and fire, the path, the vehicle. He has constructed machines for transportation and for manufacture. The story of Man's ingenuity and perseverance in that field is gloriously varied and exciting.

Third, we men have made a social order, or many social orders. We have invented the home, the church, the school, the press, the State. We have made customs, laws, authorities of many sorts. We have devised the factory, the office, the dining-room, the labor union, and hundreds of other groupings. We have created human society —and still have much to do.

Fourth, we have invented science, philosophy, art, literature, and music. We have created worship and games. We have interpreted ourselves, have given expression in varied forms to meanings which we find within us. Man has invented ways of saying to himself and to his fellows what he has found his world, including himself, to be.

And, finally—greatest of all his achievements, making all others possible—Man has invented language. The world which, at the first, comes to him as brute, unmeaning fact, he has restated by means of words and other symbols. And in doing this he has transformed not only the "things" with which he deals, but also himself. The invention of language is, in the truest sense, Man's remaking of his own nature. As words come into use, another self-created creature comes into being. The human animal becomes a mind, a spirit, a will. Through words the human being has invented his second self.

And now, in this hasty and summary story of the strivings of a race, what is the "direction" which we had hoped to find? From what have men been fighting themselves free? Toward what have they been trying to make their way? How shall we mark the line which leads from one of these on toward the other? Is there one human purpose?

Now the assertion which I wish to urge is that a human world which, when seen from the outside, has many purposes may, when seen from within, be unified in its intention. The "things" with which a spirit deals may be disordered, precarious, and accidental, and yet the spirit which deals with them may be dominated in its own activities by principles of order, coherence and unity. And if this be true, then it is nonsense to say, without qualification, "The World is One" or "The World is Many." Both statements are true. Each has its field. The essential point is that we avoid confusing them.

I need hardly say that the outer truth of multiplicity is one which has impressed itself vividly upon the current thinking of America. It is the "scientific" point of view. As the sciences seek to know the as yet unknown, the very quality of their "facts" must be that of the "many and accidental" rather than that of the "necessary and universal." The world which is open to investigation must be one of constant surprises. For the discoverer the universe is a discrete and changing one. It is filled with the novel, the strange, the unpredictable. Every new happening brings with it new knowledge, new problems, new opportunities, new purposes. Life is not the expression of a single, already-known idea, a single dominating purpose. It is rather a flowing stream of changes, a series of ever new and unpredictable events.

And from this it follows that it is not "scientific" to claim to know, by principles formed in advance of the "facts" themselves, what those facts will be or mean. To know, prior to an inquiry, the truth for which you are inquiring, is dogmatism. To interpret new situations merely in terms of principles or purposes drawn from old experiences is a false traditionalism. We must learn as we go. We cannot know in advance. We may not impose upon an outer, objective world our old-fashioned beliefs. In our dealings with an "open" universe, we must be open-minded. We must be scientific and experimental. The world of outer fact is clearly multifarious.

But now, the curious paradox of our double nature appears in the fact that we cannot assert this multiplicity in the outer world without, by the same act, asserting the inner unity of our own thinking. The experimental attitude finds "events" and "things" to be many and varied. But in so doing it asserts with equal clearness the activity of a single mind. It forbids us to say "must" or "must not" when we are dealing with external happenings. But that very act of "forbidding" is itself a "must not." It is an assertion of necessity, of authority, of principles of order, in the inner life. I know no philosophic principle which has been asserted and imposed with more vigorous authority than the demand, "You must be scientific." That demand is laid upon every one who ventures into the field of thinking about a universe so dangerous, so difficult as ours. Its claim upon us is imperative and uncompromising. It is a principle waiting for us at the beginning of every inquiry. It says "must" and "ought" and "right" and "wrong" and "true" and "false." It approves and condemns. Nothing could more clearly express the acceptance of a single, dominating formula than the fervor with which the experimentalist insists that thinking shall be "experimentally" done. There is, he tells us, a "scientific habit of mind." There are demands of accuracy, of thoroughness, of tentativeness, of high imagination, of scrupulous checking of all hypotheses. These are the obligations of any one who thinks. To them we are committed. Throughout them all there runs a single, unchanging purpose—the human attempt to think well about its world. In a word, the denial of unity and authority in the outer universe is based upon the assertion of unity and authority in the realm of thinking.

Now the significance of this dominating principle of the "experimental method" for our discussion lies in the fact that it makes all human investigation, in all ages, in all places, into a single process. It does for our mental activities what Jesus and Socrates have done for our choices and values. If it be true that all men who study must submit themselves to the principles of "experimental inquiry," then here is a standard by which all men and all groups may be judged. Here is a universal and necessary law. We are all engaged in a common intellectual enterprise. As participants in that enterprise all individuals and all civilizations can be assessed. We can, in terms of it, estimate the intellectual quality of the child, the savage, the college graduate, the self-educated man. We can give rating to a Newton, a Darwin, a Kant, a Shakespeare. We can place the mistakes and the insights of a banker, a radical, a patriot, a sentimentalist. All these succeed or fail as thinkers according as they meet or fail to meet the universal requirements that they be "scientific" in the use of their minds. In short, human thinking, as seen from within, is a single process. It has a direction in which it is trying to go. All men, so far as they think, are struggling to make headway in that direction. They share in a common enterprise. Their society is, intellectually, a social order.

But the argument which we have thus far applied only to "scientific" activities applies with equal force to all the enterprises in which men are engaged. Throughout all the range of our human living, when it is seen as the activity of human beings, there emerges a common direction, a common purpose to go in that direction. I have listed five great fields in which the multifarious activities of men are to be found. May I now try in very summary fashion to indicate the uniting purpose by which all these inventions are dominated? And if it appears that I give two principles rather than one, I hope it will be noted that these two imply each other, that they are different aspects of a single intention. It should be noted, also, that the "scientific" activity of which we have been speaking takes its own proper place as a phase of our all-inclusive spiritual enterprise.

As we men assess each other, as we admire or despise ourselves and our fellows, our first test is, I think, that of taste. A man is a man in so far as he is aware of life, sensitive to the qualities which it offers for his experience. At this point, the one fundamental human sin is dullness. Our human world invites us to exist as minds, as wills, as spirits. It offers for our experience beauty in manifold forms. It presents fields of action in which a man may exercise his powers. It thrusts before us problems and puzzles to challenge our wits. And in the face of these there is one sure way in which life can be destroyed. It is the way of stupidity—of simply failing to see, to feel, to be aware of what the possibilities of human living are. And, on the other hand, the one sure way of creating life is that of sensitiveness. To be alive, as a human being, is to be aware of the world.

If any one doubts the statement just made, let me ask him to see in contrast the use of language by Shakespeare and the use of it in our common, lazy speech. The phrase, "Oh how much more doth beauty beauteous seem,/By that sweet ornament which truth doth give!"—that phrase thrills us into life by the exquisiteness of its perception. In it human language reaches the very top of its quality. Meanings are perceived and words are fitted to them by a sensitive apprehension which is human genius. And, as against this, by contrast with it, much of our current, vulgar phrasing seems to be nothing else than a deliberate attempt of the human spirit to avoid existence. Our words are effortless and dull and undiscriminating. They slur our possible meanings. They "get by" in the task of expression. They far too commonly express only the sullen determination of the lazy mind not to be drawn into the activities of living.

The same contrast can be found in the field of architecture. The Church of St. Ouen in Rouen is a building which can stir the human being into the richest and deepest forms of spiritual experience. Every line of that interior, every color, every space is singing the passion and beauty of adoration. To see and to feel it is to be caught up into an apprehension of what worship can be. Here again, human activity is at the top of its quality. But not very far away from that building in Rouen one can find the depths of human life as well. People are living in hovels designed, it would seem, to dull and stupefy them. In those places, unfit for human habitation, every instinctive reaction must be that of avoiding life, of refusing to see its ugliness, of resisting the brutality of an environment from which one cannot physically escape. Just as the Church is seeking to save, to create, so is the social order about it—for which the Church, too, is responsible—seeking to drive human beings out of human existence. From their birth they are under sentence of death.

The same contrast can be found in every field of experience. On one side is Socrates facing even death with eager, questioning, excited, laughing eyes. On the other side is the financial trickster, so arranging his "business deal" that he dare not let his mind dwell upon it but must rather, out of business hours, dull that mind with crude and meaningless enjoyments. There is, in human life, the way of taste and sensitiveness. And there is also the way of dullness, of death. And human life really exists so far, and only so far, as it rises above one of these and makes its way in the direction of the other.

Our second test for the inventing of life is, I think, that of intelligence. It includes, but is much wider than, that "experimental method" of which I have spoken. It is the counterpart, the other side, of taste. Men must not only appreciate their world, savor its quality. They must also interpret their appreciations, understand them, weave them together into systems of ideas which give them order and coherence for the serving of the purposes which are inherent in them. And here, too, we both succeed and fail. On the one side is mere mental sluggishness, the avoiding of mental effort. All of us, in some measure, take life as it comes, with blind acceptance, with no attempt at understanding it. But on the other hand, such men as Socrates and Jesus, Lincoln and Gandhi, Darwin and Newton, Shakespeare and Lenin, Isaiah and Loeb—these men really live as minds. They have imaginations which rush out from every present experience and go ranging through the entire universe in search for meanings which will reveal to that experience its own character. They are passionate in their search for truth, but cool and objective in their judgments about it. They find the realization of their own purposes by giving themselves utterly to a cause which runs through all the ages, in relation to which their own achievements, however great, can be only one small contribution to the work on which their hearts are set. The lives of men, so far as they are really lived, are dominated by the patient, eager, joyous, dispassionate attempt at right thinking. On the creative side, this is what human living is. So far as men do not engage in it, they are not alive, as men.

And now, at last, we are brought by our argument to the point for which it has been seeking. The essential trouble with the outer view of life and of the world is that it does not mean anything. It does not make sense. If a man devotes his energies solely to the making of a fortune, his life is, in the end, foolishness. If a nation takes as its goal the acquiring of wealth and power, that goal slips and slides away into incoherent and self-destructive acquisitions which serve no essential purpose. The outer world, taken by itself, has no meaning. That is why the growing externalization of the American mind has wrought such havoc among us. It is not that we are lacking in eager and generous spiritual impulses. It is rather that, in such a world as we interpret ours to be, such impulses seem to be out of place; they cannot fail to be silly and sentimental and ill-founded. There is no human venture in whose cause they may enlist. But if, on the other hand, the human spirit becomes aware of its own quality, if it undertakes to dominate the world and itself for the extension and enrichment of that quality, then both the world and the self are taken up into a grand, magnificent adventure which runs through all the ages, within which each man and each nation may seek to find its proper place. The Spirit of Man has direction. To have the sense of that direction is to be a man. So far as we are alive as human beings, we are together committed to the doing of something which is worth while. That is what it means to live the inner life.

What I have just said may be put into different words if we say that democracy is of necessity a spiritual principle. It simply cannot be stated in external, material terms. It is a gospel which no materialist can understand. And from this it follows that a people whose imagination is dominated by external aims, external methods, external ideas, cannot be democratic in its view of life, its behavior toward life. As we Americans have thus far used them, the sciences and the technologies have persistently and inevitably undermined all the democratic foundations upon which American society is built. And they have done this not because they intend to do so but because we have misinterpreted them, have allowed them to get out of hand. A democracy is not a multifarious collection of human bodies seeking satisfaction of their desires. It is a unity of the spirit among a multitude of persons who are made one by common ties of admiration and devotion to common ideals. It is a people which knows itself to be one in purpose, whatever may be the multiplicities and variations in the midst of which its many lives are lived. The essential mark of any democracy is the domination exercised over all its members by a single spiritual intention.

SUGGESTED FURTHER READINGS

ARISTOTLE. *Politics.* Translated by J. E. C. WELLDON. 1883.

BELLAMY, EDWARD. *Looking Backward.* 1887.

BOSANQUET, B. *The Philosophical Theory of the State.* New York: The Macmillan Co., 1899.

DEWEY, JOHN. *Freedom and Culture.* New York: G. P. Putnam's Sons, 1939.

HAMILTON, ALEXANDER; JAY, JOHN; MADISON, JAMES. *The Federalist Papers.* ed. E. M. EARLE. New York: Modern Library Inc., 1941.

HOBBES, THOMAS. *The Leviathan.* London: Oxford University Press, 1929. Part I, Chap. xiii, to Part II, Chap. xix.

LOCKE, JOHN. *Second Treatise on Civil Government.* Oxford: Basil Blackwell & Mott, Ltd., 1946.

MacIVER, R. M. *The Modern State.* London: Oxford University Press, 1930.

MacKAYE, JAMES. *Americanized Socialism; A Yankee View of Capitalism.* New York: Liveright Publishing Corp., 1916.

MEIKLEJOHN, ALEXANDER. *What Does America Mean?* New York: W. W. Norton & Co., Inc., 1935.

MILL, JAMES. *An Essay on Government.* 1828.

MILL, J. S. *On Liberty.* (Everyman ed.) New York: E. P. Dutton & Co., Inc., 1928.

——. *Representative Government.* (Everyman ed.) New York: E. P. Dutton & Co. Inc., 1928.

PLATO. *The Republic.* 4th ed. Translated by BENJAMIN JOWETT. Vol. II.

ROUSSEAU, J. J. *The Social Contract.* (Everyman ed.) New York: E. P. Dutton & Co., Inc., 1936.

SMITH, T. V. *The Demoocratic Way of Life.* Chicago: The University of Chicago Press, 1926.

TAWNEY, R. H. *The Acquisitive Society.* New York: Harcourt, Brace & Co., Inc., 1920.

CHAPTER 7

The Arts

THE ARTISTIC PROCESS

Between early January and late February 1787, Wolfgang Amadeus Mozart spent the winter in Prague, and during that time made a contract with Bondini, the director of the Opera Company, to write a new opera for the coming season for a hundred ducats. Returning to Vienna, Mozart and his librettist, Lorenzo da Ponte, seized upon an old and very bad plot about a libertine dragged down to hell by a stone statue. It had recently been revived by Bertati and set to music under the title "The Stone Guest." Da Ponte stole shamelessly from Bertati and for this new patchwork Mozart composed the music. A contemporary tells of Mozart's method of composing:

Mozart wrote everything with such ease and speed as might at first be taken for carelessness or haste; also he never went to the pianoforte while composing. His imagination held before him the whole work clear and lovely once it was conceived. His great knowledge of composition made easy for him the general harmonic panorama. One seldom finds in his scores improved or erased passages. But it does not follow that he merely sketched out his works hastily. The composition had long been finished in his head before he sat himself at his writing-desk. When he received the text for a vocal work he went about with it for some time, thought himself thoroughly into it, and gave it all the power of his fantasy. Then he worked out his ideas fully on the pianoforte and then for the first time sat down to write. Consequently the writing was for him an easy task during which he often joked and chattered. . . .

Late in the summer of 1787 Mozart took the largely finished score with him to Prague again and there, in the summer-house in the vineyard of his friend Duscheck, he completed the work. But just in the nick of time! Legend has it that on the day before the performance he sat up all night writing the overture. Be that as it may, on October 29, 1787, the opera *Don Giovanni* was first performed. The aged Casanova came from the nearby town of Dux just to hear it, the opera house was full, and the work was heard with delight and received with enthusiasm.

Ten years later the great Goethe, having just heard a performance of *Don Giovanni* in Weimar wrote to the poet Schiller: "Your hopes for opera are richly fulfilled in *Don Giovanni* but the work stands absolutely alone and Mozart's death prevents any prospect of its example being followed." Greater praise and a greater judgment of worth the opera could hardly have had.

The story of *Don Giovanni* is the story of many a work of art, and it illustrates the three stages in the natural history of every artistic process. Between March and October 1787 occurred *the act of artistic creation*. On the evening of October 29, 1787 with the aid of orchestra, singers, scenery, occurred for the enthusiastic audience (and for Mozart himself) *the act of artistic enjoyment*. Ten years later in the admiring letter of Goethe to Schiller occurred *the act of artistic judgment*. These are the three "moments" in the total artistic experience, and their reflective consideration provides the subject-matter of *aesthetics*.

It is clear that in the artistic process (as in the moral situation) we can distinguish elements, and these are (1) the artist, (2) the work of art, (3) the audience, and (4) the critic. To this perhaps ought to be added (5) the social and artistic tradition within which the artist works, and in some cases (2) needs to be expanded into two elements, (a) the work as it is in an abstract form and (b) the work as it is embodied in the sensuous medium by its interpreters. This last is not an esoteric distinction; it is simply occasioned by the difference between, on the one hand, the plastic arts and literature, and, on the other, the theatre arts (or arts of performance)—music, dance, and drama, with their compound forms, ballet and opera. A novel, a painting, or piece of sculpture is simply what it is and immediately available to be seen or read. But a tragedy or a symphony, as a written script or score, is rather the work of art as a permanent possibility of performance, and is to be distinguished from the orchestral performance or acted play which is the work of art in actuality, given to the audience through sight and sound.

Two further distinctions are needed to round out the picture. Although there is a very close relation between art and the value which we speak of as "the beautiful," the latter is wider than the former, for it applies to nature and its nonpurposive embodiments of beauty. A waterfall over a steep cliff or a human face or body may be beautiful, but they belong to nature and not to art. We may learn to find beautiful the song of the warbler or the graceful gait of a child crossing the street but this is "accidental" beauty and cannot rightfully be called either music or the dance. Art is not nature, and although its materials and, often, its subject is taken from or inspired by nature, it is an artificial and man-made product.

But if it is the case that not all beautiful things are man-made, it is also the case that not all man-made objects are beautiful. Partly this represents a failure to achieve the beautiful, but partly also the fact that not all man-made objects aspire to the beautiful. There are "artistic values" and there are "values in use." A Haydn quartet or a Modigliani portrait can hardly be used for anything. On the other hand a kitchen gas range or an old umbrella have almost no artistic value. Most man-made objects are neither so useless as a Haydn quartet nor so ugly as an old umbrella. They somehow combine (and in various proportions) artistic values and values in use. Benvenuto Cellini, the Renaissance goldsmith, made for the king of France a small golden bowl with a Greek god and goddess upon the rim; he made it as a saltcellar. It is now in an art museum in Vienna, probably the only saltcellar in that august institution. All of the crafts (or applied arts) such as weaving, costume making, pottery, jewelry making, and one of the fine arts, architecture, produce functional products—rugs, clothes, bowls, cups, jewelry, buildings.

The distinction between the arts and crafts or, as one should say, between the fine arts and the useful arts was unknown in the ancient world. Stonemason or architect, shoemaker or potter, all were "makers" or "artisans." And although those who made with the mind and with words alone could be distinguished from those who made with materials or "matter," there was little consciousness of art separated from the purposes and functions of daily life.

Since the Renaissance it has been different. The difference between the fine arts (painting, sculpture, music, poetry, for example) and the useful arts is a Renaissance distinction; since that time the artist has been less concerned with the construction of a useful object than in creating "beauty" or expressing his insight into the world. Thus the artistic process as here described in its divisions of creation, enjoyment, and judgment, while applicable to any form of "making," will inevitably be used largely as it relates to the fine arts.

THE ACT OF ARTISTIC CREATION

The artistic process begins with the artist who produces the work. This work is in turn presented to an audience for their enjoyment and, at a later stage, perhaps for their criticism. Artist and audience are linked by the work of art itself.

Some time around 1928, Henri Matisse arranged on an old green chest in his studio a platter, a crumpled table cloth, a blue and white pitcher, a fruit knife, a glass two-thirds full of water, and five ripe peaches, and set to work. The result is a lovely and serene work entitled "Still life with green buffet" in which the lunar green of the buffet, the sky blue of the wall behind, the white of the platter and the pitcher, and the light blue of the tablecloth form a rich color harmony against which stand out the five rosy peaches, four in the white platter, one to the side on the light blue table-cloth. The painting first passed into the hands of a private collector but now is in the Musée d'Art Moderne in Paris, where it has been a favorite of the many who visit that institution.

The painting in process in Matisse's studio is the active first step; the "Still life with green buffet" is the work of art, and as it now hangs in the Musée d'Art Moderne it is the focal point of an experience in which many interested viewers participate. What is the "Still life with green buffet"? From one point of view it is a medium-sized canvas, thinly painted, which hangs in a long white building on the bank of the Seine near the Trocadero. But from the aesthetic point of view it is the point of intersection, the *place of meeting* of the mind and emotion of Matisse and the minds and emotions of his viewers. It is, as Plato would say, the middle link in the chain of inspiration which passes from the poet to his audience. But this is to assimilate the artistic experience to the way in which we use language. It is to see in it *an act of communication.*

A mechanical view of language would put it this way. Between one human mind and another there is no mental bridge. You do not know directly what takes place in my mind nor I what takes place in yours. This is where language comes in. To a meaning in my mind I attach a word and speak it. You hear the word and from it extract or infer the meaning. The meaning has been com-municated from my mind to yours and words have been the medium of this communication. The artistic process is the same. Its creator attaches a meaning to the work of art and, upon observing the work of art, the spectator extracts the meaning. Through the work of art has occurred an act of aesthetic communication. But let us be clear. Aesthetic communication is not like scientific communication. That "meaning" which the work of art conveys is not a logical or informative or intellectual "meaning." But what kind of meaning is it then? To this matter we shall turn in just a moment.

As Henri Matisse sits in his studio before the green chest and the five peaches and other objects which he has arranged upon the chest, with his blank canvas upon the easel and his colors before him, what does he do? Of course he dips his brushes in the pigments and transfers these pigments to the canvas, and slowly that previously white surface becomes a colored surface which begins to resemble (but with distortion and not photographically) the arranged objects on the green chest. It is clear that he has begun with "an idea" and that idea has something to do with that green chest and that platter and those five peaches and the way he has arranged them. He plans to make a statement about those peaches and their relation to the pitcher and to the blue tablecloth and that statement is about objects in space. But he also plans to make a statement about the blue of the wall and its relation to the blue of the tablecloth and the relation of those two blues to the white of the platter and the green of the chest and the relation of all this to the pink-orange of the peaches. Naturally those two statements are not to be made with words, but with pigment upon canvas. Thus to the idea implicit in the arrangement of his *subject* must also be added the *materials*—blank linen canvas stretched tight on a wooden frame, pigments, oil, and brushes made of pig bristles or horse hair.

Now, one tradition, which is as old as Aristotle, describes the creative process in these terms. It is an impositon of form upon matter, it is to begin with an idea and to express it in a medium. To the blank potentiality of the canvas Matisse gives an actuality of color and shapes which expresses his idea, and this is true equally of the sculptor imposing form upon the unworked block of marble, the writer imposing form upon the possibilities of his native language, or the composer imposing structure upon the language of sound.

Naturally the work of art has been pondered, thought about, brooded over before being made. Matisse found five peaches more to the purpose than three or six. Perhaps he spent some time in the arrangement of the subject to be painted and surely he searched for the colors which should provide the proper contrast and the proper harmony. For the work was not a mere copy (and so an "imitation") of the objects which he chose; it was to be a *presenta-*

tion of those objects in the light of his own imagination of their natures and ideal properties. All along, the emergence of the painting was controlled by the direction pointed by his "idea."

The theory of artistic creation which we are sketching recognizes that art as the imposition of form upon matter requires technique, that is, great skill and mastery of his craft by the artist. He must know how to use brushes upon the canvas or chisel upon the stone in order to produce a great and successful work, but the "art" lies less in the skill than in the "idea" which the artist wishes to realize. Technical skill is in fact not the art at all, but the condition that removes the impediment of clumsiness which might prevent the work of art from coming into being. True art lies in the mind and imagination of the artist. It is his idea.

This view of artistic creation (which for convenience can be called the Aristotelian theory) is very intellectual. It makes the particular virtue of the artist reside in his intellect, and it suggests that, since his control of his medium is in the service of his intellectual vision, to lose that control is to condemn his art to mere sensualty and confusion. Of course the artist has feeling, and he must be in love with what he is doing, but his love is a love of order and the kind of order which he imposes upon matter is an expression of a kind of *artistic knowledge.*

It is precisely this view of artistic creation which Plato denies. For him the artist does not have knowledge. He has inspiration. When Matisse sits down before his easel and starts to paint feverishly the still life, which an unerring instinct has caused him to arrange in an instant, his mind is blank and it is his feelings which rush over him and into his work. He feels the reality of his pitcher and his peaches as if they were living things. They appeal to him with the immediacy of a child to its mother and in his work he conveys to others like a "medium" the way in which these objects "cry out." Sometimes he works smoothly and without error. On these days he has the sense that it is not he, but some higher power, which is guiding his hand, as if a creative force is working through him and using him for its own inscrutable ends. On other days, the hand is clumsy, nothing seems to work, he throws down the brush with disgust, the green buffet seems ugly, and even the peaches, now over a week old, are unappetizing and slightly rotting fruit.

This is the modern vision of Plato's theory of art as inspiration (see p. 387). The artist creates because he is inspired and possessed. In making the work of art he is the loadstone or magnetic source of a feeling which like a contagion spreads later to the spectators of the work of art. And since this theory of "creation through emotion" is in opposition to the Aristotelian doctrine of an imposition of an idea upon matter, there is another consequence too. It is that if you ask the artist what he has been doing, or trying to do, he will be inarticulate. He will not really know. Or at any rate, he will only be able to point to what he has done and permit the art object to speak for itself. When Socrates asks the reciter of Homer, Ion, about his craft and about that very poet Homer whom he interprets, Ion shows his intellectual weakness, he can make no critical judgments. And probably if Socrates would have been able to ask Homer himself, no answer, no aesthetic theory would have been forthcoming.

Some years ago Sidney Janis produced a book of reproductions of paintings, *Abstract and Surrealist Art in America*. He asked each of the artists to explain his picture, what it meant, what he thought he had been doing, what was his idea. One of the pictures was by Georgia O'Keeffe entitled "White Barn, Canada," and was of a long clean rectangular barn with two big doors and a full sloping roof. It was as serene and quiet a painting as Matisse's "Still life with green buffet" and presented its object with the same candor and straightforwardness. Many of the artists spoke of their pictures, pretentiously, complicatedly, glibly. But Miss O'Keeffe's comment about hers was as stark and as unadorned as the painting itself. "*White Barn, Canada* is nothing but a simple statement about a simple thing. I can say nothing about it in words, that I have not said with paint." Socrates would have been disappointed with Miss O'Keeffe's answer. But Plato would have been satisfied, for it would have confirmed him in his belief that creation is not intellectual but inspired, and that the artist cannot really know wherefrom his creation comes.

The Act of Artistic Enjoyment

The artistic object is the product of the encounter between the artist and his materials, and, whether one thinks of it, Aristotelian-wise, as the imposition of a form upon matter or, Platonically, as the expression of emotion through inspiration, the artist's relation to it ceases when it is created and he sends it out into the world as a mother sends out her child to shift for itself. The act of artistic creation ends with the work of art. And with the work of art the act of artistic enjoyment begins.

When the visitor to the Musée d'Art Moderne in Paris stands before Matisse's "Still life with green buffet" we are in the presence of a second encounter, this time between the spectator and the work of art. What is the nature of this encounter? And what is its effect upon the spectator himself? The very title which we have given to this encounter provides the first clue. It is an act of *artistic enjoyment.*

To say that the spectator "enjoys" the work is to say that the work gives pleasure, but it is not the same kind of pleasure as attaches to the satisfaction of the needs of the body. If Matisse's half-filled glass of water suddenly makes the spectator thirsty, or if the five peaches makes the viewer long to bite into their juicy flesh, then, whatever his enjoyment, it is not artistic enjoyment. For the pleasure which the peaches guarantee for the observer is a pleasure of the eyes and of the mind, a pleasure in roundness and solidity, in the contrast of orange-pink with blue and green and the effect of this pleasure is not to arouse desire, but to induce a certain quietness in the spectator.

There is obviously an important sensuous element in artistic enjoyment, for how else explain the appeal of forms and the lure of color, but it is a sensuous element abstracted and enjoyed for its own sake and not one which leads to anything beyond itself, or to a bodily act.

Thus, to the pleasure which initially defines the act of artistic enjoyment we must now add two other characteristics: first, that it is a *contemplative* experience and, second, that it is an experience which points to nothing beyond itself, in short, that it is not a means but an end, that it is *self-justifying.* Such an experience is not come by easily. It makes heavy demands. upon the spectator. He cannot take it lightly, finish it quickly, give to it only the surface of his attention. To say that the act of artistic enjoyment is by nature pleasurable, contemplative, self-justifying means something for the quality of the attention which makes it possible.

The demands which the work of art make upon the spectator are, although different *in kind,* hardly less than those which it has made upon its creator. For, artistic appreciation and enjoyment requires that the spectator both submit to the object (that is, neither pass it by nor critically reject it before it is understood) and cooperate with it. This cooperation is intuitive. It means that the viewer (in the language of Bergson) does not so much "walk around" the work of art as try to "enter into it." Knowledge on this level does not come without effort. It is like our acquaintance with persons, which begins superficially and may pass on to deep knowledge and even to love. The achievement of real artistic enjoyment requires time and, probably, that we return to the object again and again. It is surely the case that the Prague audience at the first performance of *Don Giovanni* "enjoyed" the work. It is probably true also that they enjoyed just those elements which are most easily accessible, the excitements of the duel and the descent into hell, the charm of the Don's love songs, and the sheer gorgeousness of sound of the quartet and sextet harmonies. But to "enter into the work," to cooperate with it so as to truly intuit what Mozart was trying to communicate (to enjoy, for example the meaningful scales in D minor which are a part of the overture, and to listen for the wicked notes in the violins which accompany the catalogues aria) is to experience the work repeatedly and with the rapt attention which it so richly deserves.

But suppose that this condition is fulfilled, that the spectator of *Don Giovanni* or "Still life with green buffet" enters into it, and that the experience is both pleasurable and contemplative. In what does the pleasure consist? And just what is it that is contemplated?

The Aristotelian theory of creation has an answer to both questions. For, if the act of creation is the imposition of form upon matter and if the work of art is the expression or revelation of the "idea" of the artist, then the pleasure of the spectator must be an intellectual pleasure derived when he recognizes the form which the artist has imposed upon the work, and his contemplation is of the "idea" which is revealed in it.

The formal element in the work of art, the appreciation of which is the source of artistic enjoyment, is expressed by what we call organization or structure. In a musical work like *Don Giovanni* where part follows part and sound succeeds sound it is *a structure in time*. In a painting like "Still life with green buffet," which is created on a surface with length and breadth and where all is viewed simultaneously, it is *a structure in space*. To deal with the structure of *Don Giovanni* in purely musical terms is beyond our scope, but the way in which it preserves a balance between contrasting vocal elements is a miracle of the operatic art. It has two acts and each of these has thirteen different "numbers." Each act has three duets, one trio, one quartet or sextet, and six or seven arias, and they are organized in such a way as to realize maximum effect. As one hears the opera, only the incredible variety of vocal effects somehow unified into an organic whole is intuited. But an analysis of the score and the numbers makes abundantly clear the formal element which is more directly perceived in the experience itself.

Something analogous holds for "Still life with green buffet." The line made by the front edge of the buffet cuts the canvas in two, and all of the objects are placed in the upper half along the top surface of the buffet—platter, peaches, pitcher, knife, glass. It would be difficult for an unskilled painter to provide for the horizontal movement a vertical counterbalance, but Matisse has done it. At the left is a strip of woodwork that runs the full length of the canvas from top to bottom and in the middle of the bottom half of the canvas the two doors of the green buffet open outward providing a broad, black line pointing directly to the platter of peaches which is the picture's central focus. Subject is important, but it is form and structure which gives to a subject its unity and its life. There is nothing more trying to achieve than a notable still life, for the objects are dead and all too often they stand in mute incongruity. It is to Matisse's great skill with structure that the success of this work is due, for he has made of his miscellaneous items not a collection but a "family" of objects. And it is the apprehension of this formal element which provides the true artistic enjoyment.

The enjoyment of form is but one element in the act of artistic enjoyment. There is also the refreshment which comes from a new vision of the world. If the artistic process is rightfully to be described as an act of communication, then there is a pleasure rightfully to be derived from a widening of horizons and a new sense of vision. This is what Tolstoi means when he says (see p. 376) that "a true work of art is the revelation of a new conception of life arising in the artist's soul." The new conception may be the discovery of the artist which he imposes upon the artistic object, but when from that object the spectator has himself extracted the discovery, he feels like Adam on the morning of the first creation.

"Still life with green buffet" is probably too decorative, too merely "surface" to convey a vision of the world, but it may show us in a peach what we have never seen before. *Don Giovanni* has greater depths. It is a treatment of sensuality which raises it almost to a spiritual level and it shows the erotic life, not merely as an immoral accident, but as a demonic force which dominates the life of mankind with the urgency of the sea and of the wind. And all this is shown not merely in the drama but chiefly in the music. The gentle persuasiveness of seduction and the surging power of lust are all in Mozart's music and they reveal something in experience which is ours to discover, whether we accept or reject its implications. It is a terrible opera, but a profoundly truthful one and Mozart's power of illumination heightens our pleasure as we sense its honesty. What Mozart has done superbly in music, and Matisse in painting, Wallace Stevens speaks of also for the poem.

The poem refreshes life so that we share,
For a moment, the first idea. . . .

The poem, through candor, brings back a power again
That gives a candid kind to everything.

JUDGMENT AND CRITICISM IN ART

The act of artistic judgment is the third stage of the artistic process. It presupposes that the artist has created the work of art and that the spectator has responded to it. It now raises the question of the *value* of the work of art, whether it is rightly constructed, whether it is beautiful, whether it is worthy of being enjoyed. The act of artistic judgment is therefore properly cool, properly intellectual, properly critical in its nature.

But it is not precisely clear what the basis of criticism in the arts ought to be. Nor whether there is a standard of beauty which all competent critics can be brought to acknowledge. Nor whether judgments of the work of art can properly be said to express standards which make an objective claim or whether they are simply the subjective preferences of the critics.

The question as to whether judgments of artistic worth are objective or subjective offers no problems which are essentially different than those raised by any questions of value whatsoever. We as well could ask whether truth or falsity are objective or subjective, or whether our judgments of moral worth have one or the other of those characteristics. Granting therefore that this, in all its applications, is one of the persistent problems of philosophy, let us turn to some questions which more particularly concern judgments of artistic worth.

The relation of the act of artistic judgment to the act of artistic enjoyment is not merely that of posteriority in time. It is also one of logical dependence. For it is natural that our judgments of art should follow our interpretations of art. If one believes (with Santayana) that art is primarily an instrument for the production of pleasure, then the test of the value of a work of art is whether indeed it produces the kind and quantity of pleasure desired in the spectator. If one believes (with Schopenhauer) that art is a penetration to the reality of the universe at its deepest level, then the test of the work of art is whether in fact it does express a metaphysical truth of this sort. And if one believes (with Dewey) that art is an intensified and focused expression of man's ordinary experience, then the test of the work of art is whether it actually embodies such an intensified expression of experience. One could, by further examining each of these interpretations of what a work of art ought to be, arrive at more detailed tests which would enable us to judge whether *Don Giovanni* and "Still life with green buffet" are "beautiful," "significant," or "great" works of art.

It appears, therefore, that the necessity for artistic judgment is analogous to the necessity for moral judgment and that they end in the same activity. For the appeal to moral standards we simply substitute the appeal to artistic standards. But two reservations should be noted. First, artistic judgments are independent of moral judgments. Second, artistic judgments, while related to judgments of skill, are not themselves judgments of skill.

When one tries to separate "good" art from "bad" art one uses accidentally moral terms, but one does not mean to employ them morally. When, on the other hand, one speaks of moral and immoral art, one means to imply an ethical judgment, to say that contact with the artistic object stimulates sexual feelings or encourages criminal activity. But if this is so, it is precisely because the object is not producing an artistic enjoyment. Artistic objects may accidentally have inartistic consequences but as artistic objects they are not subject to moral judgments.

Although there is considerable disagreement in judgments of artistic worth, there is a high degree of agreement about the skill displayed in works of art. Of Matisse's "Still life with green buffet," Picasso might have said that he found the subject trivial and the composition merely decorative, but he could not with professional conscience have called it badly painted. Of Mozart's *Don Giovanni* Beethoven (who was somewhat prudish in these matters) might have said that the subject was immoral and its implications disgusting, but he would have found it impossible to deny the musical skill and the melodic inventiveness. But admission of craftsmanship or technical competence in the work of art, a matter of general agreement among the experts in any art, is not itself a judgment of the beauty or the worth of the artistic product.

But how does the appeal to artistic standards take place? An illustrative case in point, although by no means the only one possible, is to be found in Tolstoi (see p. 376). Tolstoi sets himself two problems concerning the definition of the arts; first, to separate art from non-art and, second, to distinguish good art from bad. The first attempt is to delimit the field in which artistic judgment is relevant. The second is to show what standards are to be applied.

Tolstoi's definition of art is not entirely satisfactory, but at least it is definite. *Art is the creation of something new, and it attempts to communicate this something new to others.* Novel creation plus communication equals art. Tolstoi's concept of art is in one respect similar to the Aristotelian, for it sees the artist as discovering a new idea and making it available to others.

It is within this area that artistic judgment is to take place and Tolstoi asserts that there are three tests upon which a judgment of artistic worth may be founded: Is the new idea important to mankind? Is the new idea expressed clearly and understandably in the work of art? Is the author motivated by an inner need rather than external inducements? The three tests of the goodness of a work of art are, then, (1) *importance* (as opposed to triviality), (2) *clarity* (as opposed to obscurity), and (3) *sincerity* (as opposed to opportunism). The first is really a judgment of the content of the work of art, the second of its form, the third of the motive of the artist who produced it.

If we should attempt to judge our two works of art, *Don Giovanni* and "Still life with green buffet," by these tests, what would be the result? I mean by these standards understood generally, not simply as Tolstoi would have applied them. For Tolstoi was in matters of art a very biased and one-sided critic and he would certainly have called any decorative still life utterly trivial and any opera whatsoever (an art form for which he expresses continual contempt) opportunistic and insincere.

Although there are still-lifes before Matisse and operas before Mozart, no one would deny that each has brought something significantly new to the particular art form. Each is therefore art. And if the idea expressed by "Still life with green buffet" is less profound and more concerned with surface qualities than the complexities of *Don Giovanni*, its clarity and starkness of presentation is great. There were some in Mozart's own time who claimed to be perplexed by *Don Giovanni*; it is hardly conceivable that the most hardened artistic conservative could call "Still life with green buffet" an example of "unintelligibility" in modern art. As to the last test (a kind of Kantianism in the realm of the artistic) there can be little doubt in either case. The life of Mozart is a complete dedication to the musical experience. The life of Matisse is a single ponderous devotion to the plastic arts.

The following selections, "On Art" by Leo Tolstoi, "Art and Knowledge" by Plato, "Art as Wholeness" by John Dewey, and "The Nature of Beauty" by George Santayana are all examples of philosophizing about the arts. With the exception of Plato from ancient times, all are modern writers, Tolstoi writing toward the end of the nineteenth century, Santayana following him closely, and Dewey writing in the first decades of this century. The selections are typical meditations upon the nature of the arts and of the beautiful. Tolstoi has been included because he presents straightforward criteria for the artistic judgment, Plato because of his view of the act of artistic creation, Dewey because he expresses so well the unity of the work of art, and Santayana because of the way he roots beauty in the qualities of human nature.

• Leo Tolstoi (1828-1910)

On Art [1]

Leo Tolstoi, although known primarily as one of the great Russian novelists (*Anna Karenina, War and Peace,* etc.), spent most of the later part of his life in religious, social, and artistic speculations. After having become famous for his novels and stories, at fifty he turned aside from literature and, troubled and aloof, spent the next eight years of his life pondering and writing upon religion. Not long before his seventieth birthday he published *What Is Art?,* a long work but a diffuse one. The following selection *On Art* is the complete draft of one of the preparatory studies which he made before writing the larger work. It is not so meaty as the larger work but has the advantage of being more crisply written and equally straightforward in what it has to say. Tolstoi died as a very old man in 1910 and by this time had become world-famous as a religious sage, radical social reformer, and advocate of pacifism.

In our life there are many insignificant or even harmful activities which enjoy a respect they do not deserve, or are tolerated merely because they are considered to be of importance. The copying of flowers, horses, and landscapes, such clumsy learning of musical pieces as is carried on in most of our so-called educated families, and the writing of feeble stories and bad verses, hundreds of which appear in the newspapers and magazines, are obviously not artistic activities; and the painting of indecent, pornographic pic-

[1] From Leo Tolstoi, *On Art* (1895-97), trans. Aylmer Maude (The World Classics ed.). By permission of The Oxford University Press.

tures stimulating sensuality, or the composition of songs and stories of that nature, even if they have artistic qualities, is not a worthy activity deserving of respect.

And therefore, taking all the productions which are considered among us to be artistic, I think it would be useful, first, to separate what really is art from what has no right to that name; and secondly, taking what really is art, to distinguish what is important and good from what is insignificant and bad.

The question of how and where to draw the line separating Art from Non-Art, and the good and important in art from the insignificant and evil, is one of enormous importance in life.

A great many of the wrong-doings and mistakes in our life result from our calling things Art which are not Art. We accord an unmerited respect to things which not only do not deserve it, but deserve condemnation and contempt. Apart from the enormous amount of human labour spent on the preparation of articles needed for the production of art—studios, paints, canvas, marble, musical instruments, and the theatres with their scenery and appliances— even the lives of human beings are actually perverted by the one-sided labours demanded in the preparation of those who train for the arts. Hundreds of thousands if not millions of children are forced to one-sided toil, practising the so-called arts of dancing and music. Not to speak of the children of the educated classes who pay their tribute to art in the form of tormenting lessons—children devoted to the ballet and musical professions are simply distorted in the name of Art to which they are dedicated. If it is possible to compel children of seven or eight to play an instrument, and for ten or fifteen years to continue to do so for seven or eight hours a day; if it is possible to place girls in the schools for the ballet, and then to make them cut capers during the first months of their pregnancy, and if all this is done in the name of art, then it is certainly necessary to define, first of all, what really is art—lest under the guise of art a counterfeit should be produced—and then also to prove that art is a matter of importance to mankind.

Where then is the line dividing art, an important and necessary matter valuable to humanity, from useless occupations, commercial productions, and even from immorality? In what does the essence and importance of true art lie?

•　　•　　•　　•　　•

One theory—which its opponents call "tendentious"—says that the essence of true art lies in the importance of the subject treated of:

that for art to be art, it is necessary that its content should be something important, necessary to man, good, moral, and instructive.

According to that theory the artist—that is to say the man who possesses a certain skill—by taking the most important theme which interests society at the time, can, by clothing it in what looks like artistic form, produce a work of true art. According to that theory religious, moral, social, and political truths clothed in what seems like artistic form are artistic productions.

Another theory, which calls itself "aesthetic," or "art for art's sake," holds that the essence of true art lies in the beauty of its form; that for art to be true, it is necessary that what it presents should be beautiful.

According to that theory it is necessary for the production of art that an artist should possess technique, and should depict an object which produces in the highest degree a pleasant impression; and therefore a beautiful landscape, flowers, fruit, a nude figure, and ballets, will be works of art.

A third theory—which calls itself "realistic"—says that the essence of art consists in the truthful, exact, presentation of reality: that for art to be true it is necessary that it should depict life as it really is.

According to that theory, it follows that works of art may be anything an artist sees or hears, all that he is able to make use of in his function of reproduction, independently of the importance of the subject or beauty of the form.

Such are the theories; and on the basis of each of them so-called works of art appear which fit the first, the second, or the third. But, apart from the fact that each of these theories contradicts the others, not one of them satisfies the chief demand, namely, to ascertain the boundary which divides art from commercial, insignificant, or even harmful productions.

In accordance with each of these theories, works can be produced unceasingly, as in any handicraft, and they may be insignificant or harmful.

As to the first theory ("tendency"), important subjects—religious, moral, social, or political—can always be found ready to hand, and therefore one can continually produce works of so-called art. Moreover, such subjects may be presented so obscurely and insincerely that works treating of the most important of them will prove insignificant and even harmful, the lofty content being degraded by insincere expression.

Similarly according to the second theory ("aesthetic") any man having learned the technique of any branch of art can incessantly produce something beautiful and pleasant, but again this beautiful and pleasant thing may be insignificant and harmful.

Just in the same way according to the third theory ("realistic"), every one who wishes to be an artist can incessantly produce objects of so-called art, because everybody is always interested in something. If the author is interested in what is insignificant and evil, then his work will be insignificant and evil.

The chief point is that, according to each of these three theories, "works of art" can be produced incessantly, as in every handicraft, and that they actually are being so produced. So that these three dominant and discordant theories not merely fail to fix the line that separates art from non-art, but on the contrary they, more than anything else, serve to stretch the domain of art and bring within it all that is insignificant and harmful.

● ● ● ● ●

Where then is the boundary dividing art that is needful, important, and deserving of respect, from that which is unnecessary, unimportant, and deserving not of respect but of contempt—such as productions which have a plainly depraving effect? In what does true artistic activity consist?

To answer this question clearly we must first discriminate between artistic activity and another activity (usually confused with it), namely, that of handing on impressions and perceptions received from preceding generations—separating such activity as that, from the reception of new impressions: those, namely, which will thereafter be handed on from generation to generation.

The handing on of what was known to former generations, in the sphere of art as in the sphere of science, is an activity of teaching and learning. But the production of something new is creation—the real artistic activity.

The business of handing on knowledge—teaching—has not an independent significance, but depends entirely on the importance people attach to that which has been created—what it is they consider necessary to hand on from generation to generation. And therefore the definition of what a creation is, will also define what it is that should be handed on. Moreover, the teacher's business is not usually considered to be artistic; the importance of artistic activity is properly attributed to creation—that is, to artistic production.

What then is artistic (and scientific) creation?

Artistic (and also scientific) creation is such mental activity as brings dimly-perceived feelings (or thoughts) to such a degree of clearness that these feelings (or thoughts) are transmitted to other people.

The process of "creation"—one common to all men and therefore known to each of us by inner experience—occurs as follows: a man surmises or dimly feels something that is perfectly new to him, which he has never heard of from anybody. This something new impresses him, and in ordinary conversation he points out to others what he perceives, and to his surprise finds that what is apparent to him is quite unseen by them. They do not see or do not feel what he tells them of. This isolation, discord, disunion from others, at first disturbs him, and verifying his own perception the man tries in different ways to communicate to others what he has seen, felt, or understood; but these others still do not understand it as he understands or feels it. And the man begins to be troubled by a doubt as to whether he imagines and dimly feels something that does not really exist, or whether others do not see and do not feel something that does exist. And to solve this doubt he directs his whole strength to the task of making his discovery so clear that there cannot be the smallest doubt, either for himself or for other people, as to the existence of that which he perceives; and as soon as this elucidation is completed and the man himself no longer doubts the existence of what he has seen, understood, or felt, others at once see, understand, and feel as he does, and it is this effort to make clear and indubitable to himself and to others what both to others and to him had been dim and obscure, that is the source from which flows the production of man's spiritual activity in general, or what we call works of art—which widen man's horizon and oblige him to see what had not been perceived before.

It is in this that the activity of an artist consists; and to this activity is related the feeling of the recipient. This feeling has its source in imitativeness, or rather in a capacity to be infected, and in a certain hypnotism—that is to say in the fact that the artist's stress of spirit elucidating to himself the subject that had been doubtful to him, communicates itself, through the artistic production, to the recipients. A work of art is then finished when it has been brought to such clearness that it communicates itself to others and evokes in them the same feeling that the artist experienced while creating it.

What was formerly unperceived, unfelt, and uncomprehended by them, is by intensity of feeling brought to such a degree of clearness that it becomes acceptable to all, and the production is a work of art.

The satisfaction of the intense feeling of the artist who has achieved his aim gives pleasure to him. Participation in this same stress of feeling and in its satisfaction, a yielding to this feeling, the imitation of it and infection by it (as by a yawn), the experiencing in brief moments what the artist has lived through while creating his work, is the enjoyment those who assimilate a work of art obtain.

Such in my opinion is the peculiarity that distinguishes art from any other activity.

•   •   •   •   •

According to this divison, all that imparts to mankind something new, achieved by an artist's stress of feeling and thought, is a work of art. But that this mental activity should really have the importance people attach to it, it is necessary that it should contribute what is good to humanity, for it is evident that to a new evil, to a new temptation leading people into evil, we cannot attribute the value given to art as to something that benefits mankind. The importance, the value, of art consists in widening man's outlook, in increasing the spiritual wealth that is humanity's capital.

Therefore, though a work of art must always include something new, yet the revelation of something new will not always be a work of art, it is necessary:

(1) That the new idea, the content of the work, should be of importance to mankind.
(2) That this content should be expressed so clearly that people may understand it.
(3) That what incites the author to work at his production should be an inner need and not an external inducement.

And therefore that in which no new thing is disclosed will not be a work of art; and that which has for its content what is insignificant and therefore unimportant to man will not be a work of art however intelligibly it may be expressed, and even if the author has worked at it sincerely from an inner impulse. Nor will that be a work of art which is so expressed as to be unintelligible, however sincere may be the author's relation to it; nor that which has been produced by its author not from an inner impulse but for an external aim, however important may be its content and however intelligible its expression.

That is a work of art which discloses something new and at the same time in some degree satisfies the three conditions: content, form, and sincerity.

And here we come to the problem of how to define that lowest degree of content, beauty, and sincerity, which a production must possess to be a work of art.

To be a work of art it must, in the first place, be a thing which has for its content something hitherto unknown but of which man has need; secondly, it must show this so intelligibly that it becomes generally accessible; and thirdly, it must result from the author's need to solve an inner doubt.

A work in which all three conditions are present even to a slight degree, will be a work of art; but a production from which even one of them is absent will not be a work of art.

But it will be said that every work contains something needed by man, and every work will be to some extent intelligible, and that an author's relation to every work has some degree of sincerity. Where is the limit of needful content, intelligible expression, and sincerity of treatment? A reply to this question will be given us by a clear perception of the highest limit to which art may attain: the opposite of the highest limit will show the lowest limit, dividing all that cannot be accounted art from what is art. The highest limit of content, consequently, will be such as is not needed by men, and is a bad and immoral content. The highest limit of expression will be such as is always intelligible to all men. What is thus intelligible is that which has nothing in it obscure, superfluous, or indefinite, but only what is clear, concise, and definite—what is called beautiful. Conversely, the lowest limit of expression will be such as is obscure, diffuse, and indefinite—that is to say formless. The highest limit of the artist's relation to his subject will be such as evokes in the soul of all men an impression of reality—the reality not so much of what exists, as of what goes on in the soul of the artist. This impression of reality is produced by truth only, and therefore the highest relation of an author to his subject is sincerity. The lowest limit, conversely, will be that in which the author's relation to his subject is not genuine but false. All works of art lie between these two limits.

A perfect work of art will be one in which the content is important and significant to all men, and therefore it will be moral. The expression will be quite clear, intelligible to all, and therefore beautiful; the author's relation to his work will be altogether sincere and heartfelt, and therefore true. Imperfect works, but still works of art, will be such productions as satisfy all three conditions though it be but in unequal degree. That alone will be no work of art, in which either the content is quite insignificant and unnecessary to man, or the expression quite unintelligible, or the relation of the author to the work quite insincere. In the degree of perfection attained in each of these respects lies the difference in quality between all true works of art. Sometimes the first predominates, sometimes the second, and sometimes the third.

All the remaining imperfect productions fall naturally, according to the three fundamental conditions of art, into three chief kinds: (1) those which stand out by the importance of their content, (2) those which stand out by their beauty of form, and (3) those which stand out by their heartfelt sincerity. These three kinds all yield approximations to perfect art, and are inevitably produced wherever there is art.

Thus among young artists heartfelt sincerity chiefly prevails, coupled with insignificance of content and more or less beauty of form. Among older artists, on the contrary, the importance of the content often predominates over beauty of form and sincerity. Among laborious artists beauty of form predominates over content and sincerity.

All works of art may be appraised by the prevalence in them of the first, the second, or the third quality, and they may all be subdivided into (1) those that have content and are beautiful, but have little sincerity; (2) those that have content, but little beauty and little sincerity; (3) those that have little content, but are beautiful and sincere, and so on, in all possible combinations and permutations.

All works of art, and in general all the mental activities of man, can be appraised on the basis of these three fundamental qualities; and they have been and are so appraised.

The differences in valuation have resulted, and do result, from the extent of the demand presented to art by certain people at a certain time in regard to these three conditions.

So for instance in classical times the demand for significance of content was much higher, and the demand for clearness and sincerity much lower than they subsequently became, especially in our time. The demand for beauty became greater in the Middle Ages, but on the other hand the demand for significance and sincerity became lower; and in our time the demand for sincerity and truthfulness has become much greater, but on the other hand the demand for beauty, and especially for significance, has been lowered.

· · · · ·

The evaluation of works of art is necessarily correct when all three conditions are taken into account, and inevitably incorrect when works are valued not on the basis of all three conditions but only of one or two of them.

And yet such evaluation of works of art on the basis of only one of the three conditions is an error particularly prevalent in our time, lowering the general level of what is demanded from art to what can be reached by a mere imitation of it, and confusing the minds of critics, and of the public, and of artists themselves, as to what is really art and as to where its boundary lies—the line that divides it from craftsmanship and from mere amusement.

This confusion arises from the fact that people who lack the capacity to understand true art, judge of works of art from one side only, and according to their own characters and training observe in them the first, the second, or the third side only, imagining and assuming that this one side perceptible to them—and the significance of art based on this one condition—defines the whole of art. Some see only the importance of the content, others only the beauty of form, and others again only the artist's sincerity and therefore truthfulness. And according to what they see they define the nature of art itself, construct their theories, and praise and encourage those who, like themselves, not understanding wherein a work of art consists, turn them out like pancakes and inundate our world with foul floods of all kinds of follies and abominations which they call "works of art."

Such are the majority of people and, as representatives of that majority, such were the originators of the three aesthetic theories already alluded to, which meet the perceptions and demands of that majority.

All these theories are based on a misunderstanding of the whole importance of art and on severing its three fundamental conditions; and therefore these three false theories of art clash, as a result of the fact that real art has three fundamental conditions of which each of those theories accepts but one.

The first theory, of so-called "tendentious" art, accepts as a work of art one that has for its subject something which, though it be not new, is important to all men by its moral content, independently of its beauty and spiritual depth.

The second ("art for art's sake") recognizes as a work of art only that which has beauty of form, independently of its novelty, the importance of its content, or its sincerity.

The third theory, the "realistic," recognizes as a work of art only that in which the author's relation to his subject is sincere, and which is therefore truthful. The last theory says that however insignificant or even foul may be the content, with a more or less beautiful form the work will be good, if the author's relation to what he depicts is sincere and therefore truthful.

．　　　．　　　．　　　．　　　．

All these theories forget one chief thing—that neither importance, nor beauty, nor sincerity, provides the requisite for works of art, but that the basic condition of the production of such works is that the artist should be conscious of something new and important; and that therefore, just as it always has been, so it always will be, necessary for a true artist to be able to perceive something quite new and important. For the Artist to see what is new, it is necessary that he should observe and think, and not occupy his life with trifles which hinder his attentive penetration into, and meditation on, life's phenomena. In order that the new things he sees may be important ones, the artist must be a morally enlightened man, and he must not live a selfish life but must share the common life of humanity.

If only he sees what is new and important he will be sure to find a form which will express it, and the sincerity which is an essential content of artistic production will be present. He must be able to express the new subject so that all may understand it. For this he must have such mastery of his craft that when working he will think as little about the rules of that craft as a man when walking thinks of the laws of motion. And in order to attain this, the artist must not look round on his work and admire it, must not make his technique his aim—as one who is walking should not contemplate and admire his gait—but should be concerned only to express his subject clearly, and in such a way as to be intelligible to all.

Finally, to work at his subject not for external ends but to satisfy his inner need, the artist must rise superior to motives of avarice and vanity. He must love with his own heart and not with another's, and not pretend that he loves what others love or consider worthy of love.

And to attain all this the artist must do as Balaam did when the messengers came to him and he went apart awaiting God so as to say only what God commanded; and he must not do as that same Balaam afterwards did when, tempted by gifts, he went to the king against God's command, as was evident even to the ass on which he rode, though not perceived by him while blinded by avarice and vanity.

• • • • •

In our time nothing of that kind is demanded. A man who wishes to follow art need not wait for some important and new perception to arise in his soul, which he can sincerely love and having loved can clothe in suitable form. In our time a man who wishes to follow art either takes a subject current at the time and praised by people who in his opinion are clever, and clothes it as best he can in what is called "artistic form"; or he chooses a subject which gives him most opportunity to display his technical skill, and with toil and patience produces what he considers to be a work of art; or having received some chance impression he takes what caused that impression for his subject, imagining that it will yield a work of art since it happened to produce an impression on him.

And so there appear an innumerable quantity of so-called works of art which, as in every mechanical craft, can be produced without the least intermission. There are always current fashionable notions in society, and with patience a technique can always be learnt, and something or other will always seem interesting to some one. Having separated the conditions that should be united in a true work of art, people have produced so many works of pseudo-art that the public, the critics, and the pseudo-artists themselves, are left quite without any definition of what they themselves hold to be art.

The people of today have, as it were, said to themselves: "Works of art are good and useful; so it is necessary to produce more of them." It would indeed be a very good thing if there were more; but the trouble is that you can only produce to order works which are no better than works of mere craftsmanship because of their lack of the essenital conditions of art.

A really artistic production cannot be made to order, for a true work of art is the revelation (by laws beyond our grasp) of a new conception of life arising in the artist's soul, which, when expressed, lights up the path along which humanity progresses.

• Plato (427–347 B.C.)

Art and Knowledge [2]

Plato is extremely ambivalent in his attitude toward the arts. Himself one of the greatest literary figures among philosophers, he found it necessary to place poetry and music under a rigid censorship in his ideal state, portrayed in *The Republic,* and, in the last chapter of that work (Book X), renewed his criticism on the grounds that art as an "imitation" of reality provides inferior knowledge. In the *Ion,* the dialogue which comprises the following selection, Plato treats art as an irrational phenomenon, made and communicated inspirationally and therefore also to be distinguished from rational knowledge. Other works of Plato which deal with art besides the *Ion* and *The Republic* (III, X), are *Phaedrus* and *Hippias Major.*

Persons of the Dialogue
SOCRATES   ION

Socrates. Welcome, Ion. Are you from your native city of Ephesus?

Ion. No, Socrates; but from Epidaurus, where I attended the festival of Asclepius.

Soc. And do the Epidaurians have contest of rhapsodes at the festival?

Ion. O yes; and all sorts of musical performers.

Soc. And were you one of the competitors—and did you succeed?

Ion. I obtained the first prize of all, Socrates.

Soc. Well done; and I hope that you will do the same for us at the Panathenaea.

Ion. And I will, please heaven.

Soc. I often envy the profession of a rhapsode, Ion; for you have always to wear fine clothes, and to look as beautiful as you can is a part of your art. Then, again, you are obliged to be continually in

[2] From Plato, *Ion,* trans. Benjamin Jowett (1871).

the company of many good poets; and especially of Homer, who is the best and most divine of them; and to understand him, and not merely learn his words by rote, is a thing greatly to be envied. And no man can be a rhapsode who does not understanding the meaning of the poet. For the rhapsode ought to interpret the mind of the poet to his hearers, but how can he interpret him well unless he knows what he means? All this is greatly to be envied.

Ion. Very true, Socrates; interpretation has certainly been the most laborious part of my art; and I believe myself able to speak about Homer better than any man; and that neither Metrodorus of Lampsacus, nor Stesimbrotus of Thasos, nor Glaucon, nor any one else who ever was, had as good ideas about Homer as I have, or as many.

Soc. I am glad to hear you say so, Ion; I see that you will not refuse to acquaint me with them.

Ion. Certainly, Socrates; and you really ought to hear how exquisitely I render Homer. I think that the Homeridae should give me a golden crown.

Soc. I shall take an opportunity of hearing your embellishments of him at some other time. But just now I should like to ask you a question: Does your art extend to Hesiod and Archilochus, or to Homer only?

Ion. To Homer only; he is in himself quite enough.

Soc. Are there any things about which Homer and Hesiod agree?

Ion. Yes; in my opinion there are a good many.

Soc. And can you interpret better what Homer says, or what Hesiod says, about these matters in which they agree?

Ion. I can interpret them equally well, Socrates, where they agree.

Soc. But what about matters in which they do not agree?—for example about divination, of which both Homer and Hesiod have something to say,—

Ion. Very true:

Soc. Would you or a good prophet be a better interpreter of what these two poets say about divination, not only when they agree, but when they disagree?

Ion. A prophet.

Soc. And if you were a prophet, would you not be able to interpret them when they disagree as well as when they agree?

Ion. Clearly.

Soc. But how did you come to have this skill about Homer only, and not about Hesiod or the other poets? Does not Homer speak of the same themes which all other poets handle? Is not war his great argument? and does he not speak of human society and of intercourse of men, good and bad, skilled and unskilled, and of the gods conversing with one another and with mankind, and about what happens in heaven and in the world below, and the generations of gods and heroes? Are not these the schemes of which Homer sings?

Ion. Very true, Socrates.

Soc. And do not the other poets sing of the same?

Ion. Yes, Socrates; but not in the same way as Homer.

Soc. What, in a worse way?

Ion. Yes, in a far worse.

Soc. And Homer in a better way?

Ion. He is incomparably better.

Soc. And yet surely, my dear friend Ion, in a discussion about arithmetic, where many people are speaking, and one speaks better than the rest, there is somebody who can judge which of them is the good speaker?

Ion. Yes.

Soc. And he who judges of the good will be the same as he who judges of the bad speakers?

Ion. The same.

Soc. And he will be the arithmetician?

Ion. Yes.

Soc. Well, and in discussions about the wholesomeness of food, when many persons are speaking, and one speaks better than the rest, will he who recognizes the better speaker be a different person from him who recognizes the worse, or the same?

Ion. Clearly the same.

Soc. And who is he, and what is his name?

Ion. The physician.

Soc. And speaking generally, in all discussions in which the subject is the same and many men are speaking, will not he who knows the good know the bad speaker also? For if he does not know the bad, neither will he know the good when the same topic is being discussed.

Ion. Yes.

Soc. And you say that Homer and the other poets, such as Hesiod and Archilochus, speak of the same things, although not in the same way; but the one speaks well and the other not so well?

Ion. Yes; and I am right in saying so.

Soc. And if you knew the good speaker, you would also know the inferior speakers to be inferior?

Ion. That is true.

Soc. Then, my dear friend, can I be mistaken in saying that Ion is equally skilled in Homer and in other poets, since he himself acknowledges that the same person will be a good judge of all those who speak of the same things; and that almost all poets do speak of the same things?

Ion. Why then, Socrates, do I lose attention and go to sleep and have absolutely no ideas of the least value, when any one speaks of any other poet; but when Homer is mentioned, I wake up at once and am all attention and have plenty to say?

Soc. The reason, my friend, is obvious. No one can fail to see that you speak of Homer without any art or knowledge. If you were able to speak of him by rules of art, you would have been able to speak of all other poets; for poetry is a whole.

Ion. Yes.

Soc. And when any one acquires any other art as a whole, the same may be said of them. Would you like me to explain my meaning, Ion?

Ion. Yes, indeed, Socrates; I very much wish that you would: for I love to hear you wise men talk.

Soc. O that we were wise, Ion, and that you could truly call us so; but your rhapsodes and actors, and the poets whose verses you sing, are wise; whereas I am a common man, who only speak the truth. For consider what a very commonplace and trivial thing is this which I have said—a thing which any man might say: that when a man has acquired a knowledge of a whole art, the enquiry into good and bad is one and the same. Let us consider this matter; is not the art of painting a whole?

Ion. Yes.

Soc. And there are and have been many painters good and bad?

Ion. Yes.

Soc. And did you ever know any one who was skilful in pointing out the excellences and defects of Polygnotus the son of Aglaophon, but incapable of criticizing other painters; and when the work of any other painter was produced, went to sleep and was at a loss, and had not ideas; but when he had to give his opinion about Polygnotus, or whoever the painter might be, and about him only, woke up and was attentive and had plenty to say?

Ion. No indeed, I have never known such a person.

Soc. Or did you ever know of anyone in sculpture, who was skilful in expounding the merits of Daedalus the son of Metion, or of Epeius the son of Panopeus, or of Theodorus the Samian, or of any individual sculptor; but when the works of sculptors in general were produced, was at a loss and went to sleep and had nothing to say?

Ion. No indeed; no more than the other.

Soc. And if I am not mistaken, you never met with any one among flute-players or harp-players or singer to the harp or rhapsodes who was able to discourse of Olympus or Thamyras or Orpheus, or Phemius the rhapsode of Ithaca, but was at a loss when he came to speak of Ion of Ephesus, and had no notion of his merits or defects?

Ion. I cannot deny what you say, Socrates. Nevertheless I am conscious in my own self, and the world agrees with me in thinking that I do speak better and have more to say about Homer than any other man. But I do not speak equally well about others—tell me the reason of this.

Soc. I perceive, Ion; and I will proceed to explain to you what I imagine to be the reason of this. The gift which you possess of speaking excellently about Homer is not an art, but, as I was just saying, an inspiration; there is a divinity moving you, like that contained in the stone which Euripides calls a magnet, but which is commonly known as the stone of Heraclea. This stone not only attracts iron rings, but also imparts to them a similar power of attracting other rings; and sometimes you may see a number of pieces of iron and rings suspended from one another so as to form quite a long chain; and all of them derive their power of suspension from the original stone. In like manner the Muse first of all inspires men herself; and from these inspired persons a chain of other persons is suspended, who take the inspiration. For all good poets, epic as well as lyric, compose their beautiful poems not by art, but because they are inspired and possessed. And as the Corybantian revellers when they dance are not in their right mind, so the lyric poets are not in their right mind when they are composing their beautiful strains: but when falling under the power of music and metre they are inspired and possessed; like Bacchic maidens who draw milk and honey from the rivers when they are under the influence of Dionysus but not when they are in their right mind. And the soul of the lyric poet does the same, as they themselves say; for they tell us that they bring songs from honeyed fountains, culling them out of the gardens and dells of the Muses; they, like the bees, winging their way from flower to flower. And this is true. For the poet is a light and winged and holy thing, and there is not invention in him until he has been inspired and is out of his senses, and the mind is no longer in him: when he has not attained to this state, he is powerless and is unable to utter his oracles. Many are the noble words in which poets speak concerning the actions of men; but like yourself when speaking about Homer, they do not speak of them by any rules of art: they are simply inspired to utter that to which the Muse impels them, and that only; and when inspired, one of them will make dithyrambs, another hymns of praise, another choral strains, another epic or iambic verses—and he who is good at one is not good at any other kind of verse: for not by art does the poet sing, but by power divine. Had he learned by rules of art, he would have known how to speak not of one theme only, but of all; and therefore God takes away the minds of poets, and uses them as his ministers, as he also uses diviners and holy prophets, in order that we who hear them may know them to be speaking not of themselves who utter these priceless words in a state of consciousness, but that God himself is the speaker, and that through them he is conversing with us. And Tynnichus the Chalcidian affords a striking instance of what I am saying: he wrote nothing that any one would care to remember but the famous paean which is in every one's mouth, one of the finest poems ever written, simply an invention of the Muses, as he himself says. For in this way the God would seem to indicate to us and not allow us to doubt that these beautiful poems are not human, or the work of man, but divine and the work of God; and that the poets are only the interpreters of the Gods by whom they are severally possessed. Was not this the lesson which the God intended to teach when by the mouth of the worst of poets he sang the best of songs? Am I not right, Ion?

Ion. Yes, indeed, Socrates, I feel that you are; for your words touch my soul, and I am persuaded that good poets by a divine inspiration interpret the things of the Gods to us.

Soc. And you rhapsodists are the interpreters of the poets?

Ion. There again you are right.

Soc. Then you are the interpreters of interpreters?

Ion. Precisely.

Soc. I wish you would frankly tell me, Ion, what I am going to ask of you: When you produce the greatest effect upon the audience in the recitation of some striking passage, such as the apparition of Odysseus leaping forth on the floor, recognized by the suitors and casting his arrows at his feet, or the description of Achilles rushing at Hector, or the sorrows of Andromache, Hecuba, or Priam—are you in your right mind? Are you not carried out of yourself, and does not your soul in an ecstasy seem to be among the persons or places of which you are speaking, whether they are in Ithaca or in Troy or whatever may be the scene of the poem?

Ion. That proof strikes home to me, Socrates. For I must frankly confess that at the tale of pity my eyes are filled with tears, and when I speak of horrors, my hair stands on end and my heart throbs.

Soc. Well, Ion, and are we to say of a man who at a sacrifice or festival, when he is dressed in holiday attire, and has golden crowns upon his head, of which nobody has robbed him, appears weeping or panic-stricken in the presence of more than twenty thousand friendly faces, when there is no one despoiling or wronging him;—is he in his right mind or is he not?

Ion. No indeed, I must say that, strictly speaking, he is not in his right mind.

Soc. And are you aware that you produce similar effects on most of the spectators?

Ion. Only too well; for I look down upon them from the stage, and behold the various emotions of pity, wonder, sternness, stamped upon their countenances when I am speaking: and I am obliged to give my very best attention to them; for if I make them cry I myself shall laugh, and if I make them laugh I myself shall cry when the time of payment arrives.

Soc. Do you know that the spectator is the last of the rings which, as I am saying, receive the power of the original magnet from one another? The rhapsode like yourself and the actor are intermediate links, and the poet himself is the first of them. Through all these the God sways the souls of men in any direction which he pleases, and makes one man hang down from another. Thus there is a vast chain of dancers and masters and under-masters of choruses, who are suspended, as if from the stone, at the side of the rings which hang down from the Muse. And every poet has some Muse from whom he is suspended, and by whom he is said to be possessed, which is nearly the same thing; for he is taken hold of. And from these first rings, which are the poets, depend others, some deriving their inspiration from Orpheus, others from Musaeus; but the greater number are possessed and held by Homer. Of whom, Ion, you are one, and are possessed by Homer; and when any one repeats the words of another poet you go to sleep, and know not what to say; but when anyone recites a strain of Homer you wake up in a moment, and your soul leaps within you, and you have plenty to say; for not by art or knowledge about Homer do you say what you say, but by divine inspiration and by possession; just as the Corybantian revellers too have a quick perception of that strain only which is appropriated to the God by whom they are possessed, and have plenty of dances and words for that, but take no heed of any other. And you, Ion, when the name of Homer is mentioned have plenty to say, and have nothing to say of others. You ask, "Why is this?" The answer is that you praise Homer not by art but by divine inspiration.

Ion. That is good, Socrates; and yet I doubt whether you will ever have eloquence enough to persuade me that I praise Homer only when I am mad and possessed; and if you could hear me speak of him I am sure you would never think this to be the case.

Soc. I should like very much to hear you, but not until you have answered a question which I have to ask. On what part of Homer do you speak well?—not surely about every part.

Ion. There is no part, Socrates, about which I do not speak well: of that I can assure you.

Soc. Surely not about things in Homer of which you have no knowledge?

Ion. And what is there in Homer of which I have no knowledge?

Soc. Why, does not Homer speak in many passages about arts? For example, about drivings; if I can only remember the lines I will repeat them.

Ion. I remember, and will repeat them.

Soc. Tell me then, what Nestor says to Antilochus, his son, where he bids him be careful of the turn at the horserace in honour of Patroclus.

Ion.
Bend gently, he says, in the polished chariot to the left of them, and urge the horse on the right hand with whip and voice; and slacken the rein. And when you are at the goal, let the left horse draw near, yet so that the nave of the well-wrought wheel may not even seem to touch the extremity; and avoid catching the stone.

Soc. Enough. Now, Ion, will the charioteer or the physician be the better judge of the propriety of these lines?

Ion. The charioteer, clearly.

Soc. And will the reason be that this is his art, or will there be any other reason?

Ion. No, that will be the reason.

Soc. And every art is appointed by God to have knowledge of a certain work; for that which we know by the art of the pilot we do not know by the art of medicine?

Ion. Certainly not.

Soc. Nor do we know by the art of the carpenter that which we know by the art of medicine?

Ion. Certainly not.

Soc. And this is true of all the arts;—that which we know with one art we do not know with the other? But let me ask a prior question: You admit that there are differences of arts?

Ion. Yes.

Soc. You would argue, as I should, that when one art is of one kind of knowledge and another of another, they are different?

Ion. Yes.

Soc. Yes, surely; for if the subject of knowledge were the same, there would be no meaning in saying that the arts were different,— if they both gave the same knowledge. For example, I know that here are five fingers, and you know the same. And if I were to ask whether I and you became acquainted with this fact by the help of the same art of arithmetic, you would acknowledge that we did?

Ion. Yes.

Soc. Tell me, then, what I was intending to ask you,—whether this holds universally? Must the same art have the same subject of knowledge, and different arts other subjects of knowledge?

Ion. That is my opinion, Socrates.

Soc. Then he who has no knowledge of a particular art will have no right judgment of the sayings and doing of that art?

Ion. Very true.

Soc. Then which will be a better judge of the lines which you were reciting from Homer, you or the charioteer?

Ion. The charioteer.

Soc. Why, yes, because you are a rhapsode and not a charioteer.

Ion. Yes.

Soc. And the art of the rhapsode is different from that of the charioteer.

Ion. Yes.

Soc. And if a different knowledge, then a knowledge of different matters?

Ion. True.

Soc. You know the passage in which Hecamede, the concubine of Nestor, is described as giving to the wounded Machaon a posset, as he says, "Made with the Pramnian wine; and she grated cheese of goat's milk with a grater of bronze, and at his side placed an onion which gives a relish to drink." Now would you say that the art of the rhapsode or the art of medicine was better able to judge of the propriety of these lines?

Ion. The art of medicine.

Soc. And when Homer says "And she descended into the deep like a leaden plummet, which, set in the horn of ox that ranges in the fields, rushes along carrying death among the ravenous fishes"— will the art of the fisherman or of the rhapsode be better able to judge whether these lines are rightly expressed or not?

Ion. Clearly, Socrates, the art of the fisherman.

Soc. Come now, suppose that you were to say to me: "Since you, Socrates, are able to assign different passages in Homer to their corresponding arts, I wish that you would tell me what are the passages of which the excellence ought to be judged by the prophet and prophetic art"; and you will see how readily and truly I shall answer you. For there are many such passages, particularly in the Odyssee; as, for example, the passage in which Theoclymenus the prophet of the house of Melampus says to the suitors:—

Wretched men! what is happening to you? Your heads and your faces and your limbs underneath are shrouded in night; and the voice of lamentation bursts forth, and your cheeks are wet with tears. And the vestibule is full, and the court is full, of ghosts descending into the darkness of Erebus, and the sun has perished out of heaven, and an evil mist is spread abroad.

And there are many such passages in the Iliad also; as for example in the description of the battle near the rampart, where he says:

As they were eager to pass the ditch, there came to them an omen: a soaring eagle, holding back the people on the left, bore a huge bloody dragon in his talons, still living and panting; nor had he yet resigned the strife, for he bent back and smote the bird which carried him on the breast by the neck, and he in pain let him fall from him to the ground into the midst of the multitude. And the eagle, with a cry, was borne afar on the wings of the wind.

These are the sort of things which I should say that the prophet ought to consider and determine.

Ion. And you are quite right, Socrates, in saying so.

Soc. Yes, Ion, and you are right also. And as I have selected from the Iliad and Odyssee for you passages which describe the office of the prophet and the physician and the fisherman, do you, who know Homer so much better than I do, Ion, select for me passages which relate to the rhapsode and the rhapsode's art, and which the rhapsode ought to examine and judge of better than other men.

Ion. All passages, I should say, Socrates.

Soc. Not all, Ion, surely. Have you already forgotten what you were saying? A rhapsode ought to have a better memory.

Ion. Why, what am I forgetting?

Soc. Do you not remember that you declared the art of the rhapsode to be different from the art of the charioteer?

Ion. Yes, I remember.

Soc. And you admitted that being different they would have different subjects of knowledge?

Ion. Yes.

Soc. Then upon your own showing the rhapsode, and the art of the rhapsode, will not know everything?

Ion. I should exclude certain things, Socrates.

Soc. You mean to say that you would exclude pretty much the subjects of the other arts. As he does not know all of them, which of them will he know?

Ion. He will know what a man and what a woman ought to say, and what a freeman and what a slave ought to say, and what a ruler and what a subject.

Soc. Do you mean that a rhapsode will know better than the pilot what the ruler of a sea-tossed vessel ought to say?

Ion. No; the pilot will know best.

Soc. Or will the rhapsode know better than the physician what a sick man ought to say?

Ion. He will not.

Soc. But he will know what a slave ought to say?

Ion. Yes.

Soc. Suppose the slave to be a cowherd; the rhapsode will know better than the cowherd what he ought to say in order to soothe the infuriated cows.

Ion. No, he will not.

Soc. But he will know what a spinning-woman ought to say about the working of wool?

Ion. No.

Soc. At any rate he will know what a general ought to say when exhorting his soldiers?

Ion. Yes, that is the sort of thing which the rhapsode will be sure to know.

Soc. Well, but is the art of the rhapsode the art of the general?

Ion. I am sure that I should know what a general ought to say.

Soc. Why, yes, Ion, because you may possibly have a knowledge of the art of the general as well as of the rhapsode; and you may also have a knowledge of horsemanship as well as of the lyre: and then you would know when horses were well or ill managed. But suppose I were to ask you: By the help of which art, Ion, do you know whether horses are well managed, by your skill as a horseman or as a performer on the lyre—what would you answer?

Ion. I should reply, by my skill as a horseman.

Soc. And if you judged of performers on the lyre, you would admit that you judged of them as a performer on the lyre, and not as a horseman?

Ion. Yes.

Soc. And in judging of the general's art, do you judge of it as a general or a rhapsode?

Ion. To me there appears to be no difference between them.

Soc. What do you mean? Do you mean to say that the art of the rhapsode and of the general is the same?

Ion. Yes, one and the same.

Soc. Then he who is a good rhapsode is also a good general?

Ion. Certainly, Socrates.

Soc. And he who is a good general is also a good rhapsode?

Ion. No; I do not say that.

Soc. But you do say that he who is a good rhapsode is also a good general.

Ion. Certainly.

Soc. And you are the best of Hellenic rhapsodes?

Ion. Far the best, Socrates.

Soc. And are you the best general, Ion?

Ion. To be sure, Socrates; and Homer was my master.

Soc. But then, Ion, what in the name of goodness can be the reason why you, who are the best of generals as well as the best of rhapsodes in all Hellas, go about as a rhapsode when you might be a general? Do you think that Hellenes want a rhapsode with his golden crown, and do not want a general?

Ion. Why, Socrates, the reason is, that my countrymen, the Ephesians, are the servants and soldiers of Athens, and do not need a general; and you and Sparta are not likely to have me, for you think that you have enough generals of your own.

Soc. My good Ion, did you never hear of Apollodorus of Cyzicus?

Ion. Who may he be?

Soc. One who, though a foreigner, has often been chosen their general by the Athenians: and there is Phanosthenes of Andros, and Heraclides of Clazomenae, whom they have also appointed to the command of their armies and to other offices, although aliens, after they had shown their merit. And will they not choose Ion the Ephesian to be their general, and honour him, if he prove himself worthy? Were not the Ephesians originally Athenians, and Ephesus is no mean city? But, indeed, Ion, if you are correct in saying that by art and knowledge you are able to praise Homer, you do not deal fairly with me, and after all your professions of knowing many glorious things about Homer, and promises that you would exhibit them, you are only a deceiver, and so far from exhibiting the art of which you are a master, will not, even after my repeated entreaties, explain to me the nature of it. You have literally as many forms as Proteus; and now you go all manner of ways, twisting and turning, and, like Proteus, become all manner of people at once, and at last slip away from me in the disguise of a general, in order that you may escape exhibitng your Homeric lore. And if you have art, then, as I was saying, in falsifying your promise that you would exhibit

Homer, you are not dealing fairly with me. But if, as I believe, you have no art, but speak all these beautiful words about Homer unconsciously under his inspiring influence, then I acquit you of dishonesty, and shall only say that you are inspired. Which do you prefer to be thought, dishonest or inspired?

Ion. There is a great difference, Socrates, between the two alternatives; and inspiration is by far the nobler.

Soc. Then, Ion, I shall assume the nobler alternative; and attribute to you in your praises of Homer inspiration, and not art.

• John Dewey (1859–1952)

Art as Wholeness[3]

John Dewey, the most influential American philosopher of the twentieth century, wrote extensively on all branches of philosophy during the course of his extraordinary life (he died at the age of ninety-three in 1952). Noted as logician, epistemologist, educator, social philosopher, and moralist, his brand of pragmatism is perhaps more respected and universally acclaimed than any other philosophical product of twentieth-century America. A personal friend and teacher of the noted art collector Albert Barnes, Dewey learned about works of art through immediate experience and his *Art As Experience,* from which the following selection is taken, is a classic in modern aesthetics. Always interested in relating art to common life it was natural for Dewey to emphasize both functionalism in the work of art and (like Tolstoi) sincerity in the artist. What one is somewhat unprepared for in this selection is the implied mysticism; the emphasis upon the intuition of wholeness in the work of art and the sense of a larger mysterious whole lying back of the experience of art and indicated by it. The work of art for Dewey became almost a symbol of the world's organic unity.

What subject-matter is appropriate for art? Are there materials inherently fit and others unfit? Are there none which are common and unclean with respect to artistic treatment? The answer of the arts themselves has been steadily and progressively in the direction

[3] From John Dewey, *Art As Experience* (New York, 1934), pp. 187–95. Copyright, 1934, by G. P. Putnam's Sons.

of an affirmative answer to the last question. Yet there is an enduring tradition that insists art should make invidious distinctions. A brief survey of the theme may accordingly serve as an introduction to the special topic of this chapter, namely, the aspects of the matter of art that are common to all the arts.

I had occasion in another connection to refer to the difference between the popular arts of a period and the official arts. Even when favored arts came out from under patronage and control of priest and ruler, the distinction of kinds remained even though the name "official" is no longer a fitting designation. Philosophic theory concerned itself only with those arts that had the stamp and seal of recognition by the class having social standing and authority. Popular arts must have flourished, but they obtained no literary attention. They were not worthy of mention in theoretical discussion. Probably they were not even thought of as arts.

Instead, however, of dealing with the early formulation of an invidious distinction among the arts, I shall select a modern representative, and then indicate briefly some aspects of the revolt that has broken down the barriers once set up. Sir Joshua Reynolds presents us with the statement that since the only subjects fit for treatment in painting are those "generally interesting," they should be "some eminent instance of heroic action or heroic suffering," such as "the great events of Greek and Roman fable and history. Such, too, are the capital events of Scripture." All the great paintings of the past, according to him, belong to this "historical school," and he goes on to say that "upon this principle, the Roman, the Florentine, the Bolognese schools have formed their practice and by it they have deservedly obtained the highest praise"—the omission of the Venetian and Flemish schools, side by side with the commendation of the eclectic school, being a sufficient comment from the strictly artistic side. What would he have said if he had been able to anticipate the ballet girls of Degas, the railway-coaches of Daumier—actually third class—or the apples, napkins, and plates of Cezanne?

In literature the dominant tradition in theory was similar. It was constantly asserted that Aristotle had once for all delimited the scope of tragedy, the highest literary mode, by declaring that the misfortunes of the noble and those in high place were its proper material, while those of the common people were intrinsically fit for the lesser mode of comedy. Diderot virtually announced a historic revolution in theory when he said there was need for bourgeois tragedies, and that, instead of putting on the stage only kings and princes, private persons are subject to terrible reverses which inspire pity and terror. And again he asserts that domestic tragedies, although having another tone and action than classic drama, can have their own sublimity—a prediction assuredly fulfilled by Ibsen.

At the beginning of the nineteenth century, following the period that Housman calls one of sham or counterfeit poetry, verse masquerading as poetry, "The Lyrical Ballads" of Wordsworth and Coleridge ushered in a revolution. One of the principles that animated its authors was stated by Coleridge as follows: "One of the two cardinal points in poetry consists of faithful adherence to such characters and incidents as will be found in every village and its vicinity when there is a meditative and feeling mind to seek after them, or to notice them when they present themselves." I hardly need point out that long before Reynolds' day a similar revolution was well along in painting. It took a long stride when the Venetians in addition to celebrating the sumptuousness of the lives about them gave nominally religious themes a distinctly secular treatment. Flemish painters, in addition to Dutch genre painters, Breughel the elder, for example, and French painters like Chardin, turned frankly to ordinary themes. Painting of portraits was extended from nobility to wealthy merchants with the growth of commerce, and then to men less conspicuous. Toward the end of the nineteenth century all lines were swept away as far as plastic arts are concerned.

The novel has been the great instrument of effecting change in prose literature. It shifted the center of attention from the court to the bourgeoisie, then to the "poor" and the laborer, and then to the common person irrespective of station. Rousseau owes most of his permanent enormous influence in the field of literature to his imaginative excitement about "le peuple"; certainly no more to that cause than to his formal theories. The part played by folk-music, especially in Poland, Bohemis, and Germany, in the expansion and renewal of music is too well known to require more than notice. Even architecture, the most conservative of all the arts, has felt the influence of a transformation similar to that the other arts have undergone. Railways stations, bank buildings and post-offices, even churches, are no longer exclusively built as imitations of Greek temples and medieval cathedrals. The art of established "orders" has been influenced as much by revolt against fixation in social classes as by technological developments in cement and steel.

This brief sketch has only one purpose: to indicate that, in spite of formal theory and canons of criticism, there has taken place one of those revolutions that do not go backward. Impulsion beyond all limits that are externally set inheres in the very nature of the artist's work. It belongs to the very character of the creative mind to reach out and seize any material that stirs it so that the value of that material may be pressed out and become the matter of a new experience. Refusal to acknowledge the boundaries set by convention is the source of frequent denunciations of objects of art as immoral. But one of the functions of art is precisely to sap the moralistic timidity that causes the mind to shy away from some materials and refuse to admit them into the clear and purifying light of perceptive consciousness.

The interest of an artist is the only limitation placed upon use of material, and this limitation is not restrictive. It but states a trait inherent in the work of the artist, the necessity of sincerity; the necessity that he shall not fake and compromise. The universality of art is so far away from denial of the principle of selection by means of vital interest that it depends upon interest. Other artists have other interests, and by their collective work, unembarrassed by fixed and antecedent rule, all aspects and phases of experience are covered. Interest becomes one-sided and morbid only when it ceases to be frank, and bcomes sly and furtive—as it doubtless does in much contemporary exploitation of sex. Tolstoi's identification of sincerity as the essence of originality compensates for much that is eccentric in his tractate on art. In his attack upon the merely conventional in poetry, he declares that much of its material is borrowed, artists feeding like cannibals upon one another. Stock material consists, he says, of "all sorts of legends, sagas and ancient traditions; maidens, warriors, shepherds, hermits, angels, devils of all sorts; moonlight, thunder, mountains, the sea, precipices, flowers, long hair; lions, lambs, doves, nightingales—because they have often been used by former artists in their productions."

In his desire to restrict the material of art to themes drawn from the life of the common man, factory worker and especially peasant, Tolstoi paints a picture of the conventional restrictions that is out of perspective. But there is truth enough in it to serve as illustration of one all-important characteristic of art: Whatever narrows the boundaries of the material fit to be used in art hems in also the artistic sincerity of the individual artist. It does not give fair play and outlet to his vital interest. It forces his perceptions into channels previously worn into ruts and clips the wings of his imagination. I think the idea that there is a moral obligation on an artist to deal with "proletarian" material, or with any material on the basis of its bearing on proletarian fortune and destiny is an effort to return to a position that art has historically outgrown. But as far as proletarian interest marks a new direction of attention and involves observation of materials previously passed over, it will certainly call into activity persons who were not moved to expression by former materials, and will disclose and thus help break down boundaries of which they were not previously aware. I am somewhat skeptical about Shakespeare's alleged personal aristocratic bias. I fancy that his limitation was conventional, familiar, and therefore congenial to pit as well as to stalls. But whatever its source, it limited his "universality."

Evidence that the historic movement of the art has abolished restrictions of its subject-matter that once were justified on alleged rational grounds does not prove that there is something common in the matter of all the arts. But it suggests that with the vast extension of its scope to take in (potentially) anything and everything, art would have lost its unity, dispersed into connected arts, till we could not see the woods for the trees nor a single tree for its branches, were there not a core of common substance. The obvious reply to this suggested inference is that the unity of the arts resides in their common form. Acceptance of this reply commits us, however, to the idea that form and matter are separate, and leads us therefore to return to the assertion that an art product is formed substance, and that what appears upon reflection as form when one interest is uppermost appears as matter when change of interest gives another turn to direction.

Apart from some special interest, every product of art is matter and matter only, so that the contrast is not between matter and form but between matter relatively unformed and matter adequately formed. The fact that reflection finds distinctive form in pictures cannot be set against the fact that a painting consists simply of pigments placed on canvas, since any arrangement and design they have is, after all, a property of the substance and of nothing else. Similarly, literature as it exists is just so many words, spoken and written. "Stuff" is everything, and form a name for certain aspects of the matter when attention goes primarily to just these aspects. The fact that a work of art is an organization of energies and that the nature of the organization is all important, cannot militate against the fact that it is energies which are organized and that organization has no existence outside of them.

The acknowledged community of form in different arts carries with it by implication a corresponding community of substance. It is this implication which I now propose to explore and develop. I have previously noted that artist and perceiver alike begin with what may be called a total seizure, an inclusive qualitative whole

not yet articulated, not distinguished into members. Speaking of
the origin of his poems, Schiller said: "With me the perception is
at first without a clear and definite object. This takes shape later.
What precedes is a peculiar musical mood of mind. Afterwards
comes the poetical idea." I interpret this saying to mean something of the kind just stated. Moreover, not only does the "mood"
come first, but it persists as the substratum after distinctions emerge;
in fact they emerge as its distinctions.

Even at the outset, the total and massive quality has its unique-
ness; even when vague and undefined, it is just that which it is
and not anything else. If the perception continues, discrimination
inevitably sets in. Attention must move, and, as it moves, parts,
members, emerge from the background. And if attention moves
in a unified direction instead of wandering, it is controlled by the
pervading qualitative unity; attention is controlled by it because
it operates within it. That verses are the poem, are its substance,
is so truistic that it says nothing. But the fact which the truism
records could not exist unless matter, poetically felt, came first, and
came in such a unified and massive way as to determine its own
development, that is its specification into distinctive parts. If the
percipient is aware of seams and mechanical junctions in a work
of art, it is because the substance is not controlled by a permeating
quality.

Not only must this quality be in all "parts," but it can only be
felt, that is, immediately experienced. I am not trying to describe
it, for it cannot be described nor even be specifically pointed at—
since whatever is specified in a work of art is one of its differentia-
tions. I am only trying to call attention to something that every
one can realize is present in his experience of a work of art, but
that is so thoroughly and pervasively present that it is taken for
granted. "Intuition" has been used by philosophers to designate
many things—some of which are suspicious characters. But the
penetrating quality that runs through all the parts of a work of art
and binds them into an individualized whole can only be emotionally "intuited." The different elements and specific qualities of a
work of art blend and fuse in a way which physical things cannot
emulate. This fusion is the felt presence of the same qualitative
unity in all of them. "Parts" are discriminated, not intuited. But
without the intuited enveloping quality, parts are external to one
another and mechanically related. Yet the organism which is the
work of art is nothing different from its parts or members. It is
the parts as members—a fact that again brings us to the one pervasive quality that remains the same quality in being differentiated.

The resulting sense of totality is commemorative, expectant, insinuating, premonitory.

There is no name to be given it. As it enlivens and animates, it is the spirit of the work of art. It is its reality, when we feel the work of art to be real on its own account and not as a realistic exhibition. It is the idiom in which the particular work is composed and expressed, that which stamps it with individuality. It is the background which is more than spatial because it enters into and qualifies everything in the focus, everything distinguished as a part and member. We are accustomed to think of physical objects as having bounded edges; things like rocks, chairs, books, houses. Trade, and science, with its efforts at precise measurement, have confirmed the belief. Then we unconsciously carry over this belief in the bounded character of all objects of experience (a belief founded ultimately in the practical exigencies of our dealings with things) into our conception of experience itself. We suppose the experience has the same definite limits as the things with which it is concerned. But any experience, the most ordinary, has an indefinite total setting. Things, objects, are only focal points of a here and now in a whole that stretches out indefinitely. This is the qualitative "background" which is defined and made definitely conscious in particular objects and specified properties and qualities. There is something mystical associated with the word intuition, and any experience becomes mystical in the degree in which the sense, the feeling, of the unlimited envelope becomes intense—as it may do in experience of an object of art. As Tennyson said:

> Experience is an arch wherethro'
> Gleams that untravell'd world, whose margin fades
> Forever and forever when I move.

For although there is a bounding horizon, it moves as we move. We are never wholly free from the sense of something that lies beyond. Within the limited world directly seen, there is a tree with a rock at its foot; we fasten our sight upon the rock, and then upon the moss on the rock, perhaps we then take a microscope to view some tiny lichen. But whether the scope of vision be vast or minute, we experience is as a part of a larger whole and inclusive whole, a part that now focuses our experience. We might expand the field from the narrower to the wider. But however broad the field, it is still felt as not the whole; the margins shade into that indefinite expanse beyond which imagination calls the universe. This sense of the including whole implicit in ordinary experiences is rendered intense within the frame of a painting or poem. It, rather, than any special purgation, is that which reconciles us to the events of tragedy. The symbolists have exploited this indefinite phase of art; Poe spoke of "a suggestive indefiniteness of vague and therefore spiritual effect," while Coleridge said that every work of art must have about it something not understood to obtain its full effect.

About every explicit and focal object there is a recession into the implicit which is not intellectually grasped. In reflection we call it dim and vague. But in the original experience it is not identified as the vague. It is a function of the whole situation, and not an element in it, as it would have to be in order to be apprehended as vague. At twilight, dusk is a delightful quality of the whole world. It is its appropriate manifestation. It becomes a specialized and obnoxious trait only when it prevents distinct perception of some particular thing we desire to discern.

The undefined pervasive quality of an experience is that which binds together all the defined elements, the objects of which we are focally aware, making them a whole. The best evidence that such is the case is our constant sense of things as belonging or not belonging, of relevancy, a sense which is immediate. It cannot be a product of reflection, even though it requires reflection to find out whether some particular consideration is pertinent to what we are doing or thinking. For unless the sense were immediate, we should have no guide to our reflection. The sense of an extensive and underlying whole is the context of every experience and it is the essence of sanity. For the mad, the insane, thing to us is that which is torn from the common context and which stands alone and isolated, as anything must which occurs in a world totally different from ours. Without an indeterminate and undetermined setting, the material of any experience is incoherent.

A work of art elicits and accentuates this quality of being a whole and of belonging to the large, all-inclusive, whole which is the universe in which we live. This fact, I think, is the explanation of that feeling of exquisite intelligibility and clarity we have in the presence of an object that is experienced with esthetic intensity. It explains also the religious feeling that accompanies intense esthetic perception. We are, as it were, introduced into a world beyond this world which is nevertheless the deeper reality of the world in which we live in our ordinary experiences. We are carried out beyond ourselves to find ourselves. I can see no psychological ground for such properties of an experience save that, somehow, the work of art operates to deepen and to raise to great clarity that sense of an enveloping undefined whole that accompanies every

normal experience. This whole is then felt as an expansion of ourselves. For only one frustrated in a particular object of desire
upon which he had staked himself, like Macbeth, finds that life is
a tale told by an idiot, full of sound and fury, signifying nothing.
Where egotism is not made the measure of reality and value, we
are citizens of this vast world beyond ourselves, and any intense
realization of its presence with and in us brings a peculiarly satisfying sense of unity in itself and with ourselves.

• George Santayana (1863-1952)

The Nature of Beauty [4]

George Santayana, born in Spain and educated at Harvard,
taught philosophy at Harvard until shortly before the First World
War when he returned to Europe, first to England, then to Italy.
A poet and writer of polished essays, he was noted for his literary
style, his urbanity, and his knack of combining a naturalistic view of
the world with an interest in myth and metaphor. Among his best-
known philosophical works are *The Life of Reason* (5 volumes)
Realms of Being (4 volumes), *Three Philosophical Poets, Scepticism and Animal Faith,* and *The Sense of Beauty,* from which the
following selection is taken. True to his naturalism, Santayana sees
beauty itself as rooted in the emotional part of our nature but also
as a quality of things, and he presents here his well-known theory
that beauty is "pleasure objectified."

It would be easy to find a definition of beauty that should give
in a few words a telling paraphrase of the word. We know on excellent authority that beauty is truth, that it is the expression of the
ideal, the symbol of divine perfection, and the sensible manifestation of the good. A litany of these titles of honour might easily be
compiled, and repeated in praise of our divinity. Such phrases
stimulate thought and give us a momentary pleasure, but they
hardly bring any permanent enlightenment. A definition that
should really define must be nothing less than the exposition of

[4] From George Santayana, *The Sense of Beauty* (1896), Pt. I.

the origin, place, and elements of beauty as an object of human experience. We must learn from it, as far as possible, why, when, and how beauty appears, what conditions an object must fulfil to be beautiful, what elements of our nature make us sensible of beauty, and what the relation is between the constitution of the object and the excitement of our susceptibility. Nothing less will really define beauty or make us understand what aesthetic appreciation is. The definition of beauty in this sense will be the task of this whole book, a task that can be only very imperfectly accomplished within its limits.

The historical titles of our subject may give us a hint towards the beginning of such a definition. Many writers of the last century called the philosophy of beauty *Criticism*, and the word is still retained as the title for the reasoned appreciation of works of art. We could hardly speak, however, of delight in nature as criticism. A sunset is not criticised; it is felt and enjoyed. The word "criticism," used on such an occasion, would emphasise too much the element of deliberate judgment and of comparison with standards, Beauty, although often so described, is seldom so perceived, and all the greatest excellences of nature and art are so far from being approved of by a rule that they themselves furnish the standard and ideal by which critics measure inferior effects.

This age of science and of nomenclature has accordingly adopted a more learned word, *Aesthetics*, that is, the theory of perception or of susceptibility. If criticism is too narrow a word, pointing exclusively to our more artificial judgments, aesthetics seems to be too broad and to include within its sphere all pleasures and pains, if not all perceptions whatsoever. Kant used it, as we know, for his theory of time and space as forms of all perception; and it has at times been narrowed into an equivalent for the philosophy of art.

If we combine, however, the etymological meaning of criticism with that of aesthetics, we shall unite two essential qualities of the theory of beauty. Criticism implies judgment, and aesthetics perception. To get the common ground, that of perceptions which are critical, or judgments which are perceptions, we must widen our notion of deliberate criticism so as to include those judgments of value which are instinctive and immediate, that is, to include pleasures and pains; and at the same time we must narrow our notion of aesthetics so as to exclude all perceptions which are not appreciations, which do not find a value in their objects. We thus reach the sphere of critical or appreciative perception, which is, roughly speaking, what we mean to deal with. And retaining the word "aesthetics," which is now current, we may therefore say that aesthetics is concerned with the perception of values. The meaning and conditions of value are, then, what we must first consider.

Since the days of Descartes it has been a conception familiar to philosophers that every visible event in nature might be explained by previous visible events, and that all the motions, for instance, of the tongue in speech, or of the hand in painting, might have merely physical causes. If consciousness is thus accessory to life and not essential to it, the race of man might have existed upon the earth and acquired all the arts necessary for its subsistence without possessing a single sensation, idea, or emotion. Natural selection might have secured the survival of those automata which made useful reactions upon their environment. An instinct of self-preservation would have been developed, dangers would have been shunned without being feared, and injuries revenged without being felt.

In such a world there might have come to be the most perfect organisation. There would have been what we should call the expression of the deepest interests and the apparent pursuit of conceived goods. For there would have been spontaneous and ingrained tendencies to avoid certain contingencies and to produce others; all the dumb show and evidence of thinking would have been patent to the observer. Yet there would surely have been no thinking, no expectation, and no conscious achievement in the whole process.

The onlooker might have feigned ends and objects of forethought, as we do in the case of the water that seeks its own level, or in that of the vacuum which nature abhors. But the particles of matter would have remained unconscious of their collocation, and all nature would have been insensible of their changing arrangement. We only, the possible spectators of that process, by virtue of our own interests and habits, could see any progress or culmination in it. We should see culmination where the result attained satisfied our practical or aesthetic demands, and progress wherever such a satisfaction was approached. But apart from ourselves, and our human bias, we can see in such a mechanical world no element of value whatever. In removing consciousness, we have removed the possibility of worth.

But it is not only in the absence of all consciousness that value would be removed from the world; by a less violent abstraction from the totality of human experience, we might conceive beings of a purely intellectual cast, minds in which the transformations of nature were mirrored without any emotion. Every event would then be noted, its relations would be observed, its recurrence might even be expected; but all this would happen without a shadow of desire, of pleasure, or of regret. No event would be repulsive, no situation terrible. We might, in a word, have a world of idea without of a world of will. In this case, as completely as if consciousness were absent altogether, all value and excellence would be gone. So that for the existence of good in any form it is not merely consciousness that is needed. Observation will not do, appreciation is required.

PREFERENCE IS ULTIMATELY IRRATIONAL

We may therefore at once assert this axiom, important for all moral philosophy and fatal to certain stubborn incoherences of thought, that there is no value apart from some appreciation of it, and no good apart from some preference of it before its absence or its opposite. In appreciation, in preference, lie the root and essence of all excellence. Or, as Spinoza clearly expresses it, we desire nothing because it is good, but it is good only because we desire it.

It is true that in the absence of an instinctive reaction we can still apply these epithets by an appeal to usage. We may agree that an action is bad or a building good, because we recognise in them a character which we have learned to designate by that adjective; but unless there is in us some trace of passionate reprobation or of sensible delight, there is no moral or aesthetic judgment. It is all a question of propriety of speech, and of the empty titles of things. The verbal and mechanical proposition, that passes for judgment of worth, is the great cloak of ineptitude in these matters. Insensibility is very quick in the conventional use of words. If we appealed more often to actual feelings, our judgments would be more diverse, but they would be more legitimate and instructive. Verbal judgments are often useful instruments of thought, but it is not by them that worth can ultimately be determined.

Values spring from the immediate and inexplicable reaction of vital impulse, and from the irrational part of our nature. The rational part is by its essence relative; it leads us from data to conclusions, or from parts to wholes; it never furnishes the data with which it works. If any preference or precept were declared to be ultimate and primitive, it would thereby be declared to be irrational, since mediation, inference, and synthesis are the essence of rationality. The ideal of rationality is itself as arbitrary, as much dependent on the needs of a finite organisation, as any other ideal. Only as ultimately securing tranquillity of mind, which the philosopher in-

stinctively pursues, has it for him any necessity. In spite of the
verbal propriety of saying that reason demands rationality, what
really demands rationality, what makes it a good and indispensable
thing and gives it all its authority, is not its own nature, but our
need of it both in safe and economical action and in the pleasures
of comprehension.

It is evident that beauty is a species of value, and what we have
said of value in general applies to this particular kind. A first
approach to a definition of beauty has therefore been made by
the exclusion of all intellectual judgments, all judgments of matter
of fact or of relation. To substitute judgments of fact for judgments of value, is a sign of a pedantic and borrowed criticism. If
we approach a work of art or nature scientifically for the sake of
its historical connexions or proper classification, we do not approach
it aesthetically. The discovery of its date or of its author may be
otherwise interesting; it only remotely affects our aesthetic appreciation by adding to the direct effect certain associations. If the
direct effect were absent, and the object in itself uninteresting, the
circumstances would be immaterial. Moliere's *Misanthrope* says
to the court poet who commends his sonnet as written in a quarter
of an hour, *Voyons, monsieur, le temps ne fait rien a l'affaire*, and
so we might say to the critic that sinks into the archaeologist, show
us the work, and let the date alone.

In an opposite direction the same substitution of facts for values
makes its appearance, whenever the reproduction of fact is made
the sole standard of artistic excellence. Many half-trained observers
condemn the work of some naive or fanciful masters with a sneer,
because, as they truly say, it is out of drawing. The implication
is that to be correctly copied from a model is the prerequisite of
all beauty. Correctness is, indeed, an element of effect and one
which, in respect to familiar objects, is almost indispensable, because its absence would cause a disappointment and dissatisfaction
incompatible with enjoyment. We learn to value truth more and
more as our love and knowledge of nature increase. But fidelity
is a merit only because it is in this way a factor in our pleasure.
It stands on a level with all other ingredients of effect. When a
man raises it to a solitary pre-eminence and becomes incapable of
appreciating anything else, he betrays the decay of aesthetic capacity. The scientific habit in him inhibits the artistic.

That facts have a value of their own, at once complicates and
explains this question. We are naturally pleased by every perception, and recognition and surprise are particularly acute sensations. When we see a striking truth in any imitation we are there-

fore delighted, and this kind of pleasure is very legitimate, and enters into the best effects of all the representative arts. Truth and realism are therefore aesthetically good, but they are not all-sufficient, since the representation of everything is not equally pleasing and effective. The fact that resemblance is a source of satisfaction justifies the critic in demanding it, while the aesthetic insufficiency of such veracity shows the different value of truth in science and in art. Science is the response to the demand for information, and in it we ask for the whole truth and nothing but the truth. Art is the response to the demand for entertainment, for the stimulation of our senses and imagination, and truth enters into it only as it subserves these ends.

Even the scientific value of truth is not, however, ultimate or absolute. It rests partly on practical, partly on aesthetic interests. As our ideas are gradually brought into conformity with the facts by the painful process of selection,—for intuition runs equally into truth and into error, and can settle nothing if not controlled by experience,—we gain vastly in our command over our environment. This is the fundamental value of natural science, and the fruit it is yielding in our day. We have no better vision of nature and life than some of our predecessors, but we have greater material resources. To know the truth about the composition and history of things is good for this reason. It is also good because of the enlarged horizon it gives us, because the spectacle of nature is a marvellous and fascinating one, full of a serious sadness and large peace, which gives us back our birthright as children of the planet and naturalises us upon the earth. This is the poetic value of the scientific *Weltanschauung*. From these two benefits, the practical and the imaginative, all the value of truth is derived.

Aesthetic and moral judgments are accordingly to be classed together in contrast to judgments intellectual; they are both judgments of value, while intellectual judgments are judgments of fact. If the latter have any value, it is only derivative, and our whole intellectual life has its only justification in its connexion with our pleasures and pains.

Contrast Between Moral and Aesthetic Values

The relation between aesthetic and moral judgments, between the spheres of the beautiful and the good, is close, but the distinction between them is important. One factor of this distinction is that while aesthetic judgments are mainly positive, that is, perceptions of good, moral judgments are mainly and fundamentally negative, or perceptions of evil. Another factor of the distinction is that whereas, in the perception of beauty, our judgment is necessarily intrinsic and based on the character of the immediate experience, and never consciously on the idea of an eventual utility in the object, judgments about moral worth, on the contrary, are always based, when they are positive, upon the consciousness of benefits probably involved. Both these distinctions need some elucidation.

Hedonistic ethics have always had to struggle against the moral sense of mankind. Earnest minds, that feel the weight and dignity of life, rebel against the assertion that the aim of right conduct is enjoyment. Pleasure usually appears to them as a temptation, and they sometimes go so far as to make avoidance of it a virtue. The truth is that morality is not mainly concerned with the attainment of pleasure; it is rather concerned, in all its deeper and more authoritative maxims, with the prevention of suffering. There is something artificial in the deliberate pursuit of pleasure; there is something absurd in the obligation to enjoy oneself. We feel no duty in that direction; we take to enjoyment naturally enough after the work of life is done, and the freedom and spontaneity of our pleasures are what is most essential to them.

The sad business of life is rather to escape certain dreadful evils to which our nature exposes us,—death, hunger, disease, weariness, isolation, and contempt. By the awful authority of these things, which stand like spectres behind every moral injunction, conscience in reality speaks, and a mind which they have duly impressed cannot but feel, by contrast, the hopeless triviality of the search for pleasure. It cannot but feel that a life abandoned to amusement and to changing impulses must run unawares into fatal dangers. The moment, however, that society emerges from the early pressure of the environment and is tolerably secure against primary evils, morality grows lax. The forms that life will farther assume are not to be imposed by moral authority, but are determined by the genius of the race, the opportunities of the moment, and the tastes and resources of individual minds. The reign of duty gives place to the reign of freedom, and the law and the covenant to the dispensation of grace.

The appreciation of beauty and its embodiment in the arts are activities which belong to our holiday life, when we are redeemed for the moment from the shadow of evil and the slavery to fear, and are following the bent of our nature where it chooses to lead us. The values, then, with which we here deal are positive; they were negative in the sphere of morality. The ugly is hardly an exception, because it is not the cause of any real pain. In itself it is rather a source of amusement. If its suggestions are vitally repulsive, its presence becomes a real evil towards which we assume a practical and moral attitude. And, correspondingly, the pleasant is never, as we have seen, the object of a truly moral injunction.

• • • • •

THE DEFINITION OF BEAUTY

We have now reached our definition of beauty, which, in the terms of our successive analysis and narrowing of the conception, is value positive, intrinsic, and objectified. Or, in less technical language, Beauty is pleasure regarded as the quality of a thing.

This definition is intended to sum up a variety of distinctions and identifications which should perhaps be here more explicitly set down. Beauty is a value, that is, it is not a perception of a matter of fact or of a relation: it is an emotion, an affection of our volitonal and appreciative nature. An object cannot be beautiful if it can give pleasure to nobody: a beauty to which all men were forever indifferent is a contradiction in terms.

In the second place, this value is positive, it is the sense of the presence of something good, or (in the case of ugliness) of its absence. It is never the perception of a positive evil, it is never a negative value. That we are endowed with the sense of beauty is a pure gain which brings no evil with it. When the ugly cease to be amusing or merely uninteresting and becomes disgusting, it becomes indeed a positive evil: but a moral and practical, not an aesthetic one. In aesthetics that saying is true—often so disingenuous in ethics—that evil is nothing but the absence of good: for even the tedium and vulgarity of an existence without beauty is not itself ugly so much as lamentable and degrading. The absence of aesthetic goods is a moral evil: the aesthetic evil is merely relative, and means less of aesthetic good than was expected at the place and time. No form in itself gives pain, although some forms give pain by causing a shock of surprise even when they are really beautiful: as if a mother found a fine bull pup in her child's cradle, then her pain would not be aesthetic in its nature.

Further, this pleasure must not be in the consequence of the utility of the object or event, but in its immediate perception; in other words, beauty is an ultimate good, something that gives satisfaction to a natural function, to some fundamental need or capacity of our minds. Beauty is therefore a positive value that is intrinsic; it is a pleasure. These two circumstances sufficiently separate the sphere of aesthetics from that of ethics. Moral values are generally negative, and always remote. Morality has to do with the avoidance of evil and the pursuit of good: aesthetics only with enjoyment.

Finally, the pleasures of sense are distinguished from the perception of beauty, as sensation in general is distinguished from perception; by the objectification of the elements and their appearance as qualities rather of things than of consciousness. The passage from sensation to perception is gradual, and the path may be sometimes retraced: so it is with beauty and the pleasures of sensation. There is no sharp line between them, but it depends upon the degree of objectivity my feeling has attained at the moment whether I say "It pleases me," or "It is beautiful." If I am self-conscious and critical, I shall probably use one phrase: if I am impulsive and susceptible, the other. The more remote, interwoven, and inextricable the pleasure is, the more objective it will appear; and the union of two pleasures often makes one beauty. In Shakespeare's LIVth sonnet are these words:

> O how much more doth beauty beauteous seem
> By that sweet ornament which truth doth give!
> The rose looks fair, but fairer we it deem
> For that sweet odour which doth in it live.
> The canker-blooms have full as deep a dye
> As the perfumed tincture of the roses,
> Hang on such thorns, and play as wantonly
> When summer's breath their masked buds discloses.
> But, for their beauty only is their show,
> They live unwooed and unrespected fade;
> Die to themselves. Sweet roses do not so:
> Of their sweet deaths are sweetest odours made.

One added ornament, we see, turns the deep dye, which was but show and mere sensation before, into an element of beauty and reality; and as truth is here the co-operation of perceptions, so beauty is the co-operation of pleasures. If colour, form, and motion are hardly beautiful without the sweetness of the odour, how much more necessary would they be for the sweetness itself to become a beauty! If we had the perfume in a flask, no one would think of calling it beautiful: it would give us too detached and controllable a sensation. There would be no object in which it could be easily incorporated. But let it float from the garden, and it will add another sensuous charm to objects simultaneously recognised, and help to make them beautiful. Thus beauty is constituted by the objectification of pleasure. It is pleasure objectified.

SUGGESTED FURTHER READINGS

ALEXANDER, SAMUEL. *Beauty and Other Forms of Value.* London: Macmillan & Co., Ltd., 1933.

BOSANQUET, B. *Three Lectures on Aesthetics.* London: Macmillan & Co., Ltd., 1915.

CARRITT, E. F. *The Theory of Beauty.* New York: The Macmillan Co., 1914.

CROCE, B. *Aesthetics.* London: Macmillan & Co., Ltd., 1909.

DEWEY, JOHN. *Art as Experience.* New York: G. P. Putnam's Sons, 1934.

DUCASSE, C. J. *The Philosophy of Art.* New York: Dial Press, Inc., 1929.

GREENE, T. M. *The Arts and the Art of Criticism.* Princeton: Princeton University Press, 1947.

HEGEL, G. W. *The Philosophy of Art.* London: George Bell & Sons, Ltd., 1930.

MARITAIN, JACQUES. *Art and Scholasticism.* Translated by J. F. SCANLAN. New York: Charles Scribner's Sons, 1930.

MUNRO, T. *The Arts and Their Interrelations.* New York: Liberal Arts Press, 1949.

PEPPER, STEPHEN. *The Bases of Criticism in the Arts.* Cambridge: Harvard University Press, 1945.

PRALL, D. W. *Aesthetic Judgment.* New York: The Thomas Y. Crowell Co., 1929.

SANTAYANA, G. *The Sense of Beauty.* New York: Charles Scribner's Sons, 1936.

THISELIN, BREWSTER. *The Creative Process.* Berkeley: University of California Press, 1952.

CHAPTER 8

History

MEANING IN HISTORY

All philosophizing about nature ends with some theory of the cosmos. All philosophizing about human experience ends with some theory about history. The one represents our attempt to unify the experiences of matter, life, and mind in terms of some wider doctrine of space. The other represents our attempt to unify the human experiences of individual decision, social living, and the arts in terms of some wider doctrine of time.

There is one part of our reflection about history which has to do with the nature of historical writing itself. We may ask: What do we mean by an event in history? How is it possible to describe a process of historical change? Is it possible for the historian to be as objective about the facts which he describes as the scientist about the facts which he describes? What kinds of bias, personal, racial, national, philosophical, afflict historians? Does the writing of history itself affect the course of history? All of these questions are really questions about method. They relate to what the historian does, just as questions of scientific method relate to what the scientist does. And, interesting as they are, they are less significant than questions about the content of history, about what conclusions we come to when we try to make sense out of the historical process as a whole, about the tendency of human life in general which is expressed in the acts of peoples, cultures, nations.

Of course, the conception of "the historical process as a whole" is quite abstract and secondary; it is something to which we come when we grow philosophical in the sense defined by Socrates, namely, when we attempt to be spectators of all time and all existence. The historical consciousness does not originate in this fashion. It begins by being something much more specific. It begins in what we understand as "tradition."

417

All life requires some degree of orientation. This means that we must look around, take our bearings, and ask where we are. But this is a process which involves both space and time. Everyone has sometime had the experience of "being lost." Historical ignorance is the sign that one is "lost" in time rather than in space. Tradition supplies the first approximation to an orientation in time by making a reference to the "presentness" of the past. Every medium-sized Southern town in the United States has on its courthouse lawn a monument to the Confederate dead. Every school child in the United States knows that there is a holiday on July Fourth. Every calendar in the western world measures its time by an event which occurred in the Middle East almost two thousand years ago and which it is unwilling to forget. Monuments, holidays, calendars: these are the agents of tradition. They signify the survival of the past into the present and they keep alive those memories which every society needs to make it aware of the meaning of its life.

Fortunately, or unfortunately, what tradition provides is always a selective view, and by definition this means what is local and provincial. Nations and religions are the great conservers of tradition. The best proof of this is the calendar. A calendar is the measure of historical time, and almost without exception it tells us that event which is most meaningful in the culture of a people. The Greek calendar begins in the year 776 B.C., the date of the first recorded Olympiad, a festival at once racial, cultural, and religious, celebrating the unity of ancient Greece in language, belief, and aspiration. The Roman calendar begins in the year 753 B.C., the mythical date of the founding of the city and a political date fit for the measure of time by a great political power. The Christian calendar measures time before and after that date which gives ultimate significance to the world and the Islamic calendar does likewise, although its pivotal date is not the birth of Christ, but the Hejira, the flight of the Prophet from Mecca to Medina in A.D. 632.

The calendars of cultures are the measures of their religious beliefs. The holidays of modern nations, with few exceptions date no further back than the eighteenth century; they are, of course, political, and they celebrate some epochal achievement of liberty, independence, or national unification. July 4, 1776, when the Declaration of Independence was signed, is commemorated every year in our national holiday. December 1, 1918, the Unification Day marking the creation of modern Yugoslavia, is commemorated by a national holiday. August 15, 1947, India's Independence Day, recent and unforgettable, is celebrated by a national holiday.

The time of religious calendars and national holidays is a very "warm" time. It is a time given its importance by the emotion of races, peoples, and nations. It registers the loves and the hates and the deepest commitments of groups and individuals. This kind of history is "uncritical." It is largely untouched by skepticism or scholarship. It represents less an objective consideration of the past than society's need to remember. It is the history of those who participate in history.

The time of historical writing itself, of a Thucydides, or a Gibbon, or a Mommsen is a very "cool" sort of time. It is a time in which too much emotion is a matter for suspicion and where too deep a personal involvement calls "objectivity" into question. In the type of history written in this fashion the historian almost considers himself a kind of scientist, a spectator of the historical process, coolly describing the happening of events, relating them in time, and trying to discover in history relations of cause and effect. It is, of course, not merely a question of whether one actually participates in the history which one writes. It is more a question of attitude, of objectivity. Thucydides was an Athenian general in that very Peloponesian War which his history describes. On the other hand, in Gibbon's narration of the "decline and fall" of the Roman Empire, the events of which he wrote were already over a thousand years in the past. But both Thucydides and Gibbon had before them the ideal of fact, of that impartiality which is the hallmark of science. And, although probably no historian can be completely true to this ideal, although prejudice and feeling inevitably creep in, for the "cool" sort of history this is a weakness to be deplored rather than an ideal aim to be acknowledged.

But between the "warm" history of tradition and the "cool" history of scientific chronology there is another possibility. Let us call it the "lukewarm" middle ground of *the philosophy of history*. It is warm to the extent that it does not ask so much about the facts as about *their significance for human life*. But it is cool to the extent that it tries to go beyond the provincialism of any particular religion, nation, or culture and interpret the *historical process as a whole*. Philosophy in general is a reflection upon experience, and the philosophy of history is a reflection upon historical experience, but this reflection is both contemplative and questioning. The philosopher of history tries therefore to be as systematic as possible, to provide an interpretation for the whole of historical experience, and in this interpretation to use some principle which will fit the multiplicity and variety of the actual historical events into a single ultimate meaning.

I call the philosophy of history "lukewarm" because it falls between two extremes; the concern with values which is one of the chief characteristics of religion, and the attempt to predict the future according to a logic of probability, which is one of the chief characteristics of science. Religion, to the extent that it has been concerned with the relation between God and the world in which human beings live and act, has often seen human history as a revelation of the ways of God to man, as a process in which God intervenes, and where all that happens is somehow the expression of the will of God. But science sees it otherwise. Social science, or the study of man in society, tries to formulate the laws of social change and its effort to chart the direction or *the long range trends in history* is an enterprise which comes very close to what the philosophy of history must also be. The philosophy of history, therefore, may be influenced by religion on one side and social science on the other, and the chief philosophies of history generally lean in one direction or the other.

But is there a pattern in history taken as a whole? Is it possible to say that there is some structure, or direction, or long-range trend which takes in all separate historical events and somehow gives them a unity and a meaning? And if so what is the nature of this pattern or structure? To these questions there are several answers and these answers are the most influential alternative theories which the philosophy of history presents. If one wished to name them metaphorically one could call them respectively the "rocket" theory, the "merry-go-round" theory, and the "idiot" theory of the meaning of history. The rocket theory in turn is divisible into two types, depending upon whether one views it as a slow steady rise upward into outer space, or as a kind of Fourth of July rocket which bursts into a succession of explosions as it travels toward the sky. In a more sober language the alternatives are (1) a theory of progress with this achievable in two ways, (a) through evolution and (b) through revolution; (2) a theory of historical cycles, and (3) a theory which denies that there is any meaning to history at all.

THE THEORY OF PROGRESS

The theory of progress in history is the child of the eighteenth century, but it grew into real prominence in the nineteenth century and today it is perhaps the most commonly accepted of all of the philosophies of history. Its thesis is simple. It says that all historical change exhibits a direction and that that direction is toward the future. It says that the general course of change is in the direction of an increase of value, so that the present is better than the past, and the future will be better than the present. As the world continues, its value properties intensify. The question at once arises: What particular value properties? And if the world grows "better," better in what sense? It is in answering this question that theories of progress divide into quite different theories of value.

The doctrine of progress arises in the eighteenth century, and it is the product of that century's boundless optimism. The devastating wars of the seventeenth century were over and the great scientific advances of the seventeenth century were beginning to be appreciated. A relative prosperity settled upon Europe, the arts flourished, and there came to be felt a boundless confidence in the powers of human reason. The age saw itself as a period of real "enlightenment" and looked upon the past as a time of feudalism or barbarism. Also it looked toward the future with a confidence that its own achievements would be multiplied and expanded. In a sense the age had some reason for its optimism. When it looked for proofs of the triumph of reason, it could turn to an area where reason had indeed triumphed—to science. The real cumulative advance of science has always been the best single argument for a doctrine of historical progress.

But the eighteenth century went further. From the area of science it appropriated the notion of progressive change and it tried in turn to apply this doctrine to the development of human society. Just as the social sciences only came of age after they adopted methods which had proved their worth in the natural sciences, so the eighteenth century thought that reason, which had worked such wonders with nature, could do the same for society. This notion began in France with Turgot and Condorcet, but it is also expressed (and in a fashion which is particularly valuable for our purposes) in the work of Immanuel Kant.

Kant's *Idea of A Universal History* appeared in 1784, and it summed up many of the ideas of a progressive philosophy of history. The first and most important point is that history is purposive. History, according to Kant, aims at unfolding to our view a regular stream of tendency. Even if, superficially, history seems but a senseless current of human actions, behind this lies an important natural purpose. Human nature contains certain seeds which finally bud and develop, so that in history one would expect to find a slow but steady development of certain aspects of our nature. And nations, as well as individuals, unconsciously follow the guidance of a great natural purpose. In some ways this reminds one of an earlier Christian conception of history as a slow revelation of the will of God in time, but neither Kant nor his immediate predecessors presents the idea in this way. They are not hostile to religion, but neither do they need God as a principle of explanation. They find that what history expresses is not exactly God's, but nature's purpose.

But in the case of society, what can nature's ultimate purpose be? The answer is simple—an urge toward perfection. Thus history can be read as the unravelling of a hidden plan of nature for accomplishing a perfect state of civil constitution for society. But does our experience support this conclusion? Do we see society growing more perfect before our very eyes? A little, says Kant. Civil liberty is growing. Restrictions upon individuals recede more and more. The enlightenment of men is increasing. War seems to grow less prevalent as the dangers attendant to it increase. There is something in the nature of things which seems to be preparing for a great world state.

Is this unfounded optimism on Kant's part? From the standpoint of the time in which he wrote, it was not so. That age, with Kant, found it possible to construct "a universal history" of mankind, to see that what might appear to be an incoherent aggregate of actions was really a systematic and progressive unity. For it was impossible to conceive that Nature had not proceeded with a plan and a final purpose. They could see the passage from Greece to Rome and from Rome to their own times as a regular improvement in the structure of society. And this reading of the past offered nothing but grounds for optimism as to the future.

This progressive view of history, which originated in the eighteenth century with men like Turgot and Kant, reached its height in the nineteenth century in the ideas of Hegel and Comte. In Comte, especially, the idea of progressive development in history seemed persuasive and reasonable. For Comte based his argument on those facts which could support his thesis most strongly; the facts of the history of science.

Pondering the beginnings of science among primitive people, and noting the changes through which science passed in Greek and mediaeval times, Comte was led to formulate his famous *law of the three stages*. The first tendency of all thought, said Comte, is to be religious or *theological*. All primitive peoples find in nature forces, like rain and lightning, sun and flood, which they are unable to control. Instead of seeking the causes for these events, they recognize their mystery and attribute them to the power of spirits, demons, and, finally, gods. Of these powers they stand in awe, but they have concerning them little of what later generations call curiosity. It was the particular genius of Greek thought that it should (as Aristotle noted) substitute curiosity for awe, the wonder at the regularity of natural events for a religious sense of their mysteriousness. And when this happened, thought in Comte's terms became not religious, but *metaphysical*.

Thought is metaphysical when a concept of nature replaces the domain of the gods, when things happen because of forces or qualities which are viewed as teleological or expressive of nature's purposes. But although the Greeks are interested in nature, they did not really produce a developed science. For, says Comte, science only comes into existence when the search for purposes is given up and men become interested in describing the ordered sequence of events and using these noted regularities to predict the future. Science is concerned neither with gods nor with nature's purposes; it leaves the "why" of things to others and only concentrates on their "how." And when thought has reached the stage where it is concerned only with laws of sequence, then the *positive or scientific* stage of thinking has been reached. Every science, from physics to sociology, has gone through this process of progressive change. It has begun by being religious, then become metaphysical, and finally turned into genuine science.

Comte's law of the three stages, the passage from theology to metaphysics and on to science, is a law which applies to all the intellectual products of the human mind and it is a law of progress. Comte therefore sees the historical evolution of mankind as based also upon this law. All history demonstrates the progressive enlightenment of the human mind, the process whereby religious superstition is left behind and scientific clarity takes its place. But to this doctrine of merely intellectual progress, Comte adds two others, a moral and a social. Selfishness is the primitive ethics and it slowly turns into altruism and love for humanity. And, in the same way, warfare is the occupation of primitive society and it slowly turns into peace and the development of industry. There is something enormously comforting in Comte's account of social progress, for it sees all disvalue in the past. Superstition, selfishness, war are slowly changing into science, altruism, and peaceful industry. It was certainly enormously comforting for the nineteenth century. The only question is: Is it true?

A very different theory of progress (which also originated in the nineteenth century) is that of Karl Marx. Only it does not view progress as a slow, steady, evolutionary process, but rather as a series of tensions which are repressed, built up, and finally explode in revolutionary behavior in society. The progress of Comte comes about through slow enlightenment within the mind; the progress of Marx comes about through violent action in society. And this is because while for Comte the greatest of values is enlightenment, for Marx it is freedom.

Marx sees the history of every society as a history of class struggle, of the conflict which always results from those gradations of rank which every society supports. For, abandoning the organic idea of Plato that there must be a division of labor within society, and that some must rule, some must fight, some must work, Marx sees society as a conflict between classes which grows, not from a recognition of a common area of cooperation, but from a consciousness of diverse purpose. The upper class always wants to enjoy the goods of life and to do this it must keep the lower in subjection. The lower class also wishes to enjoy these goods but is duped or forced into its subordinate role. As a result there exists (says Marx) the gross inequalities within society where the upper classes, a tiny minority, exist in a state of over-consumption while the lower classes, the vast majority, exist in a state of under-consumption and poverty. This is to say that class difference means class hostility and that, with the proper preparation, class hostility may turn into civil war.

Society through the ages, as Marx sees it, has always been divided into two great hostile camps; in the ancient world patricians and slaves, in the middle ages lords and serfs, in the modern world bourgeoisie and proletarians. But there is progress in this sense; that the conditions slowly come about in which the proletarians realize their situation and have means at their disposal to bring about a revolutionary change. But this situation has only existed since the industrial revolution and it is to an analysis of how this change has come about that Marx devotes himself.

The great change which takes place with the birth of the modern world out of the middle ages is that markets grow, machines are invented, and industry becomes massively organized. Along with this comes the rise of towns, nationalism, and the capitalistic way of life. It is the bourgeoisie which puts forward the capitalistic scheme of values with its emphasis upon private property, religion (which Marx sees as a mere promise of bliss in the life to come, the purpose of which is to reconcile the lower classes to their inferiority in this life), and excessive patriotism (this latter directed against foreign nations in order to turn aside criticism of the capitalist leaders). But in the end the exploited proletariat will rise against its capitalist masters, and this is due to the inevitable evolution of capitalism itself.

For, despite the superficial prosperity which capitalism seems to bring, inside, says Marx, it is rotten and this becomes clear in its constant crises of over-production and depression. In bad times the machinery slows down, millions are thrown out of work, and the kind of revolutionary situation develops in which finally the violent overthrow of the bourgeoisie becomes possible.

Marx saw this process as inevitable. For the employment of capital demands wage-labor; laborers compete with one another for employment until it occurs to them to band together in large labor unions for their own protection. And, once large combination of workers occurs, the victory of the proletariat is assured and the bourgeoisie will be found to have been their own gravediggers.

It is surely not necessary to point out the defects in this theory; how it originated in the nineteenth century and could not foresee certain basic changes in society which the twentieth century was to bring; how it grew out of a European situation and was therefore totally inapplicable to the New World; how above all it underestimated the degree to which different social classes could share the same values. But this criticism is out of place here for we are not considering Marxism as a social theory, but as a philosophy of history. But, needless to say, among large population groups it is a philosophy of history which is believed to be true. And, as a philosophy of history which looks toward the final overthrow of capitalism and the liquidation of social inequalities (always in the future), it is a revolutionary variant of the old eighteenth-century doctrine of progress.

THE THEORY OF CYCLES

The theory of progress which so fascinated the eighteenth and nineteenth centuries, whether in the evolutionary version of Kant or Comte or in the explosive version of Karl Marx, is not the most characteristic philosophy of history of our own age. It has been supplanted by a cyclical theory which substitutes for the unity of history in the west a plurality of diverse cultures each with its own historic importance and its own problems. The two names associated with this new cyclical philosophy of history are the German Oswald Spengler, who died in the early years of the Hitler regime, and the Englishman Arnold Toynbee. Toynbee's massive *A Study of History* (ten volumes) was completed only a few years ago. Spengler's work, *The Decline of the West,* was published at the end of the First World War. The temperaments and ideals of the two men are very different; Spengler is both pessimistic and without religious belief, while Toynbee is on the surface more optimistic and he is militantly Christian. But, despite this difference, the ideas underlying their work are very similar. Toynbee's volumes are full of digressions and are very pedantic in their scholarship; Spengler's are repetitious and oracular. But despite Toynbee's great popularity and the recent neglect of Spengler, it is Spengler who has undoubtedly the more brilliant and original mind and it is to his version of the cyclical philosophy of history that we will turn.

The shift from viewing history as a single line of development to viewing it as a series of successive great cultures is partly due to the increasing cosmopolitanism of the modern world. When remote parts of the earth are no longer isolated, when we are newly aware of the teeming population of China and India, it is no longer possible to neglect their historical antecedents. Spengler's first point of strategy is to attack the limited and provincial view of history held by western Christian culture, and to substitute for it the idea of "world history." He declares that the traditional scheme of western history, ancient, mediaeval, modern, is nonsense. For it assumes that the only history of real consequence begins with the Greeks and follows the fortunes of the Christian community of western Europe. What of Egypt? It is a mere prologue to Greece. What of China and India? They are mere footnotes to the European middle ages. What of the Aztec culture of the New World? Again, it is a footnote to the colonization of America. Such an historical perspective is childishly naive. Like the Ptolemaic astronomy, it takes the West as the center of the universe and sees all else as satellites of its central fixity. But a true view of history would view each culture in its own terms.

Spengler sees world history as the drama of a series of mighty cultures each one arising, enduring, and finally dying. About 3,000 B.C. on the Nile and the Euphrates arose the earliest cultures, the Egyptian and the Babylonian. About 1,500 years later arose three others, the Indian, the Chinese, and the ancient Greek. And about another 1,500 years later began the Arabian culture in the Old World and the Aztec in the New World. The final culture which Spengler distinguishes is the Western; beginning around the time of the Crusades, ripening with Calvin and Galileo, reaching its height with Goethe and Kant, and now already beginning to decay. Those eight cultures (Egyptian, Babylonian, Indian, Chinese, Greek, Arabian, Aztec, Western) are the basic materials for Spenglerian history.

But what is most important for Spengler's philosophy of history is the idea of biological growth which he applies to each of these separate great cultures. Like an organism each culture is born, grows youthfully, reaches its peak of maturity, and then slowly dies. Or, to use the analogy of the seasons which Spengler appropriated, each culture has its springtime of growth, its summer of early flowering, its autumn of maturity, and finally its winter of old age. Every culture, no matter how long it lives, repeats the same cycle of development.

It is from this analogy that both Spengler's pessimism and his ideas on the decline of the Western World spring. For like the individual, the destiny of any culture is that it will some day die. And for our own Western culture (which Kant and Comte believed would go on endlessly toward improvement and enlightenment) Spengler predicts the same conclusion. He already sees the West in the early winter of its decline, with all creative art a thing of the past, its originality gone, living out its last days amid gigantic wars and imperialisms, enormous city populations, a materialistic and money-oriented point of view.

The important moment for any culture, according to Spengler, is the moment when its mature vitality turns into something fixed and rigid, when artistic intuition becomes systematic philosophy, when the relation of peoples to the land and the countryside is lost and populations are concentrated more and more in enormous cities. This is the passage to a state of civilization. Spengler uses the term "civilization" in a derogatory sense, and he holds that the Western World (whether communistic or democratic, since for him ideologies are less important than conditions of life) is now in such a phase. Whatever our beliefs about a progressive future, we are, thinks Spengler, like the Greeks and the Egyptians, doomed. No culture, however powerful and optimistic, can escape its inevitable decay.

After the optimistic hopes of the progressive philosophy of history the pessimistic conclusions of Spengler's theory of cycles are somewhat dampening. But worse is to come. It is not only that the West is doomed, but that the system of values by which it lives cannot be granted validity beyond its own cultural boundaries. One of the ideas which has sustained philosophers in Western culture is the belief that the values of truth, goodness, and beauty to which it adheres are not just prejudices of Western man but hold universally for all men at all times and places. The idea of beauty as harmonious proportion should hold for the Taj Mahal, the great temple at Peking, the Parthenon, the temple of Luxor, and Chartres Cathedral equally well. The idea of mutual respect among men should be as applicable to Buddhists, Confucians, and Mohammedans as to Christians. The science of medicine should heal in Mexico and Ceylon as well as in London and Paris. But in a sense this is just what Spengler does deny. For between the great cultures there is no real relation. Each culture has its own values and its own experiences and it talks a separate language which no other culture really understands. This means that the Western philosophers are wrong in their strivings toward historical unity. You cannot formulate categories for all mankind or a system of values which can hold universally. There is no plan or aim for "Mankind." There is only the separateness of great historical entities and a complete relativity of values.

HISTORICAL SKEPTICISM

The theory of progress views the events of history as falling within a linear series ascending ever upward and onward. The theory of cycles views the events of history as endlessly repetitive as the planets in their orbits or the waves beating upon the shore. The theory of progress is an optimistic reading of the historical future. The theory of cycles, when it deals with a culture in its late maturity, has only the hopelessness of decay and death to look forward to. But, however the emotional flavor of the two theories of history differ, they are alike in one crucial respect; they do find a meaning and a pattern in history.

Perhaps it is noteworthy that philosophers of history (Kant, Comte, Marx, Spengler) are not themselves necessarily professional historians. These latter, with a certain narrow attentiveness to their craft are often least at home, least comfortable, with those grandiose reflections upon history proper which constitute the philosophy of history. In the preface to his sober and intelligent three-volume A History of Europe, H. A. L. Fisher confessed: [1]

One intellectual excitement has, however, been denied me. Men wiser and more learned than I have discerned in history a plot, a rhythm, a pre-determined pattern. These harmonies are concealed from me. I can see only one emergency following upon another, as wave follows wave, only one great fact with respect to which, since it is unique, there can be no generalizations, only one safe rule for the historian: that he should recognize in the development of human destinies the play of the contingent with the unforeseen.

Many an historian would agree with Fisher. Many have been unable to discern in history "a plot, a rhythm, a pre-determined

[1] H. A. L. Fisher, A History of Europe (3 vols.; Boston: Houghton Mifflin Co., 1935-36), I, p. vii.

pattern." They are accustomed to seeing history as toward the
end Macbeth saw life:

> . . . it is a tale
> Told by an idiot, full of sound and fury,
> Signifying nothing.

Therefore to the "rocket theory" of the philosophy of history (progress) and the "merry-go-round theory" (cycles) we must add the
"idiot theory" which in more respectful language is *the theory of
historical skepticism.*

The theory of historical skepticism denies that history has any
pattern. And it denies this on two grounds; (1) that events simply
happen and that any order which is discovered in them is not *extracted from* the facts but *imposed upon* the facts, and (2) that history is so much the record of "international crime and mass murder"
that to find it orderly and moral is itself an act of the grossest immorality. These two arguments are combined in the work of Karl
Popper (see p. 458).

If history has no meaning it is because "history" as most people
speak of it simply does not exist. There is no history of the common
life of mankind, no records of everyday existence passed on from
generation to generation. The history that one learns in schools is
the history of political power, of kings and queens, of generals and
dictators, of wars and assassinations. It is the record of unjust taxation, brutal conquest, immoral annexation, war after war, in which
the gains are a strip of land or a people bound in virtual slavery.
And this history has perennial fascination precisely because men
worship power.

If this (as Popper believes) is the customary content of history,
then it is also clear why any religious interpretation of history is
bound (also from his point of view) to be immoral. For to say
that God reveals himself in this kind of history is idolatry, blasphemy, and superstition. History is not a work of art. It is not a
play which God has written. It is a bloody tale which historians
have written under the supervision of generals, kings, and dictators. To believe that the course of a history so written was the result of God's intervention in the affairs of the world would be to
make worldly success the moral test of human actions.

The result of Popper's denial that history has a meaning is not
complete skepticism, although it is skepticism about history. It
does not deny values, although it denies that values naturally emerge
from the pages of history. For unlike Hegel, Popper believes, not

that history is the judge, but that it is up to the individual to judge history. It remains the duty of statesmen to cure the evils of society and for teachers to stimulate an interest in values. But these values do not come from history. And here is where the first argument for historical skepticism comes to reinforce the second. The events of history "happen" much like the events in nature, even though they concern men and societies rather than things or animals. Events as such are neutral. Only men have values and in their striving they may indeed affect the course of history. But history proper has no ends but those which we as human beings may impose upon it. Historical skepticism is suspicious of all the grandiose philosophies of history which have been developed, whether linear and progressive or cyclical. For it does not believe that these conceptions are actually implicit in the "facts." Meaning lies not in history but in us. And although "history" has no meaning, we can give it a meaning.

The philosophy of history is an interpretation of the passage of the human race through time. And, as such, it might be compared with the meditated course of any individual human life. A person viewing the long life of a friend recently dead might say of it: (1) "He grew constantly in wisdom and understanding as long as he lived"; or (2) "His whole life he repeated over and over again the same tragic mistakes"; or (3) "There seems to have been no meaning and no purpose to his existence." The first view is linear, the second cyclical, and the third skeptical, and there is a sense in which individual lives lend themselves to just such alternative interpretations. To be sure, an individual is not a whole culture and the analogy is not exact, but so long as men live, they will speculate upon the pattern of the past and of the future.

The following selections, "Universal History" by Immanuel Kant, "Bourgeois and Proletarians" by Karl Marx, "What Is World History?" by Oswald Spengler, and "History Has No Meaning" by Karl Popper are all attempts to contribute to the philosophy of history. And, since this field has only received particular attention since the eighteenth century, one of the selections is from this period, another from the nineteenth century, and two are from our own time. The selections from Kant and Marx represent extreme variants of the doctrine of historical progress. That from Spengler has been included as a typical modern representation of the theory of cycles. The selection from Popper represents the view of historical skepticism which has been gaining ground among philosophers and historians alike.

• Immanuel Kant (1724–1804)

Universal History [2]

Immanuel Kant, besides being one of the most original thinkers in modern philosophy, was also a typical product of the eighteenth century. He showed that century's optimism and its faith in reason. Besides his interest in theory of knowledge and ethics, he was interested in social questions as well. Two of his little pamphlets in these fields have become classics, the *Perpetual Peace* and the *Idea of a Universal History*, from which the following selection is taken. In this essay Kant develops a theory of social progress, tries to identify a purposive element in history, and reads purpose as the slow approach to a perfect state of civil society.

Whatever difference there may be in our notions of the *freedom of the will* metaphysically considered,—it is evident that the manifestations of this will, viz. human actions, are as much under the control of universal laws of nature as any other physical phenomena. It is the province of history to narrate these manifestations; and let their causes be ever so secret, we know that history, simply by taking its station at a distance and contemplating the agency of the human will upon a large scale, aims at unfolding to our view a regular stream of tendency in the great succession of events; so that the very same course of incidents, which taken separately and individually would have seemed perplexed, incoherent, and lawless, yet viewed in their connexion and as the actions of the human *species* and not of independent beings, never fail to discover a steady and continuous though slow development of certain great predispositions in our nature. Thus for instance deaths, births, and marriages, considering how much they are separately dependent on the freedom of the human will, should seem to be subject to no law according to which any calculation could be made beforehand of their amount: and yet the yearly registers of these events in great coun-

[2] From Immanuel Kant, *Idea of a Universal History* (1784), trans. De Quincey (1824), Props. viii, ix.

tries prove that they go on with as much conformity to the laws of nature as the oscillations of the weather: these again are events which in detail are so far irregular that we cannot predict them individually; and yet taken as a whole series we find that they never fail to support the growth of plants—the currents of rivers—and other arrangements of nature in a uniform and uninterrupted course. Individual men, and even nations, are little aware that, whilst they are severally pursuing their own peculiar and often contradictory purposes, they are unconsciously following the guidance of a great natural purpose which is wholly unnoticed by themselves; and are thus promoting and making efforts for a great process which, even if they perceived it, they would little regard.

Considering that men, taken collectively as a body, do not proceed like brute animals under the law of an instinct, nor yet again, like rational cosmopolites, under the law of a preconcerted plan,— one might imagine that no systematic history of their actions (such for instance as the history of bees or beavers) could be possible. At the sight of the actions of man displayed on the great stage of the world, it is impossible to escape a certain degree of disgust: with all the occasional indications of wisdom scattered here and there, we cannot but perceive the whole sum of these actions to be a web of folly, childish vanity, and often even of the idlest wickedness and spirit of destruction. Hence at last one is puzzled to know what judgment to form of our species so conceited of its high advantages. In this perplexity there is no resource for the philosopher but this—that, finding it impossible to presume in the human race any *rational* purpose of its own, he must endeavor to detect some *natural* purpose in such a senseless current of human actions; by means of which a history of creatures that pursue no plan of their own may yet admit a systematic form as the history of creatures that are blindly pursuing a plan of nature. Let us now see whether we can succeed in finding out a clue to such a history; leaving it to nature to produce a man capable of executing it. Just as she produced a Kepler who unexpectedly brought the eccentric courses of the planets under determinate laws; and afterwards a Newton who explained these laws out of a universal ground in nature. . . .

The history of the human species as a whole may be regarded as the unravelling of a hidden plan of nature for accomplishing a perfect state of civil constitution for society in its internal relations (and, as the condition of that, by the last proposition in its external relations also) as the sole state of society in which the tendencies of human nature can be all and fully developed.—This proposition is an inference from the preceding. A question arises upon it—whether experience has yet observed any traces of such an unravelling in history. I answer—some little: for the whole period (to speak astronomically) of this unravelling is probably too vast to admit of our collecting even the form of its orbit or the relation of the parts to the whole from the small fraction of it which man has yet left behind him; just as little as it is possible from the astronomical observations hitherto made to determine the course which our sun together with the whole system of planets pursues amongst the heavenly host; although upon universal grounds derived from the systematic frame of the universe, as well as upon the little stock of observation as yet accumulated, enough is known to warrant us in asserting that there *is* such a course. Meantime our human nature obliges us to take an interest even in the remotest epoch to which our species is destined, provided we can anticipate it with certainty. So much less can *we* be indifferent to it, inasmuch as it appears within our power by intellectual arrangements to contribute something towards the acceleration of the species in its advance to this great epoch. On this account the faintest traces of any approximation in such a direction become of importance to us. At present all states are so artificially inter-connected, that no one can possibly become stationary in its internal culture without retrograding in power and influence with respect to all the rest; and thus if not the progress yet the non-declension of this purpose of nature is sufficiently secured through the ambition of nations. Moreover, civil liberty cannot at this day any longer be arrested in its progress but that all the sources of livelihood, and more immediately trade, must betray a close sympathy with it, and sicken as *that* sickens; and hence a decay of the state in its external relations. Gradually too this liberty extends itself. If the citizen be hindered from pursuing his interest in any way most agreeable to himself, provided only it can co-exist with the liberty of others, in that case the vivacious life of general business is palsied, and in connexion with that again the powers of the whole. Hence it arises that all personal restriction, whether as to commission or omission, is more and more withdrawn; religious liberty is established; and thus by little and little, with occasional interruptions, arises *Illumination;* a blessing which the human race must win even from the self-interested purposes of its rulers, if they comprehend what is for their own advantage. Now this illumination, and with it a certain degree of cordial interest which the enlightened man cannot forbear taking in all the good which he perfectly comprehends must by degrees mount upwards even to the throne, and exert an influence on the principles of government. At present, for example, our governments have no money disposable for national education, because the estimates for the next war have absorbed the whole by anticipation: the first act, therefore, by which the state will express its interest in the advancing spirit of the age, will be by withdrawing its opposition at least to the feeble and tardy exertions of the people in this direction. Finally, war itself becomes gradually not only so artificial a process, so uncertain in its issue, but also in the after-pains of inextinguishable national debts (a contrivance of modern times) so anxious and burthensome; and, at the same time, the influence which any convulsions of one state exert upon every other state is so remarkable in our quarter of the globe—linked as it is in all parts by the systematic intercourse of trade,—that at length, those governments, which have no immediate participation in the war, under a sense of their own danger, offer themselves as mediators—though as yet without any authentic sanction of law, and thus prepare all things from afar for the formation of a great primary state-body, or cosmopolitic Areopagus, such as is wholly unprecedented in all preceding ages. Although this body at present exists only in rude outline, yet already a stirring is beginning to be perceptible in all its limbs—each of which is interested in the maintenance of the whole; even now there is enough to justify a hope that, after many revolutions and remodellings of states, the supreme purpose of nature will be accomplished in the establishment of a cosmopolitic state as the bosom in which all the original tendencies of the human species are to be developed.

A philosophical attempt to compose a universal history in the sense of a cosmopolitical history upon a plan tending to unfold the purpose of nature in a perfect civil union of the human species (instead of the present imperfect union) is to be regarded as possible, and as capable even of helping forward this very purpose of nature.— At first sight it is certainly a strange and apparently an extravagant project—to propose a history of man founded on any idea of the course which human affairs would take if adjusted to certain reasonable ends. On such a plan it may be thought that nothing better than a romance could be the result. Yet, if we assume that nature proceeds not without plan and final purpose even in the motions of human free-will, this idea may possibly turn out very useful; and, although we are too short-sighted to look through the secret mechanism of her arrangements, this idea may yet serve as a clue for connecting into something like *systematic* unity the great abstract of human actions that else seem a chaotic and incoherent *aggregate*. For, if we take our beginning from the Grecian history—as the depository or at least the collateral voucher for all elder or synchronous history; if we pursue down to our own times its influence upon the formation and malformation of the Roman people as a political body that swallowed up the Grecian state, and the influence of Rome upon the barbarians by whom Rome itself was destroyed; and if to all this we add, by way of episode, the political history of every other people so far as it has come to our knowledge through the records of the two enlightened nations above-mentioned; we shall then discover a regular gradation of improvement in civil polity as it has grown up in our quarter of the globe, which quarter is in all probability destined to give laws to all the rest. If further we direct an exclusive attention to the civil constitution, with its laws, and the external relations of the state, in so far as both, by means of the good which they contained, served for a period to raise and to dignify other nations and with them the arts and sciences, yet again by their defects served also to precipitate them into ruin, but so that always some germ of illumination survived which, being more and more developed by every revolution, prepared continually a still higher step of improvement:—in that case, I believe that a clue will be discovered not only for the unravelling of the intricate web of human affairs and for the guidance of future statesmen in the art of political prophecy (a benefit which has been extracted from history even whilst it was regarded as an incoherent result from a lawless freedom of will),—but also such a clue as will open a consolatory prospect into futurity, in which at a remote distance we shall discover the human species seated upon an eminence won by infinite toil where all the germs are unfolded which nature has implanted—and its destination upon this earth accomplished. Such a justification of nature, or rather of providence, is no mean motive for choosing this cosmopolitical station for the survey of history. For what does it avail to praise and to draw forth to view the magnificence and wisdom of the creation in the irrational kingdom of nature, if that part in the great stage of the supreme wisdom, which contains the object of all this mighty display, viz. the history of the human species—is to remain an eternal objection to it, the bare sight of which obliges us to turn away our eyes with displeasure, and (from the despair which it raises of ever discovering in it a perfect and rational purpose) finally leads us to look for such a purpose only in another world?

My object in this essay would be wholly misinterpreted, if it were supposed that under the idea of a cosmopolitical history which to a certain degree has its course determined *a priori,* I had any wish to discourage the cultivation of *empirical* history in the ordinary sense: on the contrary, the philosopher must be well versed in history who could execute the plan I have sketched, which is indeed a most extensive survey of history, only taken from a new station. However the extreme, and, simply considered, praise-worthy circumstantiality, with which the history of every nation is written in our times, must naturally suggest a question of some embarrassment. In what way our remote posterity will be able to cope with the enormous accumulation of historical records which a few centuries will bequeath to them? There is no doubt that they will estimate the historical details of times far removed from their own, the original monuments of which will have long perished, simply by the value of that which will then concern themselves—viz. by the good or evil performed by nations and their governments in a *cosmopolitical* view. To direct the eye upon this point as connected with the ambition of rulers and their servants, in order to guide them to the only means of bequeathing an honorable record of themselves to distant ages; may furnish some small motive (over and above the great one of justifying Providence) for attempting a Philosophic History on the plan I have here explained.

• Karl Marx (1818-83)

and

• Friedrich Engels (1820-95)

Bourgeois and Proletarians [3]

Karl Marx, perhaps the most controversial figure of the nineteenth century, and the one who (for good or for evil) has perhaps had the profoundest effect upon the modern world was born in Treves, Germany. He studied at the universities of Bonn and Berlin and began his career as a radical journalist. Finally forced to flee from Germany, he lived for a few years in Paris and then migrated to England where he died in 1883. The middle years of his life were spent in writing and in active political incitement, his last years in the writing of his scholarly and original *Capital*. His most famous pamphlet *The Communist Manifesto* is reprinted in part as the following selection. In this work Marx puts forward his doctrine of the class struggle, of the inevitable decay of capitalist society, and of the progressive revolution which will lead to the ascendancy of the proletariat.

The history of all hitherto existing society is the history of class struggles.

Freeman and slave, patrician and plebeian, lord and serf, guild-master and journeyman, in a word, oppressor and oppressed, stood in constant opposition to one another, carried on uninterrupted, now hidden, now open fight, a fight that each time ended, either in a revolutionary re-constitution of society at large, or in the common ruin of the contending classes.

In the earlier epochs of history we find almost everywhere a complicated arrangement of society into various orders, a manifold gradation of social rank. In ancient Rome we have patricians, knights,

[3] From Karl Marx and Friedrich Engels, *The Communist Manifesto* (1848), trans. Samuel Moore (1888), Sec. i.

plebeians, slaves; in the middle ages, feudal lords, vassals, guild-masters, journeyman, apprentices, serfs; in almost all of these classes, again, subordinate gradations.

The modern bourgeois society that has sprouted from the ruins of feudal society, has not done away with class antagonisms. It has but established new classes, new conditions of oppression, new forms of struggle in place of the old ones.

Our epoch, the epoch of the bourgeoisie, possesses, however, this distinctive feature; it has simplified the class antagonisms. Society as a whole is more and more splitting up into two great hostile camps, into two great classes directly facing each other: Bourgeoisie and Proletariat.

From the serfs of the middle ages sprang the chartered burghers of the earliest towns. From these burgesses the first elements of the bourgeoisie were developed.

The discovery of America, the rounding of the Cape, opened up fresh ground for the rising bourgeoisie. The East Indian and Chinese markets, the colonization of America, trade with the colonies, the increase in the means of exchange and in commodities generally, gave to commerce, to navigation, to industry, an impulse never before known, and thereby, to the revolutionary element in the tottering feudal society, a rapid development.

The feudal system of industry, under which industrial production was monopolized by closed guilds, now no longer sufficed for the growing wants of the new market. The manufacturing system took its place. The guild-masters were pushed on one side by the manufacturing middle-class: division of labor between the different corporate guilds vanished in the face of division of labor in each single workshop.

Meantime the markets kept ever growing, the demand ever rising. Even manufacture no longer sufficed. Thereupon, steam and machinery revolutionized industrial production. The place of manufacture was taken by the giant, Modern Industry, the place of the industrial middle-class, by industrial millionaires, the leaders of whole industrial armies, the modern bourgeois.

Modern industry has established the world market, for which the discovery of America paved the way. This market has given an immense development to commerce, to navigation, to communication by land. This development has, in its turn, reacted on the extension of industry; and in proportion as industry, commerce, navigation, railways extended, in the same proportion the bourgeoisie developed, increased its capital, and pushed into the background every class handed down from the Middle Ages.

We see, therefore, how the modern bourgeoisie is itself the product of a long course of development, of a series of revolutions in the modes of production and of exchange.

Each step in the development of the bourgeoisie was accompanied by a corresponding political advance of that class. An oppressed class under the sway of the feudal nobility, an armed and self-governing association in the mediaeval commune, here independent urban republic (as in Italy and Germany), there taxable "third estate" of the monarchy as a counterpoise against nobility and, in fact, corner stone of the great monarchies in general, the bourgeoisie has at last, since the establishment of Modern Industry and of the world-market, conquered for itself, in the modern representative State, exclusive political sway. The executive of the modern State is but a committee for managing the common affairs of the whole bourgeoisie.

The bourgeoisie, historically, has played a most revolutionary part.

The bourgeoisie, wherever it has got the upper hand, has put an end to all feudal, patriarchal, idyllic relations. It has pitilessly torn asunder the motley feudal ties that bound man to his "natural superiors," and has left no other nexus between man and man than naked self-interest, than callous "cash payment." It has drowned the most heavenly ecstasies of religious fervor, of chivalrous enthusiasm, of Philistine sentimentalism, in the icy water of egotistical calculation. It has resolved personal worth into exchange value, and in place of the numberless indefeasible chartered freedoms, has set up that single, unconscionable freedom—Free Trade. In one word, for exploitation, veiled by religious and political illusions, it has substituted naked, shameless, direct, brutal exploitation.

The bourgeoisie has stripped of its halo every occupation hitherto honored and looked up to with reverent awe. It has converted the physician, the lawyer, the priest, the poet, the man of science into its paid wage laborers.

The bourgeoisie has torn away from the family its sentimental veil, and has reduced the family relation to a mere money relation.

The bourgeoisie has disclosed how it came to pass that the brutal display of vigor in the Middle Ages, which reactionists so much admire, found its fitting complement in the most slothful indolence. It has been the first to show what man's activity can bring about. It has accomplished wonders far surpassing Egyptian pyramids, Roman aqueducts and Gothic cathedrals; it has conducted expeditions that put in the shade all former Exoduses of nations and crusades.

The bourgeoisie cannot exist without constantly revolutionizing the instruments of production, and thereby the relations of production, and with them the whole relations of society. Conservation of the old modes of production in unaltered form was, on the contrary, the first condition of existence for all earlier industrial classes. Constant revolutionizing of production, uninterrupted disturbance of all social conditions, everlasting uncertainty and agitation distinguish the bourgeois epoch from all earlier ones. All fixed, fast frozen relations, with their train of ancient and venerable prejudices and opinions, are swept away, all new formed ones become antiquated before they can ossify. All that is solid melts into the air, all that is holy is profaned, and man is at last compelled to face with sober senses, his real conditions of life, and his relations with his kind.

The need of a constantly expanding market for its products chases the bourgeoisie over the whole surface of the globe. It must nestle everywhere, settle everywhere, establish connections everywhere.

The bourgeoisie has through its exploitation of the world-market given a cosmopolitan character to production and consumption in every country. To the great chagrin of reactionists, it has drawn from under the feet of industry the national ground on which it stood. All old-established national industries have been destroyed or are daily being destroyed. They are dislodged by new industries, whose introduction becomes a life and death question for all civilized nations, by industries that no longer work up indigenous raw material, drawn from the remotest zones; industries whose products are consumed, not only at home, but in every quarter of the globe. In place of the old wants, satisfied by the productions of the country, we find new wants, requiring for their satisfaction the products of distant lands and climes. In place of the old local and national seclusion and self-sufficiency, we have intercourse in every direction, universal interdependence of nations. And as in material, so also in intellectual production. The intellectual creations of individual nations become common property. National onesidedness and narrowmindedness become more and more impossible, and from the numerous national and local literatures there arises a world-literature.

The bourgeoisie, by the rapid improvement of all instruments of production, by the immensely facilitated means of communication, draws all, even the most barbarian nations into civilization. The cheap prices of its commodities are the heavy artillery with which it batters down all Chinese walls, with which it forces the barbarians' intensely obstinate hatred of foreigners to capitulate. It compels all nations, on pain of extinction, to adopt the bourgeois mode of production; it compels them to introduce what it calls civilization into their midst, i.e., to become bourgeois themselves. In a word, it creates a world after its own image.

The bourgeoisie has subjected the country to the rule of the towns. It has created enormous cities, has greatly increased the urban population as compared with the rural and has thus rescued a considerable part of the population from the idiocy of rural life. Just as it has made the country dependent on the towns, so it has made barbarian and semi-barbarian countries dependent on civilized ones, nations of peasants on nations of bourgeois, the East on the West.

The bourgeoisie keeps more and more doing away with the scattered state of the population, of the means of production, and of poverty. It has agglomerated population, centralized means of production, and has concentrated property in a few hands. The necessary consequence of this was political centralization. Independent, or but loosely connected provinces, with separate interests, laws, governments, and systems of taxation, became lumped together in one nation, with one government, one code of laws, one national class interest, one frontier and one customs tariff.

The bourgeoisie, during its rule of scarce one hundred years, has created more massive and more colossal productive forces than have all preceding generations together. Subjection of Nature's forces to man, machinery, application of chemistry to industry and agriculture, steam-navigation, railways, electric telegraphs, clearing of whole continents for cultivation, canalization of rivers, whole populations conjured out of the ground—what earlier century had even a presentiment that such productive forces slumbered in the lap of social labor?

We see then: the means of production and of exchange on whose foundation the bourgeoisie built itself up, were generated in feudal society. At a certain stage in the development of these means of production and of exchange, the conditions under which feudal society produced and exchanged, the feudal organization of agriculture and manufacturing industry, in one word, the feudal relations of property became no longer compatible with the already developed productive forces; they became so many fetters. They had to burst asunder; they were burst asunder.

Into their places stepped free competition, accompanied by social and political constitution adapted to it, and by economical and political sway of the bourgeois class.

A similar movement is going on before our own eyes. Modern

bourgeois society with its relations of productions, of exchange and of property, a society that has conjured up such gigantic means of production and of exchange, is like the sorcerer, who is no longer able to control the powers of the nether world whom he has called up by his spells. For many a decade past, the history of industry and commerce has been but the history of the revolt of modern productive forces against modern conditions of production, against the property relations that are the conditions for the existence of the bourgeoisie and of its rule. It is enough to mention the commercial crises that by their periodical return put on its trial, each time more threateningly, the existence of the entire bourgeois society. In these crises a great part not only of the existing products, but also of the previously created productive forces, are periodically destroyed. In these crises there breaks out an epidemic that, in all earlier epochs, would have seemed an absurdity—the epidemic of overproduction. Society suddenly finds itself put back into a state of momentary barbarism; it appears as if a famine, a universal war of devastation, had cut off the supply of every means of subsistence; industry and commerce seem to be destroyed; and why? Because there is too much civilization, too much means of subsistence, too much industry, too much commerce. The productive forces at the disposal of society no longer tend to further the development of the conditions of the bourgeois property; on the contrary, they have become too powerful for these conditions by which they are fettered, and as soon as they overcome these fetters they bring disorder into the whole of bourgeois society, endanger the existence of bourgeois property. The conditions of bourgeois society are too narrow to comprise the wealth created by them. And how does the bourgeoisie get over these crises? On the one hand by enforced destruction of a mass of productive forces; on the other, by the conquest of new markets, and by the more thorough exploitation of the old ones. That is to say, by paving the way for more extensive and more destructive crises, and by diminishing the means whereby crises are prevented.

The weapons with which the bourgeoisie felled feudalism to the ground are now turned against the bourgeoisie itself.

But not only has the bourgeoisie forged the weapons that bring death to itself; it has also called into existence the men who are to wield those weapons—the modern working-class—the proletarians.

In proportion as the bourgeoisie, i.e., capital, is developed, in the same proportion is the proletariat, the modern working-class, developed, a class of laborers who live only so long as they find work, and who find work only so long as their labor increases capital.

These laborers, who must sell themselves piecemeal, are a commodity, like every other article of commerce, and are consequently exposed to all the vicissitudes of competition, to all the fluctuations of the market.

Owing to the extensive use of machinery and to division of labor, the work of the proletarians has lost all individual character, and, consequently, all charm for the workman. He becomes an appendage of the machine, and it is only the most simple, most monotonous and most easily acquired knack that is required of him. Hence, the cost of production of a workman is restricted almost entirely to the means of subsistence that he requires for his maintenance, and for the propagation of his race. But the price of a commodity, and also of labor, is equal to its cost of production. In proportion, therefore, as the repulsiveness of the work increases the wage decreases. Nay more, in proportion as the use of machinery and division of labor increases, in the same proportion the burden of toil increases, whether by prolongation of the working hours, by increase of the work enacted in a given time, or by increased speed of the machinery, etc.

Modern industry has converted the little workshop of the patriarchal master into the great factory of the industrial capitalist. Masses of laborers, crowded into factories, are organized like soldiers. As privates of the industrial army they are placed under the command of a perfect hierarchy of officers and sergeants. Not only are they the slaves of the bourgeois class and of the bourgeois state, they are daily and hourly enslaved by the machine, by the overlooker, and, above all, by the individual bourgeois manufacturer himself. The more openly this despotism proclaims gain to be its end and aim, the more petty, the more hateful and the more embittering it is.

The less the skill and exertion or strength implied in manual labor, in other words, the more modern industry becomes developed, the more is the labor of men superseded by that of women. Differences of age and sex have no longer any distinctive social validity for the working class. All are instruments of labor, more or less expensive to use, according to their age and sex.

No sooner is the exploitation of the laborer by the manufacturer, so far at an end, that he receives his wages in cash, than he is set upon by the other portions of the bourgeoisie, the landlord, the shopkeeper, the pawnbroker, etc.

The lower strata of the middle class—the small tradespeople, shopkeepers and retired tradesmen generally, the handicraftsmen and peasants—all these sink gradually into the proletariat, partly because their diminutive capital does not suffice for the scale on which Modern Industry is carried on, and is swamped in the competition with the large capitalists, partly because their specialized skill is rendered worthless by new methods of production. Thus the proletariat is recruited from all classes of the population.

The proletariat goes through various stages of development. With its birth begins its struggle with the bourgeoisie. At first the contest is carried on by individual laborers, then by the workpeople of a factory, then by the operatives of one trade, in one locality, against the individual bourgeois who directly exploits them. They direct their attacks not against the bourgeois conditions of production, but against the instruments of production themselves; they destroy imported wares that compete with their labor, they smash to pieces machinery, they set factories ablaze, they seek to restore by force the vanished status of the workman of the Middle Ages.

At this stage the laborers still form an incoherent mass scattered over the whole country, and broken up by their mutual competition. If anywhere they unite to form more compact bodies, this is not yet the consequence of their own active union, but of the union of the bourgeoisie, which class, in order to attain its own political ends, is compelled to set the whole proletariat in motion, and is moreover yet, for a time, able to do so. At this stage, therefore, the proletarians do not fight their enemies, but the enemies of their enemies, the remnants of absolute monarchy, the landowners, the non-industrial bourgeois, the petty bourgeoisie. Thus the whole historical movement is concentrated in the hands of the bourgeoisie, every victory for the bourgeoisie.

But with the development of industry the proletariat not only increases in number; it becomes concentrated in greater masses, its strength grows and it feels that strength more. The various interests and conditions of life within the ranks of the proletariat are more and more equalized, in proportion as machinery obliterates all distinctions of labor, and nearly everywhere reduces wages to the same low level. The growing competition among the bourgeois, and the resulting commercial crisis, make the wages of the workers even more fluctuating. The unceasing improvement of machinery, ever more rapidly developing, makes their livelihood more and more precarious; the collisions between individual workmen and individual bourgeois take more and more the character of collisions between two classes. Thereupon the workers begin to form combinations (Trades' Unions) against the bourgeois; they club together in order to keep up the rate of wages; they found permanent as-

sociations in order to make provision beforehand for these occasional revolts. Here and there the contest breaks out into riots.

Now and then the workers are victorious, but only for a time.
The real fruit of their battle lies not in the immediate result but in
the ever-expanding union of workers. This union is helped on by
the improved means of communication that are created by modern
industry, and that places the workers of different localities in contact with one another. It was just this contact that was needed to
centralize the numerous local struggles, all of the same character,
into one national struggle between classes. But every class struggle
is a political struggle. And that union, to attain which the burghers
of the Middle Ages with their miserable highways, required centuries, the modern proletarians, thanks to railways, achieve in a few
years.

This organization of the proletarians into a class, and consequently into a political party, is continually being upset again by
the competition between the workers themselves. But it ever rises
up again, stronger, firmer, mightier. It compels legislative recognition of particular interests of the workers by taking advantage of
the divisions among the bourgeoisie itself. Thus the ten hours' bill
in England was carried.

Altogether collisions between the classes of the old society further, in many ways, the course of development of the proletariat.
The bourgeoisie find itself involved in a constant battle. At first
with the aristocracy; later on, with those portions of the bourgeoisie
itself whose interests have become antagonistic to the progress of
industry; at all times, with the bourgeoisie of foreign countries.
In all these battles it sees itself compelled to appeal to the proletariat, to ask for its help, and thus, to drag it into the political arena.
The bourgeoisie itself, therefore, supplied the proletariat with its
own elements of political and general education; in other words, it
furnishes the proletariat with weapons for fighting the bourgeoisie.

Further, as we have already seen, entire sections of the ruling
classes are, by the advance of industry, precipitated into the proletariat, or are at least threatened in their conditions of existence.
These also supply the proletariat with fresh elements of enlightenment and progress.

Finally, in times when the class-struggle nears the decisive hour,
the process of dissolution going on within the ruling class—in fact,
within the whole range of an old society—assumes such a violent,
glaring character that a small section of the ruling class cuts itself
adrift and joins the revolutionary class, the class that holds the

culture in its hands. Just as, therefore, at an earlier period, a section of the nobility went over to the bourgeoisie, so now a portion of the bourgeoisie goes over to the proletariat, and in particular, a portion of the bourgeois ideologists, who have raised themselves to the level of comprehending theoretically the historical movements as a whole.

Of all the classes that stand face to face with the bourgeoisie today the proletariat alone is a really revolutionary class. The other classes decay and finally disappear in the face of modern industry; the proletariat is its special and essential product.

The lower middle class, the small manufacturer, the shopkeeper, the artisan, the peasant, all these fight against the bourgeoisie, to save from extinction their existence as fractions of the middle class. They are therefore not revolutionary, but conservative. Nay, more; they are reactionary, for they try to roll back the wheel of history. If by chance they are revolutionary, they are so only in view of their impending transfer into the proletariat; they thus defend not their present, but their future interests; they desert their own standpoint to place themselves at that of the proletariat.

The "dangerous class," the social scum, that passively rotting mass thrown off by the lowest layers of old society, may, here and there, be swept into the movement by a proletarian revolution; its conditions of life, however, prepare it far more for the part of a bribed tool of reactionary intrigue.

In the conditions of the proletariat, those of the old society at large are already virtually swamped. The proletarian is without property; his relation to his wife and children has no longer anything in common with the bourgeois family relations; modern industrial labor, modern subjection to capital, the same in England as in France, in America as in Germany, has stripped him of every trace of national character. Law, morality, religion, are to him so many bourgeois prejudices, behind which lurk in ambush just as many bourgeois interests.

All the preceding classes that got the upper hand sought to fortify their already acquired status by subjecting society at large to their conditions of appropriation. The proletarians cannot become masters of the productive forces of society, except by abolishing their own previous mode of appropriation. They have nothing of their own to secure and to fortify; their mission is to destroy all previous securities for and insurances of individual property.

All previous historical movements were movements of minorities, or in the interest of minorities. The proletarian movement is the self-conscious, independent movement of the immense majority. The proletariat, the lowest stratum of our present society, cannot stir, cannot raise itself up without the whole superincumbent strata of official society being sprung into the air.

Thought not in substance, yet in form, the struggle of the proletariat with the bourgeoisie is at first a national struggle. The proletariat of each country must, of course, first of all settle matters with its own bourgeoisie.

In depicting the most general phases of the development of the proletariat, we traced the more or less veiled civil war, raging within existing society, up to the point where that war breaks out into open revolution, and where the violent overthrow of the bourgeoisie lays the foundations for the sway of the proletariat.

Hitherto every form of society has been based, as we have already seen, on the antagonism of oppressing and oppressed classes. But in order to oppress a class, certain conditions must be assured to it under which it can, at least, continue its slavish existence. The serf, in the period of serfdom, raised himself to membership in the commune, just as the petty bourgeois, under the yoke of feudal absolutism managed to develop into a bourgeois. The modern laborer, on the contrary, instead of rising with the progress of industry, sinks deeper and deeper below the conditions of existence of his own class. He becomes a pauper, and pauperism develops more rapidly than population and wealth. And here it becomes evident that the bourgeoisie is unfit any longer to be the ruling class in society, and to impose its conditions of existence upon society as an over-riding law. It is unfit to rule, because it is incompetent to assure an existence to its slave within his slavery, because it cannot help letting him sink into such a state that it has to feed him, instead of being fed by him. Society can no longer live under this bourgeoisie; in other words, its existence is no longer compatible with society.

The essential condition for the existence, and for the sway of the bourgeois class, is the formation and augmentation of capital; the condition for capital is wage labor. Wage labor rests exclusively on competition between the laborers. The advance of industry, whose involuntary promoter is the bourgeoisie, replaces the isolation of the laborers, due to competition, by their involuntary combination, due to association. The development of Modern Industry, therefore, cuts from under its feet the very foundation on which the bourgeoisie produces and appropriates products. What the bourgeoisie therefore produces, above all, are its own grave diggers. Its fall and the victory of the proletariat are equally inevitable.

• Oswald Spengler (1880–1936)

What Is World History? [4]

Oswald Spengler was born in Germany and educated at Halle, Munich, and Berlin. He studied natural science, philosophy, and history and later taught in secondary schools until he retired to devote himself to writing. His great work, *The Decline of the West*, from which the following selection is taken, was published just after the First World War and brought him immediate fame. He received two calls to a university professorship, both of which he refused. He had hopes of being a spiritual leader in German politics, and it was believed at first that he would be sympathetic to Hitler. But this did not happen. He died three years after the Nazis came to power. In this selection Spengler attacks the usual periodization of history, puts forward his theory of the succession of great cultures, and states his theory of the relativity of values.

What, then, is world-history? Certainly, an ordered presentation of the past, an inner postulate, the expression of a capacity for feeling form. But a feeling for form, however definite, is not the same as form itself. No doubt we feel world-history, experience it, and believe that it is to be read just as a map is read. But, even today, it is only forms of it that we know and not the form of it, which is the mirror-image of our own inner life.

Everyone of course, if asked, would say that he saw the inward form of History quite clearly and definitely. The illusion subsists because no one has seriously reflected on it, still less conceived doubts as to his own knowledge, for no one has the slightest notion how wide a field for doubt there is. In fact, the lay-out of world-history is an unproved and subjective notion that has been handed down from generation to generation (not only of laymen but of professional historians) and stands badly in need of a little of that scepticism which from Galileo onward has regulated and deepened our inborn ideas of nature.

Thanks to the subdivision of history into "Ancient," "Mediaeval"

---

[4] From Oswald Spengler, *The Decline of the West* (2 vols.; New York, 1926-28), Introduction, Secs. vi-viii. Copyright, 1926-28, by Alfred A. Knopf, Inc.

and "Modern"—an incredibly jejune and meaningless scheme, which has, however, entirely dominated our historical thinking—we have failed to perceive the true position in the general history of higher mankind, of the little part-world which has developed on West-European soil from the time of the German-Roman Empire, to judge of its relative importance and above all to estimate its direction. The Cultures that are to come will find it difficult to believe that the validity of such a scheme with its simple rectilinear progression and its meaningless proportions, becoming more and more preposterous with each century, incapable of bringing into itself the new fields of history as they successively come into the light of our knowledge, was, in spite of all, never whole-heartedly attacked. The criticisms that it has long been the fashion of historical researchers to level at the scheme mean nothing; they have only obliterated the one existing plan without substituting for it any other. To toy with phrases such as "the Greek Middle Ages" or "Germanic antiquity" does not in the least help us to form a clear and inwardly-convincing picture in which China and Mexico, the empire of Axum and that of the Sassanids have their proper places. And the expedient of shifting the initial point of "modern history" from the Crusades to the Renaissance, or from the Renaissance to the beginning of the 19th Century, only goes to show that the scheme per se is regarded as unshakably sound.

It is not only that the scheme circumscribes the area of history. What is worse, it rigs the stage. The ground of West Europe is treated as a steady pole, a unique patch chosen on the surface of the sphere for no better reason, it seems, than because we live on it—and great histories of millennial duration and mighty far-away Cultures are made to revolve around this pole in all modesty. It is a quaintly conceived system of sun and planets! We select a single bit of ground as the natural centre of the historical system, and make it the central sun. From it all the events of history receive their real light, from it their importance is judged in perspective. But it is in our own West-European conceit alone that this phantom "world-history," which a breath of scepticism would dissipate, is acted out.

We have to thank that conceit for the immense optical illusion (become natural from long habit) whereby distant histories of thousands of years, such as those of China and Egypt, are made to shrink to the dimensions of mere episodes while in the neighbourhood of our own position the decades since Luther, and particularly since Napoleon, loom large as Brocken-spectres. We know quite well that the slowness with which a high cloud or a railway train in the distance seems to move is only apparent, yet we believe that the tempo of all early Indian, Babylonian or Egyptian history was really slower than that of our own recent past. And we think of them as less substantial, more damped-down, more diluted, because we have not learned to make the allowance for (inward and outward) distances.

It is self-evident that for the Cultures of the West the existence of Athens, Florence or Paris is more important than that of Lo-Yang or Pataliputra. But is it permissible to found a scheme of world-history on estimates of such a sort? If so, then the Chinese historian is quite entitled to frame a world-history in which the Crusades, the Renaissance, Caesar and Frederick the Great are passed over in silence as insignificant. How, from the morphological point of view, should our 18th Century be more important than any other of the sixty centuries that preceded it? Is it not ridiculous to oppose a "modern" history of a few centuries, and that history to all intents localized in West Europe, to an "ancient" history which covers as many millennia—incidentally dumping into that "ancient history" the whole mass of the pre-Hellenic cultures, unprobed and unordered, as mere appendix-matter? This is no exaggeration. Do we not, for the sake of keeping the hoary scheme, dispose of Egypt and Babylon—each as an individual and self-contained history quite equal in the balance to our so-called "world-history" from Charlemagne to the World-War and well beyond it—as a prelude to classical history? Do we not relegate the vast complexes of Indian and Chinese culture to foot-notes, with a gesture of embarrassment? As for the great American cultures, do we not, on the ground that they do not "fit in" (with what?), entirely ignore them?

The most appropriate designation for this current West-European scheme of history, in which the great Cultures are made to follow orbits round us as the presumed centre of all world-happenings, is the Ptolemaic system of history. The system that is put forward in this work in place of it I regard as the Copernican discovery in the historical sphere, in that it admits no sort of privileged position to the Classical or the Western Culture as against the Cultures of India, Babylon, China, Egypt, the Arabs, Mexico—separate worlds of dynamic being which in point of mass count for just as much in the general picture of history as the Classical, while frequently surpassing it in point of spiritual greatness and soaring power.

The scheme "ancient-mediaeval-modern" in its first form was a creation of the Magian world-sense. It first appeared in the Persian and Jewish religions after Cyrus, received an apocalyptic sense in the teaching of the Book of Daniel on the four world-eras, and was developed into a world-history in the post-Christian religions of the East, notably the Gnostic systems.

This important conception, within the very narrow limits which fixed its intellectual basis, was unimpeachable. Neither Indian nor even Egyptian history was included in the scope of the proposition. For the Magian thinker the expression "world-history" meant a unique and supremely dramatic act, having as its theatre the lands between Hellas and Persia, in which the strictly dualistic world-sense of the East expressed itself not by means of polar conceptions like the "soul and spirit," "good and evil" of contemporary metaphysics, but by the figure of a catastrophe, an epochal change of phase between world-creation and world-decay.

No elements beyond those which we find stabilized in the Classical literature, on the one hand, and the Bible (or other sacred book of the particular system), on the other, came into the picture, which presents (as "The Old" and "The New," respectively) the easily-grasped contrasts of Gentile and Jewish, Christian and Heathen, Classical and Oriental, idol and dogma, nature and spirit with a time connotation—that is, as a drama in which the one prevails over the other. The historical change of period wears the characteristic dress of the religious "Redemption." This "world-history" in short was a conception narrow and provincial, but within its limits logical and complete. Necessarily, therefore, it was specific to this region and this humanity, and incapable of any natural extension.

But to these two there has been added a third epoch, the epoch that we call "modern," on Western soil, and it is this that for the first time gives the picture of history the look of a progression. The oriental picture was at rest. It presented a self-contained antithesis, with equilibrium as its outcome and a unique divine act as its turning-point. But, adopted and assumed by a wholly new type of mankind, it was quickly transformed (without anyone's noticing the oddity of the change) into a conception of a linear progress: from Homer or Adam—the modern can substitute for these names the Indo-German, Old Stone Man, or the Pithecanthropus—through Jerusalem, Rome, Florence and Paris according to the taste of the individual historian, thinker or artist, who has unlimited freedom in the interpretation of the three-part scheme.

This third term, "modern times," which, in form asserts that it is the last and conclusive term of the series, has in fact, ever since the Crusades, been stretched and stretched again to the elastic limit at which it will bear no more. It was at least implied if not stated in so many words, that here, beyond the ancient and the mediaeval, something definitive was beginning, a Third Kingdom in which, somewhere, there was to be fulfilment and culmination, and which had an objective point.

As to what this objective point is, each thinker, from Schoolman to present-day Socialist, backs his own peculiar discovery. Such a view into the course of things may be both easy and flattering to the patentee, but in fact he has simply taken the spirit of the West, as reflected in his own brain, for the meaning of the world. So it is that great thinkers, making a metaphysical virtue of intellectual necessity, have not only accepted without serious investigation the scheme of history agreed "by common consent" but have made of it the basis of their philosophies and dragged in God as author of this or that "world-plan." Evidently the mystic number three applied to the world-ages has something highly seductive for the metaphysician's taste. History was described by Herder as the education of the human race, by Kant as an evolution of the idea of freedom, by Hegel as a self-expansion of the world-spirit, by others in other terms, but as regards its ground-plan everyone was quite satisfied when he had thought out some abstract meaning for the conventional threefold order.

On the very threshold of the Western Culture we meet the great Joachim of Floris (c. 1145-1202), the first thinker of the Hegelian stamp who shattered the dualistic world-form of Augustine, and with his essentially Gothic intellect stated the new Christianity of his time in the form of a third term to the religions of the Old and the New Testaments, expressing them respectively as the Age of the Father, the Age of the Son and the Age of the Holy Ghost. His teaching moved the best of the Franciscans and the Dominicans, Dante, Thomas Aquinas, in their inmost souls and awakened a world-outlook which slowly but surely took entire possession of the historical sense of our Culture. Lessing—who often designated his own period, with reference to the Classical as the "after-world" (Nachwelt)—took his idea of the "education of the human race" with its three stages of child, youth and man, from the teaching of the Fourteenth Century mystics. Ibsen treats it with thoroughness in his *Emperor and Galilean* (1873), in which he directly presents the Gnostic world-conception through the figure of the wizard Maximus, and advances not a step beyond it in his famous Stockholm address of 1887. It would appear, then, that the Western consciousness feels itself urged to predicate a sort of finality inherent in its own appearance.

But the creation of the Abbot of Floris was a mystical glance into the secrets of the divine world-order. It was bound to lose all meaning as soon as it was used in the way of reasoning and made a hypothesis of scientific thinking, as it has been—ever more and more frequently—since the 17th Century.

It is a quite indefensible method of presenting world-history to begin by giving rein to one's own religious, political or social convictions and endowing the sacrosanct three-phase system with tendencies that will bring it exactly to one's own standpoint. This is, in effect, making of some formula—say, the "Age of Reason," Humanity, the greatest happiness of the greatest number, enlightenment, economic progress, national freedom, the conquest of nature, or world-peace—a criterion whereby to judge whole millennia of history. And so we judge that they were ignorant of the "true path," or that they failed to follow it, when the fact is simply that their will and purposes were not the same our ours. Goethe's saying, "What is important in life is life and not a result of life," is the answer to any and every senseless attempt to solve the riddle of historical form by means of a programme.

It is the same picture that we find when we turn to the historians of each special art or science (and those of national economics and philosophy as well). We find:

"Painting" from the Egyptians (or the cave-men) to the Impressionists, or

"Music" from Homer to Bayreuth and beyond, or

"Social Organization" from Lake Dwellings to Socialism, as the case may be,

presented as a linear graph which steadily rises in conformity with the values of the (selected) arguments. No one has seriously considered the possibility that arts may have an allotted span of life and may be attached as forms of self-expression to particular regions and particular types of mankind, and that therefore the total history of an art may be merely an additive compilation of separate developments, of special arts, with no bond of union save the name and some details of craft-technique.

We know it to be true of every organism that the rhythm, form and duration of its life, and all the expression-details of that life as well, are determined by the properties of its species. No one, looking at the oak, with its millennial life, dare say that it is at this moment, now, about to start on its true and proper course. No one as he sees a caterpillar grow day by day expects that it will go on doing so for two or three years. In these cases we feel, with an unqualified certainty, a limit, and this sense of the limit is identical with our sense of the inward form. In the case of higher human history, on the contrary, we take our ideas as to the course of the future from an unbridled optimism that sets at naught all historical, i.e. organic, experience, and everyone therefore sets himself to discover in the accidental present terms that he can expand into some striking progression-series, the existence of which rests not on scientific proof but on predilection. He works upon unlimited possibilities—never a natural end—and from the momentary top-course of his bricks plans artlessly the continuation of his structure.

"Mankind," however, has no aim, no idea, no plan, any more than the family of butterflies or orchids. "Mankind" is a zoological expression, or an empty word. But conjure away the phantom, break the magic circle, and at once there emerges an astonishing wealth of actual forms—the Living with all its immense fullness, depth and movement—hitherto veiled by a catchword, a dry-as-dust scheme, and a set of personal "ideals." I see, in place of that empty figment of one linear history which can only be kept up by shutting one's eyes to the overwhelming multitude of the facts, the drama of a number of mighty Cultures, each springing with primitive strength from the soil of a mother-region to which it remains firmly bound throughout its whole life-cycle; each stamping its material, its mankind, in its own image; each having its own idea, its own passions, its own life, will and feeling, its own death. Here indeed are colours, lights, movements, that no intellectual eye has yet discovered. Here the Cultures, peoples, languages, truths, gods, landscapes bloom and age as the oaks and the stone-pines, the blossoms, twigs and leaves—but there is no ageing "Mankind." Each Culture has its own new possibilities of self-expression which arise, ripen, decay, and never return. There is not one sculpture, one painting, one mathematics, one physics, but many, each in its deepest essence different from the others, each limited in duration and self-contained, just as each species of plant has its peculiar blossom or fruit, its special type of growth and decline. These cultures, sublimated life-essences, grow with the same superb aimlessness as the flowers of the field. They belong, like the plants and the animals, to the living Nature of Goethe, and not to the dead Nature of Newton. I see world-history as a picture of endless formations and transformations, of the marvellous waxing and waning of organic forms. The professional historian, on the contrary, sees it as a sort of tapeworm industriously adding on to itself one epoch after another.

But the series "ancient-mediaeval-modern history" has at last exhausted its usefulness. Angular, narrow, shallow though it was as a scientific foundation, still we possessed no other form that was not wholly unphilosophical in which our data could be arranged, and world-history (as hitherto understood) has to thank it for filtering our classifiable solid residues. But the number of centuries that the scheme can by any stretch be made to cover has long since been exceeded, and with the rapid increase in the volume of our historical material—especially of material that cannot possibly be brought under the scheme—the picture is beginning to dissolve into a chaotic blur. Every historical student who is not quite blind knows and feels this, and it is as a drowning man that he clutches at the only scheme which he knows of. The word "Middle Age," invented in 1667 by Professor Horn of Leyden, has today to cover a formless and constantly extending mass which can only be defined, negatively, as every thing not classifiable under any pretext in one of the other two (tolerably well-ordered) groups. We have an excellent example of this in our feeble treatment and hesitant judgment of modern Persian, Arabian and Russian history. But, above all, it has become impossible to conceal the fact that this so-called history of the world is a limited history, first of the Eastern Mediterranean region and then,—with an abrupt change of scene at the Migrations (an event important only to us and therefore greatly exaggerated by us, an event of purely Western and not even Arabian significance),—of West-Central Europe. When Hegel declared so naively that he meant to ignore those peoples which did not fit into his scheme of history, he was only making an honest avowal of methodic premisses that every historian finds necessary for his purpose and every historical work shows in its layout. In fact it has now become an affair of scientific tact to determine which of the historical developments shall be seriously taken into account and which not. Ranke is a good example.

Today we think in continents, and it is only our philosophers and historians who have not realized that we do so. Of what significance to us, then, are conceptions and purviews that they put before us as universally valid, when in truth their furthest horizon does not extend beyond the intellectual atmosphere of Western Man?

Examine, from this point of view, our best books. When Plato speaks of humanity, he means the Hellenes in contrast to the barbarians, which is entirely consonant with the ahistoric mode of the Classical life and thought, and his premisses take him to conclusions that for Greeks were complete and significant. When, however, Kant philosophizes, say on ethical ideas, he maintains the validity of his theses for men of all times and places. He does not say this in so many words, for, for himself and his readers, it is something that goes without saying. In his aesthetics he formulates the principles, not of Phidias's art, or Rembrandt's art, but of Art generally. But what he poses as necessary forms of thought are in reality only necessary forms of Western thought, though a glance at Aristotle and his essentially different conclusions should have sufficed to show that Aristotle's intellect, not less penetrating than his own, was of different structure from it. The categories of the Westerner are just as alien to Russian thought as those of the Chinaman or the ancient Greek are to him. For us, the effective and complete comprehension of Classical root-words is just as impossible as that of Russian and Indian, and for the modern Chinese or Arab, with their utterly different intellectual constitutions, "philosophy from Bacon to Kant" has only a curiosity-value.

It is this that is lacking to the Western thinker, the very thinker in whom we might have expected to find it—insight into the historically relative character of his data, which are expressions of one specific existence and one only; knowledge of the necessary limits of their validity; the conviction that his "unshakable" truths and "eternal" views are simply true for him and eternal for his worldview; the duty of looking beyond them to find out what the men of other Cultures have with equal certainty evolved out of themselves. That and nothing else will impart completeness to the philosophy of the future, and only through an understanding of the living world shall we understand the symbolism of history. Here there is nothing constant, nothing universal. We must cease to speak of the forms of "Thought," the principles of "Tragedy," the mission of "The State." Universal validity involves always the fallacy of arguing from particular to particular.

But something much more disquieting than a logical fallacy begins to appear when the centre of gravity of philosophy shifts from the abstract-systematic to the practical-ethical and our Western thinkers from Schopenhauer onward turn from the problem of cognition to the problem of life (the will to life, to power, to action). Here it is not the ideal abstract "man" of Kant that is subjected to examination, but actual man as he has inhabited the earth during historical time, grouped, whether primitive or advanced, by peoples; and it is more than ever futile to define the structure of his highest ideas in terms of the "ancient-mediaeval-modern" scheme with its local limitations. But it is done, nevertheless.

Consider the historical horizon of Nietzsche. His conceptions of decadence, militarism, the transvaluation of all values, the will to power, lie deep in the essence of Western civilization and are for the analysis of that civilization of decisive importance. But what, do we find, was the foundation on which he built up his creation? Romans and Greeks, Renaissance and European present, with a fleeting and uncomprehending side-glance at Indian philosophy—in short "ancient, mediaeval and modern" history. Strictly speaking, he never once moved outside the scheme, nor did any other thinker of his time.

What correlation, then, is there or can there be of his idea of the "Dionysian" with the inner life of a highly-civilized Chinese or an up-to-date American? What is the significance of his type of the "Superman"—for the world of Islam? Can image-forming antitheses of Nature and Intellect, Heathen and Christian, Classical and Modern, have any meaning for the soul of the Indian or the Russian? What can Tolstoi—who from the depths of his humanity rejected the whole Western world-idea as something alien and distant—do with the "Middle Ages," with Dante, with Luther? What can a Japanese do with Parzeval and "Zarathustra," or an Indian with Sophocles? And is the thought-range of Schopenhauer, Comte, Feuerbach, Hebbel or Strindberg any wider? Is not their whole psychology, for all its intention of world-wide validity, one of purely West-European significance?

How comic seem Ibsen's woman-problems—which also challenge the attention of all "humanity"—when, for his famous Nora, the lady of the North-west European city with the horizon that is implied by a house-rent of 100 to 300 a year and a Protestant upbringing, we substitute Caesar's wife, Madame de Sevigne, a Japanese or a Turkish peasant woman! But, for that matter, Ibsen's own circle of vision is that of the middle class in a great city of yesterday and today. His conflicts, which start from spiritual premises that did not exist till about 1850 and can scarcely last beyond 1950, are neither those of the great world nor those of the lower masses, still less those of the cities inhabited by non-European populations.

All these are local and temporary values—most of them indeed limited to the momentary "intelligentsia" of cities of West-European type. World-historical or "eternal" values they emphatically are not. Whatever the substantial importance of Ibsen's and Nietzsche's generation may be, it infringes the very meaning of the word "world-history"—which denotes the totality and not a selected part —to subordinate, to undervalue, or to ignore the factors which lie outside "modern" interests. Yet in fact they are so undervalued or ignored to an amazing extent. What the West has said and thought, hitherto, on the problems of space, time, motion, number, will, marriage, property, tragedy, science, has remained narrow and dubious, because men were always looking for the solution of the question. It was never seen that many questioners implies many answers, that any philosophical question is really a veiled desire to get an explicit affirmation of what is implicit in the question itself, that the great questions of any period are fluid beyond all conception, and that therefore it is only by obtaining a group of historically limited solutions and measuring it by utterly impersonal criteria that the final secrets can be reached. The real student of mankind treats no standpoint as absolutely right or absolutely wrong. In the face of such grave problems as that of Time or that of Marriage, it is insufficient to appeal to personal experience, or an inner voice, or reason, or the opinion of ancestors or contemporaries. These may say what is true for the questioner himself and for his time, but that is not all. In other Cultures the phenomenon talks a different language, for other men there are different truths. The thinker must admit the validity of all, or of none.

How greatly, then, Western world-criticism can be widened and deepened! How immensely far beyond the innocent relativism of Nietzsche and his generation one must look—how fine one's sense for form and one's psychological insight must become—how completely one must free oneself from limitations of self, of practical interests, of horizon—before one dare assert the pretension to understand world-history, the world-as-history.

• Karl R. Popper (1902–   )

History Has No Meaning [5]

Karl Popper, born in Vienna at the turn of the century and educated at the University of Vienna is now Professor of Logic and Scientific Method at the University of London. His chief work is *The Open Society and Its Enemies*, published in 1945, and it is from this work that the following selection is taken. In it Popper states the case for the belief that history has no meaning. His assumptions are positivistic, but he is not unsympathetic to our giving a meaning to history, provided that we acknowledge ourselves rather than history as the source of value.

[5] From Karl Popper, *The Open Society and Its Enemies* (2 vols.; London, 1945), chap. xxv. Copyright, 1945, by Routledge and Kegan Paul Ltd.

But is there such a clue? *Is there a meaning in history?*

I do not wish to enter here into the problem of the meaning of "meaning"; I take it for granted that most people know with sufficient clarity what they mean when they speak of the "meaning of history" or of the "meaning of life." And in this sense, in the sense in which the question of the meaning of history is asked, I answer: *History has no meaning.*

In order to give reasons for this opinion, I must first say something about that "history" which people have in mind when they ask whether it has meaning. So far, I have myself spoken about "history" as if it did not need any explanation. That is no longer possible; for I wish to make it clear that *"history" in the sense in which most people speak of it simply does not exist;* and this is at least one reason why I say that it has no meaning.

How do most people come to use the term "history"? They learn about it in school and at the University. They read books about it. They see what is treated in the books under the name "history of the world" or "the history of mankind," and they get used to looking upon it as a more or less definite series of facts. And these facts constitute, they believe, the history of mankind.

But we have already seen that the realm of facts is infinitely rich, and that there must be selection. According to our interests, we could, for instance, write a history of art; or of language; or of feeding habits; or of typhus fever (see Zinsser's *Rats, Lice, and History*). Certainly, none of these is the history of mankind (nor all of them taken together). What people have in mind, when they speak of the history of mankind, is rather the history of the Egyptian, Babylonian, Persian, Macedonian, and Roman empires, and so on, down to our own day. In other words: They speak about a *history of mankind,* but what they mean, and what they have learned about in school, is the *history of political power.*

There is no history of mankind, there are only many histories of all kinds of aspects of human life. And one of these is the history of political power. This is elevated into the history of the world. But this, I hold, is an offence against every decent conception of mankind. It is hardly better than to treat the history of embezzlement or of robbery or of poisoning as the history of mankind; for *the history of power politics is nothing but the history of international crime and mass murder* (including, it is true, some of the attempts to suppress them). This history is taught in schools, and many of the greatest criminals are presented as heroes.

But is there really no such thing as a universal history in the sense of a concrete history of mankind? There can be none. This must be the reply of every humanitarian, I believe, and especially that of every Christian. A concrete history of mankind, if there were any, would have to be the history of all men. It would have to be the history of all human hopes, struggles, and sufferings. For there is no one man more important than any other. Clearly, this concrete history cannot be written. We must make abstractions, we must neglect, select. But with this we arrive at the many histories; and among them, at that history of international crime and mass murder which has been advertised as the history of mankind.

But why has just the history of power been selected, and not, for example, that of poetry? There are several reasons. One is that power affects us all, and poetry only a few. Another is that men are inclined to worship power. But there can be no doubt that the worship of power is one of the worst kinds of human idolatries, a relic of the time of the cage, of human servitude. The worship of power is born of fear, an emotion which is rightly despised. A third reason why power politics has been made the core of "history" is that those in power wanted to be worshipped and could enforce their wishes. Many historians wrote under the supervision of the generals and the dictators.

I know that these views will meet with the strongest opposition, especially from some apologists for Christianity; for although there is hardly anything in the New Testament to support this view, it is often considered a Christian dogma that God reveals Himself in history; that history has meaning; and that its meaning is the purpose of God. Historicism is thus held to be a necessary element of religion. But I do not admit this. I contend that this view is pure idolatry and superstition, not only from the point of view of a rationalist or humanist but from the Christian point of view itself.

What is behind this religious historicism? With Hegel, it looks upon history as a stage, or rather, as a kind of lengthy Shakespearean play; and the audience conceive either the "great historical personalities," or mankind in the abstract, as the heroes of the play. Then they ask, "Who has written this play?" And they think that they give a pious answer when they reply, "God." But they are mistaken. Their answer is pure blasphemy, for the play was not written by God, but, under the supervision of generals and dictators, by the professors of history.

I do not deny that it is as justifiable to interpret history from a Christian point of view as it is to interpret it from any other point of view; and it should certainly be emphasized, for example, how much of our Western aims and ends, humanitarianism, freedom, equality, we owe to the influence of Christianity. But at the same time, the only rational as well as the only Christian attitude even towards the history of freedom is that we are ourselves responsible for it, in the same sense in which we are responsible for what we make of our lives, and that only our conscience can judge us, not our worldly success. The theory that God reveals Himself and His judgement in history is indistinguishable from the theory that worldly success is the ultimate judge and justification of our actions; it comes to the same thing as the doctrine that history will judge, that is to say, that future might is right; it is the same as what I have called "moral futurism." To maintain that God reveals Himself in what is usually called "history," in the history of international crime and mass murder, is indeed blasphemy; for what really happens within the realm of human lives is hardly ever touched upon by this cruel and at the same time childish affair. The life of the forgotten, of the unknown individual man; his sorrows and his joys, his suffering and death, this is the real content of human experience down the ages. If that could be told by history, then I should certainly not say that it is blasphemy to see the finger of God in it. But such a history does not and cannot exist; and all the history which exists, our history of the Great and Powerful, is at best a shallow comedy; it is the opera buffa played by the powers behind reality (comparable to Homer's opera buffa of the Olympian powers behind the scene of human struggles). It is what one of our worst instincts, the idolatrous worship of power, of success, has led us to believe to be real. And in this not even man-made, but man-faked "history," some Christians dare to see the hand of God! They dare to understand and to know what He wills when they impute to Him their petty historical interpretations! "On the contrary," says K. Barth, the theologian, in his *Credo*, "we have to begin with the admission . . . that all that we think we know when we say 'God' does not reach or comprehend Him . . . , but always one of our self-conceived and self-made idols, whether it is 'spirit' or 'nature', 'fate' or 'idea' . . ." (It is in keeping with this attitude that Barth characterizes the "Neo-Protestant doctrine of the revelation of God in history" as "inadmissible" and as an encroachment upon "the kingly office of Christ".) But it is, from the Christian point of view, not only arrogance that underlies such attempts; it is, more specifically, an anti-Christian attitude. For Christianity teaches, if anything, that success is not decisive. Christ "suffered under Pontius Pilate." I am quoting Barth again: "How does Pontius Pilate get into the Credo? The simple answer can at once be given: it is a matter of date." Thus the historical power which was successful at that time, plays here the purely technical rôle of indicating when these events happened. And what were these events? They have nothing to do with power-political success, with "history". They are not even the story of an unsuccessful non-violent nationalist revolution (à la Gandhi) of the Jewish people against the Roman conquerors. The events are nothing but the sufferings of a man. Barth insists that the word "suffers" refers to the whole of the life of Christ and not only to His death; he says: "Jesus *suffers*. Therefore He does not conquer. He does not triumph. He has no success . . . He achieved nothing except . . . His crucifixion. The same could be said of His relationship to His people and to His disciples." My intention in quoting Barth is to show that it is not only my "rationalist" or "humanist" point of view from which the worship of historical success appears as incompatible with the spirit of Christianity. What matters to Christianity is not the historical deeds of the powerful Roman conquerers but (to use a phrase of Kierkegaard's) "what a few fishermen have given the world." And yet all theistic interpretation of history attempts to see in history as it is recorded, i.e. in the history of power, and in historical success, the manifestation of God's will.

To this attack upon the "doctrine of revelation of God in history," it will probably be replied that it *is* success, His success after His death, by which Christ's unsuccessful life on earth was finally revealed to mankind as the greatest spiritual victory; that it was the success, the fruits of His teaching which proved it and justified it, and by which the prophecy "The last shall be first and the first last" has been verified. In other words, that it was the historical success of the Christian Church through which the will of God manifested itself. But this is a most dangerous line of defence. Its implication that the success of the Church is an argument in favour of Christianity clearly reveals lack of faith. The early Christians had no worldly encouragement of this kind. (They believed that conscience must judge power, and not the other way round.) Those who believe that the history of the success of Christian teaching reveals the will of God should ask themselves whether this success was really a success of the spirit of Christianity; and whether this spirit did not triumph at the time when the Church was persecuted, rather than at the time when the Church was triumphant. Which Church incorporated this spirit more purely, that of the martyrs, or the victorious Church of the Inquisition?

There seem to be many who would admit much of this, insisting as they do that the message of Christianity is to the meek, but who still believe that this message is one of historicism. An outstanding representative of this view is J. Macmurray, who, in *The Clue to History*, finds the essence of Christian teaching in historical prophecy, and who sees in its founder the discoverer of a dialectical law of "human nature." Macmurray holds that, according to this law, political history must inevitably bring forth "the socialist commonwealth of the world. The fundamental law of human nature cannot be broken . . . It is the meek who will inherit the earth." But this historicism, with its substitution of certainty for hope, must lead to a moral futurism. "The law *cannot* be broken." So we can be sure, on psychological grounds, that whatever we do will lead to the same result; that even fascism must, in the end, lead to that commonwealth; so that the final outcome does not depend upon our moral decision, and that there is no need to worry over our responsibilities. If we are told that we can be *certain*, on scientific grounds, that "the last will be first and the first last," what else is this but the substitution of historical prophecy for conscience? Does not this theory come dangerously close (certainly against the intentions of its author) to the admonition: "Be wise, and take to heart what the founder of Christianity, who was a great psychologist of human nature and a great prophet of history, tells you; join the last; for according to the laws of human nature, this is the surest way to come out first!" Such a clue to history implies the worship of success; it implies that the meek will be justified because they will be on the winning side. It translates Marxism, and especially what I have described as Marx's historicist moral theory, into the language of a psychology of human nature, and of religious prophecy. It is an interpretation which, by implication, sees the greatest achievement of Christianity in the fact that its founder was a forerunner of Hegel—a superior one, admittedly.

My insistence that success should not be worshipped, that it cannot be our judge, and that we should not be dazzled by it, and in particular, my attempts to show that in this attitude I concur with the teachings of Christianity, should not be misunderstood. They are not intended to support the attitude of "other-worldliness" which I have criticized in the last chapter. Whether Christianity is other-worldly, I do not know, but it certainly teaches that the only way to prove one's faith is by rendering practical (and worldly) help to those who need it. And it is certainly possible to combine an attitude of the utmost reserve and even of contempt towards worldly success in the sense of power, glory, and wealth, with the attempt to do one's best in this world, and to further the ends one

has decided to adopt with the clear purpose of making them succeed; not for the sake of success or of one's justification by history,
but for their own sake.

A forceful support of some of these views, and especially of the
incompatibility of historicism and Christianity, can be found in
Kierkegaard's criticism of Hegel. Although Kierkegaard never
freed himself entirely from the Hegelian tradition in which he was
educated, there was hardly anybody who recognized more clearly
what Hegelian historicism meant. "There were," Kierkegaard wrote,
"philosophers who tried, before Hegel, to explain . . . history. And
providence could really not but smile when it saw these attempts.
But providence did not laugh outright, for there was a human,
honest sincerity about them. But Hegel—! Here I need Homer's
language. How did the gods roar with laughter! Such a horrid
little professor who has simply seen through the necessity of anything and everything there is, and who now plays the whole affair
on his barrel-organ: listen, ye gods of Olympus!" And Kierkegaard
continues, referring to the attack by the atheist Schopenhauer upon
the Christian apologist Hegel: "Reading Schopenhauer has given
me more pleasure than I can express. What he says is perfectly
true; and then—it serves the Germans right—he is as rude as only
a German can be." But Kierkegaard's own expressions are nearly
as blunt as Schopenhauer's; for Kierkegaard goes on to say that
Hegelianism, which he calls "this brilliant spirit of putridity," is the
"most repugnant of all forms of looseness"; and he speaks of its
"mildew of pomposity," its "intellectual voluptuousness," and its "in-
famous splendour of corruption."

And, indeed, our intellectual as well as our ethical education is
corrupt. It is permeated by the admiration of brilliance, of the
way things are said, which takes the place of a critical appreciation
of the things that are said (and the things that are done). It is permeated by this romantic idea of the splendour of the State of History
on which we are actors. We are educated to act with an eye to
the gallery.

The whole problem of educating man to a sane appreciation of
his own importance relative to that of other individuals is thoroughly muddled by these ethics of fame and fate, by a morality
which perpetuates an educational system that is still based upon
the classics with their romantic view of the history of power and
their romantic tribal morality which goes back to Heraclitus; a
system whose ultimate basis is the worship of power. Instead of a
sober combination of individualism and altruism (to use these labels
again), that is to say, instead of a position like "What really matters

are human individuals, but I do not take this to mean that it is I who matters very much," a romantic combination of egoism and collectivism is taken for granted. That is to say, the importance of the self of its emotional life and its "self-expression" is romantically exaggerated, and with it, the tension between me and the group, the collective; which replaces the other individuals, the other men, and which does not admit of reasonable personal relations. "Dominate or submit" is, by implication, the device of this attitude; either be a Great Man, a Hero wrestling with fate and earning fame ("the greater the fall, the greater the fame," says Heraclitus), or submit yourself to leadership and sacrifice yourself to the higher cause of your collective. There is definitely a neurotic, a hysterical element in this exaggerated stress on the importance of the tension between the self and the collective, and I do not doubt that this hysteria, this reaction to the strain of civilization, is the secret of the strong emotional appeal of the ethics of hero-worship, of the ethics of domination and submission.

At the bottom of all this there is a real difficulty. While it is fairly clear that the politician should limit himself to fighting against evils, instead of fighting for "positive" or "higher" values, such as happiness, etc., the teacher, in principle, is in a different position. Although he should not *impose* his scale of "higher" values upon his pupils, he certainly should try to *stimulate* their interest in these values. He should care for the souls of his pupils. (When Socrates told his friends to care for their souls, *he* cared for them.) Thus there is certainly something like a romantic or aesthetic element in education, such as should not enter politics. But though this is true in principle, it is hardly applicable to our educational system. For it presupposes a relation of friendship between teacher and pupil, a relation which, as emphasized in chapter 24, each party must be free to end. (Socrates chose his companions, and they him.) The very number of pupils makes all this impossible in our schools. Accordingly, attempts to impose higher values not only become unsuccessful, but it must be insisted that they lead to *harm* —to something much more concrete and public than the ideals aimed at. And the principle that those who are entrusted to us must, before anything else, not be harmed, should be recognized to be just as fundamental for education as it is for medicine. "Do no harm" (and, therefore, "give the young what they most urgently need, in order to become independent of us, and to be able to choose for themselves") would be a very worthy aim for our educational system, and one whose realization is very far away, even though it sounds modest. Instead, "higher" aims are the fashion, aims which are typically romantic and indeed nonsensical, such as "the full development of the personality."

It is under the influence of such romantic ideas that individualism is still identified with egoism, as it was by Plato, and altruism with collectivism (i.e. with the substitution of group egoism for the individualist egoism). But this bars the way even to a clear formulation of the main problem, the problem of how to obtain a sane appreciation of one's own importance in relation to other individuals. Since it is felt, and rightly so, that we have to aim at something beyond our own selves, something to which we can devote ourselves, and for which we may make sacrifices, it is concluded that this must be the collective, with its "historical mission." Thus we are told to make sacrifices, and, at the same time, assured that we shall make an excellent bargain by doing so. We shall make sacrifices, it is said, but we shall thereby obtain honour and fame. We shall become "leading actors," heroes on the Stage of History; for a small risk we shall gain great rewards. This is the dubious morality of a period in which only a tiny minority counted, and in which nobody cared for the common people. It is the morality of those who, being political or intellectual aristocrats, have a chance of getting into the textbooks of history. It cannot possibly be the morality of those who favour justice and equalitarianism; for historical fame cannot be just, and it can be attained only by a very few. The countless number of men who are just as worthy, or worthier, will always be forgotten.

It should perhaps be admitted that the Heraclitean ethics, the doctrine that the higher reward is that which only posterity can offer, may in some way perhaps be slightly superior to an ethical doctrine which teaches us to look out for reward now. But it is not what we need. We need an ethics which defies success and reward. And such an ethics need not be invented. It is not new. It has been taught by Christianity, at least in its beginnings. It is, again, taught by the industrial as well as by the scientific cooperation of our own day. The romantic historicist morality of fame, fortunately, seems to be on the decline. The Unknown Soldier shows it. We are beginning to realize that sacrifice may mean just as much, or even more, when it is made anonymously. Our ethical education must follow suit. We must be taught to do our work; to make our sacrifice for the sake of this work, and not for praise or the avoidance of blame. (The fact that we all need some encouragement, hope, praise, and even blame, is another matter altogether.) We must find our justification in our work, in what we are doing ourselves, and not in a fictitious "meaning of history."

History has no meaning, I contend. But this contention does not imply that all we can do about it is to look aghast at the history of political power, or that we must look on it as a cruel joke. For we can interpret it, with an eye to those problems of power politics whose solution we choose to attempt in our time. We can interpret the history of power politics from the point of view of our fight for the open society, for a rule of reason, for justice, freedom, equality, and for the control of international crime. Although history has no ends, we can impose these ends of ours upon it; and *although history has no meaning, we can give it a meaning.*

SUGGESTED FURTHER READINGS

BURCKHARDT, JACOB. *Force and Freedom.* New York: Pantheon Bks., Inc., 1943.

COHEN, M. R. *The Meaning of Human History.* La Salle, Ill.: The Open Court Publishing Co., 1947.

COLLINGWOOD, R. G. *The Idea of History.* London: Oxford University Press, 1946.

COMTE, AUGUST. *The Positive Philosophy.* London: Chapman & Hall, Ltd., 1890. Introduction.

CONDORCET. *Sketch of the Procession of the Progress of the Human Spirit.* Hanover, N. H.: The Sociological Press, 1928.

HEGEL, G. W. *The Philosophy of History.* New York: John Wiley & Sons, Inc., 1944.

LÖWITH, KARL. *Meaning in History.* Chicago: University of Chicago Press, 1949.

MARX, KARL. *Capital.*

———, and FRIEDRICH ENGELS. *The Communist Manifesto.* Translated by SAMUEL MOORE, 1888.

MACMURRAY, JOHN. *The Clue to History.* New York: Harper & Brothers, 1939.

POPPER, KARL. *The Open Society and Its Enemies.* 2 vols. London: Routledge and Kegan Paul Ltd., 1945.

ST. AUGUSTINE. *The City of God.* London: J. M. Dent & Sons, Ltd., 1931.

SPENGLER, OSWALD. *The Decline of the West.* 2 vols. New York: Alfred A. Knopf, Inc., 1926-28.

TOYNBEE, A. J. *A Study of History.* 10 vols. New York: Oxford University Press, 1934–54.

TURGOT, A. R. J. *Discourse on the Progress of the Human Spirit.* Hanover, N. H.: The Sociological Press, 1926.

WHITEHEAD, A. N. *Adventures of Ideas.* New York: The Macmillan Co., 1933. Part I.

CHAPTER 9

Religion

The Nature of Religious Experience

We have now come to the final area set off upon our map of experience, the realm of things above man. This is the realm of God in his allegedly perfect and all powerful nature, of his acts, and of the events which follow from His will. It is also the realm of the transcendent values of truth, goodness, and beauty, less as these enter into human experience than as they may be in their own nature, guaranteed and authorized by God. It is fitting that we should return to this area at the end of our inquiry into the varieties of experience and the philosophical meditation upon them. For, as that area which is of greatest ultimate concern to man, it is the coping stone of all the rest. Just as the consideration of what it means to be a cosmos is the summit of all philosophizing about nature, and just as the consideration of the meaning of history is the summit of all philosophizing about human experiences, so the consideration of God and ultimate values summarizes all that might be said both of nature and of man.

Candor, however, requires one to add that if this is the most significant of all areas of philosophizing, it is at the same time the most uncertain, the most productive of disagreement, the fullest of hostile and even irreconcilable beliefs about its subject matter. For, in philosophy, the ironic truth seems to be that men agree most about what matters least and agree least about what matters most.

The disagreement over God and ultimate values is of a particularly difficult sort. There may be many different philosophies of nature, but there is no one who denies that nature exists. There may be many different philosophies of human experience, but there is no one who denies that human experience exists. But there are many different philosophies about God and ultimate values, and some of them absolutely deny that there is any domain of things above man and nature which exists. The denial of God and the supernatural is one of the theories which must, then, here be taken into account.

The most comprehensive attack comes not from within the field of philosophy itself, not from those who deny faith as a method of knowing or the supernatural as a possible object of experience. It comes from those outside the field of philosophy proper, from psychologists and anthropologists, whose effect is to cast doubt, not merely upon the "existence" of God, but upon the usefulness or the "value" of any religious experience whatsoever.

The attack upon the value of religious experience rests upon two separate but related analogies; one with the childhood of the human race, the other with the childhood of the individual man. The spectacle of what religion has been in the past is a humiliation to reasonable men and when one learns the facts of how closely contemporary religious ritual is related to it, there may come uneasiness if not disgust. Suppose the anthropologist is right. Then religion originates as magic and superstition. Primitive man tries to coerce nature to do his bidding and he does this through magic rites of prayers and sacrifice. This may rest upon the most absurd nonsense as to what the gods are, and it may end with acts of human sacrifice, of gross immorality, of crude torture. We can understand such behavior (although we cannot condone it) by attributing it to "primitive mentality," inferior races, or days gone by. But that means that humanity should by now have outgrown such superstitions. But modern religion (say the anthropologists), though it may have outlived the crudities, is based upon the same superstitions. Modern man still celebrates in springtime the dying of his God and symbolically eats His body and drinks His blood. Or he observes the most primitive forms of food taboo in the name of piety. Or he performs meaningless acts of penance to a demanding deity. But if human social evolution has any meaning, should it not be the progress that the eighteenth and nineteenth century read into it; from superstition to reasonableness, from primitive magic to enlightenment, from religion to science? So runs the first argument.

The second argument rests upon the childhood of the individual man. It says: when we are children we need our parents to satisfy our needs, tell us what to do, smooth our relations with the outside world, serve as authority for our acts. But when we grow up, we renounce the authority of our parents, recognize that we must now guide our lives by our own standards and, if we are mature, become realistic and self-dependent. Now, religion has all of the qualities of the dependence of a child. The idea of God with one stroke explains all of our perplexities about the origins of man and of the world, and we give to God the same status of omnipotence as we give to our parents before we discover the facts of their limitations. Religion gives to man the sense that there is a protecting power watching over him; who always acts for the best, and who will guarantee his immortality beyond the disappointments of this life. Naturally, the ordinary man in visualizing this power imagines it in the form of a loving, protecting, and wise father, and all the artists of the Western World have followed this convention. God, in this view, is a great "father-figure" who understands the needs of His sons and daughters, and He can be softened by their prayers and moved by the demonstration of their remorse. But obviously (runs this second argument) this is a sign of infantilism, it is based on wishful thinking and a kind of pathetic dependence; and above all it has nothing to do with "the facts of life." It is necessary, then, for men to grow up emotionally as they do physically, to put aside childish hopes and romantic notions which serve only as crutches to the weak, and to begin to see the universe frankly as a place with no special regard for human purposes and values. This is real maturity and it means the conscious abandonment of the illusions of religion.

The recognition that religion has originated in superstition and savagery and that it does, indeed, often use for its keenest imagery the relation of a father to his children distresses some minds, but for most it is not decisive. Because, however we interpret it, there has never been a society without religion. So persuasive a phenomenon, even if it is not scientific, even if it is more akin to fiction or to the "myth-making" faculty in man, must fulfill some deeply felt need within the human species. What this need is becomes clearer when we ask: What is the nature of religious experience?

Perhaps the most satisfactory answer to this question is that provided by William James in *The Varieties of Religious Experience* (see p. 483). James, after a painstaking examination of all kinds of religious phenomena including conversion, saintliness, and mysticism, was finally able to state the chief characteristics of the religious life. And he found it to include the following three beliefs and two psychological qualities.

1. That the visible world is part of a more spiritual universe from which it draws its chief significance
2. That union or harmonious relation with that higher universe is our true end

3. That prayer or inner communion with the spirit thereof—be that spirit "God" or "law"—is a process wherein work is really done and spiritual energy flows in and produces effects psychological or material, within the phenomenal world
4. A new zest which adds itself like a gift to life, and takes the form either of lyrical enchantment or of appeal to earnestness and heroism
5. An assurance of safety and a temper of peace, and, in relation to others, a preponderance of loving affections

James was less concerned with the definition of God than the concrete nature of religious experience, and from these beliefs and qualities we discover the essence of religion. It is first of all a sense that back of nature and human experience there is a "something More." The world reaches further than appears on the surface, and it is possible for man to somehow identify with or relate himself to that "something More." The chief consequence of a lack of religious belief is a sense of alienation from the world, a sense of not being in tune with the nature of things, an isolation and a loneliness. The chief consequence of religious belief is that the universe seems friendly to man because these are cosmic values with which he can identify. It is this which gives zest to life and which assures him of safety and of peace.

But James, true to his pragmatic beliefs, is interested less in truth than in consequences, and he sees that the religious experience puts the individual in contact with the divine in such a way that "work is really done," energy flows in, and the world of everyday life is transformed. The significance of this view of religion is that it minimizes religious knowledge. The "truths" of religion become less significant than the needs of man. And this, of course, is why religion is universal. [Religion strikes men in terms of their personal concerns.] Not general truths, but private and personal phenomena are the most real to human beings, and the most genuine questions we ask are those about our destiny in this world and after.

The distrust of general truths helps us also to find amidst the diversity of religious creeds and sects, a unity of religious experience. For religion is found in feeling, not in "belief," and, whereas when religion is expressed as doctrine, doctrines differ, the feelings and conduct of the members of the great religions are substantially the same. Religion is a state of feeling called "faith" plus a formulated creed to which faith is then added, and the significant aspect here is the "faith-state" and not the creed. Religion obviously includes a concept of God, but definition for James is less important than the life consequences of faith in His existence. "Where God is," says James, "tragedy is only provisional and partial and shipwreck and dissolution are not the absolutely final things."

THE EXISTENCE AND ATTRIBUTES OF GOD

The religious experience is primary, but still it is not the main concern of the philosophy of religion, for this latter deals less with the emotional than the rational elements in religion. It is interested in the details of religious belief, the forms of knowledge through which our religious beliefs are justified, and whether or not these beliefs are true. It asks what can be said for faith as a method of knowing, how any belief in the supernatural can be validated, and what is the relation between the natural and the supernatural worlds.

But above all, the philosophy of religion is concerned with God; what can we infer concerning His nature, what are His attributes, what are the rational arguments for and against His existence? Here again philosophy is less the experience itself than the reflection upon experience. And that means that the philosophy of religion by itself is probably powerless either to give one faith or to destroy the faith which one already has. Religious believers may use reason to support the series of beliefs which they hold upon other grounds, unbelievers may appeal to reason to substantiate their unbelief. And, therefore, the very question of whether man's reason supports or denies the beliefs which are accepted primarily on other grounds is one of the crucial questions of the philosophy of religion. St. Thomas Aquinas argued that although some of the mysteries of the divine nature are too great for the human mind to deal with, yet it would be strange indeed if truths of faith were in direct conflict with the truths of reason. Therefore he taught that in many respects faith and reason coincide. David Hume took exactly the opposite position. Our reason, he said, was meant to deal with matters of fact, with the normal course of events, with recurrent laws of nature. But with the superhuman, reason almost by definition can have nothing to do. Any account of God's miraculous works must be in conflict with our reason, for it is our reason which convinces us of the uniformity of our experience, and any miracle is a violation of the uniform and the expected.

However they disagree on the relation of faith and reason, there is one point upon which St. Thomas and Hume do agree. And that is that if God is known, it is not directly and through the senses. We have no direct sensations of the divine nature; God is not see-able, hearable, touchable. And if this is so, apart from the dogmatic statements of revelation and the sacred writings, God must be known indirectly, or, as St. Thomas says, by analogy. But, whether by revelation or by indirect inference, when we think of God, what are the qualities or attributes with which we endow Him? It is this question concerning the divine nature which is at the center of the philosophy of religion, and the answers which have been given to it indicate the vast range of the possible beliefs about God.

We have seen very early in our study (Chapter 2) that there are three modes of knowing which divide the allegiance of those interested in philosophical problems: rationalism, empiricism, intuitionism. And this distinction is very useful for the philosophy of religion because here too are three methods of knowing which, when applied to God, provide three rather different pictures of God's nature. The method of intuition has been the source of the picture of God which has been given by the great religious mystics. But it is a confused and contradictory picture because it claims somehow to give *a direct account* of God's nature, although it is forced to use a finite medium of reporting, that is, language, to report about an infinite and transcendent being. For this reason, mysticism, although it must be recognized as a position, can give no "reasonable" account of God's nature.

With rationalism and empiricism it is otherwise, and these two can almost be said to provide the great traditional (and largely opposed) pictures of God. Rationalism has given the great theistic accounts of the middle ages and the seventeenth century. Empiricism has given the more qualified accounts of the eighteenth and nineteenth centuries. It is a difference illustrated by St. Thomas and Hume on the issue of faith and reason. And, in the matter of the attributes of God, it is interestingly illustrated by the difference between the seventeenth-century rationalist Leibniz and the nineteenth-century empiricist John Stuart Mill.

For Leibniz (see p. 499) God has just those qualities which have traditionally been associated with the Christian faith. He is an absolutely perfect being who acts metaphysically and morally in the most satisfactory manner imaginable. Although we are far from understanding God's reasons, our love for Him demands that we be satisfied with all that He has done. Those who are discontented with the divine guidance of the world are no better than rebels; what God demands of us is not merely that we acquiesce in His will but truly believe in the goodness of the past and do our best to act for the future according to the presumed will of God.

It is self-evident that God does all for the best and that no injury can come to those who love Him. To know God's reasons (why, for example, He permits sin) naturally passes the ability of any finite mind. But yet we have but to examine the world to recognize His many excellences.

Leibniz was himself a great mathematician, and it was not unnatural that he should find in the author of the universe just those qualities of simplicity and economy which characterize a good mathematical demonstration. God Himself is like an excellent geometrician, a good architect who manages all for the best. He always employs the simplest and most effective methods and, since He does nothing disorderly, He has created a world whose orderliness but reflects His own divine habits. Leibniz lived before Hume and so he could not know the latter's argument against miracles as a violation of the reasonable laws of nature. But he has already produced an argument with which to refute Hume. For he would say that miracles are themselves within the order of nature. If nature is only a habit of God's which He can change at will, then, if a miracle occurs, it must always be because God has found a strong enough reason to change His habitual course of action.

Leibniz depends heavily upon what is usually called the teleological argument for God's existence; he believes that the divine wisdom is shown in the excellence of the mechanical structure of bodies and of the world. And this is the same as saying that nature can be accounted for both by efficient and by final causes. Above all God is the agent through which the human individuals may experience the world. He is the only immediate external object for us all, and He gives us objects to perceive. Long ago Plato had used a similar metaphor. To see, said Plato, demands not merely an eye and an object, but also the light which bathes the object and gives sight to the eye. And for Leibniz this is precisely the function of God. He is the cause of all our perceptions. In Him alone is our light.

Leibniz was a mathematician and a rationalist, but he was also an optimist and a more or less traditional spokesman for orthodox Christianity. John Stuart Mill was none of these. He was an empiricist, hopeful but realistic in his estimates of the world, far removed from orthodox Christianity. And his view of the powers of God as inferable from the world of nature as we know it was very Greek. This means that he sensed the limited powers of any God who had created the world.

If, says Mill (see p. 504), we inquire what sort of God exists, we shall have to say that although He must be far superior in power to even the greatest of men, yet He is neither all powerful nor everywhere existent in the universe. Rather it seems as though in creating the world, God worked under serious limitations. For matter and force do not seem to have been created by God (nor does He seem to have the power to alter them). If we simply examine what we see, without prejudice and without commitment as to the nature of God, we will be willing to assert that most natural objects have defects. Wonderful as are the mechanisms of minerals, plants, and animals, it is possible to say that they could have been more perfect. They seem to have certain capacities for a limited quantity of endurance. After that they dissolve, decay, wither away, or die.

But, above all, no one not intimidated by the force of conformity or prejudice could ever with Leibniz assert that this is the best of all possible worlds. Human misery is a fact; starvation, suffering, cruelty, terrible disease, death, and sadness are not to be denied. Where did these evils come from? Who is responsible for their existence? There is no evidence whatsoever, says Mill, that they are the product of some devil or evil intelligence. But since they are obvious evils, they must be due to some insufficiency of knowledge or some limitation of the power of God.

To say (as the Judeo-Christian tradition does say) that God is eternal, one, omnipotent, orderly, purposeful, supremely good, everywhere, and supremely intelligent is, in the face of real evil, to assert incompatible characteristics of His nature. For in an imperfect and in some ways monstrous world like ours, an omnipotent God must have some sympathy with evil, or a supremely good deity must have felt some limitation of His power. Mill sees only too well "the impossible problem of reconciling infinite benevolence and justice with infinite power in the Creator of such a world as this." And Mill continues indignantly: "The attempt to do so not only involves absolute contradiction in an intellectual point of view, but exhibits to excess the revolting spectacle of a jesuitical defense of moral enormities."

The problem of evils suggests to Mill, as it has to many before and after the nineteenth century, the necessity of recognizing either a limitation of God's power or of His goodness. And of the two he is more in sympathy with the former. Although no "moral purpose" can be derived from our observations of the world, still as feeling beings we are able to experience pleasure and even the pains which we feel have a certain preservative tendency. It does seem therefore that the Creator desired the pleasure of his creatures, and at least a limited benevolence may be attributed to Him.

The outcome of Mill's investigation of the attributes of God is thus very different from that of Leibniz's. He concludes that God is a being of great but limited powers, perhaps with unlimited intelligence, and surely with some regard for human happiness, but unfortunately without either moral purpose or a passion for justice. Any other view of the matter, intimates Mill, comes either from wishful thinking or imaginary revelation.

Leibniz's views of the attributes of God are those of a man who seems genuinely unwilling to ask any questions of so exalted a being. Mill, with critical persistence, almost with detachment, tries to hold this being accountable for those imperfections which his intelligence finds in the world. Thus these two views are representative of quite different approaches to the matter of God's nature and attributes. They do not, of course, exhaust the possibilities. God has also been thought of as existing apart from the world which he has created and separate from it (transcendent) and as the spirit of the world itself and represented in everything which happens (immanent). He has been called, on the one hand, Universal Mind or Spirit or even "The Absolute," and, on the other, the soul which informs the world which is in turn God's body (pantheism). He has been called cold, aloof and superhuman and, on the other hand, he has been called influential, responsive to man, and supremely worthful.

Although the question of the attributes of God is one of the central problems of the philosophy of religion, another which has been historically equally important is the problem of the proof of God's existence. For those with faith, the existence of God is self-evident. But it has been held (notably by St. Thomas Aquinas) that the existence of God, even insofar as it is not self-evident to us, can be demonstrated indirectly, that is, through the effects which God has created. This, of course, is not direct acquaintance with God's nature, it is only inferential knowledge by which from what we experience we infer that power which must have made the experience possible.

There have been many such attempted "proofs." But the three which have stood up best against the many opposing arguments are, respectively, the cosmological argument, the teleological argument, and the moral argument for God's existence. To each of these we will very briefly turn.

The Cosmological Argument. This is the argument which best satisfies the eternal human propensity to question origins. The world we live in gives evidence of great age. Where did it come from? All our experience shows us that effects have causes and that in the world there is a never-ending causal chain. Who first set this chain of causation in motion? Two alternative possibilities the human mind finds it impossible to accept; (1) that there was no one to start the motion and causal series of the world, and (2) that the chain of causation goes back infinitely without any beginning at all. Therefore, it is argued, God is the being who first communicated movement to the universe, who "set it going." And He is also the first efficient cause in the great chain of cause and effect. As first mover and as first cause, God's existence is necessary to account for the world as we know it.

The Teleological Argument. This is the argument which Leibniz presented, the argument from design. It satisfies the eternal human desire to account for the lawful and the orderly in existence. It caused Sir James Jeans to assert that if there is a God, He is certainly an excellent mathematician. And it caused Newton to find God in the beauties of the motions of the heavenly bodies. It is based upon the supposition that to be chaotic and disorderly is to be without purpose, and that where on the contrary there is regularity, order, coordinated activity, harmony, and progressive growth, there surely is the evidence of planning and purpose. Now the facts of nature illustrate just such a regularity, harmony, and progressiveness. The behavior of matter in motion is regular, the movements of the heavens illustrate a cosmic harmony, the course of biological evolution shows the course of a purposive development and the continual emergence of higher forms. Every form of order in nature is, therefore, an argument for the existence of a God who not only has set the world in motion, but who, by his imposition of form upon it, shows that he has made it according to his own mysterious purposes.

The Moral Argument. One form of this argument was put forward by Kant, and, as its title suggests, it is the argument which satisfies the continuing human need to find human aspirations expressed in the very structure of existence. What is the origin of our sense of right and wrong? How does it happen that our consciences tell us so absolutely what our duty is? When we ask such questions it is difficult to escape the conviction that were it not the agent of God, our conscience would not possess such absolute authority. It is then but a step to say: (1) Conscience is the voice of God in the soul of man; (2) the absolute values of goodness and rightness come from God and would not be authoritative unless they did; (3) in a world where the unjust are not immediately punished nor the good rewarded, there must be a further system of rewards and punishments over which God presides. Since we demand authority for conscience, objectivity for values, and ultimate justice for the universe, these can only be secured granted the existence of a God. Therefore if the world is to be moral, it presupposes the divine nature.

HUMANISTIC AND NATURALISTIC RELIGION

The attempts to determine the attributes of God and the efforts to demonstrate His existence all follow from the orthodox Christian conception of what religion means. And it means, at the very least, a belief in a supernatural being and an unshakable conviction of the truth of certain beliefs which are held upon the grounds of faith. But, although this is one form which religion takes, it is not the only one. Increasingly in the modern world there is an effort on the part of philosophers to turn away from supernaturalism and to construct a theory of religion that is both compatible with the conclusions of modern science and at the same time grounded in those human aspirations which make religion a necessity of man's being. Such a theory of religion minimizes the supernatural element and emphasizes the natural and the human, and its groundwork has been laid by two of the most admired American philosophers of the present century, George Santayana and John Dewey.

The great discovery of Santayana is that between "the truths of religion" and the "truths of science" there is no basic conflict. And this is the case, he maintains, because it is only metaphorically that we can speak of "truths of religion." Only science can provide us with truth in the sense of fact and where religion has gone astray is in its claim to furnish factual truth. But religion is not a substitute for science, it is a species of poetry, and, in saying this, Santayana is not trying to trivialize religion, but, on the contrary, to re-establish its dignity at that very place where its claim is exclusive and powerful, in the realm of ideal aspiration.

Religion is poetry. When it tries to be reasonable, it is a reasonableness of the imagination which it has in mind. Religious writings have the same value as any mythology or epic poetry; their "truth" consists in the interpretation of life which they provide and in the symbolic form in which they clothe the moral experience which they are trying to illuminate. And, in the same way, the ritual associated with any religion is the same in substance with drama, that is, an imaginative portrayal of an attitude toward the world. It is, therefore, inaccurate to speak of one set of sacred scriptures as true and another as false (as, for example, one speaks of one scientific theory as outmoded, and another as applicable). One religion may indeed be superior to another, but only in the sense that it provides a richer symbolism and a higher moral truth.

According to Santayana religion contains two different, but basic, elements—a moral purpose, and a mythological conception of the world. It is deeply symbolic and it uses its symbolism in the service of a certain moral attitude toward life. It is practical in the most obvious sense of that word. For it seeks to capture the mind and the imagination of its followers and to transfer to them by means of myth, parable, and story the moral lessons of experience which it has distilled. When seen in this light the conflict between science and religion will dissolve in thin air, and the hostilities between different religions will evaporate. For they will represent, not truth versus falsehood, but a series of diversified imaginations and a series of different levels of moral value.

It is clear that Santayana's conception of religion is far from that which is traditionally held; not so much in a difference of attitude as in a difference of belief. And this comes out most clearly in the difference of the understanding of God. For historic Christianity God is a being, an actual *person,* and the personality of God is the center of religious attention. But for Santayana "God" does not designate a person but an ideal. It is a symbol for what we take to be the supreme values. And our reverence for God is therefore not the expression of our submission to a physical power in the universe, but rather the expression of our acknowledgment of those moral ideals by which we intend to live.

Such a view of God obviously means a change also in attitude toward certain other customary religious concepts—prayer, piety, spirituality, and the like. If God is not a being, then prayer to God cannot be a utilitarian function in which the human individual seeks gifts from a power competent to grant them. This smacks too much of primitive magic and superstition. But prayer, in Santayana's own sense, does have a most important meaning; it is the way the human soul retires into its privacy in order to define its values, the way it reconciles itself to what must be, the way it may grow by the contemplation of its ideals. Piety and spirituality will now also have somewhat different meanings. Piety grows out of human relations and only slowly grows cosmic, that is, takes the entire universe for its object. And finally, to be spiritual does not mean to be otherworldly in the ordinary sense but to look constantly toward perfection as the guide of our life. "To be spiritual is to live in view of the ideal." And this means not any single value, but the entire constellation of values unified and harmonized in conception.

Although the outlooks of Santayana and Dewey are, in general, quite different, they are alike in their emphasis upon the natural and human characteristics of religion as opposed to the usual beliefs of supernaturalism. Neither Santayana nor Dewey find the traditional sects of orthodox Christianity satisfactory, although Santayana is somewhat more tolerant of them than Dewey. For, to Santayana, they are so many different modes of poetry. But to Dewey they express certain unfortunate elements of sectarian narrowness. The chief difference between the two men is this: whereas Santayana views religion almost as a mode of art, Dewey sees it as a social enterprise. But their similarity is greater than their difference, and it consists in their view of religion as the medium for the expression of men's highest values.

Perhaps the chief clue to Dewey's concept of religion is the distinction he makes between *having a religion* and *being religious*. Having a religion means to be a member of a group which has a traditional mode of observance and a definite creed. It is religion in its most social, most dogmatic, most fixed form. But being religious means to have a certain attitude or way of looking at the world. Being religious requires no church, no priesthood, no ritual. It can be put in another way. We have already in this chapter spoken of "the nature of religious experience," and by doing so we have taken for granted that there is a kind of experience which differs in quality from moral experience, artistic experience, or historical experience. But just this Dewey would deny. He would not talk about a kind of religious experience in which we commune with God or are given evidence of religious truths. He would talk about "the religious in experience," by which he would mean that attitude or quality which enters our experience when we deal with matters of ultimate human concern, when we raise questions about the goals toward which our life is directed, when, in short, we try to unify and harmonize the many purposes we experience into an orderly whole. Whenever there is the search for unified ideals, there exists a religious attitude.

Dewey's mistrust of organized religion in its traditional forms springs from two sources, the confinement of its dogmatism and the divisiveness of its sectarian ideals. Traditional religions have fixed systems of belief to which one must adhere. They do not provide for growing, developing beliefs. And, similarly, by defining God as both good and existing, they include goodness in the very nature of the universe without providing sufficiently for that human struggle which causes a goodness to emerge that did not previously exist. Finally no religion can truly exist in isolation. Religious ideals are shared ideals and they express "a common faith." Therefore, any form of sectarianism which restricts the access to values and emphasizes the separateness of divisions of humanity militates against the idea of the continuous human community of which we are all a part.

THE FUNCTIONS OF RELIGION

Despite the attacks upon religion made obliquely by the interpretations of anthropology and of psychology, religion seems to be a permanent ingredient in human culture. And, despite the profound differences which traditionalists and nontraditionalists find in the attributes of God, and the differences between orthodox supernaturalists on the one hand and naturalists and humanists on the other, it seems to be the case that religious experience is of many kinds and that the field is broad enough to include points of view which are extremely diverse. The same could, of course, be said of art or the field of moral experience.

If one asks, therefore, somewhat in the manner of William James (but with perhaps an even broader base of comparison), what is the chief function of religion, it might be possible to answer in this way. The function of religious experience in human life seems to be threefold: (1) It provides a picture of the universe which puts together or integrates the various strands of all human experience, (2) it celebrates in some ultimate way the ideal values or aspirations toward which all human lives are directed, and (3) it expresses the human reliance upon powers or spirits beyond its clear understanding, that is, it indicates the human dependence upon a "something More" which in some ways is always mysterious or problematical.

Expanding these in such a way that they may include matters which it has traditionally been impossible to separate from science and philosophy, one could add that religions often claim to provide for their adherents:

1. An explanation of how the universe originated
2. An explanation of what the universe aims at
3. An assertion of the values by which we ought to live
4. A guarantee of immortality
5. A unified theory of the meaning of human life
6. A glimpse of the ultimate mystery

There is perhaps one major difficulty in this account. It emphasizes the purely theoretical side of the philosophy of religion and it neglects the essence of the religious experience. And this essence, a theologian like Paul Tillich would say (in opposition to

Dewey), lies in a very special kind of *encounter with reality*, and it is to this encounter with reality that we give the name religion. That which is to be described with theoretical detachment belongs to the philosophy of religion. That in which one is deeply involved (Tillich calls it "existentially involved") is the religious or theological experience. The religious experience has two aspects. On the one hand there is God or the absolute element in the experience, a being who is transcendent and with whom our relationship is so serious as to be decisive. And, on the other hand, there is the concrete and universal "concerns" of man which lead him into this experience. Participation in a religious reality is the presupposition of any theology, for it must consider propositions which refer to the foundations of our being and upon which the meaning of our existence depends. The importance of Tillich's conception of theology is that it returns religion from theoretical speculation back to its center—the issues of human life and the universe which matter most.

But at the same time even Tillich's own emphasis upon the religious man's *encounter with reality* (or God) raises speculative issues. For, unless his meaning is purely mystical, man's encounter with reality produces not only mere feeling, but has also some cognitive content. For the religious individual to *acknowledge* God means also that he has some *knowledge* of God. And this raises all the issues of intuitive versus scientific knowing which we have encountered before.

But God and our knowledge of Him is only one term of the religious encounter as Tillich sees it. The other is the human concern which projects man—almost literally *throws* him—into the path of belief. Just as there is a need for men to interpret historical experience, so the confrontation with suffering, tragedy, and death yields a rich harvest of religious faith.

The following selections, "Religious Experience" by William James, "The Nature and Perfection of God" by G. W. Leibniz, "The Attributes of God" by J. S. Mill, and "The Method of Theology" by Paul Tillich, are all concerned with the problem of religions. Leibniz wrote during the seventeenth century, Mill and James during the nineteenth. Tillich is a contemporary. The selection from James has been included to throw light upon the religious experience, those from Leibniz and Mill to show two contrasting views of the attributes of God, one rationalist, the other empiricist. The brief selection from Tillich is meant to suggest the "existentialist" position in theology.

• William James (1842–1910)

Religious Experience [1]

William James here considers the nature of the religious experience. The selection is taken from *The Varieties of Religious Experience,* delivered by James as The Gifford Lectures at Edinburgh
in 1901-2. It is the last chapter of these lectures where, after having presented the various manifestations of the religious life, James
sums up the chief characteristics of religion. James's account follows the point of view for which he is famous, a method which uses
all the resources of science, but ends with a great sympathy for faith,
feeling, and the romantic side of life.

The material of our study of human nature is now spread before
us; and in this parting hour, set free from the duty of description,
we can draw our theoretical and practical conclusions. In my first
lecture, defending the empirical method, I foretold that whatever
conclusions we might come to could be reached by spiritual judgments only, appreciations of the significance for life of religion,
taken "on the whole." Our conclusions cannot be as sharp as dogmatic conclusions would be, but I will formulate them, when the
time comes, as sharply as I can.

Summing up in the broadest possible way the characteristics of
the religious life, as we have found them, it includes the following
beliefs:

1. That the visible world is part of a more spiritual universe
   from which it draws its chief significance;
2. That union or harmonious relation with that higher universe
   is our true end;
3. That prayer or inner communion with the spirit thereof—be
   that spirit "God" or "law"—is a process wherein work is really
   done and spiritual energy flows in and produces effects, psychological or material, within the phenomenal world.

Religion includes also the following psychological characteristics:

[1] From William James, *The Varieties of Religious Experience,* Chap. xx, with
omissions. Copyright by Paul R. Reynolds and Son.

4. A new zest which adds itself like a gift to life, and takes the form either of lyrical enchantment or of appeal to earnestness and heroism.

5. An assurance of safety and a temper of peace, and, in relation to others, a preponderance of loving affections.

. . . . .

We have next to answer, each of us for himself, the practical question: what are the dangers in this element of life? and in what proportion may it need to be restrained by other elements, to give the proper balance?

But this question suggests another one which I will answer immediately and get it out of the way, for it has more than once already vexed us. Ought it to be assumed that in all men the mixture of religion with other elements should be identical? Ought it, indeed, to be assumed that the lives of all men should show identical religious elements? In other words, is the existence of so many religious types and sects and creeds regrettable?

To these questions I answer "No" emphatically. And my reason is that I do not see how it is possible that creatures in such different positions, and with such different powers as human individuals are, should have exactly the same functions and the same duties. No two of us have identical difficulties, nor should we be expected to work out identical solutions. Each, from his peculiar angle of observation, takes in a certain sphere of fact and trouble, which each must deal with in a unique manner. One of us must soften himself, another must harden himself; one must yield a point, another must stand firm—in order the better to defend the position assigned him. If an Emerson were forced to be a Wesley, or a Moody forced to be a Whitman, the total human consciousness of the divine would suffer. The divine can mean no single quality, it must mean a group of qualities, by being champions of which in alternation, different men may all find worthy missions. Each attitude being a syllable in human nature's total message, it takes the whole of us to spell the meaning out completely. So a "god of battles" must be allowed to be the god for one kind of person, a god of peace and heaven and home, the god for another. We must frankly recognize the fact that we live in partial systems, and that parts are not interchangeable in the spiritual life. If we are peevish and jealous, destruction of the self must be an element of our religion; why need it be one if we are good and sympathetic from the outset? If we are sick souls, we require a religion of deliverance; but why think so much of deliverance, if we are healthy-

minded? Unquestionably, some men have the completer experience
and the higher vocation, here just as in the social world; but for
each man to stay in his own experience, whate'er it be, and for
others to tolerate him there, is surely best.

But, you may now ask, would not this one-sidedness be cured if
we should all espouse the science of religions as our own religion?
In answering this question I must open again the general relations
of the theoretic to the active life.

Knowledge about a thing is not the thing itself. You remember
what Al-Ghazzali told us in the Lecture on Mysticism—that to understand the causes of drunkenness, as a physician understands
them, is not to be drunk. A science might come to understand
everything about the causes and elements of religion, and might
even decide which elements were qualified, by their general harmony with other branches of knowledge, to be considered true; and
yet the best man at this science might be the man who found it
hardest to be personally devout. *Tout savoir c'est tout pardonner.*
The name of Renan would doubtless occur to many persons as an
example of the way in which breadth of knowledge may make one
only a dilettante in possibilities, and blunt the acuteness of one's
living faith. If religion be a function by which either God's cause
or man's cause is to be really advanced, then he who lives the life
of it, however narrowly, is a better servant than he who merely
knows about it, however much. Knowledge about life is one thing;
effective occupation of a place in life, with its dynamic currents
passing through your being, is another.

For this reason, the science of religions may not be an equivalent
for living religion; and if we turn to the inner difficulties of such a
science, we see that a point comes when she must drop the purely
theoretic attitude, and either let her knots remain uncut, or have
them cut by active faith. To see this, suppose that we have our
science of religions constituted as a matter of fact. Suppose that
she has assimilated all the necessary historical material and distilled
out of it as its essence the same conclusions which I myself a few
moments ago pronounced. Suppose that she agrees that religion,
wherever it is an active thing, involves a belief in ideal presences,
and a belief that in our prayerful communion with them, work is
done, and something real comes to pass. She has now to exert her
critical activity, and to decide how far, in the light of other sciences
and in that of general philosophy, such beliefs can be considered
true.

Dogmatically to decide this is an impossible task. Not only are
the other sciences and the philosophy still far from being completed,

but in their present state we find them full of conflicts. The sciences of nature know nothing of spiritual presences, and on the whole hold no practical commerce whatever with the idealistic conceptions towards which general philosophy inclines. The scientist, so-called, is, during his scientific hours at least, so materialistic that one may well say that on the whole the influence of science goes against the notion that religion should be recognized at all. And this antipathy to religion finds an echo within the very science of religion itself. The cultivator of this science has to become acquainted with so many groveling and horrible superstitions that a presumption easily arises in his mind that any belief that is religious probably is false. In the "prayerful communion" of savages with such mumbo-jumbos of deities as they acknowledge, it is hard for use to see what genuine spiritual work—even though it were work relative only to their dark savage obligations—can possibly be done.

The consequence is that the conclusions of the science of religions are as likely to be adverse as they are to be favorable to the claim that the essence of religion is true. There is a notion in the air about us that religion is probably only an anachronism, a case of "survival," an atavistic relapse into a mode of thought which humanity in its more enlightened examples has outgrown; and this notion our religious anthropologists at present do little to counteract.

This view is so widespread at the present day that I must consider it with some explicitness before I pass to my own conclusions. Let me call it the "Survival theory," for brevity's sake.

The pivot round which the religious life, as we have traced it, revolves, is the interest of the individual in his private personal destiny. Religion, in short, is a monumental chapter in the history of human egotism. The gods believed in—whether by crude savages or by men disciplined intellectually—agree with each other in recognizing personal calls. Religious thought is carried on in terms of personality, this being, in the world of religion, the one fundamental fact. To-day, quite as much as at any previous age, the religious individual tells you that the divine meets him on the basis of his personal concerns.

Science, on the other hand, has ended by utterly repudiating the the personal point of view. She catalogues her elements and records her laws indifferent as to what purpose may be shown forth by them, and constructs her theories quite careless of their bearing on human anxieties and fates. Though the scientist may individually nourish a religion, and be a theist in his irresponsible hours, the days are over when it could be said that for Science herself the heavens declare the glory of God and the firmament showeth his handiwork.

Our solar system, with its harmonies, is seen now as but one passing case of a certain sort of moving equilibrium in the heavens, realized by a local accident in an appalling wilderness of worlds where
no life can exist. In a span of time which as a cosmic interval will
count but as an hour, it will have ceased to be. The Darwinian
notion of chance production, and subsequent destruction, speedy or
deferred, applies to the largest as well as to the smallest facts. It
is impossible, in the present temper of the scientific imagination, to
find in the driftings of the cosmic atoms, whether they work on the
universal or on the particular scale, anything but a kind of aimless
weather, doing and undoing, achieving no proper history, and leaving no result. Nature has no one distinguishable ultimate tendency
with which it is possible to feel a sympathy. In the vast rhythm of
her processes, as the scientific mind now follows them, she appears
to cancel herself. The books of natural theology which satisfied the
intellects of our grandfathers seem to us quite grotesque, representing, as they did, a God who conformed the largest things of
nature to the paltriest of our private wants. The God whom science
recognizes must be a God of universal laws exclusively, a God who
does a wholesale, not a retail business. He cannot accommodate
his processes to the convenience of individuals. The bubbles on the
foam which coats a stormy sea are floating episodes, made and un-
made by the forces of the wind and water. Our private selves are
like those bubbles—epiphenomena, as Clifford, I believe, ingeniously
called them; their destinies weigh nothing and determine nothing
in the world's irremediable currents of events.

You see how natural it is, from this point of view, to treat religion as a mere survival, for religion does in fact perpetuate the
traditions of the most primeval thought. To coerce the spiritual
powers, or to square them and get them on our side, was, during
enormous tracts of time, the one great object in our dealings with
the natural world. For our ancestors, dreams, hallucinations, revelations, and cock-and-bull stories were inextricably mixed with facts.
Up to a comparatively recent date such distinctions as those between what has been verified and what is only conjectured, between
the impersonal and the personal aspects of existence, were hardly
suspected or conceived. Whatever you imagined in a lively manner, whatever you thought fit to be true, you affirmed confidently;
and whatever you affirmed, your comrades believed. Truth was
what had not yet been contradicted, most things were taken into
the mind from the point of view of their human suggestiveness, and
the attention confined itself exclusively to the aesthetic and dramatic aspects of events.

How indeed could it be otherwise? The extraordinary value, for explanation and prevision, of those mathematical and mechanical modes of conception which science uses, was a result that could not possibly have been expected in advance. Weight, movement, velocity, direction, position, what thin, pallid, uninteresting ideas! How could the richer animistic aspects of Nature, the peculiarities and oddities that make phenomena picturesquely striking or expressive, fail to have been first singled out and followed by philosophy as the more promising avenue to the knowledge of Nature's life? Well, it is still in these richer animistic and dramatic aspects that religion delights to dwell. It is the terror and beauty of phenomena, the "promise" of the dawn and of the rainbow, the "voice" of the thunder, the "gentleness" of the summer rain, the "sublimity" of the stars, and not the physical laws which these things follow, by which the religious mind still continues to be most impressed; and just as of yore, the devout man tells you that in the solitude of his room or of the fields he still feels the divine presence, that inflowings of help come in reply to his prayers, and that sacrifices to this unseen reality fill him with security and peace.

Pure anachronism! says the survival-theory;—anachronism for which deanthropomorphization of the imagination is the remedy required. The less we mix the private with the cosmic, the more we dwell in universal and impersonal terms, the truer heirs of Science we become.

In spite of the appeal which this impersonality of the scientific attitude makes to a certain magnanimity of temper, I believe it to be shallow, and I can now state my reason in comparatively few words. The reason is that, so long as we deal with the cosmic and the general, we deal only with the symbols of reality, but *as soon as we deal with private and personal phenomena as such, we deal with realities in the completest sense of the term.* I think I can easily make clear what I mean by these words.

The world of our experience consists at all times of two parts, an objective and a subjective part, of which the former may be incalculably more extensive than the latter, and yet the latter can never be omitted or suppressed. The objective part is the sum total of whatsoever at any given time we may be thinking of, the subjective part is the inner "state" in which the thinking comes to pass. What we think of may be enormous—the cosmic times and spaces, for example—whereas the inner state may be the most fugitive and paltry activity of mind. Yet the cosmic objects, so far as the experience yields them, are but ideal pictures of something whose existence we do not inwardly possess but only point at outwardly,

while the inner state is our very experience itself; its reality and
that of our experience are one. A conscious field *plus* its object as
felt or thought of *plus* an attitude towards the object *plus* the sense
of a self to whom the attitude belongs—such a concrete bit of personal experience may be a small bit, but it is a solid bit as long as
it lasts; not hollow, not a mere abstract element of experience, such
as the "object" is when taken all alone. It is a *full* fact, even though
it be an insignificant fact; it is of the *kind* to which all realities
whatsoever must belong; the motor currents of the world run
through the like of it; it is on the line connecting real events with
real events. That unsharable feeling which each one of us has of
the pinch of his individual destiny as he privately feels it rolling
out on fortune's wheel may be disparaged for its egotism, may be
sneered at as unscientific, but it is the one thing that fills up the
measure of our concrete actuality, and any would-be existent that
should lack such a feeling, or its analogue, would be a piece of
reality only half made up.

If this be true, it is absurd for science to say that the egotistic
elements of experience should be suppressed. The axis of reality
runs solely through the egotistic places—they are strung upon it like
so many beads. To describe the world with all the various feelings
of the individual pinch of destiny, all the various spiritual attitudes,
left out from the description—they being as describable as anything
else—would be something like offering a printed bill of fare as the
equivalent for a solid meal. Religion makes no such blunder. The
individual's religion may be egotistic, and those private realities
which it keeps in touch with may be narrow enough; but at any
rate it always remains infinitely less hollow and abstract, as far as
it goes, than a science which prides itself on taking no account of
anything private at all.

A bill of fare with one real raisin on it instead of the word "raisin,"
with one real egg instead of the word "egg," might be an inadequate meal, but it would at least be a commencement of reality.
The contention of the survival-theory that we ought to stick to non-
personal elements exclusively seems like saying that we ought to
be satisfied forever with reading the naked bill of fare. I think,
therefore, that however particular questions connected with our individual destinies may be answered, it is only by acknowledging
them as genuine questions, and living in the sphere of thought which
they open up, that we become profound. But to live thus is to be
religious; so I unhesitatingly repudiate the survival-theory of religion, as being founded on an egregious mistake. It does not follow, because our ancestors made so many errors of fact and mixed

them with their religion, that we should therefore leave off being religious at all. By being religious we establish ourselves in possession of ultimate reality at the only points at which reality is given us to guard. Our responsible concern is with our private destiny, after all.

You see now why I have been so individualistic throughout these lectures, and why I have seemed so bent on rehabilitating the element of feeling in religion and subordinating its intellectual part. Individuality is founded in feeling; and the recesses of feeling, the darker, blinder strata of character, are the only places in the world in which we catch real fact in the making, and directly perceive how events happen, and how work is actually done. Compared with this world of living individualized feelings, the world of generalized objects which the intellect contemplates is without solidity or life. As in stereoscopic or kinetoscopic pictures seen outside the instrument, the third dimension, the movement, the vital element, are not there. We get a beautiful picture of an express train supposed to be moving, but where in the picture, as I have heard a friend say, is the energy or the fifty miles an hour?

Let us agree, then, that Religion, occupying herself with personal destinies and keeping thus in contact with the only absolute realities which we know, must necessarily play an eternal part in human history. The next thing to decide is what she reveals about those destinies, or whether indeed she reveals anything distinct enough to be considered a general message to mankind. We have done as you see, with our preliminaries, and our final summing up can now begin.

I am well aware that after all the palpitating documents which I have quoted, and all the perspectives of emotion-inspiring institution and belief that my previous lectures have opened, the dry analysis to which I now advance may appear to many of you like an anticlimax, a tapering-off and flattening out of the subject, instead of a crescendo of interest and result. I said awhile ago that the religious attitude of Protestants appears poverty-stricken to the Catholic imagination. Still more poverty-stricken, I fear, may my final summing up of the subject appear at first to some of you. On which account I pray you now to bear this point in mind, that in the present part of it I am expressly trying to reduce religion to its lowest admissible terms, to that minimum, free from individualistic excrescences, which all religions contain as their nucleus, and on which it may be hoped that all religious persons may agree. That established, we should have a result which might be small, but would at least be solid; and on it and round it the ruddier additional be-

liefs on which the different individuals make their venture might
be grafted, and flourish as richly as you please. I shall add my own
over-belief (which will be, I confess, of a somewhat pallid kind,
as befits a critical philosopher), and you will, I hope, also add your
over-beliefs, and we shall soon be in the varied world of concrete
religious constructions once more. For the moment, let me dryly
pursue the analytic part of the task.

Both thought and feeling are determinants of conduct, and the
same conduct may be determined either by feeling or by thought.
When we survey the whole field of religion, we find a great variety
in the thoughts that have prevailed there; but the feelings on the
one hand and the conduct on the other are almost always the same,
for Stoic, Christian, and Buddhist saints are practically indistinguishable in their lives. The theories which Religion generates, being
thus variable, are secondary; and if you wish to grasp her essence,
you must look to the feelings and the conduct as being the more
constant elements. It is between these two elements that the short
circuit exists on which she carries on her principal business, while
the ideas and symbols and other institutions form loop-lines which
may be perfections and improvements, and may even some day
all be united into one harmonious system, but which are not to be
regarded as organs with an indispensable function, necessary at all
times for religious life to go on. This seems to me the first conclusion which we are entitled to draw from the phenomena we have
passed in review.

The next step is to characterize the feelings. To what psychological order do they belong?

· · · · ·

The faith-state may hold a very minimum of intellectual content.
We see examples of this in those sudden raptures of the divine
presence, or in such mystical seizures as Dr. Bucke described. It
may be a mere vague enthusiasm, half spiritual, half-vital, a courage, and a feeling that great and wondrous things are in the air.

When, however, a positive intellectual content is associated with
a faith-state, it gets invincibly stamped in upon belief, and this explains the passionate loyalty of religious persons everywhere to the
minutest details of their so widely differing creeds. Taking creeds
and faith-state together, as forming "religions," and treating these as
purely subjective phenomena, without regard to the question of
their "truth," we are obliged, on account of their extraordinary influence upon action and endurance, to class them amongst the most

important biological functions of mankind. Their stimulant and anaesthetic effect is so great that Professor Leuba, in a recent article, goes so far as to say that so long as men can *use* their God, they care very little who he is, or even whether he is at all. "The truth of the matter can be put," says Leuba, "in this way: *God is not known, he is not understood; he is used*—sometimes as meat-purveyor, sometimes as moral support, sometimes as friend, sometimes as an object of love. If he proves himself useful, the religious consciousness asks for no more than that. Does God really exist? How does he exist? What is he? are so many irrelevant questions. Not God, but life, more life, a larger, richer, more satisfying life, is, in the last analysis, the end of religion. The love of life, at any and every level of development, is the religious impulse."

At this purely subjective rating, therefore, Religion must be considered vindicated in a certain way from the attacks of her critics. It would seem that she cannot be a mere anachronism and survival, but must exert a permanent function, whether she be with or without intellectual content, and whether, if she have any, it be true or false.

We must next pass beyond the point of view of merely subjective utility, and make inquiry into the intellectual content itself.

First, is there, under all the discrepancies of the creeds, a common nucleus to which they bear their testimony unanimously?

And second, ought we to consider the testimony true?

I will take up the first question first, and answer it immediately in the affirmative. The warring gods and formulas of the various religions do indeed cancel each other, but there is a certain uniform deliverance in which religions all appear to meet. It consists of two parts:—

1. An uneasiness; and
2. Its solution.

1. The uneasiness, reduced to its simplest terms, is a sense that there is *something wrong* about us as we naturally stand.

2. The solution is a sense that *we are saved from the wrongness* by making proper connection with the higher powers.

In those more developed minds which alone we are studying, the wrongness takes a moral character, and the salvation takes a mystical tinge. I think we shall keep well within the limits of what is common to all such minds if we formulate the essence of their religious experience in terms like these:—

The individual, so far as he suffers from his wrongness and criticises it, is to that extent consciously beyond it, and in at least possible touch with something higher, if anything higher exist. Along with the wrong part there is thus a better part of him, even though it may be but a most helpless germ. With which part he should identify his real being is by no means obvious at this stage; but when stage 2 (the stage of solution or salvation) arrives, the man identifies his real being with the germinal higher part of himself; and does so in the following way. *He becomes conscious that this higher part is conterminous and continuous with a MORE of the same quality, which is operative in the universe outside of him, and which he can keep in working touch with, and in a fashion get on board of and save himself when all his lower being has gone to pieces in the wreck.*

It seems to me that all the phenomena are accurately describable in these very simple general terms. They allow for the divided self and the struggle; they involve the change of personal centre and the surrender of the lower self; they express the appearance of exteriority of the helping power and yet account for our sense of union with it; and they fully justify our feelings of security and joy. There is probably no autobiographic document, among all those which I have quoted, to which the description will not well apply. One need only add such specific details as will adapt it to various theologies and various personal temperaments, and one will then have the various experiences reconstructed in their individual forms.

So far, however, as this analysis goes, the experiences are only psychological phenomena. They possess, it is true, enormous biological worth. Spiritual strength really increases in the subject when he has them, a new life opens for him, and they seem to him a place of conflux where the forces of two universes meet; and yet this may be nothing but his subjective way of feeling things, a mood of his own fancy, in spite of the effects produced. I now turn to my second question: What is the objective "truth" of their content?

The part of the content concerning which the question of truth most pertinently arises is that "MORE of the same quality" with which our own higher self appears in the experience to come into harmonious working relation. Is such a "more" merely our own notion, or does it really exist? If so, in what shape does it exist? Does it act, as well as exist? And in what form should we conceive of that "union" with it of which religious geniuses are so convinced?

It is in answering these questions that the various theologies perform their theoretic work, and that their divergencies most come to light. They all agree that the "more" really exists; though some of them hold it to exist in the shape of a personal god or gods, while others are satisfied to conceive it as a stream of ideal tendency embedded in the eternal structure of the world. They all agree, moreover, that it acts as well as exists, and that something really is effected for the better when you throw your life into its hands. It is when they treat of the experience of "union" with it that their speculative differences appear most clearly. Over this point pantheism and theism, nature and second birth, works and grace and karma, immortality and reincarnation, rationalism and mysticism, carry on inveterate disputes.

At the end of my lecture on Philosophy I held out the notion that an impartial science of religions might sift out from the midst of their discrepancies a common body of doctrine which she might also formulate in terms to which physical science need not object. This, I said, she might adopt as her own reconciling hypothesis, and recommend it for general belief. I also said that in my last lecture I should have to try my own hand at framing such an hypothesis.

The time has now come for this attempt. Who says "hypothesis" renounces the ambition to be coercive in his arguments. The most I can do is, accordingly, to offer something that may fit the facts so easily that your scientific logic will find no plausible pretext for vetoing your impulse to welcome it as true.

The "more" as we called it, and the meaning of our "union" with it, form the nucleus of our inquiry. Into what definite description can these words be translated, and for what definite facts do they stand? It would never do for us to place ourselves offhand at the position of a particular theology, the Christian theology, for example, and proceed immediately to define the "more" as Jehovah, and the "union" as his imputation to us of the righteousness of Christ. That would be unfair to other religions, and, from our present standpoint at least, would be an over-belief.

We must begin by using less particularized terms; and, since one of the duties of the science of religions is to keep religion in connection with the rest of science, we shall do well to seek first of all a way of describing the "more," which psychologists may also recognize as real. The *subconscious self* is nowadays a well-accredited psychological entity; and I believe that in it we have exactly the mediating term required. Apart from all religious considerations, there is actually and literally more life in our total soul than we are at any time aware of. The exploration of the transmarginal field has hardly yet been seriously undertaken, but what Mr. Myers said in 1892 in his essay of the Subliminal Consciousness is as true as when it was first written: "Each of us is in reality an abiding psychical entity far more extensive than he knows—an individuality which can never express itself completely through any corporeal manifestation. The Self manifests through the organism; but there is always some part of the Self unmanifested; and always, as it seems, some power of organic expression in abeyance or reserve." Much of the content of this larger background against which our conscious being stands out in relief is insignificant. Imperfect memories, silly jingles,, inhibitive timidities, "dissolutive" phenomena of various sorts, as Myers calls them, enters into it for a large part. But in it many of the performances of genius seem also to have their origin; and in our study of conversion, of mystical experiences, and of prayer, we have seen how striking a part invasions from this region play in the religious life.

Let me then propose, as an hypothesis, that whatever it may be on its *farther* side, the "more" with which in religious experience we feel ourselves connected is on its *hither* side the subconscious continuation of our conscious life. Starting thus with a recognized psychological fact as our basis, we seem to preserve a contact with "science" which the ordinary theologian lacks. At the same time the theologian's contention that the religious man is moved by an external power is vindicated, for it is one of the peculiarities of invasions from the subconscious region to take on objective appearances, and to suggest to the Subject an external control. In the religious life the control is felt as "higher"; but since on our hypothesis it is primarily the higher faculties of our own hidden mind which are controlling, the sense of union with the power beyond us is a sense of something, not merely apparently, but literally true.

This doorway into the subject seems to me the best one for a science of religions, for it mediates between a number of different points of view. Yet it is only a doorway, and difficulties present themselves as soon as we step through it, and ask how far our transmarginal consciousness carries us if we follow it on its remoter side. Here the over-beliefs begin: here mysticism and the conversion-rapture and Vedantism and transcendental idealism bring in their monistic interpretations and tell us that the finite self rejoins the absolute self, for it was always one with God and identical with the soul of the world. Here the prophets of all the different religions come with their visions, voices, raptures, and other openings, supposed by each to authenticate his own peculiar faith.

Those of us who are not personally favored with such specific revelations must stand outside of them altogether and, for the present at least, decide that, since they corroborate incompatible theological doctrines, they neutralize one another and leave no fixed results. If we follow any one of them, or if we follow philosophical theory and embrace monistic pantheism on non-mystical grounds, we do so in the exercise of our individual freedom, and build out our religion in the way most congruous with our personal suscepti- bilities. Among these susceptibilities intellectual ones play a de- cisive part. Although the religious question is primarily a question of life, of living or not living in the higher union which opens itself to us as a gift, yet the spiritual excitement in which the gift ap- pears a real one will often fail to be aroused in an individual until certain particular intellectual beliefs or ideas which, as we say, come home to him, are touched. These ideas will thus be essential to that individual's religion;—which is as much as to say that over- beliefs in various directions are absolutely indispensable, and that we should treat them with tenderness and tolerance so long as they are not intolerant themselves. As I have elsewhere written, the most interesting and valuable things about a man are usually his over-beliefs.

Disregarding the over-beliefs, and confining ourselves to what is common and generic, we have in *the fact that the conscious person is continuous with a wider self through which saving experiences come*, a positive content of religious experience which, it seems to me, *is literally and objectively true as far as it goes.* If I now pro- ceed to state my own hypothesis about the farther limits of this extension of our personality, I shall be offering my own over-belief —though I know it will appear a sorry under-belief to some of you— for which I can only bespeak the same indulgence which in a con- verse case I should accord to yours.

The further limits of our being plunge, it seems to me, into an altogether other dimension of existence from the sensible and merely "understandable" world. Name it the mystical region, or the super- natural region, whichever you choose. So far as our ideal impulses originate in this region (and most of them do originate in it, for we find them possessing us in a way for which we cannot articulately account), we belong to it in a more intimate sense than that in which we belong to the visible world, for we belong in the most in- timate sense wherever our ideals belong. Yet the unseen region in question is not merely ideal, for it produces effects in this world. When we commune with it, work is actually done upon our finite personality, for we are turned into new men, and consequences in the way of conduct follow in the natural world upon our regenera- tive change. But that which produces effects within another real- ity must be termed a reality itself, so I feel as if we had no philo- sophic excuse for calling the unseen or mystical world unreal.

God is the natural appellation, for us Christians at least, for the supreme reality, so I will call this higher part of the universe by the name of God. We and God have business with each other; and in opening ourselves to his influence our deepest destiny is fulfilled. The universe, at those parts of it which our personal being constitutes, takes a turn genuinely for the worse or for the better in proportion as each one of us fulfills or evades God's demands. As far as this goes I probably have you with me, for I only translate into schematic language what I may call the instinctive belief of mankind: God is real since he produces real effects.

The real effects in question, so far as I have as yet admitted them, are exerted on the personal centres of energy of the various subjects, but the spontaneous faith of most of the subjects is that they embrace a wider sphere than this. Most religious men believe (or "know," if they be mystical) that not only they themselves, but the whole universe of beings to whom the God is present, are secure in his parental hands. There is a sense, a dimension, they are sure, in which we are *all* saved, in spite of the gates of hell and all adverse terrestrial appearances, God's existence is the guarantee of an ideal order that shall be permanently preserved. This world may indeed, as science assures us, some day burn up or freeze; but if it is part of his order, the old ideals are sure to be brought elsewhere to fruition, so that where God is, tragedy is only provisional and partial, and shipwreck and dissolution are not the absolutely final things. Only when this farther step of faith concerning God is taken, and remote objective consequences are predicted, does religion, as it seems to me, get wholly free from the first immediate subjective experience, and bring a *real hypothesis* into play. A good hypothesis in science must have other properties than those of the phenomenon it is immediately invoked to explain, otherwise it is not prolific enough. God, meaning only what enters into the religious man's experience of union, falls short of being an hypothesis of this more useful order. He needs to enter into wider cosmic relations in order to justify the subject's absolute confidence and peace.

That the God with whom, starting from the hither side of our own extra-marginal self, we come at its remoter margin into commerce should be the absolute world-ruler, is of course a very considerable over-belief. Over-belief as it is, though, it is an article of almost every one's religion. Most of us pretend in some way to prop it upon our philosophy, but the philosophy itself is really propped upon this faith. What is this but to say that Religion, in her fullest exercise of function, is not a mere illumination of facts already elsewhere given, not a mere passion, like love, which views things in a rosier light. It is indeed that, as we have seen abundantly. But it is something more, namely, a postulator of new *facts* as well. The world interpreted religiously is not the materialistic world over again, with an altered expression it must have, over and above the altered expression, *a natural constitution* different at some point from that which a materialistic world would have. It must be such that different events can be expected in it, different conduct must be required.

This thoroughly "pragmatic" view of religion has usually been taken as a matter of course by common men. They have interpolated divine miracles into the field of nature, they have built a heaven out beyond the grave. It is only transcendentalist metaphysicians who think that, without adding any concrete details to Nature, or subtracting any, but by simply calling it the expression of absolute spirit, you make it more divine just as it stands. I believe the pragmatic way of taking religion to be the deeper way. It gives it body as well as soul, it makes it claim, as everything real must claim, some characteristic realm of fact as its very own. What the more characteristically divine facts are, apart from the actual inflow of energy in the faith-state and the prayer-state, I know not. But the over-belief on which I am ready to make my personal venture is that they exist. The whole drift of my education goes to persuade me that the world of our present consciousness is only one out of many worlds of consciousness that exist, and that those other worlds must contain experiences which have a meaning for our life also; and that although in the main their experiences and those of this world keep discrete, yet the two become continuous at certain points, and higher energies filter in. By being faithful in my poor measure to this over-belief, I seem to myself to keep more sane and true. I *can*, of course, put myself into the sectarian scientist's attitude, and imagine vividly that the world of sensations and of scientific laws and objects may be all. But whenever I do this, I hear that inward monitor of which W. K. Clifford once wrote, whispering the word "bosh!" Humbug is humbug, even though it bear the scientific name, and the total expression of human experience, as I view it objectively, invincibly urges me beyond the narrow "scientific" bounds. Assuredly, the real world is of a different temperament—more intricately built than physical science allows. So my objective and my subjective conscience both hold me to the over-belief which I express. Who knows whether the faithfulness of individuals here below to their own poor over-beliefs may not actually help God in turn to be more effectively faithful to his own greater tasks?

• G. W. Leibniz (1646–1716)

The Nature and Perfection of God [2]

G. W. Leibniz the great seventeenth-century mathematician and philosopher was born in Leipzig and educated at the University of Jena. He lived most of his life as court councilor and librarian in Hannover. Most of his philosophical writings (he wrote in Latin, French, German) consisted of short essays. The most famous are *The New System of Nature, New Essays Concerning Human Understanding, The Monadology,* and *Discourse on Metaphysics,* from which the following selection is taken. In this work Leibniz presents his view of the perfection and orderliness of the divine nature and brings his mathematical interests into the service of an optimistic view of God's world.

Concerning the divine perfection and that God does everything in the most desirable way. The notion of God which is the most common and meaningful is satisfactorily experienced in these words: *God is an absolutely perfect being.* But the consequences of this are not often enough considered; for example, one should note that there are many different kinds of perfection all of which God possesses, and each one pertains to him in the highest possible degree.

We must also know what perfection is and here is a sure sign that one does; to know that those forms or natures which are not susceptible of it to the highest degree (as for example the nature of numbers or of figures) are not really perfect. This is because the greatest of all numbers (which is the sum of all numbers) and also the greatest of all figures implies contradiction while the greatest knowledge and omnipotence contain no impossibility. In consequence power and knowledge can be perfect and insofar as they pertain to God, they have no limits.

Whence it follows that God who possesses supreme and infinite wisdom acts in the most perfect manner not only in a metaphysical sense but also morally speaking, and it can be said with respect to ourselves that the more we are enlightened and informed about the

[2] Selections from G. W. Leibniz, *A Discourse on Metaphysics* (1678), trans. by the author.

works of God, the more we will be disposed to find them excellent and conforming entirely to what we might have wished.

That the love of God demands from us complete satisfaction with and acquiescence in that which he has done. The general recognition of this great truth that God always acts in the most perfect and the most desirable manner possible is, in my opinion the foundation of the love which we owe to God in all things; for, one who loves seeks his satisfaction in the happiness or perfection of the object loved and in his actions. And I believe that it is difficult to love God truly if one having the power to change himself, is not of the disposition to desire that which God desires. In fact those who are not satisfied with what God does, seem to me like discontented subjects whose intentions are not very different from those of rebels.

I hold therefore that following these principles, to act in accordance with the love of God, it is not enough to force oneself to have patience, but we must be truly satisfied with all that happens to us by his will. I am referring to what has happened in the past. For, as for the future, one ought not to be resigned nor to wait ridiculously with arms folded for what God will do according to the sophism which the ancients called "the lazy reason." But it is necessary to act according to the presumed will of God so far as we are able to judge it and trying with all our might to contribute to the general welfare and particularly to the armantation and the perfection of that which teaches us or of that which is near us and so to speak at hand. For, while the future may perhaps show that God has not wanted our good intention to have its way, it does not follow that he has not wished us to act as we have done. On the contrary since he is the best of all masters, he always demands merely the right intention, and it is for him to know the hour and the place proper to make good designs succeed.

In what the principles of perfection of the divine guidance consist and that the simplicity of the means is equal to the richness of the effort. It suffices then to have this confidence in God, that he does all for the best and that no injury can come to those who love him: but to know in particular the reasons which have caused him to choose this order of the universe, to permit sin, to dispense his saving grace in a certain manner, all this passes the ability of a finite mind and particularly when such a mind has not yet arrived at the joy of a vision of God.

Yet one can make certain general remarks concerning the course of providence in the government of things. One can say, therefore, that he who acts perfectly is like an excellent geometrician who knows how to find the best constructions for a problem; like a good architect who manages his site and the funds destined for the building in the most advantageous manner, allowing nothing shocking or what might detract from the beauty of which it is capable; like a good head of the household who employs his property so that there may be nothing uncultivated or sterile; or like a clever machinist who makes his product by the most facile means possible; and like an intelligent author who captures the most reality in the least amount of space. Now, the most perfect of all beings (who occupy the least space and interfere with one another least) are just those spirits whose perfections are virtues. That is why it cannot be doubted that the felicity of such spirits is the principal aim of God and that he executed this purpose as far as the general harmony permits. Of which more later.

Reference to the simplicity of God's ways always concerns the methods which he employs, just as on the contrary when the reference is to variety, richness and abundance, it concerns the ends or effects. And the one ought to be equal to the other as the cost of a building ought to be equal to the grandeur and beauty that one expects of it. It is true that nothing costs God anything (just as there is no cost for a philosopher who makes hypotheses for the construction of his imaginary world) because God has only to make decrees in order to bring an actual world into being; but, in matters of wisdom the decrees or hypotheses equal the expenses in the degree that they are more mutually independent; for the reason wishes to avoid multiplicity of hypotheses or principles much as the simplest system is always preferred in Astronomy.

That God does nothing that is not orderly and that it is not possible even to imagine events which are not orderly. The desires or acts of God are commonly divided into ordinary and extra-ordinary. But it is good to remember that God does nothing disorderly. Thus, that which passes for extraordinary is so only with respect to a particular order established among created things. For as regards the universal order; everything conforms to it. This is so true that not only does nothing occur in the world which is absolutely irregular, but it is not even possible to imagine such an occurrence. For, let us suppose for example that one puts down on a piece of paper a number of dots at random as do those who exercise the ridiculous art of Geomancy. I say that it is possible to find a geometric line whose notion shall be constant and uniform, following a certain rule such that the line shall pass through all the dots and in the same order as the hand has marked them down.

And if someone should trace continuously a line sometimes straight sometimes circular or of any other nature, it is possible to find a notion or rule or equation common to all the points of this line according to which the changes of direction must occur. There is for example, no face whose contour does not constitute part of a geometric line and which cannot be traced entirely by a certain regular movement. But when the formula is very complicated, that which conforms to it is called irregular.

Thus one can say that in whatever manner God might have created the world it would in any case have been regular and orderly. But God has chosen the most perfect, that is to say, the one at the same time the most simple in hypothesis and the most rich in phenomena as would be a geometric line whose construction was easy and whose properties and effects were remarkable and of great significance. I use these comparisons to draw a certain imperfect resemblance to the divine wisdom and to say that which may at least bring our minds to conceive in some fashion that which could not be otherwise stated. But I do not pretend thus to explain the great mystery upon which the whole universe depends.

That miracles conform to the general order although they go against subordinate rules and concerning that which God wishes or permits by general or particular wishes. Now since nothing can be done which is not orderly, we may say that miracles are also within the order of natural operations that one terms natural because they conform to certain subordinate rules which we call the nature of things. For it can be said that this nature is only a custom of God's which he can change for a stronger reason than the one which moved him to use these rules. As for general or particular intentions, according as one sees it, it may be said that all is in accordance with his most general intention, which conforms best to the most perfect order he has chosen. But one can also say that he has particular intentions which are exceptions to the subordinate rules mentioned above, for the most general of God's laws (which rules the entire course of the universe) is without exception.

One can also say that God wills everything which is an object of his particular intention, but as for the objects of his general intentions, such as the actions of creatures, particularly those who are reasonable with whom God wishes to cooperate, a distinction is necessary; for if the action is good in itself, we may say that God wishes it and at times commands it even though it does not take place, but if it is bad in itself and becomes good only by accident and particularly after punishment and reward have corrected its evil and rewarded the evil with interest in such a way that more perfection results in all the consequences than if the ill had not occurred, then one can say that God permits the evil and not that he desired it although he has cooperated by means of the laws of nature which he has established and because from them he knows how to bring about the greatest good result.

If mechanical laws depended merely upon geometry alone without metaphysical influences, the phenomena would be quite different from what they are. Now, since the wisdom of God has always been recognized in the detail of the mechanical structure of certain bodies, it should also be shown in the general economy of the world and in the constitution of laws of nature. So true is this that one notices the plans of this wisdom even in the laws of motion in general. For, if bodies were only extended masses and motion were only change of place and if everything could be deduced by geometric necessity from merely these two definitions, it would follow, as I have shown elsewhere that the smallest body on contact with a very large one at rest would communicate to it its own velocity without losing any of its own. Also a quantity of other such rules wholly contrary to the formation of a system would have to be admitted. But the decree of the divine wisdom in preserving always the same force and the same direction has provided such a system. I find even that many of the effects of nature can be doubly accounted for, that is both by a consideration of efficient causes and also by a consideration of final causes. As example is God's decree of always producing the effect in the easiest and most determinate way as I have shown elsewhere in giving the reason for the laws of catoptrics and dioptrics of which more later.

God alone is the immediate object of our perceptions which exist outside of us, and in him only is our light. From the point of view of metaphysical truth there is no external cause which acts upon us except God and he alone affects us directly by virtue of our continual dependence upon him. It follows from this that there is no other external object which affects our soul and causes our perceptions. So we have in our soul ideas of everything only because of the continual action of God upon us, that is, because every effect expresses its cause and therefore the essence of our soul is a certain imitation or image of divine essence, thought and will and everything therein contained. One can say, then, that God is the only immediate external object for us and that we see all things through him. For example, when we see the sun and the stars, it is God who gives us and preserves in us these ideas and who causes us to think by his concurrence along those certain lines according to the laws which he has established. God is the sun and the light of souls. . . .

• John Stuart Mill (1806–73)

The Attributes of God[3]

J. S. Mill here states a view of God's attributes very different from Leibniz's. Mill was not raised in any religious belief, but neither was he hostile to the religious point of view. His attitude here is to take the standpoint of "natural religion," that is, to examine religion reasonably and without depending upon any revelation, in order to see what kind of attributes God has as suggested by nature itself.

It is next to be considered, given the indications of a Deity, what *sort* of a Deity do they point to? What attributes are we warranted, by the evidence which Nature affords of a creative mind, in assigning to that mind?

It needs no showing that the power if not the intelligence, must be so far superior to that of Man, as to surpass all human estimate. But from this to Omnipotence and Omniscience there is a wide interval. And the distinction is of immense practical importance.

It is not too much to say that every indication of Design in the Kosmos is so much evidence against the Omnipotence of the Designer. For what is meant by Design? Contrivance: the adaptation of means to an end. But the necessity for contrivance—the need of employing means—is a consequence of the limitation of power. Who would have recourse to means if to attain his end his mere word was sufficient? The very idea of means implies that the means have an efficacy which the direct action of the being who employs them has not. Otherwise they are not means, but an in-

[3] From J. S. Mill, *Theism* (1874), Pt. II.

cumbrance. A man does not use machinery to move his arms. If he did, it could only be when paralysis had deprived him of the power of moving them by volition. But if the employment of contrivance is in itself a sign of limited power, how much more so is the careful and skilful choice of contrivances? Can any wisdom be shown in the selection of means, when the means have no efficacy but what is given them by the will of him who employs them, and when his will could have bestowed the same efficacy on any other means? Wisdom and contrivance are shown in overcoming difficulties, and there is no room for them in a Being for whom no difficulties exist. The evidences, therefore, of Natural Theology distinctly imply that the author of the Kosmos worked under limitations; that he was obliged to adapt himself to conditions independent of his will, and to attain his ends by such arrangements as those conditions admitted of.

And this hypothesis agrees with what we have seen to be the tendency of the evidences in another respect. We found that the appearances in Nature point indeed to an origin of the Kosmos, or order in Nature, and indicate that origin to be Design but do not point to any commencement, still less creation of the two great elements of the Universe, the passive element and the active element, Matter and Force. There is in Nature no reason whatever to suppose that either Matter or Force, or any of their properties, were made by the Being who was the author of the collocations by which the world is adapted to what we consider as its purposes; or that he has power to alter any of those properties. It is only when we consent to entertain this negative supposition that there arises a need for wisdom and contrivance in the order of the universe. The Deity had on this hypothesis to work out his ends by combining materials of a given nature and properties. Out of these materials he had to construct a world in which his designs should be carried into effect through given properties of Matter and Force, working together and fitting into one another. This did require skill and contrivance, and the means by which it is effected are often such as justly excite our wonder and admiration: but exactly because it requires wisdom, it implies limitation of power, or rather the two phrases express different sides of the same fact.

If it be said, that an Omnipotent Creator, though under no necessity of employing contrivances such as man must use, thought fit to do so in order to leave traces by which man might recognize his creative hand, the answer is that this equally supposes a limit to his omnipotence. For if it was his will that men should know that they themselves and the world are his work, he, being omnipotent, had only to will that they should be aware of it. Ingenious men have sought for reasons why God might choose to leave his existence so far a matter of doubt that men should not be under an absolute necessity of knowing it, as they are of knowing that three and two make five. These imagined reasons are very unfortunate specimens of casuistry; but even did we admit their validity, they are of no avail on the supposition of omnipotence, since if it did not please God to implant in man a complete conviction of his existence, nothing hindered him from making the conviction fall short of completeness by any margin he chose to leave. It is usual to dispose of arguments of this description by the easy answer, that we do not know what wise reasons the Omniscient may have had for leaving undone things which he had the power to do. It is not perceived that this plea itself implies a limit to Omnipotence. When a thing is obviously good and obviously in accordance with what all the evidences of creation imply to have been the Creator's design, and we say we do not know what good reason he may have had for not doing it, we mean that we do not know to what other, still better object—to what object still more completely in the line of his purposes, he may have seen fit to postpone it. But the necessity of postponing one thing to another belongs only to limited power. Omnipotence could have made the objects compatible. Omnipotence does not need to weight one consideration against another. If the Creator, like a human ruler, had to adapt himself to a set of conditions which he did not make, it is as unphilosophical as presumptuous in us to call him to account for any imperfections in his work; to complain that he left anything in it contrary to what, if the indications of design prove anything, he must have intended. He must at least know more than we know, and we cannot judge what greater good would have had to be sacrificed, or what greater evil incurred, if he had decided to remove this particular blot. Not so if he be omnipotent. If he be that, he must himself have willed that the two desirable objects should be incompatible; he must himself have willed that the obstacle to his supposed design should be insuperable. It cannot therefore *be* his design. It will not do to say that it was, but that he had other designs which interfered with it; for no one purpose imposes necessary limitations on another in the case of a Being not restricted by conditions of possibility.

Omnipotence, therefore, cannot be predicated of the Creator on grounds of natural theology. The fundamental principles of natural religion as deduced from the facts of the universe, negative his omnipotence. They do not, in the same manner, exclude omniscience: if we suppose limitation of power, there is nothing to contradict the supposition of perfect knowledge and absolute wisdom. But neither is there anything to prove it. The knowledge of the powers and properties of things necessary for planning and executing the arrangements of the Kosmos, is no doubt as much in excess of human knowledge as the power implied in creation is in excess of human power. And the skill, the subtlety of contrivance, the ingenuity as it would be called in the case of a human work, is often marvellous. But nothing obliges us to suppose that either the knowledge or the skill is infinite. We are not even compelled to suppose that the contrivances were always the best possible. If we venture to judge them as we judge the works of human artificers, we find abundant defects. The human body, for example, is one of the most striking instances of artful and ingenious contrivance which nature offers, but we may well ask whether so complicated a machine could not have been made to last longer, and not to get so easily and frequently out of order. We may ask why the human race should have been so constituted as to grovel in wretchedness and degradation for countless ages before a small portion of it was enabled to lift itself into the very imperfect state of intelligence, goodness and happiness which we enjoy. The divine power may not have been equal to doing more; the obstacles to a better arrangement of things may have been insuperable. But it is also possible that they were not. The skill of the Demiourgos was sufficient to produce what we see; but we cannot tell that this skill reached the extreme limit of perfection compatible with the material it employed and the forces it had to work with. I know not how we can even satisfy ourselves on grounds of natural theology, that the Creator foresees all the future; that he foreknows all the effects that will issue from his own contrivances. There may be great wisdom without the power of foreseeing and calculating everything: and human workmanship teaches us the possibility that the workman's knowledge of the properties of the things he works on may enable him to make arrangements admirably fitted to produce a given result, while he may have very little power of foreseeing the agencies of another kind which may modify or counteract the operation of the machinery he has made. Perhaps a knowledge of the laws of nature on which organic life depends, not much more perfect than the knowledge which man even now possesses of some other natural laws, would enable man, if he had the same power over the materials and the forces concerned which he has over some of those of inanimate nature, to create organized beings not less wonderful nor less adapted to their conditions of existence than those in Nature.

Assuming then that while we confine ourselves to Natural Religion we must rest content with a Creator less than Almighty; the question presents itself, of what nature is the limitation of his power? Does the obstacle at which the power of the Creator stops, which says to it: Thus far shalt thou go and no further, lie in the power of other Intelligent Beings; or in the insufficiency and refractoriness of the materials of the universe; or must we resign ourselves to admitting the hypothesis that the author of the Kosmos, though wise and knowing, was not all-wise and all-knowing, and may not always have done the best that was possible under the conditions of the problem?

The first of these suppositions has until a very recent period been and in many quarters still is, the prevalent theory even of Christianity. Though attributing, and in a certain sense sincerely, omnipotence to the Creator, the received religion represents him as for some inscrutable reason tolerating the perpetual counteraction of his purposes by the will of another Being of opposite character and of great though inferior power, the Devil. The only difference on this matter between popular Christianity and the religion of Ormuzd and Ahriman, is that the former pays its good Creator the bad compliment of having been the maker of the Devil and of being at all times able to crush and annihilate him and his evil deeds and counsels, which nevertheless he does not do. But, as I have already remarked, all forms of polytheism, and this among the rest, are with difficulty reconcilable with an universe governed by general laws. Obedience to law is the note of a settled government, and not of a conflict always going on. When powers are at war with one another for the rule of the world, the boundary between them is not fixed but constantly fluctuating. This may seem to be the case on our planet as between the powers of good and evil when we look only at the results; but when we consider the inner springs, we find that both the good and the evil take place in the common course of nature, by virtue of the same general laws originally impressed—the same machinery turning out now good, now evil things, and oftener still, the two combined. The division of power is only apparently variable, but really so regular that, were we speaking of human potentates, we should declare without hesitation that the share of each must have been fixed by previous consent. Upon that supposition indeed, the result of the combination of antagonist forces might be much the same as on that of a single creator with divided purposes.

But when we come to consider, not what hypothesis may be conceived, and possibly reconciled with known facts, but what supposition is pointed to by the evidences of natural religion; the case is different. The indications of design point strongly in one direction, the preservation of the creatures in whose structure the indications are found. Along with the preserving agencies there are destroying agencies, which we might be tempted to ascribe to the will of a different Creator; but there are rarely appearances of the recondite contrivance of means of destruction, except when the destruction of one creature is the means of preservation to others. Nor can it be supposed that the preserving agencies are wielded by one Being, the destroying agencies by another. The destroying agencies are a necessary part of the preserving agencies: the chemical compositions by which life is carried on could not take place without a parallel series of decompositions. The great agent of decay in both organic and inorganic substances is oxidation, and it is only by oxidation that life is continued for even the length of a minute. The imperfections in the attainment of the purposes which the appearances indicate, have not the air of having been designed. They are like the unintended results of accidents insufficiently guarded against, or of a little excess or deficiency in the quantity of some of the agencies by which the good purpose is carried on, or else they are consequences of the wearing out of a machinery not made to last for ever: they point either to shortcomings in the workmanship as regards its intended purpose, or to external forces not under the control of the workman, but which forces bear no mark of being wielded and aimed by any other and rival Intelligence.

We may conclude, then, that there is no ground in Natural Theology for attributing intelligence or personality to the obstacles which partially thwart what seem the purposes of the Creator. The limitation of his power more probably results either from the qualities of the material—the substances and forces of which the universe is composed not admitting of any arrangements by which his purposes could be more completely fulfilled; or else, the purposes might have been more fully attained, but the Creator did not know how to do it; creative skill, wonderful as it is, was not sufficiently perfect to accomplish his purposes more thoroughly.

We now pass to the moral attributes of the Deity, so far as indicated in the Creation; or (stating the problem in the broadest manner) to the question, what indications Nature gives of the purposes of its author. This question bears a very different aspect to us from what it bears to those teachers of Natural Theology who are incumbered with the necessity of admitting the omnipotence of the Creator. We have not to attempt the impossible problem of reconciling infinite benevolence and justice with infinite power in the Creator of such a world as this. The attempt to do so not only involves absolute contradiction in an intellectual point of view but exhibits to excess the revolting spectacle of a jesuitical defence of moral enormities.

On this topic I need not add to the illustrations given of this portion of the subject in my Essay on Nature. At the stage which our argument has reached there is none of this moral perplexity. Grant that creative power was limited by conditions the nature and extent of which are wholly unknown to us, and the goodness and justice of the Creator may be all that the most pious believe; and all in the work that conflicts with those moral attributes may be the fault of the conditions which left to the Creator only a choice of evils.

It is, however, one question whether any given conclusion is consistent with known facts, and another whether there is evidence to prove it; and if we have no means for judging of the design but from the work actually produced, it is a somewhat hazardous speculation to suppose that the work designed was of a different quality from the result realized. Still, though the ground is unsafe we may, with due caution, journey a certain distance on it. Some parts of the order of nature give much more indication of contrivance than others; many, it is not too much to say, give no sign of it at all. The signs of contrivance are most conspicuous in the structure and processes of vegetable and animal life. But for these, it is probable that the appearances in nature would never have seemed to the thinking part of mankind to afford any proofs of a God. But when a God has been inferred from the organization of living beings, other parts of Nature, such as the structure of the solar system, seemed to afford evidences, more or less strong, in confirmation of the belief: granting, then, a design in Nature, we can best hope to be enlightened as to what that design was, by examining it in the parts of Nature in which its traces are the most conspicuous.

To what purpose, then, do the expedients in the construction of animals and vegetables, which excite the admiration of naturalists, appear to tend? There is no blinking the fact that they tend principally to no more exalted object than to make the structure remain in life and in working order for a certain time: the individual for a few years, the species or race for a longer but still a limited period. And the similar though less conspicuous marks of creation which are recognized in inorganic Nature, are generally of the same character. The adaptations, for instance, which appear in the solar system consist in placing it under conditions which enable the mutual action of its parts to maintain instead of destroying its stability, and even that only for a time, vast indeed if measured against our span of animated existence, but which can be perceived even by us to be limited: for even the feeble means which we possess of exploring the past, are believed by those who have examined the subject by the most recent lights, to yield evidence that the solar system was once a vast sphere of nebula or vapour, and is going through a process which in the course of ages will reduce it to a single and not very large mass of solid matter frozen up with more than Arctic cold. If the machinery of the system is adapted to keep itself at work only for a time; still less perfect is the adaptation of it for the abode of living beings since it is only adapted to them during the relatively short portion of its total duration which intervenes between the time when each planet was too hot and the time when it became or will become too cold to admit life under the only conditions in which we have experience of its possibility. Or we should perhaps reverse the statement, and say that organization and life are only adapted to the conditions of the solar system during a relatively short portion of the system's existence.

The greater part, therefore, of the design of which there is indication in Nature, however wonderful its mechanism, is no evidence of any moral attributes, because the end to which it is directed, and its adaptation to which end is the evidence of its being directed to an end at all, is not a moral end: it is not the good of any sentient creature, it is but the qualified permanence, for a limited period, of the work itself, whether animate or inanimate. The only inference that can be drawn from most of it, respecting the character of the Creator, is that he does not wish his works to perish as soon as created; he wills them to have a certain duration. From this alone nothing can be justly inferred as to the manner in which he is affected towards his animate or rational creatures.

After deduction of the great number of adaptations which have no apparent object but to keep the machine going, there remain a certain number of provisions for giving pleasure to living beings, and a certain number of provisions for giving them pain. There is no positive certainty that the whole of these ought not to take their place among the contrivances for keeping the creature or its species in existence; for both the pleasures and the pains have a conservative tendency; the pleasures being generally so disposed as to attract to the things which maintain individual or collective existence, the pains so as to deter from such as would destroy it.

When all these things are considered it is evident that a vast deduction must be made from the evidences of a Creator before they can be counted as evidences of a benevolent purpose: so vast indeed that some may doubt whether after such a deduction there remains any balance. Yet endeavouring to look at the question without partiality or prejudice and without allowing wishes to have any influence over judgment, it does appear that granting the existence of design, there is a preponderance of evidence that the Creator desired the pleasure of his creatures. This is indicated by the fact that pleasure of one description or another is afforded by almost everything, the mere play of the faculties, physical and mental, being a never-ending source of pleasure, and even painful things giving pleasure by the satisfaction of curiosity and the agreeable sense of acquiring knowledge; and also that pleasure, when experienced, seems to result from the normal working of the machinery, while pain usually arises from some external interference with it, and resembles in each particular case the result of an accident. Even in cases when pain results, like pleasure, from the machinery itself, the appearances do not indicate that contrivance was brought into play purposely to produce pain: what is indicated is rather a clumsiness in the contrivance employed for some other purpose. The author of the machinery is no doubt accountable for having made it susceptible of pain; but this may have been a necessary condition of its susceptibility to pleasure; a supposition which avails nothing on the theory of an Omnipotent Creator but is an extremely probable one in the case of a contriver working under the limitation of inexorable laws and indestructible properties of matter. The susceptibility being conceded as a thing which did enter into design, the pain itself usually seems like a thing undesigned; a causal result of the collision of the organism with some outward force to which it was not intended to be exposed, and which, in many cases, provision is even made to hinder it from being exposed to. There is, therefore, much appearance that pleasure is agreeable to the Creator, while there is very little if any appearance that pain is so: and there is a certain amount of justification for inferring, on grounds of Natural Theology alone, that benevolence is one of the attributes of the Creator. But to jump from this to the inference that his sole or chief purposes are those of benevolence, and that the single end and aim of Creation was the happiness of his creatures, is not only not justified by any evidence but is a conclusion in opposition to such evidence as we have. If the motive of the Deity for creating sentient beings was the happiness of the beings he created, his purpose in our corner of the universe at least, must be pronounced, taking past ages and all countries and races into account, to have been thus far an ignominious failure; and if God had no purpose but our happiness and that of other living creatures it is not credible that he would have called them into existence with the prospect of being so completely baffled. If man had not the power by the exercise of his own energies for the improvement both of himself and of his outward circumstances, to do for himself and other creatures vastly more than God had in the first instance done, the Being who called him into existence would deserve something very different from thanks at his hands. Of course it may be said that this very capacity of improving himself and the world was given to him by God, and that the change which he will be thereby enabled ultimately to effect in human existence will be worth purchasing by the sufferings and wasted lives of entire geological periods. This may be so; but to suppose that God could not have given him these blessings at a less frightful cost, is to make a very strange supposition concerning the Deity. It is to suppose that God could not, in the first instance, create anything better than a Bosjesman or an Andaman islander, or something still lower; and yet was able to endow the Bosjesman or the Andaman islander with the power of raising himself into a Newton or a Fenelon. We certainly do not know the nature of the barriers which limit the divine omnipotence; but it is a very odd notion of them that they enable the Deity to confer on an almost bestial creature the power of producing by a succession of efforts what God himself had no other means of creating.

Such are the indications of Natural Religion in respect to the divine benevolence. If we look for any other of the moral attributes which a certain class of philosophers are accustomed to distinguish from benevolence, as for example Justice, we find a total blank. There is no evidence whatever in Nature for divine justice, whatever standard of justice our ethical opinions may lead us to recognize. There is no shadow of justice in the general arrangements of Nature; and what imperfect realization it obtains in any human society (a most imperfect realization as yet) is the work of man himself, struggling upwards against immense natural difficulties, into civilization, and making to himself a second nature, far better and more unselfish than he was created with. But on this point enough has been said in another Essay, already referred to, on Nature.

These, then, are the net results of Natural Theology on the question of the divine attributes. A Being of great but limited power, how or by what limited we cannot even conjecture; of great, and perhaps unlimited intelligence, but perhaps, also, more narrowly limited than his power: who desires, and pays some regard to, the happiness of his creatures, but who seems to have other motives of action which he cares more for, and who can hardly be supposed to have created the universe for that purpose alone. Such is the Deity whom Natural Religion points to; and any idea of God more captivating than this comes only from human wishes, or from the teaching of either real or imaginary Revelation.

• Paul Tillich (1886–)

The Method of Theology[4]

Paul Tillich was educated at Berlin, Tübingen, and Breslau. He taught in German universities before coming to the United States in 1933. Here he has taught at Union Theological Seminary and later at Harvard. Tillich is one of the most famous contemporary theologians, orthodox in temperament, who has applied the principles of "existential philosophy" to the problems of theology. Works of his are *The Religious Situation, Systematic Theology,* and *The Interpretation of History.*

We encounter reality—or reality imposes itself upon us—sometimes in a more complex way, sometimes in definite and distinguishable elements and functions. Whenever we encounter reality in the one or the other way, it challenges our cognitive power and brings it into action. The way in which the cognitive power works is dependent on three factors: its own structure, the structure of the reality it encounters, and the relation of the two structures. In a methodical approach these three factors are noticed, analyzed, and evaluated. But the *prius* of all this is the encounter itself; and nothing is more destructive for knowledge than the establishment of methods which, by their very nature, prevent the actual encounter or prejudice its interpretation. (It is my opinion that the term "encounter" is more adequate for our pre-theoretical relation to reality than the term "experience," which has lost so much of its specific meaning that it needs to be "saved," namely, restricted to a theoretically interpreted encounter.)

4 From Paul Tillich, "The Problem of Theological Method," *The Journal of Religion,* Jan. 1947. By permission of The University of Chicago Press.

The presupposition of theology is that there is a special encounter with reality—or a special way in which reality imposes itself on us—which is ordinarily called "religious." And it is the presupposition of this paper that "having a religious encounter with reality" means "being ultimately concerned about reality."

THEOLOGY AND PHILOSOPHY OF RELIGION

The ultimate concern or the religious encounter with reality can be considered in two ways. It can be looked at as an event beside other events, to be observed and described in theoretical detachment; or it can be understood as an event in which he who considers it is "existentially" involved. In the first case the philosopher of religion is at work, in the second the theologian speaks. The philosopher of religion notices the ultimate concern, which he cannot help finding in the history of religion as a quality of practically all representative personalities, symbols, and activities that are called "religious." But in his dealing with this characteristic of religion he himself is only theoretically, but not existentially, concerned. The religious concern is not his concern in so far as he is a philosopher of religion. He points to it, he explains it, but his work is not an expression of the religious encounter with reality. This is different in the theologian. He applies his ultimate concern to everything, as an *ultimate* concern demands—even to his theoretical interpretation of the religious encounter. For the theologian the interpretation of the ultimate concern is itself a matter of ultimate concern, a *religious* work.

But this distinction is not unambiguous. There is an element in every philosophy (not only in every philosopher) which is "existential," i.e., which has the character of an ultimate decision about the meaning of reality. The less technical and the more creative a philosophy is, the more it shows, at least implicitly, an ultimate concern. No creative philosophy can escape its religious background. This is the reason for the tremendous influence that philosophy has had not only on theology but also on the history of religion and vice versa; for, as the philosopher cannot escape his theological background, so the theologian cannot escape his philosophical tool. Those who try to do so deceive themselves: their language, which is shaped through philosophy, betrays them (as even Barth has admitted).

Nevertheless, the distinction between theology and philosophy of religion is valid and cannot be obliterated without dangerous consequences. It is very unfortunate that the so-called "Continental" theology has brought into disregard the function of an independent philosophy of religion, thus creating an intolerable theological absolutism; and it is equally unfortunate that American (nonfundamentalistic) theology was not able to protect itself from being dissolved into a general philosophy of religion, thus producing a self-destructive relativism.

Theology is the existential and, at the same time, methodical interpretation of an ultimate concern. The interpretation of an ultimate concern is "existential" if it is done in the situation of concern. The interpretation of an ultimate concern is methodical if it relates the concern rationally to the whole of experience. Theology, literally and historically, unites these two elements. Theological propositions, therefore, are propositions which deal with an object in so far as it is related to an ultimate concern. No object is excluded from theology if this criterion is applied, not even a piece of stone; and no object is in itself a matter of theology, not even God as an object of inference. This makes theology absolutely universal, on the one hand, and absolutely definite, on the other hand. Theology has to deal with everything, but only under the theological criterion, the ultimate concern.

The concept "ultimate concern" is itself the result of a theological procedure. It expresses two sides of the religious experience: (1) The one side is the absolute or unconditional or ultimate element in religious experience. Every religious relation, attitude, symbol, and action is unconditionally *serious; decisive* in an absolute sense; *transcending* any preliminary, transitory, and dependent value. The whole history of religion confirms this side of religious experience. Where there is a living religion, it makes an absolute claim; it claims the "whole heart"; it does not admit anything ultimate besides itself. (2) The other side is the dynamic presence of the "ultimate" as a continuous, never ceasing, concrete, and universal concern, always demanding and giving, always threatening and promising. As an actual concern it expresses itself in the actualities of life, qualifying every section of existence and using every section of existence for its own embodiment in symbols and actions; for the religious or ultimate concern refers to the ultimate foundation of our being and the ultimate meaning of our existence. Therefore, we can formulate the abstract criterion of every theological work in this way: Those propositions are theological which deal with a subject in so far as it belongs to the foundation of our being and in so far as the meaning of our existence depends on it.

The Positive Element in the Theological Method

The ultimate concern is a concrete concern; otherwise it could not be a concern at all. Even mysticism lives in concrete traditions and symbols in order to express, in action and thought, that which transcends everything concrete. Theology, therefore, must interpret the totality of symbols, institutions, and ideas in which an ultimate concern has embodied itself; theology is, first of all, positive. It works on the basis, in the material, and for the purpose of an actual religion. The participation in a religious reality is a presupposition of all theology. You have to be within the circle of a concrete religion in order to interpret it existentially. This is the "theological circle" which theology cannot (and never should try to) escape. This circle is not vicious, but its denial is dishonest, for it could be denied only in the name of an assumedly higher ultimate, which immediately would establish the same circle.

The Element of Immediacy in the Theological Method

The positive element in theology, as discussed above, gives the *content* of theological work; the rational element, to be discussed later, gives the *form* of theological work; and the element of immediacy, to be discussed now, gives the *medium* of theological work. Without participation in the reality within which theology speaks, no theology is possible; it is the air in which theology breathes. We call this participation "experience" in the larger sense of the word, in which it covers the mere encounter as well as the cognitively conscious encounter. "Experience" in both senses is the medium, the element in which theology lives. But the religious experience of the theologian is not a positive source and not a norm of systematic theology. Everybody's religious experience is shaped by the denominational group to which he belongs. The education in his own church opened the door to religious reality for every theologian. Later he has personal experiences which confirm or transform his earlier ones. But his intention should never be to make his earlier or later experiences the content of his theology; they certainly will enter into it, but this is an event, not an intention. It is the function of the medium to mediate, not to hold fast. It was the danger of Schleiermacher's theology that his concept of "religious consciousness" became confused with "experience." But it contradicts the basic principle of the Reformation to look at one's self instead of looking beyond one's self at the new reality which liberates man from himself. Our experience is changing and fragmentary; it is not the source of truth, although without it no truth can become *our* truth.

It might be said that the whole history of religion, including the biblical religion and the development of Christianity, is the reservoir of man's religious experience and that the positive element of theology is identical with the contents of this experience. Such a statement is correct, but ambiguous. A content, e.g., of the experience of the prophet Isaiah, is the paradoxical acting of God in history. This divine acting transcends every immediate experience. It has become manifest to the prophet in a situation which we should call "revelation." Of course, the prophet is aware of this situation, and to that extent it is an "experience." Not the experiential side, however, is significant for the prophet and for the theologian, but the revelatory side. The word "revelation" has been distorted into "supra-natural communication of knowledge"; it is hard to save the word (and many others) from this state of corruption into which it has been brought by both supra-naturalism and naturalism. Nevertheless, "revelation" points to something for which no other adequate word is available—certainly not "religious experience." Revelation is the manifestation of the ultimate ground and meaning of human existence (and implicitly of all existence). It is not a matter of objective knowledge, of empirical research or rational inference. It is a matter of ultimate concern, it grasps the total personality and is effective through a set of symbols. Revelation is not restricted to a special period of history, to special personalities or writings. It occurs wherever it "wills." But we can speak of it only if it has become revelation *for* us, if we have experienced it existentially. Not experience, but revelation received *in* experience, gives the content of every theology.

Suggested Further Readings

BERGSON, HENRI. *The Two Sources of Morality and Religion.* New York: Henry Holt & Co., Inc., 1935.

DEWEY, JOHN. *A Common Faith.* New Haven: Yale University Press, 1934.

FRAZER, J. G. *The Golden Bough.* New York: The Macmillan Co., 1951.

FREUD, SIGMUND. *The Future of an Illusion.* New York: Liveright Publishing Corp., 1949.

HOCKING, W. H. *The Meaning of God in Human Experience.* New Haven: Yale University Press, 1912.

HUME, DAVID. *Dialogues Concerning Natural Religion.* New York: Hafner Pub. Co., Inc., 1948.

JAMES, WILLIAM. *The Varieties of Religious Experience.* New York: Modern Library Inc., 1935.

LEIBNIZ, G. W. *Discourse on Metaphysics.* Translated by the author. 1678.

MILL, J. S. *Three Essays on Religion.* London: Longmans, Green & Co., Ltd., 1874.

MONTAGUE, W. P. *Belief Unbound.* New Haven: Yale University Press, 1930.
RUSSELL, BERTRAND. *Mysticism and Logic.* New York: Longmans, Green & Co.,
   Inc., 1918. "A Free Man's Worship."
ST. THOMAS AQUINAS. *Summa Theologica.* New York: Benziger Bros., 1910. Vol. I.
SANTAYANA, GEORGE. *Reason In Religion.* New York: Charles Scribner's Sons, 1905.
TEMPLE, WILLIAM. *Nature, Man and God.* New York: The Macmillan Co., 1934.

Index